The GREAT INDIAN GENIUS HAR DAYAL

BHUVAN LALL

INDIA · SINGAPORE · MALAYSIA

Notion Press

Old No. 38, New No. 6
McNichols Road, Chetpet
Chennai - 600 031

First Published by Notion Press 2020
Copyright © Bhuvan Lall 2020
All Rights Reserved.

ISBN 978-1-64760-796-8

Dedicated to my late mother

Vijai Laxmi Lal

whose life and love for poetry taught me that

the dash of a pen is more significant than

the use of a sword

"Here's to the crazy ones, the misfits, the rebels, the troublemakers, the round pegs in the square holes, the ones who see things differently - they're not fond of rules. You can quote them, disagree with them, glorify or vilify them, but the only thing you can't do is ignore them because they change things, they push the human race forward and while some may see them as the crazy ones, we see genius, because the ones who are crazy enough to think that they can change the world, are the ones who do"

Steve Jobs

CONTENTS

1

IN SEARCH OF HAR DAYAL

"Lala Har Dayal was one of India's noblest children and who in
happier times would have done wonders with his gigantic intellectual power.
For his mind was one of the greatest I have ever known and his character also
was true and pure…"

Reverend Charles F. Andrews
Missionary and Educator

It was the onset of summer and remarkably bright morning on Wednesday, July
5th, 1933 in London.

Chaman Lal, the chief reporter for *The Hindustan Times,* walked into the
Thomas Cook's office at 45, Berkeley Street in the leafy neighborhood of Mayfair
in the heart of the city. He was in town to attend the World Economic Conference
organized by the League of Nations that was aimed at reviving global trade. It was
his last day in London and he was in the travel agency's office to collect his mail
before departing for the United States later that evening.

Lal, the twenty-eight-year-old newsperson with already over a decade of
journalistic experience behind him, defied easy categorization. He claimed to be
moderate in his political views yet was the secretary of the Delhi Branch of a
radical organization named Naujawan Bharat Sabha. The Hukumat-i-Britannia
(Government of British India) believed him to be a 'dangerous customer' and a
'live revolutionary'.

Five years earlier on February 18th, 1928, Lal, who was originally from Sargodha
in Punjab, had observed a heated debate on India's right to independence from
the press gallery in the Central Assembly of Delhi. Then in a moment of passion,
the young man dramatically flung his attaché case towards the head of Sir Basil
Phillott Blackett, the finance member of the British Viceroy's executive council.
Though the attaché case missed its intended target, Lal was immediately arrested
for attempted assault. He was later released after a fine of Rs. 200 as Blackett

sportingly dismissed the entire episode and even invited him for tea at his home. Nevertheless, largely due to his daredevilry he became an overnight sensation in India and a marked man. Everyone including Philip Crawford Vickery, the head of the Indian Political Intelligence (IPI) from October 1926 to August 1947, hereafter referred to him as 'Chaman Lal of Basil Blackett fame'. His movements were under surveillance and he was considered, "an excitable creature who is capable of doing any wild act under the stimulus of his feelings".

Chaman Lal lived up to his reputation and was directly involved in undercover revolutionary activities. He was present in the Central Assembly Hall on that fateful day, April 8th, 1929, as his compatriots Bhagat Singh and Batukeshwar Dutt hurled two bombs - "a big bang to wake up the deaf". On December 23rd, 1929, he covertly participated in the attempt by revolutionaries to derail the train of the British Viceroy Lord Edward Irwin, 1st Earl of Halifax, by triggering off bombs on the railway tracks. The Department of Criminal Investigation (DCI) suspected the incorrigible journalist of revolutionary tendencies and jailed him three times. Later after his release, he requested for a British Indian passport to travel abroad for further education. He was deemed sufficiently trustworthy only after he became a father on March 15th 1933 and granted permission to travel to Europe and the United States.

However Chaman Lal, on his first overseas trip in June 1933, held a secret close to his heart. He was on a mission to cautiously seek out his childhood hero and a man he had never met or even seen a photograph of - the reclusive Indian patriot Har Dayal (1884–1939), also known as Lala Har Dayal M.A. or Dr. Har Dayal.

Immediately after his arrival in England, Lal made several inquires about Har Dayal who was reported to be lodged somewhere in London's suburbs. He combed the large city of London for a month but could not locate him. There was no residential address, telephone number or any other link to Har Dayal. None of Lal's acquaintances or prominent Indians living in England could provide him with the celebrated Dilliwallah's whereabouts in London. It seemed no Indian had met or heard from the Indian revolutionary for decades. There were no recent pictures or known friends either. Lal then got himself interviewed and photographed by the *Daily Herald*, a popular newspaper of London in the hope that it might draw the attention of Har Dayal. But that too came to naught. After a month-long investigation, all of his sources dried up. It was a huge set back for the uncompromising nationalist who like millions of other young Indians grew up in India hearing about the electrifying exploits of Har Dayal before and during WWI. At this stage, he despairingly gave up all expectations of ever tracing his idol.

In London on that July morning, Lal gathered his correspondence from the Thomas Cook mail window on the first floor and sat down in the foyer to read his letters. He found himself seated next to Anthony Isar, a British civil servant and former City Magistrate of Delhi. This sudden meeting brought back unpleasant memories, as Isar had dispatched Lal to Hukumat-i-Britannia's prisons on three occasions in India. For Isar's exceptional service record, His Majesty's Government conferred upon him the honor of a Member of the British Empire whereas Lal's press pass was confiscated.

Then suddenly, a shabbily dressed Indian in severely soiled shoes with a house key hanging from his crumpled jacket's front pocket walked through the large metal doors into the hallway of the elegantly appointed global travel agency's office. The slightly stocky man, about five feet five inches tall with a thinning hairline and somewhat trimmed mustache wore a pair of thick steel-rimmed circular frame glasses that gave him the intense appearance of a well-read professor. But it was the penetrating eyes and the serenity on the smiling face of the Indian that distinguished him from the well-attired crowd in the busy lobby. He just stood there waiting for the elevator.

In his book, *The Vanishing Empire*, Chaman Lal recounted the entire episode. He described that on sighting this sage-like figure he had an intuition and conveyed to Isar, "I feel that he is the great Lala Har Dayal... let me pay him my respects..."

Isar restrained Lal. He gently educated him about the British etiquette of not approaching strangers without a formal introduction, "It is against the etiquette to ask anybody if he is so and so. Don't do that..." Lal was in no mood to accept the advice to his erstwhile tormentor and readily flouted British protocol, asserting, "You keep your etiquette with yourself – I am going to ask him..." Lal rushed forward to enter the elevator along with him to go to the mail department and following Indian traditions respectfully touched the feet of the man.

Lal then inquired, "Are you Lala Har Dayal?"

Though taken aback by the abruptness the astounded man acknowledged being Har Dayal, himself.

Har Dayal, who was forty-eight years old now, recognized Chaman Lal straightaway from his picture that had appeared in the *Daily Herald* exclaimed, "You are Chaman Lal. I have seen your picture though we have not met". He warmly embraced the much younger Indian from his hometown Delhi. They proceeded to a small cafeteria on the first floor of the office. Lal was thunderstruck after serendipitously coming face to face with his favorite patriot and the intellectual giant from India. In the last few hours at his disposal in London, his lifelong desire was realized and he discussed the affairs of the world with the elusive Har Dayal.

Unknown to the rest of the crowd in the cafeteria of the Thomas Cook office on that summer day in London, the soft-spoken and well-mannered Indian that Chaman Lal randomly encountered was once a fierce revolutionary who was still banned in India.

Who was Har Dayal?

Decades before Jawaharlal Nehru acknowledged India's tryst with destiny, much before Subhas Chandra Bose faced the British Empire on the battlefield and even before Mahatma Gandhi unleashed *satyagraha* in India there was 'Har Dayal'.

A model for other Indian revolutionaries worldwide, the charismatic Har Dayal in November 1913, at the age of twenty-eight, took center stage in Indian history as the foremost leader of the Ghadr Party in California. Today the former headquarters of the Ghadr Party at 5 Wood Street is in a quite neighbourhood in San Francisco, close to the Silicon Valley that has in recent years seen an influx of entreprenuers, information technology engineers and code writers from India. However over a century ago, Har Dayal powered the vaguely known second Indian war of independence and an entire era of the Indian freedom struggle from this city and its university campuses. With India as his battleground, the ripples from his audacious and rebellious campaigns spread far and wide among the non-resident Indians across the world. The economic prosperity and the democratic institutions of the United States, a former British colony, inspired Har Dayal and the Ghadr movement. It eventually led to India's independence in 1947 and the formation of the largest democracy in the history of humankind.

India's struggle for independence from Hukumat-i-Britannia was multilayered. It contained both the martial elements as well as the spirit of *ahimsa* (nonviolence). But in our history publications, the role of the revolutionaries was minimized and patriots like Har Dayal were deliberately painted out of the picture. An inventor of innovative ideas and unique ideologies he was one of the original disrupters from India like Aurobindo Ghosh before him. And the Ghadr Party, only a brief episode in the life of Har Dayal, laid the foundation for the political efforts of both Mahatma Gandhi, the pacifist and Subhas Chandra Bose, the leader of the Indian National Army.

Today, Har Dayal whose life and genius inspired generations of Indians has come and gone. That name, 'Har Dayal' means almost nothing to Indians or present day world. Despite his striking revolutionary activities and breathtaking scholastic feats, he is largely unknown in modern-day India. In the twenty-first century, his contributions to India's independence and modern thought are locked away somewhere within the dusty files inside the vaults of government records. He is not counted amongst the forerunners of the Indian freedom movement. Besides, his brand of ethical internationalism does not find representation in the prevailing political dialogue globally. Irrespective of the verdict on him, Har Dayal is a historical figure of our nation and in world history. He is too important to be left in the obscurity of the archives or as the hyperbole of legend.

The person behind the name

On October 14th, 2017, my life partner, Arti Mathur and I met Har Dayal's granddaughter, Ms. Shubh Paul, in Delhi. She and her husband E. Jaiwant Paul have written Har Dayal's biography. Dr. Emily Brown (1911–2001) and Dr. Dharmavira too have produced exhaustively researched biographies of Har Dayal that were published over half a century ago. There have been similar efforts in Hindi by historians and researchers. Yet I feel with the passage of time more specifics are now available and the intricate life of this rare man deserves further analysis.

As a biographer of Har Dayal, it was extremely problematic for me to explore the life of a loner who was on the move across continents over a hundred years ago, conducted himself in an unorthodox manner with no real job throughout his life, a man who endlessly searched for a new image for himself and one who mostly lived in seclusion. The first two decades of twentieth-century, the period of extensive action for Har Dayal, have yet to be completely explored by writers in the context of Indian nationalism. Other than a few books, some Government reports, British Secret Service records, limited newspaper stories plus few private letters, to our immense regret, the world-class intellectual left almost nothing behind about himself. The study of his lifespan has huge gaps, years that were enormously difficult to cover, almost no notes of his arrivals and departures, mostly no home or workplace addresses and little else in terms of his memoirs. In his multiple books and articles he wrote more about the world, India, and humankind than seemed imaginable but for some unimaginable reason did not attempt an autobiography. He had a few lifelong friends but mostly distant devotees, detached admirers, and absolutely no close associates left to interview due to passage of time.

The distance of history did not deter me from visiting his known places of residence, study and work in India, United Kingdom, Europe, Canada, and California to write this book. I approached the libraries, collections, and archives at the University of Delhi, St. John's College, Oxford University, Cambridge University, Stanford University, the University of California at Berkeley and Rydal Museum as well as Viskadalen folkhögskola outside Goteborg, Sweden who have all kept some of the official records about him and his life intact. There is a considerable amount of information about Har Dayal deposited in the private collections and Government archives of India, Great Britain, Sweden, Germany, America, and Canada. Utilizing the material from all these resources I have tried to faithfully reconstruct the life and times of a fascinatingly complex man.

This book charts the dramatic rise of a miracle boy walking in the lanes of Delhi who went on to travel the world and become many things including an enigmatic global legend in his lifetime. The book focuses on his spectacular mind that operated in puzzling political environs a century ago. I have additionally endeavored to disseminate the historic elements and put our nation's independence movement in its proper frame of reference without depreciating the struggles of other Indian leaders just as Har Dayal would have intended it to be.

Through these pages as I retrace the footsteps of Har Dayal, the reader will travel on a roller-coaster of the extraordinary life of an unsung protagonist bursting with supreme academic abilities, patriotic zeal, and internationalism at the same time. There are nonetheless several aspects of his life that we will never understand but hopefully can aspire to get closer to the person behind that name - Har Dayal.

The Great Indian Genius

Finally the title of the book, *The Great Indian Genius*, is not an exaggeration nor a hagiographic account or worship of a super brilliant man but designed to stress the unmatched refinement and the overwhelming power of Har Dayal's intellect. This unique feature was universally acknowledged across the world during his lifetime and even after he has departed. Needless to add, to study his life's work was an education by itself.

The Great Indian Genius is the untold story of an inspiring Indian icon, a thought-provoking chronicle of the lost chapter of the Indian freedom struggle and a portrait of a man who came from nothing and by his own intellect, courage, determination, initiative, and destiny forged a legendary life. Eight decades since Har Dayal crossed the great divide it is time to rescue this rare man from oblivion and shine a light on him. He belongs not only to India but also to the entire humanity and his life's work must be brought back into recognition. I offer this story here as a dramatic new chapter in the history of colonization of India and believe that Har Dayal is a real-life hero for our collective future as a world civilization.

Bhuvan Lall

New Delhi

November 18th 2019

2

THE GHADR OF 1857 IN DELHI

"Ai vaaye inqilaab zamaane ke jaur se
Dilli Zafar ke haath se pal mein nikal gayi"

(Alas! What a revolution, due to the cruelty of the age,
Delhi slipped out of Zafar's hands in a moment)

Bahadur Shah 'Zafar'
Mughal Shehenshah

Tuesday, September 22nd, 1857 was a dark day in the history of Delhi.

That stifling afternoon, the victorious cavalryman, a perfect swordsman and a temperamental firangi, Captain William Stephen Raikes Hodson (1821–1858) rode towards Delhi - the captured capital city of Mughliyah Saltanat along with a hundred armed men. A bullock drawn carriage slowly trailed them with the three Mughal princes, Mirza Mughal, Mirza Khizr Sultan and Mirza Abu Bakr, held by armed guards as prisoners. They were commanders of a force of rebel sipahis. They surrendered to Captain Hodson of the 1st European Fusiliers and the officiating Deputy Assistant Quartermaster General under the impression that he would guarantee their lives.

Enroute to the devastated imperial city, at the Delhi Darwaza, a crowd of Dilliwallahs (residents of Delhi) followed them and even more people collected near the entrance. A panicked Hodson feared the rescue of the Mughal Shahzadas (princes) and an attack against his hundred-odd men. He decided that the three Shahzadas must be executed there and then. He ordered the three young men to disembark from the carriage and strip. The guards quickly seized their ceremonial jeweled swords. Against the glow of the twilight, the bare-chested Shahzadas were lined up in a clear vision of Hodson.

For the next few minutes, there was an eerie silence. Legend has it that Mirza Moghul at this moment asked Hindus and Muslims to remember what they could achieve with unity.

Then Hodson pulled out his loaded Colt revolver and aimed at the heart of Mirza Mughal, son of the Shehenshah. Two shots rang out and blood spluttered out of the chest of the Shahzada as he collapsed. Mirza Khizr Sultan, one of the leaders responsible for the deaths of European women and children was the next to fall. He was shot through his neck. And finally Prince Abul Bakr, heir to the throne was executed in cold blood.

The large crowd stood speechless. With the merciless murders of the three Shahzadas the limited power of the once great Mughal shahi- gharana was gone forever.

Next Hodson the cold-blooded killer calmly removed the signet rings and the turquoise armlets from the three corpses that were thrown into a cart. On a later date, in a letter to his sister Hodson gave his version of the events, "In twenty-four hours, therefore, I disposed of the principal members of the house of Timur the Tatar. I am not cruel, but I confess I did rejoice at the opportunity of ridding the earth of these wretches. I intended to have had them hung, but when it came to a question of 'they' or 'us' I had no time for deliberation". Hodson, later accused of financial impropriety, left behind a pool of blood and rode away through Delhi Darwaza with the seized jewels and swords. The naked bodies of the dead Shahzadas were left to rot in the sun in front of the kotwali, in the heart of the city for the next three days before being buried in dishonored graves.

Within six months of the execution on March 9th, 1958, in Lucknow, a bullet hit Hodson in his chest. The firangi succumbed to the injuries. But on that ill-fated September day of 1857 Hodson had sent a powerful message to the Dilliwallahs. He demonstrated the feringih's unlimited capacity for brutality. The exact spot where the three Mughal Shahzadas were slaughtered came to be known as '*Khooni Darwaza*' (the Bloody Gate).

This ruthlessness and violence marked Hukumat-i-Britannia's reign of terror over the next ninety years in India.

The Company Bahadur

The story of Hukumat-i-Britannia's triumphant landing in far off India started two hundred and fifty-seven years earlier on a cold winter morning in London on December 31st, 1600. On that day, The East India Company was started by an assorted group of two hundred and eighteen merchants. It was granted a Royal

Charter and a monopoly of trade to the east of the Cape of Good Hope, signed by Queen Elizabeth I (1533–1603). Its primary mission was to trade with the Mughliyah Saltanat as the magnificence of the court the Mughal Shehenshah had attained legendary status in the East as well as the West. The first representative of East India Company to the Mughliyah Saltanat, Sir Thomas Roe, astounded by the opulence of the Mughal Shehenshah Jahangir's (1569–1627), jewels, described him as "the treasury of the world". In a letter to Prince Charles on October 30, 1616 he reported, "In jewells (which is one of his felicityes) hee is the treasury of the world, buyeing all that comes, and heaping rich stones as if hee would rather build then weare them."

Once the East India Company managed to subdue their principal rivals, the Portuguese forces in India and deal with the French Compagnie des Indes Orientales, Thomas Roe artfully managed to obtain the permission to trade from the mighty Mughliyah Saltanat. His Majesty Jahangir's naiveté and egocentricity are reflected well in the firman:

"Upon which assurance of your royal love I have given my general command to all the kingdoms and ports of my dominions to receive all the merchants of the English nation as the subjects of my friend; that in what place soever they choose to live, they may have free liberty without any restraint; and at what port soever they shall arrive, that neither Portugal nor any other shall dare to molest their quiet; and in what city soever they shall have residence, I have commanded all my governors and captains to give them freedom answerable to their own desires; to sell, buy, and to transport into their country at their pleasure…"

"For confirmation of our love and friendship, I desire your Majesty to command your merchants to bring in their ships of all sorts of rarities and rich goods fit for my palace; and that you be pleased to send me your royal letters by every opportunity, that I may rejoice in your health and prosperous affairs; that our friendship may be interchanged and eternal." *(Sir George Birdwood's The Register of Letters)*

For the next hundred years, the company brought spices, tea and exotic articles from India to Europe. By 1707, Jahangir's powerful grandson and Indian monarch Aurangzeb (1618–1707) was dead and the great Mughal shahi gharana was reduced to nothing but a puppet show. On April 10th, 1717, John Surman, the chief of the mission to Delhi obtained the firman of Mughal Shehenshah Farrukhsiyar (1683–1719), that has been regarded as the *Magna Carta* of the English trade in India. With this firman the Company had the unqualified rights of trading in India's richest province Bengal only by paying Rs. 3000 annually.

The fading power of the Mughliyah Saltanat granted India's foreign settlers a chance to expand their trade and garrisons unchecked. They fuelled their arsenals at the handful of Indian trading outposts with the help of the British navy. A company member Robert Clive's (1725–1774), victory at the Battle of Plassey on June 23rd, 1757, marked East India Company's ambition to take over India. Clive later recognised the Battle of Plassey as "a Revolution scarcely to be parallel'd in history". After defeating the combined forces of Shah Alam II, Mir Qasim and Shuja-ud-Daulah at the Battle of Buxar on October 22nd, 1764, the company gained supremacy over northern India as a whole. The fundamentally flawed Clive used a combination of treachery, cunning, and naked military power in his quest to rule India. He finally returned to Britain in 1767 with a personal fortune then valued at £234,000 that made him one of the wealthiest men in Europe. He defended his immoral earning in India by stating; "I stand astonished at my own moderation." On November 22nd, 1774, at the age of forty-nine, Clive, possibly under the influence of opium stabbed himself to death with a penknife. By then the Indian slang for plunder, "loot" was making its way into the British lexicon.

Subsequently, the ravenous East India Company distinctively attacked by British statesman Edmund Burke as a "state in the disguise of a merchant", faithfully followed the business model perfected by Clive. The wily British traders exploited one homegrown power or population against the other. They ejected local Maharajas, Nawabs and Sultans and turned the commercial enterprise into a kingdom. Slowly they formed an Empire on the subcontinent that stretched further east and south and then northwest, than any precursor in India's recent history. At the beginning of 1857, the East India Company had successfully transformed itself into the most powerful military and economic force the world had ever seen. But in the heat and dust of May in 1857 the greedy multinational corporation met its the biggest military challenge yet - one that ultimately led to its liquidation.

The Indian Insurrection

On Thursday, March 19th, 1857, Mangal Pandey (1827–1857), a sipahi of the 34th Bengal Regiment broke ranks to incite his fellow regimental mates in Barrackpore, near Calcutta (Kolkata now) to protest against defiled kartoos. The kartoos were laced with cow and pig fat and there were rumors that local religious observances were being disregarded on purpose by the firangis. Confronted by his officers Pandey put his toe into the trigger of his musket and madly fired upward at his breast. He survived the suicide attempt but in the early hours of April 8th, 1857, in front of all fellow sipahis of the 34th Bengal Regiment he was hanged. The legend of his sacrifice, though an isolated act of rebellion, was repeated endlessly and gained fervor. It ultimately sparked a insurrection among the sipahis.

In the searing heat of Sunday, May 10th, 1857, in Meerut, the Indian sipahis of the 3rd Native Light Cavalry inspired by Mangal Pandey, refused orders and attacked their superior officers. The insurrection was fueled by discontent within the ranks, fear of the firangi rule and the use of tainted kartoos. The rage produced acts of severe violence. They left a trail of blood all over the military cantonment in Meerut and dashed off to Delhi some fifty kilometers away with the rallying call; *'Dilli Chalo'* (onwards to Delhi). In the early hours of May 11th, the sipahis crossed the Jamuna river and entered the Lal Qila (Red Fort also referred to as Qila Mubarak or Qila-e-Mulla - the exalted fortress) and demanded an audience with the Mughal Shehenshah.

The rebellious sipahis offered the existing representative of the great Mughal dynasty, Shehenshah Abu Zafar Sirajuddin Mohammed Bahadur Shah 'Zafar' (1775–1862) titular leadership of the insurrection. Their mission was to reinstate Zafar as Badshah of the entire nation. And under the flag of the once-great Mughliyah Saltanat, the Hindu and Muslim sipahis declared their intention to finish off the firangi. By accepting Zafar as their leader the rebel sipahis acknowledged that the long-standing war between the Hindus and the Muslims had ended.

Zafar was born in 1775 when the almost two-century-old British East India Company, was still a coastal power in India clinging to the Indian shores. He was a member of the dynastic line that extended back to Turco Mongol lineage of warlord Timur and and an empire founded by his forefather Shehenshah Zahiruddin Babar (1483–1530) that once stretched from Kabul to Madras. During a hundred-year period of power and glory (1556–1657) under the reigns of Babar's grandson Shehenshah Jalaluddin Akbar and his two successors, Jahangir, a great connoisseur of gemstones, and Shah Jahan, who achieved fame as the builder of the Taj Mahal, the Mughliyah Saltanat of India was renowned worldwide for its imperial vision and lavishness. Their descendant Zafar lived long enough to see the great Mughal shahi gharana that once ruled India with unmatched splendor reduced to humiliating inconsequentiality. After General Gerard Lake's forces defeated the Maratha warriors on September 11th, 1803, the East India Company answerable to only its shareholders and board of directors in London ruled over the last bastion of the Mughals - Delhi. The eighty-two-year-old Shehenshah received an allowance from the local British Resident who held the real power.

Now all of a sudden, the political nonentity Zafar, shocked by the slaughter and looting in Delhi committed the fatal error of accepting the leadership of the revolt that was foisted on him by the sipahis. On the morning of May 12th, 1857, the end of the rule of firangis and revival of the Mughliyah Saltanat was announced with the booming of the guns at the Lal Qila. The war against the rule of the East India Company had begun under Zafar's unenthusiastic direction and with Delhi as its nerve- center. The rebellion also posed a considerable threat to East India Company supremacy in India as it represented the spectacle of Hindu-Muslim unity. The ensuing insurrection between the firangis and the rebel sipahis was to become the bloodiest in the history of the British Empire and came to be identified as the Ghadr of 1857 (Rebellion of 1857).

The Fall of Delhi

The firangi fauj identified by their red coats, enraged by the massacre of their comrades in Meerut, swore dire vengeance and rushed towards Delhi. The loss of Delhi was a severe blow to the prestige of the British Empire. The firangis laid a long siege outside the gates of the capital city. Richard Baird-Smith, the Chief Engineer of the East India Company, avowed, "We must not release our hold of Delhi even by an inch! Our noose, fallen round her neck like cruel death, must be constant and thorough! If we raise the siege of Delhi, the Punjab will be out of hand, India will be gone, and the Empire ruined forever". From May 1857 onwards for the next hundred and thirty-four days, the brave sipahis fought off the firangi fauj around Delhi.

June 23rd, 1857, the hundredth anniversary of Robert Clive's victory at the Battle of Plassey was a challenging day for the firangi fauj. A prophecy circulated in the bazaar folklore of Delhi, that the firangis would be driven out of India on that day. By now the sipahis had risen against their superiors in Nimach, Jhansi, Lucknow, Bareilly, Benaras, Kanpur, Allahabad and the Ghadr had spread widely over North India. Consequently, there was an exceptionally ferocious attack on the ridge outside Delhi. Brigadier General Archdale Wilson had 4,023 infantrymen, 1,293 cavalrymen, as well as 1,602 artillerymen and engineers - a total of 6,918 operational troops under his command. The firangis drove the attackers back to their Delhi ramparts and won the day.

The siege of Delhi was a fight to the end between the relics of the Mughliyah Saltanat and the bourgeoning global superpower. As the artillery bombarded the beautiful capital of the Mughliyah Saltanat, thousands of helpless civilians were caught up in the horrors. There were unimaginable casualties, with both sides famished, the city left without water, and the combatants on both sides were driven to the limits of extreme physical and mental endurance. Wild stories circulated freely in the panic-stricken atmosphere of 1857. Fearing for their lives scores of Dilliwallahs in a state of panic fled through the Delhi Darwaza on the south end of the walled city before all the gates could be locked.

By early September 1857, the striking-looking, six feet two inches tall Irishman Brigadier General John Nicholson (1821–1857) had dashed down the Grand Trunk high road from Punjab to Delhi. He decided to finish off any further challenges to firangi rule by Indian sipahis. With a coldblooded hatred for the rebel sipahis in his heart, he convinced his generals that, "Delhi must be taken and it is absolutely essential that this should be done at once". At 0300 hrs on September 14th, the five thousand men strong firangi fauj with a column led by Nicholson launched a four-pronged attack to end the four-month-long siege and regain control over Delhi.

Saheb-i-Alam Bahadur (Lord Governor-General), Bakht Khan (1797–1859), an experienced artillery officer defended Delhi with an estimated thirty thousand Indian fighters under his command. Eleven kilometers of a seven-meter high wall encircled the city and fortified Delhi. It was reinforced by several bastions and fourteen gates, all surrounded by a twenty five-foot-deep dry moat.

Nevertheless, on the morning of September 14th, Lieutenants Duncan Charles Home and Philip Salkeld of Bengal Sappers and Miners, under a heavy fire of musketry blew open a hole at the Kashmiri Darwaza one of the gates protecting Delhi and gained an entry point into the city's impregnable wall. Fierce and determined street-to-street warfare raged between the firangis and the well-entrenched Indian defenders with no quarter given on either side. The firangi fauj fought under a constant rain of fire by the Indians. After six hours the firangis lost 66 officers and 1,104 men. The fierce-eyed racist warrior, Nicholson waving his sword overhead led an assault to lift the siege of Delhi at the Lahori Darwaza.

He was fired on from point-blank range from a window and was incapacitated. He succumbed to his injuries a few days later in the prime of his life and became the Victorian "Hero of Delhi".

For the next five days, it was a desperate situation and the fate of the British East India Company rested on seizing Delhi from the Indians. On September 18th, there was a solar eclipse. For superstitious Indian sipahis, it signified more evil to come. Finally, on Sunday, September 20th, 1857 the soldiers of 52nd (Oxfordshire and Buckinghamshire) Light Infantry and the 75th Highlanders blew the gates of the Lal Qila and entered the official residence of the Mughal Shehenshah. But the seat of the Mughliyah Saltanat was deserted. Zafar and his sons frightened by defeat had slipped out and sought refuge in their forefather Humayun's (the son of Babar, the founder of the dynasty) tomb on the outskirts of Delhi.

Just before dawn on Monday, September 21st, upon military command the guns from across the bloodstained battlements of Delhi thundered a royal salute in honor of Queen Victoria (1819–1901) the monarch of Britain. The cannon fired in precise motion a hundred and one times. There was vibration and the earth shook under the feet of the Dilliwallahs with each roar. Tall proud firangis in bright red uniforms with somber faces and white gloves shouted commands. The firing reverberated through the city and sent a cloud of white smoke into the air. The uninterrupted roar of the guns announced to all within an earshot that the city of Delhi had fallen and been taken over by the army of retribution. The strange community of firangis from a distant island of wool merchants, shopkeepers and sailors were victorious. They were masters in Delhi and had captured the city for the second time in the century. They regarded Delhi as particularly important for symbolic and tactical reasons since it was the traditional capital of the Mughliyah Saltanat and was for several centuries considered the heart of India by many rulers. After winning the battle of Delhi, the weary firangis now rested their feet in the famous 'Elysium on Earth', the Diwan-i-Khas of the Lal Qila.

That morning, a sleep-deprived Zafar heard the royal salute loud and clear. He at once knew that the peaceful life that permitted him to write poetry in his luxurious palace was over. Later in the afternoon of September 21st, Captain Hodson along with fifty armed warriors entered the magnificent tomb of red sandstone surmounted by a perfect white marble dome. After a tense two-hour wait, he successfully negotiated Zafar's surrender on a promise that his life would be spared. He boldly stepped forward and brought back a stunned Zafar to his former home - the Lal Qila as a prisoner. On his return to Delhi, Hodson was feted as a hero for his actions. The next day, Hodson executed the three Mughal Shahzadas at point-blank range in cold blood. *The Illustrated London News* justified Hodson's summary dispatch of the princes and remarked, "The Royal scoundrels were known to have taken throughout the most active share in the rebellion".

In Delhi, Mirza Ghalib (1796–1869) one of India's greatest poet in a note to a friend lamented: "The light has gone out of India." It is said that the poet was arrested by the vengeful firangis and presented before the Military Governor of Delhi, Colonel Pelham Burn (1807–1882) who had taken residence in a haveli of Kutubuddin Sowdager. When the Colonel enquired about the poet's religion, Ghalib, with his usual wit intact replied, "I am half firangi and half Muslim since I consume alcohol…" On that rare occasion Colonel Burn, who retired in 1861 as a Major General, appreciated the sense of humor of the poet and let him return unharmed to his haveli in Qasimjan.

Elsewhere the drunken firangis unleashed a war of reprisal on the Dilliwallahs. It was hell everywhere in the city intended by Mughal architects to be the mirror image of the heavens. Gallows were set up in every neighborhood. Several entirely blameless Indians who found themselves amid the Ghadr were bludgeoned and some even blown off from the mouth of the canons. Thousands of sipahis and Dilliwallahs were forced to clean bloodied stones with their tongues, then flogged and summarily hanged. Countless women while saving their honor committed suicides by jumping into the wells. There were heaps of corpses all over. Numerous streets, lanes, and wells were filled with bloated corpses of men and animals. A horrible stench hung in the air. The city was virtually depopulated by the invading firangis and left an empty ruin. The beautiful city with opulent palaces, large mansions, water fountains, flower gardens, and teeming bazaars was reduced to a city of death. The inhuman massacre on an unprecedented scale by the firangis in Delhi eclipsed the notorious mass murder and plunder of Dilliwallahs by the Persian raider Nadir Shah who decamped with most of the Mughal treasures in a trail of blood in March 1739, and even the seven blood-soaked invasions of the Afghan Ahmad Shah Abdali between 1748 and 1767.

British historian, Michael Edwards, inscribed in *My Indian Mutiny Diary 1957*, "From the first murder of European civilians at Meerut and Delhi, the English threw aside the mask of civilization and engaged in a war of such ferocity that reasonable parallel can be seen in our times with the Nazi occupation of Europe and in past, with the hell of the Thirty Years War".

The End of the Mughliyah Saltanat

From January 27th, 1858 to March 9th, 1858, a farcical trial of the frail Bahadur Shah Zafar was held at the Lal Qila. He was charged with sedition during the 'mutiny of 1857'. Zafar was not amenable to the fiat of a British Court as he was himself a sovereign and not a British subject. At the end of the trial, held in an environment of horror, the Court did not pronounce judgment on his arguments but gave a terse finding: "The Court, on the evidence before them, are of opinion that the Prisoner Muhammad Bahadur Shah, Ex-King of Delhi, is guilty of all and every charge preferred against him."

The firangis escorted Zafar; the slave rather than the master of circumstances to Rangoon (now Yangon). Zafar's wife Zeenat Mahal (1823–1886), their son Jawan Bakht (1841–1884), a couple of other wives and servants, accompanied him. Broken-hearted Mughal Shehenshah Bahadur Shah Zafar breathed his last in exile on the morning of Friday, November 7th, 1862, in the captivity of Hukumat-i-Britannia. He was 87.

A minor poet himself (Zafar was his takhallus or pen-name), he usually spent his time writing pessimistic verses. Sadly, in his last days, he was even deprived of paper and pencil to write. He scribbled his epitaph on the wall with a burnt stick.

"Kitna hai badnaseeb Zafar, dafn ke liye,
Do gaz zameen bhi na mili kuu-e-yaar mein"

(How unlucky is Zafar, for his burial,
Did not get even two yards of land on the street of the beloved)

The last Mughal Shehenshah of India reduced to a mere shadow of a name was buried anonymously and forgotten as a footnote in history. However, the mausoleum of Zafar remained one of India's most visible symbols of the Ghadr of 1857 and an inspiration for future revolutionaries. In Zafar's hometown Delhi, the Union Jack fluttered on his erstwhile home, the Lal Qila. The Dilliwallahs gradually returned to their homes after sanity returned. Yet the full social, cultural, economic and political impact of the Ghadr still lay in the future.

Ironically at the end of 1945, the Indian National Army trials at the same Lal Qila (the Red Fort trials) decided the fate of the Hukumat-i-Britannia in India and around the world.

The First Indian War of Independence

The Ghadr that began on May 10th, 1857, in the military cantonment of the town of Meerut, even after the fall of Delhi escalated into a violent Ghadr largely in the upper Gangetic plain and central India, with the major hostilities in present-day Uttar Pradesh, Bihar, and northern Madhya Pradesh. The sparks of grand resistance became flames that shook India like a severe earthquake, with its epicenter in Delhi. Over the next year, the firangi fauj launched a military campaign for winning back their lost jurisdiction.

On June 17th, 1858, the valiant Rani Lakshmi Bai of Jhansi met a warrior's death on the battlefield and a few days later with the fall of Gwalior, the firangis won the last battle of the Ghadr.

The fourteen months-long Ghadr from early May 1857 to the end of June 1858 left the nation burning. It produced a galaxy of legendary Indian superheroes like Rani Laxmi Bai, Mangal Pandey, Mirza Mughal, and Bakht Khan, Tantia Tope, Nana Sahib, Rao Tula Ram, Kunwar Singh, Narayan Singh, and Khan Bahadur who went to war to stop the alien East India Company from enslaving an entire nation. Their legacies remained in the hearts and minds of millions of Indians in the decades to come.

Subsequently, entire populations in villages were murdered and countless innocent Indians lost their lives. Orthodox historians claimed only 100,000 Indian sipahis were slaughtered during the Ghadr in British Empire's barbarity but it is accepted that almost ten million Indians were killed over ten years beginning in 1857.

The Ghadr was the 'Indian holocaust'.

For the firangis, the Ghadr of 1857 was the defining event in British imperial history and came as a greater shock than the loss of the American colonies. Thereafter British Indian history in the nineteenth century was divided into two halves, separated by the great watershed of 1857. The Ghadr of 1857 was also known in Britain as the great rebellion, the Indian rebellion, the Indian mutiny, the revolt of 1857, the rebellion of 1857, the uprising of 1857, the sepoy rebellion, the Indian insurrection, and the sepoy mutiny. But for the Indians, the year '1857' became symbolic as the first Indian war of independence.

In Britain, the scale of the insurrection profoundly stunned the public opinion. Taking great pride in British imperialism, William Howard Russell (1820–1907), an Irish reporter with *The Times*, recorded in, *My diary in India*, "Never was the strength and courage of any race tried more severely any one year since the world began than was the mettle of the British in India in 1857. And yet, it must be admitted that with all their courage they would have been quite exterminated if the natives had been all and altogether hostile to them..."

The indiscriminate killing by avenging sipahis and firangi troops outraged the population of Great Britain. One hundred and eighty-two members of the British Armed personnel and civilians were awarded the Victoria Cross – the most prestigious and the highest award in Britain for averting the danger posed to the dominance of British in India. Some of the firangi officer's deeds as violent bullies, contemptuous of Indian life and dignity made them British heroes and were celebrated in memoirs, biographies, statues, and memorials, both in India and at home in Britain.

Brigadier Nicholson's gallant service and untimely passing were commemorated at an octagonal, four-story tower on the Ridge in Delhi that lists the names of the officers and soldiers who died during the siege. The plaque reads: "On 21st September the city was evacuated of the enemy." Nicholson, a soldier whose courage was matched only by his brutality, was celebrated in Rudyard Kipling's (1865–1936), immortal novel *Kim*, "And they fared out from the gloom of the mango tope, the old man's high, shrill voice ringing across the field, as wail by long-drawn wail he unfolded the story of Nikal Seyn (Nicholson) – the song that men sing in the Punjab to this day."

Major Hodson became known as "Hodson of Hodson's Horse" and a memorial of black marble, and a white and colored stone was erected in Lichfield Cathedral, Great Britain. The memorial portrayed the last Mughal Shehenshah's historic surrender to Hodson. It also served as a reminder of how Hodson played an important part in ending the Ghadr by depriving the rebel sipahis of their chosen figurehead. The iconography in its four allegorical panels reads, 'Justice, Fortitude, Temperance and Mercy'. Hodson's widow presented Queen Victoria Shehenshah Zafar's Sword and the monarch honored her with an apartment at Hampton Court Palace in consideration for her husband's distinguished services.

Hukumat-i-Britannia's domination over India

In the aftermath of the Ghadr, British attitudes toward Indians generally, including toward Indians in Britain, changed. The old order gave way to the new as India came under the direct rule of the British Crown. The East India

Company's military and political supremacy in India was terminated. The era of the military campaigns of Robert Clive and the wars fought by the Duke of Wellington for the British in India was over. Even the historic East India Company was dismantled on June 1st, 1874.

The British Parliament enacted the Government of India Act, 1858. All rights and powers in India now lay with the British Crown to be exercised in its name by the Government of India (Hukumat-i-Britannia). The office of the Secretary of State was created in place of the President of the Board of Control of the East India Company, to rule India and the army and civil administration were reorganized. Lord Edward Stanley was appointed as the first Secretary of State for India and the India Office housed in Westminster in London, administered India. Calcutta was named as the new capital of the Hukumat-i-Britannia. Delhi, the former capital city of Mughliyah Saltanat was reduced to a nonentity for its role in the Ghadr of 1857 and became another provincial town of the Punjab province in North India. The British Indian army was prudently restructured after the Ghadr. The proportion of firangi officers and soldiers to Indian sipahis in the army was raised and fixed at one to two in the Bengal army.

The Ghadr of 1857 cost the British treasury £36 million before it ended. The detractor of the East India Company, British economist, Adam Smith had previously denounced the Company as a bloodstained monopoly: "burdensome", "useless" and responsible for grotesque massacres in Bengal. Before it was put out of its misery, the Company ruled over ninety million Indians, controlled 243,000 square kilometers of land, issued its coins, complete with the Company crest, and supported an army of two hundred thousand armed soldiers and officers. German philosopher, economist, historian and sociologist, Karl Marx (1818–1883) in an article in *New-York Daily Tribune*, July 15th, 1857, foresaw, "it is only the prologue of a most terrible tragedy that will have to be enacted."

Away from Delhi, the shadow of famine was darkening over India. A series of disastrous crop failures lead to wide-scale starvation and epidemics. The scarcities during the reign of Hukumat-i-Britannia affected a large population of India and millions were thought to have died, conditions being worse because of the shortage of food. It is undeniable that during their rule Hukumat-i-Britannia systematically kept India poor while it was a wealthy nation when they arrived. And by the time the firangis would depart from India it would have achieved zero per-capita economic growth. Hukumat-i-Britannia's imperial policies lead to widespread poverty, low life expectancy, and illiteracy.

Indians in Blood and Color but English in Taste

Education was regarded by Hukumat-i-Britannia as a prime mover to justify the conquest. Ruthless imperialism was rebranded as a 'civilizing mission'.

On February 2nd, 1835, Thomas Babington Macaulay (1800–1859), a member of the East India Company's ruling council as well as a historian had stated in his minute on Indian education, "A single shelf of a good European library was worth the whole native literature of India and Arabia." Advocating the provision of English language education and the advancement of European learning, especially the sciences, in India, the committed racist, Macaulay's Minute clearly expressed his intentions: education was to "form a class who may be interpreters between us and the millions whom we govern; a class of persons, Indian in blood and color, but English in taste, in opinions, in morals, and in intellect".

After the Ghadr of 1857, there exited a fear in some quarters that the educated elite would eventually become resentful, restless agitators, ambitious of power and official distinction, and possessed of the most disloyal sentiments towards that Hukumat-i-Britannia which, in their eyes, had usurped all the influence that rightly belonged to Indians. Nevertheless, Sir William Wilson Hunter as the Chairman of the first Indian Education Commission in 1882 introduced the three-tier educational system with a focus on the English language in the schools and at university, level. By the end of the nineteenth century, the entire fabric of the indigenous Indian educational system was shattered to pieces. The emphasis in Delhi's education syllabus was on the teaching of the English language as against Sanskrit, Hindi, Urdu, Persian, and Arabic and imparting European ideas. As a result, the free intellectual growth of the Indians based on time-tested ancient traditions was stunted and several generations of Anglicized Indians dominated India's elite society. Though the English language dominated Indian education yet literacy rates in India remained poor. And even as late as 1941, the literate represented barely 16% of pre-independent India's population.

After the bloodbath of 1857, Hukumat-i-Britannia tightened their stranglehold over Delhi. In 1867, C. Dooran, the British inspector of schools in Delhi, mooted plans to open English language educational facilities for the growing city. In the 1870s, Bishop Henry Alexander Douglas of Bombay (Mumbai now), recommended that the Universities of Oxford and Cambridge send out men of high scholarship who would live in a religious community and work amongst the educated classes of India. Cambridge University carried his idea forward and set up the English medium Cambridge Mission School in Delhi in 1865. The school was promoted to high school standards in 1876–77.

With India under the firm grip of Hukumat-i-Britannia, the city's anatomy was carefully readjusted. The entire parts of the city were destroyed and the city changed beyond recognition. Many symbols of Mughliyah Saltanat were demolished and most of its treasures stolen. The famed Lal Qila was turned into a magazine and a garrison for firangi troops. Architecturally delicate marble pavilions were pulled down to create ugly army barracks. The Delhi railway station was built after further demolition inside the Lal Qila. Soon a clock tower appeared at the center of Chandni Chowk and a brand new Town Hall was erected in 1863 on the main street, initially known as Lawrence Institute and later the Municipality corporation. New roads like 'Nai Sarak' were created to provide easy access to the firangi fauj in case of another 'Ghadr'. Countless residences of Dilliwallahs were forcefully removed to suit the new masters. A new city within a city was created in the posh Civil Lines.

In 1863, Hukumat-i-Britannia erected a Victory Memorial at the Ridge, which records the number of soldiers who died or were wounded in the battle for Delhi. The casualties among the firangis were recorded by name and the sacrifice of their Indian brothers-in-arms was mentioned only as fourteen "native" sipahis. And at this moment, the past was erased and new history books were introduced. The historians dropped the eyewitness accounts of the orgy of blood and terror undertaken by the firangis. Alternatively, efforts were made to suggest that the Indians had invited them to rule over India. The new colonial masters, the commercially astute Hukumat-i-Britannia combined a policy of co-operation and conciliation with a policy of coercion and force and altered the character of the city of Delhi.

During the Mughliyah Saltanat, the astonishing and accidental intermingling of peoples, cultures, and ideas gave birth to the *Ganga-Jamuni Tehzeeb* of India – a distinctive way of life spawned by the coming together of two great oceans – India and Islam. Sir John Hubert Marshall, who was the Director-General of the Archaeological Survey of India from 1902 to 1928 had appropriately remarked, "Seldom in the history of mankind has the spectacle been witnessed of two civilizations so vast and so strongly developed, yet so radically dissimilar as the Muhammadan and Hindu, meeting and mingling together".

In all of history, it is said there is not a more dramatic tale.

Devoid of a major role in governance, the last Mughal Shehenshah Zafar presided over a creative and literary court – a culture of artists and scholars. In this period, recognized as the Delhi renaissance, the famed city of the Mughals grew intellectually and science, humanities and Urdu Shayari thrived. The culture of Shayari in Delhi represented the erudite elite and part of the compositeness of North Indian cultural sophistication. By the mid-nineteenth century, the Shayari of Mir Taqi Mir, Momin Khan Momin, Ibrahim Zauq and Mirza Asadullah Khan Ghalib reached the peak of refinement for its imaginative vision, the exactness of observation and aptness of style.

The significance of Hindu-Muslim unity as indicated by the Ghadr of 1857 and Delhi's famed *Ganga-Jamuni Tehzeeb* from the reign of the Mughliyah Saltanat was not lost on the firangis. Lord John Elphinstone, Governor of Bombay in 1858, remarked, "Divide et impera was the old Roman motto and it should be ours." A systematic strategy of fomenting separate consciousness between the two main communities – the Hindus and the Muslims was launched. The seeds of division were sown to thwart a unified nationalist movement that could overthrow the Hukumat-i-Britannia. There began to emerge a new realization of separate interests and separate identities among the Hindus and Muslims.

After the annus horribilis of 1857 many eminent horror-struck Dilliwallahs including the leading poets of Delhi unable to accept the new rulers relocated to other parts of India. Officially the population declined from an estimated 152,000 persons living in the walled city alone in 1853–54 to 142,000 in the entire region of Delhi by 1864. *(Cambridge Economic History of India)*

There was a greater realization that the damage done by the Hukumat-i-Britannia to the culture of India was irreversible.

Sazaa-e-Kalapani – The Devil's Island

Two hundred Indian convicts disembarked at Ross Island, the smallest of the five hundred and seventy-six islands that form the Andaman and Nicobar archipelago on March 10th, 1858 abroad the frigate 'Semiramis'. The men were under the overall responsibility of the Superintendent, Dr. James Pattison Walker, who was supported in his undertaking by a guard of sixty naval brigade men, two doctors, and an overseer. Surrounded by hundreds of kilometers of ocean in every direction the 'Sazaa-e-Kalapani' provided no hope of escape and was designed with the sole purpose of keeping the men in isolation. The penal colony was a 'devil's experiment' that involved torture, medical tests, forced labor and for many the ultimate escape – death.

After the Ghadr of 1857, among Hukumat-i-Britannia's first acts in 1858 was to set up a penal colony on the remote Andaman Islands of Bay of Bengal and start exiling political prisoners to it. The penal settlement on the Andamans is the darkest chapter in the history of Hukumat-i-Britannia's ninety-year rule over India that is filled with several brutal and dark chapters.

Based on a mythical Indian story about the faithful being parted from their souls by crossing the sea Hukumat-i-Britannia created a psychological gulag based around the Sanskrit term *'Kala Paani'* (black waters or waters of death). It took days of travel on the seas and crossing the forbidden 'black waters', and it was not only physically challenging, but the banished prisoners additionally felt immense guilt for abandoning India at the time of colonial rule and severe famine. Leaving the Indian soil and the regenerating waters of the Holy Ganges meant the end of the reincarnation cycle for millions of Indians and the possibility of never reaching a higher caste status. In the godless Andamans, they would lose their religious observations and become part of a living hell. Short of capital punishment 'Sazaa-e-Kalapani' was the cruelest sentence reserved for special prisoners for it not only demoralized the men but also completely broke them.

On February 8th, 1872, the British Viceroy of India, Richard Bourke, 6th Earl of Mayo (1822–1872), the third most powerful person in the British Empire after Queen Victoria and Prime Minister William Ewart Gladstone, stopped off in the Andaman Islands. Prison reform was one of Lord Mayo's areas of interest. Heavily protected by his security detail he made an impromptu and unplanned stop to admire the view at Mount Harriet. As he began to walk up the pier leading to his boat with evening darkness coming on, the kitchen knife-wielding convict Sher Ali Afridi fastened like a tiger on the British Viceroy's back and stabbed him twice. Within minutes Lord Mayo lay dead. Sher Ali Afridi who was a former orderly to the Commissioner of Peshawar did not attempt to escape and was hanged on March 11th, 1873.

Britain was saddened by the ghastly crime and there was a general feeling of horror at the act across the Empire. At the same time the sensational news excited

Indians as no British Viceroy, the representative of the power of Hukumat-i-Britannia, had ever been assassinated or seriously threatened.

Too Big to Fail

Twenty years following the Ghadr of 1857, on the morning of first day of January 1877, after a roar of guns, a fanfare of trumpeters and a display of firecrackers, British Viceroy Lord Lytton (1831–1891) sitting on a magnificently decked tall elephant marched in procession through Delhi with Lady Edith Villiers Lytton by his side.

At exactly noon he walked across eight hundred feet of the red carpet to enter the Durbar at the Coronation Park – a newly erected site in northwest Delhi. The Proclamation Durbar in Delhi was the most extravagant spectacle in the subcontinent's living memory in a city. Delhi was chosen as the site of the pompous ceremony 'forever bound up with the history of India'. Thirty-four years later Lord Lytton's son in law the architect Edwin Lutyens (1869–1944) would transform Delhi into an imperial city – the Rome of Hindustan.

After inspecting a guard of honor, Lord Lytton entered an opulent blue tent specially raised for the occasion. As he took his imperial seat he was surrounded by the heads of every department of Government, 1,200 of the noble band of civil servants, 14,000 splendidly equipped and disciplined firangi troops and Indian sipahis and seventy-seven of the ruling Maharajas of India representing territories as large as Great Britain, France and Germany combined plus some 84,000 Dilliwallahs. Major Osmond Barnes of the Tenth Bengal Cavalry and the Chief Herald, stepped forward and read the Imperial Proclamation in English, announcing the assumption of the Imperial title by British Queen Victoria, as the *'Qaiser-e-Hind'* (Empress of India) in absentia.

At its conclusion hundred and one salutes of artillery, intermingled with feuz de joie from the assembled firangi troops and Indian sipahis were fired. The Royal Standard was hoisted in the heart of India and the bands again played, 'God Save the Queen' as all the guests stood in attention.

Then Lord Lytton as part of his speech for the day read out a telegraphic message from the Queen who was to succeed the Shehenshahs of the Mughliyah Saltanat, stating, "We Victoria by the grace of God of the United Kingdom, Queen, Empress of India send though our Viceroy to all our officers, civil and military and to all Princes, chiefs and the people now at Delhi assemble our Royal and Imperial greeting and assure them of the deep interest and earnest affection with which we regard the people of our Indian Empire... We have witnessed with heartfelt satisfaction the reception they have accorded to our beloved son, and have been touched by the evidence of their loyalty and attachment to our House and Throne. We trust the present occasion may tend to unite in bonds of yet closer affection ourselves and our subjects, that from the highest to the humblest all may feel that under our rule the great principles of liberty, equity, and justice are secured to them and that to promote their happiness, to add to their prosperity, and advance their welfare, are the ever-present aims and objects of our Empire." Thereafter audience rose to their feet as a flourish of trumpets and richly caparisoned elephants trumpeted behind them.

After the proclamation of Queen Victoria, as the 'Qaiser-e-Hind', Britain became the most powerful nation in the world. In the Victorian age, Britain surpassed all its competitors in Europe in accomplishing world domination. The mighty British Empire ruled over one-sixth of the world. Never before in the history of humankind, there was a comparable kingdom with the extent, wealth, discipline or control of the British Empire. It ruled the waves and it took a domineering role in determining the future of humankind. The British saw themselves as the masters abroad and a peaceful commercial nation at home.

Meanwhile, Queen Victoria who never visited India and ruled from her palace in faraway London delighted in her new dignity as the 'Qaiser-e-Hind' took lessons in Urdu from her Indian attendants. But for her Indian subjects, the British Imperial history was the tragic story of oppression, prejudice, and conquests by brute force. Any Indian who opposed Hukumat-i-Britannia's economic and administrative policies was labeled as a 'traitor' and there were dreadful consequences including a life term of the 'Sazaa-e-Kalapani'.

In Delhi, the Dilliwallahs who endured the brunt of the firangi atrocities held on to the memories of the Ghadr of 1857 and the inspirational poetry from the reign of the last Mughal Shehenshah Bahadur Shah Zafar. Half a century later the events of the Ghadr of 1857 and the first Indian war of independence remained the prime-motivating factor for the second Indian war of independence – Ghadr Party of India and as well as for the Azad Hind Fauj (Indian National Army), the third and final Indian war of independence with the city of Delhi serving as a backdrop.

3

THE MIRACLE BOY FROM INDIA

"He (Har Dayal) was then quite a young boy of 16 or 17 years reading
at St. Stephens College and both of us were amazed to meet the young
man who at that age had read so extensively and had such clear cut ideas…"

Sir Tej Bahadur Sapru
Indian Lawyer and Political Leader

The particularly cold and snowy evening of Tuesday, January 22nd, 1901, in London was a fateful day for the British Empire.

That evening, Sir Frank Green, the Lord Mayor of London received an important message from Albert Edward, The Prince of Wales (1841–1910) that disclosed, "My beloved mother the Queen has just passed away, surrounded by her children and grandchildren".

The city of London calmly received the distressing news of the death of Queen Victoria. London was the city of the dead. It was as if everyone in Britain had lost a father or a mother. In her passing, Britain lost a monarch whose rule in the annals of history is incomparable. Her demise brought an end to the sixty-three-year reign, the longest in British history. She governed over a global Empire in a period of great events, manifold changes and unsurpassed national prosperity. She had additionally seen the growth of an Empire on which the sun never set. With her departure almost coinciding with the end of the nineteenth century a long chapter of peace within the British Empire also ended.

It was the beginning of a new age for Hukumat-i-Britannia. An era where the existence of the British rule in India came under threat. This was the seedtime for a revolution that would shake the foundation of the Empire and challenge its complacency and raison d'etre like never before.

The Pen is Mightier than the Sword

On the day of national mourning in Great Britain, in another part of the British Empire, a subject of Hukumat-i-Britannia, the sixteen-year-old Har Dayal sat next to a flickering lamp in his house in Delhi engrossed in reading a thick book. Far removed from the mourning for the 'Qaiser-e-Hind' in distant London and the great demonstrations of sorrow that were to follow across India, the young Dilliwallah was consumed by his quest to expand his mind in the shadows of the Mughal monuments of Delhi.

Born on Tuesday, November 18ᵗʰ, 1884 just over a quarter-century after the Ghadr of 1857, Har Dayal was the son of Bholi Rani and Gauri Dayal Mathur. (Har Dayal's date of birth is often mistaken as October 14ᵗʰ, 1884 but his University admission form in his handwriting records November 18ᵗʰ, 1884)

Har Dayal's grandfather Lala Bhawani Shankar was employed in the court of Neemrana State, a small region within Alwar State. (*Lala* is an honorific used particularly in North India with connotations ranging from 'Respected Brother' to a 'Learned' person'. Har Dayal in the course of his life would also be known as Lala Har Dayal). His father Gauri Dayal Mathur, the youngest of four brothers (Lakshmi Narayan, Madho Narayan, and Bishambar Dayal) was a scholar of Persian and Urdu. He was employed by the Hukumat-i-Britannia as a reader in the District Court of Delhi. He had a large family of seven children – four sons and three daughters. Har Dayal was the youngest of the four brothers, Kishan Dayal, Bhairo Dayal, and Manohar Lal. They belonged to a socially progressive and literate family of the time-worn metropolis of Delhi.

The Dayal family home was in the neighborhood of Cheera Khana off Nai Sarak in Delhi. The main street came to be called 'Nai Sarak' because it was a relatively newer, broader street built after the Ghadr of 1857 and connected the older Chawri Bazaar market to the newly built Town Hall in Chandni Chowk. Nai Sarak was officially named Egerton Road, in honor of a British civil servant, Philip H. Egerton – the Deputy Commissioner of Delhi.

The population of the seventeenth-century city had steadily declined after the Ghadr of 1857 and by 1901 the total population of Delhi according to *Cambridge Economic History of India* was 208,000, in comparison to close to 847,796 people that lived in the capital city of Calcutta. In that era, clusters in the city of Delhi were based on occupation, community or religion. With its web of intermingling lanes and bagichis, the residential area of Cheera Khana was predominantly a bastion of Kayathas (the community of scribes in India). Har Dayal's family too belonged to the social sect of scribes. Cut-off from the traditions of the Indian caste system, the community of scribes were neither warriors, priests nor traders but freethinking intellectuals. Pen, paper, and service were intimately part of their identity and consequently, vocations based on high literacy became their domain expertise. Besides they retained a strong sense of culture; were cosmopolitan, sophisticated, affluent, politically pragmatic, linguistically gifted and spiritually inclined. The scribe community in India is still symbolized by a divine figure wielding a pen, inkpot, and a sword.

This community considers the dash of a pen as more significant than the counter use of a lance.

From the earliest period of Indian history, the scribes kept the enormous administrative machinery of the various Maharajas from Rajput kingdoms to the Mughliyah Saltanat well oiled. At its height, the Mughliyah Saltanat (1526 to 1707) was the richest Empire on the planet. The Saltanat was as much a standing military cantonment as it was a *kaghazi raj* and the scribes skillfully governed this centralized vibrant state. In the reign of Mughal Shehenshah Jalaluddin Akbar (1556–1605) the community of scribes emerged as among the 'nine gems' of the Mughal courts. The scribes were appointed as the *Munshis* and occupied center stage in the emerging discourse on the *munshi khana* of the Mughliyah Saltanat. They managed the official correspondence of the Mughliyah Saltanat – *the Dar-ul-Insha* that was believed to be the largest in the world in the age of Mughal governance. Significantly these scribes were also recognized as a representation of the harmony between Hindus and Muslims.

In Delhi, after the Ghadr of 1857, living in the times of Hukumat-i-Britannia the relatively small community of scribes were able to keep their original culture intact and at the same time reluctantly accept the British as the new rulers of India. They survived and even flourished through a combination of political flexibility, non-sectarian spiritualism and a continuing commitment to education and intellectual life. Soon complete fluency over English and Persian in addition to Sanskrit, each with its script, became synonymous with the community of scribes. The Hukumat-i-Britannia officially recorded that the community was well represented in the revenue offices, the courts of justice and the literary professions in Upper India.

The Miracle Boy

On a regular day, a small boy barely into his teens walked into the small library at the Cambridge Mission School in Delhi to return the thick books he had borrowed to read the week before. The librarian at his school wondered at his ability to read so many books meant for older people at one time. After returning the books the young Har Dayal could astonishingly recall the entire text verbatim. As a school student, he had read everything he could get his hands on and it was widely reported amongst his fellow students and teachers that he could remember the contents of each volume in excruciating detail. He had inherited his love for books from his erudite father and his deep insights into spirituality from his devout mother. At school, he was engrossed in the primers published by the Royal Society of England and even terse books written by British thinkers like John Stuart Mills, Herbert Spencer and Thomas Huxley. Har Dayal's natural gifts and a nurturing environment provided him the motivation and tenacity to read biographies of Alexander, Napoléon and to comprehend the works of Socrates and Plato. He similarly amazed his family members, fellow students, and teachers when by grade six he read the editorials of the newspaper *Tribune* and the magazine *Harbinger* and reproduced the texts perfectly.

It was clear that Har Dayal had the gift of eidetic memory, (photographic memory). Not surprisingly, with no tools at his disposal other than the force of his intellect, he completed his schooling at the Cambridge Mission School at fourteen and had an academic record like no one else in India at that time.

Author and journalist Khushwant Singh (1915–2014) reminisced about Har Dayal in a newspaper article published in *Tribune* (August 16th, 2003). He wrote, "While I was still at school, the one name that was on all lips as the paradigm of the ultimate in scholarship was that of Har Dayal. His name was always prefixed by two words, the great: he was the great Har Dayal. Stories of his greatness as a student multiplied. He had a phenomenal memory: he had to read a book once and he could reproduce its contents word for word; he was not only a topper in every subject, but he also broke previous records with wide margins in every exam he took. Though this was not absolutely correct because at times he was beaten by other examinees to the second place, but people refused to believe it."

Across Delhi, the young Har Dayal was celebrated as the 'miracle boy'.

The miracle boy initial education was impacted by the remnants of the famed Delhi renaissance and he grew intellectually and culturally within the space of the walled city. In that era, the lives of the Dilliwallahs revolved around its beautiful main thoroughfare, Chandni Chowk. Like all the Dilliwallahs, the young Har Dayal lived the four seasons in the city, walked through the maze-like lanes of Delhi, played near the ancient monuments, learnt swimming in the river Yamuna, flew kites from the roof, relished the Delhi cuisines, adored the intense chess competitions, appreciated the local poet's ghazals and bait bazi and was the resident expert in the sport of pigeon flying. After school, he would gather all the youngsters of his neighborhood and teach them English and Mathematics. Among the young kids was Hanwant Sahai (1881–1975), who was Har Dayal's classmate but dropped out of school and later joined the nationalist movement along with him. The young children would often ask him to read the English alphabets or recite the mathematics tables in reverse and he would astonish them with his intellectual feats.

Har Dayal developed a life-long attachment to the city and its *Ganga-Jamuni Tehzeeb* was strongly reflected in the cultured demeanor throughout his life. It was a distinctive city at that time best expressed in the words of the poet Mir Taqi Mir –

"Dilli jo ek sheher tha, aalam mein intekhaab,
Rehte thay muntakhab hi jahaan rozgaar ke"

(Delhi, that was a city unique on the globe
Where lived only the chosen of the time)

Har Dayal's parents recognized his academic talents and encouraged him to pursue higher studies like his elder brothers who became lawyers. He didn't have a choice. His father and his elder brothers followed the dictum of the community of scribes, *'Kayastha Bachcha, ya padha bhala ya mara bhala'* (A Kayastha child will study or perish).

Har Dayal following the family tradition entered the reputed St. Stephen's College (locally called the Mission College), to study Sanskrit in the Bachelor of Arts program and his Sanskrit teacher was Pandit Raghubir Dayal, a nationalist. An extension to the Cambridge Mission School, St. Stephen's College had opened its doors on February 1st, 1881 with just five students and three teachers in an eighteenth-century haveli called Sheesh Mahal in Kinari Bazar in Delhi. The college was affiliated to the University of Punjab in Lahore and began building a formidable reputation in academics. Initially, it taught the four-year Bachelor's degree course at Calcutta University in English, History, Geography,

General Science and study of The Bible. In 1885, the College, for the first time introduced the Bachelor of Arts degree, and Makkhan Lall became the first graduate. The resumption of Sanskrit learning was one of Principal Reverend Samuel Scott Allnutt's most cherished hopes and Pandit Bihari Prasad Dube was recruited to teach Sanskrit. By December 8th, 1891, it moved to a newly constructed building in Kashmiri Gate that was inaugurated by Lt. Governor of Delhi, Sir James Lyall.

At St. Stephen's for the first time, Har Dayal came in direct contact with the ruling class of India, as the Christian missionaries were his teachers. Reverend George Hibbert-Ware, a gentle and unassuming man of deep sensitivity and sympathy, taught at St. Stephens from 1898 to 1906 and was the third Principal of the college (1902–07). He was a keen footballer and joined the nascent nationalist movement with expansive enthusiasm. He broke new ground by making systematic visits to the homes of students. Har Dayal was inspired by the social commitment, religious pluralism, and selflessness of these educators from Cambridge and Oxford. At St. Stephens, he became a member of the Young Men's Christian Association.

Though he suffered from health issues, Har Dayal showed great promise while at St. Stephens College and acquired astonishing fluency in English, Hindi, Sanskrit, Urdu, and Persian. A dazzling product of Delhi's famed *Ganga-Jamuni Tehzeeb*, the Dilliwallah enjoyed the Persian and Urdu poetry. He was also captivated with Edwin Arnold's *The Light of Asia* and memorized it from beginning to end during his first year at St. Stephen's College, as he could not afford to buy a copy.

His legend spread across India through his writings and scholastic feats during his college days. Sir Tej Bahadur Sapru (1875–1949), an illustrious lawyer of India, decades later in an article in *The Tribune* (September 17th, 1938), recalled being introduced to the boyish Har Dayal, "The first time that I knew of him was so far back as 1902 or 1903 when he wrote a remarkable article in *The Hindustan Review*. My friend Mr. Sachchidanand Sinha (a distinguished educationist, lawyer, and journalist who published *The Hindustan Review* and *Kayastha Samachar* from Allahabad) and I happened to go shortly after to Delhi and then we made his acquaintance. He was then quite a young boy of 16 or 17 years reading at St. Stephens College and both of us were amazed to meet the young man who at that age had read so extensively and had such clear cut ideas."

The Most Eligible Bachelor

In 1900 at the age of sixteen, Har Dayal was one of the most eligible bachelors of Delhi. Following the established social practice at that time in an arranged match he was married to Sunder Rani, the attractive and talented daughter of the aristocratic Diwan Gopal Chand, one of the three Naib Nazims (Magistrate/Sessions Judge), in the princely state of Patiala. Sunder Rani was six years younger than Har Dayal. Apart from belonging to the social community of Har Dayal, Sunder Rani's grandfather originally from Meerut was a Diwan of Patiala State. The charismatic Maharaja Sir Bhupinder Singh was the ruler of Patiala State, a self-governing princely state outside British India during the British rule in India.

At this stage, a bright young boy, Gobind Behari Lal (1889–1982) who was Diwan Gopal Chand's cousin and as well as an uncle of Sunder Rani came into contact with Har Dayal. Gobind's (referred to in this book as Gobind or Gobind Behari Lal) father, Bishan Lal Mathur was a *Tehsildar* (civil servant) in the state of Bikaner and spent his initial years there. Gobind considered Har Dayal his 'Guru' (mentor) and reminisced later, "I came under the influence then of a senior student, five years older than me, and a classmate of one of my brothers. He was the most important friend in my life, in a way… He was closely related to me, my family." Gobind subsequently joined Har Dayal in his nationalist enterprises and became his lifelong admirer.

Har Dayal furthermore founded the Delhi Kayastha Sabha for elderly persons of his community in Chelpuri neighborhood of Delhi that was part of the nationwide association – the Kayastha Sadar Sabha Hind (National association of the community of scribes). The objective of the Kayastha Sadar Sabha Hind was to promote education within the community by founding schools, publishing books, advancing female education, hindering wedding extravagances and revising the age for marriage that was as low as 11–13 years at that time.

The Nationalistic Impulse

At the turn of the century, though barely out of his teens and still a student of St. Stephen's College, Har Dayal knocked at the door of a large house, 'Prem Dham' at Dariba Kalan then a fashionable area of Delhi. On stating the password he was allowed entry to attend a secret meeting. It was the house of Amir Chand (1869–1915), a highly respected Dilliwallah and his teacher at the Cambridge

Mission School. Amir Chand later published books and also an Urdu weekly, the *Imperial Fortnightly Advertisers* and *Akash* as well as a religious journal called *Thundering Dawn*. Amir Chand's house was the rendezvous for a group of revolutionaries including the distinguished teachers at St. Stephens, Pandit Raghubir Dayal and Syed Haider Raza. Another Dilliwallah Master Awadh Behari, a University gold medalist in Mathematics who had joined St. Stephens as a Professor in 1904 was part of this group. Har Dayal attended the meetings of the secret society that promoted revolutionary work in North India.

The reminiscences of the Ghadr of 1857 even after close to five decades reverberated in the minds of the Dilliwallahs. Time and history could not destroy a collective storehouse of memories of the atrocities committed by the firangis. The youngsters of Delhi grew up hearing stories of Hukumat-i-Britannia's massacres as they were passed on from father to son. The legends of merciless murders and fates worse than death were a constant theme in the family tales. Even the mere sight of a man in a European hat in Delhi was enough to scatter a crowd and send everyone away shuddering. Those who had witnessed or participated in the Ghadr against the British were venerated as kind of demigods.

After the formal takeover of India in 1859, the reforming influence of the Hukumat-i-Britannia in India was not limited to its locomotives and law books. On December 28th, 1885, the first session of the Indian National Congress, a forum for emerging nationalist sentiment, was held in the hall of Gokuldas Tejpal Sanskrit College at Bombay. Allan Octavian Hume (1829–1912) a fifty-six-year-old British civil servant serving in India, had founded the Indian National Congress. As Magistrate and Collector of Etawah district during the Ghadr of 1857, Hume had led an irregular force of 650 Indian sipahis in defense of the area and kept a daily record of skirmishes with the mutineers. Hume wanted the Indian National Congress to be a 'safety valve' to prevent the repeat of a mass upheaval like the Ghadr. In its first decade, the Indian National Congress became a pressure group of Indian notables seeking no more than colonial self-government and greater political autonomy within the British Empire. Its members were a set of articulate professionals – lawyers, journalists, doctors and business magnets that had emerged as anglophiles and were called 'Macaulay's children'.

At the 1896 session of the Indian National Congress held in Calcutta, poet Rabindranath Tagore (1861–1941) sang the poem, *'Bande Mataram'* (Hail Mother India). It had originally appeared in *Anandamath*, a novel published in 1882 by writer Bankim Chandra Chattopadhyaya (1838–1894). It partial translation in English read:

"Mother, I bow to thee!
Rich with thy hurrying streams,
bright with orchard gleams,
Cool with thy winds of delight,
Dark fields waving Mother of might,
Mother free.
Glory of moonlight dreams,
Over thy branches and lordly streams,
Clad in thy blossoming trees,
Mother, giver of ease
Laughing low and sweet!
Mother I kiss thy feet,
Speaker sweet and low!
Mother, to thee I bow...."

'Bande Matram' gripped the imagination of Indians and became theme song of India's freedom movement. It was reflected in the greetings and rallying cries of the anti-Hukumat-i-Britannia forces working secretly and underground.

One such group of anti-colonial nationalists regularly gathered at Amir Chand's 'Prem Dham' in Delhi to discuss political ideas and events. It was a difficult time for the nationalists serving in the Hukumat-i-Britannia's institutions as even the staff members of St. Stephens's college referred to their Indian colleagues as 'natives'. Across British ruled India Indians were regular recipients of insults and violence and were treated like second-class citizens in their motherland. During these years political protests were unknown and non-existent. Most Indians pretended to be loyal to the British King and were conscious of the fact that they were subservient to the dreaded Hukumat-i-Britannia. At Amir Chand's house during the secret meeting a few fiery revolutionaries began expressing, "We want the British out," "We want home rule," and "we want 'Indianization".

However unknown to Har Dayal, Hukumat-i-Britannia's spies were aware of these clandestine undertakings and had opened a confidential file on him. Fearing the possibility of a Russian incursion into India, the first British Indian

Secret Service (intelligence) department was established by Hukumat-i-Britannia in 1878 at Simla. According to the National Archives of India (NAI) documents in 1902, the Police Commission under the Lt. Governor of Bengal, Sir Andrew Henderson Leith Fraser (1848–1919) recommended the creation of a central Department of Criminal Intelligence (DCI). The existing staff of the Thugee Department was absorbed in the DCI and it was headquartered in Simla and an initial secret service fund of Rs. 12,000 was assigned to the department. The DCI was assisted by the Criminal Investigation Department in each province in British India, under a Deputy Inspector General of Police. It was for "collating and distributing information regarding organized crime and to assist in the investigation of crimes when they are of special character." These clandestine departments staffed by the best British or Anglo Indian police officers in British India effectively monitored the revolutionary activity against the Hukumat-i-Britannia in India.

From now onwards British Secret Service operatives trailed Har Dayal for the rest of his life. Then an event held in Delhi overwhelmed all the Dilliwallahs including the miracle boy.

The Greatest Power in the World

On Monday, December 29th, 1902, the historic capital of India – Delhi, became the scene of incomparable magnificence and splendor and all the Dilliwallahs witnessed the unbridled power of Hukumat-i-Britannia.

Oxford-educated Lord George Nathaniel Curzon, 1st Marquess Curzon of Kedleston (1859–1925), the British Viceroy of India since 1899, relished the medieval pomp and ceremony that came with his job and he decided to hold a Mughal style Durbar in the Mughal capital to recognize Edward VII as the new Emperor of India. He was a convinced imperialist who believed the notion of Britain's "civilizing mission" in India and also wanted to publically endorse that India was firmly under the control of His Majesty's Government. According to Nicholas Mansergh's *The Commonwealth Experience,* Lord Curzon had written, "As long as we rule India, we are the greatest power in the world. If we lose it, we shall drop straight away to a third-rate power."

On the cold December morning in 1902, Lord and Lady Mary Victoria Curzon along with British Royalty, Prince Arthur, the Duke of Connaught and the third son of Queen Victoria, and Princess Louise Margaret, Duchess of Connaught, reached Delhi by train. They took part in a state procession through the famed central avenue of Chandni Chowk and out to the Durbar site on an elephant witnessed by thousands of Dilliwallahs including Har Dayal. They entered the Durbar amid a salute of thirty-one guns. The British National Anthem, "God Save the King", was played with full gusto. Over three hundred veterans of the Ghadr of 1857 attended the main ceremony. Lord Curzon summoned over a hundred Maharajas of India, and they made their attendance visible to the world by arriving on elephants caparisoned in gold and flashing with gems. In a group photograph taken at the event, Lord Curzon is seen seated with Dukes, Lords, and Generals beside a hundred and fifteen British subjects.

Lord Curzon's unparalleled display of splendor eclipsed even the mightiest Shehenshahs of the Mughliyah Saltanat. The entire pageant was a combination of oriental exuberance and wealth with western precision of organization. He lined up a procession of his army along with military bands to send a message that it was greater indeed than any army in the neighborhood The reverberations of the booming cannons sent the message loud and clear – the British had replaced the Mughals as the legitimate rulers of India and any sign of resistance would be crushed with overwhelming power.

It was heard far and wide.

Though, from the perspective of the spectators, the timing of the Durbar was erroneous as it was preceded by a horrible famine. In 1899–1900, the areas of Agra, Oudh, Bengal, Central Provinces, Rajputana, and Gujarat were under the grip of a severe famine that claimed millions of lives. The opulence displayed at the Durbar was seen as an insult to the feelings of millions of Indians. Lord Curzon brazenly faced the disapproval from the Indian press.

Hukumat-i-Britannia was akin to a military-backed dictatorship over Indians who were now aware that British merchants looted their nation's wealth while it's military and civilian officials sought power and privilege. The nationalist leader from Poona (Pune now), Bal Gangadhar Tilak (1856–1920), wrote an editorial in his magazine *Kesari* stating that instead of this unjustified ostentatious expenditure, if the Government had remitted the debts of the cultivators, the expenses would have been much less and the people would have blessed the Government. He added that it should be remembered that the very ground on which this Durbar took place in Delhi, had seen so many Empires reduced to ashes. *The Review of Reviews* reminded the participants of the Durbar that, behind the glitter of the Maharaja's jewelry and diamonds there were millions of invisible hungry and destitute Indians. *Kayastha Samachar,* in an editorial note, ridiculed the Maharaja of Rewa for bringing a white elephant for the Delhi Durbar while thousands of his subjects had taken shelter in Delhi during the famine.

There goes Har Dayal

At the end of winter in 1903, Har Dayal impeded by illhealth, traveled to Lahore, the capital of the state of Punjab, by train to appear in the final examinations for the Bachelor of Arts degree. A local legend claimed, he was asked to answer any six of the twelve questions of the subject within three hours in the form of essays. Amazingly he answered all and wrote a note that the examiner could choose to grade any six. The results of the Bachelor of Arts final examination at the University of Punjab were announced in the summer of 1903. Though Har Dayal secured the first division, for the first time in his school and his academic career, he dropped to the second place. Nevertheless, his facility with multiple languages, his phenomenal memory, profound reading, and an incredibly sharp mind enabled him to finish his Bachelor of Arts examinations at St. Stephen's College at a young age of eighteen.

A few months later, Har Dayal was back in Lahore along with his heavy trunks and baskets. Having been surpassed by a student from Lahore in the final BA examination he wanted to pursue a Master's degree at the Punjab University in Lahore. He entered the prominent Government College, Lahore and the subject for his Master of Arts degree was English Literature.

Punjab University came into existence in 1882. Earlier in 1879, British Viceroy Lord Lytton presided over the convocation of 'Punjab University College' held in its convocation hall. As maintained by the *Punjab Census Report of 1901,* the proportion of educated persons was one in twenty-six and the percentage was still low as compared to other provinces. In Bengal, 1,039 students passed their intermediate and 329 completed their graduation in 1900–1901 and their number was 244 and 127 respectively in Punjab. Dr. Gothlieb Wilhelm Leitner (1840–1899) an educationist and diplomat had set up Lahore's Government College in 1864. The majestic college building designed in Gothic style by William H. Purdon, Superintendent Engineer and constructed in 1877 under the supervision of Executive Engineer Kannhaiya Lal. It was an old structure and in the year 1903 gates and fences were put up to give the grounds the appearance of an educational building. Reflecting the neo-gothic tradition, the building had grandeur and design that adapted to the climate of Lahore. The classrooms with high ceilings were accessed from a deep and wide verandah that also protected from the strong sun. The two-story residential hostel for students had six dining rooms; three storerooms and three separate kitchens. Besides having its graduates join as civil servants in the Hukumat-i-Britannia the college built a decent reputation in sports with an excellent cricket team. A Scotsman, Professor Samuel Robson of the Bengal Educational Service was the Principal of Government College and the Professor of English since 1898 having relocated from Dacca College.

After his enrollment at the University, Har Dayal was initially awarded a stipend based on his previous academic performance. Within months he was additionally the recipient of the highly prized 'Aitchison – Ramrattan Sanskrit Scholarship' of Rs. 15 per month at Punjab University for two consecutive years (1903–1905). A believer in austerity, he lived simply and never drank or smoked. Among his college mates, he was known as *'haft zuban'* (master of seven languages) for his knowledge of Sanskrit, Hindi, Persian, Urdu, English, and Punjabi to which he now added Pashto.

At the University, Har Dayal was soon considered the most brilliant man in the province of Punjab. He was first in everything, his memory was phenomenal and he could remember entire books by heart. He spent long hours studying in the college library and he could recite William Shakespeare's 'Othello' in its entirity without glancing at his notes.

An American academic, Dr. Hervey DeWitt Griswold (1860–1945), the Professor of Philosophy at Forman Christian College and its librarian, was stunned by the extraordinary memory skills of the university student. He recorded in his book, *Insights into Modern Hinduism*, "He (Har Dayal) attended my lectures on Tennyson's *In Memoriam* in the Forman Christian College, Lahore, an arrangement existing between these two Lahore colleges of the Punjab University for joint lectures in MA English subjects. Along with his fellow students he sought to master the text of *In Memoriam*, and at the same time, as a work of supererogation, he committed a large part of the poem to memory. One evening he gave a public exhibition of his powers of memory. Eight or ten masses of strange, unconnected material, including several long sentences in Pashto, were successively sounded into his ears for him to assimiliate and reproduce. Everything came out in the order in which it went in, and perfectly. It was an example in modern India of the high development in ancient India of the same faculty, by which, for example, the whole text of the Rigveda could be carried in the memory of those who were in a very real sense living manuscripts." Har Dayal's English Professor and the College Principal, Samuel Robson (1853–1914) was reported to have warned him quite earnestly that such mental strain would result in permanent brain damage. But nothing stopped Har Dayal. According to a much-repeated tale, on being informed about the existence of a man with a spectacular brain in south India, the young prodigy gave a public demonstration of his intellectual gifts; he repeated verses in Sanskrit and English that were being recited by his friends, solved a mathematical problem, counted the ringing of the bell at a nearby temple and won a game of chess all at the same time and with a smile!

In March 1880 in an article in *Athenoeum*, the celebrated Sanskrit Professor Sir Monier-Williams had written about the mind-boggling multi-tasking power of memory of Indians, called 'Satavadhani', persons who could concentrate on a hundred things at once. He also described the 'Trinsadavadhanis', persons who could do thirty tasks at a time and also the 'Ashtavadhanis' or people capable of simultaneously attending to eight jobs at once. The Polish-American mathematician Mark Kac (1914–1984) delineated the bifurcation of human brilliance by degree and termed two kinds of geniuses; the ordinary and the magicians. His appreciation of the magicians pertains to Har Dayal and he wrote, "An ordinary genius is a (person) that you and I would be just as good as, if we were only many times better. There is no mystery as to how his mind works... It is different with the magicians.... Even after we understand what they have done, the process by which they have done it is completely dark. They seldom, if ever, have students because they cannot be emulated and it must be terribly frustrating for a brilliant young mind to cope with the mysterious ways in which the magician's mind works."

After consuming several books his brain was already roaming far beyond his age. It was slowly becoming apparent that this budding genius would make a mark in history and win legendary popularity. Dr. Dharmavira, in his biography, *Lala Har Dayal and Revolutionary Movements of His Times*, has verified, "wherever he went about in town, students would point at him – there goes Har Dayal."

The pen must retain what the sword had won

Bigger than Delhi, Lahore, the capital of Punjab, was a culturally and politically vibrant city of North India at that time with a population of over two hundred thousand people. This walled city stood on the Grand Trunk Road that since antiquity had linked the Indian subcontinent to Asia. It was often said, *Jisne Lahore Nai Dekhya O Jamyai Nai* (Anyone who has not seen Lahore hasn't really lived).

A statue of Sir John Lawrence (1811–1879), the British hero of the Ghadr of 1857, built by Sir Edgar Boehm, was raised on Mall Road in Lahore, in March 1887, paying homage to the former British Viceroy of India. He was the man who was responsible for subjugating the province of Punjab during the Ghadr in 1857. The inflammatory inscription on its base read, "Will you be governed by the pen or the sword". A few years later, Har Dayal observed in a series of essays in the Lahore based newspaper *The Punjabee*, "It conceals the truth that we are governed by both sword and pen" and added, "The British clearly recognized that the pen must retain what the sword had won".

For all the young students including Har Dayal's elder brothers arriving from Delhi and other smaller towns of North India, Lahore was a place of marvelous complexity and romance. Away from home and his wife Sunder Rani for the first time, Har Dayal's years at Lahore were crucial for him because it was here, he came into contact with a new set of political, social, religious and academic activists. Being distanced from his kinsmen and family members he broadened his social outlook and became more cosmopolitan rather than just remain confined to the community of scribes. Lahore famous for its colleges, newspapers, and politics had a multiethnic culture. Unlike Delhi, the choice of lifestyles for the white-collar educated Punjabi professionals was not dictated by caste, place of birth or inheritance. It was also home to the largest print and publishing industry with over fifty printing presses operating in the district.

Har Dayal during his student days in Lahore equated himself with men of great intellect. He admired the civil servant turned historian and political leader, Romesh Chandra Dutt (1848–1908). Dutt qualified for the much-admired Indian Civil Service (ICS) 'but always retained his national dignity'. Even when he was in the ICS, he earned a reputation as a first-rate orator and a man who was not afraid to express independent views. After retirement, he taught History at the University of London, but returned to India and became a most effective Diwan of Baroda State. In three years Dutt introduced far-reaching reforms and made Baroda under the great Gaekwar ruler Maharaja Sayaji Rao a model state. His writings and books including *The Economic History of India in the Victorian Age*, published in 1902 were extremely popular among the new generation of educated Indians. In his writings, he detailed evidence of deliberate economic destruction at the behest of British business of India's world-leading textile industry in the eighteenth century. Dutt was elected President of the Indian National Congress at Lucknow in 1899. As a successful civil servant, top leader, scholarly historian, and author, Dutt was all that the rising Indian intelligentsia aspired to be and for Har Dayal, he was "the ideal civil servant who never gave up the love of his country".

Another role model for Har Dayal was Sir Raghunath Purushottam Paramjpye (1876–1966) in whom he saw 'the ideal academician.' Paranjpye attended St. John's College, Cambridge University under a Government scholarship where he held a brilliant academic record and became the first Indian to be bracketed, senior wrangler. He gave up the opportunity of joining the Hukumat-i-Britannia's civil service and opted for a career in academics in India. He later became the Vice-Chancellor of Bombay University and founder of the Rationalist Association of India. In the academic environment of the Government College of Lahore Har Dayal also became a member of the Rational Society and he remained interested in this movement throughout his life.

At the end of the nineteenth century, a reform movement within Indian society and religion had made a great impact across India. A sage and great scholar, Dayanand Saraswati (1824–1883) founded the Arya Samaj institution dedicated to the promulgation of Vedantic traditions. He became instrumental in a big way for India's regeneration and renaissance. The reformist Arya Samaj opposed the fourfold *Varna* system (caste system), untouchability, child marriage, and supported widow remarriage and inter-caste marriages. The Arya Samaj furthermore stood for equal rights of man and woman in social and educational matters.

The young Har Dayal saw faith as a cultural and social movement and formed long-lasting friendships in Lahore with followers of the Arya Samaj who had a profound influence on him.

Lala Lajpat Rai (1865–1928), the dynamic nationalistic leader was the most impressive person Har Dayal met in Lahore. Originally from Hissar in North India, Lajpat Rai, born on January 18th, 1865 had shifted to Lahore in 1894 where he became a prolific writer on nationalistic issues and a distinguished lawyer. Popularly known as *'Punjab Kesri'* (Lion of Punjab), he authored several books including the biographies of Italian revolutionaries Giuseppe Garibaldi and Giuseppe Mazzini and edited the newsletter, *The People*. A top-ranking leader of the nationalist movement Lajpat Rai stressed upon the idea of self-reliance for Indians at the Indian National Congress session held in Lahore from December 27th–29th, 1900. Blessed with exceptional organizing abilities and oratorical skills, he founded the Servants of the People Society and instigated in Indian youth the seed for striving for India's independence. His peers referred to him as 'Lalaji' and Har Dayal along with scores of young men in North India considered him their leader.

Har Dayal associated with another prominent resident of Lahore, Lala Hans Raj (1864–1938) who was the President of the Arya Samaj's Dayanand Anglo-Vedic (DAV) College and was reputed to have one of the finest libraries in Punjab. The DAV College in Lahore was established precisely to provide some independence from the British University system and to introduce the youthful minds into modes of life coherent with India's spirit and character. Har Dayal later referred to Hans Raj as Mahatma (Great Soul).

Among the tiny university student community of Lahore Har Dayal was enormously popular and he befriended a fellow student, Bhai Parmanand (1876–1947). He was later an instructor of History at the DAV College in Lahore and a staunch opponent of the caste system. They remained close friends for the rest of their lives. Two years senior to him, Khudadad Khan Chaudhuri of Jassarwal, Sialkot who was studying Chemistry at the Punjab University was his confidante too. Khudadad later completed a Ph.D. in Organic Chemistry from Munich and set up a factory in Dehradun.

Our India is better than the rest of the World

In 1904, Muhammad Iqbal (1877–1938), who was briefly an Assistant Professor of English at the Government College in Lahore, at the invitation of his favorite student Har Dayal, came to preside over the first anniversary of 'The Young Men's Indian Association of Lahore'. Har Dayal, after a verbal altercation resigned from the membership of 'Young Men's Christian Association' and had founded the rival association.

Iqbal, the famed poet and philosopher, who was later knighted by the Hukumat-i-Britannia, displaying his intellectual and literary gift, rather than deliver a lecture chose to recite a patriotic song written in Urdu for the first time. It was titled, "*Saare Jahan Se Accha Hindustan Hamara*" (Our India is better than the rest of the world).

"*Saare jahaan se achha hindostaan hamaraa,
Hum bulbulain hai iskee, ye gulsitan hamaraa,*

Parbat vo sabse unchaa hum saaya aasma kaa,
Vo santaree hamaraa, vo paasbaan hamaraa,
Godee mein khel ti hain is kee hazaaron nadiyaan,
Gulshan hai jinke dum se, rashke janna hamaraa,
Mazhab nahee sikhataa apas mein bayr rakhnaa,
Hindee hai hum, vatan hai hindostaan hamaraa...”

(Our India is better than the rest of the world,
We are its nightingales and this is our garden,
That mountain most high, neighbor to the skies,
It is our sentinel; it is our protector,
A thousand rivers play in its lap,
Gardens they sustain, the envy of the heavens is ours,
Faith does not teach us to harbor grudges between us,
We are all Indians and India is our homeland...)

Nationalist passion was slowly consuming Har Dayal. The twenty years old was now identified both in Delhi and Lahore for his academic brilliance as well as political activism. This reputation earned him constant police surveillance by the British Secret Service even as a student.

Visiting Faculty at St. Stephen's College

Reverend Charles Freer Andrews (1871–1940), a thirty-three-year-old priest and a Fellow of Pembroke College, Cambridge, landed in Delhi on March 20th, 1904; on a day he called his 'Indian Birthday'. Armed with a cricket bat and a tripos each in classics and theology he was to teach English at St. Stephens College from October 1904. Known for his scholarship in Latin and Greek, Andrews was marked as a 'literary man'. Hugh Tinker in his biography, *The Ordeal of Love: C. F. Andrews and India* has observed, "The actual environment of the Delhi where he arrived around March 1904 was dominated by events which had occurred almost fifty years before – the siege and capture of Delhi, the climactic event of the Indian mutiny. Delhi had never forgotten the Mutiny.... Indians and the British hugged their memories. Indians remembered departed greatness. The British remembered the killing of their countrymen, the heroism of John Nicholson and the others who had recaptured Delhi: 'Never Again' was their watchword."

The prospect of a repeat of 1857 haunted the British.

In 1906 Principal Hibbert Ware went on home leave and resigned. Andrews turned down the opportunity to succeed him so that for the first time an Indian, Professor Sushil Kumar Rudra (1861–1925) who was teaching for close to two decades could be elevated to that position. Professor Rudra had joined the College staff in 1886 and was the fourth Principal and the first Indian Principal from 1906 to 1923 with Andrews as Vice-Principal from 1907 to 1914. In 1907, Andrews founded the St Stephen's College Magazine that was later renamed *The Stephanian*. He became interested in Yoga after witnessing the dramatic yogic performances of a wandering Indian swami.

An unusual man, Andrews during his stay in India, went on to become one of those extremely rare personalities who were respected both within Indian nationalist circles and official British ones. His conduct raised the prestige of the Englishmen in India and earned the respect of Indians. Later Andrews entered the fold of Indian nationalism and in some measure determined its course.

Through 1904–05, Har Dayal often returned to Delhi from Lahore, to meet his wife Sunder Rani and family members. On a visit to St. Stephens College, the restless ever-smiling man was introduced to Andrews. Andrews became his ardent admirer and later recorded in *The Modern Review* (Lala Har Dayal: A Noble Patriot and Truth Lover, *The Modern Review*, LXVII: April 1940), "Lala Har Dayal was never actually my own pupil he always regarded me as one of his teachers: for I came to St. Stephen's College, Delhi, just after he had left his old and dearly loved college in Delhi in order to take his final M.A. course in Lahore. When I came to Delhi early in 1904, he used to come over from Lahore and visit me: for Principal S. K. (Sushil Kumar) Rudra was very dear to him indeed, and his home was in Delhi." Andrews' amazing personality and his abounding love for all humanity revealed his intense inner ordeal that captivated the younger man. Har Dayal was enthralled with Andrew's scholarship of Latin and Greek as well as his knowledge of English poets and their poetry.

But on the night of April 3rd, 1905, these peaceful visits were disrupted when the animals in the Lahore Zoo were reported to be extremely agitated. The next morning, a little after 0600 hrs, the ground shook in three jolts over three minutes and a massive earthquake wrecked the Dharamshala-Kangra area in the lower Himalayas, north of Lahore. The aftershocks were felt all across North Punjab. It was considered the deadliest earthquake in the recorded history of India. Close to twenty thousand people were killed though the full measure of catastrophe could not be ascertained. Nevertheless, Lajpat Rai along with some of his followers including Har Dayal left immediately for the hills – the scene of the worst devastation. There he worked to the point of exhaustion and helped in organizing relief for the affected.

From his early years, he was willing to give or do whatever he could and never take advantage of any person or position for himself. *Dr. Dharmavira in his biography* has included an incident that his childhood friend Hanwant Sahai recalled "in winter evening on return from high lands, Har Dayal took off his new woolen coat and giving it to a beggar said that, – your need is greater than mine. Have it."

As he was keen on academics Har Dayal was offered the position of the Principal of Dayal Singh College in Lahore on completion of his Master's degree. He fleetingly considered being the head of the institution but eventually walked away from the idea finding it difficult to work within a system. This characteristic of non-conformity would be visible regularly throughout his life.

The Brightest Star of the Punjab University

In early June 1905, the twenty-year-old Har Dayal appeared before the committee of the syndicate of the Punjab University in Lahore for obtaining the state-financed three-year scholarship to study further in the top universities of Britain. The NAI documents record that the distinguished committee comprised of Justice P.C. Chatterji, Vice-Chancellor of Punjab University, Barrister Mian Muhammad Shah Din, Dr. James Caruthers Rhea Ewing, the American Principal of the Forman Christian College, Samuel Robson, Principal of Government College and the renowned Sanskrit scholar, Professor Alfred Cooper Woolner, the Principal of Oriental College.

The members of the high profile committee were interviewing Har Dayal, the boy who had earned the title of 'the brightest star of the Punjab University.'

At the end of the academic year 1905, Har Dayal had topped the Master of Arts course with record-breaking ninety-one percent marks. He secured the first-ever 'First Class' Master of Arts in English awarded at the Punjab University and was the recipient of the Arnold Gold Medal thus creating a matchless record. The university retained all his examination answer sheets as models of excellence for future students. The Professors of Punjab University told him they could not teach him anything further and he should go to Britain for advanced education. They recommended his name for the prestigious Government scholarship awarded annually by the Hukumat-i-Britannia.

From 1886 onwards Government scholarships were awarded to bright and deserving students from the Indian Universities. The prestige of the Government scholarship was largely due to the fact the impartial imperial system itself had picked them out. It was explained that the object of creating the scholarships was to encourage Indians to resort more freely to Britain to perfect their education and study for the various learned professions or the civil service system. The members of the committee had to choose one candidate from five universities in India (Calcutta, Bombay, Madras, Punjab, and Allahabad). The committee also had to consider the suitability of the student for eventually joining the Hukumat-i-Britannia as an Indian civil servant after his education at Oxford or Cambridge.

The members of the committee were charmed by the striking clean-shaven bespectacled youth with a chiseled nose, strong chin and penetrating eyes that were sharp and probing. He demonstrated complete fluency over English among other languages and possessed a hearty laugh. His smile could disarm his opponents and his habit of sliding his steel-rimmed spectacles up the bridge of his nose was copied by many of his young followers. Though his attire left much to be desired it gave him the appearance of a keen scholar. But by far his most outstanding features as his colossal intellectual prowess accompanied by soaring modesty. His responses to the committee's questions descended like an avalanche of thoughts, ideas, and quotations with great clarity. According to a family legend, one member of the committee asked him what was the key to Hukumat-i-Britannia's administrative success. Har Dayal smiled enigmatically and retorted, "Divide et impera – this much we have learned from you." Har Dayal's magnificent performance at the St. Stephen's College and Punjab University ensured that this brazenness was overlooked.

However, in addition to Har Dayal's terrific academic achievements the members of the committee were privy to a secret file that was a complete record of his nationalistic activities from his meetings at Amir Chand's Prem Dham to his association with Lajpat Rai, Hans Raj and Muhammed Iqbal as also his launch of 'The Young Men's Indian Association of Lahore'. A confidential report filed in Lahore about Har Dayal indicated, "a sense of revolt had taken deep root in his mind and had even permeated strongly a select circle of friends." James Campbell Ker (1878–1961) a senior member of the British Secret Service had branded him "something of a firebrand in politics".

A private letter (written later on July 18th, 1907), from Sir Harold Arthur Stuart (1860 – 1923) Director, DCI to Sir Charles Lyall, India Office, London, reveals that at the time Har Dayal was interviewed for one of the Government scholarships, he was, "suspected of disloyalty to the British Government and a reference was accordingly made to the Principal of the Mission College, in which he was educated, but that gentleman, (a letter from Professor Sushil Kumar Rudra), reported that the accusation of disloyalty appeared to be groundless." The Committee on receipt of the secret report and reference letters buried all the initial objections and other background checks in files bundled in red tape. There was unanimity in the views of members regarding Har Dayal.

And on Thursday, June 15th, 1905, Har Dayal broke yet another record as being the first student from Punjab University and the first student from North India to be awarded the £600 scholarship to be paid in quarterly installments over three years and was provided round trip passage to study in the best universities of Britain. (The scholarship of £600 in 1905 would be approximately worth £80,000 today). Significantly, the contract required a bond in the amount of Rs. 3,400 if a recipient of such a scholarship did not fulfill the terms of his contract.

Har Dayal was now considered the finest product from the university system of India in that year. The added prestige was due to the fact the Hukumat-i-Britannia's committee had picked him out as especially worthwhile and talented. Hukumat-i-Britannia was trying to introduce him into the sacred fortress of the Indian Civil Service (ICS) system, based on the Roman pro-consul or Chinese Mandarin. He pledged, as a condition of the scholarship, to serve the Hukumat-i-Britannia on his return. His Indian and English mentors predicted a great responsibility for him in the affairs of his country and his overjoyed family members thought he would return to India as a London trained barrister or a Deputy Commissioner and an eminent member of the ICS. He was asked to furnish details of his family background, complete address and state the date of his departure to Britain. He notified the Registrar, Punjab University, on 26th June 1905, that he would be sailing from Bombay on September 2nd, 1905 by the P&O Steam Navigation Company's mail steamer *S.S. Egypt.*

On August 10th, 1905, Sir Stuart, officiating as the Home Secretary informed Sir Arthur Godley (1847–1932), His Majesty's Permanent Under-Secretary of State for India, "Lala Har Dayal is not at present prepared to say at which university he will elect to study but he will report to the Secretary of State his choice of university, college and of the course of study which he will pursue soon after his arrival in England."

Ready to leave for further studies in Britain, Har Dayal traveled second class from Delhi by Punjab Bombay Mail and arrived in Bombay disembarking at Victoria Terminus on August 29th at 1320 hours. At this young age, Har Dayal felt perfectly equipped for the life ahead of him. From his knowledgeable mind to the power of his speech and from the attractiveness of manner to the application of his talents – nothing appeared to be missing. At just twenty years, his brain unraveled the complex and intertwined qualities of intellect, imagination, determination and simple decent behavior that usually entwined to create a human being capable of changing the world. In totality, he was an up-and-coming intellectual and the world was his oyster. Throughout history, rare individuals like him have stood out for their spectacular contributions. Yet at that stage, it was difficult to foresee that this brilliant young man would one day challenge the might and mind of His Majesty's Government, the biggest empire the world had ever known. And the empire on which the sun could not set punished him for his audacity.

4

THE OXFORD SCHOLAR

"Har Dayal had a great reputation among the Indians but he was at Oxford a little before my time at Cambridge. I met him once or twice in London during my Harrow days."

Jawaharlal Nehru
First Prime Minister of India

Monday, October 16th, 1905 was a day of national mourning in India. Bonfires of British clothes and products were ablaze across the nation. People fasted and observed a general strike. Shops, colleges, and schools were shut down. Leaders in Bengal urged the people to boycott British goods. Fires were lit across India where British manufactured onlookers threw the British made clothes they were wearing into the fire. The streets of Calcutta echoed with Tagore's composition, "*Amar Sonar Bangla*". The slogan of the dawn of Indian nationalism was '*Bande Mataram*'. Thousands refrained from meals, suspended business and walked barefoot to the banks of the Hoogly for a dip in the holy river amidst thunderous cries of '*Bande Mataram*'. Subsequently, on November 8th, 1905, Percy Comyn Lyon, Chief Secretary of East Bengal and Assam banned the use of the intensely passionate song and slogan in public places. It had the opposite effect to that intended and turned out to be the war cry for India's independence from the Hukumat-i-Britannia.

At Har Dayal's alma mater Government College in Lahore, the students went on strike in defiance of the Principal Samuel Robson's order that all of them should wear British made blazers. The students went back to the classes only after the order was withdrawn and they were allowed to wear Indian clothes. In Delhi, a small group of lawyers led by Shankar Nath, Barrister-at-law, and assisted by Har Dayal's elder brother Kishan Dayal initiated the early political movement.

Previously on July 7th, 1905, the self-obsessed Lord Curzon not rattled with the famines of 1899–1900 that killed an estimated million Indians went a step further and set the Muslim community against Hindus with the partition of Bengal. His controversial plan to partition the state of Bengal into East and West Bengal, largely on time tested Hukumat-i-Britannia's principle of *divide et impera* (divide and rule) came into effect on October 16th, 1905. Lord Curzon, the architect of the partition, knew that splitting Bengal, a state that was as large as France, would weaken the influence of the nationalist movement.

But the partition of Bengal turned out to be a huge blunder. The British Viceroy in one stroke provided the first light to the fire of Indian nationalism. The partition became the principal vehicle of the nationalist movement and acquired new strength, mass-orientation, and multi-dimensional character. It also marked the 'arrival of the bomb' on the Indian political scene as young men and women took to individual acts of violence. India had not witnessed such public agitation since the Ghadr of 1857. To deal with the rising political agitation, the Hukumat-i-Britannia passed a series of politically repressive acts that prohibited political meetings, closed printing presses, shut down newspapers and imprisoned anyone who threatened the interests of the British Crown.

With the state of Bengal in political chaos in mid-August 1905, Lord Curzon abruptly resigned from the position of British Viceroy that he had long considered, "the noblest gift of the British nation and that it ought to be looked upon as a prize to be awarded only to its greatest statesmen." Never was discontent in India more acute and extensive than the date when Lord Curzon laid down the reins of office. The pompous man left due to an unbearable conflict with Lord Horatio Herbert Kitchener (1850–1916), Commander-in-Chief of the British Indian to enorce the subordination of the military to the civil authority. He left India, an angry and embittered man and asserted, "Should the day ever come when the British Viceroy would be treated as the mere puppet of the Home Government, the justification for the post would cease to exist." In his farewell speech at Bombay, he remarked, "Let India be my judge". After returning from India, Lord Curzon became His Majesty's Foreign Secretary and was elected Chancellor of Oxford University in March 1907, holding the post till his death on March 20th, 1925. As years went by he lamented, "I must be entirely forgotten or have no friends left." Both declarations were partially true. Few British Viceroys had experienced such extreme vicissitudes of triumph and defeat.

The partition of Bengal was to be the turning point in Hukumat-i-Britannia's history. From the Battle of Plassey in 1757 to the Ghadr of 1857 it was a century, and from the Ghadr to *Bande Mataram* half a century more. The Hukumat-i-Britannia was no longer in its youth. The meridian had long been traversed and the crucial years of the Hukumat's dominance over India were over.

Passage to Britain

Just over a month before the partition of Bengal, on Saturday, September 2nd, in 1905, the Peninsular and Oriental Steam Navigation Company's ship *S.S. Egypt* set sail from Bombay docks for Britain. Har Dayal backed by the scholarship from the Hukumat-i-Britannia, and the free passage from India worth £34, (Rs. 456) settled down in a second (B) saloon. It was for the first time in his life that he had seen a ship and the sea on which it sailed. He was fascinated with the scenes of embarkation, the swirling waves, and the moving away of the steamship from the dock. Slowly the dark spires and gothic buildings of Bombay stood out in sharp relief. Then as the *S.S. Egypt* moved towards the high seas the coast lights blazed out.

By the time Har Dayal embarked, P&O had been operating in the high seas for nearly sixty-eight years. Though free to travel within the Empire on a British Indian passport, Har Dayal additionally carried a Hukumat-i-Britannia issued certificate of identity that contained information about family background, pecuniary status, and objective of the visit. It was an attempt by the Hukumat-i-Britannia's India Office to exercise some supervision and control over Indian students. The voyage from India to Britain via the Cape of Good Hope took six months at least but by early 1900 the passage by ship to London was down to less than three weeks due to the opening of the Suez Canal. The ships were luxuriously fitted out with a high standard of accommodation for both the First class as well as the Second class passengers.

As the *S.S. Egypt* sailed west Har Dayal felt the pangs of separation. His departure from India was emotionally intense. Sea voyages like the issue of the dowry (transfer of gifts and wealth at the time of marriage of a daughter) was a social reform issue of some concern for the community of scribes in North India in the early part of the twentieth century. Quoting ancient texts the elders of the community considered overseas travel inauspicious. The prohibition against sea voyage curiously seemed to apply only to Britain and both Andaman Islands and Japan were exempt. The men who had made seas voyages to England and foreign lands were excommunicated from the *biradari* (clan/community) and faced social persecution. Normally they would be ostracized and not allowed to perform the funeral of their parents. They were furthermore not permitted to eat meals with other members of the community and had to atone for their 'sins' by performing purification rites on the banks of the river Ganges for taking such a journey. There were further threats of disinheritance. Har Dayal benefited from the ongoing debates regarding the foreign travel dispute within the Kayastha Sadar Sabha Hind conference in 1905 held at Gazipur. The leaders of the community decided in favor of overseas travel for higher education and abandoned the old-fashioned views held in the past.

On the *S.S. Egypt,* Har Dayal spent his time mostly in walking and reading, with a little conversation with fellow-passengers for variation. He admired the uninterrupted vastness and unbounded expanse of the sea and endured the peculiar smell of the boat and the seawater. Before departing he had finished a crash course in English social etiquette including table manners, using the art of cutlery and tableware from those who had lived overseas before. Also, like all young Indian students who ventured overseas in that period, he was given strong moral lectures and warned about loose women and the influence of liquor. He had additionally got his medical tests and insurance done.

During meals, his thoughts flew to his home and his mother's tearful face, and the catch in her voice as she struggled to say a prayer before his departure. His scholarship to study at Oxford was a exceptionally proud moment for his family and similarly for all the Dilliwallahs. His name had appeared on the front pages of all the major local newspapers of the time. Yet he was distraught on leaving his wife Sunder Rani behind in Delhi. Outdated Indian social practices debarred women from traveling overseas. Women were expected to remain in strict purdah and within *zenana* (ladies section) of the house – virtually imprisoned indoors the four walls of the house. Though Har Dayal belonged to a progressive family, Sunder Rani's parents, as well as his brothers, had put their foot down and refused her permission to travel with her husband.

Har Dayal who had lost his father was also traveling far from next of kin and his three brothers Kishan Dayal, Bhairon Dayal and Manohar Dayal who were all lawyers practicing in courts in North India. He was closest to his eldest brother Kishan Dayal, who he called Kishan dada. A prominent lawyer in Delhi with offices in Dariba, Kishan Dayal participated in the Indian nationalist movement and his son Bhagwat Dayal later became a leading barrister in Delhi.

The ship sailed leisurely to Aden leading to the Red Sea. For youthful Indian it was instructive to see the Arab homeland; desert, oasis, camel ride, searing dusty gusts and clamorous bazaars. From there the ship crossed the Suez Canal into the Mediterranean, docking at Naples and then reaching Marseilles. The ship went past Gibraltar (Jebel-el-Tariq) onto Tilbury Dock on the north bank of the River Thames in Essex a week later.

The Greatest Capital City in the World

Almost three hundred years ago the arrival of the first Indian in 1614 had caused a stir in London. As the young man walked down the streets, he was shadowed by youngsters glaring at him open-jawed and women watched him through tiny cracks in their doors. Now in 1905, dressed in a hastily stitched new coat and trousers Har Dayal landed in a strange country and unfamiliar surroundings. He was the poster child of the Hukumat-i-Britannia and ostensibly ordained to scale the peaks of imperial fame and fortune. For a student of English acquainted with the literature of Britain, his education in Oxford would expose him to a world of professional and personal opportunities.

By the time Har Dayal landed in London, the imperial city was "the greatest capital of the world", at the heart of an equally expansive Empire. In the first decade of the new century, Britain was a global superpower and a nation particularly comfortable with educational elitism, with elaborate hierarchies and tight power networks. It was estimated that the British Monarch, Edward VII, affectionately called Bertie, ruled a fifth of the world map, and one in five persons on the planet were his subjects. Britain's playboy king had waited for nearly six decades to get his chance to rule. When he finally ascended the British throne in 1901, at age fifty-nine, he had a well-earned reputation for debauchery. A notorious gambler, glutton, and philanderer he took advantage of his royal entitlements to travel, hunt, entertain, over-indulge and bed a string of mistresses and married women in addition to his wife. He loved the luxuries of life and his main excitement was for uniforms (he liked to strut in a Field Marshal's outfit). His reign affirmed at the dawn of a new century "there'll always be an England." The Edwardian era took not only its name but also much of its character from its monarch.

London was the nexus of the Empire's political authority, financial power, and commercial dominance. It was unquestionably the richest, largest, most populous city the world had ever seen – immense, vast and endless. Its population at seven million was greater than that of Paris, Berlin, St. Petersburg and Moscow combined. It had seen fifteen decades of expansion, prosperity and civic grandeur funded by the loot of the British Empire. It was moreover the meeting point for an extraordinary slice of humankind from across the world.

Har Dayal was awestruck by the size and opulence of London with its meticulously dressed men in bowler hats and rolled umbrellas. He later told his friends about the lack of color in British fashion, "When I first went to London it was distressing to see so much black and white in the costumes of the people in the streets". He walked on the charming streets and looked into the well-dressed shop windows, the eating and drinking places where men and women went together. There were also some serious modern advances, unlike India. The roads were filled with horse carriages and early motorcars and there were underground trains, electricity (nearly every house in London had electricity by this point) and advances in photography and flying machines. It was during this period that politician Winston Churchill (1874–1965) declared that Great Britain was the best country in the world to live in.

Visitors from India flocked to the Trafalgar Square to feed the pigeons but rarely recognized that the two statues of rather austere-looking men erected there had a history in their country. The bronze sculpture of Major General Sir Henry Havelock who won fame in Britain during the Ghadr of 1857 where he recaptured Cawnpore (Kanpur) but died at Lucknow, read 'Soldiers! Your Labours Your Durations Your Sufferings And Your Valour Will Not Be Forgotten By A Grateful Country'. The former Commander-in-Chief of India, Sir Charles James Napier was the other bronze statue in Trafalgar Square. He was clad in a military uniform and held a scroll symbolizing his Governorship of Sind.

For the moment, the Russia – Japanese War in 1905 was the turning point for Britain's image as a global power. The Indians were elated at the news of the defeat of Russia at the hands of Japan. After the fall of Delhi in the Ghadr of 1857 Indians now construed this as the symbol of the rise of the East. The Japanese victory had demonstrated the possibility of a non-white race prevailing against European armed forces.

Senior British official and future member of the British parliament Sir Reginald Henry Craddock lamented: "I believe that things would have been much quieter in India had Japan met defeat from Russia." He commented, "It was Japan's victory that started the idea of Swaraj in India". Valentine Chirol (1852–1929) the perceptive British journalist, reporting for *The Times*, observed, "it would not be surprising if Indian nationalists were to seek Japanese guidance and assistance for the liberation of their motherland."

And in Delhi, Charles Andrews recorded the effect of the Russo-Japanese War upon the peoples of Asia; "it was clear to those who were watching the political horizon that great changes were impending in the East. Storm clouds had been gathering thick and fast. The air was full of electricity. The war between Russia and Japan had kept the surrounding peoples on the tiptoe of expectation. A stir of excitement passed over the North of India. Even the remote villagers talked over the victories of Japan as they sat in their circles and passed round the huqqa at night. A new chapter was being written in the book of the world's history. Delhi was a meeting-point of Hindus and Muslims, where their opinions could be noted and recorded" *(The Renaissance in India by C. F. Andrews, Young People's Missionary Movement, 1912).*

This was just the beginning of the twentieth century. It was a pivotal age about to witness revolutions in technology, religion, industry, and global politics. It was moreover a time when Britain was at the forefront of big and bold ideas that would transform the world like never before.

An Indian Scholar Up at Oxford

After a stopover in glitzy London, on Friday, October 13th, 1905, the government scholar Har Dayal filled the form at St. Johns College, Oxford for enrollment. St. Johns College was founded in 1555 by Sir Thomas White and was primarily a producer of Anglican clergymen in the previous periods of its history but over time gained a reputation in both law and medicine. On the enrollment form Har Dayal, in his handwriting, gave his date of birth as November 18th, 1884 and place of birth as Delhi. He added that he was "the fourth son of Mr. Gauri Dayal, Government Service (Reader)" who was 'Deceased'. He chose a dual-track course in Economics and Modern History, specifically the later period of Europe and British India. Later he also added Political Science and Sanskrit.

Har Dayal chose Oxford over Cambridge though Charles Andrews wanted him to go to the later. Oxford was famous globally for its prestigious University, the oldest in the English-speaking world. Located at a distance of 80 km north of London to study at Oxford was a dream come true for every young scholar within the British Empire. Admission to Oxford was much more difficult than Cambridge. Students from India had to take a preliminary examination in

English, Greek or Latin for admission in Oxford while Cambridge had no such requirement. Oxford authorities had a racially motivated quota system as they were under pressure from British undergraduates to restrict admissions to Indians students at their University.

The first Indian students arrived in Oxford in 1871 and over the next two decades about fifty graduated. For the handful of Indian scholars, the degree at Oxford was to become a passport for an academic career with the universities of the Hukumat-i-Britannia. Cornelia Sorabji (1866–1952) who was in residence at Somerville College from 1889 to 1892 became the first woman of any nationality to read law at Oxford and later was India's first female advocate. By the time Har Dayal reached Oxford the number of Indians at Oxford was less than half at Cambridge. As specified in a Hukumat-i-Britannia report in 1907, there were about seven hundred Indian students in Britain – three hundred and eighty lived and studied in London with three hundred and twenty enrolled in Law, a hundred and fifty studying in Edinburgh, eighty-five enrolled at Cambridge and thirty-two attending Oxford.

Har Dayal had reached Oxford in time for the Michaelmas session and the academic year started on the first Monday of October 1905. The university town appeared more beautiful than the postcards he had seen. Housed amidst historic buildings with stunning architecture and beautiful gardens it provided efficient access and resources to study for international students. Oxford with its spires, domes, quaint streets and weathered college buildings looked lovely at that time of the year. The trees were planted between buildings as if a Sunday painter had spent ages rendering each street scene in pastels. At the beginning of the university year, there were trunks everywhere with shouts of recognition in the lanes while bespectacled freshmen like Har Dayal bought fountain pens and stationary. Porters carried the luggage from the train station to the doorstep of the residents. It felt like the university town was being recharged with so much activity all around.

The education at Oxford would give Har Dayal a new outlook; confident, internationalist, intellectually flexible and above all a macro view of the wider world. Oxford was also placed with a particularly strong character – too rooted in history to be affected by the changing political climate or at least it was assumed so.

The Power of Swadeshi

On November 18th, 1905, the S. S. Peninsula docked in Bombay and Gilbert John Elliot-Murray-Kynynmound, 4th Earl of Minto (1845–1914), a British aristocrat and politician, arrived as Lord Curzon's successor. The new British Viceroy of India, with the personal motto 'Mildly and Firmly', took charge at a time of apprehensions on the political future of Hukumat-i-Britannia. His first task was taking charge of the British royal the future King George V (1865–1936), then still the Prince of Wales, who landed in India with his wife on November 10th, 1905, as part of an official tour of the British Empire. He would come back six years later as the only King of India to attend his own Delhi Durbar. On their first tour of India, they visited Delhi on December 12th, 1905 and visited the sites of the Ghadr of 1857 including the Red Fort and the Humayun's Tomb. Silent film shot during the tour shows the couple in royal procession through the streets of Bombay, lined with onlookers and accompanied by a military parade. It was arguably the most intense and ambitious Royal visit ever conducted by the Royal Family.

While the Royals were busy visiting Indian cities, Indian National Congress emerged as the leading resistance group against Hukumat-i-Britannia's policies in India. At its meeting on August 7th, 1905, held in Calcutta, it had adopted a resolution to boycott British goods and now in December 1905, the message of 'Swadeshi' was adopted in Benaras under the Chairmanship of a respected member, Gopal Krishna Gokhale (1866–1915). The thirty-nine-year-old Gokhale, a known social reformer had previously resigned as Professor of History and Political Economy at Fergusson College in Poona to enter politics. On June 12, 1905, he had formed, 'The Servants of India Society' in Pune "to train national missionaries for the service of India and to promote by all constitutional means the true interests of the Indian people". As the youngest President-elect in Congress history, in his presidential address on December 27th, 1905, in Benaras, Gokhale condemned Lord Curzon and termed the upheaval of popular feeling in Bengal a landmark in the history of national progress. He advocated moderate and constitutional methods of agitation and gradual reform.

Another man about to assume leadership in India was Aurobindo Ghosh (1872–1950) the brilliant intellectual and future spiritual leader who held a senior classical scholarship to King's College, Cambridge. Son of Dr. Krishna Dhun Ghosh, a civil surgeon, in 1890 Ghosh had passed the examination for the ICS though at the end of two years of probation failed to present himself at the riding examination and was disqualified for the Service. Favoring militant nationalism Ghosh later launched the paper *Bande Mataram* in August 1906 and transformed the political thought of India. His was a clear attempt to stir up the youth to take part in revolutionary activity and free the country from the foreign yoke. Ghosh was in favor of extending the nationalist movement to the rest of India.

At the end of 1905, there was a change of Government in Britain. The Conservatives were replaced by a Liberal Ministry under Sir Henry Campbell-Bannerman, with Lord John Morley (1838–1923) as Secretary of State for India. Lord Morley had always been well known for his anti-imperialist and radical views and had once stood out strongly for Irish Home Rule. Indian politicians, therefore, had high hopes of him. The Prince of Wales on his return from the Indian tour had a long exchange with Lord Morley, in which he gave a thought-provoking interpretation of his impressions in India. He thought that Indians needed to be treated with wider sympathy and the English administrators had an ungracious bearing on the local population.

Both Lord Morley and Lord Minto knew that Hukumat-i-Britannia had to safeguard its interest from ambitious, semi-educated and able men, who would risk life to overthrow British dominion, and who enjoyed the passive sympathy of the majority. They had the means to defeat such attempts with the cavalry, the telegraph, and command over endless spies. Hukumat-i-Britannia was confident of ensuring the surrender, betrayal or death of any Indian insurgency. They had armed police and soldiers that could effectively block all the escape routes. There was always the trial for treason that would lead to the increase to the population of the Andamans' ghastly Cellular Jail – Hukumat-i-Britannia's own Alcatraz.

An Exemplary Student

At the Bodleian Library in Oxford, the librarians became familiar with Har Dayal the academically inclined not very tall Indian (he was five feet five inches in height) could be observed doing extensive reading and making notes sometimes over the weekends. From St. Stephens in Delhi to St. John's in Oxford was a dramatic shift for him. He began his studies under famous India born Orientalist, Arthur Anthony Macdonell (1854–1930) who was the Professor of Sanskrit and Keeper of the Indian Institute at Oxford. His academic choices at Oxford were spectacularly eclectic; in addition to prowess in Sanskrit and English, Har Dayal absorbed himself in vast reading every week, writing essays that synthesized and summarized his ideas. A voracious reader since childhood he now further refined his writing style in Oxford and displayed a faculty for subtle analytical criticism in his essays. He arrived at his final arguments with precision without sweeping statements that were a mark of a mature and healthy mind at work. Legend has it that his essays and tutorials at Oxford were considered exceptional and his Professors regularly remarked that they could neither add nor improve upon them.

Settling down itself was no problem but he had to take part in too many Oxford routines. Unlike the Oxford undergraduates, the somewhat ascetic Har Dayal didn't care too much about fashionable clothes but as specified by University norms, he ordered full-dress suits, dinner jacket, ties, plain shirts, and a Norfolk jacket. For the winter he purchased woolen underwear and overcoat. Thereafter he got used to the roll call in the morning in the dining hall and dinners in the vast paneled hall with portraits of notables. He never smoked or drank alcohol. He had embraced twin objectives of knowledge and service and from all accounts was the personification of perfect and winning manners. Due to the spirit of renunciation and sacrifice, the twenty-one year old was held in high esteem both by the teachers and the students. He gradually made his presence felt at Oxford and many students considered him an exemplary personality.

At the end of 1905, Charles Andrews was in London to consult a specialist for ear trouble. He took the opportunity to do a language course at Cambridge and visited Har Dayal at Oxford. He noted that, "… when I met Har Dayal at Oxford but he was busy with his studies and made his requirements very less for living, he used to live in a small house, in nature he was like saints". On another occasion, the former students of St. Stephens hosted a dinner in honor of Professor Rudra at Cambridge. Har Dayal attended that dinner along with Andrews and the group photograph of that evening decorated the wall of the Principal's office at St. Stephens for several years.

Majlis – The Council of Indians

The academic atmosphere of Oxford was enlightening for Indian scholars but they had to suffer the racial prejudices resulting from the unnatural relationship between Great Britain and India. The leadership of Britain was imperialistic in attitude – proud of the Empire and its ability to civilize the world. At the end of the year 1889, a young British writer named Rudyard Kipling arrived in London, the literary center of the British Empire with some of his ballads to sell. The December number of *Macmillan's Magazine* contained one of his ballads that set the British Empire on fire, with words charged with racism, which are not likely to be forgotten:

"Oh, East is East, and West is West, and never the twain shall meet,
Till Earth and Sky stand presently at God's great Judgment Seat"

These lines implied that the peoples on opposite sides of the world were so different that they would never appreciate each other until the Day of Judgment. Despite his jingoism, the Bombay born British writer Kipling was noticed at once for his immense gift for using words and much acclaim followed. The imperialists propagated that Britain had done more for India in the last hundred years than India had done over a thousand years. India they claimed was a geographical term and no more a nation than the equator. Since Britain had staked a great deal of money into India she could claim to own it and India owed her a debt of gratitude. They also felt that India did not deserve self-government and was in any case not ready for it. The imperialist attitude was that India had no democratic ideals and no national unity. They held that the true comparison between India and the western world was best obtained by remembering that India was as big as the whole of Europe excluding Russia but that it was more divided racially, linguistically, and religiously than the whole of Europe. The generally propagated opinion was that if Britain left India it would be constantly torn by civil and military wars.

For every positive attitude toward Indians at Oxford, there existed a negative one and racial discrimination had crept in for the Indians by the turn of the twentieth century. Stereotypes prevailed as Indians were looked upon as snake charmers or theosophists or as degenerate descendants of rebels from the banks of the Ganges. The students from India faced widespread prejudice when they rented a place to stay or entered a restaurant to eat. Indians at Oxford were aware of their position as they sauntered down the High street after dinner and sometimes exchanged uncomplimentary racial remarks and even blows with English students. Indians would often be asked to go back to their black country. For the politically conscious the stay at Oxford was expected to enhance their respect and loyalty towards the British Empire. However the Irish, Egyptian, Turkish and Russian students freely interacted with Indians making them conscious of the movements in their part of the world.

Previously in late October 1905, the Special Branch, the British police national security wing (British Secret Service) had intercepted a communication from Har Dayal to his friend Khudadad Khan from Oxford. In the letter he had written, "the more I think about it, the more I realize that half measures are of no use politically...Our object is not to reform Government, but to reform it away, leaving, if necessary, only nominal traces of its existence." In another intercepted post he wrote that he wanted to start a college in Punjab as a feeder of a society of selfless workers to create a cadre of Indian Sanyas Service (ISS) for Indians as a nationalist alternative to Hukumat-i-Britannia's Indian Civil Service.

At Oxford, using his supreme organizational ability, Har Dayal transformed the Oxford Indian Club into the Oxford Majlis and was elected its President. Rather than use a name in Sanskrit, the Dilliwallah adopted the name 'Majlis', a Urdu word for the council to embrace all the Indians at Oxford irrespective of religion. The Majlis was not only restricted to Indian students; Ceylonese and Burmese students were an integral part of the 'Indian student' community. From a vague institution for tea and cakes on a Sunday afternoon imitating the British lifestyle, this association of Indians became the center for all kinds of revolutionary debates at Oxford. Indian students normally known for their self-conscious timidity in Britain would convene on Sunday evenings to hold formal debates and let off steam. They were at Oxford at a time when the world was resonating with revolution and thinking aloud. Old regimes were breaking down, science was undermining religious authority every day and the effects of the partition of Bengal were felt even as far as London. They would additionally hold other social events such as music, dancing, and lectures from invited speakers from India who were visiting Britain.

The Majlis helped Har Dayal shape into an eloquent orator. Addressing the Oxford students he soared high and opened the floodgates of passion through the imagery of his heartfelt speeches. His motivational words and incredible knowledge had a warm impact on his audience. Gifted with a sense of humor and a hearty laugh he straightaway drew the attention of fellow students. Famous for his idealistic vigor and strong determination, Har Dayal became a force to reckon with in debating circles at the university.

As it was at St. Stephens College in Delhi and later at Government College in Lahore, Har Dayal's popularity and fame extended far beyond Oxford. Jawaharlal Nehru (1889–1964), the young son of the famous Indian lawyer, Motilal Nehru (1861–1931) had enrolled at the expensive boarding school Harrow in Britain on September 21st, 1905 to complete his schooling. The future Indian leader and India's first Prime Minister recollected in his *Autobiography*, "Har Dayal had a great reputation among the Indians but he was at Oxford a little before my time at Cambridge. I met him once or twice in London during my Harrow days."

Most of the Indians took part in the anti-imperialism political discussions yet some would later serve the Hukumat-i-Britannia in India as senior civil servants. Renowned Indian diplomat and a member of the ICS, K. P. S. Menon, who was elected president of the Oxford Majlis in 1920, recalled in his *Autobiography* that even after fifteen years, "the memory of Har Dayal, an Oxford man... still lingered in the Majlis."

The India Office and New Scotland Yard kept an eye on the Majlis and were particularly concerned about their nationalist sympathies.

The Indian Sociologist

In early 1906, Bhai Parmanand, clad in a warm overcoat stood on Har Dayal's doorstep and the college friends reunited after several months. After teaching as a Professor at Dayanand College in Lahore, he visited Nairobi and Mombassa in Kenya, Durban and Johannesburg in South Africa to teach under the auspices of the Arya Samaj. He arrived in London from Cape Town.

During his visit to South Africa in August 1905, he had met and stayed for a month with Mohandas Karamchand Gandhi (1869–1948), later known as Mahatma Gandhi at his house in Johannesburg. Mahatma Gandhi was the most important figure of the anti-colonial movement in South Africa at that time. Just over a decade ago, on the night of June 7th, 1893, Mahatma Gandhi, the twenty-three-year-old London trained Barrister was thrown off the train's first-class "whites-only" section at Pietermaritzburg station in South Africa for declining to give up his legimate seat. Even though he possessed a valid first-class ticket, he was forced to stay at the station that night shivering in cold. That bitter racial incident played a major role in Mahatma Gandhi's decision to stay on in South Africa and fight the discrimination being faced by Indians there. Bhai Parmanand in his autobiography, *The Story of my Life*, later remarked, "His (Mahatma Gandhi) simple life and asceticism left a deep impression on me even then".

Bhai Parmanand planned to write a thesis for a Masters's degree titled, 'The Rise of British Power in India' later published as a book with a title, *Tarikh-i-Hind*. He stayed with Har Dayal and spent time at Oxford for an independent study of Indian history. He also found a home at the residence of Kareshi Ram on 53 Northumberland Place in London and visited the British Museum and Library for his research.

In April 1906, Bhai Parmanand introduced Har Dayal to the distinguished Indian resident of Britain, Shyamji Krishna Varma (1857–1930) in London. Previously Mahatma Gandhi had written a letter of introduction to Krishna Varma for Bhai Parmanand. The serious-looking and bearded Sanskritist and thinker, Krishna Varma was the first Indian to gain a Master's degree from Oxford University, where he worked under the Sanskrit Professor Sir Monier-Williams. He acquired a deep knowledge of Sanskrit for which he was awarded the title of 'Pandit'. He was also a barrister from the Inner Temple and had amassed a small fortune from his investments in cotton mills while he worked for several princely states in India. A self-made multi-millionaire he eventually owned shares in countless companies from Moroccan railways to Berlin power plants and traded on the stock exchanges of Europe.

In 1897, upset with the autocratic, exploitative and oppressive regime of Hukumat-i-Britannia, Krishna Varma had returned to Britain with his wife Bhanumati, the daughter of a rich merchant, Seth Chhabildas Lalubhai of Bombay. In the year 1900, he bought a luxurious house, 9 Queenswood Street (now 60 Muswell Hill Road) in the northern suburbs of London and became a zealous follower of the enormously influential English philosopher and sociologist Herbert Spencer (1820–1903). The author of the much acclaimed nine-volume, *A System of Synthetic Philosophy,* Spencer was recognized as a major figure in the intellectual life of the Victorian era and he coined the term 'survival of the fittest'. In 1902, Spencer, the former sub editor of *The Economist*, received a nomination for the Nobel Prize for literature, but did not win it, and died on December 8th, 1903 at the age of eighty-three years having already seen much of his fame and influence fade away. At Spencer's cremation, Krishna Varma announced an endowed lectureship of £1,000 in Spencer's name at Oxford. Later on March 9th, 1905, Fredric Harrison, an honorary fellow of Wadham College, delivered the first Herbert Spencer lecture established at Oxford University by Krishna Varma.

Since January 1905, Krishna Varma published the anti-colonialist English language newspaper, *The Indian Sociologist* with the subtitle, 'An Organ of Freedom and Political, Social, and Religious Reform' that was intended to galvanize many more intellectual revolutionaries into action through its nationalist writings. In the 'Editor's Statement' of the first issue itself Krishna Varma described himself as an 'Indian Sociologist' and explained that the paper would refer back to sociological texts in its work and as the basis of many of its arguments." He placed two quotations from Spencer at the top of every issue: "Every man is free to do that which he wills, provided he infringes not the equal freedom of any other man," and "Resistance to aggression is not simply justifiable but imperative. Non-resistance hurts both altruism and egoism."

The first issue of *The Indian Sociologist* additionally published the scheme of six Herbert Spencer Indian Fellowship of Rs. 1,000 each to encourage young Indian students to complete their education in Britain. But the scholarship came with a stiff clause that the candidate was not expected to "accept any post, office, emoluments or service under the British Government after his return to India".

The India House Nationalists

On Saturday, July 1st, 1905, one of Karl Marx's earliest English supporters, Henry Hyndman of the Social Democratic Federation was welcomed into a building on a leafy residential street 65 Cromwell Avenue in London. Hyndman, the epitome of an upper-class gentleman, from his silk top hat to his silver-topped cane who had met Marx in the 1870s, unveiled the building purchased by Krishna Varma as 'India House'. In his speech, Hyndman foresaw the significance of setting up the India House and remarked, "As things stand, loyalty to Great Britain means treachery to India... From England itself, there is nothing to be hoped for. It is an immoderate man, the determined man, the fanatical man who will work out the salvation of India by himself. The institution of this India House means a great step in that direction of Indian growth and Indian emancipation, and some of those who are here this afternoon may witness the first fruits of its triumphant success."

Krishna Varma anticipated the necessity of starting a hostel for a large number of Indian students who were denied boarding and food due to racial discrimination. Located not far from the Highgate cemetery where Karl Marx was buried and Spencer was cremated, the India House accommodated twenty-five residents and included a reading room, lecture hall, and library.

One of the attractions was the Indian kitchen there making it one of the first places in London to popularize Indian cuisine. Almost a century ago, in 1810, Dean Mahomet (later Sake Dean Mahomed) had opened the first Indian-owned London curry house, Hindoostane Dinner and Hookah Smoking Club, also known as the Hindostanee Coffee House, at 34 George Street, near Portman Square. Its handwritten menu included more than twenty-five dishes, including chicken and lobster curries and a selection of bread. The Hindostanee Coffee House was furnished with bamboo chairs and Hookha and ran for two years before going bankrupt. In the years 1906 to 1910, an Indian entrepreneur Nizamuddin had at various stages opened three restaurants in London, near Chancery Lane, 9 Uxbridge Road, and 36 Ledbury Road and according to British Secret Service reports Indian extremists frequented them.

As predicted by Hyndman within months of its launch, India House became a radical center of Indian nationalism outside India during the Hukumat-i-Britannia. Har Dayal would often escape 'the city of dreaming spires' on holidays and weekends, to go to London and meet other like-minded Indians. The limited news of political upheavals in India spearheaded by Gokhale and Aurobindo Ghosh greatly agitated Har Dayal's mind. Krishna Varma had also inaugurated a new organization in London called 'The Indian Home Rule Society'. The first meeting laid out the society's aims: securing home rule for India, carrying on propaganda in Britain to achieve it, and spreading information about freedom and national unity in India. The fascination for India's liberation was of growing interest to Har Dayal. After discussing politics and social issues at India House on the weekends he would travel back along the twisting country roads to Oxford in the evening.

The star attraction for youngsters like Har Dayal and Bhai Parmanand was the eighty-year-old Indian political leader Dadabhai Naoroji (1825–1917) also known as the 'Grand Old Man of India' who lived in London. The Parsi cotton trader was a great public figure and the first Indian Member of Parliament in the United Kingdom's House of Commons representing Central Finsbury for the Liberal Party. He was furthermore one of the founders of the Indian National Congress and became its president three times in 1886, 1893 and later in 1906. Naoroji's work focused on the drain of wealth from India into Britain during the colonial rule of British in India. He regularly voiced the grievances of the Indian people and proclaimed their aims, ideals, and aspirations to the world at large.

In his presidential address at Lahore in 1893, Naoroji had articulated the multicultural vision for India; "Let us always remember that we are all children of our mother country. Indeed, I have never worked in any other spirit than that I am an Indian, and owe a duty to my country and all my countrymen. Whether I am a Hindu, a Mohammedan, a Parsi, a Christian, or any other creed, I am above all an Indian. Our country is India; our nationality is Indian."

On the evening of Monday, April 30th, 1906, the President of the Indian National Congress, Gokhale reached London to meet the British Members of Parliament and other officials of the India Office. The train was late by two hours, yet about fifty Indians led by Dadabhai Naoroji waited at the Victoria Station to receive him. At a dinner of the London Indian Society, on May 5ᵗʰ, 1906, Gokhale hit hard at the repressive acts of Sir Bampfylde Fuller, Lt. Governor of East Bengal and demanded his recall. During his visit to London, the 'Anti-Imperialist League of America' invited Gokhale to the United States to deliver a series of lectures on India. The Hukumat-i-Britannia's politicians and officials viewed Gokhale as the most eminent Indian statesman of his time, with 'mellow wisdom and quiet strength'. Later in 1914, Gokhale turned down the offer of a knighthood and in the words of his biographer, B. R. Nanda, "he wanted to turn the encounter with the Raj into an opportunity for building a secular, modern and democratic society."

Bhai Parmanand introduced Har Dayal to Gokhale at the India House and a short discussion on motivating Indians for freedom from Hukumat-i-Britannia followed. Gokhale reportedly tried to explain his stance on an "evolution" toward independence, Har Dayal cut him short, protesting that this was no way to "enthuse people for freedom." Gokhale then tried to recruit the young man into the Servants of India Society, but he politely declined to state that he did not agree with the Society's principle of supporting the British Empire. Gokhale commented, "For him, freedom is an obsession, he thinks of nothing else."

Another Indian student at the India House who thought of nothing else but freedom of India was the twenty-three-year-old multi-dimensional young man from Pune, Vinayak Damodar Savarkar (1883–1966), who had recently appeared in London to become a barrister. In July 1906, Har Dayal got acquainted with Savarkar at the India House. Still, in his early twenties, Savarkar impressed everyone with his fierce and incendiary nationalism. Similar in age and outlook Har Dayal and Savarkar became close compatriots. He even became an active member of Savarkar's Abhinav Bharat. Savarkar was inspired by the life and work of Giuseppe Mazzini, the Italian revolutionary who lived in London and spearheaded the revolutionary movement in his homeland. He celebrated Indian festivals in London and organized meetings of Indians on Sunday afternoons at the India House.

Amogn the other noteworthy person Har Dayal met at India House was the inscrutable Virendranath Chattopadhyaya (1880–1937), the younger brother of Sarojini Naidu, 'the nightingale of India'. A member of a famous Indian family, his father Professor Aghorenath Chattopadhyaya was the principal of Nizam College in Hyderabad. Virendranath (also called Chatto) had originally come to

London to appear in the ICS examination but he failed twice and then assisted Krishna Varma in editing *The Indian Sociologist*. He had additionally joined the Inns of Court at Middle Temple to become a barrister and was counted among the group of brilliant young Indian patriots in London.

Decades later Indian nationalist leader, Sarat Chandra Bose, referred to the historical significance of India House in the Indian freedom movement; "I feel proud to call to mind the glorious traditions that Shyamji Krishna Varma and his comrades established in their fight for India's freedom. They dreamt of and fought for Indian Independence when most of the present leaders of the Congress, who assumed power as a result of a compromise with the British Imperialists of acquiescing in British Imperialist rule, were in political nurseries with their ideas unformed."

5

THE YOUNG PATRIOT IN HIS MAJESTY'S BRITAIN

"It is needless to say that even in England, he (Har Dayal) maintained his reputation for brilliant scholarship, but what is remarkable is that it was here he became a nationalist".

Lala Lajpat Rai
Indian Nationalist

In the summer of 1906, hundreds of people at the platform of the railway station in Ghaziabad in India accosted a man appearing to run away with someone's wife. Before the incident could turn ugly the man loudly claimed that his name was Har Dayal and the woman Sunder Rani was his wife.

Just a month before, to the utter surprise of his relatives and friends, Har Dayal had unexpectedly landed at his house in Delhi from Britain. He had previously applied to the India Office for permission to travel to India during the vacation at Oxford and it was reluctantly granted. Indians studying in Britain rarely returned before completing their degrees or getting a job as the costs of a sea voyage were exorbitant. They usually came back due to extraordinary family circumstances or for financial or health reasons. But Har Dayal simply wanted to meet his family. Though the family was delighted to see him, a 'London returned' Har Dayal kept his mission a secret. While he was expanding his intellect at Oxford and getting involved with Indian nationalism, his personal love life was in turmoil. His wife Sunder Rani was always on his mind. With the irregular correspondence and the busy study schedule he immensely missed her in Britain.

Har Dayal was aware that in contrast to women in India, it was normal for British women to have an outdoor life, use public transport to travel independently and shop at the markets. The latest inventions of the typewriter, the telephone, and new filing systems offered women of Britain increased employment opportunities.

There was also a whole range of new professions including doctors, nursing and academics with the rapid expansion of hospitals and schools. The past year in Britain was additionally the start of the militant phase of the Suffrage movement. Cries of "deeds, not words" and "votes for women" were adopted as campaign slogans for the right to cast a ballot. At a meeting addressed by British politician Sir Edward Grey in Manchester, Christabel Pankhurst and Annie Kenney had repeatedly shouted, "will the Liberal Government give votes to women?" Both of them were asked to leave and later arrested in the name of suffrage for women.

Har Dayal's secret reason for returning home to Delhi was rather ambitious in the year 1906. The headstrong individual wanted to take his wife Sunder Rani back with him to Oxford to show her the best of British life, education, and culture especially the evolving role of women in modern society. In the first two years of their marriage, they had lost a son in infancy and Har Dayal felt that the young couple should stay together to build a family. Sunder Rani's family vehemently opposed Har Dayal's proposal for taking her to Britain and some members still believed in the age-old custom that traveling the seven seas amounted to sacrilege.

A disappointed Har Dayal bided his time and briefly taught at the St Stephen's College as a lecturer in History and Economics in place of Professor Rudra who was visiting Britain. At St. Stephens, he started '*the Ramayan society*' based on the text written by Romesh Chandra Dutt who had provided an English translation of the ancient Sanskrit epic. He also gave his distant relative Gobind Behari Lal, a subtle hint about not appearing in the forthcoming ICS examination. Gobind was stunned, as this seemed to defy all logic, as a brilliant Indian student like Har Dayal was naturally expected to join the Indian Civil Service after his studies at Oxford.

In the interval, anticipating that Har Dayal may be up to some mischief, the family head Lala Gopal Chand clandestinely sent Sunder Rani from Delhi to their family home in Meerut till her husband was around. A cousin Mahabir Chand escorted her to Meerut by train.

Har Dayal got to know about this from his family circles and put his plans into action. He along with some of his friends including Amir Chand and Khudadad Khan, now a lecturer in Chemistry in the Roorkee Engineering College, intercepted the train en route at Ghaziabad. Har Dayal dramatically jumped into his wife's compartment and bundled her out onto the platform. Her cousin Mahabir came out in hot pursuit and there was a major altercation at the railway station. The onlookers got the wrong impression that Har Dayal was kidnapping someone's wife and intervened in the affair. To avert a hostile situation Har Dayal announced that the woman was his lawfully wedded wife and Sunder Rani also had to loudly declare that she was Har Dayal's wife. At this moment Khudadad Khan though just five feet six inches tall forcibly held Mahabir back while Har Dayal and Sundar Rani bolted. They later got on a train heading to Bombay.

The exasperated relatives of his wife, as well as his brother Kishan Dayal, followed the couple to Bombay. Har Dayal kept Sunder Rani concealed in a man's disguise and changed hotels in Bombay. Finally, the couple was safely on the French ship Messageries Maritimes *S.S. Ville de la Ciotat*. Sunder Rani's relatives rushed to the dock to make a last-ditch effort to rescue her. As the ship slowly departed from Bombay, the Dilliwallah appeared on the deck to wave goodbye to his relatives and shouted, "All is fair in love and war". The couple sailed away to Marseilles on the triple expansion engine liner. He had liberated Sunder Rani from the decadent customs of India. Aboard the French ship, the couple had two weeks of romantic solitude. Later they landed in France and then traveled to Paris by train before finally reaching his home in Oxford.

On arrival in Oxford, the couple set up a small household in a pretty townhouse on 97 Southmoor Road even though the expenses were high. Britain was to be the home for the couple for the next one and a half years. Unlike in India, the Dayals lived in an atmosphere of freedom at Oxford and he resolved that his wife, Sundar Rani, should take to the work of regeneration of Indian womanhood. Accordingly, he began teaching her history and political science at Oxford.

Back in India, Har Dayal's father-in-law Lala Gopal Chand was left red in the face in the presence of his family and colleagues. Har Dayal's biographers Shubh Paul and E Jaiwant Paul, have disclosed in *Har Dayal, The Great Revolutionary*, that Gopal Chand was furious and shouted, "That mad genius is going to ruin himself and my daughter's happiness..."

Days later the whole episode appeared in the Lahore daily, *The Punjabee* under the headline, "Wife Kidnapped by Husband!" Later other newspapers in India including *The Civil and Military Gazette* of Lahore and *The Pioneer* of Allahabad praised Har Dayal for his 'moral courage'. Following Har Dayal's example, another Oxford student Lala Chandu Lal was inspired to break the centuries-old strict laws and he too smuggled his wife from Delhi to Britain. Chandu Lal's wife after reaching Britain developed a close friendship with Sunder Rani being the only two Indian women in Oxford at that time.

This was the first act of rebellion by Har Dayal – a revolt against the archaic social mindset of the Indian community.

The Future Leader of India

On October 20th, 1906, a thirty-seven-year-old, Mahatma Gandhi arrived in Southampton with a South African Indian delegation to meet Lord Morley and get the 'Black Acts' repealed. This was Mahatma Gandhi's first visit since he had left Britain after completing his law studies in 1891. Influenced by Leo Tolstoy he had launched a peaceful agitation based on passive resistance seeking cooperation from the South African authorities. During the Boer War (1899–1901) he organized an ambulance corps for the British army and commanded a Red Cross unit.

On this visit to London, he spent two nights at India House. Krishna Varma's self-fashioning as an ascetic nationalist and setting up India House impressed Mahatma Gandhi. In his London travelogue penned for his journal *Indian Opinion*, Mahatma Gandhi describing the revolutionary from Kutch penned, "He decided to spend his earnings on the benefit of the country. With this end in view, he came to Britain and settled there. He lives on the land, which he has purchased. Though he can afford to live in comfort he lives in poverty. He dresses simply and loves like an ascetic. His mission is service to his country." It is recorded that Sunday morning (October 21st) was spent meeting young Indians at India House.

Later accompanied by Bhai Parmanand, Mahatma Gandhi also visited influential Jewish business figure Joesph Polak and stayed with him for the day at his home on 28 Grosvenor Road. Polak took him to the House of Commons to meet various Liberal Members of Parliament.

Har Dayal was fifteen years junior to Mahatma Gandhi but no record exists of their meeting in London.

Unrest in Indian Politics

By the end of 1906, a year after the partition of Bengal in India, Viceroy Minto first instigated the demand and then cunningly accepted Sir Aga Khan-led Muslim delegation's request for the protection of the rights of the minorities against the assertion of the numerically larger Hindu population. The seeds of communal hatred were sown by Hukumat-i-Britannia via its *divide et impera* strategy to protect its commercial and political interests.

At the Calcutta session of the Indian National Congress held from December 26–30, 1906, there was a dispute between moderate and extremist wings of the party regarding appointing the President of the session. Tilak emerged as 'The father of the Indian unrest'. He was proud of his country's heritage and wrote about its culture, which had attracted the West. The fact that Indians wanted to abandon their own culture and ape the West disturbed him. His famous slogan, "Swaraj is my Birthright and I shall have it" had become extremely popular in India. The combination of Lala Lajpat Rai, Bal Gangadhar Tilak and Bipin Chandra Pal (1858–1932), represented East, West, and North India and formed a new triumvirate called Lal Bal Pal.

At last the former Indian member of the British Parliament, Dadabhai Naoroji was declared the president for the third time. Under the leadership of Naoroji, Congress adopted 'Swaraj as the Goal of Indian people'. But the resolution was toned down and it was agreed, "self-government means that obtaining the self-governing British Colonies." Thus the definition of Swaraj demanded by the extremists was altered. The moderates by clever maneuvering defeated the extremists and the difference became apparent.

The Indian National Congress was now set to split.

Nevertheless, Naoroji in his speech claimed, "We need a body of half a dozen at least if not a dozen enthusiastic and well qualified Indians for the work of the Committee here and for propagandism by our organ, literature, and lectures to be permanent residents in England. These may be either well educated and competent well to do men who can live on their means or well to do should supply the means to enable such well-qualified men to live here. Our success must depend upon our own proper men and sufficient means. Indians must make up their minds for large sacrifices both personal and pecuniary…" At the end of the address Naoroji, quoted the words of Sir Henry Campbell Bannerman, "Good government could never be a substitute for government by the people themselves."

Dominus Illuminatio Mea (Lord is My Light)

The weather in Oxford in late December 1906 was mild and the maximum temperature was close to 13°C. Then bitterly cold east winds developed the day after Christmas and temperatures fell. Oxford had its first snowfall. It barely covered the ground and was gone by the afternoon but Har Dayal and Sunder Rani knew it was only a prelude to what was coming. Sunder Rani was upset with the fog and winter. She did not know many people in Oxford and was not yet fluent in the English language. The idea of studying politics, history, and philosophy under the guidance of her husband was not working out. His plans to involve her in his future revolutionary enterprise seemed vague. In early 1907 the temperature dropped further and there was snow everywhere. Sunder Rani unable to adject with the cold fell ill in Oxford. Har Dayal rented an apartment in the seaside town of Brighton for his wife. The couple lived at 19, Wyndham Street (Marine Parade), Brighton for almost two months in the winter while he traveled back and forth from Oxford. A little later the couple moved to number 65 Wyndham Street and stayed there till the last week of April before returning to better weather in Oxford.

Har Dayal as a student at Oxford was attracted to men of great intellect. He serendipitously was in Britain during the real golden age of British culture in that first decade of the twentieth century with writers such as J.M. Barrie, P.G. Wodehouse, Joseph Conrad, Arthur Conan Doyle, H. G. Wells, Rudyard Kipling, George Bernard Shaw, E.M. Forster and Beatrix Potter amongst others. Har Dayal went to meet the poet laureate Robert Bridges in his home, Chilswell House in Boars Hills, five kilometers southwest of Oxford. Bridges afterward remembered the young Indian and spoke to Sir Tej Bahadur Sapru in the highest terms, both of his character and his intellectual attainments. Har Dayal also paid a visit to the famous dramatist George Bernard Shaw at his house in the small village of Ayot St Lawrence outside London.

On January 22nd, 1907, the trustees at St John's College fascinated by Har Dayal's intellectual assets awarded him an additional £30 as the Casberd Exhibitioner taking his scholarship to £230 per year. The news of this award was published in the London newspapers including *The Guardian* (January 23rd, 1907) and it was the first time his name appeared in the British media.

Next Har Dayal appeared in a tough written examination conducted to elect a Sanskrit scholar for the Foundation of Colonel Boden at the Indian Institute Rooms, Broad Street in Oxford. The prestigious scholarship was established in 1833 to support students learning Sanskrit and was tenable only for two years, with the possibility of extension to a third year. Previously only one Indian student Brajendranath De was a Boden Sanskrit Scholar at Oxford who later qualified for the ICS. The examiners communicated to the Vice-Chancellor that they "recommend for the election of Har Dayal of St. John's College as the Boden Sanskrit Scholar at Oxford". On May 18th, 1907, the official *Oxford magazine* declared the result of the Boden scholarship and congratulated Har Dayal on his accomplishments. It printed, "It is announced tonight that the Boden Sanskrit scholarship has been gained by Mr. Har Dayal, of St. John's College. The scholarship is tenable for four years with an annual stipend of £50".

The total value of British scholarship to Har Dayal was now an astronomical sum of £840. (The scholarship of £840 in 1907 would be approximately worth £99,500 or Rs. 1 Crore today). This was an unparalleled record in the history of Oxford for an Indian student. Har Dayal's exceptional success at Oxford amplified an interesting distinction between intelligence and genius.

Sattavanche Dohale

On Saturday, May 11th, 1907, Savarkar stood before an audience of young Indian students at Tilak House, 78 Goldsmith Avenue in Acton in London. They had accepted his invitation that read, "Under the auspices of the Free India League it is decided to commemorate the golden jubilee of the patriotic rising of 1857. This meeting is to be held on Saturday the 11th of May, the day of the Declaration of Independence. Your presence is earnestly solicited with your friends."

The celebration of Martyrs' Day named '*Yaadgari Diwas*', (Remembrance Day celebrations) to commemorate the Ghadr of 1857 began with Savarkar's fiery speech. Reading from his essay, 'Sattavanche dohale' (Longing for '57) Savarkar declared, "The Nation that has no consciousness of its past has no future. Equally true it is that a nation must develop its capacity not only claiming a past but also of knowing how to use it for the furtherance of its future." Invoking the martyrs of 1857, he asserted, "The war begun on the 10th of May 1857 is not over on the 10th of May 1907, nor can it ever cease till a 10th May to come sees accomplished and our Motherland stands free!" The spirit of 1857 was still alive, he proclaimed and the revolutionaries would continue the struggle of the rebel leaders.

Savarkar added, that the two great principals of swadharma and swaraj remained the unifying features throughout the war of independence. He reiterated the religious unity of the revolutionaries "men of different religions, men of different caste, people following widely different professions – not able any longer to bear the sight of the persecution of the Mother brought about the avenging revolution in an incredibly short time".

In his speech, he specified that India needed inspirational heroes from the Ghadr of 1857 and the nation needed to be roused. He effectively told the story of men and women who had sacrificed their lives for India's liberty in 1857. In his speech, he debunked all the self-serving theories of British historians like Charles Ball, John Kaye and George Bruce Malleson for whom the dominant narrative was the 'mutiny' and all the rebels were portrayed as selfish, petty and naïve. Savarkar presented the Ghadr of 1857 in a brand new manner that could inspire its second coming.

Thunderous applause followed. The event to commemorate the Ghadr of 1857 concluded with the distribution of *'Parshad'* (ritual offering) in the form of a *chapatti* – (Indian bread used as a secret messaging system in North India that had spooked the Hukumat-i-Britannia during the Ghadr of 1857). The Indians furthermore wore badges with the legend *'Honour to the Martyrs of 1857'*. After consulting the historiographies at the British Library, Savarkar later enlarged his essay into a published book, *The Indian War of Independence*.

Additionally, Krishna Varma gave fiery speeches in the free atmosphere of Hyde Park in London, calling for the support of progressive and sympathetic Britons in the right cause of India's emancipation. In early 1907, a question was raised in the House of Commons enquiring whether the Government proposed to take any action against Krishna Varma. Valentine Choril, the editor of *The Times,* regarded India House, the unassuming Victorian building in a quiet, well-off side street of London, "the most dangerous organization outside India." An editorial in *The Times* submitted Krishna Varma should be prosecuted for preaching "disloyal sentiments" to the Indian students staying at India House on Cromwell Avenue. But soon after the 'Yaadgari Diwas' in London sometime in June 1907 Krishna Varma secretly left for Paris leaving the management of the India House to the able Savarkar.

In a subsequent issue of *The Indian Sociologist*, a change of address was listed as, '10 Avenue Ingres, Passy, Paris, France'. Also, Krishna Varma remarked in the September 1907 issue: "On the earnest advice of some of our friends, we left England, practically for good, during the early part of June last, seeing that mischief was brewing." According to *Shyamji Krishna Varma: Sanskrit, Sociology, and Anti-Imperialism*, written by Harald Fischer-Tiné, the real reason for his relocation was that British Secret Service was on his trail. He had met an American by the name of O'Brien at the India House who had contacted him claiming to be a staff member of New York's *Gaelic American*, a prominent

Irish-Catholic newspaper owned and operated by the Irish nationalist John Devoy who supported the Indian independence movement. O'Brien turned out to be a detective of Scotland Yard. Dreading the British Secret Service operatives Krishna Varma thought it prudent to leave Britain.

In his book, *Policing Transnational Protest*, Daniel Brückenhaus had revealed, "In the years between 1905 and 1909, the Special Branch increasingly tried to infiltrate meetings at India House and attempted to obtain information on Indians' activities. In order to do so, white British policemen were sometimes used; howerever this situation was dangerous because of the anticolonialists' concerted efforts to expose them. The police detective Harold Brust for instance, was beaten severely several times by Indians he was shadowing in Cambrdige, Oxford and London…. After all, Brust remarked, "most of us S.B. men held a sneaking admiration for the adrour of these lads who mistakenly believed themselves the appointed saviours of their down trodden country".

Apostrophizing the Martyrs of 1857

Fifty years since the Ghadr, back in India at an enormous gathering at Lyallpur on March 3rd, 1907, Banke Dayal, introduced his song, "Pagdi sambhal Jatta, Pagdi Sambhal oye". The song became the very symbol and soul of the Pagdi sambhal Jatta movement led by the former schoolmaster and Indian revolutionary leader, Ajit Singh (1881–1947) and his Bharat Mata society in North India.

Even though the Hukumat-i-Britannia was at its very pinnacle in India in 1907, it faced the greatest threat of internal unrest due to the revival of the memories of 1857. The British Viceroy Minto considered the idea of the celebration of the fiftieth anniversary of the events of 1857 in India as dangerous. On the occasion, he unveiled a large statue of Brigadier-General John Nicholson showing him with a naked sword in hand and surrounded by mortars that were erected facing the battered walls of Delhi at Kashmiri Darwaza. He justified it by stating that it was raised to the memory of a soldier worshipped as a hero by both British and Indian troops, but "to celebrate the jubilee of 1857 would be an inexcusable mistake".

The year 1907 was also a hundred and fifty years after the Battle of Plassey. For Lord Curzon in Britain, it seemed appropriate for India to erect a memorial to Clive associated with the anniversary of Plassey. In Minto's opinion, "Anything of the sort is…utterly out of the question. I cannot imagine anyone, who has ever thought twice about it, making such a proposal. The story of the Mutiny is a splendid page in our history – a story of magnificent courage and endurance which our Indian troops in many cases faithfully shared with us, but I cannot say how wrong I feel it would be to revive the memory of those times throughout India above all, at the present moment".

Preceding this a London newspaper suggested that the superstitious people of India attached great importance to dates and therefore the Government should take special care in case some wholesale disturbance occurred on the anniversary. Consequently, the British Secret Service looked at May 10th, 1907, with some apprehension. After the celebrations in London, copies of Savarkar's essay in the form of a leaflet 'Oh Martyrs' were sent to various addresses in India and later appeared in the newspaper *Vihari* on June 10th, 1907. The leaflet was soon in the possession of Charles James Stevenson-Moore (1866–1947) the Director of DCI in Simla. He informed the Hukumat-i-Britannia about the leaflet, "which apostrophizes the mutineers of 1857 and prophesies a revolution in 1917."

Sir Denzil Charles Jelf Ibbetson, the Cambridge educated ICS officer, posted as the Lt. Governor of Punjab, faced series of riots, and murders challenging the British rule. Sir Ibbetson communicated to the British Viceroy Lord Minto that he feared a great conspiracy similar to the Ghadr of 1857 was afoot. There was also a growing fear of an Afghan – Russian – Punjabi alliance to create unrest. Previously, firangi troops were drafted into Lahore when a mob protesting against the arrest of Indian barristers partly burned the bungalow of P. D. Agnew the District Magistrate and destroyed his furniture and papers. Horrifically Europeans were attacked on the main streets in Lahore. There were several strikes among revenue clerks and the North-Western State Railway too went on strike.

Lord Horatio Herbert Kitchener, Commander-in-Chief of the British Indian army communicated that the Indian newspapers and journals were disseminating rebellion in India. The devastating consequences of a replay of the Ghadr of 1857 alarmed Lord Minto, as well as Lord Morley in London. Both men recognized that fresh measures were needed to encourage and reward loyalty to the Hukumat-i-Britannia in India. The sadhus and fakirs were considered the harbingers of sedition and steps were taken to prevent them from entering the British Indian army cantonments.

It was alleged that the popular leader Lajpat Rai was the mastermind and the organizer-in-chief of the underground activities. The other name mentioned as a seditionist was that of Ajit Singh. He along with his brother Kishan Singh (father of revolutionary Bhagat Singh) had worked among the people at the grassroots in famine-stricken regions of India and also in flood-and-earthquake-affected areas. Both Lajpat Rai and Ajit Singh had seized on the momentum generated by the unrest in Punjab. Lajpat Rai's newspaper, *The Punjabee*, published stirring nationalistic articles and Ajit Singh gave fiery speeches. Riots against British rule broke out in the cities of Amritsar, Lahore, and Rawalpindi.

On May 3rd, the Hukumat-i-Britannia issued emergency measures in the state of Punjab and press censorship was enforced. Then on May 9th, the Hukumat-i-Britannia issued warrants under Regulation III of 1818 for the arrest and deportation of Lajpat Rai without a trial till November 12th, 1907 to Mandalay in Burma. On June 3rd similar orders were issued for Ajit Singh. This lead to nation-wide protests in India the impact of which was felt as far as Britain.

Young Nehru then in his final years at Harrow mentioned in his *Autobiography*, "Right through the years 1906 and 1907 news from India had been agitating me. I got meager enough accounts from the English papers but even that little showed big events were happening at home in Bengal, Punjab, and Maharashtra. There was Lala Lajpat Rai's and S. Ajit Singh's deportation, and Bengal seemed to be in an uproar, and Tilak's name was often flashed from Poona and there were Swadeshi and boycott. All this stirred me tremendously..." He added, "From 1907 onwards for several years India was seething with unrest and trouble. For the first time since the Revolt of 1857 India was showing fight and not submitting tamely to foreign rule...."

The Anarchist Politics in Britain

At Oxford, the young Har Dayal greatly disturbed by the deportation of Lajpat Rai and Ajit Singh and influenced by the events at the India House was attracted to anarchist politics in Britain. Around the same time, he made the pilgrimage to see Pyotr Alexander Kropotkin (1842–1921), the Russian born leader of highbrow anarchism in his home at 6 Crescent Road, Bromley, a remote suburb in South London. Kropotkin had fled from Russia and used his house to lecture college students, anarchist exiles, young anarchists and British socialists. He was a man of worldwide repute and his writings had been translated into every European language.

The Indian nationalist in Har Dayal emerged as he became disillusioned with Oxford's education that celebrated and idealized occidental imperialism. Later he recollected that he discovered real patriotism among the British for their nation in Oxford. He had found that at the university, his fellow English students were intensely preoccupied with the political and economic problems of the British nation and the Empire. When the news had arrived that the British had at last beaten the Boers, the Oxford boys had torn off doors and burned them in bonfires, celebrating the victory. He recalled that he was amazed at the intense, profound nationalism of the Englishman. His predilection was towards anarchism of Kropotkin at this stage. He began to share Kropotkin's unwavering faith in the revolutionary potential of the masses. He developed a distrust of the state and a young man's faith in revolution and rationalism.

Over the years many Russian like Kropotkin including Mikhail Alexandrovich Bakunin, Alexander Berkman, and Emma Goldman had escaped from Russia and appeared in Britain and the United States. The activities these political refugees were directed at their homeland. There were all kinds of anarchist currents in Britain, from an exiled group of literati out of touch with the popular mood to militant revolutionaries. Political activity was enhanced by propaganda, aimed at affecting emigrant's newspapers. The anarchists in Russia had resorted to the use of bombs and in Paris, the Hindi speaking Russian anarchist Nicholas Safranski was sought by Indian activists to teach the secret art of making explosives and bombs. Copies were made of the twenty-nine-page bomb-making manual and distributed to various members of the group. One such copy reached Har Dayal. The idea was to send the booklet and information to compatriots in India.

To Hell with ICS

Har Dayal was expected to follow the path taken by young Indians educated at Oxford or Cambridge. With his academic record and a state scholarship, he was a natural candidate for the famed ICS.

In 1907 the British Empire was the closest example of World Government humankind had ever known. To govern effectively the empire a small group of Indian Civil officers was created usually filled with Oxford and Cambridge graduates. Their compensation was in proportion to their power and they were paid the highest salaries in India along with great privileges. A tiny cadre of just over a thousand, governed over more than three hundred million Indians in a land some thirteen thousand kilometers away from London. The languages, the religions and the castes combined with a huge population and the complexities of India were tremendously difficult to understand. This required local Indian expertise and ICS was opened to Indians by the Hukumat-i-Britannia in 1861. The largely British ICS accepted just four or six Indians through a exceedingly tough entrance examination held in London but made it possible for an exceptionally bright Indian to enter the world of a well-appointed lifestyle. The best Indian students competed for these positions and Satyendranath Tagore, became the first Indian to qualify the ICS in 1863. By 1902, of the total number of 1067 ICS officers, there were only forty Indians. In those days to be an ICS officer for an Indian was to rise to the level of the "Gods of Simla". Some equated the ICS with Plato's guardians. Several ICS officers had received a knighthood after a successful career in India.

Har Dayal, with his outstanding scholastic gifts, was poised to join the ranks of the ICS. He had to choose ten subjects and appear in nineteen written plus four practical examinations that would take the whole of August. The British Empire would have welcomed an officer like him with open arms in the much-venerated Indian Civil Service. His friends, family members and in-laws in Delhi looked forward to his selection in the ICS as a non-white "Burra Sahib" in Hukumat-i-Britannia; as a district head or a judge.

In the previous year, another Government of India scholar, Panna Lall from Agra, a graduate of Calcutta University, who was at Cambridge was called to the Bar at the Gray Inn on November 18th, 1906 and was placed first in the final list of selected candidates from India in the ICS entrance examination. He went on to distinguish himself in the ICS as a scholar of great learning.

However, the Indian nationalist movement in London, the work of international anarchists and the recent events in India including the deportation of his heroes to Mandalay had a deep impact on the twenty-two-year-old Har Dayal's mind. He was brilliant enough to have easily passed the ICS entrance examination but he vehemently denounced the well-trodden path of the western-educated Indian. Unlike other Indians, he shockingly favored the challenging life of a revolutionary to the soft life of a member of the elite. The fervent nationalist in a flash of clarity – his eureka moment, gave up the chance of a lifetime and refused to appear for the entrance examination.

Proud of his ferocious intellect and with the bold conviction of youth the Dilliwallah is reported to have dramatically exclaimed, "To hell with ICS".

An Act of Complete Rebellion

In early September 1907, Har Dayal attended his last lecture at St. John's College. He was a man of strong impulses and once an idea got into his head he was unlikely to relent. After relinquishing the opportunity to become an ICS officer, in the middle of his last term at Oxford, the patriotic and idealistic man decided to even resign from his hard-won Indian Government and Oxford scholarships on ideological grounds. He declared, "No Indian who really loves his country ought to compromise his principle and barter his rectitude for any favor whatever at the hands of alien oppressive rulers of India."

Bhai Parmanand tried to dissuade him even suggesting that he should at least finish his studies at Oxford and not depart midstream after concluding 5/6th of the course. He also felt that the cost of living with his wife in Britain would be quite a bit and the ongoing scholarship would help. But the headstrong and rebellious Har Dayal had already made up his mind. In his autobiography, *The Story of My Life*, Bhai Parmanand remembered, "He would say that these degrees are for us just what the degree of Pandit would be to an Afghan, whom, after conquering Afghanistan we had brought to Benares for education." *Dr. Dharmavira in his biography* has written, "Har Dayal did not complete his studies in Oxford, "because he maintained that this was going against the principle he had set before himself. This was unheard of and unequaled."

Har Dayal's decision to leave Oxford shocked the imperialist and the academic community at the University. James Bellamy, the President of St. Johns College and former Vice-Chancellor of the University of Oxford came up with an offer to pay the fees instead of the Government's scholarship and tried to dissuade the particularly adamant young man. The process continued for over months. He was called to the India Office and the issue of his resignation was discussed at length. As no other Oxford scholarship holder had ever resigned in the history of the University, Members of Parliament came to meet him in Oxford and tried to reason with him but to no avail. There were yet other ways of negotiating. The recently knighted Sir William Hutt Curzon Wyllie (1848–1909), who was the political Aide-de-Camp for Lord Morley, remarked that "as he (Har Dayal) will fail to complete three years residence in this country he may be held to be liable to the penalty attached to the forfeiture of this scholarship".

The NAI documents record that Lord Morley received a missive from Har Dayal where he announced his resignation. "...I beg to resign the scholarship which was awarded to me in accordance with article 6 of the said 'Agreement' this resignation to take effect from September 18, 1907. I beg to inquire if I should make any payment to the Secretary of State for India under article 7 of the above mentioned agreement in order that the bond given by me and two sureties in accordance with Article 8 of the same agreement may be null and void. I beg to state that the scholarship had not been 'forfeited' but has been resigned by me. I also beg to state that the cost of my 'free passage' from India to England in September 1905 amounted to nearly £34 (thirty-four pounds). I was given a second-class ticket from Delhi to Bombay (G.I.R.R.) and a second (B) saloon ticket from Bombay to London by the P and O's Egypt. I am not certain if I traveled from Delhi to Bombay at the expense of the Government of India. I beg the favour of your informing me of the exact sum that help resents the cost of my free passage from India to England..."

Har Dayal straightaway returned the money that was paid for his passage to Britain. Consequently, he lost the much-needed stipend and audaciously walked away without completing his degree.

The news of Har Dayal's unprecedented resignation from Oxford and sidestepping the ICS examination was received with absolute disbelief at his home in Delhi. The Civil Service and working for the ruling dispensation was the original job profile of the community of scribes. By his inexplicable actions, he had shattered the expectations of his family and his three elder brothers who looked forward to his professional success as an ICS officer. His father-in-law Gopal Chand was particularly upset at his reckless behavior. He could not fathom how a man of his astounding competence and learning could be convinced about being 'a burning nationalist'. But clearly, the brainpower of Har Dayal was meant for a much larger canvas.

After resigning from Oxford the prodigy from India plunged full time into the Indian freedom movement with single-minded devotion to end the degrading injustice imposed on India. Previously in the May 1907 issue of *The Indian Sociologist*, Har Dayal in an article had recalled verses of the *Bhagwad Gita*, *"Karmanyevadhikaraste ma phaleshi kadachana"* (do your duty regardless of consequences). And months later Har Dayal decided to use his matchless intellectual prowess to solve the greatest problem of his era, the complete dissolution of the British Empire.

Dip the Pen in my Heart's Blood

In November 1907, just over two years since he arrived in Britain, now freed from the burden of an Oxford degree and entering the ICS, Har Dayal came back to his home at 97 Southmoor Road in Oxford where he still lived with Sunder Rani. Despite the economic difficulties after quitting the scholarship he was deeply committed to the cause of India's self-determination and seemed to be evolving into an amazing Indian leader. The ideas of sacrifice, martyrdom, resurrection, and redemption had tremendous appeal for Indians. In Indian ethos, the act of personal sacrifice was the highest attainment in life and considered far higher than the act of accumulation that the society generally accepted as a sign of success. Har Dayal was furthermore influenced by the devotion to duty of the Christian missionaries like Charles Andrews as well as contemporary western democratic and libertarian movements.

After quitting the Oxford scholarship and with his name removed from the St. John's books, Har Dayal had no financial support or immediate job prospects. He requested Krishna Varma for the sustenance of 16 shillings per week for one year. Krishna Varma's promises were partially fulfilled. Nevertheless, Har Dayal made India House in London as his base for future political adventures. Here he applied his colossal mind in authoring ideas for India's independence and competently writing for the magazines The *Indian Sociologist* in Paris and *The Modern Review*, a leading journal of the progressive Indian intelligentsia published by Ramanand Chatterjee in Calcutta. He also produced an incredible 'constitution of India' like document, 'A Sketch of a Complete Political Movement for the Emancipation of India,' that he submitted to Krishna Varma. He even spearheaded the effort at India House to collect funds for the Lajpat Rai – Ajit Singh Fund. Additionally, he made plans to launch a magazine, *Swarjaya*, modeled on *The Indian Sociologist*. Har Dayal dramatically announced, "When I write, I shall dip my pen in my heart's blood and write what I feel and think."

Besides attacking the Hukumat-i-Britannia's education system in India, Har Dayal focused his energies on disseminating the economic reality of India under foreign rule. He began an independent study of the history of revolutionary movements and the socio-economic condition of India, preparing a textbook on Indian politics, and getting a closer look at the work of radical emancipatory movements in America, England, Ireland, and on the Continent. Through his writings he exposed that India was being used as a captive market for British goods and services and this kind of economic racism was impeding the growth of

India's economy. The cost of the large British Indian army, as well as the ICS, was also being borne by the Indians. With each passing day, India was growing poorer while Britain was getting richer and had become a world economic power.

In another drastic move despite extreme weather conditions he even gave up wearing western clothes and was seen walking around London in Indian pagri, kurta, and dhoti wrapped in a warm shawl. His struggle with the wintery windy conditions was real and he frequently caught pneumonia and bronchial disorders. "We are helpless before the fantastic obstinacy of Har Dayal", commented his colleague Vinayak Savarkar.

In his mind, Har Dayal was now a rebel at war with the British Empire and possibly a man of destiny.

6

THE FIREBRAND POLITICAL MISSIONARY IN INDIA

"About this time one of the most sinister figures in the revolutionary movement appeared on the scene. This was Har Dayal, a native of Delhi...He was back in Lahore in 1906 and stayed for some time with Lajpat Rai with a party of young men, whose characters he was forming by preaching passive resistance and boycott, thus anticipating Gandhi by ten years..."

Sir Michael Francis O'Dwyer
Lt. Governor of Punjab

On the extremely cold Monday evening of December 23rd, 1907, the deeply etched memories of the "Ghadr of 1857", also called the Sepoy Mutiny by British historians, were brought back to London.

Albert Hall, an impressive concert venue in the heart of the city was decorated with sketches of the Kashmiri Gate of Delhi, and the Residency at Lucknow, and the Well at Cawnpore. Lord Edward Levy-Lawson Burham, the proprietor of *The Daily Telegraph* had funded the banquet for the veterans of the Indian mutiny of 1857 as "The golden commemoration of the Indian Mutiny Veterans". In the audience were 250 of the surviving officer veterans and 544 soldier veterans of the British military campaigns of 1857–58. The youngest among the veterans was sixty-five years of age. He was a drummer boy during the mutiny. The many distinguished guests besides the veterans included the winner of Victoria Cross, General Sir Dighton Probyn, and Rudyard Kipling, who had recently returned from Stockholm with the Nobel Prize for Literature valued at £ 7,700.

That memorable evening, an elegantly attired former British Viceroy of India, Lord Curzon got up from his seat and proposed a toast to "the Survivors of the Indian Mutiny". In one of the best speeches of his career, he described the banquet at Albert Hall as the natural sequel to the memorable entry of the veterans of the mutiny at the Delhi Durbar in 1902.

Next, the band of the 1st Duke of Cornwall's Light Infantry, the old 32nd Foot, the defenders of Lucknow, played a selection of music. The Cawnpore born, Field Marshal Lord Frederick Sleigh Roberts (1832–1914), former Commander-in-Chief in India and a veteran of 1857, presided at the long table. He was mentioned seven times in dispatches for hand-to-hand combat in the recapture of Delhi and had won the Victoria Cross for his actions. He read a cordial message from King Edward VII and in his speech recalled the bravery of his fellow officers drawing from his immensely popular autobiography, *Forty-One Years in India* (1897). His address featured a roll call of the heroic British Generals of 1857, Field Marshal Sir Colin Campbell, Lt. General Sir James Outram, Brigadier General James Neill, and Major General Sir Henry Havelock. He especially evoked the roles of Sir Henry Lawrence, the defender of Lucknow and Brigadier John Nicholson, the hero of Delhi. All those present in the Albert Hall stood while the 'Last Post' was sounded. Finally, Lewis Waller in his golden voice recited the deeply moving verses, 'The Veterans' written by Kipling, admirably reflecting the spirit of a memorable and affecting celebration. The proceedings closed with 'Auld Lang Syne' sung by Muriel Foster and Ben Davies.

In the days leading up to the event, the local newspapers of Britain had carried long accounts to bring back the memories of the insurrection to the fore. The celebrated military hero Field Marshal Sir Evelyn Wood penned an eighteen-part account entitled, 'The Revolt in Hindustan' in *The Times*. Besides, there were theatrical plays in London that dramatized the events and favorably showcased the glory of the British armed forces in 1857. Central to the spectacle was the noble martyrdom of the British army in the cause of the Empire. The theatres in London shook with applause in the end as the rebels were blown from cannons. Despite the bravado and the façade of celebration and remorseless accounts, in their hearts, the civil servants and the military leaders of the Hukumat-i-Britannia feared a replay of the Ghadr of 1857 in India and acknowledged the grave danger in ruling over a large mass of people across the seas. Away from the atmosphere of jubilation in London commemorating the victory of 1857, the British Empire was facing a new kind of threat in Bengal and Punjab in distant India.

Hukumat-i-Britannia Under Attack in India

On Friday, December 6th, 1907, Lt. Governor Andrew Fraser was traveling on a local train in his carriage. Fraser was on the hit list of the Indian revolutionaries for his role in planning the partition of Bengal. A few weeks before in November 1907, two futile attempts were made between Chandernagore and Maukundu to bomb the trains in which the Lt. Governor was traveling. He had escaped unhurt on both occasions. This time, as the train neared Narayangarh at Midnapore in Bengal, a small blast blew up the train tracks. Despite the twisted rails and a five feet wide crater the Lt. Governor's carriage miraculously did not derail. The assassination attempt on the life of Fraser by Indian revolutionaries failed for the third time.

The 26th session of the Indian National Congress was to be held on December 26th, 1907 at Surat, on the banks of the river Tapti. Three days prior on December 23rd, Dacca's (Dhaka) District Magistrate, Basil Copleton Allen was waiting at the Goalundo railway station and was attacked by Indian revolutionaries. He was shot at but did not die. At the Whitehall in London, Lord Morley was not surprised. On December 26th, he wrote to Lord Minto, "It has long been evident that Indian antagonism to Government would run slowly into the usual grooves, including assassination."

At the Indian National Congress's annual session in Surat, the murderous attack on Allen created a sensation among the delegates. The extremists within the party were disturbed by the rumors that the moderates wanted to scuttle the four resolutions adopted at the Calcutta session in 1906. The moderates were deeply hurt by the ridicule and venom poured on them. The delegates, thus, met in an atmosphere surcharged with anger and the session was marred by disturbances. Extremist leaders like Bal Gangadhar Tilak, Lajpat Rai, and Bipin Chandra Pal pushed for resolutions on swaraj, boycott and national education while the moderate leaders like Surendranath Banerjea and Gopal Krishna Gokhale backed a softer attitude. With no meeting ground between the two sections, the Surat session disintegrated into confusion and eventually had to be suspended sine die.

Just ten years before, on September 2nd, 1897, Lord George Francis Hamilton, the Secretary of State for India, had written to then British Viceroy Lord Curzon, "I think the real danger to our rule in India, not now but say fifty years hence, is the gradual adoption and extension of western ideas of agitation and organization, and, if we could break the educated Hindu party into two sections holding widely different views, we should, by such a division, strengthen our position against the subtle and continuous attack which the spread of education must make upon our present system of Government."

The other major political development at that time was the formation of the Hindu Mahasabha under the leadership of Madan Mohan Malaviya (1861–1946) and Lajpat Rai which emerged from a combination of the regional Hindu Sabhas, the first of which was established in Punjab in 1907. Previously a political party with the object of protecting the rights of Indian Muslims, 'All-India Muslim League' was founded in December 1906 at Dacca.

Har Dayal Returns

In early February 1908, Har Dayal and Sunder Rani boarded the *S. S. Golconda* and left Britain for Madras via Port Said, Suez, and Aden. At the beginning of 1908 with the onset of the dreaded winter months of Britain, Har Dayal was cheerful that his wife was expecting their child. A son had been born two years after their marriage but the infant had sadly lived for only ten months. Considering the costs of living in Britain and the health condition of his wife, he decided to return to India.

A single second-class ticket was sent by Gopal Chand to enable Sunder Rani to return to India for a family wedding. Short on funds, Har Dayal exchanged the single second-class ticket for two third-class tickets on *S. S. Golconda,* a British India Steam Navigation Co. Ltd ship to India that connected London to Madras. He wanted to return to India to arouse his countrymen against Hukumat-i-Britannia. In the many trunks, the couple had packed part of Har Dayal's library and a lot of revolutionary literature. It included the manual of bomb-making and several editions of *The Indian Sociologist*. In September 1907 the Hukumat-i-Britannia had banned the publication or distribution of *The Indian Sociologist* in India. Further, the Sea Customs Act of 1878 allowed the Hukumat-i-Britannia to "prohibit or restrict the bringing or taking by sea or by land goods of any specified description into or out of India across any customs frontier as defined by the Central Government."

Sunder Rani had a premonition that the British Secret Service may search their luggage on arrival in Madras so she advised her husband to destroy the banned material. As they first glimpsed the coast of India, and the harbor of Tuticorin with its majestic cocoa palms and its yellow-sanded beach came into view, the couple destroyed all the inflammatory journals, books, leaflets and newspapers they had in their possession. It is probable Har Dayal with his eidetic memory skill had retained the contents of the journals before consigning them to the sea.

After landing in Madras, Har Dayal planned to travel by train through the nation stopping at various places to meet major political leaders and assess the political climate. Introducing himself as a 'political missionary' the twenty-three-year-old met the veteran leaders Tilak and Gokhale in Poona. In his autobiography, *Majhi janmathepa – My Transportation for Life*, Savarkar later recorded Har Dayal's version of the meeting, "While in India Har Dayal once went to Poona to pay a visit to Tilak. And then he paid a similar visit to his rival Gokhale. He had traveled all over India paying visits to the leaders of India in opposite camps. And he had heard from them nothing but abuse and misrepresentation of one another. But Tilak and Gokhale were free from this foible. Each of them tried in his own way to persuade Har Dayal to join his own party, but not a word they breathed about each other, to reduce character or misrepresent work. Not a word of malice or vilification escaped their mouth. On the other hand, what they spoke of one another was full of appreciation and reverence."

Tilak said, "Do see Gokhale once." And Gokhale said, "You have done well in seeing Tilak." And he added, "That you have put up with him is as it should be, for the next generation is going to be his." In turn, Tilak was awestruck by the young revolutionary and mentioned to Krishna Varma that in the times to come he expected Har Dayal to develop into a major leader in Punjab and that he would "prove a tower of strength to the Nationalist Party generally."

Finally, Har Dayal reached his in-laws' mansion in Meerut clad in a simple dhoti, kurta, pagri, and shawl dressed like a simple Indian villager instead of the customary Savile Row stitched three-piece suit, Oxford tie, and hat for a 'London returned' Indian gentleman. For a man whose community is known for its upper-class lifestyle and its love for alcohol and non-vegetarian cuisine he had turned into a strict vegetarian and abstained from drinking alcohol.

Gopal Chand, a much-respected Judge, was by now convinced that his daughter Sunder Rani's life was crumbling. On receiving his daughter in his home he confronted the young radical and termed him inconsistent, inconsiderate, impetuous, and wrongheaded. *Dr. Dharmavira notes in his biography*, that Lala Gopal Chand was livid and told Har Dayal that he had devastated his daughter's life, "You could have had a brilliant career, you could have joined the ICS, you could have been anything, but instead you have chosen a path which will lead straight to prison."

Though in the long run Gopal Chand was proven wrong his disappointment with his son-in-law at that juncture was not unfounded. Har Dayal with his unique and rare intellectual gifts could have risen in the ICS to the highest positions. With his reputation as one of the most brilliant Indians of his times, a Knighthood or even Lordship was well within his reach. He even politely turned down offers from Maharajas across India including Kashmir and Rajputana to be the Diwan. Instead, he chose the path less traveled and lived in direct opposition to the ruling dispensation of the day.

Gopal Chand moved Sunder Rani back into his family home and prohibited Har Dayal from seeing her. Despite the outrage and insults thrown at him in the presence of all his family members, Har Dayal remained calm. The wannabe 'Buddha' looked at the love of his life with his intense dark eyes and with a tender smile, sought permission to live like an ascetic. Sunder Rani accepted what fate held for her. The young couple sacrificed their relationship and did know at that time that they would never meet again. Har Dayal walked out of his in-laws' mansion to serve the land of his birth and expected no rewards in return. He was a true 'Karma Yogi' like Swami Vivekananda and Sri Aurobindo before him and Mahatma Gandhi and Netaji Subhas Chandra Bose later.

The Society of Political Missionaries

On a temperate March evening, Narayan Prasad Arora encountered a familiar-looking person at the Bhagwat Ghat in Kanpur. He immediately recognized that the man was 'The Great Har Dayal', walking in ordinary clothes. Har Dayal along with four young men dressed in homespun clothing of khaddar and carrying lathis was enjoying their evening on the banks of the Ganges. Arora claimed he was astonished to see this well-known public intellectual dressed like an *aam admi* (common man) as he defied the norm of being 'a suited booted English speaking Indian'. After interacting with the humble and cheerful leader Arora instantly enrolled in his ashram the following day.

After leaving his expectant wife in Meerut at her parent's home, Har Dayal had reached Kanpur. Here Manohar Lal Chak, the father of a friend from his London days, provided Har Dayal with a house and Amir Chand put up the funds to set up the ashram. He set up a revolutionary organization in India and called it Desh Bhakt Samaj governed by a Desh Sewak Samiti (political missionaries council). The idea of this council had emerged on February 23rd, 1907, at the annual meeting of the Indian Home Rule Society held in London and Krishna Varma announced a donation of Rs. 10,000 to establish a society of political missionaries in India called 'Deshbhakta Samaj or Society of Political Missionaries'. Har Dayal had worked out the sketch for the 'Society of Political Missionaries' in an article first published in *The Indian Sociologist* in May 1907. It was also an extension of ideas he expressed to Khudadad Khan from Oxford in 1905.

The objective of the 'Society of Political Missionaries' was to stimulate a healthy national pride by impressing the idea of national continuity and unity. Har Dayal wanted the Hukumat-i-Britannia to leave India at any cost and if a revolution was required so be it. He wanted to constructively prepare a new generation of selfless political leaders as an alternative to the ICS for the diplomatic or military struggle against the evil Hukumat-i-Britannia. He rejected the idea of large-scale meetings and mass movement and his modus operandi was to work only with a small exclusive group of 'clever students, sons of landlords and sons of rich merchants'.

Many parents at that time considered Har Dayal a great patriot, but a real danger for their families and a bad influence on their sons. Nonetheless, he collected nearly half a dozen young men including Gobind Behari Lal, Amir Chand, Avadh Behari, Hanwant Sahai, Dinanath and Dwarka Nath Bose of Meerut. Another member of the 'Society of Political Missionaries' was Charanji Lal, who was a student in the Forman Mission School in Lahore.

Among his early associates of the 'Society of Political Missionaries' was Tara Chand (1888–1973), who was married to Sunder Rani's sister Maha Devi. A brilliant student at Muir Central College in Allahabad he was the son of Lala Kripa Narain. Influenced at that stage to drop his studies by Har Dayal, Tara Chand later studied at Oxford and became an eminent educationalist, historian and eventually served as the Vice-Chancellor of Allahabad University (1945–47) as well an Ambassador of India to Iran (1951–58).

Har Dayal's friend from Punjab University, Dr. Khudadad Khan, was sacked at Roorkee College for refusing to apologize to Lt.-Colonel Philson whom he had abused. Khan introduced him to the revolutionary Jitendra Mohan Chatterji, son of a lawyer from Saharanpur. The 'Society of Political Missionaries' successfully connected the revolutionaries of North India with the activities of Bengal and helped each other in a variety of ways. Later the charismatic Rash Behari Bose (1886–1945) also joined this group. Bose had worked at the Pasteur Institute of Kasauli and was employed as a laboratory assistant in the Chemistry Department in the Forest Research Institute. Chatterji later recalled that for Har Dayal, "the only dream he saw was the liberation of his country". He preached the relevance of passive resistance as a weapon for driving the British out of India.

All the youngsters took the solemn oath that they would devote themselves to the service of the country. Gobind at this point as a twenty-year-old decided to not get married after joining his mentor. He strongly felt that there was no need or place for a wife and children in the liberation movement. He agreed with his guru that the best way forward was to adopt the state of 'Brahmacharya' for the rest of his life. 'Brahmacharya' as a form of self-restraint was regarded as a virtue and even ancient Indian scriptures had scores of examples of Indian heroes who followed this path and conduct.

According to the constitution of the society, the membership was open to all Indians without any discrimination of religion or gender. Further, no political missionary was to accept or persuade others to accept directly or indirectly any office, title, pension or emolument from the Hukumat-i-Britannia. They planned Hindi classes in all the principal cities of India, Madras, Bombay, Calcutta, and gradually expand to other cities to promote national unity. The great secret of success, according to Har Dayal, was, first the study of foreign languages particularly French; secondly, education in European University; thirdly, the remodeling of the social life of upper and middle classes in India and lastly the study of sociology.

By the end of April 1908, after having been at Manohar Lal Chak's house in Kanpur for barely six weeks Har Dayal went to Haridwar and Dehradun and then moved to Lahore with his group. Gobind left for Allahabad where Motilal Nehru was hosting a Congress conference to heal the Surat breach between the moderates and extremists. Narayan Prasad Arora claimed the twenty-two days he spent with Har Dayal in March and April 1908 in Kanpur were the finest days of his life.

He later profiled the famous Dilliwallah in a book and maintained that in his life he, "met a lot of national leaders in India but no one could match Har Dayal – he was what is described in English as a – Genius".

No Englishmen Allowed

A few months later Professor Rudra, now the Principal of St. Stephens College, Delhi, traveled to Lahore to specifically meet Har Dayal at his one-room ashram at Sutar Mandi. Rudra was shocked to see that Har Dayal had daringly posted a notice in Hindi, 'No Englishmen allowed', outside his ashram. As a head of Christian Mission College, Rudra walked a razor's edge. He was deeply committed to the national movement but was respectful to the Hukumat-i-Britannia too. He wore a British style three-piece suit and tie and his favorite student refused to see him. Eventually, Professor Rudra accepted the bizarre conduct and changed his dress to be accepted in the ashram.

In Lahore, Har Dayal followed much the same pattern of life he had established at Kanpur except that it was even more austere. He dressed in a white dhoti and shirt with a saffron cloth. Away from his family, Har Dayal adopted the ancient Indian routine of austerity – 'simple living and high thinking'. His one-room home and ashram had two Peshawari mats – one for sleeping on the floor and another for guests to sit. Besides the clothes, the only furniture was a wooden rack full of books.

During the meeting with his teacher, Har Dayal, now a hardened radical declined to have a conversation in English. Despite being very European in his manners and taste he became an enthusiastic advocate of Indian nationalism and lifestyle. His ideology stemmed from his belief in Pan-Hinduism as a solution to ending British imperialism. He held that the British were not simply subjugating India, but were also slowly destroying the ancient religions of India. For Har Dayal, Hinduism was India's history and future and he believed in the abandonment of everything western to gain independence. He furthermore endorsed the reign of ancient religion in a united India of the future. His extensive writings in the nationalist press about the revival of Indian ethos in response to centuries of persecution of Indians by invading armies from the western frontier were avidly read. He first discarded British food, then British dress and finally English language itself. Though he knew many languages he deliberately talked in Indian languages to everyone he met. He replied only in Hindi or Sanskrit to scores of letters that he received in English and refused to use Hukumat-i-Britannia's postage stamps. He reverted to the Hindu calendar as against the globally accepted Christian calendar. He had cast-off what he called 'all badges of slavery'.

Though the Buddha was his life long ideal and his rationalism had made him skeptical of visiting temples he seemed to have become a fanatic propagandist of Indian and Vedic culture. He strongly felt that the cow was central to the Indian spiritual beliefs and "the cow is the flag of the Hindu nation". Later in a significant piece of writing he called for the establishment of cow protection societies in every city and town and recommended a four-point plan that included introduction of a monthly magazine, a nationwide campaign for spreading the gospel of cow protection, establishment of cow shelters and requesting Indian holy men to assist in propaganda and inspection of cow shelters.

Professor Rudra realized that his former student was now a completely transformed individual from the one he knew. On being told by Professor Rudra that he too was a product of the best of the western education system that he was now rejecting, Har Dayal replied that he was what he was despite the education imparted by the foreigners. Har Dayal thought that no Indian who really loved his nation ought to compromise his principles and barter his rectitude for any favor whatsoever at the hands of an alien oppressor.

A supporter of reverse colonization, the radical thinker wished to organize a conquest of Britain to colonize the colonizer. He wanted to introduce his ideas of education in Britain so that the imperialists could learn Sanskrit and be aliented from their own language and culture. Consequently he felt that they would never be able to dream of liberty and independence. He had turned Lord Macaulay's idea of "Indians in blood and color but English in taste in opinions, in morals and in intellect" on its head and wanted to create 'Englishmen in blood and color but Indian in taste, in opinions, in morals, and in intellect.'

One of the Most Sinister Figures

Michael Francis O'Dwyer (1864–1940), who had a first in jurisprudence from Balliol College, Oxford, joined the ICS in 1885 and remained one of the most hated figures in the history of Hukumat-i-Britannia. He had a well-earned reputation for dictatorial rule, tyranny, and intimidation. O'Dwyer, in his memoirs, *India as I Knew it: 1885–1925,* claimed, "about this time one of the most sinister figures in the revolutionary movement appeared on the scene…(Har Dayal), he threw up this scholarship in 1907 (state scholar) and thenceforward devoted his undoubted talents to revolutionary work was back in Lahore in 1908 and stayed for some time with Lajpat Rai with a party of young men, whose character he was forming by preaching passive resistance and boycott thus anticipating Gandhi by ten years". In addition, Indian The NAI records reveal that Police official David Petrie (1879–1961) later noted, "Har Dayal, after his return got together a party of some thirty or forty students to whom he expounded his own extreme views. It is not known whether in those early days Har Dayal actually preached assassination…"

The British Secret Service kept a close watch on the nationalistic Har Dayal's fledging enterprise of disruption. Though he often associated with armed revolutionaries there was no evidence that he was personally involved in any acts of violence. From Lahore, Har Dayal tried to connect with Aurobindo Ghosh and

Jugantar, a secret revolutionary society operating in Bengal but that did not work out. He was successful in re-establishing a working relationship with Lajpat Rai and Ajit Singh after they were released from detention in Mandalay.

Lajpat Rai was the first to identify the young man as a political agent for a free India of the future. Watching him from a distance, Lajpat Rai, did not approve of this hard-edged stance of the young rebel and insisted, "Lala Har Dayal appeared on the scene and took up the task of forming a cadre of political missionaries. But I did not like his scheme nor his way of working. Those who were involved in this controversy know this fact." Lajpat Rai also remarked about Har Dayal's brief enchantment with this divisive thought process, "For a time he was a strict Hindu in form, though not in religion…"

Har Dayal became a sort of wandering monk of Indian nationalism in Punjab. Self-denial in everyday life was seen as a precondition for those involved in seeking India's freedom. Sacrifice in the cause of the nation was deeply respected in India. As disclosed by the British Secret Service report, his fame was spreading nationwide. As he walked the streets of Lahore residents of the area would stand up to respectfully greet him whom he modestly acknowledged with a smile. Scores of young Indians who met Har Dayal in Lahore were influenced by his revolutionary thoughts. In continuation of his mission, Har Dayal appealed to the young Indians who sought employment with the Hukumat-I-Britannia Government, not to serve the British in any capacity. He advocated the rejection of the British books at educational institutions and even asked the young lawyers in Lahore and Delhi not to accept work from the Hukumat-i-Britannia.

The Rulers and the Ruled

At this stage, Har Dayal was an absolute firebrand. Influenced by the French Revolution, Dante Alighieri and Robespierre on one hand and the ancient spiritual philosophies of India on the other, he wanted to reinterpret the history of India and the lives of Indian heroes. He began to publish political tracts and regularly contributed articles to *The Punjabee* and *Hindustan* in Lahore and the reputed *The Modern Review*, about the exploitation by the Hukumat-i-Britannia.

In an article titled, 'The Rulers and the Ruled', published in *Hitkari* on June 1st, 1908, he alleged that Englishmen knew very little about India but what they did know, they turned to good account. "They know that India has come down to them as a heritage and that its people are to be ruled for the benefit of Anglo-

Indians. They regard the country as another El Dorado and look upon the ICS as a foundation stone for future eminence and fame." He recognized that every Englishman dreaded the thought of losing India, "He knows that England's greatness as a power in the world is mainly due to her possession of India, and consequently Englishmen are loth to give full liberty to the country".

The Arya Gazette ran an article by Har Dayal in which he claimed that India had civilized the entire world and taught mankind the different arts and sciences. It was a religious obligation for Indians, therefore, to study the ancient wisdom to know themselves. He added, "I should have written in Sanskrit to appeal to my countrymen in Bengal, Bombay or Madras (an aspiration which has not altogether been abandoned)". He extended this ethical analysis of lost authenticity to the Indian National Congress. "As for our 'Congress-men,' they seem to have lost the primary instincts of self-respecting nations, accepting their lot of an inferior status to Englishmen."

Har Dayal held that education was the central mode of progress. He strongly felt that the education policy of the Hukumat-i-Britannia was to support enslavement to the state. He observed that the Hukumat-i-Britannia's permanence was guaranteed because education had done the work of pacification. In this period he identified, "A nation ceases to maintain its entity and integrity if it begins to ape the manners... of its masters... the British educational system is one huge octopus which is sucking out the moral lifeblood of the nation... The British teach our boys what is really a caricature of history... that we are an incapable race...Woe to the nation that allows its children to read such history". He added, "We must place the gradual evolution of the sense of duty to mankind as the primary object of a healthy educational system." Otherwise, India would be a nation of "moral and intellectual pygmies, contemptible creatures whose lives are short, miserable and brutish."

In the book, *Our Educational Problem*, written by Har Dayal, and published in March 1922, Lajpat Rai penned the foreword stating, "In 1908, when Lala Har Dayal wrote these articles for *The Punjabee* I labored under the belief that some kind of education was better than no education, but my opinions have since undergone a great change and now I feel that while up to a certain point this education did us a certain amount of good, for some years backward however it has been productive of positive harm. It has helped in the multiplication of intellectual and economic parasites and retarded our progress towards freedom.... Mr. Har Dayal's articles are therefore, of great use in enlightening people on the merits of this question."

In the summer of 1908, Har Dayal was a unique figure in India, an action-driven thinker who moved fast, wrote constantly and was listened to intently by the youth with a great deal of respect. Lajpat Rai later commented, "His (Har Dayal's) cult at that time was a wholesale boycott of British Government and British institutions. He aimed at establishing an order of Hindu ascetics, to preach his ideas and to spread his propaganda…. He lived a life of purity and wanted others to do the same. At that time he did not believe in or preach violence. He discussed, argued, preached and wrote for the press. His writings began to attract attention and so did his activities and it was feared that the government would soon find some means of putting him out of the way…"

This period witnessed the fanatical deployment of the colonial sedition law by the Hukumat-i-Britannia that made convicts out of political players and swiftly dispatched them to the black waters of the Cellular Jail in the Andamans. Har Dayal was for a long time a 'man of interest' for the British Secret Service. Detectives kept an eye on him day and night and all his mail was intercepted.

The Kingsford Incident

On the moonless night of Thursday, April 30th, 1908, two brave Indian revolutionaries eighteen-year-old, Khudiram Bose (1889–1908) and nineteen-year-old, Prafulla Chaki (1888–1908) set out on a difficult mission in Muzaffarpur, a remote area in Bihar. Hidden in their clothes were three revolvers and a bomb. At about 2000 hrs they positioned themselves beside a tree outside the British station club and waited for their target. The man they wanted to execute was Douglas Kingsford who was the former chief presidency magistrate of Calcutta and had become a hated figure in nationalist circles since he ordered intense flogging of political agitators for defying the police of Hukumat-i-Britannia. A carriage appeared thirty minutes later and mistaking it for Douglas's transport Khudiram hurled the bomb.

The two youngsters fled the scene but the mission failed. Kingsford had escaped as he was not in the carriage but two English women Pringle Kennedy and her daughter Grace were blown apart. The bomb manual of Nicolas Safranski was having an overwhelming impact on the Indian revolutionary movement. After the failed assassination attempt, two policemen arrested Khudiram Bose within a day while Prafulla Chaki, when cornered at a railway station by Nandalal Banerjee, a police inspector, put a bullet to his own head. Khudiram Bose after a trial was sentenced to death and the court ordered the hanging to be completed by August 11th, 1908. The daring revolutionary act by the teenagers disturbed the entire country. Almost simultaneously widespread arrests as part of a nationwide mission of ruthless repression took place across India.

In the very early hours of the morning of May 2nd, 1908, Hukumat-i-Britannia's police with pistols in hand forcibly entered a house at 48 Grey Street in Calcutta. The party led by Superintendent of Police Richard Cregan served an arrest warrant to Aurobindo Ghosh. Soon it was revealed that Hukumat-i-Britannia had also arrested his brother Barindra Ghosh along with scores of young revolutionaries including Sudhir Kumar Sarkar (1889–1974) on suspicion. Ghosh was charged with 'conspiracy' or for 'waging war against the King', the equivalent of high treason.

The British Regime in India is Doomed

Fifty years after the end of Ghadr of 1857, at about 1800 hrs on June 24th, 1908, Hukumat-i-Britannia's police reached the entrance of Sardar Griha, Fancy Buildings near Crawford Market in Bombay. Indian leader Bal Gangadhar Tilak was arrested on the orders of A.H.S. Aston the Chief Presidency Magistrate of Bombay on charges of sedition, glorifying violence and approving murder. In the May 12th, 1908 edition of his newspaper *Kesari*, Tilak had defended the two brave Indian revolutionaries Khudiram Bose and Prafulla Chaki involved in the Kingsford incident and called for immediate '*swaraj*' (freedom).

In the court, a dashing thirty-two-year-old London trained Anglophile barrister Mohammed Ali Jinnah (1876–1948), who was an eminent member of the Indian National Congress rose to defend Tilak and moved a bail application that was turned down. Later in his life Jinnah, then a self-confessed Indian nationalist, turned into a champion of mass agitation for a separate Muslim nation.

On July 22nd, 1908, just after an eight-day long trial, Tilak was sentenced to a six-year jail term in Mandalay in Burma. Accepting the outcome, the fifty-three-year-old Tilak asserted, "In spite of the verdict of the Jury, I maintain that I am innocent. There are higher powers that rule the destiny of men and nations and it may be the will of providence that the cause which I represent may prosper more by my suffering than my remaining free."

For the next six days, the city of Bombay came to a standstill with the public protesting, all markets and mills shut down and all businesses on hold. Thirty-eight people died in Hukumat-i-Britannia's police action. The British Secret Service reports have revealed that Raghubir Dayal, Chandu Lal, and Amir Chand along with Raza were considering holding a large meeting in Delhi under the patronage of Lajpat Rai to express indignation at the conviction of Tilak.

In another part of the world, Russian leader Vladimir Lenin (1870–1924) visited the India House with British communist Guy Aldred (1886–1963) and was made aware of the Indian revolutionary movement. Lenin was yet to emerge on the world stage as the leader of the Russian revolution and lived in London at 21 Tavistock Place. In his first published article about international affairs on July 23rd, 1908, he alleged that the British angered by the mounting revolutionary struggle in India are "demonstrating what brutes" the European politician can turn into when the masses rise against the colonial system. Lenin pointed out, "Nowhere in the world – with the exception, of course of Russia – will you find such abject mass poverty, such chronic starvation among the people. The most liberal and radical personalities of free Britain…become regular Genghis Khans when appointed to govern India, and are capable of sanctioning every means of 'pacifying' the population in their charge, even to the extent of flogging political protestors!" Lenin predicted, "The infamous sentence pronounced by the British jackals on the Indian democrat Tilak", and with the Indians having got a taste of political mass struggle, the "British regime in India is doomed". The life and work of Lenin were to have a deep impact on the Indian revolutionaries across the spectrum during the freedom movement. Back in November 1907, Har Dayal had agreed with Russian revolutionaries and written in *The Indian Sociologist*, "Every Indian must be convinced that if Russian methods are carried on in our country rigorously by our oppressors the so-called British rulers, we must meet it with a measure for measure"

The Indian residents in Britain in a protest meeting held on August 1st, at Caxton Hall, in London sympathized with Tilak and the members of his family in their misfortune and suffering and desired to give expression to their indignation and grief at the unfair trial and the monstrous sentence inflicted on him.

Escape from Hukumat-i-Britannia

In early August 1908, Har Dayal due to severe financial difficulties moved to a house in Nawan Kot located a few kilometers southwest of the Civil Lines in Lahore. One night he got a secret communication from Lajpat Rai. He was informed that all of his seditious writings had attracted the attention of Stevenson-Moore, Director of DCI and plans were afoot to take him into custody and dispatch him to the Andamans. An Indian member of the British Viceroy Lord Minto's executive council disclosed to Lajpat Rai that after the Douglas Kingsford incident, Har Dayal's name was being discussed at the highest level as a problematic agitator. Further, there was a strong likelihood that in a police crackdown following Tilak and Aurobindo Ghosh's arrest there was a warrant out for him to be detained soon. The advice received by Lajpat Rai and subsequently passed on to Har Dayal was, "Send him abroad to save his valuable life."

But Har Dayal was reluctant to travel overseas as his covert revolutionary activity in Punjab was attracting a lot of interest and participation of the youth. His harsh yet intellectually sound articles were read widely and inspired Indians against the British imperialism. Additionally, he was anxious about Sunder Rani's heath and the imminent birth of their child. Nevertheless, to protect himself from the dreaded British Secret Service and in the larger interest of the nationalist movement, he decided to leave India for a short while till the threat of arrest declined. Evading the police, he noiselessly boarded an express train from Lahore railway station to Delhi. For financial aid, he turned to Professor Rudra at St. Stephens College. Notwithstanding his discourteous conduct in their last meeting in Lahore, Rudra still held him in high regard and gave him a substantial amount of money from his savings to fund his escape to Europe. At the Delhi Railway Station before leaving town for Bombay Har Dayal entrusted Amir Chand with the responsibility of his underground organization. Anticipating a hasty departure, he had previously told Chatterji in Lahore that they would correspond by mail and he should establish contact with Amir Chand who would lead the group in his brief absence. He expected to return to India shortly to resume his role as the leader of the Deshbhakta Samaj. His colleagues Hanwant Sahai and Syed Haider Raza kept his departure a secret from all the relatives and friends some of who were in the pay of Hukumat-i-Britannia as police informants and spies.

In mid-September, British Secret Service discovered to their shock thet the Dilliwallah they wanted to imprison had sailed for Britain on the Navigazione Generale Italiana, S.S. *Rubattino* a month earlier on August 15th, 1908. Har Dayal disembarked at Naples via Ceylon (Sri Lanka) in early September and then made his way to Britain after spending a few days in Paris. He had successfully hoodwinked the British Secret Service.

On the emotional front, Har Dayal was distressed that he could not meet his wife Sunder Rani before leaving or see the face of their daughter Shanti Devi who was born on Saturday, August 8th, 1908. Lala Gopal Chand had deliberately banned him from visiting his daughter. It was beyond his imagination that he would never meet his immediate family or set foot on the land of his forefathers again. The twenty-three-year-old Indian revolutionary was exiled from India forever at this early age and from August 15th, 1908 till his last day on earth he remained an Indian outside India mostly without a passport or nationality. He chose to suffer this fate for he was a feverish Indian patriot who wanted complete freedom for his motherland.

Such was his predicament that decades later in his book *Hints for Self Culture* he quoted the views of Henry Facet, "To die is nothing but to live and not to see the dear ones that is calamity".

7

THE INTERCONTINENTAL NATIONALIST

"Whether as an Indian nationalist or an anarchist internationalist,
he (Har Dayal) was a revolutionist at every moment with a shrewd
psychological knowledge of the value of the martyr's role for attracting and
retaining disciples to carry out his work… India was always on his mind…
nationalism was his ruling passion".

Van Wyck Brooks
Author and Literary Critic

On Wednesday, October 7th, 1908, a middle-aged Barrister from India re-entered Transvaal while returning from Natal in South Africa and created history.

Mahatma Gandhi was unable to show his registration papers to the officials as he had burnt them. He was immediately taken into custody and on October 14th he was imprisoned with hard labor in the border town of Volksrust with seventy-five other Indian supporters. This was the second time in his life that he was arrested. On January 10th, 1908, Mahatma Gandhi was arrested for the first time for failing to register or to leave Transvaal in South Africa and sentenced to two months of simple imprisonment.

Two days later in London, Sir Muncherjee Bhownagree, the second Indian to sit in the British Parliament and the man who had assisted Mahatma Gandhi on his visit in 1906, presided over a protest meeting against his imprisonment in South Africa. Lajpat Rai led the protest in India stating, "Mr. Gandhi in his goal had the satisfaction of knowing that he was making history". Bipin Chandra Pal added, "Go on brother Gandhi." The meeting ended with the singing of '*Bande Mataram*'. Mahatma Gandhi was finally released from prison

on December 12th, 1908, and his stature as a prominent Indian nationalist had
grown amongst Indians in London as well as in India.

The Political and Military Conquest of Britain

A month before Mahatma Gandhi's arrest in South Africa, on Friday, September
11th, 1908, Har Dayal was back in Oxford, to continue his political activism.
Estranged from his wife's family and having destroyed his chances of a career in
the ICS he now had no source of regular income. His brother Kishan Dayal in
India and Bhai Parmanand sent him some money to survive in Britain. A single
man, he rented a room at his old Southmoor Road address and ate his meals at the
house of his friends Chandu Lal and Kashi Prasad Jayaswal or sometimes cooked
himself. He received several congratulatory messages via his secret network from
his family members and friends in India on becoming a father. He wrote letters
to Sunder Rani that were sent to his brother-in-law, Richpal Chand's address at
Kunwar Niwas in Pipal Mandi in Agra, hoping that he could be reunited with his
wife and newborn daughter. He wished that they could join him in Britain. The
family after his departure was continually under surveillance by the British Secret
Service and this affected his correspondence with them. In her later years, Shanti
Devi reminisced in *Dr. Emily Brown's biography*, that even as a very small child she
was warned never to mention her father's name.

While London was decked up for the 1908 Olympic games, Har Dayal was
homesick, lonesome and surviving on less than six-pence a day. Over the next six
months of his life, Har Dayal separated from his comrades and isolated from his
organization in India had only his books for company. He declared that 'Gautama
Buddha' was his model and began the study of all religions besides sleeping on
the floor. He also proclaimed the need for celibacy as the highest ideal in the
service of the nation, an idea he explained as a note in Krishna Varma's *The Indian
Sociologist*.

Contrary to his claims to be a pacifist Buddhist, a secret report from the British
Secret Service revealed that on Sunday, September 13th, 1908, an unusually angry
Har Dayal made a startling speech at India House calling for "the political, social
and military conquest of Britain" and to take back by force what was robbed from
India by the firangis. He furthermore spoke about 'Hindu Sangathan' and the
defense of India's northwestern borders in a united India of the future. His speech
caused a commotion and many Indians protested especially against the sectarian

aspects of his talk. The students at India House considered this unexpected speech from a known Dilliwallah bestowed with *Ganga-Jamuni Tehzeeb* dangerous for the growth of the nationalist revolutionary movement and intervened to stop him. Some of these controversial thoughts many years later appeared in *Pratap* (1925) as his political testament. Due to his extremist ideas about the political and military conquest of Britain, Har Dayal faced alienation from his friends like Lajpat Rai, Savarkar and the Indian students in British universities and Indians earning a livelihood in London. British Secret Service described his sectarian thoughts as "enthusiastic," but "rather foolish".

Har Dayal quickly realized his vision of 'a united India under one religion' had no takers and he was courting pointless religious controversies. Lajpat Rai, confirmed, "He went to England with the idea of preaching his gospel among the Indian students in England. He stayed there for some time and found out there was not much scope for his type of nationalism…"

The Member of the Cosmopolitan Club

No longer part of the Oxford student's circle and a bit traumatized by his exclusion from the Indian network after his contentious lecture at the India House, Har Dayal did a *volte-face* and joined the Cosmopolitan Club in Oxford.

Alain LeRoy Locke (1885–1954) founded the Oxford Cosmopolitan Club. He was an exquisitely brilliant intellectual and the first African-American Rhodes Scholar, who was denied admission to several colleges at the University of Oxford because of his race. Locke finally gained entry into Hertford College, where he studied from 1907 to 1910 and later gained fame as the father of the Harlem Renaissance. Locke respected Har Dayal, as the Indian intellectual though they were not friends. In the years to come, Har Dayal borrowed Locke's favorite term, 'renaissance', to symbolize the intellectual awakening he wanted in the world.

The Club held its meetings at 14 Beaumont Street and its philosophical conundrum debated on possible way to be non-essentialist about race and simultaneously promote self-expression of color-conscious ethnic and racial groups. Besides Har Dayal, it attracted many young international Oxford students who heard papers, held debates and discussions in order 'to promote mutual knowledge'. Among the members were D. B. Burckhardt of Norway; Hamid-el-Alaily (future president of the Egyptian Society of England) and Pixley Ka Isaka Seme, a South African (who later helped form the South African Native

National Congress). Satyavarta Mukerjea, an Indian student of Modern History at Exeter College, Oxford, who later entered Baroda State Service in India, was also part of the club. These nationalists from around the world saw themselves as developing cosmopolitanism among their people when they returned homes. They were painfully aware of the disparity between European and colonial social development, yet sensitive to the destruction of their native culture. Members associated with the club promoted ideas of collective identity.

The membership of the club opened Har Dayal's mind to other world cultures and shortly thereafter he progressed to a more balanced outlook. Har Dayal introduced the members to the truly revolutionary view of the future that could go beyond the politics of Britain's domination of India. He contributed articles to the second issue of the club magazine. He additionally presented a paper, 'Obstacles to Cosmopolitanism,' (November 1908), arguing that "nationalism, and intellectual bigotry – the demand that others conform to our ideas of group politics or be rejected – kept humanity from embracing the central idea of cosmopolitanism that we should love one another regardless of our beliefs or affiliation." He further argued, that the love of the nation cannot be completely eradicated but national and racial identity can be deemphasized. He wanted to replace nationalistic history with world history. He wanted the members of the club to travel around the continent of Europe preaching and living cosmopolitanism. For the members of the club, Har Dayal's powerful critique was nothing short of revolutionary and for him, it was a total reversal of his previous beliefs as a political missionary in India. It was moreover a dress rehearsal of ideas of world citizenship that would emerge even more strongly later in his mind. Though his ideas changed emphatically much too often, Har Dayal managed to go deep into the concepts and emerge with one of the most superior treatises and understanding of these contradictory ideas and stances. With the added knowledge of cosmopolitanism, he made a surprise appearance at the large gathering of Indians at Cadby Hall, Kensington. Here he made a startling speech along with Lajpat Rai in favor of 'swaraj'.

Blood and Thunder Type of Indian Patriots

In Calcutta on November 7th, 1908, Lt. Governor Fraser entered Overtown Hall at the Young Man's Christian Association to attend a lecture by Dr. Ernest DeWitt Burton, a biblical scholar from the University of Chicago. As Fraser entered the hall and walked towards the platform a nineteen-year-old student Jitendra Nath

Rai Chowdhury raised a revolver to shoot at him. The weapon was no more than six inches from the Lt. Governor's chest. He pulled the trigger twice but the revolver misfired.

An American B. C. Barber, the General Secretary of the Young Men's Christian Association (YMCA) daringly threw himself at the assailant and struggled with him to save the life of Fraser. At that moment without a thought, Majaraja Bijay Chand Mahtab Bahadur of Burdwan interposed himself between Fraser and the assassin's gun at the risk of his own life. Hukumat-i-Britannia's police took Chowdhury into custody and Fraser proceeded to preside over the meeting. Later Maharaja of Burdwan was awarded the Knight Companionship of the Indian Empire for his act of devotion and courage.

Two days after the failed assassination of Fraser, on the evening of November 9th, Indian revolutionaries in Calcutta gunned down Nandalal Banerjee, the Inspector of Police, who by trying to arrest Prafulla Chaki at Muzaffarpur in the Kingsford incident had led him to commit suicide in 1908.

On the evening of January 12th, 1909, Sir William Lee-Warner (1846–1914), the Under Secretary of State for India stepped out of his Whitehall office and headed to the exclusive Athenaeum Club on Pall Mall. An Indian living in London, Basudev Bhattacharya, who was once editor of the revolutionary newspapers like *Sandhya* and *Jugantar*, approached him. He was denied an appointment until then by Sir Lee Warner and deterred from presenting a petition to Lord Morley, at the India Office. Nonetheless, Basudev insisted on walking along with him. An altercation of sorts ensued and Sir Lee-Warner used some derogatory words against Indians. Next, Basudev assaulted Sir Lee Warner on his leg with a stick on the steps of the Athenaeum club. A month later, Basudev was produced before a magistrate at Bow Street and fined £10 and awarded six months imprisonment. It was also established that he was a regular visitor to India House.

After the unexpected attack on Sir Lee Warner, His Majesty's Government took effective measures to control the suspected revolutionary activities at the India House. Security was enhanced outside the home of Lord Morley and Scotland Yard detectives accompanied Sir Lee Warner. Additionally, Scotland Yard's Special Branch received orders to undertake surveillance of Indian subversives in Britain and covertly began shadowing Indian students in London. In the February 1908 issue of *The Indian Sociologist*, there was an article on the presence of a plain-clothes policeman posted outside India House.

Sir Lee-Warner sounded Lord Morley that reports were emerging from Stevenson-Moore of DCI, about possible attempts to assassinate British civil servants and officials as well as plans to smuggle arms and explosives into India. Having been attacked, Sir Lee-Warner felt Scotland Yard was not equipped to handle this kind of work. In any case Sir Edward Henry, the Police Commissioner was not keen on employing surveillance beyond London. Lord Morley was surprised to learn that Scotland Yard had organized no apparatus for establishing "the existence and the ramifications of a regular dynamite and dagger confederacy in London, Paris, Berlin and New York." Lord Morley, ridiculed the surveillance operations in London and warned Lord Minto, that the "ordinary square-toed English constable was wholly useless in the case of Indian conspirators". Any surveillance over Indians required a specialist familiar with languages, habits, and names. The Hukumat-i-Britannia was asked to seek the services of a retired police officer for watching the growing Indian student population in Britain. Early in 1909, a British Secret Service operative, 'C,' arrived in London to collect information about nationalist activities among the Indians. 'C' was successful in providing information that Scotland Yard had failed to accumulate.

Previously, His Majesty's Government had set up the Sir Lee-Warner committee comprising of three senior officials – Sir William Lee-Warner, Theodore Morison and Sir Curzon Wyllie to evaluate the political climate amongst the migrant students. *The Indian Sociologist* had described Sir Lee Warner and Sir Curzon Wyllie as "old unrepentant foes of India who have fattened on the misery of the Indian peasant ever (sic) since they began their career." Based on oral and written testimonies taken from thirty-five Indians and sixty-five Europeans in London, Oxford, Cambridge, and Edinburgh, the findings appeared in a detailed departmental report that was considered inflammatory by the India Office and marked secret. It cited British Secret Service reports that students were being lured towards Highgate (India House) as soon as they got to London: "Representatives of the India house visit the railway stations at which Indian students arrive, and offer them the advantages of…cheap lodgings," they warned. "On reaching India House (new arrivals) are plied with the arguments of Mr. Krishna Varma's adherents, and are no doubt frequently converted to his view." William Lee-Warner pointed out the existence of "a blood and thunder type of Indian patriots", who wanted to cultivate things that cannot but lead to outrage and anarchy and hoped for the expulsion of the British from India.

Later, on February 23, 1909, Lord Morley, gave his great speech on Indian constitutional reform in the House of Lords. He announced a reform program that was enshrined in 'the Indian Councils Act of 1909'. In the proposed reforms the Viceroy's executive council was to be expanded to include sixty Indian representatives that brought about a limited increase in the involvement of Indians in governance for Hukumat-i-Britannia. Additionally, Lord Morley appointed two Indians to his London-based group of advisers. Lord Minto, responding to Lord Morley's urging to act similarly, appointed Satyendra Sinha, the advocate-general of Bengal.

Hidden in the final draft of 'the Indian Councils Act of 1909' was the Hukumat-i-Britannia's time tested policy of *divide et impera*. The act granted separate electorates for the Hindu and Muslim communities ostentatiously for balanced representation in the new council. The Muslim League welcomed Hukumat-i-Britannia's superficial intention to safeguard Muslim interests. The Indian National Congress, as a national party rejected the identification of voters with a particular community and opposed it. Lord Morley revealed his thoughts in a statement at the House of Lords, "There are three classes of people whom we have to consider in dealing with a scheme of this kind. These are the extremists who nurse fantastic dreams that someday they will drive us out of India. The second group nourishes no hopes of this sort but hopes for autonomy or self-government of the colonial species and pattern. And then the third section of this classification asks for no more than to be admitted to co-operation in our administration."

An Extremist who nurses Fantastic Dreams

Clearly, the revolutionary-minded Har Dayal was considered one of the extremists who wanted to end Hukumat-i-Britannia.

The British Secret Service verified that on December 21st, the Nationalist Conference (annual session of Indian National Congress) was held at Caxton Hall in London. At the session, an intense Har Dayal refused to speak on any resolution and objected to the presence of Dr. Ananda Kentish Muthu Coomaraswamy, a young Ceylonese Tamil philosopher and an early interpreter of Indian culture to the West. Son of a South Asian father and British mother, Dr. Coomaraswamy had married a British national; Alice Ethel Richardson who used the stage name Ratan Devi to perform Indian songs. Afterwards in a long letter published in *The Indian Sociologist*, Har Dayal gave his defense and reasoned that, "I owe it to my friends and acquaintances to explain my conduct in refusing to speak on any resolution at the Nationalist Conference held at Caxton on the evening of December 21; now this gentleman is a Eurasian and has married an English woman although he possesses an Indian name and wears a turban. As soon as I realized that it would injure our movement if we elected such a man to preside at a nationalists' meeting I held back".

There was an intelligence report stating that a week later on December 29th, Har Dayal was back at Caxton Hall to passionately speak at the celebration of the birth anniversary of Guru Gobind Singh. Bipan Chander Pal presided over the meeting that was attended by a hundred and fifty people. Among the audience were Lajpat Rai Gokul Chand Narang, G.S. Khaparde and Ram Bhuj Dutt. Narang exhorted the Indian students in Britain to abandon their studies and work for the liberation of their country.

By the end of February 1909, Har Dayal was diagnosed with pneumonia and had moved to 29, Poplar Grove, Shepherd's Bush in London. Barely surviving, he was unwell, totally penniless and his mind was in a disruptive mood. Krishna Varma wrote to him from Paris to take care of his health first and possibly move to a place with a warmer climate. He even offered to send him funds for his immediate expenses. Har Dayal sensed that his unique talents were being wasted in Britain and the Hukumat-i-Britannia would arrest him if he stayed there any longer. After considering enrolling at Harvard University in the United States for higher education, he boarded a ferry along with his suitcases filled with all his books and instead traveled to Geneva.

Thus began another chapter in the transnational revolutionary life of Har Dayal that overlapped and engaged with the momentous events of the early twentieth century. And the British Secret Service operatives effectively sabotaged the Indian nationalist's life and aspirations at every turn in such a fashion that this remarkable man was forced to live in exile like a wandering patriot for the rest of his life.

The Paris India Group

Har Dayal relocated to Paris from Switzerland in the spring of 1909 once his health showed improvement. He accepted the Indian Martyrs Scholarship offered by Indian revolutionary leader and benefactor Madame Bhikaji Rustom Cama (1861–1939). She had met him in October 1908 in London and troubled by his dire financial condition requested him to move to Paris. He got a new office at Madame Cama's spacious home at 25, rue de Ponthien Champs Elysees in Paris.

Madame Cama, an independently wealthy Parsi woman from Bombay, came to Britain in 1901 for medical treatment and was inspired by the work of Krishna Verma. She later moved to the French capital as some Parsis had started arriving there at the turn of the century. Many prominent Indians in Europe had relocated from London to be away from Hukumat-i-Britannia's jurisdiction.

Madame Cama along with Manchershah Barjorji Godrej, a businessman with interest in automobiles and accessories, and a prince Sardarsinghji Rewabhai Rana (1870–1957), a scion of the ruling family of Limbdi State, formed the Paris India Group. They held regular meetings and an annual dinner get-together during Diwali. This was one occasion where Indians residing in or traveling through Paris celebrated the festival of lights together.

At one of the most important political events in Europe, the International Socialist Conference held at Stuttgart, Germany on August 21st, 1907, Madame Cama and S. R. Rana unfurled the first version of the Indian national flag – a tricolor of green, saffron, and red stripes. 'Bande Mataram' was written across the central saffron stripe in Hindi. On the bottom red stripe, a half-moon was on the right and the rising sun on the left, indicating the Hindu and Muslim faiths. The fiery lady then announced, "This is the flag of independent India. I appeal to all gentlemen to stand and salute the Flag." At least a thousand delegates stood up and saluted the flag. Invited to speak at the conference, Madame Cama rose to condemn the effects of British imperialism, "the dreadful miseries – the food shortages, rates of death, and epidemics". Despite objections from British participants, she succeeded in moving a resolution in favor of India's freedom.

At a Paris India Group meeting, Har Dayal found a lifelong friend in the financially well-positioned S. R. Rana who lived with a German, Therese Liszt, at 46 rue Balanche. Rana was the life and soul of the Paris India Group.

Har Dayal also reconnected with Krishna Varma who operated from Paris and still published *The Indian Sociologist*. Since his arrival in Paris in June 1907, Krishna Varma had rented a large flat on the Avenue Ingres, situated in the upper-class neighborhood of Passy, part of the noble sixteenth arrondissement. Though he lived a fairly frugal life he employed a British butler and a secretary. Hukumat-i-Britannia had issued a warrant for his arrest and unsuccessfully tried to have him extradited from France. But he had gained the support of many top French politicians. He received assorted important French personalities at his flat and was sympathetically considered, "*linguiste et homme politique Hindou – de grandes aptitudes intellectuelles*" (Indian linguist and politician with great intellectual skills). Indian revolutionaries and young patriots met every Sunday afternoon at his flat to discuss political issues. In February 1909, Krishna Varma sent a note to *The Times* newspaper responding to attacks on the India House. He pointed out that both John Milton, the great poet and George Washington, the first President of United States, who had advocated the violent overthrow of tyrannical governments, were honored in Britain. Nevertheless Benchers of the Inner temple stuck off his name from the register of barristers on April 30th, 1909, and the Hukumat-i-Britannia withdrew the Herbert Spencer endowment at Oxford. The once venerated Sanskrit scholar suddenly became a persona-non-grata in Britain.

Bande Mataram

Madame Cama requested Har Dayal's help in editing her new revolutionary journal, *Bande Mataram* – a monthly organ of Indian independence. Finding his raison d'etre, he single-handedly edited the journal with great enthusiasm and turned it into an instrument of the "new party." It revived the title of the Calcutta broadsheet that was founded by Bipin Chandra Pal and later edited by Aurobindo Ghosh. The purpose of *Bande Mataram* in Har Dayal's own words, was to, "recognize that the importation of revolutionary literature into India from foreign countries is the sheet-anchor of the party – and the center of gravity of political work has shifted from Calcutta, Poona and Lahore to Paris, Geneva, Berlin, London and New York." The journal was to be printed in Geneva to avoid prosecution for publishing seditious material similar to the Russians who were getting everything printed in Switzerland. Har Dayal planned to smuggle it into India through the French city of Pondicherry.

The dynamic lady and the talented wordsmith combined their resources and branded themselves as campaigners for open rebellion. They were under constant surveillance by British Secret Service operatives. The other Indian businessmen living in Paris and on the 'to be watched list' of the British Secret Service and French intelligence agents were Krishna Varma, S. R. Rana, Hiralal Banker, Dalichand Bhavsar, Hiralal Shah and Mahadeo Rao.

Har Dayal had reached Paris during the Belle Époque; the "beautiful time" between the late nineteenth century and the outbreak of the World War (WWI). Paris had become an international center for painting, dance, music, theater, and publishing. The construction of Gustav Eiffel's tower for the 1889 world's fair had made it the "city of light". The city could boast many of the world's foremost medical and scientific institutions of the day, and Europe's most modern manufacturing facilities. The face of the future, many believed, could be seen in Parisian leadership in such brand-new fields as motion pictures, automobile manufacturing, and aviation. It had the best cafes, theatres and the Louvre – the best museum in the world. London, Vienna, Berlin, and Rome could not compete. The French capital and the nation that invented, 'liberté, egalité, fraternité' thrived on art and politics.

For Har Dayal, the avant-garde lifestyle of Paris revealed layer upon layer of political movements and its streets were littered with monuments of social upheaval. He later adviced, "You must feel what the French call the joy of living in every nerve and fiber of your being". Besides, Paris was the center of revolutionary activity and he slowly mastered the French language. He plunged into the entire range of revolutionary literature at the bibliothèque at Sorbonne University. He also engaged with revolutionary networks comprised of the crème de la crème of social democrats, Marxists, socialist revolutionaries, anarchists and various veterans of revolutionary movements in Russia, Ireland, and Egypt. He additionally came into close contact with Karl Marx's grandson Jean-Laurent Longuet (1876–1938), a socialist lawyer who was the founder and editor of the newspaper *L' Humanite and* a critique of the British imperialism.

Then an event in London sent shock waves around the world.

The Shots that Shook the Empire

On Thursday, July 1st, 1909, a twenty-five year old mechanical engineering student from India entered 'Fairyland', a shooting range owned by Henry Stanton Morley, situated on the top floor at 92 Tottenham Court Road in London, a stone's throw from the British Museum, with his automatic magazine Colt pistol in his coat pocket. He was a regular visitor, appearing three times per week, for the past three months. He had acquired a gun license and would fire twelve practice shots. On that day he fired his customary twelve practice shots and hit the target eleven times displaying considerable proficiency.

At around 2000 hrs dressed in a formal dark lounge suit and a blue turban, the young Indian left his front room on the ground floor of the lodging house owned by Mini Harris, on 106, Ledbury Road in the Bayswater neighborhood of London. Half an hour later he walked into the Jehangir Hall of Imperial Institute in South Kensington to attend a reception hosted by the National Indian Association. At the end of the meeting at about 2300 hrs, Sir Curzon Wyllie, the infamous British official, and the Political Aide-de-Camp to the Secretary of State for India walked out. The Indian student stepped forward near the landing and removed a loaded automatic pistol from his right coat pocket. Unexpectedly the muzzle of the Colt almost touched the head of Sir Curzon Wyllie. The young Indian then fired. The four bullets shot at point-blank range into the face of Sir Curzon-Wyllie killed him instantaneously. A Parsi resident of Shanghai, Dr. Cawas C. Lalcaca (1862–1909), on a year-long sabbatical to Britain, tried to intervene and save Sir Curzon Wyllie but the man fired at him as well. One of the bullets went through the back shoulder and into the right lung of Dr. Lalcaca and he fell backward writhing in agony. He died a few minutes later of hemorrhage and shock from the bullet injuries.

In the ensuing chaos, the man tried to put a bullet to his head but was wrestled down to the ground as his gold-rimmed spectacles fell. Police Constable Fredrick Nicholls arrived and arrested the Indian who was then removed to Walton Street police station. Dr. Thomas Neville who examined him found him calm and collected and his pulse normal. He was later produced before Horace Smith, the Magistrate of Westminster Police Court, and told him clearly, "I do not plead for mercy: nor do I recognize your authority over me..." The police found two picture postcards in his room in London, the first depicting the blowing of Indian rebels from the mouths of cannons during the Ghadr of 1857, and the second a portrait of Lord Curzon with 'Heathen Dog', penciled on it.

The name of the Indian student enrolled in University College, London to study engineering, was Madan Lal Dhingra (1887 – 1909) the sixth of seven children of a civil surgeon Dr. Ditta Mal Dhingra.

Fired by Savarkar's charged personality and plans for India's freedom, the young Amritsar born Dhingra was among the enlisted students of the secret society at India House. Savarkar's meetings attracted Indians living in France and Switzerland along with other revolutionaries from Ireland, Russia and Egypt living in London. A law student at the time, Asaf Ali (1888–1953) of Delhi, later recalled "a flaming ring of violent revolutionism" had built around Savarkar, who was "by far the most arresting personality" among the Indian student community in London. Savarkar had passed the final examinations for Bar-at-Law in Gray's Inn but the Inn Benchers declined to confer the degree on him. On appeal, it was ruled that the degree would be conferred if Savarkar would give a written undertaking not to participate in Indian politics. Savarkar refused to bow before the British Empire and Gray's Inn decided not to confer the degree. His elder brother, Ganesh Damodar Savarkar (1879–1945) was arrested previously in India on the thin grounds of publication of a provocative poem and on June 8th, 1909 sentenced to 'Sazaa-e-Kalapani'.

Savarkar along with his Indian activists continued with the secret activities with increased zest and even undertook the preparation of a treatise on explosives. The bomb-making manual had reached India and was to be employed by the activists to deadly effect in the years to come. Some had tried to work in the arms and ammunition factories in Germany disguised as Englishmen. They planned to smuggle pistols to India. One of the objectives of Savarkar's group of London based revolutionaries was to inspire a revolt just like 1857.

The political assassination of Sir Curzon Wyllie on that evening, was not only disconcerting for citizens of London, faced with political assassination by an Indian for the first time on British soil, but also extremely distressing for Scotland Yard and the British Secret Service community.

It represented their greatest fear.

Four days after the killing of Sir Curzon Wyllie, on July 5th, 1909, a public meeting was held in Caxton Hall in London to condemn the act. It was chaired by Sir Agha Khan and many Indian luminaries such as Sir Mancherji Bhavnagri, Sir Surendranath Banerjee, Maharaj Kumar of Cooch Behar, the Maharaj Kumar of Bobili, Sir Din Shah, Mr. Fazalbhoy Currimbhoy (Chairman of the Bombay Mill Owners) and Bipin Chandra Pal were in attendance. Theodore Morrison conducted Bhajan Lal, Madan Lal Dhingra's younger brother, studying in Edinburgh to the stage in the packed Caxton Hall. It was announced that the Dhingra family had completely distanced itself from Madan Lal's actions and Bhajan Lal had joined the meeting to "show before his fellow countrymen that he disassociated himself from the murderer." In the presence of a massive audience, Bhajan Lal was overcome by emotions and could hardly speak. Thereafter, Bipin Chandra Pal submitted a vote of condolence to the family of Dr. Lalcaca.

At Caxton Hall, the speakers denounced Dhingra's act and termed it unforgivable, inhuman and uncivilized. As the motion for condemnation was about to be passed almost unanimously one hand rose up in opposition. It was the hand of Savarkar, who got up and protested, "No, not unanimously. There are opponents of the motion as well. Takedown my name, Savarkar. I oppose the motion." There was a great uproar at Caxton Hall. There were loud and indignant cries of, "Put him out". And in the emotionally charged atmosphere, Edward Palmer, an Indian from Hyderabad, rushed and assaulted Savarkar as he was stating his opposition. British police rushed in and the meeting ended in disarray.

Eight days after the assassination, Mahatma Gandhi landed in London to familiarize Hukumat-i-Britannia with the *satyagraha* of the Indians of the Transvaal. He alleged that those inciting Dhingra were guiltier than Dhingra, who had committed his deed "in a state of intoxication". He reemphasized that these assassinations would not expel the British from India. (*Indian Opinion, August 14, 1909*).

On July 10th, Dhingra was charged with double murder and the only statement he made to the Magistrate, was, "...I want to say is that there was no willful murder in the case of Dr. Lalcaca. I did not know him. When he advanced to get hold of me I simply fired in self-defense". *The New York Times* in an editorial titled, "British Complacency and Crime," on July 19th, 1909, not only found fault in India House and Dhingra but also in British political policy towards Indian students in the period leading up to the assassination.

After the shortest trial in British history, on August 17th, 1909, Madan Lal Dhingra was hanged at the Pentonville Prison, in London and became the first Indian nationalist to be hanged in Britain. Dhingra's final statement was as inspiring as his actions; "I believe that a nation held down in bondage with the help of foreign bayonets is in a perpetual state of war...the only lesson required in India at present is to learn how to die, and the only way to teach it is by dying ourselves. My only prayer to God is that I may be re-born of the same mother and I may re-die in the same sacred cause till the cause is successful. *Bande Mataram*".

And despite his hostility to Indian nationalism, Sir Winston Churchill, future Prime Minister of Britain, saw Dhingra as a romantic figure. Though he supported Dhingra's execution he quoted his last speech from memory and claimed that it was "the finest ever made in the name of patriotism". Sir Churchill even predicted that Dhingra would be remembered in two thousand years, "as we remember Regulus and Caractacus and Plutarch's heroes".

The second Indian war for independence had begun.

La Plume Est Plus Forte Que L'épée

Dhingra's valor infuriated British monarch Edward VII and in a memo dated August 17th, 1909 he suggested to Lord Morley that Indians be barred from coming to England without a valid reason.

The NAI records show that on August 20th, 1909, His Majesty's Government ordered the seizure of all the copies of the August issue of *The Indian Sociologist*. Four days later, Chief Inspector John McCarthy led a team of New Scotland Yard officers to arrest Guy Aldred who secretly used the 'Bakunin Press' at his home on 35 Stanlake Road, Shepherd's Bush to publish the journal. The British police seized 396 copies of the August issue. It contained articles by Krishna Varma advocating the view that "political assassination is no murder," and proclaiming Dhingra "a martyr in the cause of Indian independence"; it also contained a violent article by Dhingra himself, justifying the methods of Indian "Nationalists." Detectives Harold Brush and Mathew MacCoughlin gave evidence against him. In his defense, Aldred claimed that he had printed *The Indian Sociologist* because he claimed the right of an enlightened race to have a free press. On September 10th, 1909, the court of Justice Bernard Coleridge convicted him of seditious libel declaring: "Guy Alfred Aldred, you are young, vain, and foolish; you little know that others regard your statements far more seriously than they deserve. The sentence of this Court is twelve months imprisonment in the First Division."

Aldred became the first Englishman to court imprisonment for the cause of India's freedom.

At the end of August with his nerves getting strained under pressure in Paris, Har Dayal took a short holiday for health reasons to Montreux in Switzerland. He arrived later at 'Societe de l'imprimerie Moderne'; rue du Rhone 52–54 in Geneva to take the delivery of the latest issues of *Bande Mataram* from Kirchhofer, the sole owner of the printing press. One thousand copies of the first issue were handed over to him in person while the other issues were sent for security reasons to an address of a colleague of Madame Cama in Paris – Madame Cadiou at 114 Boulevard Montparnasse.

As a writer, Har Dayal remained par excellence. In the first issue of the journal, *Bande Mataram,* dated September 10th, 1909 the penman of the Indian independence movement paid a glowing tribute to the ultimate sacrifice of Madan Lal Dhingra. He penned, "Dhingra, the immortal has behaved at each stage of his trial like a hero of ancient times. He has reminded us of the history of medieval Rajputs and Sikhs, who loved death like a bride. England thinks she has killed Dhingra, in reality, he lives forever and has given the death blow to English Sovereignty in India."

In the introduction to the journal, Har Dayal mantained, "We do not look before and after when we pen out our message bearing passion laden words." He added, "Three stages of every national movement must be passed through. History cannot alter its course... Virtue and wisdom first, then war and finally independence..."

Exhorting patriotism Har Dayal added, "We must recognize at present that the importation of revolutionary literature into India is the sheet-anchor of the party.... The circulation of revolutionary leaflets, journals, and manifestoes should be looked upon as a sacred duty by all patriots. We are not exaggerating the importance of this work when we use that expression. Let us look upon every leaf of revolutionary literature with almost superstitious veneration and try to make it reach India by all means in our power."

In spite of the article in admiration of Dhingra, Lajpat Rai felt that Har Dayal was not an advocate of the use of a bomb or the revolver for killing individuals, even though he admired and glorified those who had risked their lives using the same. Later Har Dayal admitted that he knew Dhingra during his days in London as a morbid and an unbalanced man. But the acts of Indian revolutionaries, without doubt, were inspirational for the youth in the days of the freedom movement. Their desperate deeds, daring devices, and indifference to death won them a lasting place in the memory of the nation. Decades later on December 12th, 1976, Madan Lal Dhingra's coffin was exhumed in the presence of Natwar Singh, then Acting High Commissioner for India and was flown back to India.

Next Har Dayal wrote an article from Paris, provocatively titled, 'The Social Conquest of the Hindu Race' and it was published in *The Modern Review* in September 1909. In this article, he argued that one of the primary means through which Britain had accomplished its social conquest was by taking control of India's fundamental institutions, its schools, and universities in particular and by burying its national literature and history. He argued "the decay of the moral fiber of a country paves the way for extraneous powers which, in turn accelerates the process of decline by its very existence. How did one revitalize a fallen race?" It was, "the leaders and thinkers of a fallen race that had to achieve this". He contended, "Sooner or later, the unsubdued heart and mind of the sturdy race will seek its outward sign and symbol, its embodiment in the world of fact, viz, a national state. The great duty of a subject people consists of guarding the Promethean spark of national pride and self-respect, lest it should be extinguished by the demoralizing influences that emanate from foreign rule".

Predictably Hukumat-i-Britannia banned the article under the Press Act and the Sea Customs Act.

Finding it difficult to fund his stay in Paris and with no financial offer available, Har Dayal left for Salsomaggiore Terme in Italy in mid-October 1909 where he found cheaper accommodation. In a message to S. R. Rana on October 18th, he requested him to look for a place in Paris for four to five francs a day during December. (*Letters of Lala Har Dayal*)

His Majesty's Indian Secret Service

On the morning of Saturday, November 13th, 1909, Lord Minto and his wife Lady Mary, on an official visit drove from the railway station through the streets of Ahmedabad towards the Raipur gate in an open carriage. The streets of the city were packed with hundreds of onlookers when unexpectedly a large white ball was hurled at the British Viceroy's carriage. Sergeant Spenser of the Inniskilling Dragoons, who was riding beside the Viceroy's carriage in an ingenious display of alertness, blocked the missile with his saber. Another missile hit the wrist of the Viceroy's Jamadar who was holding an umbrella over Lady Minto out he dropped the projectile safely to the ground. The Viceregal Party unhurt and unmoved drove on and finished the drive through the city without grasping that the two missiles were coconuts filled with explosives wrapped in a white paper. Later an explosion was reported from the site after the carriage had passed away. In London, the attempt to assassinate the British Viceroy evoked a feeling of profound horror mingled with intense relief at the failure of the plot.

The probable assassins were never found.

For the moment the murder of a high-ranking British official of the stature of Sir Curzon Wyllie, in the heart of London at the hands of Dhingra led to a drastic change in the modus operandi of the British Secret Service. After the murder, Lord Morley had his retinue of three Special Branch detectives shadowing him to and from work at the India Office. The Hukumat-i-Britannia's policy after the execution of Madan Lal Dhingra was to crush the extremists and rally the moderates to their side for stamping out extremism.

Another wing of the British Secret Service called the "Indian Political Intelligence Office" (IPI) was created in London that dispersed its operatives throughout Great Britain and Western Europe. The IPI would be a precursor to the highly sophisticated British military intelligence organizations of the WWI. IPI was run by the Secretary of State for India through the India Office's Public and Judicial Department in Whitehall and reported directly to the Director of DCI in distant Simla.

In India, an Oxford man, Charles Rait Cleveland (1866–1929), ICS, took over from Stevenson Moore as the Director of DCI from February 1910 and the tenure lasted till his retirement in September 1919. This arrogant and forceful character chose Superintendent of Police, John Arnold Wallinger or 'W' of the Imperial Police (Bombay cadre) as the person to head the new outfit in London. By January 1910, the cold-blooded and aloof Wallinger had arrived in Central London and taken over as the 'itinerant officer' charged with setting up the British Indian Secret Service network in Europe. His father, W. H. A. Wallinger, had served with the Indian Forest Service and John Wallinger was a member of the Imperial Indian Police since 1896. Early in 1909, he had distinguished himself as a detective while working up evidence against a revolutionary conspiracy in one of the Indian States. Wallinger possessed a considerable linguistic aptitude, speaking three Indian languages including Marathi and Gujarati and was intimately acquainted with many Gujarati merchants who traded across Europe. Under Wallinger, IPI's immediate assignment was to "watch anti-British conspiracies in England and Europe, so far as they affect Indian interests." He quickly applied his diplomatic and detective skills to the recruitment of informants and the establishment of close personal ties with police officials in London, Paris and elsewhere throughout the continent. His three-room attic office was co-located with the newly formed Secret Service Bureau (later MI5) and the Secret Intelligence Service (later MI6) at 64 Victoria Street in London. IPI operated with a permanent staff of atleast seven.

IPI also worked secretly out of a nondescript office in Delhi and was a key element in enforcing His Majesty's Government's rule in India. Simultaneously in January 1910, a special department was formed in Bengal for the suppression of political crime in the office of the Inspector General. Since September 1909, the political branch and the Special branch was lodged at 7 Kyd Street in Calcutta.

Under instructions from Lord Morley, there was a severe crackdown on Indian revolutionaries living in Britain. Additional policemen were posted outside the India Office, meant to tail any Indian students who entered and looked suspicious. IPI increased the number of detectives to watch over the India House. Soon British Secret Service operatives had totally infiltrated the India House. It was closed down in the fall of 1909 and Savarkar moved to a room over a small Indian restaurant in Red Lion Passage. Krishna Varma's wife Bhanumati traveled to London alone and stayed for three weeks to arrange for the sale of India House.

London was no longer a safe place to indulge in revolutionary activities.

Hukumat-i-Britannia's Most Wanted

On December 21st, 1909, Arthur Jackson, the well-known Sanskrit scholar who was the British magistrate in Nasik entered Vijayanand theatre to attend a performance organized as part of his farewell function. An Indian revolutionary Anant Kanhere (1892–1910) pumped four bullets into Jackson and murdered him. The eighteen-year-old Kanhere was hanged in the Thane Prison on 19th April 1910, a mere four months after the murder.

The Browning pistol that was used by Kanhere to murder Jackson was traced back to a batch of twenty pistols that Savarkar in London had smuggled through an intermediary into India using a suitcase with a false bottom. After being pursued by Scotland Yard, Savarkar shifted to Paris on January 6th, 1910 and stayed at the Hotel de Holland, rue Cadet. Here he reconnected with Madame Cama and Har Dayal just as the "flood of the century" left its mark on the city of lights.

By the beginning of 1910, the Hukumat-i-Britannia was particularly worried by the presence of Savarkar in Paris as he was out their jurisdiction. They had recorded statements in India that implicated him in the murder of Jackson. They wanted to imprison him for all times to come. His Majesty's Government reacted to Savarkar's departure immediately, issuing a warrant for his arrest under the Fugitive Offenders Act and charging him with five crimes, the most important of which was: "delivering seditious speeches in India from January 1906 and in London from 1908–1909".

Then, Wallinger began his top-secret mission in France where a large number of Indian revolutionaries including Savarkar, Krishna Varma, Madame Cama, Rana, Godrej, and Har Dayal had established a base. IPI planned surveillance on all the Indian revolutionaries and collated systematic records of their activities and regularly sent them to Simla. These classified documents contained extremely useful information. Rare group-photographs were printed at Simla as 'Memorandum on the Anti-British Agitation among the Natives of India in England and France.'

Largely due to Wallinger's intervention IPI cultivated friendly relations and established a working relationship with Celestin Hennion, director of the French Sûreté Générale (the Paris political police) that had a force of 8,835 men. The French-British Entente Cordiale – partial cooperation between His Majesty's Government and the French police was in place since 1904 due to the 'German threat'. Savarkar was under tremendous emotional pressure to return to London. He later recalled, "My dear and near relatives were arrested. They were being tortured to disclose our names. I was very restless. Every day some news would trickle in and make me more unhappy. Har Dayal used to console me, but really my mind was in two thoughts. I used to say to myself: My friends, my own brothers are rotting in prisons, whereas I am sauntering here in Paris Gardens! Oh what a life this?" Har Dayal used to restrain me by saying; No, you cannot go! You must not go! If you go, it will be the end of everything! You are the soul of the organization. If you are removed, the movement will lose its force!"

On Sunday, March 13th, 1910, Savarkar was at the Paris Gare du Nord ready to embark on the boat train to Calais-Maritime and then onwards to Dover Marine and London. Madame Cama also arrived at the platform along with Har Dayal with the hope that Savarkar would change his mind at the last minute and not advance towards 'the jaws of death'. As a law student, he was confident that since there was no precedent for deportation based only on the charge of political radicalism he would be lodged in a jail in Britain and not be sent to India. Savarkar later reminisced, "Amongst them, I saw two faces outwardly calm but in fact, very sad – one of Madame Cama, the other of Har Dayal" almost as if they had a foreboding of what was to come." He regretted, "That was my last sight of my dearest friend Har Dayal".

Then the unflinching Savarkar overriding Har Dayal's concern for his personal safety left Paris for the British Empire's capital city. British Secret Service operatives were already at the Victoria Station on a lookout for "a small man with an intelligent face and a nervous manner". The moment Savarkar stepped off the boat train in London he was surrounded and immediately taken into custody by Scotland Yard to be lodged in Brixton jail by Hukumat-i-Britannia's police. He was arrested under a telegraphic warrant from the Government of Bombay under the Fugitive Offenders Act. The next day British courts accused him of "offenses of sedition and abetment to murder". It was ruled that he should be sent to India to stand trial.

Savarkar's arrest was a huge feather in the cap for Wallinger's IPI.

After the arrest of Savarkar, the manuscript of the original '1857 Marathi book' was handed over to Madam Cama in Paris. She kept it in her safe in the Bank of France beyond the reach of the British Secret Service operatives.

Then on the afternoon of Monday, April 4th, 1910, Le Dupleix, a steamer reached the Pondicherry pier from Calcutta. Aurobindo Ghosh disembarked from the steamer in French India to retire from active politics and pursue a spiritual and literary lifestyle thereafter. In his later years, he would be nominated for the Nobel Prize for Literature as well as Peace. French-occupied India had for long been the refuge for civil debtors and other malefactors seeking to escape the clutches of the Hukumat-i-Britannia's police. In September 1908, poet, writer and activist Subramania Bharati fearing arrest had reached Pondicherry and sought political asylum there.

In Delhi, Lord Minto in a dispatch to Lord Morley, on May 26th, 1910, describing Ghosh, stressed, "he is the most dangerous man we now have to reckon with...Surely you cannot hope that such a man should remain at large? We had to consider two courses of the procedure against him – deportation and prosecution in accordance with the law." Despite their best efforts the Hukumat-i-Britannia's police never got to arrest Ghosh.

With both Savarkar and Ghosh out of activism, the Hukumat-i-Britannia now focused its energies on the firebrand Har Dayal living in Paris.

A Retreat in Algeria

Paris had endured the epic flood of 1910 and thousands had evacuated in January due to water levels rising in the Seine. Har Dayal faced an extremely cold winter as the electricity failed. The metro had finally opened only in April. He was given the carte blanche by Madame Cama to do what he liked with the journal but he was dismayed by the recent arrest of Savarkar. There were serious political and personal differences in the Paris India Group between Krishna Varma and Madame Cama. She regarded Krishna Varma as a difficult person who wanted to dominate the proceedings among the Indians in Paris. She indirectly attacked his stilted style of writing, imperious manners, and materialism. Besides, he was no longer providing financial support to the revolutionaries including Har Dayal.

Feeling stifled in Paris, Har Dayal got hold of an atlas at the bibliothèque to locate a place within the French-controlled territories where he could stay without spending much money. He did not want to travel to any part of the British Empire due to a probable attack by the British Secret Service operatives who now followed him all around Paris. His other consideration was a warmer climate that suited his fragile health. Then suddenly on April 5th, 1910, with the small amount of money saved by him, Har Dayal bid au revoir to Paris for an unknown destination. He debated going to Japan via America and then finally headed towards Algiers.

From the ship, the long line of the blue African coast was mysterious and dim. The white terraces of the town gleamed in the sunshine from the harbor and the French touch dominated everything from wide streets, electric trams, motorcars, cafes, bars, shops, architecture, and the road signage. Algiers itself was a city of contrasts and Arabs called it, 'a diamond in an emerald frame'.

Har Dayal informed S. R. Rana that Algiers reminded him of Bombay and numerous international tourists were staying at the first-class white-colored hotels with gardens in the Mustapha quarter with views of the bay. The town itself had only ten Indians residing there and a lot of small-time businessmen from Italy, Spain, and Greece. He noticed the oriental dress and barefoot people and veiled ladies and summer clothing. He set out to learn Arabic though he found the Bibliotheque in Algiers very limited. The local university also disappointed him. It was "a sort of school for the Arabs," he observed. (*Letters of Lala Har Dayal*)

While His Majesty's leading adversary was in Algiers in distant London, at 2330 hrs GMT on Friday, May 6th, 1910, the British Monarch Edward VII, passed away at the Buckingham Palace. His final words, to his son the Prince of Wales and heir, were, "I am very glad", in response to the news his horse had won at Kempton Park. King George V who succeeded him immediately informed the Lord Mayor about the loss of his father. His telegram read: "I am deeply grieved to inform you that my beloved father, the King passed away peacefully at 11:45 tonight. GEORGE".

Edward VII had waited a long time to become the King but his reign was so eventful that it would become known as an "era" of its own. To everyone's great amazement, this playboy prince had sobered up and by the time he died after only nine years on the throne he had proven to be an extremely efficient leader and an ace diplomat, at home and abroad. The Edwardian era in British history was the inauguration of a new world in many political, social and artistic respects, especially in the attitudes towards women that took an important turn. Writing a eulogy to King Edward VII as a wise dedicated monarch who had served his people well, Nobel Laureate Kipling offered a poem, 'The Dead King', to several newspapers including *The Morning Post, The Daily Telegraph* and *The Times*. The funeral procession of Edward VII was taken out in an impressive procession from Westminster Hall on its journey to Windsor.

As the streets of London were packed with awed mourners, Har Dayal sent a letter to S. R. Rana from Algiers requesting him to invite Indian revolutionaries V.V.S. Aiyer (1881–1925) and Virendranath Chattopadhyaya from London to Paris to help with the publication of *Bande Mataram*. He was also in correspondence with Dadabhai Naoroji granddaughter Perin Naraoji who lived in Paris and wrote extensively to her about Algiers. In his letters, he claimed that the cost of living was much higher than he expected and the Hotel de la Californie on rue Charlemagne was noisy and dishonest. On June 4th, 1910, he shifted to the hilly suburb of El Biar near Algiers laid out in European lines for foreign visitors. He continued to live like an ascetic and meditated. Later in his correspondence with Rana, he depressingly remarked about disillusionment and premonition of death. In Algiers he even faced a threat to his life. His message to Rana revealed his acute state of depression, "I often find relief in crying. It is good for me." He added he had taken up playing the mandolin on a local doctor's advice. *(Letters of Lala Har Dayal)*

By July 1910, he had had enough of Algeria and wound up his meditative and mandolin practice. The restless man still wanted to go to Japan via America as it was a proud independent nation but sailed back to Marseilles and caught a train to Paris to return to Rana's apartment. Here he discussed with Rana's German companion, Therese Liszt, the serious possibility of moving to Berlin considering it "the capital of the country which at present is most hostile in spirit to England." With the future in his mind, he wanted to cultivate friendly relations with the powerful German nation.

Savarkar's Leap of Liberty

On July 1st, 1910, exactly one year after Madan Lal Dhingra's assassination of Sir Curzon Wyllie, Savarkar accompanied by a dozen police officers, including Indian constables was led in handcuffs on board the *S.S. Morea*, a P&O ocean liner. He was bound for India and the steamship had a refueling stop at Marseilles. Earlier, the British police had thwarted an attempt by Indian and Irish revolutionaries to extricate him from jail. Wallinger established a strong enough connection with the French Sûreté Générale and they assured him that they would 'avoid any incident' in Marseilles. They also promised that they would prevent any Indian without a valid ticket from entering the ship.

On the morning of Friday, July 8th, while the *Morea* was docked in Marseilles harbor, Savarkar decided to take his fate into his own hands. He bravely leaped into the cold sea and swam ashore toward French soil. But he was promptly caught by a French brigadier of the Maritime Gendarmerie and rushed back to the ship sparking a diplomatic dispute. This extraordinary attempt at escape in Marseilles led to a heroic elevation of him in India and across the world.

In Paris, Har Dayal back from his sojourn in Algeria at the end of July 1910, frantically worked for his friend's release claiming that His Majesty's Government had illegally abducted Savarkar on French soil. In protest, Jean Longuet, editor of *L' Humanite* asserted, "This Indian stepped into the soil of France being harassed by British... From information kindly furnished to us by Madam Cama, editor of the *Bande Mataram* and a young Hindu living in Paris named Mr. Har Dayal, we are able to give some details of Savarkar's life and character." Later *Gouvernement de la République française* (Government of France) protested before the Permanent Court of Arbitration in The Hague, which ruled that, despite the "irregularity" in the arrest, the British did not have to hand its prisoner back.

Savarkar was 'illegally' transported to Bombay on July 22nd, 1910 and was soon charged with plotting to wage a war against the King and providing weapons used to assassinate a British citizen. Hukumat-i-Britannia sought to portray the killings of Sir Curzon Wyllie and Arthur Jackson as Savarkar's personal vendetta rather than as a higher nationalist cause. He was sentenced to an unprecedented two life terms – fifty years – in prison. The Governor of Bombay, Sir George Sydenham Clarke described him as "one of the most dangerous men that India has produced". He was packed off to 'Sazaa-e-Kalapani' in Andaman Island where three suicides of convicts a month had become the norm.

It was clear that the Hukumat-i-Britannia sought to physically eliminate the main masterminds and principal challengers to their Empire failing which they were to be transported for life to the Devil's Island or exiled from India.

The Alliance between Indian and Egyptian Revolutionaries

Hukumat-i-Britannia unable to arrest Krishna Varma and Madame Cama decided to attach their properties and cut their funding. Madame Cama lived in Paris with negligible personal assets in India and Krishna Varma had divested himself of all his investments in Britain yet Hukumat-i-Britannia was determined to, "to hit them in their pockets if we can do so".

In Paris, Jean Longuet introduced the leaders of the Egyptian movement to the Paris India Group and the nationalists of the two nations planned their respective upcoming conferences. British Secret Service operatives and French intelligence agents recorded the visits of a man in a motorcar, identified as "Farid Bey the Egyptian revolutionist" to the home of Madame Cama. The Egyptian National Party planned to hold its second congress from September 22nd to 26th 1910, at Hotel des Societies Savantes in Paris. Muhammad Loutfi Goumah, one of Egypt's famous lawyers and Hamid-el-Alaily, an acquaintance of Har Dayal from the Cosmopolitan Club at Oxford, were the two secretaries of the Congress. Armed with the additional asset of the Arabic language, Har Dayal became a keen participant in this enterprise.

On the eve of the conference, Wallinger and British Secret Service operatives were able to influence the *Gouvernement de la République française* to issue a pre-dated order of September 16th, 1910, that prohibited the holding of the Egyptian conference by the '*exile politique*'. At the last minute largely due to the well-funded Egyptian movement the conference was relocated to Brussels and all the delegates traveled as guests of the organizers from Paris Gare de Nord by the 8:20 am express train. The Indian delegation wearing badges and Egyptian rosettes of red and white ribbons included Madame Cama, Har Dayal, Virendranath and Asaf Ali. Indian revolutionary Aiyer who had recently relocated to Paris from London wore a Fez cap just like the hosts and a button with the engraving, 'in memory of the martyrs of 1857'. The two granddaughters of Dadabhai Naoroji, Perin and Goshi who were close to Madame Cama also accompanied the delegation.

Egyptians had come from all over Europe including Britain, Germany, Italy, Russia, and Switzerland besides Egypt. Among the other notable speakers who attended the Congress were Mustafa Kamal Pasha's brother, Ali Kamel Fahmy, a fine orator in Arabic; the fiery Irish activist Charlotte Despard and James Keir Hardie a Scottish coal miner who became a Labour Party leader. He was a thickset Englishman of medium height with somewhat rebellious hair and wore a black silken sash in place of a belt around his girth. His speeches in India during his visit in 1907 were misrepresented in the British Press and he was accused of stirring up sedition.

Asaf Ali made a mention of Har Dayal's transformation from his fiery 'Hindu religion's reign in a united India' lecture at India House in London in September 1908 to a more balanced cosmopolitan outlook. In his memoirs, *The Emergence of Modern India*, Ali observed, "Har Dayal had not only got over his anti-Muslim propensities but was at this time passionately pro-Egyptian and was actually the most energetic of the organizers of the Congress. He had formed particularly close relations with Goumah and Hamid-el-Alaily. The former was a gifted person, speaking several languages with fluency like Har Dayal himself." El-Alaily presented a paper called 'The Moral and Intellectual Aspects of the Egyptian Political Movement,' which was largely written by Har Dayal. His speech went on to appeal to the Egyptians' honor, by reminding them of their ancient historic past, their great deeds and civilization at a time when Europe had not even come into being. He asserted, "So a great past justified the claim to a great future, for the Egyptians of today were heirs of the past. The genius that reared the Pyramids and composed the Book of the Dead still remains in us like hidden fire... The remembrance of our early history assures us that we are not a radically incompetent race...and that we can, therefore, believe in the final success of our Cause."

However it was Har Dayal's paper on 'The Egyptian Army', that was a cause celebre. Delivered in his incomparable style it created a sensation and called upon Egyptians to refuse to be enlisted in the British Egyptian army. Hardie chaired that impressive session. Har Dayal ended the session by stating, "Pay attention to your army. She can and she must help you someday". The newspapers in Britain omitted his references to the army, though all the lectures delivered at the conference were published in the form of a book titled, *Œuvres du congrès national égyptien*. At the Brussels congress, it was decided that close contact be maintained between the Egyptian, Indian, and Irish nationalists. About this time Virendranath decided to hold a conference of Indian nationalists.

After his return from Brussels, the intellectually progressive Har Dayal had major differences with both Krishna Varma and Virendranath. There were constant quarrels, rivalry and mutual accusations of selfishness and treachery. Though a believer in secret or direct methods, Har Dayal could not support the policy of individual political assassinations. He observed that "half measures are of no use. They blind the people to the mighty issues that are at stake. We must lay the axe at the root of the tree. The people can never understand the figment of loyalty to a sovereign and hostility to the British Viceroy. This is a European conception, which cannot be assimilated by us." He believed in the development of strength of character and saw himself becoming more of a political propagandist rather than a leader of a great movement. British Secret Service reports recorded that, "He is apparently the ablest of the Paris party but is handicapped by ill health. Chattopadhyaya who is the second in point of ability prefers indirect and devious methods. He says that he considers it right to meet strategy with strategy and diplomacy with diplomacy..."

After being in and out of France for eighteen months and over two years since leaving India, the twenty-five-year-old Har Dayal felt his revolutionary life had reached a cul-de-sac. The Paris India Group had lost its esprit de corps and was disintegrating fast. Krishna Varma was now a fallen hero and the clash of ideas had reached a point that Har Dayal could only confide in Madame Cama, S. R. Rana or Perin Naoroji. The long hours of incessant writing and the irregular bouts of illness disheartened him. His expenditures in Paris were much more vis-à-vis the previous years. Reduced to living in utter poverty with basic meals and torn clothes, the brilliant man was distraught about beseeching Kishan Dayal for money from time to time. Besides, after the imprisonment of Savarkar, Har Dayal was dispirited about the future. In an atmosphere of severe depression, he felt that everything he had done from his rejection of Oxford and the ICS to his nationalist work in India and France had eventually amounted to nothing.

His mind focused on doing something dramatic with his life.

Renunciation in the Caribbean

Once again, Har Dayal packed his bags and books. He noiselessly disappeared from Paris on Wednesday, September 28th, 1910 and reached Marseilles. Later from Marseilles he informed S. R. Rana that he proposed to sail on October 10th for Ras Jibutil (Djibouti). He eventually boarded a ship at Le Havre bound for Martinique, the rugged French island at the southern end of the Caribbean. Before departing he secretly informed Rana that he wanted to practice Buddhism on the Caribbean island. The emulation of Buddha was a time-honored and hugely respected practice of withdrawal in Indian spiritual terms. Much like Gautam Buddha he too had left his wife and child in the pursuit of self-discovery, truth, and enlightenment. Once again in his life, the intellectual and spiritual came to the rescue of the revolutionary leader.

It took almost a month of zigzagged sea travel via Morocco as the ship crossed the tropic of cancer and the vast ocean. Across the Atlantic for the first time, Har Dayal alighted in Martinique, a spectacular island where nearly fifty percent of the landmass was a forest. Located several thousand kilometers away from his homeland India and just to the south of the United States, the French territory of Martinique was gifted with mild Caribbean weather. It was a mountainous stunner crowned by the still-smoldering Mont Pelée, the volcano that had wiped out the former capital of St-Pierre in 1902. Offering a striking diversity of landscape and atmosphere, the small island of Martinique was covered with tropical rain forests, rolling plains and grazing lands. It had a small population of about 184,000 persons and it was estimated that 3/4th of children were born out of wedlock on the island. By 1910, the number who could read and write was only 69,170. (*Annuaire de la Martinique, Fort-de-France: Imprimerie du Government*).

Fort de France, the capital city dominated by the St. Louise Cathedral and the statue of Empress Josephine had a distinct dash of Gallic joie de vivre and some of the architecture dated back to the nineteenth century. The city was built along with a series of laid-back beaches with just a few francophile restaurants and boulangeries. There was a covered market selling a dizzying array of fruits and vegetables. The architecturally magnificent Schoelcher bibliothèque was a nineteenth-century wrought iron, wood and glass library built originally in Paris for the 1889 World's Fair, which was broken down into pieces and sent to Martinique where it was reopened across from the city's central park.

The general business of the French West Indian island of La Martinique was dependent on the miles of rolling sugarcane fields. From May 6th, 1853 to 1883, indentured workers were brought from the French Indian territories of Pondicherry in India to La Martinique after an arduous three-month journey to work in the sugar industry. The Indians with or without their families came to escape socio-economic hardships and colonial occupation of their motherland. Consequently, a sizeable population of Indo-Martiniquais descendants lived on the island too and they were referred to as *"Kulas or coolie"* (the porters). They constructed a global Indo-Francophone identity – French-speaking Martiniquais or Mauritians, with close ties to Créole, Tamil, Hindi, and English. Later one of the most famous Mauritians Frantz Fanon (1925–61) identified closely with the liberation movement and his political sympathies eventually forced him out of the country so he became a propagandist and a seminal anticolonial theorist. In one of his famous works, *Black Skin, White Masks*, he psychoanalyzed the subjugated non-white persons who were perceived to be lesser beings in the White world that they lived in.

Fluent in French, Har Dayal rented a room with a local Créole speaking family in Fort de France and managed to live by teaching English to the local boys. He barely survived but the arrogance of the Indian nationalists in Paris had heightened his sense of renunciation. In Martinique, he took to penance after the manner of the Buddha and meditated surrounded by a riot of nature, tallgrass prairies, centuries-old mahogany trees, towering ferns, bamboo and a crazy array of wildflowers.

The only narrative of Har Dayal's short stay at Le Martinique originates from Bhai Parmanand's autobiography, *The Story of my Life.*

In Lahore, Bhai Parmanand was forced to resign from his position at DAV College by Hukumat-i-Britannia. Keen on practicing pharmacy at the age of thirty-four years he proceeded to the United States. On the way he traveled through Paris eager to meet Har Dayal, but the latter had already left France. Rana informed him that he had received Har Dayal's latest letters through the *'poste restante'* (care of the postmaster), from a French island in the Caribbean.

Bhai Parmanand moved on and boarded *S.S. Nieuw Amsterdam* from Rotterdam bound for New York. He landed on October 31st, 1910 and the Ellis Island register for Alien passengers arriving in the United States recorded his local address as Morris Building, 1421 Chesnut Street in Philadephia. On arrival, Parmanand discovered that he would have to wait a few months before he could start his training in pharmacy at the University of Philadelphia. Faced with racism and social isolation on the East Coast, he decided to leave for British Guiana to reach out to the community of Indians residing there as an Arya Samaj missionary. Many decades ago on January 10th, 1838, the *Whitby* had sailed from Calcutta with 249 immigrant laborers from India who arrived after a long voyage of 112 days in British Guiana to work at the sugar plantations. Bhai Parmanand deliberately chose a ship and sea route that traveled to Georgetown in British Guiana via the French island of Martinique.

On November 25th, 1910 the ship anchored at the sleepy seaside town of Fort de France for a few hours and he went ashore in search of Har Dayal in a town of twenty-seven thousand people. With almost no facility with the French language, he approached the local post office but they could hardly help as Har Dayal kept no fixed time to fetch his mail. Disappointed that he was so near and yet so far from his friend he turned back to the ship. A worker from the shipyard who spoke broken English offered to pinpoint the house where 'Indien' (Har Dayal) lived. Bhai Parmanand was led to a place where Har Dayal had rented a room and was informed that the 'Indien' had gone to the nearby hills to meditate. Ahead of Bhai Parmanand were tremendous views of the immense landscape, nearly empty hillsides and choppy waters of the Atlantic. It was a hard challenge to locate Har Dayal in this vastness before his ship departed within an hour. As it was almost time for the ship to leave, with great effort he convinced a local lad to find Har Dayal for him.

The boy searched for Har Dayal on a trekking path across from the mangrove swamp and found him on his usual place atop the hill in a clearing under the trees. On learning that '*un etranger*' (a stranger), had disembarked in Martinique and was '*cherche*' (searching) for him, Har Dayal was quite alarmed. The youngster insisted that he must return to his house at once as the 'etranger' was in a rush. Har Dayal suspected that a British Secret Service operative or an Indian policeman, after intercepting his correspondence to his friends and family, might have reached Martinique to question or arrest him.

Har Dayal approached carefully and was absolutely thrilled to see Bhai Parmanand, his friend from his Lahore days right at his doorstep in Fort de France. The two friends warmly embraced and greeted each other with the nationalistic slogan '*Bande Mataram*'. After their unexpected reunion, both friends realized that human beings may think whatever they liked about themselves but in reality, they were a product of circumstances.

Har Dayal decided on the spot that Bhai Parmanand must disembark at Martinique, as they needed to spend more time together. The next ship to British Guiana was exactly a month later. Bhai Parmanand decided to stay on in Fort de France and Har Dayal helped him remove his bags from the ship. Bhai Parmanand found Har Dayal absorbed in a minimalistic routine of study, meditation, sleeping on the floor and subsisting on boiled grain and potatoes. He was captivated with spirituality and a perpetual intellectual war raged within him. He toyed with various spiritual ideas but did not believe in the traditional form of religion and its various rituals. Har Dayal explained to Bhai Parmanand, that he intended to offer the world a new philosophy – 'Hardayalism'. Har Dayal affirmed, "the ideal social order would be the one which approximated to the legendary Vedic period of Indian history because, as, practical equality existed only in that society, where there were no governors and no governed, no priests and no laymen, no rich and no poor."

Bhai Parmanand revealed, "Lala Har Dayal wished to found a new faith and he had chosen this place for preparing himself by discipline and study for his great mission… his life at this time was really a life of asceticism…when I asked him he said that he wished like Buddha to give a new religion to the world and was preparing himself for it…"

In Har Dayal's utopian vision of a new religion, he asserted the superiority of women and declared that the ideas of patriotism and race were relics of barbarism.

He imagined a world whose motto was to be: atheism, cosmopolitanism, and moral law. As claimed by this republic would not be a state, because the latter represented force and persecution. No modification of its activity, no tinkering with parliaments and senates and parties, could bring up the republic. The latter must grow up by the side of the state, which it would undermine finally. He later put down his thoughts in an article, 'The Coming Republic' published in the March 1911 issue of *The Liberator*. In his view, the new religion would owe its origin to a man, "who should tower above others in virtue and wisdom… a man who has passed through the ordeal of temptation and come out unscathed, who possesses insight into the needs of the age and is sure of his message, imparts his fervor of conviction and optimism to others. Thus a religion takes its birth."

Over the next month after numerous long and thoughtful discussions, Bhai Parmanand successfully persuaded his friend to give up forming concepts of a new religion and his quest for a new system of belief, 'Hardayalism'. Bhai Parmanand discouraged him by saying, "My view is that all religions are a kind of fraud on mankind. You will be merely adding one more fraud." He advised the brilliant Har Dayal to use his exceptional talents and enterprise not to live like a recluse but to instill the flame of patriotism in the hearts and minds of the thousands of Indians living in North America and seek out the knowledge in American Universities.

Before departing for Georgetown in British Guiana on December 25th, Bhai Parmanand advised, "Let us have Swami Vivekananda as our ideal. Such a one is needed both by India and the rest of the world."

Seventeen years before on the afternoon of Monday, September 11th, 1893, the thirty-year-old Indian monk, Swami Vivekananda, original name Narendranath Dutta (1863–1902) gently got up from his seat on the crowded stage and walked towards the podium at the inaugural meeting of the World's Parliament of Religions in Chicago. This was the first-ever attempt at a formal international dialogue between representatives of multiple faiths. Swathed in his orange turban, a calm and determined Vivekananda greeted the gathering with the now-famous words, "Sisters and Brothers of America…". The entire hall reverberated with instant applause as all the people in attendance rose to their feet for an ovation lasting more than three minutes. This was followed by one of the most famous speeches on spirituality by an Indian on the world stage and is extensively quoted till today. In the brief but eloquent speech on day one, he riveted the audience with his call for religious tolerance and an end to fanaticism. Vivekananda became the star of the Parliament. The modern monk from India, Swami Vivekananda died on July 4th, 1902, less than nine years after his appearance at the World's Parliament of Religions. Years after his death, Vivekananda's message and his magnificent speech in Chicago had influenced, inspired and affected young Indians like Har Dayal.

By the end of 1910, Har Dayal had spent twenty-four months in Oxford as a student, six months in India as a Political Missionary and twenty-eight months as a wandering patriot in Europe, Algeria, and Martinique. Time had now moved on and the twenty-six-year-old revolutionary had a new mission in his life. After a dismal sojourn of three months in Martinique, he began to once again pack his bags and sort out his books for another life-transforming trip. His next destination the United States – the land of opportunity fascinated him. The idea of visiting the United States appealed to the Dilliwallah's intellectual curiosity and adventurous heart. He later remarked, "it soon occurred to me that I had not seen America and its institutions and there was a large number of my countrymen here". He still held the dream of completing a doctorate in Buddhism from Harvard University close to his heart. Besides, the 'New World' was "an ethical sanitarium" for anyone escaping the tyranny of the Hukumat-i-Britannia. He informed Madame Cama to say that Martinique was "a dreadful hole of a place" and he proposed to leave for the United States.

The next three years were the defining period of Har Dayal's life and the United States of America provided him a stage and an audience to promote his ideas and ideology like never before.

8

A LEARNED MAN AT STANFORD

"I know Har Dayal well... He is a man of great force of character and is greeted with genuine reverence throughout India... I have heard educated Punjabis and even Bengalis speak of him as the greatest man in India... I regard him as a learned man, a powerful man, and a very good man."

Professor Arthur Upham Pope
The University of California, Berkeley, USA

On an extremely warm Tuesday afternoon of July 25th, 1911, the citizens of Chicago still recovering from the North-Eastern American heatwave were outraged by a murderous attack on its streets.

A twenty-five-year-old Indian named Husain dressed in khaki hunting clothes with a knotted tie and armed with a Belgian rifle appeared near the Chicago Opera House. Standing diagonally across from the busy intersection of Washington and Clark Street the man ran amok. He pointed the gun at passing crowds and screamed, "I hate your America".

Then the crazed man indiscriminately clicked the trigger six times.

Each soft-nosed steel bullet from the high-powered 45-caliber rifle found its mark and eight people were injured before the magazine jammed. The shooting created a panic among hundreds of pedestrians. Patrolman M. J. Hynes on duty on an adjacent street immediately rushed at the maniac who furiously swung his jammed rifle at him. Husain attempted to fire once again but the policeman sprang on him and threw him on the sidewalk. Mounted Police officer D. Malloy arrived on the scene on his galloping horse to seize the Indian. An angry crowd collected and demanded that the man be lynched.

Taken to the safety of the Central Station, Husain, a former British Indian armyman declared that the 'tyranny of the British Government' had prompted him to shoot at crowds. The Chicago police found two incoherent letters in his jacket pocket, one addressed to United States President William Howard Taft and the other to Horace D. Nugent, the fifty-three-year-old British Consul at Chicago since 1909, asking for permission to carry out his shooting. He was charged with first-degree murder as one of his victims Archibald Hunt who was shot in the left leg succumbed to his injuries at the hospital. Later, Dr. George J. Spencer, the city physician, after conducting an examination pronounced Husain a fit subject for the mental asylum.

The next day *The Chicago Examiner* printed Husain's photograph on the front page with the heading, "Maniac Empties Rifle Into Crowds in the Loop-7 Wounded, One a Girl, in Sudden Fusillade".

As disclosed by British Secret Service reports, Husain, the son of Abdul Aziz from Jullundur district in Punjab, served as an informer for the police in India. Based on his father's loyalty to Hukumat-i-Britannia, he was sent to the United States to infiltrate the student community and to report on any political activity. It was recorded that racial discrimination and abuse during his five-year stay in the United States had caused him to lose control over his senses. Due to his insane behavior, Hukumat-i-Britannia's activities in United States escaped being compromised.

In the summer of 1911, Cleveland, Director of DCI in India, established that given the sensitive nature of the political opinions amongst Indian students in the United States there was a need for a Secret Service operative from India in New York. The best-known British resident in the United States, Frederick Cunliffe-Owen (1855–1926) masqueraded as a journalist but was an undercover British Secret Service operative since 1905. He obtained information on Indians living on the east coast and covertly attended meetings at India Club at the Vedanta Temple in New York. He also employed reporters to assist him with reporting on the society of Indian students.

In a secret meeting of Defense Chiefs in Simla, Cleveland warned His Majesty's Government that his men had uncovered a mysterious and dangerous conspiracy aimed at overthrowing British rule in India. He divulged to the gathering, "like some hidden fire this seditious movement was spreading across the country". As claimed by, the conspirators were not the usual hotheads and agitators but highly intelligent and well organized. He asked his audience, "my own impression is that it is directed and controlled by one great intellect – but whose?".

The men in the room shuddered at the thought of another bloodbath such as Ghadr of 1857. They concluded that if the DCI, one of the most competent organizations of its kind in the world had not uncovered the design of the 'politico criminal activity', there was only one explanation that the actual director of these nefarious designs was a man outside India's frontiers and beyond the reach of Cleveland's team.

An Indian in New York

Six months before the tragic shooting incident on the streets of Chicago, on the cold Thursday of February 9th, 1911 in New York, the Department of Immigration of the United States in a handwritten register recorded the arrival of an unmarried twenty-seven-year-old (he was twenty-six), bespectacled Indian named, Har Dayal. He had disembarked at the Port of New York on a small steamship *S.S. Philadelphia* as a steerage passenger sailing from San Juan, Puerto Rico and his last place of residence was recorded as St. Chaney. The man was given the passenger ID 101069090126. His final destination was recorded as Cambridge, Massachusetts. He had previously reached Puerto Rico on February 3rd, 1911 as a passenger on *S.S. President* from St. Thomas in West Indies.

For Indians and brilliant scholars like Har Dayal, America was not yet the land of dreams. Traditionally, no two nations, so far apart geographically on planet Earth, have been so intimately linked as India and the United States. Nico Slate, Professor of History at Carnegie Mellon University, in her well-researched book *Lord Cornwallis Is Dead: The Struggle for Democracy in the United States and India*, has revealed that the first person from India to have reached the United States was "an East Indian, a native of Bombay", that had married a Mashpee Indian woman and settled on Cape Cod in 1787. Some historians have recorded the arrival of a person from India in Salem in 1790 with British Captain John Gibaut. In 1799, Salem's globe tottering local merchant mariners established an East India Marine Society and in due course, Indian sailors from Calcutta arrived at regular intervals. Astonishingly there exists a record of a small number of merchant seamen from India recruited to fight in the American Civil War.

The renowned Brahmo Samaj leader, Pratap Chandra Mazumdar came on a lecture tour to the United States in August 1883 and Anandibai Joshi came to the Women's Medical College of Pennsylvania and became an MD in 1886. Rudyard Kipling accidentally found that three Parsi businessmen Allbless, Rustomjee and Byramjee from India had registered in a hotel in Philadelphia in 1889 and later met them during supper. In 1887, a detachment of sipahis passed through Canada, as they returned to India having served the Guard of Honor during the celebration of Diamond Jubilee of Queen Victoria in London. The Indian sipahis of the British Indian army in London returned via Canada decided to work in the mills, the farms and on railroad construction in British Columbia. They carried back tales of economic prosperity in Canada and the United States. Indians, mainly peasants and former sipahis from Punjab had begun relocating to the United States. Soon after a wave of immigration from North India to the Pacific Coast of America followed.

Fewer than seven hundred Indians had entered the United States during the nineteenth century and by 1900, they were reduced to five hundred. Usually, they paid $400 to complete the two-part thirty-day steamship journey from Calcutta to Hong Kong and then to Vancouver and San Francisco. As maintained by the *United States Bureau of the Census 1975* – almost seven thousand Indians were living in the United States between 1900 and 1920 out of which 5,771 persons from India arrived between 1900–1910. The migration from India was also due to the failure of crops and the severe famines in Punjab between 1905–1910.

Much before the wave of Indian immigrants, the Indian sacred texts, *The Bhagavad Gita* and *The Upanishads* reached American shores in the early years. American essayist, poet, and philosopher Ralph Waldo Emerson praised ancient India, "once illustrious in the elder time" and even imagined a future India undergoing a "godlike birth". The mystic and writer Henry David Thoreau went further and in contrast to the British imperial historians raised Hindu texts above their Western equals. He enlightened his American readers by stating, that one sentence from *The Vedas* was, "worth the state of Massachusetts many times over" and "In comparison with the philosophers of the East, we may say that modern Europe has yet given birth to none. Besides the vast and cosmological philosophy of the *Bhagavad Gita*, even our Shakespeare seems sometimes youthfully green and practical merely".

Famed American poet and journalist, Walt Whitman in his masterwork, *Leaves of Grass*, issued in 1872 included a poem 'Passage to India'. He perceived India as a "soothing cradle of man" and ancient land of history and legend, morals and religion, adventure and challenge. Whitman pointed to, "The flowing literature, tremendous epics, religions, castes, Old occult Brahma, interminably far back— the tender and junior Buddha..." American humorist Mark Twain in a grand plan to recover his professional losses traveled through India and Ceylon from January to April 1896 and was suitably impressed, to put it mildly. In his revealing 712-page book, *Following the Equator*, Twain informed American readers, "So far as I am able to judge nothing has been left undone, either by man or Nature, to make India the most extraordinary country that the sun visits on his rounds...."

Distinct from the thinkers, poets and writers there were some Americans who were not as captivated with India and President Franklin Roosevelt (1882–1945) in a speech before the Methodist Episcopal Church, Washington DC on January 18th, 1909, declared, "The successful administration of the Indian Empire by the English has been one of the most notable and most admirable achievements of the white race during the past two centuries... Indeed, if English control were now withdrawn from India, the whole peninsula would become chaos of bloodshed and violence; till the weaker peoples, and the most industrious and law-abiding, would be plundered and forced to submit to indescribable wrong and oppression; and the only beneficiaries among the natives would be the lawless, violent, and bloodthirsty..."

This political propaganda resulted in the racial bias that greeted the handful of visitors from India.

Enlightenment at Harvard

Har Dayal (his name was often misspelled as Har Dyal in the United States) appeared in America at a time when Indians due to the color of their skins were not accepted as naturalized American citizens. Startlingly the United States in its wisdom termed all the visitors from India including Hindus, Sikhs, Christians, Parsis, Buddhists, and Muslims as 'Hindoos' or 'East Indians' from Hindustan. Everything appearing from India was tagged, 'Hindoo' – Hindoo food, Hindoo music, Hindoo alphabet, and Hindoo politics to differentiate from Native American 'Indians'. The Pacific Coast of America even witnessed anti-immigrant hysteria and on September 4th, 1907, a race riot broke out in Bellingham, Washington, that shook the entire Indian community. Newspaper headlines such as, "Have we a dusky peril – Hindoo hordes invading the state" had appeared in Bellingham newspapers. There were moves to 'Keep the Hindoo out" on the Pacific Coast.

It was quite cold and dreary in the booming New York City for Har Dayal. With all its multistoried commercial and residential buildings reaching for the skies the city's population was approaching five million. The Flatiron Building, completed in 1902, was one of the tallest buildings in the world when it was built. Most New Yorkers got around on foot like all the major cities of Europe. Horse-drawn carriages had only just begun to give way to motorcars and the city's first subway line had opened. Cruise lines, commuter ferries, and tourist boats dotted the harbor. The Statue of Liberty, a popular tourist destination was an inspiration for all the immigrants and visitors from other parts of the globe.

Even in 1912 it was a busy place and a city that nearly never slept. Har Dayal later observed, "When I first went to London I was surprised by the nervous activity of the people. It seemed to me that they are using altogether too much energy in the course of the day. But on coming to this country, I found that the English seemed almost phlegmatic in comparison with the Americans..."

After a transitory stopover in New York City, Har Dayal traveled north to Boston, Massachusetts and as guided by Bhai Parmanand stayed briefly at the Vedanta Society. Har Dayal throughout his life retained a spiritual bent of mind and he met Swami Satya Dev 'Sanyasi' at the Vedanta center in Boston. A spiritual master originally from Lahore, Swami Satya Dev was on a lecture tour in the United States and had delivered speeches in Washington DC, New York, Pittsburg, and Berkeley. Har Dayal at a later date pointed out that the Indian missionaries were "representatives of that spirit of enterprise and self-denial which was transforming New India". He also thought that Swami Ram Tirtha was the greatest Hindu who ever came to America (he had visited San Francisco from 1902 to 1905) – "a real saint and sage whose life mirrored the highest principles of Hindu spirituality as his soul reflected the love of the 'Universal Spirit' whom he tried to realize."

Next Har Dayal headed to the snow-covered Harvard University campus with the intent of spending the next two years completing his Doctorate in Buddhism. The oldest institution of higher education in the United States, Harvard was established in 1636. It was named after the College's first benefactor, the young minister John Harvard of Charlestown, who upon his death in 1638 left his library and half his estate to the institution. Its fame had reached India and it was considered a fertile ground for scholarship on ancient Indian philosophies. Harvard had a historical and intellectual interest in India that went back for several decades. Back in 1847, the Harvard Library had a copy of William Ward's, *A View of the History, Literature,* and *Mythology of the Hindoos* that was used by Ralph Emerson. In 1893, John Henry Wright, a Professor of Greek at Harvard had described Swami Vivekananda as "Here is a man who is more learned than all of our learned professors put together".

The University had a strong reputation for Indian studies and the study of Sanskrit even at the turn of the century. Noted Sanskrit Professor Charles Rockwell Lanman (1850–1941) was hired as Wales Professor of Sanskrit in 1880. He lived in India and was also the Honorary Fellow of the Asiatic Society of Bengal. In the Department of Philosophy, Professor James Haughton Woods (1864–1935) played a fundamental role in making the professional study of Asia a possibility at Harvard. Woods's interest in Buddhism and Indian philosophy had led him to further study at Benares and Srinagar in India. On his return to Harvard in 1903, he was appointed Professor of the Philosophical Systems of India.

In 1911, Acharya Dharmananda Damodar Kosambi (1876–1947), Bijoy Kumar Sarkar, Jatindra Nath Seth, Narendra Nath Sengupta, and Hira Lal Roy were among the Indian students at Harvard. Kosambi, who compiled the critical edition of *Visuddhimagga* at Harvard, introduced Har Dayal to Professor Lanman and Professor Woods at Harvard. They immediately noticed the youthful Indian as a gifted student of Buddhism. He held rock-solid academic credentials of having attended St. Johns College at Oxford though he did not hold a degree. He also had copies of his published writings in India as well as the official communication stating that he was a Casberd Exhibitioner as well as a Boden Sanskrit Scholar at Oxford. He was fluent in almost ten languages. Intent on studying Buddhism and its philosophy he was permitted to research at the Harvard Union library and Professor Woods pulled out some hard to access books about India for him. Like other Indian revolutionaries, he turned to ancient Indian history in his endeavor to show that India was far superior to Britain in its great traditions. He later expressed both pleasure and surprise that Harvard students were working on translations of Patanjali's Yoga sutras. One of the students was the poet T.S. Eliot who studied Sanskrit at Harvard.

Har Dayal's temperate nature, austere habits, and excellent reading and writing skills at Harvard appealed to Professor Woods. A year later in a letter of recommendation, Professor Woods put in writing: "Har Dayal appeared last winter and planned to take a course with me in Indian philosophy. We talked informally together and I hunted up some texts for him and the library. I have heard of him from Indian friends and known nothing but good of him... My opinion is that he is a very good man."

The Political Missionary in California

The most important meeting Har Dayal had during his stay in the United States was with the charismatic Indian academic and preacher from Lahore, Sant Teja Singh (1877–1965). After graduating in English literature from Government College, Lahore, Sant Teja Singh was at Harvard for the Master of Arts degree. Having traveled across Canada and the United States, he was aware of the resentment against Hukumat-i-Britannia among the thousands of Indians working in the fields, farms, and factories on the Pacific Coast of North America. The saintly person gently advised the young scholar and patriot to pursue the cause of Indian nationalism among the Indians on the Pacific Coast instead of studying Buddhism at Harvard. Sant Teja Singh insisted that there was a need for a young leader like Har Dayal in California to stimulate the idea of freedom from British rule amongst the Indians living in North America. Har Dayal already possessed the necessary experience of India House, Society of Political Missionaries and the Paris India Group to provide him with a framework. Sant Teja Singh asserted that the greatest challenge before all Indians was to end their enslavement from the British.

Har Dayal recognized his real mission in the United States after being stirred by Sant Teja Singh. Besides, the New England winter with heavy snow was too hard on him and the sun, sand, and beaches of California were far more inviting. By end of March 1911, an inspired Indian patriot yet again decided to return to the world of revolutionaries and packed his bags and books to head out to California. Har Dayal abruptly ended his stint at Harvard and boarded the train to Chicago and then took the Overland to arrive in San Francisco, a city with a very agreeable climate.

The Sikhs, the Swamis, and the Students, with the Spies

The tenth-largest city of the United States, San Francisco was also the chief seaport on the Pacific Coast. In 1911 it was still being rebuilt after the destruction of over twenty-eight thousand buildings in the devastating earthquake and fire on the morning of April 18th, 1906. The City by the bay distanced from the older culture of the East Coast of the United States was a place open to original ideas, world-shattering opinions, and a nonconformist lifestyle.

The next three years in San Francisco became the game-changer and most productive period of Har Dayal's revolutionary life.

The scholarly man chose to locate himself at Berkeley, the site of the famous University of California (UC Berkeley). He was always comfortable in the harmonious setting of a university community like Oxford and Harvard. Mainly due to a small overseas student population residing at the university, the campuses usually provided him access to newspapers, magazines, and a vast library plus a scholarly atmosphere.

Since 1904 Indians had begun enrolling at UC Berkeley. In January 1908 sixteen students from India vehemently protested against a lecture by evangelist J. Lovell Murray who had insulted Hinduism in the past. An Indian, Girindra Mukherjee the President of the Association of Oriental Students in UC Berkeley during 1907–8 led the protest and later published an article in the April 1908 issue of *Overland Monthly*, titled, 'The Hindu in America' clearing some of the misconceptions about India held by Americans at that time.

While at Berkeley, Har Dayal heard that the hardworking Indians in California, Oregon, Washington, and British Columbia were facing racial violence and discrimination by local Governments. He finished his long article 'India in America' offering his assessment of Indians in the United States. He described the lives of his fellow countrymen in America, with an emphasis on four classes of Indians: "the Sikhs, the Swamis, and the Students, with the Spies". The article was signed off "Berkeley, California, USA", dated April 28th, 1911, and was published three months later in the July 1911 issue of *The Modern Review*. The readers in India including his friends and family were informed of his current address in the United States and the DCI of Hukumat-i-Britannia termed the article 'an excellent one'.

In his article 'India in America', Har Dayal contended that "America is perhaps the only country in the world from which a solitary wandering Hindu can send a message of hope and encouragement to his countrymen" and that India should feel drawn towards "this charming land of freedom and optimism because of the great interest America takes in India." He praised the United States over Europe for its ethical ideal and political and social freedom.

He compared the status of Indians across Europe – "Under the Union Jack, they have no status, as they are servants in the house. An Englishman never forgets that a Hindu is his 'fellow-subject.' In English colonies, they are feared on economic grounds, and persecuted and humiliated for many other reasons." As for the French, he wrote "India retains a place in their consciousness only as a country which they unluckily lost to England" and he praised the Germans, "to have learned to admire Hindu genius through Sanskrit literature, and I was surprised to find a young man of no high educational attainments had read 'Sakuntala' in translation. But the Germans seldom see a living Hindu at close quarters. There are only a few Hindu students and merchants in some towns. The educated classes certainly take a keen interest in India from political motives. Am sure that the Germans would love and admire our people".

A visionary ahead of his time, Har Dayal also recommended Universities of the United States as an ideal destination for the brilliant Indian students. According to him, "America is the land of opportunity for poor, industrious and intelligent students," and he warned that no Indian should come to the United States unless he had the assurance of his return passage. A student could earn his day-to-day living expenses "but could not anticipate saving any money". Har Dayal invited Bhai Parmanand to San Francisco to enroll at the Universities of California, as they would waive off the tuition fees for good scholars.

A Modern Rishi in Hawaii

Har Dayal rarely visited Hindu temples but he visited the Vedanta Society Center in San Francisco as it called itself, 'the only Hindu temple in the Western World'. A direct disciple of Ramakrishna Paramahansa, Swami Trigunatita (1865–1915) had established the temple on January 7th, 1906. Architecturally it was a combination of many religious places of worship (a church, a temple, a mosque, and a monastery) as well as an American residence. In 1910, Inayat Khan, musician and Sufi saint performed at the Vedanta Society Center at the invitation of Swami Trigunatita.

The visit made Har Dayal nostalgic after being away from the lanes of Lahore and Delhi. It reminded him of the spiritual centers of Haridwar and Rishikesh and in the article 'India in America' he penned, "I am trying to find a similar spot in the West, where I may perfect the process of self-development, which can be brought to fruitful issue only in a warm and equable climate, such as that which Nature has bestowed on our blessed India…". He also added, "Perhaps I shall find the long-looked-for haven of repose in Southern California, where a climate like that of India makes uninterrupted meditation possible and enables the earnest inquirer to practice the true sannyasa."

Before taking on the humungous enterprise of revolutionary work on the Pacific Coast, the spiritually minded Har Dayal decided to revitalize himself with some hard meditative practices. For the soul-uplifting atmosphere of calm solitude to perfect the process of self-development he chose the beaches of Hawaii Islands in mid-Pacific. Easily accessible beaches with overhanging coconut palms and gently rolling surf surrounded by mountain ranges and valleys created unmatched scenery in Hawaii. Famous writers from Mark Twain to Robert Louis Stevenson had celebrated the beauty of the Hawaiian Islands over decades. He boarded a steamship from San Francisco for the six-day sea voyage to Honolulu some three thousand seven hundred kilometers away.

A few days later at his Chelpuri house in Delhi, Hanwant Sahai was surprised to receive a note from his friend Har Dayal describing his life in Honolulu. According to the letter, the altruistic idea for penance and the search for truth did not leave him. He was driven to utter poverty and spent time living on bread and milk on the Waikiki beach. Much like a modern Hippie, he saved Hotel room expenses by staying in a cave on the Beach. He slept on the ground on a bed of straw and ate whole-wheat bread, boiled potatoes, and raw vegetables. He also drank milk and cocoa, which he prepared on a stove. On the Waikiki beach, there was no snow, no winter and the water was a warm 24 degrees centigrade. The native Hawaiians, the American sailors, the immigrants, and the Asian labor force made up the unique mix of people on the islands. The local fishermen regarded Har Dayal as a Buddhist sage and fed him. He found an audience for his philosophy lectures among the beach community of Honolulu.

On the premises of the Metaphysical Club in Boston in March 1911, a lady had asked Har Dayal if he could practice mental healing. He wrote: "Many rich and educated ladies affect to be enamored of the Hindu religion and burn incense before statues of Buddha placed in their drawing rooms for purpose of decorations."

Amidst his simple meditative and saintly life, the academically oriented Indian was engrossed in the study of the works of Karl Marx. During his stay in Hawaii he completed his groundbreaking work on Marxism, 'Karl Marx: A Modern Rishi'. Har Dayal's article appeared in *The Modern Review* in March 1912, more than five and a half years before the Socialist Revolution in Russia. The article was later translated in Indian languages including Urdu and Hindi, as "*Mazduron Ka Peghambar Karl Marx*".

During his student days in London, Har Dayal had visited the grave of Marx at the Highgate cemetery. Now he tried to understand how this theorist had challenged the existential crisis of his age. In a stirring commentary about Marx, the dedicated scholar and tireless revolutionary declared, "In this short essay, I propose to tell young India the story of the life and work of a great European Rishi, a saint and sage, whose name is revered today by millions of men and women in all countries of the West. Such a study will show us that saintliness does not consist only in repeating religious formulae and singing hymns and that the hardest tapas can be performed out of a penance grove and without sitting in the midst of four burning logs of wood under the burning sun. It will also lead us to the discussion of vital problems of human welfare and set us thinking. It will teach us not to confine ourselves to the writings of Kanada and Kapila, Sankaracharya and Ramanuja in our search for wisdom, but to turn to the great modern thinkers for guidance in our social, moral, intellectual and political difficulties. Modern civilization has been built up by the devoted labors of a group of heroes and heroines at the head of vast numbers of energetic people, and Marx is one of this coterie of thinkers and workers, whose names are household words in Europe."

The young revolutionary in his biographical paper on Marx, revealed, "Modern India has a personal tie too, that links Marx's name to her destiny, for Marx's favorite grandson, Mr. Jean Longuet, one of the most prominent French journalists, is a staunch champion of India's rights and aspirations and always supports new India's claims in his daily paper, *L' Humanite* of Paris. Monsieur Longuet is the son of Karl Marx's eldest daughter and used to comfort the last days of the great philosopher in the early eighties. Young India does not know the full value of Mr. Longuet's services to her cause but time will reveal all."

In a fast-evolving world, a farsighted Har Dayal predicted, "Marx's name will be cherished by generations yet unborn. And his wife and children will share his glory. When poverty and slavery are no more, and the last shreds of private capitalism are consigned to the scrapheap of the past, humanity will remember that they who brought it out of the wilderness were often faint from lack of food. Mothers will tell the story of that mother, who offered her children on the altar of the cause, so those little children should play and laugh in the golden age to come." He ended with a pertinent question to his readers, "Someone must suffer that the world may be helped. Reader, will you be that one?" Har Dayal's advice to the future generations was; "Revise your Marx frequently and appreciate the value and significance of true Marxism if you do not understand Marxism you cannot mark in the vanguard of progressive humanity".

Har Dayal's pamphlet became a part of the national revolutionary legacy of India and it facilitated several serious intellectuals to find their way to Marxism.

Indian communist leader and a pioneer of Marxist philosophy in India, Puran Chand Joshi (1907–1980), believed that Har Dayal was the first Indian to write an article on Marx. Joshi later penned a biographical note on Har Dayal, noting his contribution in popularizing Marxism, writing, "Marx and his contributions were still, as a rule, unknown in India. There was, however, a marked change in the situation by the beginning of the next decade."

From the moment of his discovery of Marx, Har Dayal's mind was clear India had to have revolution.

Sazaa-e-kalapani for Savarkar

On July 4th, 1911, a chained Savarkar was led off the steamer *S.S. Maharaja* at the docks on Andamans. The dispute over his successful escape in July 1910 in Marseilles was presented before the Permanent Court of Arbitration in The Hague. The court had ruled in Britain's favor on February 24th, 1911. The tribunal ruled that an "irregularity was committed by the arrest of Savarkar" but that "there is no rule of International Law imposing… any obligation on the Power which has in its custody a prisoner, to restore him because of a mistake committed by the foreign agent who delivered him to that Power". Sentenced to transportation for life to the Andamans, the wooden ticket around his neck stated that he had to serve two life terms of twenty-five years each (the only one of a kind), locked in the newly built Cellular Jail.

The Cellular Jail at the Andaman Islands had become the ultimate destination for the extremist forces in India. All the Indian revolutionaries who posed a threat to the Hukumat-i-Britannia were regularly tortured and hanged at this godless facility. Construction of the high-security prison had started in 1896 and was completed in 1906. It was a massive three-storied structure, shaped like a starfish with seven wings that could be watched from a central watchtower. It was the standard design of most British jails and a facility where six hundred and ninety-eight souls could be kept in solitary confinement for the crime of opposing Hukumat-i-Britannia. As Savarkar entered the jail, he later recorded, "I felt that I had entered the jaws of death. The high wall was adorned with a festoon of manacles and several similar instruments of torture were hanging down from the wall." From his 13.5 feet by 7.5 feet cell (No 52, Level Three, Yard Seven Wing), he could view the gallows where the Hukumat-i-Britannia hanged revolutionaries. He spent the next nine years and ten months locked here and scratched out his story with a nail on the walls of his cell. Both the Savarkar brothers Ganesh and Vinayak were a cause célèbre in India and considered the heroes amongst jailed revolutionaries of the Cellular Jail.

Like Aurobindo Ghosh before him, Savarkar was described by the Hukumat-i-Britannia as "one of the most dangerous men that India has produced". A fate similar to Savarkar awaited Har Dayal had the British Secret Service operatives captured him in India or Europe. But he was in Hawaii where he considered the idea of writing a biography of his associate Savarkar as well as republishing his banned book, *The Indian War of Independence* in the United States.

The arm-waving, teetotaler and clever Indian

On August 27th, 1911, Bhai Parmanand disembarked from *S.S. Voltaire* in New York and made his way to San Francisco. By the end of the summer of 1911, Har Dayal distressed by the news of Savarkar's incarceration in Andamans and the much-publicized shooting incident in Chicago was also back in Berkeley after his Hawaiian interlude. The two friends reunited after several months. Since they had last met in Fort de France, Bhai Parmanand had successfully established Arya Samaj schools and temples for the Indian population in British Guiana and Trinidad. He now enrolled at the University of San Francisco, College of Pharmacy. Initially, both Har Dayal and Bhai Parmanand shared an apartment at 810 Shrader Street next to a huge park and a short ten-minute walk from the University of San Francisco campus. Later Har Dayal placed an advertisement in the local newspapers seeking independent accommodation for himself that read: "Wanted - small unfurnished room – cheap – Write Har Dayal" and moved to Berkeley. He had to frequently advertise, as it was exceedingly hard for Indians to rent a place due to racial undercurrents.

Gradually the two old friends from Lahore created a fine network of the disparate Indians on the Pacific Coast. Two exceptionally pious and patriotic men, Baba Jawala Singh (1866–1938) and Baba Wasakha Singh (1877–1957), met Bhai Parmanand and Har Dayal at Stockton and invited them for the celebration of Gurpurab of the 10th Sikh Guru. A large number of Sikhs living in California along with thirty-five Muslims and twelve Hindus had joined the celebrations as a model of interfaith relationship. Bhai Paramand and Har Dayal were among the Indians who were connected with these events from the beginning. Almost a year later on October 24th, 1912, services began at the Gurudwara (Sikh Temple) in Stockton – the first in the United States.

Ram Nath Puri (1881–1974), an early immigrant to San Francisco who had already established a group for Indians called the Hindustan Association and brought out a Hindi periodical titled *Circular-i-Azadi* (Circular of Freedom) joined them. Tarak Nath Das (1884–1958), a talented orator, community organizer, and dynamic political activist, had evaded capture by British Secret Service operatives in India and arrived in Seattle via Japan on July 16th, 1907. He worked in Canada as a 'Hindoo interpreter' for the United States Immigration Service in Vancouver, British Columbia and studied at Norwich University in Vermont, the oldest private military university in the United States. Das reached Berkeley to get involved in the political activities of Har Dayal.

Har Dayal and his group began meeting the large number of Indian immigrants around San Francisco on the weekends and during holidays. They connected with the Indian immigrant community working as farmers, contractors, laborers, shopkeepers, spiritual figures and students and spent hours lecturing. On the farmlands of Northern California, Har Dayal preached revolution with his power talks to the Indians and at the end of sessions sang patriotic songs and danced with them with great fervor. His austerity, honesty, and sacrifice attracted the handful of Indians living in a foreign land and he became a sort of hero for them.

Har Dayal also joined some activist organizations in the San Francisco Bay Area and began to jointly deliver free speeches around the city to make inroads into the social, academic and political circles of the Pacific Coast. Bhai Parmanand recollected in his autobiography, *The Story of my Life*, "With the help of the doctor a hall was hired and I arranged for his delivering lectures on Hindu Philosophy." After the lectures, the two youngsters from India were soon rubbing shoulders with radicals of all stripes including Irish, Russian, Japanese, Chinese and Turkish. They spoke every Friday evening at the assembly hall of the Phelan building near Market and Grant Avenue under auspices of the Dionysian Society.

Bhai Parmanand details that Har Dayal's writings and speeches were of full of insight and characteristic humor and attracted a lot of interest in San Francisco, "His language, his eloquence and talent were indeed wonderful and his reputation spread… Lala Har Dayal had by his high attainments, simplicity, and capacity for sacrifice, earned for himself, both at the university and in the eyes of the press in California, unusual respect and admiration. The newspapers referred to him as the "Hindu Saint", during his stay there, however, his thoughts again began to take a new turn and this time it was in the direction of socialism and communism.

Lala Har Dayal indeed never occupied a middle position; he was always going from one extreme to another."

A popular man in San Francisco, he was viewed as a combination of an Eastern philosopher, modern journalist, defender of causes and an agent provocateur. With no equivalent in the United States, Har Dayal was invited to attend a variety of social occasions. After one such talk he got acquainted with the social crusader Charles Erskine Scott Wood and he also met Winston Churchill (1871–1947 – not related to the British politician), the best selling novelist in the United States, and befriended writer Jack London (1876–1916). Subsequently, in 1915, Jack London exalted Har Dayal in his last novel, *The Little Lady of the Big House* and created an arm-waving, teetotaler and clever Indian character called 'Dar Hyal' who questioned the "monogamic marriage institution of Western civilization".

The First University Lecturer from India

Har Dayal's reputation as a public intellectual and a skillful speaker had already captivated audiences in San Francisco and UC Berkeley took note of his presence. His talk on the subject of "The Aim and Method of Hindu Philosophy in Theory and Practice", at the Theosophical Society, 346, Pacific Building in San Francisco on December 24th, 1911 was widely discussed by the Professors of UC Berkeley.

Keen on chasing academics, Har Dayal in December 1911, met Harvard graduate, Charles Henry Rieber (1866–1948) who was Professor of Logic at the Department of Philosophy at UC Berkeley. Har Dayal gave him an outline of the talks he wished to deliver on Hindu Philosophy. Professor Rieber liked his approach and arranged for him to give a few informal lectures on Indian philosophy to the classes in that term. After the lectures, Har Dayal established a good rapport with Professor Arthur Upham Pope (1881–1969) an important faculty member at UC Berkeley. Har Dayal even sought a meeting with the celebrated chess player and Sanskrit Professor at UC Berkeley, Arthur W. Ryder (1877–1938) for his advice. *Time* magazine described Ryder as the greatest Sanskrit student of his day and added "Ten men like that would make a civilization". Decades later American scientist Robert Oppenheimer, a former student of Ryder at UC Berkeley, explaining the power of the atomic bomb test quoted from his translation of *The Bhagavad Gita*, "Now I have become Death, the destroyer of worlds".

Har Dayal met Oxford-educated Rhodes Scholar Farham P. Griffiths, Secretary to Benjamin Ide Wheeler, President of UC Berkeley to seek a job at the University. Though they were not acquainted at Oxford, Griffiths had heard about the excellent impression the Indian scholar and lecturer made at Harvard and UC Berkeley. Har Dayal enclosed his academic background and applied for the position of an instructor at UC Berkeley. He was directed to Leland Stanford Junior University that stood across the Bay from UC Berkeley as it had an emerging department of philosophy.

Stanford University was named in the memory of Leland Jr. the only child of railroad magnate and former California Governor Leland Stanford and Jane Lathrop. They bestowed a large fortune that included the 8,180-acre Palo Alto stock farm to the University. The Stanfords and founding President David Starr Jordan (1851–1931), the leading naturalist of the United States, intended their new University to be non-sectarian, co-educational and inexpensive. The University taught the conventional liberal arts as well as ran courses in modern technology and engineering. Their vision took shape on the oak-dotted fields of the San Francisco Peninsula. Founded on October 1st, 1891, it had enrolled 1700 students by 1910.

Stanford's exposure to India was limited. But the Co-Founder of the University, Jane Lathrop had visited India in November 1903 and the faculty hosted occasional talks on India by traveling Swamis and British visitors. Only two students from India, Surendra Mohan Bose, and Khagendra Chandra Das had graduated at Stanford in the Class of 1910 (Chemistry). Before returning to their country, both young nationalists continued onwards to Japan, where each gained technological knowledge that assisted them in launching their businesses - waterproofing for Bose, and pharmaceuticals for Das.

A Swiss student, Frieda Mathilda Hauswirth (1886–1974) enrolled at Stanford to study English, described the Indian students in the Universities of Northern California in her book, *A Marriage to India*, "Nationally very conscious, the majority of these students tried their best to live and work in a way that would reflect on their motherland. This was the period of keen, crude enthusiasm, cosmopolitan clubs meeting on a basis of frank comradery, the acclamation of international sympathies, denunciation of national and racial prejudices. The Hindoos felt a proud and sensitive need to do whatever they could to counteract the talks of returning missionaries, to whose money collecting interests it was to paint India black. They never missed a chance of arranging lectures by themselves or by prominent Indians who passed through San Francisco."

As maintained by *Stanford University Archives*, on January 12th, 1912, President David Starr Jordan, sought the advice of Dr. John Maxson Stillman, Chairman of the Advisory Board at Stanford University, on the application received from Har Dayal who offered to act as an instructor in Philosophy. The early days of Philosophy at Stanford were exciting and at times, tumultuous. The first fourteen years after the establishment of the university in 1885 saw only minimal instruction in philosophy but it changed when the philosopher Dr. Henry Stuart (1870–1951) joined in 1907. Professor Stuart taught courses in ethics, logic, metaphysics, epistemology, evolutionary theory, and history of philosophy.

Both Jordan and Professor Stuart sought the estimations from other academics at Harvard and UC Berkeley about Har Dayal before offering any position to the young Indian scholar.

According to the *Stanford University Archives* records, Professor Ryder of UC Berkeley in a glowing letter of approval to Stanford University for Har Dayal confirmed his proficiency, "I have seen him a number of times and had a considerable conversation with him. He has a wide and accurate knowledge of Sanskrit literature and philosophy – in some ways better than we westerners can ever hope to attain. He has also studied in Europe and knows how western scholarship proceeds. His command of English is remarkable and his acquaintance with European history and present conditions extremely good. So far as his intellectual equipment goes, he would make a most desirable addition to any University faculty..."

Another exceptional endorsement was received from Professor Pope of UC Berkeley, stating, "I know Har Dayal well and am glad of the opportunity to express my appreciation of his character and ability. He is a man of great force of character and is greeted with genuine reverence throughout India. Particularly in Punjab, he is regarded as a saint and I have heard educated Punjabis and even Bengalis speak of him as the greatest man in India... From what I know of him I regard the high esteem in which he is held as wholly deserved.... Mr. Har Dayal is also a scholarly man. In general culture and information, he surpasses most of our college teachers... I regard him as a learned man, a powerful man, and a very good man."

Similar testimonials about the Indian scholar's erudite acumen were received from Professor Lanman and Professor Woods at Harvard. Accordingly, to test the waters, Stanford invited Har Dayal to deliver two lectures at its Chapel on the evenings of February 7th and 8th, 1912. Har Dayal spoke on the subject, 'Systems of Oriental Philosophy' and 'Problems of Oriental Philosophy'. The teachers and students of philosophy at the University and all those interested in oriental subjects attended the two talks. The profundity and extensiveness of his knowledge of the domain was visible during the addresses. After the lectures in his response to Jordan, Professor Stuart pointed out, "Mr. Dayal's two lectures in the University Chapel seem to have made a very good impression... Indian philosophy is undoubtedly an interesting and instructive episode in the history of human culture and the evidence at hand seems to point to Mr. Dayal's competence as an interpreter of it."

By the end of February 1912, Jordan was enthralled with the Indian based on the recommendations received from the Professors at Harvard and UC Berkeley and his talks at the University Chapel. Jordan thought that Har Dayal was a man entirely competent as of character and scholarship to teach. He wanted Har Dayal to give a course in Sanskrit under the general direction of Professor Stuart at the Philosophy department. After serious deliberation, the final validation for Har Dayal came from Professor Stuart himself who suggested that Har Dayal be employed with the title of 'Lecturer in Indian Philosophy' for the current term January 8th to May 15th, 1912.

Then in a historic move, the visionary Jordan offered Har Dayal, a lectureship for 'Indian Philosophy' at Leland Stanford University on March 1st, 1912. An unusual clause inserted in the contract by Har Dayal was that he would accept no fees or salary for teaching. The self-sacrificing man who lived off the minor income from his writings, public lectures and support from his brothers believed in the ancient Indian principle of "vidya daan", literally meaning, "the gift of learning."

Faculty Elects a Hindu

On Tuesday, March 5th, 1912, a twenty-seven year old cultured and brainy looking youthful Indian with his round-framed spectacles, a thinning hairline and a smiling face entered room 460 at Stanford at sharp 1330 hrs in the afternoon. He began teaching a course of Indian Philosophy in English and the talk was sprinkled with his usual wit. For the first time, the student community at a university in the United States attended a course (with credits) taught by an Indian lecturer. To be back in the scholarly environment of the university classroom where he had excelled all his life was like a wish come true for Har Dayal.

The date, March 5th, 1912 will remain significant in Indo American history. On that day Har Dayal became the first Indian professional to break through the glass ceiling of white-collar occupations in the United States. This was a time when Indians were not accepted as American citizens and there were reports of racial discrimination at restaurants, hotels and public transport. For Har Dayal to be engaged as a lecturer by a well-known American University was recognition of India as an ancient land of wisdom and a farsighted decision by the academics of the United States. A man of foreign birth and possessing extensive education, his engagement at Stanford created more than ordinary interest in the United States. By not accepting any remuneration for his work as a lecturer he gained tremendous respect and his tenure at Stanford enlightened American society about the superb scholarly aptitude of educated Indians. Though Har Dayal made a small beginning it would take half a century for the entire range of Indian talent to be recognized across the United States in the form of Indian academics, actors, businesspersons, corporate executives, doctors, economists, filmmakers, engineers, entrepreneurs, information technology professionals, journalists, lawyers, media persons, military personnel, motel owners, musicians, politicians, scientists, shopkeepers, sportspersons, writers and other specialists.

The New York Times in its issue dated March 10th, published the news story with the heading, "FACULTY ELECTS A HINDU' and noted that "perhaps the first Hindu (Indian) professor to hold a position in an American college has been elected to the Stanford faculty by the Board of Trustees in the person of Har Dayal, who is to give a course in Sanskrit and to deliver Philosophies of India". The news report added that he was a graduate of Punjab University and also studied at Oxford with a fellowship in Sanskrit. Newspapers across California also carried the news. *The Stanford Daily* added, "The engagement by the trustees of Mr. Dayal is an innovation in American college circles, as no other Hindu lecturer is known to be engaged in the institutions of the United States. The students who take the new courses will doubtless receive many benefits by receiving their knowledge of the subject practically first hand."

His name and brief biography listing his professional academic career were published later in the Stanford yearbook as:

HAR DAYAL, Lecturer on Indian Philosophy. B. A., Punjab University, 1903, M. A., 1904. Aitchison-Ramrattan Sanskrit Scholar, 1903–05; Lecturer in History and Economics, St. Stephen's College, Delhi, 1905; Government of India Scholar at Oxford (History and Economics), 1905–07; Boden Sanskrit Scholar, Oxford, 1907; Casberd Exhibitioner in History, St. John's College, Oxford, 1907.

The teaching stint at Stanford was one of the high points of Har Dayal's complex life. Much to the delight of family, friends, and followers in India and around the world, with this accomplishment, he was acknowledged for finally making a worthwhile contribution to humanity and also utilizing his amazing talents in the honorable profession of academics as a University Lecturer. Back in Lahore, Lajpat Rai, an admirer of Har Dayal remarked, "Har Dayal is one of the most distinguished Indians that ever visited America…"

The Intellectual Confidante

In early April 1912, Har Dayal moved from Berkeley to Palo Alto and took up residence in a one-room studio apartment at 347 Ramona Street between the railroad tracks and Kipling Street. Here he lived like a poor labourer and furnished his dwelling with numerous books, a mat spread on the floor that served as his bed and a single chair that he kept for visitors. Eating only fruits for his meals, he lived just five kilometers from the Stanford campus, a gentle walk through a large grove of eucalyptus trees with a wide palm-lined avenue. He was close to a small post office, the powerhouse with its famous chimney and several service buildings, including a commons restaurant, the University Inn and a bookstore on Lasuen Street that he often visited.

In the course of his living in Palo Alto and teaching at Stanford, Har Dayal came across the literary critic Van Wyck Brooks (1886–1963). Son of a businessman, the superbly educated Brooks was a recent Harvard graduate (Class of 1908). He had studied literature and philosophy and clubbed around with T. S. Eliot, Walter Lippmann, John Hall Wheelock, Maxwell Perkins and other undergraduates who later became famous. Brooks chose Eliot as the quintessence of the Harvard he knew. He was chosen as an Instructor in English Literature at Harvard in September 1911 and was for several years engaged in magazine work with *The World's Work, Colliers* and other publications. Brooks, like Har Dayal, lived through his pen and for him, "not to be writing a book was not to be alive at all". He was a mystical and fervently optimistic man who deciphered signs of change in the American consciousness. Both of them also knew Alain LeRoy Locke as he was at Harvard before going to Oxford as a 'Rhodes Scholar'.

Har Dayal and Brooks, the two young literary radicals became long-term intellectual confidantes. Har Dayal was also introduced to his wife Eleanor Kenyon Stimson and was extremely fond of their son Charles. Brooks too enjoyed the company of the elegantly talkative firebrand and conceivably suspected that the Indian revolutionary was teaching Philosophy at Stanford to mask his real work as a mastermind of a rebellion. In his *Autobiography*, Brooks recalled that time: "He carried this mystification so far as to stage at my house a colloquy with an Indian professor (Bhai Parmanand) who had come from Punjab and who proclaimed his nationalism while Har Dayal boldly affirmed that the international social revolution was his only interest."

Revolutionist first and everything else afterward

The distinctive appointment of a pronounced anti-imperialist and a public intellectual like Har Dayal at an American University attracted a lot of attention in California and the United States. In the next few months, he got involved with lot of different organizations.

To pursue his revolutionary goals Har Dayal established the communist leaning 'Fraternity of the Red Flag' which merged Hindu and Buddhist asceticism and self-discipline with anarchist politics and goals. Initiation into the order required no less than a year-long term; the taking of vows of poverty, homelessness, humility, purity, and service; and faith in the "eight principles of radicalism." He ambitiously called for personal self-improvement via the abolition of private property, patriotism, racism, religion and the state along with the emancipation of women to establish Universal brotherhood. A year later, he founded the anarcho-syndicalist Bakunin Institute - the monastery of the Order of the Red Flag. It was set up in a building on gently sloping six acres of land overlooking the Ocean in Hayward worth $7,000 donated by a supporter E. Norwood. The institute began by publishing a journal, *Land and Liberty* edited by India born British citizen William C. Owen.

Simultaneously Har Dayal was attracted to San Francisco's multiethnic radical milieu and founded the Radical Club (the complete title was the 'International-Radical-Communist Anarchist Club'). A motley assortment of intelligentsias and eccentrics joined the bandwagon it met for monthly dinners at one of the many Italian restaurants of North Beach, considered to be the city's Latin Quarter. Here Har Dayal was acquainted with the anarchist leader Alexander Berkman and his life-long accomplice Emma Goldman. Being a member of the Cosmopolitan Club in Oxford, the first of its kind in Britain, he was considered a pioneer in the movement and invited by Professor Pope to be a member of the local Cosmopolitan Club at Berkeley. His first talk at the home of Dr. Payson Jackson Treat, Professor of Far Eastern History at Stanford was 'The Growth of the Cosmopolitan Movement'.

More importantly, Har Dayal became the secretary of Oakland's Industrial Workers of the World (IWW), Mixed Local 174 popularly known as the 'Wobblies'. IWW was an international labor union that was founded in Chicago on June 27th, 1905. In a much-applauded speech on the 'The future of the labor movement' at the IWW meeting, Har Dayal condemned patriotism as having been, "devised to divide the laborers into their various countries and thus into a false division of society". A positive account about his lecture appeared in, *The San Francisco Bulletin*. Though he knew that with all the high profile publicity Stanford University would know of his leanings towards anarchism he did not care. He told his friends that he was no hypocrite and he had not sold his soul to the university. Historian Kornel Chang claimed, "Within IWW circles, no figure was held in higher esteem than the South Asian revolutionary."

Still a prolific writer, in a series of articles titled, 'Some Phases of Contemporary Thought in India,' Har Dayal demanded that India should completely do away from the institution of the caste system. He clearly professed, "I do not acknowledge any caste-system, good, bad, or indifferent..." and her enemies." During this period the volatile thinker finished writing a few more articles reflecting his idealism that were published in *The Modern Review* including, 'Education in the West: A Suggestion,' (February 1912), 'Indian Philosophy and Art in the West,' (April 1912) and 'The Wealth of the Nation' (July 1912). Here Har Dayal ridiculed the gurus who confused people's minds with metaphysics while overlooking the real suffering present in India: "While so much transcendental nonsense is being perpetrated, famines are desolating the land, pestilence, and malaria hang like a pall on town and country, and there is not a single decent representative institution, technical institute, laboratory or library in the whole country."

His article 'What the World is waiting for,' appeared in an American magazine, *The Open Court*. Here he again challenged the established religious order for being dogmatic, "The new wine of science and comparative religion has burst the old bottles of established religions" and argued that in the modern world the majority of educated men and women had no definite philosophy of life. The solution according to him was, "Renunciation, and renunciation alone, will save humanity". While Har Dayal was busy impressing Americans on the Pacific Coast and his fanbase in India with his cerebral perceptions, the despotism of the British rule in India was being camouflaged in ceremonies of splendor.

The Sham Life of an Empire

The Delhi Durbar - With Our King and Queen in India, a two and a half-hour-long documentary film about the grand spectacle recorded by Charles Urban in Kinemacolor was screened in the Savoy and Cort Theatre in downtown San Francisco. As the scenes of Delhi came alive in color on the screen at the Cort Theatre on 64 Ellis Street, Har Dayal and his friend, John Daniel Barry (1866–1942), a reporter for *The San Francisco Bulletin* watched the film in the audience.

The Durbar of 1911 was the biggest news event for the young film industry and the official documentary film made on the occasion was one of the first color feature films to be seen worldwide. The film covered the fortnight-long celebration of December 1911, as the city of Delhi hosted the coronation of their Majesty King George V, the King of the United Kingdom and the British Dominions and Emperor of India. King George V made his grand entry in the Durbar on horseback that ironically led to confusion among the crowds who failed to recognize him, as they were looking for the royal to be straddling on a mammoth elephant like the Mughals. Still, the British Empire was at its pinnacle and nowhere was its power and opulence more apparent than in the Delhi Durbar of 1911. Its scale visible on the screen was astounding.

In the end, George V rose and in a clear voice reversed the partition of Bengal and the transference of the capital of Hukumat-i-Britannia to Delhi. The Durbar was then closed and the King and Queen departed. The message was clear: the British were the legitimate successors of the Mughals and the previous Indian rulers like the famous Rajput king, Prithviraj Chauhan. The new capital was intended to express the power of the Hukumat-i-Britannia, just as Shahjahan's capital had expressed the authority of the Mughliyah Saltanat for the sipahis of the Ghadr of 1857. The documentary film reinforced the image of the Hukumat-i-Britannia in the minds of the average American citizens as it ran for fifteen months in the United States and grossed a handsome amount of $750,000.

For the Dilliwallah living far away on the Pacific Coast of the United States, the Mughal era monuments reminded him of his childhood and he yearned to be back home. Har Dayal told Barry, "I am beginning to be homesick. I played in those ruins as a boy. It is uncanny to see them up there". During the Durbar his own alma mater St. Stephens College was involved and the students retained as stewards. After the screening Har Dayal told Barry, "its the sham life of an empire".

Barry communicated the progressive thoughts of the Indian revolutionary to his boss, Fremont Older (1856–1935), the managing director of *The San Francisco Bulletin* and a prominent member of the San Francisco establishment. Older greatly valued Har Dayal's intellectual acumen and between June and July 1912, *The San Francisco Bulletin* published a series of five articles by John Barry that examined the demand for a free India. The articles were based on his conversations with Har Dayal who in a preface in *The San Francisco Bulletin* wrote: "I also beg to acknowledge our indebtedness to Mr. John D. Barry, the scholar and the sage, whose pen has given to the people of America some of the greatest truths for which they have been waiting. Mr. Barry is one of the ablest and noblest men whom I have met in my travels. His charming personality is reflected in his writings, which are marked by rare dignity and sweetness. His heart goes out to you my beloved countrymen because you are weak and poor today… our voice is stifled at home but it is heard in other lands. You are not alone in your struggle…. *Satyameva viyate nanrtam* (Truth triumphs not falsehood)."

In his long piece, Barry added Har Dayal's remarks after the screening of the documentary film about the Durbar of 1911, "It shows that England is not sure of her power. And the removal of the capital from Calcutta to Delhi that is another sign… Through the Durbar they are trying to appeal to the people with imitation of the old barbaric magnificence. It had its place in its days. But it is out of place now…"

Later in 1913, Har Dayal remarked that the event was; "the dark days of shame specifically with the fostering of an illusion: The jaded King of England was trotted out to Delhi to impress the grandeur of the 'Empire' on the minds of the assembled hosts of Hindustan." A politically astute observer, he was correct in forecasting, that this was "the final culmination of the Empire-building process in India".

The Indian Scholars at Berkeley

On Monday, August 26th, 1912, the *S.S. Nile* owned by Pacific Mail Steamship Company approached the Pacific Coast of the United States. Onboard the ship, Gobind Behari Lal caught the first glimpse of California. He was among the six students from India selected for the newly launched 'Guru Gobind Singh Sahib educational scholarship' at UC Berkeley.

In 1912, there were about thirty-seven Indian students at UC Berkeley and Stanford and a hundred in the United States. They were mostly graduates from Punjab and Calcutta universities doing postgraduate study. Many had mortgaged land or borrowed money from family members to pay the third-class fare of $300 for the long sea voyage of thirty days from India to North America. The tuition at the Universities was only $15 a year and living expenses totaled to a ballpark figure of $250. But the costs were still prohibitive for Indians and there was no financial support available besides the opportunities for self-support by working part-time in the United States.

At the suggestion of Bhai Parmanand, Har Dayal devised a scheme of scholarship to bring deserving Indian students from all over India to study at UC Berkeley and Stanford as an alternative to Oxford and Cambridge in Britain. The scholarship provided Indian students with free boarding, stationery, clothes, expenses and all requisites of life on the campus of the University. A ground-breaking idea incorporated by Har Dayal was to bring 'Indian women students' to an American University. Besides, the scholarship did not discriminate on the basis on castes, religions or regions of India.

On January 25th, 1912, Har Dayal with the financial backing from a wealthy Indian farmer Baba Jawala Singh living in Moreland had announced the 'Guru Gobind Singh Sahib educational scholarship' at a press meet. It was the first Indian scholarship at an American University and the idealistic President Wheeler of UC Berkeley had given his approval. The journalists of the Bay Area were informed that the three-year scholarship for six Indians would commence from August 1912. The announcement received wide acclaim in the Californian press and newspapers across India.

Then on May 25th, 1912, the names of the six men selected under the chairmanship of Professor Arthur Pope by Baba Jawala Singh, Sant Teja Singh, Tarak Nath Das, and Har Dayal were declared. They were chosen from six hundred applications and represented the various Madras, Pune, Aligarh and Delhi Universities as well as different faiths of India. Among the selected students were Henry Edward Pandion, Nand Singh Sihra, B.S. Sharma, Darisi Chenchiah and Vaman Ramchandra Kokatnur.

A surprising inclusion was Gobind Behari Lal. He was an excellent student who had completed his Bachelor of Arts degree at St. Stephen's College, Delhi, and Masters from Punjab University and was teaching at the Hindu College at Kashmiri Gate in Delhi. He wanted to study further at Cambridge, Oxford or Edinburgh but was incensed after watching the proceedings of the Durbar of 1911 in Delhi. He resented Hukumat-i-Britannia and jumped at the scholarship from an American university. Though Gobind maintained that he was chosen strictly on merit it seems highly improbable that his relative and guru Har Dayal had no role to play in his selection for the scholarship. Nonetheless, Gobind sought a Doctorate in social sciences at UC Berkeley. After his name appeared in the list of selected candidates he left his house in Kinari Bazaar in Delhi during the monsoons in 1912. He then traveled by sea from Calcutta via Burma and Hong Kong, to board the *S.S. Nile* from Yokohama, on August 10th. He preferred the alternative and cheaper transpacific route as the sad episode of the *R.M.S. Titanic* sinking after colliding with an iceberg on its maiden voyage on April 15th, 1912 was extensively published in Indian newspapers.

Gobind alighted from *S.S. Nile* in the United States on August 26th and like most Asian immigrants witnessed that Europeans had their papers processed onboard the ship and allowed to disembark by the US Immigration Service. But the other immigrants, including Indians, Russians, Mexicans as well as those who needed to be quarantined for health reasons, were ferried to Angel Island Station, the largest island in the San Francisco Bay, for processing of medical papers and immigration interviews.

Once past the 'alien admission' paperwork, two days later Gobind was delighted to see an awkwardly outfitted but smiling Har Dayal holding a copy of *The San Francisco Bulletin* waiting to receive him at the Pier 40, South of Market Street. The two Dilliwallahs embraced and received each other with the popular Indian slogan *'Bande Mataram'*. They immediately picked up their conversation from when they had separated in Delhi in August 1908 as Har Dayal had fled from India. Gobind brought news about family, friends and the political situation of India while his mentor updated him about his global endeavors over the last four years in London, Paris, Algiers, Fort de France, Harvard, Honolulu, and San Francisco.

A week later Gobind was enrolled for higher studies at UC Berkeley. San Francisco at that time was one of the most freedom-loving and democratic places in the world. These were the golden years of Berkeley and it was considered the Athens of America personifying a spirit of freedom that had never existed in history. Gobind immediately noticed that the American professors he encountered at UC Berkeley were very friendly in contrast to the undemonstrative British inspired teachers in Indian universities. The educated Americans were compassionate towards the modern-minded, new knowledge-seeking Indians. He was also amazed that the campus was coeducational and unlike India women, students sat next to him in the classroom. His classmates included Henry Francis Grady the first United States Ambassador to India and Sun Fo, the son of famous Chinese political leader and philosopher Dr. Sun Yet-sen (1866–1925). There exist misleading accounts of Har Dayal meeting Dr. Sun Yet-sen in Honolulu. But after his sixth and last visit to Hawaii, Sen had left for Japan on May 1910, a year before Har Dayal appeared on the Pacific Islands.

After his enrollment, Gobind was told that the financial arrangement for the education scholarship was shaky due to a failed crop that summer. Consequently, on arrival, all the Indian scholars were lodged together in a self-managed rented hostel at 2273 Shattuck Avenue. Their common postal address was PO Box 455, Berkeley, California, USA. The student hotel was named 'Nalanda Hostel' by Har Dayal, after the traditional Buddhist seat of learning. The Indian scholars were informed that if they failed to study or maintain a good moral character their scholarship would be forfeited. They were debarred from smoking or consuming alcoholic beverages. Professor Pope and his wife Bertha Clark Pope who lived at 2708 Virginia Street in Berkeley came out to help the students adjust to life on the University campus.

Gobind's guru, Har Dayal was genuinely admired among the small Indian student community at UC Berkeley. According to the records in the *West Bengal State Archives*, an Indian student in the United States, Waman Sakharam Sant-Akolekar, gave a statement to Bengal CID about Har Dayal, "I knew practically nothing of this gentleman when I was in India. When I went to the United States, I heard his name very often. Almost every student of India residing in American knew about Mr. Har Dayal."

The Indian lecturer gave the young students books to read on Victor Emanuel II, Giuseppe Mazzini, Giuseppe Garibaldi, and the revolutionary movements of the world. The students heard and read about Har Dayal's lectures at Stanford and in San Francisco. Within the first year of his arrival in the United States, Har Dayal was recognized in California as a creative and versatile philosopher and a remarkable and decent man from India. He was well known among the Californian literati as also in the Indian community for his infectious humor, intelligence, charm, and simplicity.

On one occasion, Chenchiah, a scholarship student and some Indians in Berkeley offered to buy Har Dayal a new overcoat and shoes since the ones he regularly wore was full of holes. But the leader claimed it was inconsequential what he wore every day. Then while Har Dayal was asleep, Chenchiah secretly removed his old overcoat and shoes and replaced them with a brand new coat and a shining pair of shoes. Next morning Har Dayal took the new coat to the local market in Berkeley and exchanged it with a second-hand one with holes similar to the one he wore earlier but could not find a replacement for his first-hand shoes. In a recollection published in *Madhya Pradesh Chronicle* on June 2nd, 1966, by Dr. Gurdev Singh Deol titled, 'Lala Har Dayal as a revolutionary', it is revealed that if he ever got late in returning to the hostel at night, Har Dayal who often carried his blankets with him would sleep outside the front door on the stairs rather than disturb the sleep of the students inside.

Not all Indian students appreciated Har Dayal. The British Consul-General in San Francisco, Andrew Carnegie Ross took a discreet interest in the affairs of the Indian students at Berkeley and Stanford. Under Ross's influence, some students began to object to Har Dayal's domineering approach, egalitarian lifestyle and attitude of self-importance. Nevertheless, most Indians respectfully called him 'Lalaji'.

Then two controversies at Stanford nearly destroyed Har Dayal's 'saintly' reputation and cost him the only 'job' he ever held in his entire life.

Women of the West and Free Love

Writing in *The Modern Review*, Har Dayal described his impression of 'Women of the West' (published July 1911). He set out to prove that there is not much to choose for women between East and West. For him, the fact that "Western women go to college, play the piano, read the newest books, or even write a novel does not make their position any higher than that of their sisters in the East". He protested against "the hypocrisy, the misery, the contempt, the awful cruelty" to which they were constantly exposed especially "being prepared for the marriage market as were the slaves put up for sale…" For advancement, he pointed towards France and gave it high marks, calling Paris the intellectual center of the world. One of the goals of his 'Fraternity of the Red Flag' was, "the establishment of the complete economic, moral, intellectual and sexual freedom of woman, and the abolition of prostitution, marriage, and other institutions based on the enslavement of woman."

Har Dayal was a sensation among the student community of Stanford. He became so popular on campus that *The Daily Californian* even published regular editorials on his talks. The fame of his classes and lectures spread and he attracted some female fans. Stanford student Frieda Hauswirth attended a meeting of the Radical Club in Palo Alto at the house of a notable California suffragist Alice Park where Har Dayal spoke. The young Frieda had married a fellow Stanford student Arthur Lee Munger (who later qualified as a Doctor), on August 7th, 1910, in an unconventional marriage ceremony at Temple Square in Palo Alto that shocked the local community. She was now drawn to the powerful speaker whose speeches were filled with ecstasy and passion. She developed an infatuation for the radical thinking Indian lecturer and often helped type his essays on Hindu philosophy till midnight.

In her book, *A Marriage to India,* Frieda recollected, "Under the influence of my Hindu friends my interests gradually shifted from Indian philosophy and literature to the social and economic aspects of Indian life, to history and politics. Under their guidance, my reading was bound to be one-sided. Vivekananda, Margaret Noble, Savarkar, Cotton, Digby, Sunderland - these were typical of the authors I studied. While reading and the attitude of the majority of the Hindu students made me vividly realize their strong nationalist bias, and while the great historic struggle for freedom of my birth-country gave me a natural sympathy for like aspirations in all countries, still, I was, in theory at least, an internationalist. Intellectually, however, I was at this time more preoccupied with India than any other land."

Living alone in California, the young Har Dayal, professed to the principle of celibacy. His wife Sundar Rani lived in India at her parent's home with great difficulty and had raised their daughter Shanti Devi singlehandedly for the past four years. The lecturer and the 'married' student became friends. The cat was soon out of the bag. The confused relationship of Har Dayal with Frieda raised eyebrows among the student community and the faculty at Stanford and UC Berkeley where the 'angelic man' from India was a prominent figure. Allegations of moral turpitude by the Indian lecturer flew. The student community threatened to malign his flawless reputation in the United States, Europe, and India. Frieda curtly ended the matter and returned to Switzerland to her mother's home in Zurich to pursue a Ph.D. in educational methods at the Zurich University leaving behind a heartbroken Har Dayal. Following this Har Dayal himself recalled his fleeting affair with Frieda as: "I passed through a peculiar experience through my friendship with her at Palo Alto." This was not the last time Har Dayal sought female companionship.

Around the same time, in Los Angeles, twenty-one-year-old Heluiz Chandler and twenty-three-year-old Careleton Washburne, a former student of Stanford shocked America by announcing that they had signed a 'Free Love' contract. Los Angeles courthouse issued the young couple a marriage license in room 23 on Friday, September 13th, 1912. Married after just a week of acquaintance their contract stated that the marriage does not give either one control over the other, that it is not a bar to other marriages should this one prove unfruitful, that it terminates simultaneously with the death of love on either side, that neither shall have the right to restrain the other should he or she see fit to incur other parental responsibility.

This astonishing marriage set up challenges to the established and accepted marriage convention in United States. Washburne confirming the open marriage contract told the American press; "Our action is a protest against the slavery of marriage that kills". The parents of the daring couple approved their decision.

Har Dayal, who had now moved to a studio on 437 Kipling Street in Palo Alto, was the first to rally support for the young couple's seemingly outrageous act. He claimed he was always interested in variation from the normal as it indicated a new social force. The university lecturer approving the actions and the unusual document declared, "Washburne is one of my best friends and I desire to express my sincere appreciation of his courage and wisdom in defying customs and conventionality by entering into this so-called, 'free love contract' before marrying." He confirmed he was proud of Washburne's example and hoped that several other young people would follow it. The newspapers reported that 'The learned doctor of Hindu philosophy' went further and sent telegrams to the young couple – "Heartiest congratulations on marriage. May all happiness crown you brave pioneers of women's freedom".

The shocking public support of 'Free Love' contract by the high profile Indian lecturer and a distinguished public figure was widely discussed in California. Har Dayal shook up even the non-conformist San Francisco with his views on marriage, property, and government. The benefactors of Stanford who provided endowments had severe reservations about the controversial extra-curricular activities of the fierce Indian intellectual serving on the faculty of the university. Many voices had already been raised against his dangerous liaisons with anarchists and a married student. The university management too had a reputation to protect and distanced itself from the embarrassment caused by the Lecturer of Indian Philosophy.

An incorrigible rebel against the system for most of his life, Har Dayal had sacrificed the last installment of the Government Scholarship at Oxford, walked away from the prospect to be an ICS officer in India and abruptly left from being a columnist for *Bande Mataram* in Paris. On September 13th, 1912, much to the relief of Stanford, the independently minded and rebellious Har Dayal relinquished his position as lecturer at Stanford. In a long unstamped letter to Jordan, sent from Berkeley, he attributed his resignation to the conflict between his social activism and his academic responsibilities.

President of Stanford, Jordan, who took a friendly, paternalistic interest in Har Dayal accepted the resignation and informed one of the trustees of Stanford, Timothy Hopkins, "It is thus fair to Mr. Dayal to note that before any of the matters under discussion came up he had tendered his resignation from the university". Independently Har Dayal issued a press statement that appeared in the *San Francisco Call* and *The Seattle Star*. It clarified he was no longer a lecturer at Stanford University and was soon going to start a lecture tour across the country. He had plans to publish a propagandist magazine and newspaper along with John Barry to be circulated at the two universities in San Francisco. He also had his work cut out as a prominent socialist in the United States and a notable Indian revolutionary who plotted against the Hukumat-i-Britannia.

On September 19th, *The Stanford Daily* mentioned that with the resignation of Har Dayal, the Hindu student who has been giving lectures in Indian Philosophy, "Stanford loses the distinction of having on its faculty rolls the only Hindu professor in the United States". The newspaper added, "Dayal was a unique figure in American college circles. Of foreign birth, of abundant means and extensive education, his engagement here created more than ordinary interest."

An Indian Nationalist or An International Anarchist

On Friday, October 18th, 1912 (exactly seven years after the partition of Bengal) the Indian community of San Francisco celebrated India Day, at Stiles Hall on the UC Berkeley campus. Har Dayal and Bhai Parmanand organized the event. In his welcome address, the former Stanford lecturer known for his nationalistic zeal surprisingly declared himself to be an internationalist who did not believe in the "narrow views of nationalism". His introduction was followed by speeches by Professor David Prescott Barrows, Department of Political Science at Berkeley and the Chinese student of UC Berkeley, Sun Fo. There were also speeches by

Tarak Nath Das titled, 'The scope and aim of Indian nationalism', this was followed by a talk by Professor Pope, on 'American ideals and the Indian National Movement' and his wife Bertha read a paper depicting evils of British rule in India. Immediately thereafter, *'Bande Mataram'* was sung enthusiastically. The event was widely publicized in the local newspapers.

Notwithstanding the Stanford experience, by the end of 1912, the twenty-eight-year-old, Har Dayal was the most well known Indian living in the United States and a celebrity in the Indian revolutionary groups in India, France, and Britain. American intelligentsia enjoyed his talks and respected him for his humane passion. Any article authored by him had considerable readership amongst Americans and Indians. On one occasion, Edward Cahill, a popular local newspaper columnist of California, contested some of Har Dayal's political viewpoints in his weekly column, 'The Candid Friend' writing, "The lecturer does not explain how things would be improved under socialism. If as he declares the voters, as a body do not now understand the issues involved, he ought to explain how things would be improved under socialism…"

Even his movements around the Bay Area were paid attention to by the local press such as; "Har Dayal has come down from San Francisco to visit friends over the weekend". On December 13th, 1912, the newspapers reported that Har Dayal was among the prominent citizens of San Francisco who participated in the twenty four hour protest meeting against capital punishment, a campaign led by Fremont Older that began at 1800 hrs near the corner of Grant Avenue and Market street (now there exists a Museum of Ice Cream at this spot) and ended at six the following day. Throughout the night arguments were advanced to show that capital punishment does not lessen homicide. Among those who spoke that night besides Har Dayal were Fremont Older's wife, Cora Miranda Older and Dr. Harmon Titus. Nico Slate has pointed out in, *Lord Cornwallis Is Dead: The Struggle for Democracy in the United States and India (2019),* "No figure embodied that interconnected struggle more than the most famous Indian American intellectual in the first half of the twentieth century, Har Dayal."

Living in California, Har Dayal was writing, working and waiting for the right moment to position his political philosophies and launch revolutionary activities on a large scale. The Ghadr that the Indian revolutionaries and nationalists had long dreamt about was looming. An event in Har Dayal's home town Delhi was to spiral events out of the control for the Hukumat-i-Britannia and project

Har Dayal as a spearhead of the largest anti-colonial movement of the time that attempted to overthrow the British Empire by force.

It was as if the moment the Indian revolutionary had been waiting for all his life had finally come.

9

THE MOST DANGEROUS
REVOLUTIONARY IN AMERICA

"Of all the Indian agitators who have visited the United States and of all those of
whom I have knowledge, I am led to believe that Har Dayal is the most dangerous."

Charles William Hopkinson
British Secret Service Operative

It was a near-perfect winter morning on Monday, December 23rd, 1912, in Delhi.
The famed Chandni Chowk was an astonishing sight. The central boulevard of
the city was decorated beautifully and the lavish streamers stretched right up to
the Lal Qila on the far end where a Union Jack fluttered in the bright Indian sun.
There were enormous crowds and chairs were placed on either side of Chandni
Chowk. The black market rates of the front row tickets were an astronomical Rs.
300. In no city in the world could humanity be packed more closely together or
find so great a variety of perches. The flat roofs, balconies, windows, platforms, and
lodges swarmed with Dilliwallahs and young boys invaded the trees and attached
themselves to the lampposts as the multitudes massed in the roadway like a sea.

The whole of Delhi was radiant and expectant.

It was the day for the Viceroy's State Entry into Delhi, the new capital of the
Hukumat-i-Britannia in India. King George V at the Durbar of 1911 had announced
the transfer of the capital from Calcutta to Delhi. Though it upset the business
community of Calcutta the transfer of the seat of the Government was considered
a bold stroke of statesmanship that would mark a new era in the history of India.

On that December morning, the capital city awaited the arrival of the His
Excellency the fifty-four-year-old, Viceroy Lord Charles Hardinge (1858–1944)
and his wife Lady Winifred Selina Hardinge (1868–1914). Excellent arrangements
were made by the civil administration in Delhi to welcome the British Viceroy who
had succeeded Lord Minto in November 1910. Five hundred and sixty-five armed

inspectors, constables and mounted police officers guarded the entire stretch of Chandni Chowk. Several policemen not in uniform watched the crowds and kept an eye for suspicious bags, rolled up newspapers, large overcoats, umbrellas or any packages. Additionally there was a military presence on the main street of Delhi that day.

Ever since the Durbar of 1911, near-complete peace had prevailed in India. As a precaution three hundred real or suspected revolutionaries and alleged bad characters of Delhi were forcibly put behind bars. All signs of resistance were crushed with overwhelming power and the Hukumat-i-Britannia was akin to a military-backed dictatorship over Indians. Additionally, most of the troublesome agitators from North India were imprisoned or transported to the Andamans by Hukumat-i-Britannia while two of the foremost revolutionaries had relocated notably Aurobindo Ghosh to Pondicherry and Har Dayal to California.

Around 1030 hrs, the gleaming Viceregal train from Calcutta steamed into the sparkling central railway station of Delhi. Viceroy Lord Hardinge, a gentle and restrained old man, disembarked from the train and was greeted by Sir Louis William Dane, ICS, the Lt. Governor of Punjab. Next Lord Hardinge sat on a Sofa Chair as he met all the Ruling Maharajas of Punjab and received an address of welcome from the municipal committee of Delhi. His face had the appearance of a bulldog with padded cheeks and he greeted everyone in a high-pitched, hoarse English accent. Outside the railway station, the Viceroy along with Lady Hardinge mounted the ornamental silver howdah on a huge tusker gorgeously caparisoned with saddlecloths of gold and silver. The protocol was modified since the absence of an elephant had been widely noticed during the Durbar of 1911.

The state functions arranged for the occasion in Delhi were carried out with unusual pomp and grandeur. Hukumat-i-Britannia with the regular routine of Durbars and elephant processions in the former Mughal capital of Delhi and around the Lal Qila earnestly tried to establish the permanency of their Empire in the minds of the Indians. Although Viceroy Lord Hardinge sat atop the elephant stiffly, he wielded enormous lethal power as he determined and controlled the dispensation of justice; as the representative of the King of Britain in India. The British Viceroy of India had an authority so wide that no one could comprehend thoroughly what the position and job of a British Viceroy exactly were except one who was appointed the Viceroy. The position of the British Viceroy besides the pomp, pageantry had a salary worth a king's ransom and they could retire like a royal back home in Britain.

The triumphant elephant procession rode ceremoniously into Delhi from the Railway Station with thousands of spectators on the housetops and streets cheering. A battery of artillery headed the procession with the Inniskilling Dragoons following them. The Viceroy's bodyguard and staff led the enormous elephant with the Viceregal pair on top. General Sir Garrett O'Moore Creagh, VC, Commander-in-Chief in India, along with other members of the Viceroy's Council came next. They were trailed by scores of Punjab police and nobles on horseback, then came the richly dressed Punjab chiefs wearing priceless jewels and seated on the backs of fifty elephants. The procession presented a most stunning spectacle, and three English regiments along with sipahis of the British Indian army lined the route.

As the procession swaggered mid the magnificence and splendor, along the Queen's Garden and Town Hall, Viceroy Lord Hardinge had a premonition. He detailed in *My India Years* that he told his wife, "I feel quite miserable, I am sure something dreadful is going to happen." She replied, "It is only that you are tired and you always dislike ceremonies". Nevertheless, he persisted in his statement.

At 1145 hrs right in the center of Chandni Chowk just beyond the Clock Tower the crowds accorded the Viceroy Lord and Lady Hardinge an enthusiastic welcome. The never-ending rotation of Viceroys was puzzling for the Indians as they were used to the long reigns of Indian rulers in the past. In any case, a short five-year term was not enough time to govern a colony as large as India. But the crowds were ecstatic on that morning. The enormous elephant named Moti lent by the Princely State of Faridkot drew all eyes. The loud appreciation even captivated the policemen who joined in the clapping. The cheering was deafening.

By then in accordance with a well thought out plan, the two men crew of the secret society was already on the roof of the three-storied Punjab National Bank building. The men in disguise had taken positions among the hundred and fifty spectators on the densely packed roof minutes before the procession was to cross them. It was a carefully chosen spot as it had multiple points of access and egress. In the preceding few weeks they had vigilantly walked these paths, climbed these stairs, studied every inch of the building and had practiced hitting on a moving target several times. Other members of the team mixed with the cheering crowd across the Punjab National Bank had their eyes fixed on the Viceroy from various points. The chief planner stood on the rooftop of a nearby building and had the best overall view of the boulevard below. A total of ten men were ready to deliver the mightiest blow they could on the representative of King

George V, the British Emperor and the second most powerful man on Earth, Viceroy Lord Hardinge.

The main assailant held in his right hand a Wills tobacco tin can wrapped in a grey handkerchief. He lit the fuse and took careful aim with his eyes. This was going to be a single volley. He could not miss and had to hit the exact mark. His compatriot kept a lookout and momentarily distracted the spectators crowding the roof. Suddenly a missile was hurled from the roof of the Punjab National Bank aimed at the slow-moving heavily ornamented elephant. The target was the head of Viceroy Lord Hardinge.

Then the extra roar of the explosion was heard several kilometers away as it shattered the peace of a festive winter morning. An acid bomb weighing between half and three-quarters of a pound exploded against the howdah on the elephant. Pigeons flew from the rooftops in all directions. Dogs ran barking aimlessly. Chickens madly flapped and screeched in their coops. The windows rattled and some old buildings even shook. Then there was dead silence.

"Shabash!" (Bravo), an exclamatory cry was heard conveying success.

The three DCI officers in plainclothes, armed with revolvers and escorting the elephant did not realize what had happened. Viceroy Lord Hardinge's private secretary, James Houssemayne DuBoulay, ICS (1868 – 1943) turned around from his elephant and dismissed the blast as a firecracker. The procession continued moving. Lady Hardinge, who later described the incident as a "terrible experience", felt an upheaval and was thrown forward. After she recovered she was dazed and almost deaf with loud singing in her head. There was an unexpected quietness. The Viceroy's helmet was on the road. The Viceroy stopped waving as he saw some yellow powder on his hand and with icy calm told his wife, "I am afraid, that was a bomb". Viceroy Lord Hardinge looked pale. Lady Hardinge inquired, "Are you sure that you are not hurt?". He answered, "I am not sure. I had a great shock and feel as though somebody has hit me very hard in the back and had poured boiling water over me but I think I can go on." The elephant had stopped momentarily and the Chief of Police handed the Viceroy his helmet on the top of a lance and asked for orders. He was told that the procession was to proceed as before. The fifty-one elephants continued on their course down the Chandni Chowk towards the Lal Qila.

A few seconds afterward, Lady Hardinge discovered that the attendant Jamadar Mahabir Singh of Balarampur State, who held the ceremonial *palki* (Imperial umbrella), was blown to pieces. She also saw red flesh through a slit of the Viceroy's uniform near his right shoulder. The elephant was brought to a halt. Just then the Viceroy had a little convulsion and began to lose consciousness. By now he was bleeding profusely from about six wounds. There were difficulties in getting the Viceroy off the howdah as he reeled and fainted from loss of blood. Lord Hardinge later recorded "I heard afterwards that the elephant being too frightened by the bomb to kneel, it had been necessary to pile up wooden cases and that my A.D.C. Hugh Fraser had lifted me down like a baby." Eventually, the Viceroy's staff took off their splendid coats and used them as slings to lift him to the ground with the help of firefighters and their ladders. On regaining consciousness, Viceroy Lord Hardinge gave instructions to his private secretary DuBoulay and his military secretary, Colonel Francis Aylmer Maxwell for the full carrying out of the ceremony. The Viceroy's wish was that Indians should realize that nothing could deflect the Hukumat-i-Britannia from its declared intention.

On hearing about the explosion, William Malcolm Hailey, ICS, the Chief Commissioner of Delhi along with his team, rushed from the Lal Qila to the Viceroy's assistance in two motorcars. Colonel Maxwell and Dr. Robert James Blackham improvised a chair stretcher and the wounded Viceroy was placed in one of Hailey's motorcars that straightaway rushed to the city hospital. Lady Hardinge maintained her composure and followed her husband in another motorcar.

In the interval, there was pandemonium near the Punjab National Bank Building on the main boulevard of Chandni Chowk. There was a fear of another bomb waiting to explode nothing though came of it. People were madly running about and screams could be heard. Mothers grabbed their children while some spectators too shocked stood motionless.

The detectives themselves ran in random directions. Although the target was missed despite all the training it made its mark. The members of the secret society as instructed deftly run into the maze of lanes of Delhi in the chaos that followed. They stayed calm, got rid of their disguises and then disappeared into thin air.

At the Viceroy's insistence, the procession was reformed and the march to the Lal Qila continued.

After the explosion, David Petrie, the rugged Scotsman known for his immense physical and moral strength and the Directorate of Criminal Investigation's representative at the Viceroy's State Entry into Delhi appeared on the scene. He found the senior-most official Lt. Governor Sir Dane particularly excitable and unable to contain the damage. On seeing Petrie, Chief Commissioner Hailey immediately made him in-charge of the inquiry into the Bomb outrage and appointed him Additional Superintendent of Police of Delhi on the spot. The thirty-three-year-old graduate of Aberdeen University had spent just over a decade in the Indian Police and this was to be his most important assignment till then. Later in April 1941, Prime Minister Winston Churchill appointed him as the Director-General of Military Intelligence 5 (MI5), the internal security service of Britain during the Second World War (WWII). It was at the Bomb attack on British Viceroy Lord Hardinge in Delhi that he cut his teeth.

The NAI documents record that though Petrie was twenty minutes too late, on his instructions the police surrounded the Punjab National Bank building and the entire rectangular block called Katra Dhulya. Every occupant in and around was methodically questioned and British nurses examined all the women. It was revealed that besides the Indian umbrella bearer who was killed instantaneously a man and a boy among the spectators were also killed, and one of the Viceregal attendants and several bystanders were wounded. A large handkerchief full of nails and screws was collected in the streets later. Petrie ordered the systematic hunt for the assassins with raids in religious places, hotels, eating houses, gambling dens, brothels and all the usual places where suspects were known to hide. Spies were alerted and policemen were posted at the Delhi railway station. Telegraph messages were flashed from the police control room across India to look out for suspects alighting from trains from Delhi.

Though all routes in and out of the city were closed and several preventive arrests were made, it was believed that the main actors and conspirators had escaped.

At 1400 hrs in the afternoon, Sir Guy Fleetwood Wilson, the finance member of the Governor-General's council, fulfilled the Viceroy's part of the program as originally scheduled. He formally assumed possession of Delhi at the Imperial Durbar camp at the *Diwan-i-aam* of the Lal Qila (hall of public audiences). Sir Dane, Lt. Governor of Punjab, gracefully handed over the charge of the ancient capital of India that had been part of the state of Punjab since February 1858 to the Hukumat-i-Britannia. In July 1911, it was Lord Hardinge who had recommended the transfer of the capital to the ancient seat of Hindu and Mughal dynasties, writing, "Delhi is still a name to conjure with". Sir Wilson observed that he regarded the transference to Delhi of the Government of India as restoring to India one of her ancient traditions.

At the end of the proceedings, Sir Wilson read a message from the Viceroy. It disclosed that the assassination attempt of the King's representative in India had failed and he had only been slightly injured. The message was received with prolonged cheering. At the city hospital, the doctors attending Lord Hardinge discovered that he had escaped death by a hair's breadth. He had a four-inch-long deep wound that exposed the shoulder blade and his back was badly lacerated by the nails, screws and gramophone needles with which the bomb was packed. The explosion had caused temporary deafness. The doctors deemed an operation necessary. Chloroform was administered to remove the small nails and particles of iron from the right shoulder and back.

The failed assassination bid angered many Dilliwallahs. Some businessmen of Delhi closed their establishments and the shops were shuttered the next day. At the same time, the audacity of the assault won the admiration of the silent majority of India. The bomb attack on the Viceroy in Chandni Chowk was the beginning of the end of the Hukumat-i-Britannia.

The Esperanto of Revolution

The news about the assassination attempt on British Viceroy Lord Hardinge in Delhi traveled halfway across the world and reached the perceptive ears of Har Dayal in Berkeley. For Har Dayal who had just two months ago declared himself as an internationalist and departed from the "narrow views of nationalism" the dramatic event in his hometown had many undertones. On the evening of December 23rd, as the Dilliwallah stepped out of his home at 1936 Bonita Avenue and rushed to 2273 Shattuck Avenue, the house where the Indian scholarship students lived in Berkeley. Breathlessly he informed them about the incident; "Have you heard the news? What one of my men has done in India to Lord Hardinge". The shocking news about the bomb attack was received with great joy and the students at once began singing *'Bande Mataram'*. About sixteen Indian students who lived at 1907 University Avenue were also summoned to join the celebrations. The young Indians danced excitedly and then dashed to the local newspaper office to find out the latest developments coming on the Marconi Transatlantic wireless telegraph from Delhi and London. There they took turns at reading the news available and ascertained all the facts as they appeared.

Gobind on hearing the news supported the action of the Indian revolutionaries. He thought that they had thrown a challenge at Hukumat-i-Britannia that they could not take over India and there was resistance in Delhi for now. Away from his motherland for more than four years, Har Dayal then looked at Gobind and gave him an unexpected Christmas present, "I will not be able to return home now". Unknown to the rest of the world, Har Dayal was in secret correspondence with his friends in Delhi and knew that after the bomb attack if he returned to India he would be implicated and dispatched to the dark cells of the Cellular Jail in Andamans or worse, hanged by the Hukumat-i-Britannia. Gobind realized that as a close confidante of Har Dayal and a member of the secret society in Delhi he too would face a similar fate.

Given the joyful Christmas atmosphere in California, the students decided that to mark the occasion a celebratory dinner on December 25th must be arranged on the Berkeley campus for the Indian community. Har Dayal was asked to be the guest of honor and he accepted. But several Indian students including Henry Edward Pandion took exception to the feast held to commemorate the attack and refused to attend it.

The next morning on Tuesday, December 24th, Har Dayal picked up the morning newspaper *San Francisco Call* at his doorstep. The headlines credited to Paul Lambeth of London read, "VICEROY OF INDIA NEAR DEATH AS RESULT OF PLOT". He quickly went through the entire story and rushed out to get copies of other newspapers. The unbelievable news of an attempt to assassinate the British Viceroy at the greatest imperial procession on the occasion of the State Entry was published widely on the front pages of newspapers all over the world. *The New York Times* ran a big story on its third page with a photograph of Hardinge and his wife stating, 'VICEROY OF INDIA WOUNDED BY BOMB – Attacked on State Entry into Delhi – Indications of an Extensive Plot".

The banner headlines created a wave of horror, anger, and sorrow in Britain. King George V sent a message of sympathy to Lord Hardinge from London. In the following days, there were over two thousand letters and telegrams of empathy and indignation received by the British Viceroy's office. *The Times* in London in an editorial broadcast, "All reputable Indian politicians willingly recognize that they have received great concessions for which they are grateful. The act, which the empire now deplores, was unquestionably the work of some members of that implacable organization of Anarchists which haunts the purlieus of great Indian cities and remains untouched by political concessions or imperial visits… Anarchism is no new thing in India and those with knowledge are well aware that it has not disappeared…".

The murderous attack in faraway Delhi and its global impact in the waning days of 1912 plunged Har Dayal right back into nationalist activities. Since the first news of the bombing had reached him in his dismal lodgings in Berkeley he had lived for this day, which had now, miraculously, come. At the Christmas Dinner in a hall filled with about twenty Indians including Bhai Parmanand, Tarak Nath Das, Sarangadhar Das, Ranjit Singh, and Gobind, Har Dayal, in high spirits, delivered one of his finest speeches. The Dilliwallah opened with the famous couplet of Mir Taqi Mir;

"Pagari apani sambhaliyega 'Mir!'
Aur basti nahin, ye Dilli hai!!"

(Take care of your turban, Mr. Mir!
This is not just any town, this is Delhi)

Har Dayal claimed, "December 23rd, 1912 is a date that will go down in history." For him, the heroic act of throwing a bomb on the representative of the British King was a sign that Indians wanted Hukumat-i-Britannia's tyranny to end. The bomb for him was "one of the sweetest and loveliest and the harbinger of hope and courage". He held that the incident in Chandni Chowk marked the definite revival of the revolutionary movement after the short interval of inactivity. Elated by the charged-up political atmosphere in India he applauded the attack on the Viceroy. He added, "this bomb marks a red-letter day in our revolutionary annals."

Then Har Dayal made the sensational disclosure to all those present, "One of our men did it". This hint about his knowledge of the secret conspiracy in Delhi was met with uproar and followed by nationalist slogans and cries of *"Bande Mataram"* at the dinner.

The forceful speaker addressing the young Indian students wanted to start a movement from California at once to support his comrades in Delhi to drive the British out of India. He knew that the British Empire occupied much of the real estate on the planet and he would be arrested if found anywhere on their territory. He decided to launch the revolutionary movement from California and to mobilize several thousand Indians based on the Pacific Coast. He knew the distance from India would be an advantage, as it would insulate them from the British Secret Service. On this historic day, the young Indians studying in California agreed that all the Indians overseas must be united in this cause.

The patriots had their work cut out.

Later that night, Har Dayal now back in his revolutionary mode penned an impassioned tribute to the bomb thrower, in a circular titled *Yugantar*, a direct reference to a banned Bengali newspaper and the *Yugantar* (new era) ideal as expounded by the famous Indian revolutionary Jatindra Nath Banerjee (1877–1930). He mailed it to Shyamji Krishna Varma and Madame Cama in Paris for publication. Har Dayal, declared, "The incident at Chandni Chowk, had thought-provokingly interrupted the spectacle by which the British were "stepping into the shoes of the Grand Mogul…The explosion broke the hypnotic spell of the imperial state; when Caesar referred to himself as the son of God, he had to be reminded by others that he was but the son of man." In the spirit of socialism and nationalism, he added, "May durbars and bombs go together till there are no more durbars on the face of the Earth".

In addition, he commented, "The use of a bomb thus enters the service of democracy, as an indispensable instrument, speaking for the voiceless multitude, in a tongue that is the Esperanto of revolution." His inspiring words were, "Indeed this bomb was the most serviceable and successful bomb in the history of freedom all over the world. The city of Delhi had redeemed her ancient fame Delhi has spoken and the world has heard and the tyrant has heard too. And we, the devoted soldiers of freedom, in the country of abroad, have also heard the message."

Die and Build Your Nation

The day after Christmas, on December 26th, Nehru now a twenty-three-year-old London returned Barrister walked into the 28th session of the Indian National Congress at Bankipore (Bankipur). This was his first political outing and the session was overshadowed by the bomb attack on the British Viceroy. Here he met Gokhale; the much-respected Indian leader who had returned from South Africa on December 13th, 1912 after meeting Mahatma Gandhi who had expressed the desire to work in India under his leadership. Nehru too was swayed by the political thought and gravitas of Gokhale while the rest of the Congress session was, according to him, "to a large extent, the session was a great celebration of English knowing high-class people. There, from morning to evening, people wearing freshly ironed clothes were seen roaming. Actually, this was like a social festival, which contained no political zeal in their hearts…"

Despite the tremendous exertions of the revolutionaries across India, the moderate leaders of the Indian National Congress were holding annual conventions to pass ineffectual resolutions that did not draw the attention of the common Indians or cause any inconvenience to Hukumat-i-Britannia. As early as November

18th, 1900, Lord Curzon had in a dispatch to Lord Hamilton, the Secretary of State for India, anticipated, "own belief is that the Congress is tottering to its fall and one of my greatest ambitions while in India is to assist it to a peaceful demise".

The Social Dynamite

On the evening of January 18th, 1912, Har Dayal entered the Jefferson Square Hall, at 925 Golden Gate Avenue for deliver a talk before the Oakland's Industrial Workers of the World. He was greeted with a standing ovation that he acknowledged with a smile. Clearly, since his arrival in California in April 1911, he had also soared to extraordinary heights of public attention in San Francisco's liberal and trade union groups. As the Secretary of the 'Wobblies', he spoke overpoweringly to the audience about socialism, industrial exploitation, and other similar stuff. His revolutionary spirit and rhetorical fervor were revived by the attack on the Viceroy Lord Hardinge in his hometown in the course of the last few weeks.

Sitting inconspicuously among the IWW members was a lean, six feet, two inches tall and thirty-four-year-old British Secret Service operative William Charles Hopkinson (1880–1914).

The one-man Intelligence agency on the Pacific Coast, Hopkinson had the reputation of being thoroughly reliable, calm and collected in difficult and dangerous situations. The NAI records reveal that his father was a sergeant instructor at Allahabad in India who had died in the Sir Louis Cavagnieri massacre at Kabul in 1879 leaving behind his Indian mother and him in Lahore. At the age of sixteen, he was forced to join the police and moved from Mussoorie to Calcutta to work as a Sub Inspector. In 1907, he was relocated to Vancouver, British Columbia and designated as a 'Dominion Police Officer on Special Duty'. He operated undercover with a special commission to report on seditious activities in the Indian community on the Pacific Coast. He spoke fluent Hindi and Punjabi and often moved around Vancouver disguised as a poor Indian under the alias of Narain Singh with a false beard and turban. He directly reported to William Wallace Cory, the Deputy Minister of the Interior in Ottawa. And his reports were forwarded only to Cleveland of DCI in distant Simla in India. In November 1908, he had married Nellie Fryer, an English stenographer from the up-scale London Highgate who acted as his unpaid secretary. They had two daughters, Jean, born in 1908, and Constance, born four years later. They lived in a large home in Vancouver's rapidly rising Grandview neighborhoods with Nellie's family.

In the autumn of 1911, Hopkinson did a nineteen-day tour of the Pacific Coast of the United States. At that time his bête noire was Tarak Nath Das. He had established a trustworthy network of spies and connected with the anti-Indian, Captain Frank Ainsworth of the US Immigration Service at San Francisco. Ainsworth had successfully changed the immigration policy at Angel Island Station for '*Hindoos*' (the generic term with racial overtones for Indian immigrants) after forcing the removal of his boss Hart North in April 1911. Soon the proportion of the Indians who were denied immigration on arrival at Angel Island Station rose from 46 percent to 98 percent. Ainsworth maintained "these Hindoos are highly unassimilable and many communities in which they are not wanted...."

Although Hopkinson was unable to prove Das as an anarchist, he had identified the Indian anti-colonial movement in California as a serious threat. But he was rebuffed at the British Consulate since he did not have adequate documents stating his position within the Canadian Government or with His Majesty's Government. However, in October 1912, Hopkinson was alarmed by the reports about the 'India Day' celebrations organized by Har Dayal at Berkeley.

On January 8th, 1913 he returned to San Francisco at 2200 hrs and took a room at the Argonaut Hotel, the former fruit-canning factory near the waterfront at Fisherman's Wharf in the name of W. C. Hampton. He had a clear view of San Francisco from his window. The following morning Hopkinson presented his credentials to British Consul-General Ross at the British Consulate located in Room 106, Hansford Building, 268, Market Street in San Francisco. Ross who had relocated from Buenos Aires two years ago excitedly updated him about the recent undertakings of the Indian anarchist Har Dayal. Ross through his spies among the Indian students had heard that in honor of the attempt on Hardinge a celebratory feast was held at Berkeley on Christmas night where the charismatic Har Dayal made sensational claims. The "feast and jollification" at Berkeley enraged the British Secret Service operative. He swung into action.

Through the Angel Island Station, he got an appointment with special agent Clayton Herrington of the United States Department of Justice. Herrington was willing to assist him and arranged to monitor all the mail to and from India that was moving through the Berkeley and San Francisco post offices. He also hired a clerk inside the San Francisco Post Office to intercept all of Har Dayal's mail. He interviewed an Indian student of UC Berkeley, who had approached Ross for money and retained him as his mole for $ 15 per month to ensure constant surveillance of Har Dayal. Additionally, he employed an assistant, Arthur Tilton

Steele (1872–1961), code-named 'Spenser', India born American accountant, who had graduated from St. Xavier's College, Calcutta and clashed with Har Dayal in the columns of *The San Francisco Bulletin* in July 1912 at the behest of His Majesty's Government.

In the interim the Governor-General of Canada, Prince Arthur, Duke of Connaught (1850–1942), the third son of Queen Victoria sent an urgent telegram from Ottawa to James Bryce, His Majesty's Ambassador in Washington DC, to obtain the consent of the United States Government for cooperating with Hopkinson in San Francisco. It read, "Hopkinson is most desirous of securing reliable information with regard to one named Har Dial (misspelled) now Berkeley California, who is supposed to have landed in New York within the past 18 months." Ross too sent off a memo to Bryce about Har Dayal that was forwarded to Sir Edward Grey, Secretary of State for foreign affairs in London.

That evening at the IWW meeting accompanied by Steele, Hopkinson saw the Indian revolutionary in action for the first time in his life. The NAI records divulge that he recorded his impressions as; "Har Dayal then faced his audience; he is a man of about 29 years of age, height about 5'6'; weight about 150 pounds, clean-shaven, dark complexion, close-cropped hair and wears spectacles. He has a good command of the English language and speaks with very little accent".

Har Dayal's electrifying speech was met with applause and he was hailed as a leading Indian reformer and a savior of the downtrodden Indian people. He concluded his address by inviting all the members of the audience to attend his radical study lab situated between Valence and Mission streets where classes were held every Monday evening.

Hopkinson made numerous notes of his speech but was uncomfortable in the company of what he termed in his report as "very questionable class of humanity," the hall being located in the "toughest" part of San Francisco. Jefferson Square itself was known as San Francisco's Hyde Park and was known for the stormy character of its political meetings. Every shade of political and religious thought was expounded in its open-air forums. Hopkinson had already been warned by his colleagues to be careful during his visit to California, as he was a marked man. As a preemptive move, he had already left a letter of authority for Consul-General Ross to take possession of his belongings in Hotel Argonaut in case of any unforeseen mishap were to take place.

Five days later on January 12th, 1913, at a meeting held at Jefferson Square Hall, Har Dayal made a speech on "The Revolutionary Labor Movement in

France." Hopkinson and Steele were once again in the audience taking notes. Two stenographers from the US Immigration Service were assigned to take copious notes of all the speeches of Har Dayal.

The presence of recognizable faces among his audience at all venues did not go unnoticed and unsuspected but Har Dayal couldn't care less about Hukumat-i-Britannia's spies like Hopkinson. He had previously written, "We bewilder (spies) by the self-evident sincerity of our utterances. What would spies report back to the India Office, other than the importance of industrial progress; the fruits of democracy; and meanness of Theodore Roosevelt; and thankfulness for the necessity of education, liberal and technical, and for the uplift of Indians?"

To protect himself from the British Secret Service operatives Har Dayal had deviced two systems for secret coded messages, to be passed on his network of Indian friends and supporters. The first was a substitution cipher that gave each letter of the message numericals from 0–9. The other was a more complicated version that was based on the Oxford English dictionary method and also wrote messages in groups of numbers. In using this method, the first numerical in each group was the number of the page in the dictionary on which the word would be found, the second figure gave the column, and the third figure was the number of the word in the column, counting from the top of the page.

Nevertheless Hopkinson, a well trained operative, back to his old tricks, wearing a turban in the guise of 'Narain Singh', shadowed Har Dayal day and night. He closely watched Har Dayal's every move, read his articles, saw him on the campus of the UC Berkeley, heard his praise from all quarters in San Francisco, saw people come alive at the sight of him and understood his torrent of words spoken with fire, passion, and energy and yet the more he saw, the less he understood his target.

By bracketing Har Dayal just as an anarchist, Hopkinson was unable to fathom the intellectual powerhouse he was dealing with. Har Dayal's leadership went beyond the Indian circles in California and the erudite populace of San Francisco eagerly sought him. On the afternoon of February 2nd, the members of the California Club heard the knowledgeable Indian lecture on 'Modern English Literature – Robert Browning'. In a message, he informed Brooks, "I had a delightful meeting at the California Club in the city, when I gave a talk on Robert Browning." Then a few days later he lectured at the open forum of the Jefferson Square Hall on a different subject; 'Social evil fallacies'. Har Dayal continued his literary activities and invited Brooks to speak on American poet Whitman at the

Rice Institute in Oakland on Wednesday evening, February 12th, for the People's Literary League and informed him that he had read a paper on 'Anarchism and the State' before the Philosophical Union of the UC Berkeley. A prolific writer of the highest standard between his frequent speeches he also found time to pen a short essay on 'Jesus Christ' on the suggestion of John Barry.

At the end of his Californian tour, Hopkinson dispatched a full account of Har Dayal's activities including "the feast and jollification" of Christmas to DCI in Simla via Ottawa and the IPI in London. Hopkinson concluded the detailed secret report by remarking: "Of all the Indian agitators who have visited the States and of all those whom I have a knowledge, I am led to believe that Har Dayal is the most dangerous. It is unfortunate that he should be located at Berkeley among the Indian students attending the University of California, as a man of his knowledge and influence and declared anarchistic tendencies, is bound to wield a great influence on the young boys at the University."

Hukumat-i-Britannia still underestimated Har Dayal.

Like Some Hidden Fire

The attempt on the life of Viceroy Lord Hardinge, who had narrowly escaped death in the bomb attack, in the heart of the new capital within an hour of his arrival, upset a lot of powerful people in London and Delhi. This sort of sensation had not been felt since the fall of Delhi on September 20th, 1857. Days after the audacious attack on the Viceroy, the spectre of the Ghadr of 1857 hung over India. The assassination attempt was criticized by newspapers around the world even attracted denunciation in the Christmas greeting of Pope Pius X.

The brashness of the revolutionaries on that December morning was as fearful as the memories of the Ghadr of 1857. It also pointed to the existence of a powerful organization that was acting against Hukumat-i-Britannia. Suddenly leaflets appeared all over North India inciting young men for revolutionary action. One of these praised the attempt on Hardinge's life and added, "Be God's instruments. Die and build your nation. *Bande Mataram.*" The truncated event of the State Entry of the British Viceroy in Delhi was a sign that the Hukumat-i-Britannia's supremacy in India was not going to remain unchallenged.

Since the summer of 1911, there was despondency and the British civil servants were guided by the fact that the underground revolutionary movement had failed after the arrest of Savarkar and the exile of Aurobindo Ghosh and Har Dayal. The

DCI considered it perfectly safe for the King and the Queen to visit India for the Durbar of 1911. After the bombing in broad daylight in the crowded Chandni Chowk, Cleveland, the Director of DCI, came under severe criticism for his failure to prevent the attack. He had unwittingly advised that no special measure was needed for the State Entry and had brought only a few officers to Delhi. Following the criticism citing medical reasons Cleveland left India for Britain and as a result, a very angry Viceroy's Council passed a formal vote of censure on him.

In another development, Sir Dane was replaced and Sir Michael O'Dwyer was appointed the new Lt. Governor of Punjab. He took charge five months later in May 1912. In his memoirs, *India As I Knew It*, he recollected, "The Viceroy made it clear that Punjab was the Province about which the Government was then most concerned; that there was much inflammable material lying about, which required very careful handling if an explosion were to be averted…"

At the beginning of 1913, at the Delhi Police Headquarters, Petrie had his hands full. Within the Hukumat-i-Britannia there was still an atmosphere of shock and disbelief. Petrie was provided with a large grant for the inquiry into the bomb outrage. Additionally two senior policemen of outstanding ability and considerable experience joined his team. Charles Stead, Senior Superintendent of Police, Criminal Investigation Department of Punjab who was a winner of the Police Medal and Godfrey Charles Denham, Superintendent of Police from Criminal Investigation Department of Bengal who had worked on the Alipur bombing case arrived within days of the attack of the Viceroy. The best detective talent in India assisted Petrie in the investigation and almost thirty-four men reported to him.

The detectives Petrie, Stead and Denham went to work in the dark. Their information sources ranged from municipal sweepers and fringe elements of Delhi, as also gentlemen of position and influence. Still, they had no clues or possible leads connecting anyone to the assassination plot. Petrie claimed that there was scarcely a single person all over India capable of being considered a potential factor in the bomb conspiracy whose doing had not been subjected to careful scrutiny but nothing came of it. The direct consequences of the assassination attempt were that the rows of neem and peepal trees along Chandni Chowk were cut down and the centuries-old beautiful canal flowing down its center was bricked.

Petrie, though gifted with a solid-state of mind, faced an impossible task at this prestigious assignment. It was further complicated since it involved the man at the top of Hukumat-i-Britannia in India and everyone from the Viceroy in Shimla to the King in London had an interest in the results of his investigation.

At the India House, there was heavy criticism of his work as it was taking forever to find the culprits. There were additional fears that the assassination attempt could be the spark that could initiate a terrible explosion in India. There were suggestions made to procure the services of a really good detective from Scotland Yard or even a good French detective from the French enclave of Chandernagore.

An initial fund of Rs. 15,000 had been offered as a reward for the capture of the bomb-thrower and it was raised to Rs. 50,000 but no one came forward. A month later on January 24th, 1913, in desperation Hukumat-i-Britannia offered an exceptionally handsome reward of Rs. 100,000 to be paid to anyone giving information leading to the arrest and conviction of the person or persons responsible for the act. This was a large enough prize for Indians for a huge bungalow in the posh locality of Civil Lines in Delhi cost approximately Rs. 5,000 at that time. Still, no information was forthcoming, the identity of Hardinge's attacker remained a mystery and nothing could be established. Petrie and his entire department felt dismayed and the matter rested there for some time.

Then at the end of January 1913, there was a breakthrough.

Hopkinson reported from San Francisco that "Har Dayal, the well known Delhi agitator who is now in Berkeley California, had after the outrage convened a party to celebrate the event and boasted that it was done by one his men in India". The name of 'Har Dayal' sent shock waves in the corridors of power in London and Delhi. Immediately all his old companions in Delhi and Lahore were kept under observation and their mail was systematically intercepted. The police teams went out to trace the whereabouts of Ajit Singh and Khudadad Khan in Europe and also watched Har Dayal's brother-in-law, Richpal Chand in Agra. Har Dayal regularly exchanged letters with Richpal about the welfare of Sunder Rani and Shanti Devi.

Suddenly Hopkinson was given considerable importance in the security set up of the Hukumat-i-Britannia due to the crucial lead provided by him. Consul-General Ross was ordered by the British Foreign Secretary, Sir Edward Grey to cooperate with Hopkinson in California and closely monitor the activities of the Indian students at Berkeley and Stanford. Hopkinson was requested to travel to London to meet with 'W' (John Wallinger who headed IPI) at the India Office for further guidance. Wallinger who was credited with the arrest of Savarkar had served in London since 1910 and was about to end his deputation. His tenure was extended for another year to March 1914 by the Hukumat-i-Britannia because of the bomb outrage and eventually he had yearly extensions till 1916.

In April 1913, Hopkinson landed at the IPI office at 64 Victoria Street in London. After meeting "our man in California," Wallinger was impressed and described his work to Cleveland as "of a most meritorious and useful character". He informed Hopkinson of the Hukumat-i-Britannia's decision to get rid of Har Dayal from the United States. They wanted to frame a charge against him, issue a warrant and deport him to a British territory with a view to his certain arrest and a good prospect of having him convicted. Though no legislation existed in the United States under which an alien might be indicted for any kind of activity pertaining to the freedom of his homeland, Hopkinson was nevertheless asked to prepare a cast-iron case for US Immigration Service to transport him out of the United States. The NAI records reveal that Wallinger granted him an additional allowance of £60 a year as a retainer and another £60 a year to spend on acquiring information. At that time, the Canadian Government, his principal employer, paid him a salary of $125 per month and he got an additional $25 from US Immigration Service. Simultaneously Hukumat-i-Britannia sent some *Colonial Blue Books* (a yearly collection with facts, statistics and data about British in India) to Tilton Steele in California for delivering speeches comprehensively refuting the charges made against the British Empire by Har Dayal in his lectures in California.

Imperialism was about lust for power and money and ruthlessly cutting down anyone who came in its way. Hukumat-i-Britannia's campaign to deport their chief foe Har Dayal was underway.

The Power of One

At the end of May 1913, five months since the attack on Viceroy Hardinge, the great black monster railway engine of Southern Pacific Transportation Company's 'Shasta Limited' thundered through the Pacific Coast of the United States. The uniformed attendant helped Har Dayal sink into his seat as he heaved his way out of Northern California to Oregon and Washington where several Indians had invited him to deliver talks. Sohan Singh Bhakna, Tarak Nath Das, Kanshi Ram, Ram Chandra and Bhai Parmanand accompanied him on his lecture tour and roadshow. In the summer of 1913, the group traveled from farm to farm, factory to factory and town to town spreading the message of the Indian revolution. Har Dayal had already spoken to Indians at Sacramento, Stockton, Oxnard, Bridal Veil, Linton, Woodland, and Portland.

The brand new train went through amazing views of forests and valleys and distant tree-cloaked ridges and peaks. It creaked and gasped its way around the bends to reveal vast sunbaked fields of maize and parched biscuit colored hills stretched for kilometers. The roaring locomotive power, the clanking of the wheels and hissing brakes from time to time did not disturb Har Dayal who was lost in his thoughts and occasionally made notes in his large notebook.

The thinking man, Har Dayal knew the colossal task that lay ahead of him. At twenty-eight years of age, his extensive travel around the world had broadened his unique mind and his significant investment in reading and writing had helped him clarify his thoughts. He had for years been engrossed in the analysis of the philosophies and methods of great revolutionary and reform movements of history. He had studied European revolutionary literature in-depth, the Irish Nationalist Movement, the Italian undertaking of Mazzini, Garibaldi and Cavour, German Nationalist program and the making of the German Empire by Bismark, Polish Nationalism, and the French Revolution. He was also fairly well acquainted with the Rise of Japan, Egyptian Nationalism, and the Young Turkism. He could recite and act out passages in French from the works of Georges-Jacques Danton and Voltaire. Since his arrival in California, he had familiarized himself with Marxist revolutionary thought and had devoted his time to studying the American Revolution.

America's War for Independence had interesting correlations to India. The East India Company dispatched Chinese tea to Massachusetts, where its dumping in Boston harbour triggered the American war of independence. During the War on October 19th, 1781, the Eton and Cambridge educated General Charles Cornwallis leading the British army surrendered to the forces of the founding father of the United States, George Washington at Yorktown. Five years later in 1786, he was appointed Governor-General and commander-in-chief in India of the East India Company, a post he held until 1794. Tipu Sultan (1750–1799), ruler of the Indian Kingdom of Mysore had reportedly ordered a copy of *The United States Declaration of Independence,* in 1778, in a prelude to his resounding endorsement of the French Revolution. He eventually lost his empire to the forces of Lord Cornwallis in India at Seringapatam on May 4th, 1799.

Besides Har Dayal's multi track intellectual training he also had by now the benefit of almost five years of operational experience of participating in the activities of the India House and the Paris India Group, single handedly managing the publication of *Bande Mataram* and leading the Society of Political Missionaries in India. In the United States he had made the additional connections with liberals and earned respect as a lecturer at Stanford. He had gained the knowledge of unifying strategies and direct action oriented revolutionary initiative from his interaction with the local progressive factions IWW where he functioned as a Secretary. Besides the above Har Dayal had a strong network of Indian revolutionaries and secret societies in Europe, Asia and India and the support of Madame Cama and Rana in Paris and Lajpat Rai, Ajit Singh, Charles Andrews, Asaf Ali and Rash Behari Bose in India. Since leaving Oxford he had evolved as a perfect combination of a motivational speaker, avant-garde writer, and a popular public intellectual.

This heady combination was to power the next phase of the Indian freedom movement.

In his notebook, Har Dayal began to systematically articulate the principles of 'Hardayalism' a radical thought process of three successive stages of 'Education, Revolution, and Reconstruction' that an enslaved people had to pass before they could establish themselves as members of the community of nations.

The first stage was 'moral and intellectual preparation'. During this period the workers must elevate the character of the people and instruct them in the principles that govern an efficient social organization. Here the people must be purged of all cowardice, selfishness, and greed; "the spirit of the slave must disappear before slavery can be ended." Har Dayal believed that the second stage was a war where debris of the old regime must be removed. And the only agent that could accomplish this work was the sword. No subject nation could bring freedom without war with its alien rulers. And he belived that war had to be declared for the establishment of a free and sovereign state managed by the people. The final stage would be reconstruction and consolidation that would commence after the war.

Har Dayal's hyperactive brain was busy connecting the dots and finding solutions to all kinds of problems. He was aware that the Indian National Congress due to its elitist nature and high profile membership had failed to connect with the masses in India. He believed that only plain speaking in local languages "carries conviction to the heart, while sophistry only perplexes honest men".

Secondly, the greater challenge facing him at that time was to unite the Indians living in North America and to bring them on the same page to ferment a revolution in India. This was not easy. The Indians were as divided as ever. They represented four major religious groups, several languages, various castes and numerous regions of India with distinctive food habits and even formed multiple social organizations. They were viewed as hot-tempered and conflict-ridden people. He ran the risk of forming an Indian organization filled with multiple egos;

age-old prejudices and divisive thinking that could end in a shamble of blood and confusion. His vast reading from history led him to conclude that in his speeches he would have to convince Indian immigrants about the larger common good and motivate them to sacrifice some of their interests to achieve it. He needed to solve this big problem with a big idea and the power of the spoken word. Inspired by Marxism, he decided to position the Hukumat-i-Britannia as the 'haves' and the Indian population as the 'have nots'. He reasoned that they rebellion would came from a coalition of the educated youth, sipahis, peasants and workers, the so-called proletariat and led always by professional revolutionaries. He also intended to structure all the scattered elements into one powerful organization on the lines of IWW. This common front in the United States and Canada was to be his strategy to spark off the Indian freedom movement in North America.

The Rise of Raja Har Dayal, Angrezi Raj Ka Dushman

As dawn broke the Southern Pacific Transportation Company's 'Shasta Limited' pulsed with the rhythm of the blue ocean went past several small towns like the surfs pounding one empty beach after another. Then the long freight trains claimed precedence over the passenger train and passed by with infinite slowness. In this land rich with trees, mill operators had eagerly hired the newly arrived hardworking Indians who populated the settlements. The largest community of Indians developed in the out-of-the-way town of Astoria in Oregon where Har Dayal was headed.

Finally, at the Astoria station, the train grounded to a standstill. According to *An Account of the Ghadr Conspiracy 1913–15,* written by F. C. Isemonger and J. Slattery, on that June morning close to hundred and fifty Indians were at the station to receive Har Dayal, Sohan Singh Bhakna, Tarak Nath Das, Khansi Ram, Ram Chandra, and Bhai Parmanand. Outside the small station, two electric trams and two motorcars were specially hired to ferry the guests to the Indian hostel. They were decorated with placards bearing the words 'India' and 'Freedom'. Just as the bespectacled Har Dayal alighted from the train along with his local hosts Kesar Singh and Karim Bakhsh, the station of Astoria reverberated with the loud shouts of *'Bande Mataram'*. Har Dayal acknowledged the patriotic slogans with a smile on his face but unlike the usual Indian leaders, he refused to be garlanded.

On the night of Wednesday, June 4th, 1913, Har Dayal accompanied by his team reached the Finnish Socialist Hall in Astoria. The small town was called the "Helsinki of the West," as it had the largest Finnish community west of the

Mississippi. In April 1911 the Finnish community had built a five-story hall, the second largest hall in Astoria that was a hub of the town's social activities. In the days gone by, on May 30th, 1913, The Astoria Budget had printed a notice from "Munshi Ram, Secretary of the Hindu Association, Astoria, Oregon." It was an invitation to hear Har Dayal, a former Stanford professor and "noted philosopher and revolutionist in India," deliver a special "lecture on India for the American residents of Astoria" at the local Finnish Socialist Hall. The hall was filled to the brim with a large number of Indian farmers, business owners, and shopkeepers. There were also American members of the local wing of IWW who were intrigued by the presence of an interesting and intelligent Indian speaker in their town.

Munshi Ram introduced Har Dayal and he stood up to deliver the most important speech of his life.

Har Dayal began with a patriotic introduction; "India is a land of mystery and romance, of unequaled charm and historical interest. The Hindus were the pioneers of Aryan civilization. Hindu literature and philosophy have attracted the best minds in many countries for many centuries. More than half the population of the globe professes creeds that originated in India. India is the holy land of Japan and China. Her claim on the civilized world is immense." And because some of the alert audience members were Americans, he added, "The discovery of America was only a fortunate mistake made by Columbus, who wished to discover the route to India."

Focussing on the gathering of Indians, Har Dayal did some plain speaking in Urdu and alleged, "Personal liberty was unknown in India and the Government there was the worst Government on the face of the earth… Torture in prison was not uncommon and there was no justice in the courts in cases between an Indian and an Englishman. The Roman Empire, the French before the Revolution, or even the Russian Empire was not worse than the Hukumat-i-Britannia in India. It could not be reformed and it must be abolished." He predicated, "British Empire is destined to vanish from Earth as all other Empires have…".

The impassioned speaker spoke in detail about the economics of Hukumat-i-Britannia and gave the *'Angrezi Raj Ka Kachha Chittha'* (the Balance Sheet of British rule in India) claiming, "the Delhi Durbar cost five million dollars while the people went hungry… and how India was being drained of its wealth and there was no expenditure on education and health of Indians. He added an interesting comparison of salaries between Indian sipahis of the British Indian army who were paid $4 a month as against $25 paid to the British soldiers.

Har Dayal connected racism in the United States with the suppression of India by Britain. He believed that Americans would never treat Indians with respect until Britain left India as a free country. He inspired the Indians in the hall with his thoughts, "You have come to America and seen with your own eyes the prosperity of this country. What is the cause of this prosperity? Why nothing more than this, that America is ruled by its own people. In India, on the other hand, the people have no voice in the administration of the country…desist from your petty religious dissensions and turn your thoughts towards the salvation of your country. What you earn, earn for your country. What work you do, do it for your country… collect money and get the youth educated in America in order that they may become equipped to serve… prepare now to sacrifice yourselves…"

Har Dayal roared about '*Naye Zammane ke nayee adarsh*' (new ideals for a new age) and offered an innovative kind of approach: including organizing a non-sectarian party, one able to take advantage of the fresh air that only the United States could afford them. He emphasized that propaganda was to be the first step to be taken in planning a revolutionary movement. He concluded that Hindustan needed to do what the United States had accomplished: that is to overthrow Hukumat-i-Britannia and establish a "United States of India". He ended his speech with a wisecrack and called the British Empire - the British Vampire!

As stated in F. C. Isemonger and J. Slattery account, "…an American asked Har Dayal about the population of India to which the latter replied was about three hundred million. "How many Englishmen are there," asked the American. "About a hundred thousand" replied Har Dayal. The American then remarked that this small number of Englishmen could be driven out of the country with stones without difficulty. Har Dayal admitted this fact and added that Indians were gradually becoming conscious of their power."

That night the audience in Astoria was visibly moved by Har Dayal's persuasive words and gave huge applause to their guest speaker. The majority of the Indians at the Finnish Socialist Hall had journeyed to the United States from their homes in India by paying the astronomical $65 fare for a two-part thirty-day steamship journey. Some had even mortgaged their ancestral land and sold family jewels to travel across the ocean. They were well built single men aged from nineteen to fifty and some had even served as sipahis in the British Indian army. A lot of them were illiterate and just a few spoke English. Most Indians on reaching the Pacific Coast of the United States were employed in lumber mills, factories, farms, railways, and shipyards. They wanted to revolt against the organized white supremacist vigilante attacks and the blatant racial discrimination faced by them but had no political ideologies or ambitions or leadership. After days of slogging in the evenings, they would get together in their little camps and sing Indian songs and dance. They lived frugally in unbearable conditions in North America to save a few thousand dollars by the end of five years and hoped to return to their families in India with a small fortune. The prosperity and democracy in North America had instilled in them large ideas, huge hopes and great visions for their homeland.

Har Dayal's nobility, genuineness, and immense sacrifice as an indefatigable toiler for the cause of Indian freedom appealed to the Indians. He had provided them the ammunition in the form of ideological zeal and organizational structure. They felt the formidable speaker though dressed in a crumpled jacket and shabby pants was adequately articulating the feelings in their hearts. That night the wave of politicization overtook the agrarian and worker population from India and Har Dayal the revolutionary emerged as a major nationalist leader of India. For some of the Indians in Astoria, there had been only one leader - '*Britannia ka Raja*' (the King of Britain) but now they saw '*Raja Har Dayal - Angrezi Raj Ka Dushman*' (King Har Dayal - an enemy of the British rule) '- who would lead them to victory.

The local Press covered the speech that lasted over an hour and the next day *Astorian* published an article titled, 'Conditions in India – Hindu Lecturer tells of oppression of people'. Later even the His Majesty's Consul in Portland communicated to India Office that Har Dayal's speech in Astoria seemed to have had a disturbing influence on the two hundred Indians working in the lumberyards.

Hindustan Association of the Pacific Coast

Events moved swiftly after the astounding speech in Astoria. A large community of courageous Indians emerged in North America who wanted to achieve the freedom of India by organized rebellion in their motherland. The two main organizations in North America, 'the Hindustan Association of America' with established chapters on several major university campuses and 'Sikh Khalsa Diwan', provided complete support to Har Dayal. And in those days of great hope and optimism, a new political formation called, 'Hindustan Association of the Pacific Coast' (HAPC), was born.

The central objective of the HAPC was "the overthrow of the Hukumat-i-Britannia and to substitute in its place a national republic based on equality and freedom". The HAPC wanted to achieve this by an armed national revolution. Every member was declared to be honor and duty-bound to participate in the fight against slavery carried on anywhere in the world but especially to crush the British Empire. Another objective was to protect the Indian immigrant community from racism.

Notably religious discussions were to not be allowed in the meetings of the party. Religion was considered a personal matter that had no place in the new organization. Within the HAPC, no person was "to get any pay for doing work in the office of the HAPC or in the Newspaper". Every worker joining the party was required to contribute one month's pay towards its funds. Furthermore, there was a democratic framework and an annual election was to be held for the office-bearers of the HAPC.

A born leader of people with a history of participating in the protests against the Hukumat-i-Britannia in India, the forty-three-year-old, Sohan Singh Bhakna (1870–1968) was elected the first President. He had landed in the United States in April 1909 and worked at the Monarch Lumber Mill in Portland. Since his arrival in North America, he had fought against racism. Former sipahi of the British Indian army, Kesar Singh Thathgarh was made the Vice President, Lala Thakur Das Dhuri (1880–1951), the founding Joint Secretary and a labor contractor Pandit Kanshi Ram was the first Treasurer. Among the initial members of the HAPC was a fervent and passionately patriotic seventeen-year-old Kartar Singh Sarabha (1896–1915), who had arrived in California on July 28th 1912. An undergraduate student of engineering at UC Berkeley, he was inclined towards the extreme brand of nationalism.

Har Dayal the real power behind the throne was made the General Secretary of the HAPC and he remained for a very short period the organization's most visible public spokesperson and propagandist.

A few months later the executive committee of the HAPC was expanded to include Santokh Singh, Arur Singh, Pirthi Singh, Pandit Jagat Ram, Karm Singh Cheema, Nidhan Singh Chugha, Sant Vasakha Singh, Pandit Munshi Ram, Harnam Singh Kotla, and Nodh Singh. To carry out the secret and underground work of the party, a three-member commission was also constituted in HAPC that included Sohan Singh Bhakhna, Santokh Singh and Kanshi Ram. Other Indians who formed the inner circle of the HAPC were Pandurang Khankhoje (1884–1967), Vishnu Ganesh Pingle (1888–1915) and Darsi Chenchaiah (1890 – 1964).

Har Dayal hoped that the unity among the Hindus, Muslims, Sikhs, and Christians in India would defeat the objective of Hukumat-i-Britannia and result in a successful revolution in India. HAPC's non-sectarian politics also integrated an unparalleled combination of social castes and made an indelible mark on the Indian imagination and politics. Writer Hari Paul Randhawa has confirmed that Mangu Ram Muggowal (1886–1980), a Punjabi Dalit worker living in California between 1905–1915, was attracted to the HAPC and joined as a 'full-time worker' out of San Francisco. One of the two Dalit members of the HAPC, Muggowal was struck by the fact that "it was a new society; we were treated as equal."

The HAPC was largely a male-dominated affair as the Indian population on the Pacific Coast overwhelmingly consisted of men. Despite the patriarchal structure of the Indian immigrant society overseas at that time, Gulab Kaur (1890–1931) like Rani Laxmibai wasn't afraid to enter a sphere traditionally dominated by men. Punjabi Poet Amarjit Chandan has discovered that Gulab Kaur originally from Bakshiwala village, Sangrur district in Punjab, left her husband to fight for her country's independence and joined the organization in Manila, Philippines. Later Emma Goldman and Agnes Smedley became active workers in the movement.

The head office of the HAPC was initially located in San Francisco at 1324 Valencia Street and it was known as 'Yugantar Ashram' or New Era Society. Har Dayal had previously written a moving tribute to the bomb thrower in Delhi and titled his circular, 'Yugantar'. For the first time since the Ghadr of 1857, HAPC under the pioneering leadership of Sohan Singh Bhakna and Har Dayal, with its headquarters in San Francisco, became the vital center for revolutionary work and for the first time raised the demand for complete freedom of India from the rule of the Hukumat-i-Britannia.

Like Napoleon in Exile in Elba

In early June, Hopkinson's secret agent in San Francisco, Tilton Steele reached Jefferson Square Hall to hear Har Dayal speak. Since Har Dayal was not there that day and reported to be in Portland, a prominent member of IWW, Dr. Ben Lewis Reitman met an scruffily dressed Steele. The NAI records show that on June 8th, 1913, Steele testified, "I had a talk with Riteman again after the lecture. He said; H.D. was a most remarkable man, a genius in fact; that some day the world and that the British Government in India would notice of tyrannies over a people that produced such men as H.D. H.D. he said was like Napoleon in Elba in exile, from his native land, but in exile he was more dangerous than at home."

On May 17th, 1913, there was another bomb attack in Lahore aimed at G. Gordon, ICS, Assistant Commissioner of Punjab. The bomb similar to the one thrown at Lord Hardinge missed its intended target and killed an Indian by mistake. The British Secret Service finally understood the gravity of the situation and focused on Har Dayal and the Indians along the Pacific Coast over the next few months.

On Friday, October 31st, 1913, Har Dayal delivered a talk on 'The revolutionary labor movement in France: its lessons and dangers' at the Jefferson Square Hall. It was filled with IWW members as well as the United Brotherhood of Carpenters and Joiners of Northern California. His speech was listened to with marked attention and frequently interrupted with applause. At that event, Hopkinson's spies heard Har Dayal refer to the IWW as the one organization that bore the "closest resemblance" to the anarchist society to which he belonged when he lived in France. Though his wide-ranging lecture mounted a defense of politically motivated assassinations he stopped short of a eulogy on the virtues of violence. The use of dynamite, he added, might, in fact, be detrimental to the interests of the anarchists. Stenographers of the US Immigration Service present in the hall made numerous notes. Though he was still the General Secretary of HAPC, Har Dayal being able to articulate contradictory ideas spoke for internationalism, decried nationalism and declared that the anarchists stood for the flag of no country.

The audience gave him a standing ovation and an Irish lady who was a keen supporter of the IWW walked towards Har Dayal and kissed him. She announced, "Har Dayal is the bravest among them and his heart is whiter than the whitest man. It was a privilege for me to kiss him and I would remember this incident all my life". Darisi Chenchiah, one of the scholarship students at UC Berkeley, recalled, "He (Har Dayal) was the most sought after leader whether the revolutionary society was Russian, Chinese, Japanese, Turkish or Irish." He was regarded as "a great philosopher, friend and guide and "the greatest intellectual exponent of the philosophy of anarchism at San Francisco and commanded great respect in the progressive circles". His connections with Russian and Irish revolutionaries also helped the HAPC members to gain the secret knowledge of protests, propaganda and revolutionary struggle as practiced in their nations.

At every Indian immigrant meeting addressed by Har Dayal in San Francisco, its suburbs and neighbouring towns, the crowd funding went overboard. Usually, the men who heard the patriotic Indian rushed to fund the HAPC. The hard working Indians who never used a bank and carried their meager savings in their pockets poured their hard-earned dollar bills. On each occasion, cash spilled out in piles of five, ten and even one hundred dollar-bills and rose on a table in front of Har Dayal. But he refused to touch the money himself and insisted that it be entrusted to a fully transparent and accountable committee of the HAPC. The saintly Har Dayal didn't believe in personal wealth and even gave away whatever his family still sent him from Delhi while maintaining the simplicity of lifestyle by eating bread and milk and sleeping on the floor of a bare room in Berkeley. The *San Francisco Examiner's* version of his living arrangements was that he ate only fruit and slept on a board, claiming that by denying himself all things in life but the satisfaction of his ideas he would concentrate all his physical and mental powers toward the ultimate goal of overthrowing an unjust ruler. Sohan Singh Bhakhna and the members of HAPC were overwhelmed with the integrity of Har Dayal 'who lived what he preached'. He was unlike other Indians who had approached them in the years gone by for funds for the cause of freedom but had ultimately cheated them. For the thousands of Indians living on the Pacific Coast, Har Dayal was a rare phenomenon, a man of iron will and invincible energy, capable of infusing passionate faith in the freedom movement and the cause of India's liberty, and possessed of equal faith in himself.

The Empire Awakens

Right through 1913 Har Dayal's name often came up for discussion at the highest level within His Majesty's Government in London, Delhi, Simla, Ottawa and at the Embassy in Washington DC. Har Dayal's rebellious speeches, writings, and campaigns of in California gave sleepless nights to the civil servants of India Office as well as IPI in London and the DCI in Simla. The desks of British Viceroy Lord Hardinge and Robert Crewe, Secretary of State for India, were getting overloaded with secret reports and files about the Indian seditionist movement in North America. HAPC posed a growing threat to Hukumat-i-Britannia in India. The revolutionary nature of Har Dayal exasperated them and Crewe perceived him to be "the most dangerous scoundrel of the whole party".

There was no doubt in the mind of the Hukumat-i-Britannia that Har Dayal was the principal challenger to the might of the British Empire and had to be destroyed. Since there were no pending warrants for his arrest in India, debating the idea of deportation of Har Dayal, Viceroy Lord Hardinge suggested to Crew, "the advantage of removing him from Berkeley may be counterbalanced by the difficulty of keeping him further under observation." Cecil Spring-Rice, the British Ambassador thought in case deportation was achieved, Har Dayal would be repatriated to the French territory of Martinique by the US Immigration Service as it was his last known address rather than to India.

The NAI records confirm that to influence the deportation of Har Dayal from the United States, the British Secret Service relocated Hopkinson to San Francisco in early November 1913. Here he rented a house in Oakland for the next four months. The British spy persuaded Captain Ainsworth of US Immigration Service to view Har Dayal as a dangerous anarchist. Previously, Britain in 1776 had called American Revolutionists 'anarchists'. However since Leon Czolgosz had killed President McKinley in 1901, a law was passed allowing deportation within three years of entry to the United States, of any anarchist alien for whom there was "local evidence of belonging to any revolutionary society." Hopkinson also aided Captain Ainsworth in the interpretation of the statements by a large number of Indians who had alighted at Angel Island Station from Manila. One of Captain Ainsworth's assistant inspectors in a secret communication had previously reported that Indian immigrants had threatened him regarding the surveillance of Har Dayal. As claimed by him, they considered his work so important that they would kill to save him: "the Hindoos regarded Har Dayal as their Messiah - the only one who could deliver them from British bonds."

Concurrently Hopkinson's mole amongst the Indian student community disclosed that Har Dayal had moved his home from Berkeley to 187 Castro Street in San Francisco to be closer to his place of work. He was reported to be taking every precaution to keep away from those he suspected to be British spies. The mole in a secret letter divulged to Hopkinson, "this revolutionary movement, with H.D. at its head, over here on the Pacific Coast, has assumed a most menacing shape, at present; it appears to have a definite plan and purpose and recognized status. There were fears that the progressive society figures and key journalists in the Bay Area were supporting H.D.'s enterprise".

The mole further warned, "It was 'a cloud no bigger than a man's hand' to use Lord Canning's own phrase, that grew and grew to a most gruesome and ghastly affair in 1857 and this revolutionary movement, as it is engineered by H.D. over here will surely spread, and find sympathizers and adherents in larger and larger numbers in the United States if allowed to grow unchecked – what the consequences will be in India itself is hard for any one to predict."

Har Dayal (1884–1939)

Photograph provided by Nisha Grover

Sunder Rani (Mrs. Har Dayal)

Photograph provided by Nisha Grover

Shanti Dayal Narain (Har Dayal's Daughter)

Photograph provided by Nisha Grover

Shanti Dayal Narain & Shubh

Photograph provided by Nisha Grover

Gobind Behari Lal

Agda Erikson

Photograph provided by Tina Collins

Har Dayal Memorial Service in New York, USA

Ghadr Memorial San Francisco

Vår älskade syster

AGDA DAYAL

f. Erikson

född å Rydboholm 18 dec. 1884

död i Kinna 13 jan. 1940,

innerligt saknad och i ljusaste
minne bevarad av oss, två gamla trotjänarinnor, släktingar och
många vänner.

SYSKONEN.

För lycka, bröd och ära
i denna värld ej strid,
låt sorgen dig ej tära
för denna korta tid.
Det är till andra strider,
dig Herren kallat har,
det är för andra tider,
Han lönen åt dig spar.

Sv. Ps. 298.

Jordfästningen äger rum i
Kinna lördagen den 20 dennes.
De som önska övervara den-
samma torde samlas på Kinna
Hotell kl. 15.

Agda Dayal Memorial Notice

Photograph provided by Tina Collins

10

THE FOUNDER OF A STARTUP IN CALIFORNIA

"Har Dyal one of the biggest intellects of India, has long been a thorn in the side of the British government because of his effective work in spreading revolutionary ideas among his fellow countrymen. Many attempts have been made to silence Har Dyal, both in India and in this country."

Emma Goldman
Political Activist and Writer

On Saturday, November 1st, 1913, Har Dayal in his old tattered coat stood prominently in the middle of the hall of the mission-style building of the newly opened Shattuck Hotel, the top hotel in Berkeley located on the corner of Allston Way and Shattuck Avenue. The entire top leadership of HAPC headed by Sohan Singh Bhakna was present in the room. Har Dayal, struggling with health issues for the past few months, carefully scrutinized the crowd to spot British Secret Service operatives and spies in the audience. In the days gone by he had deliberately misled a few Indian students, he suspected to be British spies about the actual venue and date of the India National Day dinner that was eventually held on October 18th, 1913.

The hall was packed. Har Dayal had a network like no other Indian in North America and all his American supporters attended his events in San Francisco. Besides, the Indian farmers, students, laborers and members of HAPC, the American intelligentsias sympathetic to the Indian cause included publisher Fremont Older, journalist John Barry, Professor Pope, social crusader Charles Erskine Scott Wood and even Stanford's President Jordan.

In his hand, a smiling Har Dayal held the first issue of the *Ghadr* newspaper. It drew its inspiration and name from the first Indian war of independence in 1857. The radical newspaper was to be the prospectus and voice of the movement. The

Urdu name *Ghadr* (rebellion) was chosen by Har Dayal despite objections by some members, because, "our name and work are identical." A British dictionary of Urdu from the late nineteenth century defined it as: "perfidy, faithlessness, mutiny, rebellion, sedition, riot, disturbance, confusion, tumult, noise, bustle". He believed that a revolution was going to break out all over India and the memory of the Ghadr of 1857 was the kind of anti-colonial resistance that made the Hukumat-i-Britannia shiver. It was also a tribute to the heroes of 1857 who had crossed the Hindu Muslim divide to oust the foreign invaders. After decades of propaganda, the common folk in India were led to believe that it was Hukumat-i-Britannia's divine right to rule India and treason to fight against them. Now Har Dayal predicted the end of British rule through armed revolution.

The first issue of the Ghadr, dated November 1st, 1913, described itself as 'the enemy of the English Raj, and announced that it would be issued weekly in the Urdu language'. As the editor of the *Ghadr* newspaper Har Dayal delivered a fierce speech announcing, "In the history of today's India, a new era is set in motion. The power of 'PEN' will explode like a ball of cannon. This newspaper is the staunch enemy of the English Empire and a bugle of the challenge for the Indian youth. Wake up, take up the arms and fight for the independence of India."

Not known to hold back his words, Har Dayal, read the editorial of the first issue of the *Ghadr* newspaper and declared, "Today there begins Ghadr in foreign lands, but in our country's tongue, a war against the British Raj. What is our name? Ghadr. What is our work? Ghadr. Where will be the Revolution in India? The time will soon come when rifles and blood will take the place of pens." Har Dayal provided the movement with a philosophical base and gave a call for volunteers who would contribute *"Tan, Man, Dhan"* (body, mind, and money) for the forthcoming Ghadr.

After the formation of the HAPC, a new hand-cranked printing press manufactured by the Chandler and Price Company of Cleveland had been bought with the generous funding at their disposal and *Ghadr* was published from 436 Hill Street in San Francisco. Copies of *Ghadr* newspaper rapidly reached Har Dayal's associates in Europe and India including Krishna Varma, Lajpat Rai, Ajit Singh, Madame Cama, S. R. Rana, Charles Andrews, Khudadad Khan, Asaf Ali, Amir Chand, Avadh Behari, Rash Behari Bose, and Hanwant Sahai among others. Among the few thousand subscribers of the *Ghadr* newspaper around the world was the future Indian leader Bhimrao Ambedkar, who was at that time a student at Columbia University in New York. Soon the *Ghadr* newspapers were being read aloud among the Indian immigrants. Indian places of worship were used for meetings and articles published in the *Ghadr* newspaper were discussed after the prayers.

In due course, the HAPC began to be identified with the *Ghadr* newspaper and the two names merged to become the Hindustan Ghadr Party or simply the 'Ghadr Party' (also spelled Ghadar). The Ghadr patriots were additionally known as Ghadrites and later Ghadri Babas.

At the Shattuck Hotel, on that November 1st evening, Gobind stood at the corner of the hall and observed the continuous applause of the gathering on the launch of *Ghadr*. He was pleased with the turnout. He had financed the event with his entire savings of $200. For the Indian community in San Francisco, he was considered the younger brother of Har Dayal - a relationship akin to Horatio and Hamlet.)

Many decades later, on November 24th, 1951, Gobind, in a speech at the Ceylon India Inn in New York, reminisced among Indian and American guests the initial years of the Ghadr Party movement, "we started to collaborate with Har Dayal in an organization he had established and named the Ghadr Party... thus started a militant endeavor against British rule in India under Har Dayal with its headquarters on top of a hill in the southern region of San Francisco... For the first time, Indian Nationalism had a real operation outside of Indian and the British Empire. (Dr.) Har Dayal was a magnetic personality of the kind that attracted all sorts of people towards him, towards his ideas and his friendship... Thus he was able to rally around him not only some Hindu university scholars but all hundreds and even thousands of Punjabi-Indian farmers and workers who were busy in the fields of California, Oregon, Seattle, Arizona, and nearby states. The sturdy Sikh, Pathans, Moslems of various parts of Punjab started working with him regarding him as their great leader. The committee at the Ghadr headquarters consisted of Hindus, Moslems, Sikhs, all equally zealous for the cause of India..."

In addition to Har Dayal challenging Lord Macaulay and Rudyard Kipling's established idea of India, the non-sectarian membership of the Ghadr Party directly opposed Hukumat-i-Britannia's time tested strategy of *divide et impera* within India.

In 1952, Gobind sought the intervention of the Government of India and objected to the misrepresentations about the Ghadr Party in an official publication *The March of India* (January-February 1952). In a letter to the editor, he clarified in the interest of the countless numbers of patriots who made the supreme sacrifice for the freedom of the country, that the Ghadr Party was founded by a secular-minded, non-sectarian all Indian patriot – Har Dayal. He added, "It was an all Indian nationalist movement in which Hindus, Moslems, Sikhs, and others participated... The Sikh members did play a valiant part, so did Hindus and Muslims too." Ultimately the Ghadr Party tricolor flag that fluttered over the Ghadr Party office represented its religious pluralism, including yellow for the Sikhs, red for Hindus and blue for Muslims as advocated by the *Ghadr* newspaper. Followers around the world organized themselves under the flag of the Ghadr Party. Later in his correspondence with Indians living in the United States, Gobind often clarified, "So many fakers claiming to have been founders of the Ghadr Party! Nobody realizes that Har Dayal did it – he and he alone!"

Chitto jetha bhoyshunyo

As the Ghadr Party activities expanded much to the frustration of Hukumat-i-Britannia, on November 6th, 1913, Mahatma Gandhi who was planning on returning to India, led a protest march at Palm Ford in South Africa. Accompanied by over two thousand people including a hundred and twenty-seven women and fifty-seven children he was up against a tax known as the Indian Relief Bill that was imposed on all former indentured laborers. He was arrested afterward and released only after a month on December 18th, 1913. And the Indian Relief Bill was scrapped.

In India, Mahatma Gandhi's protest march got wide publicity and Viceroy Lord Hardinge expressed strong support for his movement in a speech he made on November 26, 1913, in Madras. Gokhale who had known Mahatma Gandhi organized funds and sent Charles Andrews of St. Stephens College to South Africa to appear in meetings with the Indian leader.

But in faraway California, there was little or no impact of Mahatma Gandhi's philosophy on the Ghadr Movement. In 1913, he was hardly a known figure in the United States and only a handful of educated Indians and Americans living in California had heard of him. Some of the Indian students because of his links with Bhai Parmanand were aware of his presence and the work he was doing in South Africa. For the Ghadr Party, a revolution was in the making in India in 1913 and Mahatma Gandhi did not figure in that plan of action.

Around the same time on November 12th, 1913, the Swedish Nobel Academy announced that the Nobel Prize in Literature 1913 was being awarded to Indian poet Rabindranath Tagore, "because of his profoundly sensitive, fresh and beautiful verse, by which, with consummate skill, he has made his poetic thought, expressed in his own English words, a part of the literature of the West." The *San Francisco Call* on November 13th, 1913, published the story on the front page titled, 'Foremost India Poet Wins 1913 Nobel Prize".

The first Asian to have won a Nobel Prize sent a telegram in response to the Academy's citation. In his collection of poetry *Gitanjali*, Tagore's poem, '*Chitto jetha bhoyshunyo*' (Where the mind is without fear) reminded Indians what kind of independent India the poet dreamed of. The Nobel Prize awarded to Tagore was a crucial blow to the British literary elite. George Bernard Shaw sneered at 'Stupendranath Begorr' in a cheap dig.

And on December 10th, 1913 in the absence of Tagore, Ambassador Robert Henry Clive, the recently appointed British charge d'affaires in Sweden and grandson of the 8th Earl of Denbigh accepted the gold medal and citation at the Nobel banquet at Grand Hotel in Stockholm. Tagore's message was read out, "I beg to convey to the Swedish Academy my grateful appreciation of the breadth of understanding which has brought the distant near, and has made a stranger a brother."

Both Mahatma Gandhi and Tagore were dignified and idealistic visionaries and their life and work had a global impact.

Echoes of the Insurrection

By the first anniversary of the assassination attempt of British Viceroy Lord Hardinge on December 23rd, 1913, Har Dayal brought out the *Ghadr* newspaper on yellow paper. In commemoration of the attack on Viceroy Lord Hardinge, he put an inscription on the top of the page, "Price per copy; the Head of an Englishman". There was also a Gurmukhi edition that had been launched on December 9th, 1913.

In the lead article, '*Hamara Kesari Labas*' (our saffron attire) Har Dayal unleashed his thoughts with, "Today for the first time we have come out dressed in saffron because in the history of India this dress has been the dress of martyrs and brave warriors". In his, Shabash pamphlet he exhorted, "Don't sit there. Death hovers near-kill or be killed, do a great deed before you pass on. In other words, why not die for a cause, since one dies anyhow… Blessed is the death of the man who suffers martyrdom for the sake of freedom."

As a leader, Har Dayal displayed great confidence in the Ghadr patriots and encouraged them to contribute poetry and articles. This led to the creation of a collection of songs and poems titled, *Ghadr di Goonj* (the echoes of the Ghadr).

Towards the end of December 1913, the twenty-nine-year-old Har Dayal had successfully crossed many milestones and created a new politically disruptive enterprise that had subscribers among the Indians living worldwide. With the spread of the two thousand copies of the *Ghadr* newspaper, the voice of the Ghadr patriots was heard throughout North America and in the far-flung Indian communities across the Americas, Africa, and Europe as well as in India weaving thousands of Indians across the globe into a large collection of revolutionaries. Soon from California to Calcutta, from Portland to Punjab, from Seattle to Singapore, and from London to Lahore, the Ghadr patriots were ready and willing to take on the Hukumat-i-Britannia. Further, the Ghadr Party openly advocated armed revolution in India against the British colonizers. This they believed would ferment a huge revolution in the rest of India and end the cruel rule of Hukumat-i-Britannia. To enthuse the Ghadr patriots Har Dayal decided to publish Savarkar's work on the Ghadr of 1857 as a book in North America.

Har Dayal's counselor Bhai Parmanand, who after completing his pharmacology education in San Francisco had opened a pharmacy in Machhi Hatta, in Lahore in December 1913, appreciated his friend's achievement in his autobiography, *The Story of my Life*, "Har Dayal had correctly felt the pulse of the Indian laborers in the United States. His purchasing a press and starting a *Ghadr* newspaper in Urdu and Hindi filled with articles directed against the British Government or advocating the equality of mankind opened the eyes of his compatriots to their real situation. Young men flocked to work under him, thousand of dollars poured in by way of subscriptions..."

In his memoirs, *India as I knew it*, Michael O'Dwyer, the Lt. Governor of Punjab emphasized, "Har Dayal found the ground prepared and at once set to work to sow the seed. The attempt on Lord Hardinge's life was claimed by him, and with some reason, as the work of his party and he invited all to help in ridding India of the 'British Vampire'. The infamous *Ghadr* newspaper which openly incited to murder and mutiny and urged all Indians to return to India with the express object of murdering the British and causing revolution by any and every means was started by Har Dayal in 1913..."

The Ghadr Party launched in the United States in 1913 became one of the great utopian movements in Indian history. It was the most significant development in the story of Indian resistance to colonial occupation since the formation of the Indian National Congress in 1885. Remarkably the Ghadr movement, also the opening salvo in the Indian nationalist endeavor in the twentieth century, began a year before the world would be engulfed in 'the Great War' and four years before the Russian Revolution. Ahead of its time, it was eight years before Hasrat Mohani and Swami Kumaranand of India moved, on behalf of the Communist Party of India, a resolution for complete independence at the Ahmedabad AICC session in 1921 that was rejected by Mahatma Gandhi. The Indian National Congress adopted its famous slogan for 'poorna swaraj' only in December 1929 at its Lahore session - a full sixteen years after the Ghadr Party first raised its demand for independence.

German philosopher Arthur Schopenhauer's (1788–1860) central premise "talent hits a target no one else can hit; Genius hits a target no one else can see", correctly explained Har Dayal's brainpower. While talented revolutionaries and leaders of the freedom movement in India could achieve what other Indians could not achieve it was Har Dayal's gifted mind that achieved what others could not imagine. The Ghadr movement was without doubt an act of genius.

And Hukumat-i-Britannia's most dangerous revolutionary, Har Dayal, was the architect of this anti-colonial undertaking. Har Dayal was also the Ghadr personified in thought and remained in action a gentleman revolutionary.

By 1913 he was a serious public intellectual to reckon with in the progressive groups of the United States as well as the most popular name among the Indians in the United States and the youth of India. His incessant energy and enthusiasm and his wide range of scholarly interests created excitement wherever he appeared. He had no regrets of giving up the Oxford degree and a stable career in the ICS and had written off the life of a civil servant, "anyone can become a Deputy Commissioner…".

After the success of setting up the Ghadr Party and the weekly newspaper in record time, Har Dayal living on the other side of the planet and thousands of kilometers away from his land of birth missed all his Indian compatriots. At this rare moment of triumph in his life, he wanted all his comrades and the committed revolutionaries from India, France, Switzerland, Japan, and Britain to formulate a common cause with the Ghadr movement for the emancipation of India.

In Delhi, Hanwant Sahai was involved in supporting women's education and widow remarriage and working towards a casteless and classless society. He received a letter from Har Dayal happily informing him about the Ghadr publishing work that had extended and expanded in all directions. Hanwant Sahai read that there was a fund of about $ 2,000 from subscriptions. This had enabled Har Dayal to establish a press, an Institute and two weekly newspapers in connection with the propaganda work. The Ghadr press was able to print over one thousand sheets an hour and tons of literature ready to be smuggled into India. Har Dayal in the letter acknowledged the help from several of his young teammates who were working at the *Ghadr* newspaper without any thoughts of financial compensation. He called them, "splendid fellows". Har Dayal advised his friend to travel to San Francisco from the Pacific route to join him in March 1914 as part of the editorial team of the *Ghadr* newspaper. He advised him on the costs and the nature of work he could do in California.

Like a pathfinder, he could sniff the winds and sense what lay ahead. Planning for all eventualities Har Dayal mentored Ram Chandra, and at a formal dinner announced that the young man from Peshawar would take over as the next editor of the *Ghadr* newspaper in case of a calamity. Originally from Peshawar, Ram Chandra had known Har Dayal from India and previously worked with *Aftab* and *Akash*, two nationalist newspapers in Delhi. He had eluded British Secret Service and arrived in San Francisco in 1913 to work with his guru.

Har Dayal also invited his contact, the distinguished revolutionary Abdul Hafiz Barkatullah (1864–1928) from Japan to the United States to shape the Ghadr Party. The multilingual Barkatullah hailed from Bhopal and was a Professor of Urdu at Tokyo University where he regularly brought out revolutionary literature including *The Islamic Fraternity* against Hukumat-i-Britannia. In his writings and speeches Barkatullah advocated close cooperation between Muslims and Hindus in the struggle for India's independence. He was a thorn in the flesh of the British Empire and the British Secret Service demanded his deportation while he wanted to return to the United States where he had worked previously.

During the Christmas break in 1913, Har Dayal once again missed being with his family and felt intellectually deserted as his friend Brooks who was away in Britain. In a message to Brooks, he affectionately remembered his son 'Charlie' and wrote, "A Happy New Year & a year of many toys, much play, continual growth, and lots of candy for Charlie. Try to convey my message to him".

The Enemy of My Enemy

In the last days of 1913, the fearless patriot left no stone unturned in chasing his goals. Under his guidance Ghadr Party had cultivated a sense of transnational anti-colonial consciousness; that, unlike the Indian National Congress, thought in terms of global socialist revolution, not simply India's independence. He now incorporated the classic advice gained from the ancient Indian work on statecraft, *Arthashastra*, "the enemy of my enemy is my friend."

Har Dayal was aware that the British Secret Service was spying on him, the Ghadr patriots and the *Ghadr* newspaper but instead of agitating he dismissed the work of their operatives as amusement and diversion in his otherwise intense and strenuous life. He opened discussions for a fresh round of fundraising in the Bay Area with diplomats of nations politically opposed to Britain. Har Dayal, who never moved a muscle without a political motive, clandestinely arrived at 2313 Hearst Avenue in Berkeley, the residence of Franz Bopp, the German Consul-General in San Francisco. Bopp had come to the United States in 1893 and married an Illinois girl, Oliva Voche two years later. They lived in Berkeley with their two sons William and Franz and the office of the Consulate was located across the Bay at 201 Sansome Street.

At Bopp's home that evening in a closed room they discussed possible collaboration and a strategic alliance of the Ghadr Party with the Auswärtiges Amt (German Foreign Office). After glancing through the recent copies of the *Ghadr* newspaper, the German diplomat offered to introduce the Indian revolutionary to the resourceful Irish revolutionary group in the United States and specifically Larry de Lacey, the Irish Republican Brotherhood leader in the Bay Area who was to be helpful in the future. Har Dayal revealed that he was a supporter of Ricardo Flores Magon and his anarcho-syndicalist Partido Liberal Mexicano and had secretly backed the cross-border mobilization to liberate Mexico from the control of capitalist warlords. He informed Bopp that an arrangement of cooperation had also been reached with Dr. Sun Yat Sen's Chinese Nationalists. The Ghadr patriots were already sending the *Ghadr* newspaper around the world.

Har Dayal then proposed an agreement of financial and military assistance from the German Consulate in San Francisco. In previous months, Ambassador Johann Heinrich von Bernstorff (1862–1939) and Captain Franz von Papen (1879–1969) the newly appointed Deutsches Reich's secret service chief at the German Embassy in Washington DC had given their full support to such an initiative. The Deutsches Reich welcomed any kind of trouble for Hukumat-i-Britannia in India because that meant the British would have to fight two wars shortly, one in Europe and one in India. Papen later revealed the German motives in his *Memoirs*; "We did not go so far as to suppose that there was any hope of India achieving her independence through our assistance, but if there was any chance of fomenting local disorders, we felt it might limit the number of Indian troops who could be sent to France and other theatres of war". In the years to come Papen was lifted to supreme importance and appointed Chancellor of Germany in June 1932. He disgraced himself by supporting the Hitler led Nazi regime and defended himself at the Nuremburg trials.

Bopp confided in Har Dayal that though he was under orders from Papen to seal this relationship he still needed the proof of concept before recommending the 'Ghadr Party' investment proposal to Berlin.

The New Hope

On New Year's Eve of Wednesday, December 31st, 1913, over a hundred Indians assembled in a huge hall, in a building on 2nd and L streets in Sacramento. They were responding to a notice in the *Ghadr* newspaper that urged all Indians to attend the gathering to hear Har Dayal speak about British atrocities in their motherland. It was the largest ever gathering of the various groups of India from California, Oregon, Washington, and members traveled from Manila and Brazil to attend the celebrations.

The event was described in detail in the January 6th, 1914 issue of *Ghadr* newspaper. At the Ghadr Party meeting, Franz Bopp sat next to Sohan Singh Bhakna and Har Dayal along with the entire Ghadr Party top leadership on the stage as a 'special guest'. The hall was strikingly decorated will pictures of Mazzini, William Tell, Lenin, Dr. Sun Yat Sen, Nanasahib Peshwa, Tatya Tope, Chapekar brothers, Khudiram Bose and Rani Laxmibai among other patriots and revolutionaries.

As Har Dayal rose to speak, the entire space echoed with cries of *'Bande Mataram'* and the assembly was overwhelmed with loud applause. This was an acknowledgment of Har Dayal's stature within the Indian community. He was immensely respected for his dedicated patriotism, scholarly knowledge, unparalleled eloquence, and unmatched virtues. His penetrating gaze lent an almost hypnotic quality to his personality and his voice carried the persuasion and genuineness of his ideas. His vision, organizing, and executive abilities were an inspiration for all Indians. This made him the most treasured Indian revolutionary of his time.

Welcoming his special guests, Har Dayal dramatically declared that a large-scale war was about to break out in Europe. He perceptibly gauged the situation more than six months before the outbreak of WWI. He wanted Indians to use this opportunity to return to India for their revolution. Typical of the well-read scholar he read aloud selections from a book by Friedrich von Bernhardi, titled, *Deutschland und der Nächste Krieg (Germany and the Next War)*, in which the arch Prussian militarist referred to the "exploitation of India" by Britain since the industrial revolution and forecast that, were England embroiled in war, "revolutions might break out in India and Egypt" thus imperiling its "World Empire." In Britain's difficulty in Europe, he saw an enormous opportunity for India's freedom movement.

Har Dayal had previously written that Berlin was "the capital of the country which at present is most hostile in spirit to England" and now he declared, "the Germans have great sympathy with our movement for liberty, for they and ourselves have a common enemy. In future Germany can draw assistance from us and also render us assistance". Before concluding he dropped a startling hint about the future and informed his audience, "if 1 am turned out of this country, 1 will prepare for the Ghadr in another country - 1 shall have to go to Germany..."

Once again to the amazement of Bopp the hall boomed with loud cheering and the entire gathering displayed a will to be free of the British rule. Then an emotionally charged Kartar Singh Sarabha jumped on to the stage and began singing, "*Chalo chaliye, desh nu yudh karen, eho akhiri vachan te farman ho gaye*" (Come! Let us go and join the battle for freedom, the final call has come, let us go). The spectators joined him in singing and dancing.

As Har Dayal's eyes met that of an appreciative Bopp the far-reaching Ghadr Party's pact with Auswärtiges Amt was sealed and the Berlin - Berkeley axis took shape at that meeting.

Indian Citizenship Bill

A month later, on February 9th, 1914, exactly three years since Har Dayal had first set foot in the United States, the US Immigration Service in Washington DC finalized the deportation case against Har Dayal in collaboration with the British Embassy. Ironically that very day itself Har Dayal had appeared in the Capital as part of a three-member delegation with Dr. Sudhindra Bose and Dr. Bishan Singh

226 | The Great Indian Genius Har Dayal

to make representations before the 'Committee of Immigration on Restrictions of Immigration of Hindu Laborers'.

They were sent by the Hindustan Association and the Khalsa Diwan Society to protest against the bill that would exclude the immigration of all Asiatics to the United States. In 1914, Indians were stigmatized, teased and persecuted for maintaining their religious customs and discriminated against in theaters, bars, restaurants and hotels in the United States. They were charged higher rents and offered the lowest wages across the nation. Till that winter the Indians never had a voice in Washington DC,

Dr. Sudhindra Bose (1883–1946) who led the delegation was an instructor in the Department of Political Science at Iowa since 1913 and along with Dr. Singh and Har Dayal in an intense lobbying effort sought meetings with United States politicians in Washington DC. They met Sir Cecil Spring-Rice, the British Ambassador to acquaint him with the issue. Sir Rice deftly explained that he would seek instructions from His Majesty's Government in London to assist in this cause. The delegates then met William Jennings Bryan, Secretary of State and William Bauchop Wilson, Secretary of Labour but President Woodrow Wilson's sudden illness led to the cancellation of the meeting at the White House. The British Secret Service operatives kept a close watch on the movements of the Indian delegates.

Attracting a lot of local attention with their gold-trimmed turbans, the delegates met many journalists at the impressive Metropolitan Hotel on the northside of Pennsylvania Avenue. In an interview, Dr. Bose claimed, "We want the opportunity for our people to come to the United States to study and travel just as Americans go to India for the same purpose". Har Dayal was described by the media as a representative of the revolutionary party in India that opposed British rule.

On February 13th, the delegates, in a closed-door meeting, appeared before the Committee of Immigration chaired by John L. Burnett and the hearing continued for four hours though no final decision was reached. Har Dayal inexplicably changed his mind and did not testify. He felt since the British Embassy had branded him as an anarchist within the US Immigration Service, his attendance could damage rather than help the cause of the Indians. Caminetti had already warned Burnett about Har Dayal's antecedents as a leading anarchist. He had also forwarded a large portion of Har Dayal's speech that was read by the committee during the hearings.

Still, Har Dayal's independent views became part of the statement by Anthony Caminetti (1854–1923), Commissioner General of Immigration, United States Department of Labor. Har Dayal was inserted in the record as a "cultured man and a graduate of Oxford University". Caminetti wrote down, "A member of the Hindu race (Har Dayal) called at the bureau the other day and suggested that a great deal of the objection to these bills concerning Hindu immigration…". Har Dayal had expressed strong objections relating to Indian laborers being bracketed with "all idiots, imbeciles, feeble-minded persons, etc."

These were pioneering efforts by Dr. Bose, Dr. Bhishan Singh, and Har Dayal and it would take thirty-two years for the Luce-Cellar Bill to become law as the Immigration Act of 1946, conferring rights of United States citizenship on the natives of India. A hundred years later over four million Indians would call United States of America their home.

Love of Liberty

On the morning of February 16th, 1914, a special team of police inspectors and constables knocked the main door of 'Prem Dham' at Dariba Kalan – the haveli of Amir Chand. Then the police party forcefully charged into the courtyard armed with a search warrant. This incursion by police, as part of four raids ordered in Delhi by Petrie, the Additional Superintendent of Police of Delhi was based on clues discovered in Raja Bazaar in Calcutta.

The NAI documents record that the house was ransacked thoroughly in the presence of Amir Chand. The policemen spotted a large trunk on the balcony. Its locks were broken and the contents poured out. In the trunk, the policemen found some brown papers of a very distinctive character and a cover containing a Hindi pamphlet dealing with the use of poison. They noticed a codebook kind of manuscript containing a list of names with an alias and a letter of the alphabet opposite each name; a list of places, next to a special letter denoting places of meeting. Amir Chand's house was called Rs. 100 and Avadh Bihari was coded as Rs. 400 with Annas and Pies indicating time. The police located what they were looking for; sixty copies of a leaflet titled, *'Love of Liberty'* advocating a general massacre of Europeans, especially the English. This was the third version of the leaflet printed in Calcutta and circulated in Punjab and Upper Provinces. There was a biscuit box containing a quantity of cotton wool with some slight yellow stains on it.

The most important discovery was an unsigned handwritten message on the letterhead of 'The University of California, Berkeley', dated September 4th, 1913. The writer had requested for addresses where the weekly newspaper could be sent from the United States. Five packages of the *Ghadr* newspaper were found along with it. The raid at Amir Chand's house also led to the interception of a letter from a person named 'Dinanath' of Lahore.

The following day, Stead from the Criminal Investigation Department of Punjab conducted a series of raids in Lahore. The former member of the Society of Political Missionaries, Dinanath was arrested and under severe torture by the police revealed the entire scheme. Thereafter, Amir Chand, the low profile and cultured Headmaster at the Anglo Sanskrit School situated at Charkewalan turned to be the central figure in the secret society of 'the workers of God'. This authoritative Dilliwallah had taken over the mantle of the Society of Political Missionaries from Har Dayal since his disappearance from India in August 1908. Amir Chand's experience, public esteem, and talents were an asset to the organization. Further, Petrie maintained that the police had taken so long to identify Amir Chand as the key suspect because Charles Andrews of St. Stephens College held him in high regard and had protected him. Amir Chand had received the Charles Andrews Award and the Anglo Indian Sanskrit school where he was the headmaster, was Cambridge protected. In the times past, Andrews at the request of Amir Chand had written the introduction to Swami Ram Tirath's four volumes of *In Woods of God-Realization*. Andrews now distanced himself from Amir Chand by claiming that Amir Chand had cut ties with him for the past three or four years. The scholarly Amir Chand was also employed by Lala Sultan Singh to teach his son Raghubir Singh who later founded the Modern School in Delhi.

Cleveland considered Amir Chand as a "bloodthirsty plotter and debaucher of youths for revolutionary purpose."

After the arrest of Amir Chand all his associates Awadh Behari, Basant Kumar Biswas, Bhai Bal Mukund, Hanwant Sahai, and six others were placed before the Delhi Magistrate for trial within a month on March 16th, 1914. Though Biswas claimed credit for having thrown the bomb it was likely that he did so to take the heat of Rash Behari who was on the run. For Hukumat-i-Britannia the main conspirator turned out to be Rash Behari Bose and Petrie concluded that; "Rash Behari had a marvelous success... as a political missionary in Punjab... Collecting the remnants of Har Dayal's society around him, Rash Behari in October 1912 visited Lahore and found the time right for the inception of a campaign of violence". It was later revealed that Rash Behari after the murderous incident had taken the evening train back to Dehradun, where he resumed his duties as a clerk at the Forest Research Institute. A few months later Viceroy Lord Hardinge came to Dehradun for treatment following the Delhi outrage. Rash Behari appeared at the Circuit House to wish him a speedy recovery. He also praised the Almighty for offering the Kings representative to India a providential escape from a deadly attack.

In his memoirs, *My Indian Years: 1910–16*, Viceroy Lord Hardinge, remembered, "when driving in a car from the station to my bungalow, I passed an Indian standing in front of the gate of his house with several others, all of whom were very demonstrative in their salaams. On my inquiring, I was told that the principal Indian there had presided two days before at a public meeting at Dehra Dun and had proposed and carried a vote of condolence with me on account of the attack on my life. It was proved later that it was this identical Indian who threw the bomb at me!"

The police could not arrest Rash Behari who went underground. He was declared a proclaimed offender and all his properties were confiscated by Hukumat-i-Britannia. He was described in a circular as a man "of about thirty years of age, fair-complexioned and tall, has large eyes, and that the third finger of one hand is stiff and scarred due to some accident."

The hunt for the revolutionaries who had orchestrated the attack on Viceroy Lord Hardinge had finally ended. It was the culmination of one of the most comprehensive police investigations ever launched in India. Denham, Deputy Director of the Special Team and Charles Augustus Tegart from CID of Bengal who was a master of disguise, had succeeded in identifying the nationalist group from the remnants of the bombs that had exploded in Sylhet, Calcutta, Lahore, and Delhi.

At the annual investiture ceremony, Petrie was conferred with the 'King's Police Medal' for cracking the 'bomb outrage' case. Even after receiving hundreds of letters of congratulations, Petrie knew his assignment was far from over. On his desk, there was an unsigned handwritten note dated September 4th, 1913, on the letterhead of 'University of California, Berkeley'. It was recovered from Amir Chand's house and handwriting experts had confirmed that it matched the handwriting of Har Dayal.

Petrie had sent for Kishan Dayal to additionally verify that it was his brother's handwriting for he believed Har Dayal to be the "presiding genius of the organization". The British Secret Service planned to remove Har Dayal from the scene to obliterate the Ghadr movement. Their strategy was to 'take off the head and the body will automatically fall to the ground'.

Silencing Har Dayal

On the evening of March 25th, 1914, at about 2015 hrs, the audience was slowly filling the Bohemian Hall, 1530 Ellis Street to hear the much sought after guest speaker – Har Dayal. Without even looking the audience knew when Har Dayal entered the room. They could literally feel the electricity. He was charged with charisma, strength and saintly energy. Cultured and highly literate he may have been, but Har Dayal also had no compunction about going to war with the British Empire. As the principal theorist behind the Ghadr movement his voice was heard and respected in California's farms, factories, university campuses, newspapers, unions and even in Washington. But the US Immigration Service considered him an undesirable alien.

As the refined orator approached the podium three men from the US Immigration Service approached him. One of them asked if his name was 'Har Dayal'. On his polite confirmation, he was taken to the side and served an arrest warrant number 53572/92 dated February 10th, 1914, for being an undesirable alien in the United States in violation of the law. Har Dayal read the contents of the arrest warrant that accused him of being an 'Anarchist' and laughed loudly. He had already anticipated Hukumat-i-Britannia's move and knew it would amount to nothing. Thinking ahead he had on January 19th, 1914, quietly applied for American Citizenship at a San Francisco court, a status that would protect him from deportation.

The three inspectors realized that the bespectacled accused with boyish looks, shining dark eyes, a grin from ear to ear and a face bright with enthusiasm was a man far more mature than his years. He certainly did not have the bearing of an anarchist that they had pictured in their mind. Further, there were almost three hundred people present to hear his lecture, which was an unusual number in California. Bearing in mind the dignity of the situation the lead inspector indicated to Har Dayal that he would not proceed with the arrest that night but insisted that he must arrive at Angel Island Station the next morning to defend himself. Har Dayal readily agreed and respectfully thanked them for their courtesy.

There was considerable commotion among the organizers of the lecture and several Americans present in the Bohemian Hall wanted to argue with the inspectors but Har Dayal calmed them by dismissing the inspector's visit as the enemy's first stroke. He then proceeded to deliver an inspiring speech. It was business as usual.

The next morning the Bay Area woke up with the sensational newspaper headlines about 'Har Dayal's arrest'. He was reported to be rather cool about the whole affair as he told the press that "everything would turn out all right."

The NAI documents recorded that as confirmed the night before, Har Dayal arrived at 1130 hrs, at the pier leading to the Angel Island Station for his deportation hearing. A group of two hundred and fifty Ghadr Party members flanked him for moral support. In the days leading to Har Dayal's arrest, there were subtle warnings given by the US Immigration Service to the Indians that his arrest was only the first in a list prepared by Hopkinson of one hundred and twelve Indians in the United States who were to be deported back to India. His followers feared the worst for their leader and believed the Government authorities may deport them to India. At the entrance to ferry dock of Angel Island Station, a calm and collected, Har Dayal assured his loving, warm and dedicated comrades that he had not broken any law and he had a very strong legal case in his favor. Then with the words, *"Bande Mataram"* on his lips, the confident young trailblazer walked through the gates of Angel Island Station to board the ferry and boldly face whatever waited for him at the other end.

At the small window-less interrogation room with armed gaurds posted outside, Captain Ainsworth, US Immigration Service, was waiting for a long grilling of the man considered, "the most dangerous Indian revolutionary in the United States". The secret file on the suspected agitator had ballooned with inputs from Hopkinson. Sitting across from Captain Ainsworth at the Angel Island Station, was a stenographer L. E. Dinklarge taking notes. No attorney was allowed. This was the first political interrogation of an Indian conducted by American officials in the United States.

Captain Ainsworth was brash and wanted to keep the disputes that plagued India away from California. The questioning began and Har Dayal answered each question posed to him coolly with his usual wit. Some of his answers were as enlightening as his public lectures. Captain Ainsworth confronted him with a translation of an article written by Har Dayal in the *Ghadr* newspaper. On seeing the Urdu transcript Har Dayal insisted, "furnishing my translation because

I know my language very well." The former Stanford lecturer wanted to translate it in English himself and modestly claimed to, "have a tolerable good knowledge of the English language…"

The primary conversation was about Har Dayal's speech at the Jefferson Square Hall on October 31st, 1913 and his revolutionary ideas. But he emphatically denied the charge that he was promoting anarchist ideology to overthrow American Government. He admitted; "at the time of my entry into the United States I had not thought much on conclusions of Government in general. My two chief interests were Buddhism and its efficiency and the nationalist movement in India. As time passed my interest in Buddhism has waned and the modern labor movement has taken its place while the nationalist movement in India retains the same hold on my affection."

The interrogator then turned to the subject of various religions and castes in India and questioned Har Dayal about their participation in the Indian freedom movement. He also asked Har Dayal to define his caste to which he replied, "I am a member of the Kayastha caste. It is a literary caste". Captain Ainsworth inquired, "These different castes – are they now laying aside some difference that they held regarding association together in this movement? Har Dayal observed, "Yes the fusion of various castes in the nationalist movement is very remarkable… The abolition of the caste system is one of the many principles of the nationalist party". He mentioned that in his lectures in the United States, "I look upon myself as more of a thinker and philosopher, if I may be so vain as to use that word, than as an agitator participating in any temporal social movement".

Captain Ainsworth after a detailed examination that lasted three-hours released Har Dayal from Angel Island Station on a bond of 1,000 dollars and ordered him to appear before a court on April 10th, 1914. It is rumored that an anonymous Irish lady, supporter of the IWW furnished the funds. In the interim Indians in British Columbia had overnight collected 880 dollars for funding the legal defense of Har Dayal.

True to his personality, soon after Har Dayal was released from Angel Island Station he rushed to Jefferson Square Hall in time to make another speech that very day for IWW, on "The problem of unemployment". The audience aware of his recent arrest greeted him with a standing ovation. He announced, "I try to organize labor on a moral basis and to present to the world ideas for a new synthetic system of philosophy. It is my ambition to excel both in thought and action."

The Leading Patriot of his Country

The next morning he was once again front-page news in the American newspapers. *The New York Times* reported, "Hindu Reformer Arrested". In the new story, it mentioned that Har Dayal was regarded as the leading patriot of his country and the immigration officers were said to have conducted the inquiry at the request of the British Government. A supporter of the Ghadr movement, Emma Goldman in her periodical, *Mother India,* commented, "…now the English government seems to have succeeded in persuading its lackeys in Washington to do its dirty work".

The abnormal strain of the two days caught up with Har Dayal and he was taken ill for a day on March 28th. He was aware that he had taken up a tremendous task and made some ruthless British civil servants his enemies. He stayed at his Hill Street address and was prevented from making a speech at the William Morris Circle where a large number of UC Berkeley students and Indians had gathered to hear the man in the news. Although in an interview with the newspapers he continued his confrontational public defense, "I am working along the same lines as the ultra respectable churches when they take up collections for the famines of India. I am fighting for free speech and free assembly in India. Respectable white men have fought for the same cause. As for my personal opinions, they amount to nothing. I am changing them all the time." Further, in an interview with *Los Angeles Times,* he revealed, "For many months I have been spied upon by British Secret Service operatives but have gone about my affairs openly and have not turned my statements or modulated my declarations because of their presence. My arrest was not a surprise; I had been expecting it for a long time."

Frank Larned, the Deputy Commissioner General of Immigration confirmed that the warrant was issued at the request of Ernest Scott, the First Secretary at the British Embassy in Washington DC. *The San Francisco Bulletin* reported, "Embassy at Washington accuses savant of plotting against Government". The British Embassy officials alleged that they had their eye on Har Dayal and requested that he be taken into custody as an undesirable alien. The official reason revealed was that an incriminating letter, bearing the monogram of the University of California, allegedly written by Har Dayal was found in a police raid in Delhi.

On March 27th, after consulting with his journalist friends, Har Dayal issued another hard-hitting press statement that claimed, "my arrest calls public attention to the despicable pro-British subservience of the United States Government which was so vivid a feature of President Wilson's foreign policy. The democratic administration is licking the boots of England as anyone can see, who observes the administration's attitude towards Great Britain on the canal tolls questions". He added that there was nothing in his writing to which a parallel could not be found in the writings of United States Secretary of State William Bryan. He argued that it was simply ridiculous that he was "being prosecuted in the United States and the twentieth century because of my ideas. I have broken no laws, and I have not advocated the breaking of any laws. The only overt act I have committed is advocating the overthrow of the British in India by an armed revolt."

Disputing him Anthony Caminetti, known for his naked Eurocentric xenophobia, in a press note maintained that Har Dayal was arrested due to the reports of his anarchical lectures in Oregon and San Francisco during 1913. He also clarified that the Government of Great Britain had not requested either directly or indirectly that action should be taken against him and that the department was not concerned with anything that might be occurring in India.

During his interrogation, Captain Ainsworth had told Har Dayal that as specified by American law if he could prove that he was in the United States for more than three years he would be discharged for he was no longer 'an alien'. Har Dayal's attorney Charles Sferlazzo discovered that technically his client could not be arrested as an undesirable alien or deported as he had already completed the required three years or thirty-six months since he first disembarked in the United States on February 9th, 1911. The US Immigration Service had overlooked this critical fact and made a false arrest. Caminetti accepted that his Department had delayed sending out the warrant to the San Francisco office by just a few days due to a mix up of the names in the immigration register. They had initially confused Har Dayal with a 'Hardial Singh' alias Hur Dyal of Vancouver. In the end, in a meeting in Washington DC, Commissioner Caminetti had to admit to an extremely disenchanted Hopkinson that the United States Immigration department had blundered. The man wanted by His Majesty's Government could not be deported as an undesirable alien and this case was clearly beyond their legal jurisdiction.

Enemy's First Blow

The news about Har Dayal's sensational arrest and subsequent release appeared in the world press including in Italy titled, "Il professore Indiano Dayal In-nanzi alla Commissione della immigrazione'. The *Ghadr* newspaper of March 31st, 1914, reported the event with a sensational headline; "Congratulations! Congratulations! Congratulations! Be on the Alert. Enemy's first blow". In this edition, Har Dayal gave an account of his arrest and interrogation.

In Paris, Madame Cama took up Har Dayal's case in an article published by Jean Longuet in *L'Humanite* of April 3rd, 1914, titled *'Le Nationalist Hindou Har Dayal arrete aux Etats Unis'* (The Hindu Nationalist Har Dayal arrested in the United States. Will he be extradited?). Longuet expressed a hope that the American Government would not prove false to its glorious traditions by handling over a patriot. S. R. Rana and Madame Cama also sent an urgent telegram to United States Secretary of State Bryan, asking him to release Har Dayal immediately. The French League of the Rights of Man similarly cabled Secretary Bryan that Har Dayal's case must be examined with the respect for fairness and international law which has always been the pride of Washington's fatherland.

As stated by the book, *Too Long a Sacrifice: The Letters of Maud Gonne and John Quinn*, Madame Cama alerted her friend Maud Gonne, English born Irish revolutionary and actor about Har Dayal's arrest. Gonne who had met Har Dayal in Paris exchanged a series of letters with John Quinn, an Irish American cognoscente of the art world and a New York City lawyer with deep connections in Washington DC. She wrote, "It is a question of his extradition. If the English gets him they will treat him like Savarkar who is imprisoned for life on the Andaman Islands. Har Dayal has been away from India for some years now. He is a most intelligent cultivated man who has devoted his life to the cause of his country...."

Quinn on his part contacted Har Dayal's attorney Sferlazzo and offered assistance. He was willing to intercede in the matter with both United States Secretary of State Bryan and Commissioner Caminetti. In due course, Sferlazzo thanked Quinn and informed him that charges against Har Dayal were barred by the statute of limitations. And that at present no assistance was required. Quinn once again informed Sferlazzo that he was available to speak with Commissioner Caminetti if there were any complications in the future.

Who is this Har Dayal?

In the lonely prison cell of Cellular Jail in Andamans in the middle of Bay of Bengal, Savarkar was summoned by the cruel jailor David Barrie, the self-declared 'God of Port Blair' asked, "Who Is this Har Dayal?"

In his autobiography, Savarkar recalled that he answered, "You know him. He is the man to whom the Home Member, Sir Reginald Craddock, had referred as the leader of the revolutionary movement in America, in his conversation with me in this jail." David Barry then proceeded to mislead Savarkar and as if pretending to passing confidential information told him that Har Dayal was brought to Bombay on the charge of murder. That broke Savarkar's heart and he wrote, "I was simply stunned by that news. That one of our great revolutionary leaders should have been so arrested and was to meet the same fate as I, was too much for me to bear. How unhappy my country was, indeed, that the same destiny that was mine should be his I recalled my arrest, my trial, my hardships, and my transportation to this jail."

Savarkar tried to ascertain the truth from the warders but they could not even remember the name, "Har Dayal'. He was aghast and recollected his feeling as, "What a miserable condition, this, of our motherland, that those who had lived in other lands and had worked there for her freedom, at tremendous risk to their own lives, should not be known even by name to her own ungrateful children! The thought almost maddened me with grief. My fellow-prisoners had to pour water over my head to cool my heated brain." David Barry revisited Savarkar's cell to confirm if he indeed knew Har Dayal. Savarkar retorted, "I had the honor of knowing him as my very intimate friend". The cigar-puffing jailor informed him that Har Dayal was accused of murder, and he had implicated himself in the bomb incident in Delhi. Later Savarkar confided with other fellow prisoners, "I told them that I knew fully well what I was doing, that we must not take it quietly when they talked in such terms of Har Dayal, that we must not disown him because he was under arrest as they had told us, about it. That would be sheer cowardice on our part and I was not the man to behave so. Har Dayal was my friend and I was prepared to suffer any punishment for saying so. The, political prisoners ought to learn this, If they did not learn anything else. That was the only way to show our gratitude to Har Dayal. Gradually I became appeased in mind and set about getting the news for myself." Within two days Savarkar heard that his friend was under arrest briefly in the United States but had been released on bail.

Wrath of the British Secret Service

Back in San Francisco, Har Dayal met his attorney Sferlazzo at his office on 4 Columbus Avenue. Har Dayal was optimistic that the case for deportation built against him by the British Embassy would amount to a hill of beans. Fremont Older had informed Har Dayal that he had received a confirmation from his friend William Wilson, the Secretary of Labour in Washington DC that his application for citizenship would be approved shortly. Politicians in San Francisco had also appealed to the Bureau of Labor on behalf of the young Indian intellectual and these representations had received due considerations.

But Sferlazzo who respected Har Dayal and considered him a modern-day saint disregarded all the promises made to his client by his allies. He was convinced that Commissioner Caminetti was a politician and at the end of the day would not honor his word. Sferlazzo was suspicious of the 'next steps' of the British Secret Service. Hukumat-i-Britannia alleged Har Dayal's complicity in the attempt on Viceroy Lord Hardinge's life and its officials were bent on his extradition or deportation under any circumstances. Har Dayal's comrades in Delhi were already in jail and were likely to be hanged. Additionally, as in Savarkar's case, His Majesty's Government had no reservations in flouting the international justice system to ensure Har Dayal's transportation to Cellular Jail in the Andamans. There was an additional possibility that the British Secret Service operatives might kidnap him to forcefully board a ship in California destined for India. Ghadr Party members in California feared that Hukumat-i-Britannia may unwisely find 'unconstitutional means' to get to him and hence on many occasions provided him with bodyguards. Sferlazzo advised him to immediately leave the jurisdiction of the United States and stay away from British ruled territory with the help of his associates in IWW, Irish revolutionary group and the German Consulate. Har Dayal concluded it was time to leave the United States and expand the Ghadr movement in Europe.

Following this, on April 4th, 1914, Har Dayal, already thinking of future academic opportunities, requested Stanford University to send him a letter at his Hill Street address that confirmed his employment as a Lecturer for Hindu Philosophy at the University from January to September 1912. On April 7th, 1914, the University Academic Secretary send him the University register of May 1912 that established his engagement and offered to send a statement of his connection with the University.

Escape from America

In early April 1914, at the train station at Oakland, a freshly shaved Har Dayal wearing a brand new hat, a long overocoat, a crisp Blue suit, shining black shoes and recently purchased gold rim glasses appeared on the platform. He looked very different and could pass off as a banker or a successful businessman. A large trunk containing his library of books and his belongings was placed next to him. It was his last day in Berkeley. Har Dayal was handed a new identity papers in the name 'Israel Aronson' and a steamship ticket booked from New York to Amsterdam for him in that name by his 'new colleagues'. He held a train ticket to New York purchased earlier from the Union Pacific's ticket office at 42 Powell Street in San Francisco. His final destination was not known as yet. It is conceivable that his friends within the progressive societies of California, the German Consulate, the Irish group and even the office of William Bryant, Secretary of State assisted him in his secret mission. Also present at the Oakland train station were Gobind and Ram Chandra. It was close to 1000 hrs and the Overland Express was about to depart. Gobind's face reflected the anxiety of the moment. He had met his guru after a gap of a week. Har Dayal himself was tense and exhausted. He was in a rush. After working in the United States for thirty-eight months the revolutionary was proceeding to his next battlefield.

According to Harold Gould's book, *Sikhs, Swamis, Students, and Spies -The India Lobby in the United States, 1900–1946,* before boarding the train Har Dayal reassured Gobind, "I am leaving the United States, but tell nobody, I am going to Switzerland. The Ghadr business can be continued; the boys have learned how to do it. I have shown the way. San Francisco is the backwater of civilization. Modern culture and civilization are in Europe...I shall maintain the closest contact with the Ghadr Party here and will go on giving advice and guidance, but in Europe, I shall be in touch with our people, with our country more than here..." Har Dayal hoped that he could be reunited with Sundar Rani and Shanti Devi in Europe. A dejected Gobind who was short on money was assured by his mentor that he would look for a possibility for him to study at the Sorbonne University in Paris or Cambridge in Britain.

Then as he had done at the Delhi railway station in August 1908 while fleeing from India, Har Dayal spent the next few minutes at the Central Station discussing the new processes to be followed after his departure. But Ghadr Party did not have the bench strength to find a successor to Har Dayal. He had managed to bridge the gap between the intellectual agitators and the majority of the North Indian migrant workers like no one else could. As the architect, he had lent dignity to the organization and achieved incredible success in a short period. Nevertheless, Har Dayal formally handed the reins of the Ghadr Party to the handsome Ram

Chandra who was also to take over as the General Secretary in the organization. Aware of Gobind's skills as a writer he asked him to assist in the publication of the *Ghadr* newspaper. That morning Har Dayal accompanied by Ram Chandra and Gobind had visited the Berkeley branch of the Oakland Bank of Savings and got his name removed as a signatory to the 'Ghadr Party' bank account. In due course, Ram Chandra took over the Ghadr headquarters at Hill Street and its press at Valencia Street in San Francisco. Two years later the Ghadr Party established new headquarters and another press at 5 Wood Street.

Then a smiling Har Dayal quickly embraced Gobind and Ram Chandra and with *Bande Mataram* on his lips boarded the train compartment. He had a sixty-eight-hour journey ahead of him to Chicago. In Harold Gould's book, Gobind recalled, "I put him on the train, the Overland Limited, and he promised to write me from New York and keep me posted from Europe... I heard nothing from him, but Ram Chandra remained in contact with him". Eighteen years would pass before the next reunion of the two Dilliwallahs.

As the Overland Limited dashed across the continent towards the East Coast, Har Dayal, who was a master of disappearing acts throughout his life, rested his feet in the cabin of the train. The journey from Oakland to New York through the vast landscape of the United States was simply a hiatus in his work as a leading Indian revolutionary. For the second time he had narrowly escaped imprisonment and the British Secret Service was clueless of his movements as yet. They communicated to their superiors in London and Simla that Irish and American sympathizers were working to assist Har Dayal. They also picked up a hint that he was out in Portland, Oregon. Though on the run Har Dayal's intellectual energy did not slacken and with a pen and paper in his hand, he braced himself to write the next chapter of the Ghadr movement.

11

THE PRESIDING GENIUS IN EUROPE

"No man in recent times has sinned more grievously against the Government... than Har Dayal".

David Petrie

Director, Department of Criminal Intelligence

It was a dark night, possibly the darkest in Canadian history.

At 0100 hrs in the morning on Sunday, July 19th, 1914, *Sea Lion*, a small tug boat, 114-feet in length with a 22-foot beam, powered by a single Mckie and Baxter triple-expansion marine steam engine made its way towards a Japanese steamer anchored on the far side of the Vancouver Harbor in British Columbia. That night, one hundred and twenty-five armed police officers and thirty-five ex-army men were aboard the *Sea Lion*. Malcolm Robert James Reid, the xenophobic Vancouver Immigration Agent, who had taken upon himself to enforce the rule of law on the Indian immigrants, led them. Supporting him in this enterprise was an equally charged, William Hopkinson who had triumphantly returned to Vancouver after his Californian sojourn and clash with Har Dayal and the Ghadr Party. Both Reid and Hopkinson were working in collaboration with Henry Herbert Stevens, a first-term Member of Parliament representing a Vancouver riding on an energetic campaign against Indian immigration.

The *Sea Lion's* white billowing smoke turned into a thick black smoke, as it pulled closer to the Japanese steamer moored near the shallow Burrard Inlet. Through the dimness of the night, the Vancouver policemen read the name etched across its bow - *Komagata Maru*.

Then the solemn silence of the night was broken. The *Sea Lion's* siren was heard from far as it approached the steamer with a threatening attitude. Over three hundred and fifty Indian passengers along with the Japanese crew were alerted and simultaneously saw the *Sea Lion* from the steamer's bridge and deck. The Indians were aware of the Vancouver police's plan to attack the Japanese steamer under the cover of darkness, board it and muscle them out of Canadian waters.

Suddenly in the middle of the calm night, Sikh, Hindu and Muslim war cry echoed in self-defence into the Vancouver skies. The lights of the *Sea Lion* revealed the weary and unarmed Indian passengers on the deck ready to defend themselves to the end.

Next a small sea battle broke out in the waters of British Columbia.

The attacking party of the *Sea Lion* armed to the teeth and equipped to board the *Komagata Maru* sprung forward but suddenly lumps of coal, bricks, wooden spears and other objects hit them. A shower of missiles was exchanged however to the advantage of the Indians, the deck of the *Sea Lion* was fifteen feet below the deck of the *Komagata Maru*. The Vancouver policemen ran, stooped, stumbled over their comrades and crawled during the bombardment. The policemen let loose the stream from a fire-hose of the *Sea Lion* on the unprotected Indians but the defence of the Japanese steamer only grew stronger. The projectiles continued dropping and policemen began to retreat onto that side of the tug furthest from the *Komagata Maru*. The *Sea Lion* was bursting with the wails and moans of defeated, agonized, injured voices of the policemen. Soon a stream of wounded policemen reeled into the captain's cabin for medical attention. The shocked reaction to the disastrous attack was recorded on the faces of Hopkinson and Reid. Despite the fact that the British Empire ruled across the world and Britannia ruled the waves the Indians on the *Komagata Maru* had not fallen to the armed assault in British Columbia.

The *Komagata Maru* was impregnable.

Finally, the *Sea Lion* on the orders of Reid cast its grappling irons.

The Vancouver Police backed away from the steamer's side, got out of the range of the shower of missiles and rushed back to the pier to seek immediate medical assistance. Fifteen minutes after the battle began the Indians had victoriously saved their lives and their ship. The attempt by the posse of Vancouver policemen under the command of a few bigoted Canadian officials to intimidate the Indians and take possession of the steamer had failed.

A few months before this face off in the seas, Gurdit Singh Sirhali (1859–1954), a wealthy Indian businessman living in Hong Kong had chartered the *Komagata*

Maru for $66,000, to take British subjects; twenty-four Muslims, twelve Hindus, and three hundred and forty Sikhs to Vancouver. He decided to challenge the passing of Canadian Order-in-Council 2642, which prohibited "the landing at any port of entry in British Columbia" of "Artisans" and "Laborers, skilled and unskilled." This Canadian law was designed to keep Indians out of Canada. Unlike the Chinese, who were barred from Canada in 1923 by the stroke of a pen, Indians were British subjects and therefore couldn't be prohibited from traveling within the British Empire. The workaround was a "continuous passage" law necessitating Indians to come uninterrupted from their native land with no stops along the way. The Canadian Government compelled steamship companies to not offer direct passenger facility from India to Canada. But the *Komagata Maru* left Hong Kong on April 4, 1914, and reached Vancouver with only permitted refueling stops in Shanghai, Moji and Yokohama thereby accomplishing a "continuous passage". Interestingly Barkatullah lived at 40 Daimichi, Akasakaku in Tokyo, at that time along with Bhai Bhagwan Singh, a former resident of Vancouver who had been forcibly deported. Both Ghadr patriots brought copies of the *Ghadr* newspaper aboard the *Komagata Maru* when it docked in Yokohama on its way to Canada.

In the summer of 1914, Vancouver looked much different than the world of today. The society was viewed as Europeans and non-Europeans and clearly segregated as "us" versus "them". The British Secret Service kept Canadian authorities informed about the steamer's progress and considered its passengers to be part of the Ghadr Party movement. Credited for ejecting Har Dayal from United States, Hopkinson appeared on the scene and convinced his colleagues in the Canadian immigration department that the *Komagata Maru* was a steamer full of illegal Indian immigrants and fiery seditionists. Previously, Cleveland in a series of notes from his office in Simla had warned about "the arrival of a Japanese ship with 400 Sikhs from India via Hong Kong at Vancouver". That put the immigration office in Vancouver into an extremely combative frame of mind. A series of inflammatory news stories were planted in the local press. *The Vancouver Daily Province* published the news report under the heading of 'Boat Loads of Hindoos on Way to Vancouver'. Another newspaper of British Columbia headlined its stories as 'Hindu Invasion of Canada'.

The *Komagata Maru* reached Vancouver on Saturday, May 23rd, 1914 but was denied entry. Immigration boats surrounded the steamer half-mile offshore and made the passengers virtual hostages. The steamer remained docked in the harbor while a legal battle waged on the shore. The steamer remained a prison – no one was allowed to disembark or board; food and water began to run low. To fight for the rights of the passengers, Ghadr patriots in Vancouver established a 'shore committee' and funds were raised. The Indian population on the entire Pacific Coast of the United States and Canada was sensitive to the issue because of the *Ghadr* newspaper. The co-operation that existed among Sikhs, Hindus, and Muslims within the Ghadr Party to support the passengers of *Komagata Maru* was noteworthy. The Indians argued that as British subjects they should have the right to immigrate to any country in the British Empire. Many of the men on board the *Komagata Maru* were veterans of the British Indian army and believed it was their right to settle anywhere in the British Empire as they had fought to defend it.

On June 21st, 1914 the Indian community combined with the Socialist Party of Canada staged a huge rally at the newly built Dominion Hall at the edge of Gastown in Vancouver attended by about eight hundred Indians and two hundred Canadians. A Canadian lawyer and Socialist Party member J. Edward Bird (1868–1948) who was engaged to represent the *Komagata Maru* in the court case addressed the meeting and suggested, "I have heard from time to time that these men are anarchists and they are all bad, all Socialists. I have myself the honor of belonging to the Canadian Socialist Party for years and I have never seen a Socialist yet who was not a decent man…don't believe all these stories that you hear about the Hindoos (Indians)…Physically they are our superiors and mentally our equals…"

But Bird, a senior partner in the Vancouver law firm of MacNeill, Bird, Macdonald and Darling was denied the right of access to his clients for weeks. After an acrid two-month face-off the Indian passengers lost and the exclusionists carried the day. The provincial authorities in British Columbia finally ordered the steamer to leave Canadian waters. In desperation, Gurdit Singh even sent out telegrams to King George V in London and Viceroy Lord Hardinge and informed them of the plight of the passengers who are being starved for food and water by the Canadian Immigration department.

By July 18th, 1914, Hopkinson realized a rapid promotion awaited him if the *Komagata Maru* were taken by force. He motivated Inspector Reid to use a firm hand and subjugate the Indians at once. Reid decided to use military power and lead an assault on the *Komagata Maru* to send the steamer back to Asia. The attack on July 19th was a disaster and the *Sea Lion* filled with bruised and wounded policemen drifted away. But the Canadian Government did not back off. Four days later, on July 23rd, 1914, *HMCS Rainbow*, a Canadian warship appeared and the *Komagata Maru* was escorted away while thousands of Vancouver residents stood on the docks and cheered. Ultimately only twenty-four Indian passengers were allowed to get off.

And with the departure of the *Komagata Maru*, the door for Indian immigrants to Canada was slammed shut for decades to come.

Israel Aaronson from Lausanne

A few months before the *Komagata Maru* episode, in the first week of May 1914, Brooks opened the mail received at his home in the London suburb of Eltham. He was surprised to see familiar handwriting on the letter and even more surprised to read its content. His friend Har Dayal had written to him from Lausanne in Switzerland on April 30th, 1914 under the assumed name of Israel Aaronson.

Brooks smiled as he read, "Here I am. You will be agreeably surprised. I escaped from the U.S. after my arrest for deportation or perhaps extradition at the request of the British Embassy..." Har Dayal informed Brooks that he was released on $1000 bail and on the advice of his friends he had left California. He requested Brooks to write to him immediately as he planned to be in Switzerland that summer. Brooks also got to know that his friend intended to do academic research since he was away from his executive duties of California.

Brooks' autobiography discloses that four days later in response to Brooks letter, Har Dayal after thinking long and hard warned him not to support or sympathize with the Indian freedom movement or its representatives if wanted to have a career in Britain, writing, "Patriotism is England's religion, & they never forgive or even tolerate a person, who doesn't worship 'the Empire'. I know it is intolerable for a man to gag himself, but reticence is the price we pay for existence in this system of society. I say this only because you may underestimate the strength of English feeling against those who are making trouble for England in India." He cautioned Brooks not to make enemies with the British as they took unrest in India very seriously. As he always did he remembered Charlie and requested Brooks to 'give him a box of chocolates'.

On reaching Geneva from New York in April 1914, Har Dayal now sported a thick mustache and lived under the adopted *nom de guerre* of 'Israel Aaronson' and later F. Sulzer and Wursten. Cognizant that the British Secret Service would shadow him, he wanted to primarily rest and recuperate from the nagging nervous affliction he had developed over the years. The spring of 1914 was a peaceful and carefree time for Europe. The continent had never been stronger, richer, picturesque and more confident of a better future. He spent his days churning out tracts in the reading room of Universite de Geneve and took his simple meals at his modest home. He took morning strolls along the Lac Leman. The beautiful alpine city was the Swiss hub for Indian revolutionaries and played host to a stream of fellow Indian, Egyptian and Russian exiles. He contacted Zurich based Indian revolutionary, Champakaraman Pillai (1891–1934) who brought out a journal called *Pro-India*. He rented three rooms and aspired to start a branch of Yugantar ashram in Switzerland. He remained in contact with his coworkers Ram Chandra in San Francisco and Rash Behari in India using the secret coded messages he had devised in California. He also continued to regularly contribute articles to the *Ghadr* newspaper and the other progressive associations in California.

In Geneva, Har Dayal worked with Egyptian journalist Dr. Mansour Rifaat, former Paris correspondent of the newspaper *El Alam* at 3 rue Versonnex. Rifaat had founded *La Patrie Égyptienne*, an organ of the Egyptian Emancipation Movement in Geneva in March 1914 and managed the Club des Patriotes Egyptiens. Har Dayal's Egyptian friends had reconnected with him and they sought his assistance in shaping an Indo-Egyptian revolutionary congress to be held at Zurich in August 1914.

Since Har Dayal's departure from the United States, Krishna Varma had also relocated to Geneva in late April 1914 and quickly received the highly coveted permis d'etablissement despite his not having a valid passport. He rented a five-room top floor flat at 1 Avenue des Vollandes with a splendid view over the lake. He met Har Dayal at Hotel Bristol and Café de la Couronne. Though they remained in social contact Har Dayal refused any financial help from him since their political differences were "irreconcilable".

In addition, Har Dayal reconnected with Ernest Douwes Dekker, an anarchist banished from Java (Indonesia) by the Dutch. He was to be one of the most hunted men in the global conspiracies of 1915. He had formerly organized the Nationalist Indian Party and published the writings of Har Dayal in Java. He was converted to the Indian revolutionary cause in Geneva and agreed to provide Dutch passports as well as arrange to distribute *Ghadr* newspaper in Java.

Besides writing to Brooks, Har Dayal reopened his correspondence with Frieda Hauswirth, his friend from Stanford, who lived with her parents in Gstaad to tempt her to work with the Ghadr movement in Europe or California. Nothing much came off it, as Frieda was not interested in pursuing a relationship with him. On her way to the United States, she was asked to carry a few letters written in Hindi and Urdu by Har Dayal addressed to Ram Chandra and Munshi Ram. She could not read the contents and destroyed the letters after informing Har Dayal. Sometime later in a letter from Geneva to Frieda who was in the United States, Har Dayal disclosed, "I am all right and busy now. Work for India is also being done successfully in many directions. Good results are expected to follow. Let us wait. There are too many hindering circumstances though…" Though the two kept in touch, Frieda fell in love with another Indian student, Sarangadhar Das after reaching Berkeley and divorced Arthur Lee Munger to marry him in 1915. She nevertheless had a long association with the Indian freedom movement that lasted most of her life. Sarangadhar Das evaluating Har Dayal described him as "an idealist, a philosopher and all that."

On July 22nd, 1914, Har Dayal informed Commissioner Caminetti in Washington DC, that "I have left the United States after my arrest at San Francisco on March 25 by orders of the Immigration Department. As the only charge against me was that of being unlawfully in the country, I hope that die exigencies of law are satisfied by my voluntary departure from the country. The only punishment for the misdemeanor charged against me was expulsion or deportation from the United States and I have left the country at my expense and on my own initiative. I ask you to consider if the Department should return the bond money ($1,000) to my lawyer, Mr. C. Sferlazzo or to the Securing Company that deposited it."

The US Immigration Service had in April 1914 written to Stanford University to confirm that Har Dayal was employed there in 1912. Since he was no longer a resident in the United States the Immigration Department locked his file. With the minor complication of Har Dayal's deportation out of his life, Commissioner Caminetti went back to maintaining that the United States Congress should halt immigration of Chinese, Japanese, Indians, and Malays because they represented the 'Asiatic menace'.

Furthermore in this period, a self-taught mathematical genius, Srinivas Ramanujam working as a shipping clerk in Madras had startled Professor Godfrey Harold Hardy of Cambridge with his work. Ramanujam landed in Cambridge in April 1914 to work on number theory and string theory and became the first Indian mathematician to become a Fellow of the British Royal Society. Hardy admitted, "I had never seen anything in the least like them before. A single look at them (mathematical equations) is enough to show that a mathematician of the highest class could only write them. They must be true because, if they were not true, no one would have the imagination to invent them." *(Quoted from The G. H. Hardy Reader, edited by Donald J. Albers, Gerald L. Alexanderson, William Dunham, 2016)*. Though Ramanujan died just six years after arriving in Cambridge, the mastermind had a lasting impact on his colleagues and in the world of mathematics.

And then in that eventful year of 1914, the first catastrophe of the twentieth century traumatized the world.

On the Brink of the Apocalypse

At 1115 hrs, on Sunday, June 28th, 1914, in the dusty Balkan town of Sarajevo, Gavrilo Princip, a nineteen-year-old high school student aiming to kill his target fired two shots from his Browning 9 mm pistol.

The first shot tore through the chest of the plucky middle-aged Archduke Franz Ferdinand of Habsburg, heir to the Austro-Hungarian throne. The second hit his wife Sophie in the abdomen. "Sophie, Sophie, don't die; live for our children", Franz Ferdinand murmured. Then he kept reiterating in a steadily more feeble voice, "It is nothing". In the next five minutes, as they bled to death, a dynasty and with it, a whole way of life toppled. The desitiny of the world changed that day in Sarajevo and this incident is considered the trigger for the Great War. In a space of just over a month, the two shots in Sarajevo plunged Europe into an unimaginable conflict that ultimately brought down four empires. The Great War also defined Britain's future and the potential of India's independence movement along with the prospects of its brave warriors and nationalists including Har Dayal.

Shocked by the assassination of his friend, Ferdinand, Germany's Kaiser Wilhelm II (1859 - 1941) the eldest grandchild of Queen Victoria imagined that a war in Europe would unite his subjects. He had a conflicting relationship with his British Royal family. On the very eve of war, he announced from the Balcony of the Royal Palace in Berlin, "A momentous hour has struck for Germany. Envious rivals everywhere force us to legitimate defense. The sword has been forced into our hands.... War will demand enormous sacrifices by the German people, but we shall show the enemy what it means to attack Germany." Later the embodiment of militarism recognized no political divisions, no political parties and asserted, "From this day on, I recognize only Germans!"

Germany and France went to war on August 3rd, 1914. Then on the warm evening of Tuesday, August 4th, 1914, George V, the King of the United Kingdom, and the British Dominions, and Emperor of India penned in his diary, "I held a Council at 10.45 to declare war with Germany. It is a terrible catastrophe but it is not our fault. An enormous crowd collected outside the Palace; we went on to the balcony both before and after dinner. When they heard that war had been declared, the excitement increased and May and I with David (the Prince of Wales) went on to the balcony; the cheering was terrific. Please, God, it may soon be over and that he will protect dear Bertie's life (George VI, serving with the Royal Navy)."

A major war of deadlocks and fear broke out that day, between two powerful rival sets; the Central Powers: Germany and Austria-Hungary on the one hand, and Triple Entente: Russia, France, and Great Britain on the other. President Wilson pledged neutrality for the United States, a position that the vast majority of Americans favored.

King George V co-opted India into his nation's war in Europe. Large scale forced enlistment was ordered across the British Empire. Mobilization started on August 8th, 1914 and the Lahore Division embarked at Karachi on August 24th with an order to proceed to Marseilles. Viceroy Lord Hardinge recorded in his autobiography, *My Indian Years*; "Within six months of the outbreak of war seven divisions of infantry and two divisions and two brigades of cavalry were sent from India overseas. ...I trusted the people of India in the great emergency that had arisen, and I told them so and my confidence was not misplaced."

The bulk of political opinion in 1914 was unified in the view that if India desired greater responsibility and self-rule, it must also be willing to share in the load of Imperial defense to gain Dominion status after the war. Indian Maharajas were pressed by King George V to send large supplies of food, money, and ammunition to support the British war effort. With the onset of the Great War, Hukumat-i-Britannia's officials in London and India were to grapple with a new threat to the British Empire – the Ghadr movement.

The Voyage of Rebels

On Sunday, August 15th, 1915, thirty-two years before India attained freedom a clarion call appeared in the *Ghadr* newspaper.

"Arise, brave ones! Quickly… we want all brave and self-sacrificing warriors who can raise revolt…"

"Salary: death
Reward: martyrdom
Pension: freedom
Field of Battle: Hindustan"

Barkatullah and Bhai Bhagwan Singh had taken charge of the Ghadr Party propaganda machine in San Francisco, on their arrival in the United States from Hong Kong on May 24th. Shortly thereafter, on July 21st, Sohan Singh Bhakna left for India and Bhai Bhagwan Singh was elected the President of the Ghadr Party while Barkatullah became the Vice President. Ram Chandra remained responsible for editing the *Ghadr* newspaper. Barkatullah now prophesied a replay of the Ghadr of 1857 in India and called for volunteers.

The Ghadr patriots had rejoiced at the news of Britain entering the Great War. They did not want to miss this opportunity with their aim of launching a revolution in India while Britain was busy fighting Germany. They realized this was the historic development that would lead to India to be proclaimed as a free and sovereign Republic. In response to the call for volunteers, the Ghadr patriots declared war against Hukumat-i-Britannia. Some of them were outstanding poets too and wrote inspirational verses. After hearing the '*Ghadr ki Goonj*' (echoes of the rebellion – a book of poems published by Ghadr Party in April 1914), thousands of zealous Indian patriots across the globe joined hands with the Ghadr patriots to fight fire with fire and returned to India with arms. Their mission was to expel the world's most powerful ruler by force from their conquered motherland. And they were ready to die as martyrs in armed combat for their nation's freedom and dignity.

On Sunday, September 27th, 1914, the *Komagata Maru* along with its weary Indian passengers made its way back to Budge Budge, thirty-two kilometers downstream from Calcutta. On its return journey the steamer had taken on a nationalistic streak when Ghadr patriots had visited the steamer in Yokohama, Japan to give lectures, weapons and distribute newspapers. The British Secret Service in India feared that the passengers landing in India might be the fearsome Ghadr patriots. 'The Ingress into India Ordinance, 1914' had been issued on September 5th, 1914, by the Hukumat-i-Britannia to restrict the movement of the persons who were considered to be prejudicial to the safety, interests or tranquility of the state.

Robert Humphreys, ICS, the Deputy Commissioner of the Hoshiarpur District in Punjab known for his tact and experience, was selected to meet the *Komagata Maru* on its return to India. The other senior official awaiting the arrival of the steamer at Budge Budge was David Petrie.

When the steamer docked, the local police tried to arrest Gurdit Singh and the other leaders as political agitators. They were forced to board a special train bound for Punjab, but several refused to disembark from the steamer. Some even decided to march to Calcutta. In the early hours of September 29th, the police panicked. Shots rang in the air and a firefight broke out. In the bloodbath that followed many '*Komagata Maru* heroes' were slaughtered in cold blood and an estimated two hundred and two were imprisoned. Both Petrie and Humphreys were hit by bullets and ended up wounded at Budge Budge. While bullets rained around him, Gurdit Singh with the assistance of local revolutionaries disappeared into the night. The passions ignited by the *Komagata Maru* incident became a rallying point for the Ghadr Party in North America.

With a reward on his head, Gurdit Singh traveled incognito across India for the next few years and remained in hiding. During this period he had to contend with the huge publicity by Hukumat-i-Britannia that highlighted the British perspective of the *Komagata Maru* tragedy. He surreptitiously met all the major nationalist leaders to tell the true story of the senseless massacre of innocent Indians at Budge Budge. Thereafter he remained a fugitive in India for seven years before he surrendered and served a five-year term in Mianwali prison in Punjab. On his release, the hero of the transpacific sea drama, Gurdit Singh settled in Calcutta where he published a book titled *Voyage of Komagatamaru: Or India's Slavery Abroad in English as also Zulmi Katha in Punjabi.*

Der Neue Orient

In early September 1914, in another part of the world, an express train with Har Dayal onboard puffed its way into the night-cloaked fields of Eastern Europe through Austria, Hungary, and Romania towards the seat of the Ottoman Empire. The Ottoman Turks, historically known in Western Europe as the Turkish Empire was a state that controlled much of Southeast Europe, Western Asia, and North Africa between the fourteenth and early twentieth centuries. The military theorists in Germany had known for years that in the event of war in Europe, India was the largest reservoir of manpower for the British Empire. Their immediate objective was to prevent the departure of Indian sipahis to the actual theatre of war in West Asia and Europe. German Chancellor Theobald von Bethmann – Hollweg grasped it as an appropriate time to launch anti-British activity in Europe, Asia, and North America. With the Great War keeping Britain occupied in Europe, the Deutsches Reich decided to cooperate with Europe based Indian nationalists and revolutionaries. Arthur Zimmermann, Deutsches Reich's Secretary of State for Foreign Affairs ensured that all the required logistics and financial support for the Indian plans were provided.

The Auswärtiges Amt appointed Max Freiherr von Oppenheim (1860–1946), an eminent German archeologist with an interest in India, as the head of the Nachrichtenstelle fur den Orient, (Newsagency for the East). Oppenheim actively summoned the Indian political émigrés and university students to Berlin, which had become the go-to European city, for all nationalists. Har Dayal topped the list of revolutionaries needed by Oppenheim and his young assistant Otto Gunther von Wesendonk, largely due to the kind of propaganda war he had unleashed in San Francisco with the eight pages of *Ghadr* newspaper and with the endorsement of the German consulate. Within months of its launch *Ghadr,* the demand for the newspaper had multiplied and it was being published in Gujarati, Hindi, Pashto, Bengali, English, German, French, and other languages. No other organization of Indian origin opposed to the British Empire had published so much literature to inform and motivate the masses.

Auswärtiges Amt archival records maintain that the Indian propagandist met Geissler, the Deutsches Reich's Consul-General in Geneva on September 2nd, 1914 with a plan to set up Ghadr Party operations in Constantinople. Har Dayal's well thought out strategy was to create a new front against Hukumat-i-Britannia from India's western border in Afghanistan via Persia in collaboration with the Deutsches Reich. He believed that once a military force of Ghadr patriots crossed the border from Afghanistan, the young Indian revolutionaries would undertake strikes in the rest of India and the country would rebel against the British. The newly opened Nachrichtenstelle fur den Orient agreed with the Indian revolutionary leader's grandiose plan and provided him a train ticket. He departed from Gare de Geneve-Cornavin for Constantinople on September 5th.

Almost simultaneously, a Halle University student, Dr. Abinash Bhattacharya, and Virendranath Chattopadhyaya who had moved to Berlin from Paris carefully negotiated an arrangement with Auswärtiges Amt. They formed the Deutscher Verein der Freunde Indien (The German Union of Friendly India) that later morphed into Das Indische Unabhängigkeits komitee (The Indian Independence Committee / Berlin India Committee) to co-ordinate revolutionary activity in India with money, arms and ammunition.

By then Har Dayal was on a train to the Turkish capital on Deutsches Reich's imperial passport as Ramalingamdass, a trader born in Dar es Salaam in German East Africa. The next morning as Har Dayal opened his eyes, his train had crossed the Danube and entered Turkey. The landscape, the dress of the peasants, bulls instead of horses drawing carts resembled those he had seen in India. He had heard a lot about Constantinople (Istanbul) while growing up as the Mughliyah Saltanat had a large contingent of cultivated Turkish noblemen in their courts in Delhi and their stories had endured.

As the train pulled into the Sirkeci railway station of the capital city of the Ottomans the Dilliawallah recorded his first impressions; "It is a great day in a young man's life when he first sees one of the ancient historic cities of the world, such as Rome, Athens, Benares or Constantinople. As I walked up the street leading from the railway station to the hotel in Stamboul my mind was in an ecstasy of delight and wonder. It was not what I saw, but what I thought of, that worked like magic in the brain. To a student of history, Constantinople…is a place of pilgrimage."

Har Dayal saw recognizable narrow lanes, covered bazaars, food stalls and watched Turks sitting around marble-topped tables, drinking coffee and smoking the narghile (hookah). There were countless handsome faces with the red fez cap that was also a familiar sight in Delhi. Unexpectedly he felt closer to home and even thought of staying in Turkey till the war ended. He enthusiastically decided to learn Turkish and recognized its remote similarity to Persian and Urdu. He held, "If your knowledge of foreign languages also helps you to make money, you gain a double advantage i.e. your mind and your money".

Dr. Emily Brown in her biography, writes that in Turkey, Har Dayal was the guest of His Highness Dr. Ahmed Fouad Pasha the Sultan of Egypt and Sudan. He stayed with Abu Saiyad of Delhi, who until 1912 had been employed as a teacher and sometimes as a clerk in Rangoon and had left for Egypt about the time of the outbreak of the Turko-Italian war. Abu Saiyad edited the journal *Jehan-i-Islam* that was started in Constantinople in May 1914 and contained articles in Arabic, Turkish and Hindi. Har Dayal contributed an article in Urdu and included anti-

British articles by Egyptian leaders, Farid Bey and Mansur Arifat. He observed, "This is the time that the Ghadr should be declared in India…"

In Constantinople, Har Dayal had a single point agenda; the establishment of a revolutionary and propaganda center with German funding. But conflicts soon emerged between Har Dayal and the Germans including Baron Hans von Wangenheim, the Deutsches Reich's ambassador to the Ottoman Empire and Wilhelm Wassmuss, the former Charge' d'affairs at Bushir, who with his flowing blonde mane wore Persian robes. Wangenheim needlessly made Har Dayal wait in the reception area of the Mission for hours before the meeting. In the meeting, Har Dayal got the impression that the German diplomats expected Indians from all over the world to travel to Turkey at their cost to join the planned secret Afghan mission. A divergence of views also surfaced with the Turkey-based Indians, the Kheiri brothers, Abdul Jabbar and Abdul Sattar. The brothers who hailed from a noble family of Delhi detested the Indian nationalist and set up a rival organization called Hind Ikhwat-ul-Anjuman that competed for the German patronage. Much to the irritation of the British, Kaiser Wilhelm II had been styling himself as "a special friend" to the 300 million Muslims of the world since 1898. Now false rumors were being spread that the Kaiser had converted to Islam.

Har Dayal opposed their prejudiced slant, as he did not want communal strife to enter the common cause of opposition to the British Empire. He also protested to Oppenheim against the religious nature of the German propaganda campaign in Turkey as he considered it not suitable for the Indian sipahis. Har Dayal saw himself as the undisputed head of the Indian operations in Turkey due to his stature as Secretary of the Ghadr Party. However the German diplomats, and the Auswärtiges Amt cared less about the means employed by the Indians and more about the ends.

Enthralled as Har Dayal was by his first visit to Turkey and the Bosporus after five-weeks, he was disappointed by the arrogant attitude of the German diplomats and the talks were abruptly broken. He attacked the German diplomats for being stingy, myopic and sectarian. A frustrated Wangenheim reported back to his superiors in Berlin, Oppenheim and Wesendonk, about Har Dayal's complete reversal of opinion and that he had returned the substantial funds offered to him and left.

The independent-minded Indian revolutionary was back on a train travelling to Gare de Geneve-Cornavin by the middle of October 1914 and held a new Turkish passport that identified him as 'Ismail Hakki Hassan of Basra' on his return journey. Disappointed with his trip to Turkey, in the two accusatory letters handed to Geissler on 19th and 24th October, Har Dayal claimed that he was inappropriate for their mission and that the Indians in Berlin did not require his assistance for their efforts. He concluded, "I also notice that while you and the authorities wish me to follow your plan in every particular, you do not wish to accede to my requests in any manner... I, therefore, desire to be excused from repeating the experience of Constantinople." Wangenheim, Wassmuss and their Indian associates in Turkey unable to fathom Har Dayal's wavering mind and assertiveness suspected him to be a traitor or even a spy.

The Death of a British Spy

On October 21st, 1914, the overconfident and seemingly clever Hopkinson stepped into the corridor of the provincial courthouse in Vancouver. A pair of eyes tracked the British Secret Service operative. The thirty-four-year-old Sikh peasant working in Canada, Mewa Singh (1881–1915), distressed about the *Komagata Maru* affair, wanted to teach a lesson to the double-dealing Hopkinson. In the months that followed the *Komagata Maru's* departure from Canadian waters, several Indians were murdered in British Columbia. Mewa Singh calmly walked towards Hopkinson who stood outside the witness room. He coolly pulled out a nickel-plated .32 caliber revolver to fire from point-blank range. Hopkinson fell to his knees and grabbed Mewa Singh around the thighs, only to receive another bullet in the region of his heart. Mewa Singh clubbed the British spy over the head with the revolver, held in his left hand and then transferred another snub-nosed revolver from his left hand to his right and continued to fire again and again.

James McCann, the Janitor of the courthouse, heard the shots and rushed to snatch the weapons from the hands of Mewa Singh. Three police officers MacDonald, Cewe, and Sustum, standing in a group at the bottom of the stairs leading to the second floor ran towards the assailant. Mewa Singh immediately yielded and simply stated, "I shoot... I go to station". By the time the two doctors of the Courthouse arrived Hopkinson lay dead in a pool of blood.

The slaying of the British Secret Service operative was the culmination of years of animosity between members of the Indian community on the Pacific Coast and the United States and Canadian Immigration Department. Local newspapers reported that Hopkinson was given a lavish send-off on the afternoon of October 24th, 1914, and his cortege was followed by more than two thousand people in one of the largest funeral processions ever seen in Vancouver. He was cremated at Mountain View Cemetery. The Department of the Interior at Ottawa paid for all the expenses relating to the funeral. In Britain, Crewe, the Secretary of State claimed, "I do not know of anyone who could fill the place of Hopkinson". And Wallinger wrote from London to Cleveland, "The blow delivered by the revolutionaries may be said to be both morally and materially a serious one. For the present, we shall be left without any information from America whatever, which I think is the most deplorable thing".

Mewa Singh was rushed to trial on October 29th 1914 where he refused to present a defense. He hesitantly accepted a lawyer E. M. N. Woods to represent him. Woods followed his wishes and called no witnesses and had no questions in cross-examination of the Crown witnesses. After a two-hour trial, the jury deliberated for just five minutes and Justice Aulay Morrison passed the judgment, "The sentence of the court is that you be taken to the prison whence you came and there on Monday, the eleventh day of January, 1915, you be hanged by the neck until you are dead."

Two months later, Mewa Singh became the first Indian to be hanged in Canada. After his execution on a rainy day, his body was taken in a hearse and carried to the British Columbia Electric Railway Depot where about five hundred Indians were standing to pray for the departed. Notwithstanding the heavy rain, they sang Indian hymns. Mewa Singh was hailed as a hero by the entire Indian community and was cremated with great honor. Thereafter every year in January the Indians in Canada and many parts of the world observed the anniversary of the martyrdom of this brave young man. The hall at the Ross Street Gurdwara (Sikh temple) was dedicated to his memory and he remained a symbol of struggle against the tyranny of Hukumat-i-Britannia.

The War to end all Wars

All hope for Germany's swift conclusion to the Great War ended after the Franco British victory in the First Battle of the Marne. The Russian steamroller of 400,000 men intimidated Berlin and Germans in turn threatened Paris. And on the battlefields of Europe, it was the sipahis of the British Indian army that faced the German advance at Ypres. On their arrival on September 26th, 1914 the sipahis left for Orleans within a month where they was deployed in the trenches. This was the first time that the British Indian army was deployed abroad on such a large scale and under settings very diverse from the Indian environment. In the next four years, 1,440,437 Indian sipahis served in Europe, Africa, and the Middle East. The British Indian army's sipahis were drawn from the 'martial races', a Victorian invention that in practice meant young men from Punjab, the Northwest Frontier, and Gurkhas from the Himalayas. Though the foot soldiers were Indian, all their superior officers were British. A half-hearted prewar effort at commissioning Indian as officers, the Imperial Cadet Corps, had not produced a single directly commissioned Indian officer by 1914. Even though there were no Indian commissioned officers in the army, about seven hundred Indian doctors held commissions as regimental medical officers in the hospitals and the field.

Mulk Raj Anand's WWI novel *Across the Black Waters*, is the tale of a sipahi Lalu, dispossessed from his land in Punjab, landing in Marseilles and negotiating European culture and fighting in a war he cannot understand, only to return to his village to find he has lost everything and everyone who counted.

On the night of October 27th, at Neuve Chapelle, the Indian sipahis of 9th Bhopal and 47th Sikhs arrived in time to rescue the British troops trapped by the German waves. Paul Kendall records in *The Battle of Neuve Chapelle: Britain's Forgotten Offensive of 1915*, that under the cover of darkness the Germans fired 3,000 shells containing sneezing powder called *Niespulver* towards the trenches occupied by the British troops and Indian sipahis. But the chemical weapons had little effect and next morning the Indian sipahis after a frantic hand-to-hand battle fought for each house secured the village. By the next day the 9th Bhopal infantary had lost 269 men and the ranks of the 47th Sikhs were redued to 68 men out of force of 289. A German soldier who was surrounded wept bitterly unmistakably thinking that he was to be bayoneted by the Indians. A stalwart Indian sipahi of 47th Sikh saved his life and patted him on the back saying, *"Daro mat"* (do not not be afraid).

Then on October 29th, 1914, an Ottoman naval sortie manned by German crews against the Russian ports in the Black Sea had led to the entry of the Ottoman Empire in the Great War. Russia and its allies Britain and France responded by declaring war on the Ottoman Empire and the Great War turned into a global conflict.

Maugham's 'Chandra Lal' – Har Dayal?

In early May 1914, Cleveland in Shimla had received confirmation from Wallinger's IPI in London that one of Britain's most formidable antagonist Har

Dayal had reached Lausanne from San Francisco. He was reported to be writing a book on philosophy and learning Spanish. His name had already appeared in the Delhi Conspiracy Case along with Amir Chand and Avadh Behari on October 6th, 1914. The IPI continued their surveillance activity and intercepted his mails in Switzerland.

Wallinger had hired writer Somerset Maugham, as a British Secret Service operative in Europe during the WWI. He wrote the thriller *Ashenden* shaped by his own experiences and created a character named 'Chandra Lal' who was based on a real Indian revolutionary. Describing him, the author wrote, "It appeared Chandra Lal was a dangerous agitator... was bitterly hostile to British rule in India... He was at the heart of plots to embarrass the British in India and so prevent them from transferring troops to the seat of war and with the help of immense sums given to him by German agents he was able to cause a great deal of trouble. He was concerned in two or three bomb outrages, which, though beyond killing a few innocent bystanders they did little harm, yet shook the nerves of the public and so damaged its morale. He evaded all attempts to arrest him, his activity was formidable, he was here and there, but the police could never lay hands on him, and they only learned that he had been in some city when, having done his work, he had left it. At last a high reward was offered for his arrest on a charge of murder, but he escaped the country, got to America, from there went to Sweden and eventually reached Berlin."

Maugham continued, "...has a wife in India and two children. He is not known to have anything to do with women. He neither drinks nor smokes. He is said to be honest. Considerable sums of money have passed through his hands and there has never been any question as to his not having made proper use of them. He has undoubted courage and is a hard worker. He is said to pride himself on keeping his word."

The writer added, "He is the most dangerous conspirator in or out of India. He's done more harm than all the rest of them put together. You know that there's a gang of these Indians in Berlin; well, he's the brains of it. If he could be got out of the way I could afford to ignore the others; he's the only one who has any guts....".

In conclusion, Maugham wrote, "Here he busied himself with schemes to create disaffection among the native troops that had been brought to Europe." In the story, the British writer revealed a resentful admiration for the target: "That Indian fellow must be a rather remarkable chap," he said. "He's got brains, of course... One can't help being impressed by a man who had the courage to take on almost single-handed the whole British power in India... After all, he's aiming at nothing for himself, is he? He's aiming at freedom for his country. On the face of it looks as though he were justified in his actions." Maugham's novel has a dramatic ending with Chandra Lal committing suicide by consuming poison to avoid being arrested. But who was Maugham's 'Chandra Lal' based on?

Indian revolutionary turned diplomat, A.C.N. Nambiar (1896–1986), who was a close associate of both Subhas Bose and Jawaharlal Nehru was convinced 'Chandra Lal' from Bengal was none other than his brother-in-law Virendranath. There exists evidence that a British Secret Service operative Donald Gullick tried to entice Virendranath to France to facilitate his arrest or assassination.

But on a closer examination the description of the character 'Chandra Lal' specially the mention of 'the brains', 'bomb outrages', 'his escape to America', 'evading arrest', 'idea of not letting Indian troops be transferred to Europe', 'wife and children in India', 'his integrity,' 'being a non smoker, teetotaler and the brains' accurately matches the profile of Har Dayal and not of Virendranath. Conceivably Maugham had both Har Dayal and Virendranath in mind and 'Chandra Lal' was erroneously identified only as Virendranath. Since then this has been an extraordinary persistence of error.

For or Against Germany

At the end of November 1914, Brooks had returned to the United States and was now living in Plainfield, New Jersey. He received a long letter from Har Dayal posted from the Petit Lancy area of Geneva. In the early months of the Great War and with the atmosphere bursting with nationalist fervor, the internationalist within Har Dayal felt "cramped and choked in this atmosphere." He observed, "People are for or against Germany. That is all."

In the rather emotional dispatch Har Dayal expressed his perplexity about the doctrine of progress, of the use of sacrifice for enlightening others (as distinguished from simplicity cultivated from enlightened hedonism) and the relation of the mass to the elite, the problem of the elite, the relative value of propaganda by word and the monastic policy of setting up a light. He was disheartened by the "dismal nationalism in Europe" at the beginning of the twentieth century and "the feudalism of America". The thoughtful man correctly predicted, "I don't know, but I think that the next half-century will be marked by great reaction all round. This war has been the grave of many reputations & movements."

In the dark days of the war, Har Dayal wished to remain independent and distanced from both the warring sides; the Triple Entente and the Central Powers. As an anarchist, he held to the ideological position that forbade him from being employed by the Government of any nation. Har Dayal informed his friend that he had once again begun his independent study of free thought and atheism and made the acquaintance of several professors at the Universite de Geneve. He could have easily joined as a Professor but had resolved that he would not be connected to any institution, "after the imbroglio at Stanford". He correctly judged himself as; "I am too erratic & explosive to be institutionalized, I think. It is best to remain a freelance".

A lucrative offer and invitation from Virendranath, Dr. Siddiqui, and Geissler to be part of the 'Das Indische Unabhängigkeits komitee' remained unopened on his desk in Geneva.

Though he had postponed bringing Sunder Rani and Shanti Devi to live with him, Har Dayal planned to stay in Switzerland for the remainder of the war period and intended to concentrate his energy to establish a newspaper in Switzerland on the lines of *Ghadr* in California. He had previously written to Barkatullah in San Francisco and asked him to launch a new newsletter attractively titled, *United States of India* from the Ghadr Party headquarters. He still took his role seriously as one of the organizers of the Ghadr Party and planned to return to San Francisco after the war was over. He had written to his friends in the United States, "if there is any legal trouble it will be seen to".

From his home and working place in Geneva, Har Dayal was in touch with both Madame Cama and S. R. Rana in France but the Paris India Group had completely collapsed by now. Asif Ali in his memoirs, *The Emergence of Modern India*, recollected, "Madam Cama, mother figure of the revolutionary party, invited me to Vichy where she had gone on medical advice. The widow of a wealthy solicitor, she was a woman of extraordinary courage and the center of gravity around whom Har Dayal, Virendranath and others moved. But the revolutionary party was now disintegrated and dispersed. Aiyer had gone back to India and was in Pondicherry… and Har Dayal was in America. Only Rana was her constant colleague in Paris. It was not a pleasant spectacle. Madam Cama appeared to be galloping into senility…" Yet Madame Cama and Rana remained deeply committed to the cause of India's freedom.

In the initital months of the war, the French police had searched the S. R. Rana's apartment in Paris and arrested him. The British officials wanted him to be deported to Britain as 'an undesirable foreigner'. Later Rana, Theresa Liszt, and son Ranjitsinh were expelled to the Caribbean island of Martinique as they posed a threat to the Triple Entente's war effort in France. Simultaneously, the aging Madame Cama was cautioned that her exertions to secure Rana's discharge were known and that she was doing damage both to herself and to Rana and that if she did not cease she would be arrested and interned. Even Jean Longuet, the pro-Indian journalist was denied permission to join as an interpreter to the British Indian army as it was presumed he would incite the sipahis to rebel.

Ultimately, the *Gouvernement de la République française* interned Madame Cama in Vichy for the rest of the war for distributing the *Ghadr* newspaper to the Indian sipahis arriving in France.

The Road to La Bassée

On December 20th, 1914, in the dead of European winter, Naik Mohammed Khan, a Pathan sipahi of the British Indian army belonging to 129th Baluchis was trapped in a major onslaught by the Deutsches Heer (Imperial German Army) in the Battle of La Bassée.

It was a fearful scene. The trees were grey; fields were green, the mud brown and the flames bright. There were barbed wires, craters, blasts, and unremitting gunfire. The air was filled with a peculiar sour, heavy and all-pervading smell of corpses. There were rotting bodies upon bodies and blood flowing everywhere. Naik Mohammed Khan stayed low, a belt full of ammunition around his body, the rifle bolt biting into his ribs and a tin hat for protection. His lightweight Khaki Drill uniform was of no use in the freezing battlefields in Europe. He and his fellow villagers were led to believe fighting for King George V and defending Hukumat-i-Britannia was the right thing to do. The majority of the sipahis serving in Europe were from the peasantry. The pay for a sipahi was a modest Rs. 11 a month but it was big enough for a hard-pressed Indian peasant's family with limited income. There were no British officers who could speak in Indian languages to them and the sipahis were constantly forced to repeat, *'Kabhi sukh and kabhi dukh – angrez ka naukar'* (Sometimes happiness, sometimes pain – the servant of the British). Naik Mohammed Khan had traveled in late September and early October 1914 on a smoky ship from Karachi via Bombay, landed in

Marseilles in France, detrained at Orleans and then marched off to the front to be cannon fodder and face German bullets and bombs.

And that night the disciplined German soldiers were relentless. They had trench mortars, searchlights, and hand grenades and launched intensive bouts of shelling and four hours of concentrated bombardment during darkness. The morale of the British soldiers with a grave shortage of officers was low. There were several incidents of insubordination on the frontline. Before orders could be passed some British soldiers ran away. They were caught in the cross fire or shot as deserters. The rest had no option but to retreat. But the under equipped sipahis of the 129th Baluchi held on. They suffered heavy losses yet crawled forward on their stomachs in an attempt to get close enough to find out what the enemy was up to. But there was no way forward. Eventually Naik Mohammed Khan was captured along with all his countrymen.

Satyagraha Reaches Indian Shores

Back home in India, on Saturday, January 9th, 1915, *S.S. Arabia*, a mail boat from London docked in Bombay. The man who was to change the destiny of India boarded a small launch that brought him to the seaboard near the newly built Gateway of India. Mahatma Gandhi, the forty-five-year-old prominent activist in South Africa, dressed in his Kathiawari turban and clothes, stepped on Indian soil after twenty-one years. He was neither a commander of great armies nor ruler of vast lands. He could boast no scientific inventions or artistic gifts. But in the decades to come this simply attired and humble Indian would become the spokesman for the conscience of humankind and a man who would make *ahimsa* and *satyagraha* (soul force) a formidable combination in the struggle for India's independence.

Weiter Nach Berlin

On a cold evening in January 1915, in the quiet environs of Geneva with fresh snow all around, a taxicab with a Swiss number plate came to a stop. An impressive looking man dressed for the weather holding an expensive case and an umbrella stepped out. He was Raja Mahendra Pratap Singh (1886–1979) a social reformer and a patriot from the princely family of Hathras in Aligarh district in India. He had left his home on December 20th, 1914 and had given up his property in India for establishing an educational institution. The twenty-eight-year-old bespectacled Prince planned to travel around the world to create awareness about the Indian independence movement. Considering him a threatening nationalist, after his departure from India, the Hukumat-i-Britannia put a reward on his head, attached his entire estate and declared him a fugitive. Unknown to them he was carrying with him letters from the heads of several Princely States of India who had offered their complete support to him for the removal of the British rulers from India.

On his arrival in Geneva, Mahendra Pratap met Krishna Varma at his flat on Avenue des Vollandes and sought the address of Har Dayal from him. He has detailed his meeting with Har Dayal who lived in frugal conditions in his memoirs, *My Life Story*, writing, "It was a long drive out in a taxi. He was living quite outside of the town. As we arrived he was baking some potatoes for his supper. We talked long about the war situation. One thing I remember very vividly that I told him very straight: why don't you go to Germany?"

Instead of accepting Mahendra Pratap's advice, Har Dayal introduced him to Consul-General Geissler in Geneva. Geissler had been unable to convince the grand old man of revolutionaries, Krishna Varma, to join the Berlin-based Indians. He was under pressure from Auswärtiges Amt to somehow persuade Har Dayal to visit Berlin. The German diplomats in Berlin realized Har Dayal's standing and influence among the Indian revolutionaries gathered from around Europe. He was also the only Indian revolutionary to have first-hand experience in the engine room of the revolutionary Ghadr Party. In the prewar years, he was the most skillfully articulate spokesman for India's independence and that gave Indians the confidence to rebel. But Har Dayal was persistent in not accepting the offer despite the sizeable financial inducement.

On meeting Geissler, the Indian Prince, who used the title 'Kunwar Raja' to display his royal status, demanded a one-on-one meeting with the Kaiser Wilhelm II as a precondition to working with the Deutsches Reich. But Geissler couldn't guarantee that. Then a week later Virendranath appeared in Geneva for the second time to convince both Har Dayal and Mahendra Pratap to join him in Berlin and become part of the Berlin India Committee. After being informed that Kaiser Wilhelm II would meet him in Berlin not once but multiple times, Mahendra Pratap accepted the offer. But Har Dayal was still adamant that he preferred Switzerland and handed Virendranath a critique of German policy in Turkey. From the contents of the hard-hitting letter it seemed, there was no turning back.

Then suddenly on January 27th, 1915, the unpredictable Har Dayal despite his past assertion; that he had no respect for the work being done in Berlin, was on a train traveling north from Gare de Geneve-Cornavin to Berlin Hauptbahnhof under the assumed name of Ramalingamdass. Virendranath traveled along with him as Mohamed Djafar and Mahendra Pratap held a Deutsches Reich passport with the name of Mohamed Pir to mislead the British Secret Service operatives. Har Dayal had finally agreed to relocate to Berlin at the request of Barkatullah who had already reached the German capital from the United States on a Deutsches Reich's passport.

In Berlin, Har Dayal stayed at 42, Leibnizstrasse, Charlottenburg with Virendranath and happily reunited with Mandayam Parthasarthi Tirumala Acharya (1887–1954), his old comrade from India House in London and the Paris India Group who had arrived from United States in December 1914. Even Tarak Nath Das, now a Ph.D. scholar at UC Berkeley and Panduranga Khankoje, an active worker of the Ghadr Party had reached Berlin from the United States in January 1915 to be part of the Indo-German effort to liberate India.

Berlin: Die Sinfonie Der Großstadt

Germany in the winter of 1915 was an industrial powerhouse and the third-largest exporter in the world with exports of over $ 2 billion in direct competition with the United States and Britain. Hamburg was one of the most important ports in Europe and the third largest in the world. By early 1913 the Germans had a fleet of 4,850 commercial ships selling German products around the world. They were also the first to built direct railroads to Asia with a train from Berlin to Bagdad.

The German capital Berlin craved a greater status, to be a 'Weltstadt' (a World City). It was a shining city and had tramways, underground railways, display windows, concert halls and cafes, smokestacks, Zepplin airships and masses of stone. In a time of horse carriages all over the world, Berlin's population of two million already had so many private cars on the roads that policemen had to direct the movement at intersections. Kaiser Wilhelm II had his own Daimler car. The Germans were the first people to undertake the systematic education of the children. They began the kindergarten and the technical training school at almost the same time. Prominent scientist Albert Einstein lived in Berlin as the director of the Kaiser Wilhelm Institute for Physics along with several other Nobel Prize winners. Writing in 1910, the sociologist Max Weber captured the tensions and the excitement of Berlin in what he called its "wild dance of impressions of sound and color".

Indo-German cultural ties went back a few centuries. Starting with Heinrich Roth and Friedrich von Schlegel, German scholars had studied Sanskrit literature and the systems of philosophy. *The Bhagavad Gita* was the first Sanskrit book printed around 1820 in Europe with a Latin translation done by Schlegel. Georg Forster translated Kalidasa's play *Shakuntalam* into German. Several Chairs of Sanskrit and departments of India studies were established in German Universities due to the history of deep interest in India and its culture. In the 1890s, Buddhism gathered impetus in Germany and famously, Arthur Schopenhauer declared himself a 'Buddhaist' in 1856. In the 1890s Theodor Schultz, a senior Prussian state employee, also avowed himself a Buddhist and published books such as *Der Buddhismus als Religion der Zukunft* (Buddhism as the Religion of the Future) in 1894.

Since the beginning of the Great War the German capital was dominated by war hysteria, ambition, and self-doubt. In 1914 Germany was recognized as having the most efficient army in the world. Its structure included universal mass conscription for short-term military service followed by a longer period in reserve. Within a week of war being declared, the reserves were called up and almost four million men were drafted in the Deutsches Heer. There were big sized placards in the city displaying, 'CROSS BRITANIEN ERKLARET UNS KRIEG' (Great Britain has declared war). Bands played patriotic tunes ceaselessly in the cafes.

Har Dayal would later describe his stay in Berlin in a chronicle, *Forty-four months in Germany and Turkey* (1920) as "There were all nations of the East in the streets of Berlin… who fancied that the triumph of German arms would redress the wrongs of their countries. Their common bond was hatred of England and France." The Indian revolutionary with a flair for foreign languages was rapidly communicating in fluent German.

Das Indische Unabhängigkeits Komitee

The newly formed Berlin India Committee with its office in a three-storied building at 38, WielandStrasse was provided a full embassy status. And the Indian revolutionaries were housed together in a four-storied building in the Schoneberg suburbs of Berlin.

From the beginning the erudite Har Dayal and the energetic Virendranath who buried their past differences were the most vocal Indians within the Berlin

India Committee. They were the interface with the senior officials of the Deutsches Reich. Baron von Wesendonk, the secretary in charge of the India section of the Auswärtiges Amt was in command of the Berlin India Committee. There was no real Chairman and Har Dayal, Virendranath, Barkatullah, Dr. Hafiz, Bhupendranath Dutta (the younger brother of Swamy Vivekanand), Champakraman Pillai and Dr. M. G. Prabhakar jointly carried out the day-to-day operations. But Har Dayal's importance was corroborated by the fact that he was recognized by General Erich Anton von Falkenhayn, the Minister of War as "the leader of the Indian nationalists in Europe".

According to *The World in World Wars:* Virendranath had travelled all over Europe to gather over a hundred Indians students, lascars, and apprentices living in Germany, Austria, Holland, and Switzerland and made them part of the Berlin India Committee. Dr. Wilhelm Mertens and Professor Salomon in Heidelberg played a critical role in gathering several Indians in Berlin. Oppenheim tended to refer to the Indians as *'Meine Inder'* (my Indians). Later on, Har Dayal's remarked, "There were all kinds of people in that association: sincere' but misguided patriots, unprincipled adventurers, self-indulgent parasites, scheming notoriety hunters, simple-minded students, and some victims of circumstance."

The Berlin India Committee envisioned three main missions – to import revolutionary propaganda, weapons and revolutionaries into India. The three chosen routes were overland through Khyber Pass via Constantinople and Baghdad, across the Pacific via Karachi and from San Francisco to Calcutta via Siam and Burma. The Indian revolutionaries were more than convinced that with the revolt among the Indians and the comprehensive defeat of Britain in WWI - freedom of their motherland was achievable in the next few years. Thus began the era of revolutionary romanticism for the Indian patriots.

The Half Moon Camp

The Great War that began on August 4th, 1914 was to end by Christmas that year. But Christmas came and Christmas went. After their capture, Naik Mohammed Khan along with the captured sipahis of the 129th Baluchi was initially taken to Lille and then removed to Halbmondlager (Half Moon camp), a British Indian army prisoners of war camp in the village of Zossen Wunstorf about nineteen kilometers from Berlin. Here the Deutsches Reich was holding French, Russian and Arab prisoners. The Indian prisoners were allotted a separate encampment and housed in new, clean, one-story barracks. There were Sikhs, Hindus, Muslims and even a small group of Christians. They were a curious sight. All big, slender and strong Indian men, walking at a brisk pace with curled beards and the wide turbans around the ears, their faces at the same time smiling and resolute.

It had taken just a few months for the British Empire and the Deutsches Reich to grasp the Great War's insatiatble appetite for flesh, blood and the wealth of their empires. Recruitment of sipahis in India was expanded. The Deutsches Heer Generals had informed Kaiser Wilhelm that the sipahis had fought valiantly against the Germans on the battlefields of Europe. Straightaway efforts were made to dissuade more of them from being recruited in the British Indian army in India. As recorded in Naik Mohammed Khan's debriefing report available at the National Archives of India, sometime in the winter of 1915, Har Dayal, Acharya, and Tarak Nath Das visited the Indian prisoners of war. These brave men who had fought valiantly for the Hukumat-i-Britannia were the prime targets for the Ghadr initiative.

In the midst of the Indian sipahis, the Dilliwallah was back in his form. Naik Mohammed Khan in a debriefing recalled, "Har Dayal was considered the leader of these Indians. He lectured and taunted us for sacrificing our lives for a foreign Government on a small pay and said that the English were oppressing the people of India and carrying away crores of rupees annually from there. He exhorted us to rise in rebellion and drive the British out of India. He also urged us to go to Turkey and fight on the side of the Turks against the British." Another Indian sipahi recalled in his debriefing that Har Dayal - a man of medium built, wheat complexion and about five feet and six inches in height spoke to the Sikhs, Hindu and Muslim sipahis and told them, "to make a common cause... in the interest of their motherland and unite with them to drive the British out". According to the debriefing reports of the Pathan sipahis, "Har Dayal and his party showed no religious prejudices and partook of our meals at times."

In his usual amiable and self-effacing style, Har Dayal distributed the *Ghadr* newspaper and '*Ghadr di Goonj*' book of poems, that inspired them to fight the Hukumat-i-Britannia for ending British rule in India instead of being on the wrong side of history. Iqbal's 'Tarana-e-Hindi' (*Saare Jahan Se Accha Hindustan Hamara*) had become an anthem of opposition to the Hukumat-i-Britannia and was effectively used by Har Dayal to sway the Indian prisoners of war. A Pathan sipahi recollected, "Har Dayal told us not to forget these lessons on our arrival in

India and try to ferment a big mutiny on reaching there. He said that India was quite ripe for a revolution and that we should lose no time to drive the English out of India....” The sipahis of the British Indian army received propaganda leaflets created by Har Dayal. These exhorted the sipahis to fight for India. They had simple slogans: ‘*Maro Angrez Ko! Germany ki Jai ho! Hindustan ki jai ho!*’ (Kill the British Army! Victory to Germany! Victory to Hindustan!) and ‘*apne labh ke liye tumhara khun bahana chahte hai*’ (the British are shedding your blood for their own gain).

The awe-inspiring speaker visited the camp multiple times and asked for volunteers for a military expedition to free India from Hukumat-i-Britannia. According to Naik Khan, “As a result of this preaching, Har Dayal succeeded in seducing some Pathan Sepoys of our regiment and forty Pathans who agreed to go to Turkey...” The rebelling sipahis were administered a new oath by the Deutsches Reich and given fresh German uniforms to wear before being dispatched to Turkey. Following this, Har Dayal wrote from Hamburg to Barkatullah that he had located two hundred and fifty Indian sailors who could potentially be recruited for the Indian National Volunteer Corps. Later due to Har Dayal's ingenuity almost three thousand recruits from the prisoner of war camps reached Baghdad to serve on the Mesopotamian and Persian fronts during WWI.

The Second Mutiny

As Har Dayal convinced the Indian sipahis in Germany to revolt, simultaneously his colleagues Ram Chandra and Gobind in San Francisco acted in close coordination with the Ghadr patriots around the world. Rash Behari was active in Lahore and Benaras to unite all the revolutionaries from Punjab to Bengal. Bhai Parmanand with his close association with the Ghadr Party in San Francisco converted his shop in Machhi Hatta in Lahore into the meeting point for the revolutionaries.

By October 1914 due to the consistent propaganda efforts from San Francisco, several thousand armed Ghadr patriots returned to India including Sohan Singh Bhakna, Jawala Singh, Kansi Ram, and Kesar Singh from around the world by sea. The Tosa Maru transported one hundred and seventy-three Ghadr patriots followed by Mashitm Maru that ferried sixty-three. Many other ships including Chag Sang, Nam Sanft, Yosaka Maru, Kitabi Narym Fushima Maru brought a large number of Ghadr patriots from Canada, Panama, Hong Kong, Singapore,

Thailand, and the Philippines. They now possessed all the three prerequisites for an effective Ghadr - men, money, and arms. Bomb factories were established in Punjab and imported arms from the United States reached Bengal. Plans were drawn to cut the telegraph lines and seize armories. Copies of the banned *Ghadr* newspaper and the *Ghadr di Goonj* books were reprinted in large quantities for distribution in India. Contacts were made even with Indian sipahis stationed at Shanghai, Hong Kong, Penang, Malaya, Burma and Singapore, and secret coded messages were sent about the forthcoming Ghadr. Their battle cry of the Ghadr of 1915 was to be '*Maro firangi ko*' (Kill the British soldiers). And the tricolor flag representing Ghadr Party's religious pluralism was to replace the Union Jack from one end of India to the other.

Dressed in an army outfit, Kartar Singh Sarabha working along with Vishnu Pingle entered the Mian Mir British Indian army cantonments at Lahore and Ferozepur to distribute the *Ghadr* newspaper newspaper. Kartar Singh Sarabha's favorite verse was;

"Seva Des di Jindrie badi aukhi, gallan krnian dher Sokhlian ne,
Jinhan Des –Seva vich pair paya, Ohna lakh Musibtan Jhallian ne"

(It is easy to talk big about it but serving the country is very difficult, Those who served had to bear countless hardships)

Other Ghadr patriots similarly targeted the cities of Meerut, Kanpur, Jacobabad, Jullundur, Allahabad, Benaras, Faizabad, and Lucknow. On reaching India, the courageous woman, Gulab Kaur, became an active comrade in places like Kapurthala, Hoshiarpur, and Jalandhar where she circulated the *Ghadr* newspaper. Employing the cover of a journalist and with a press pass in hand, she distributed arms and ammunition to other Ghadr patriots. Through these initiatives, tales of German invincibility and the entry of Afghanistan in the war against the British Empire reached the Indian sipahis.

In Lahore, the leader of the pack, Rash Behari notified Sunday, February 21st, 1915, as the date for the nationwide revolution to be launched by the 23rd Cavalry in the Lahore cantonment. Rash Behari donned an Army uniform as the stage was set for the replay of nothing less than the Ghadr of 1857. The single-minded focus of Rash Behari combined with the influence of the Ghadr Party resulted in the Singapore Mutiny of 1915.

Fifty-eight years since the Ghadr of 1857, on a stifling afternoon of February 15th, 1915, in the British colony of Singapore in the Straits Settlements, a British Indian army sipahi Ismail Khan fired the first shot at the Alexandra barracks as other Indian sipahis seized an Army lorry. This act signaled the start of a Ghadr Party inspired uprising in which the eight hundred Indian sipahis of the 5th Light Infantry of the British Indian army though sworn to an oath of loyalty to the British King George V, revolted against their British officers.

Four of the eight companies of the Light Infantry made up of Indian sipahis broke out of their barracks. Separating themselves into three groups, the armed Indian sipahis proceeded to kill ten British guards as they stormed the Tanglin barracks for ammunition. One group barged into the headquarters of the colorfully named Malay States Guides Mule Battery, a large volunteer unit, and killed its officer - Captain Moira Francis Maclean, a native of Colorado City, Texas. The thirty-year-old Captain Maclean became one of the first casualties of the Singapore uprising. The sipahis also tried to persuade the three hundred and nine German soldiers interned by the British to join them. The Germans who had already completed the work on an escape tunnel, confused by the sudden outbreak of violence decided to stay neutral but seventeen soldiers joined after some persuasion.

After seizing arms the rebels moved to Keppel Harbor and Pasir Panjang where they killed some civilians, while another group laid siege to the bungalow of their commanding officer, Lt. Colonel Edward Victor Martin blocking the route into Singapore town through the night. The armed sipahis then fanned out across the defenseless city of Singapore. As Singapore was commemorating the Chinese New Year most of the city was caught off guard. For an instant, the sipahis had jurisdiction of Singapore within their grasp. But despite liberating the German POW camp and instigating alarm on the island, the mutineers proved incapable of provoking other military and civilian groups to join them, subjugating the city, holding the Alexandra barracks or even escape from Singapore to freedom.

In response, the British Brigadier General Dudley Howard Ridout, the General Officer commanding in Singapore immediately imposed martial law. Marines from *H.M.S. Cadmus* were deployed along with British, Malay and Chinese Volunteer units and a small number of British regular troops. Vice-Admiral Sir Martyn Jerram also sent out a radio call for help to allied warships near Singapore.

By daylight the next day, February 16th, 1915, firangi troops had violently suppressed the uprising and successfully retaken the regimental barracks. There were sporadic and scattered skirmishes between the sipahis and the volunteers, sailors, and marines. Outnumbered, the sipahis' cause was lost. On February

17th, 1915, three allied ships arrived: the French cruiser *Montcalm*, the Russian auxiliary cruiser *Orel* and Japanese warships *Otowa* and *Tsushima*. With the added deployment, most of the sipahis were killed or wounded, prompting the rebellion to lose direction. The uprising was firmly quashed, several days later, by companies of the 1st/4th Battalion, King's Shropshire Light Infantry (Territorials) that had come from Rangoon along with French and Russian troops. Eventually, forty-seven British nationals died; thirteen of them civilians and a French citizen along with three Russians were wounded.

On March 22nd, 1915, a crowd of approximately 6,000 civilians turned up at Outram Prison. Five condemned sipahis from the 5th Light Infantry, Subedar Dunde Khan, Jemadar Chisti Khan, Havildar Rahmat Ali, Sepoy Hakim Ali, and Havildar Abdul Ghani were marched, by heavily armed guards, to posts in front of the prison wall. The hands and feet of the five sipahis were tied together. The supervising Major walked out and vociferously broadcast that all of the sipahis "have been found guilty of stirring up and joining a mutiny and are sentenced to death by being shot to death," and that "all these men of the Indian army have broken their oath as soldiers of His Majesty the King".

The firing squad of twenty-five men raised their rifles and fired multiple times. The sounds of bullets echoed in the Singapore skies as the crowd of civilians looked on in disbelief. Following this forty-two more sipahis were publically executed by a firing squad and two hundred Indian rebels faced court-martial. Executions were prolonged until April 18th as the last persisting sipahis were grabbed from their hiding places on the island. Most of the men belonged to the villages around Hissar, Rohtak, Gurgaon, and Karnal near the city of Delhi.

Some seventy-three Indians were given terms of imprisonment ranging from seven to twenty years while sixty-four Indians were given the Sazaa-e-Kalapani and transported to the dreaded Cellular Jail on the Andaman Islands. The rest were exiled for life to Africa to fight in the Cameroons and German East Africa even though fifty-one rebels escaped. Nearly a quarter of the regiment had been killed bringing to an end to the unexpected uprising within the British Indian army. The unforgiving reaction to the mutiny was meant to instill fear among both the Indian sipahis as well as the civilian population, and executions were made public primarily for this reason.

The formal inquiry held in the wake of the uprising blamed a lack of discipline and poor direction in the regiment as well as the activism of the Ghadr Party intent on fomenting trouble. A preacher called Nur Alam Shah and a coffee-shop owner named Kassim Mansur, the trailblazers of the 1915 uprising in Singapore, were exposed as prominent Ghadr patriots during the trial of the rebels. Gurdit Singh had lived in British Malaya and Singapore for some years before the beginning of the voyage of *Komagata Maru*. The fate of the ship was widely publicized in newspapers around the world as well as in Singapore and was used by the Ghadr patriots to exhort the sipahis.

The inquiry into the revolt held one man above all responsible - the regiment's commanding officer – Lt. Colonel Martin. After two decades in the British army, he was unceremoniously retired, with a tarnished reputation. The British Indian army downplayed the role of the Ghadr propaganda and underreported the British casualties. The four hundred-page inquiry report was never made public.

Back in Lahore, before the nationalists could carry out their plans for a nationwide Ghadr on February 21st, a traitor betrayed them at the eleventh hour and leaked the plan. The DCI in India and its large network of spies were suddenly cognizant of the scheme of the 23rd Cavalry in Lahore. On the eve of the proposed insurrection, the sipahis were disarmed, raids were conducted in known hideouts and arrests were made. Over the next few weeks' jails were filled with suspected Ghadr patriots. Some escaped arrest and decided to retreat to Afghanistan and live to fight another day but Kartar Singh Sarabha refused to bow out. He stayed the course and was eventually arrested by the police on March 2nd.

The main organizer Rash Behari successfully escaped the dragnet of the British Secret Service operatives and fled from India in the guise of Raja P.N.T. Tagore, a member of the famous Tagore family. He later recollected, "the idea of leaving my motherland mortally tormented me," and on the dark deck of the ship, "I wept alone bitterly". He arrived in the port city of Kobe on June 5th, 1915, via Singapore and then moved to Tokyo. In Japan, he used the code-name *'Thakur'* and continued to work for the Ghadr movement. He remained a major irritant for Hukumat-i-Britannia.

The Virulent Revolutionary Movement

After some successful arrests, officials of Cleveland's DCI were aware that as a Har Dayal inspired Ghadr Party was planning to ferment revolt in Punjab and Bengal. The Ghadr of 1857 remained a constant reminder for the DCI that even a small crisis could spread like wildfire. On March 11th, 1915, Cleveland brought out the secret document titled, *'Ghadr directory'* that detailed the activities of the revolutionary organization and the resumes of over five hundred revolutionaries based on their CID files.

In the introduction of the directory, Cleveland maintained, "I have included the names of many persons who have belonged to kindred movements and whose past history makes it probable that they are involved, especially as the Ghadr movement under the leadership of Har Dayal seems to have absorbed many of the minor revolutionary bodies that existed before his time. A map of the world showing the chief centers of the Ghadr movement, so far as known to us, is circulated along with this volume."

Cleveland further elaborated, "*Ghadr* - The name given by Har Dayal to the virulent revolutionary newspaper which commenced to issue in November 1913 from San Francisco. The articles in the paper are written with the open intention of inciting Indians to rise in rebellion in India. The paper is issued (weekly) in Urdu, Gurmukhi, and Gujarati… The name *Ghadr* is also applied to the revolutionary campaign which is being carried on by Har Dayal and his supporters who are to be found wherever Indians settle abroad. The Far East and the West Coast of America provide by far the larger number of adherents."

Furthermore the British Secret Service were aghast to discover that Ghadr support bases, plots, and propaganda operated throughout the diaspora; in cities and towns along the Pacific Coast of North America, the Caribbean, British Guiana, Honduras, Mexico, Panama, the Netherlands, Germany, Morocco, Madagascar, Southern Africa, Reunion, Turkey, Mesopotamia, Persia, Aden, Sudan, Egypt, Afghanistan, Australia, the Philippines, Japan, Hong Kong, Tien-Tsin, the Dutch East Indies, Singapore, Siam, Burma and almost everywhere that the Indian migrant laborers and the Ghadr patriots had reached. Within a year of its founding in San Francisco, the Ghadr Party had an estimated ten thousand registered members and seventy-two branches in North America alone. Accordingly, the British Indian army began systematically censoring letters received from the Pacific Coast of California and various places in Europe. Publications like *Ghadr* newspaper and *The Indian Sociologist* were immediately seized.

As multiple telegrams filled with stories of the bravery of the Indian sipahis on the western front in Europe reached the Viceregal Palace in Delhi, on March 19th, 1915, Sir Reginald Craddock, home member in the Viceroy's council introduced 'The Defense of India Act of 1915'. Pushed by Michael O'Dwyer, the Lt. Governor of Punjab, it was intended to smash the Ghadr movement. It was passed in a single sitting.

This draconian act entailed the suspension of the rule of law as a matter of emergency with sweeping powers for the Hukumat-i-Britannia to clampdown on the revolutionaries. This legislation combined with the 'The Ingress into India Ordinance, 1914' gave Hukumat-i-Britannia special powers to deal with the threat presented by the Ghadr Party. Together they were also the twentieth century's first imperial legislation against 'terror' and 'treason'.

War Against King Emperor

A sensational trial, 'Lahore Special Tribunal', concerning the intrigue for activating rebellion in India started in Lahore on April 26th, 1915. The Hukumat-i-Britannia was fearful of the nature of the trial and it was held in the central jail of Lahore itself.

O'Dwyer, who had been felicitated by the loyal Indian elite in a grand civic reception on March 6th, 1915, understood the dangerous nature and the outcome of the Ghadr. He recorded, "The Ghadr movement was by far the most serious attempt to subvert the British rule of India". He was determined to get all the suspects executed or banished to the Andamans. For the Hukumat-i-Britannia the scheme of an anti-colonial revolt that nearly toppled their rule in India had to be put down with a heavy hand. The other fearful idea of the Ghadr movement was replacing Hukumat-i-Britannia's colonial subjugation with a national democratic framework – this too had to be nipped in the bud. An example had to be made in the trial so that no Indian dared to challenge the might of Hukumat-i-Britannia ever again. Ghadr Party was to be ferociously crushed in Punjab.

In the first of the three trials (also known as Lahore Conspiracy or Ghadr Conspiracy trials) eighty-two revolutionaries of whom forty-one were Ghadr patriots, were charged with conspiracy to overthrow the Hukumat-i-Britannia under the Defense of India Act of 1915. At the trial Crown Prosecutor Charles Bevan Petman in his opening address, declared, "The aim and object of this formidable conspiracy was to wage war on his Majesty, the King-Emperor, to overthrow by force the Government as by law established in India, to expel the British and to establish Swadeshi or independent national government in the country". Petman named Har Dayal and recounted the details of the Ghadr Party's birth and its plan for a revolutionary led uprising in India. Hakumat Rai and Raghunath Sahai appeared on behalf of the Ghadr patriots but a large number refused to engage a lawyer or argue their cases.

While the Lahore Conspiracy trial was progressing in Lahore, on May 8th, 1915, Amir Chand and Awadh Behari, the heroic Dilliwallahs and the prime accused in the Hardinge bomb case were marched up to the site of 'Phansi Ghar' of the Central Jail of Delhi. Amir Chand embraced the noose willingly, then Avadh Behari with *'Bande Mataram'* on his lips put the noose around his neck himself. The two Stephanians were executed just a few yards away from the site of Captain William Hudson's massacre of the Mughal Shahzadas in Delhi in 1857. The city was stunned as the two sons of Delhi enjoyed high esteem in the social and intellectual circles.

Next, a twenty-year-old Basant Kumar Biswas and Bhai Bal Mukund were summarily hanged in the Ambala prison and Hanwant Sahai who was planning to relocate to Northern California to work for the Ghadr Party just a year back was shipped to the Andamans for Sazaa-e-Kalapani.

On May 13th, a company of sipahis from 23rd Cavalry (Frontier Force) was being shipped from Mian Mir, Lahore to Nagaon since they were suspected to be sympathizers of the Ghadr patriots. At the Harpalpore railway station, Dafedar Wadhawa Singh's luggage accidentally tumbled and a grenade hidden in it exploded. The British commanding officers immediately ordered the search of all the bags. Many more grenades were found concealed in the baggage. After intensive interrogation, secret links with Ghadr Party and a wider conspiracy for uprising was discovered. On September 3rd, 1915, after a court martial was held in Dagshai and subsequently twelve sipahis were hanged in Ambala Jail and others dispatched to the Cellular Jail in Andamans for the crime of 'mutiny'. This information was suppressed by the Hukumat-i-Britannia. Even Justice Sidney Rowlatt's Sedition committee report of 1918, observed: "The success attained was extremely small, but the seed sown must have cased some tragedies had not the plan for the concerted rising on 21st of February, been nipped in the bud."

Revenge of the Empire

As the Lahore Conspiracy trials progressed the Hukumat-i-Britannia was relieved but still fearful, for the Ghadr movement came within an ace of causing widespread uprising. Har Dayal with his extensive propaganda and activities was shockingly close to bringing down the enormous British Empire. Seventy-one references were made to his pivotal role in the Ghadr movement. He had become a significant threat to the security structure of the British Empire. And Hukumat-i-Britannia would have caputured him but failing that in a revengeful move they attempted the character assassination of their foremost opponent to destroy his credibility.

At the trial Har Dayal was described as: "This person is a well-known seditionist, a man of moderate position in life, who was awarded a scholarship by the Punjab Government in Oxford, which after enjoying until practically its close he made a show of resigning. He appears while in England to have become imbued with an extraordinarily passionate and unreasoning race-hatred and to have developed into a monomaniac, dangerous because he appears to have possessed a certain power of speech and because he thereafter devoted himself to inoculating others with the same views of intense race-hatred. He has apparently created an impression that he is a man of intelligence, but our mature opinion is that though he possesses cleverness of a kind, he is either a person of unbalanced mind devoid of intelligence or an unscrupulous scoundrel, who has no thought for the tools he employs in his campaign of race-hatred. No man of intelligence could possibly have conceived that there was any chance of success for the sordid conspiracy we have now to deal with, and we can only conceive that if he is to be credited with any intelligence at all he had not the slightest compunction in sending his dupes to certain destruction, provided only that in doing so he could cause to the Government in India some temporary annoyance and anxiety...".

The judgment placed evidence that it mainly wanted arms that prevented a large rising in December 1914. The Lahore Conspiracy trial claimed to have discovered that the seduction of students was carried out on all possible occasions, such inducements being offered as that "studies should be dropped as they taught only slavery; all who helped (the Ghadr) were to be given high office; the rising would be inaugurated by the arrival of leaders from foreign countries in aeroplanes; and the State would crown Har Dayal as King."

At the end of the three Lahore Conspiracy trials, twenty-eight revolutionaries were sentenced to death and a hundred were banished to Sazaa-e-Kalapani. The Hukumat-i-Britannia also confiscated all the properties of the convicted. Har Dayal's close associates Sohan Singh Bhakna, Jawala Singh and Bhai Parmanand were dispatched to the obscurity of Sazaa-e-Kalapani in the Andamans. Bhai Parmanand was initially slated for execution for the crime of receiving letters from Har Dayal but Hukumat-i-Britannia commuted it to life imprisonment for fear of public unrest. Dissatisfied by the decision, Bhai Parmanand declared, "Death is a beautiful thing... was I afraid of death? From my childhood, I had resolved to lay down my life at the altar of the motherland. I was blessed because the Almighty had given me an opportunity of welcoming death". Jawala Singh, known as the potato king of California, expected a death sentence and questioned the judges for awarding him a minor sentence of Sazaa-e-Kalapani.

Vishnu Pingle was arrested on March 23rd, 1915 after he had visited British Indian army cantonment at Meerut and according to the British Secret Service report, found in possession of "ten bombs of the pattern used in the attempt to assassinate Lord Hardinge in Delhi". He was charged with trying to "create disaffection" among the Indian sipahis and conspiring to overthrow British rule. He was sentenced to death. Ghadr Party treasurer Kanshi Ram who was operating from Ludhiana and Moga was arrested and hanged on March 27th, 1915.

Gulab Kaur who had worked with other Ghadr Party leaders such as Banta Singh Sanghwal and Harnam Singh Tundilat, suffered two years imprisonment on charges of sedition in Lahore Shahi Qila, where she underwent serious abuse and torture. Her participation in a worldwide anti-colonial movement dispelled British stereotypes about women of India being subservient, frail or submissive. Though she risked her life to kick the British out of India, Gulab Kaur remains a forgotten figure of the Indian freedom movement.

Hukumat-i-Britannia was satisfied and O'Dwyer was later able to record: "By August 1915, that is within nine months of the first outbreak, we had crushed the Ghadr rebellion. Nearly all the leaders and many of their most active adherents were in our hands awaiting trial or were brought to justice later, internal order was restored…".

Now nothing could come in the way of Hukumat-i-Britannia's large-scale mobilization of the extra manpower in the form of Indian sipahis to be shipped to the European battlefields. Though the Ghadr of 1915 ended in a disaster in India and the actual combat was brief in the Singapore uprising – it nevertheless set a precedent that would lead to the termination of the British Empire. For the revolutionaries of India, the Singapore uprising was perceived as a sequel to the Ghadr of 1857 and an important milestone in India's independence movement. Some twenty-six years from this date, Singapore would again be the location for another war for independence led by Subhas Chandra Bose.

12

THE ANTI GERMAN ORIENTAL IN BERLIN

"I was telling you about Dar Hyal... He's a revolutionist of sorts. He's dabbled in our universities, studied in France, Italy, Switzerland, is a political refugee from India and he has hitched his wagon to two stars: one, a new synthetic system of philosophy; the other, rebellion against the tyranny of British rule in India. He advocates individual terrorism and direct mass action. That's why his paper Kadar or Badar or something like that was suppressed here in California and why he narrowly escaped being deported; and that why he's up here just now devoting himself to formulating his philosophy..."

Jack London
Author

On June 29th, 1915, United States Customs officials at Hoquiam, Grays Harbor on the Pacific Coast, north of Astoria impounded the three-masted 326-ton chartered schooner, *Annie Larsen*. After boarding the ship it was discovered that it had departed from San Diego on March 8th, 1915 and its secret cargo held 4,500 Springfield rifles, 10,000 bayonets, several cases of revolvers, and 4,750,000 rounds of ammunition. The rifles had been purchased at an auction of the United States government. The mystery cargo was consigned to Juan Bernardo Bowen at Topolobampo, Mexico. The freight bill of $11,783.74 was prepaid by a check on the Guaranty Trust Company, signed by a German named Hans Tauscher. Though the vessel commanded by Captain P. H. Schulter was cleared from San Diego for Mexico the customs officials in Seattle wondered why was the ship wandering near Washington State and so far out of her course. Believing it to be another gun smuggling operation for the Mexican revolution, the Customs officials arrested the shipmates for carrying arms and ammunition in violation of United States neutrality laws. But the British Secret Service monitoring all the unusual activity on the Pacific Coast from the Consulate in San Francisco had watched the *Annie Larsen* ever since it departed from San Deigo with its suspicious cargo. They were apprehensive that the ship had a German - Ghadr connection and launched an incisive investigation.

The book *Fighting Germany's Spies* by French Strother published in 1918, revealed the entire plot. This was a German and Irish collaboration in close partnership with Ram Chandra and the Ghadr Party and the Berlin India Committee. Consul-General Bopp had employed a former German Naval officer, Fred Jebsen to charter the schooner *Annie Larsen* from Olsen and Mahoney in San Francisco and also to buy a larger steamship *Maverick*. German Embassy's Military Attache Franz von Papen in a roundabout manner along with Irish republican Joseph McGarrity had funded the arms found on *Annie Larsen*. These guns were shipped through an Irish-American shipping company to Galveston, Texas, and then by rail to San Diego to be loaded on to the *Annie Larsen* bound for Indian revolutionaries. The cargo was to be transferred on to the old Standard Oil tanker *Maverick* at a designated point on the high seas near Socorro Island three hundred and fifty miles off Mexico. The final destination of the *Maverick* was the port of Karachi, in India where small friendly fishing crafts would receive the secret cargo. The arms were directed to support the Indian revolutionaries involved in the second mutiny in Lahore and Delhi in February 1915.

Maverick commanded by Captain H. C. Nelson with American adventurer J. B. Starr-Hunt, had left San Pedro in California on April 23rd 1915, with stores sufficient to last for six months at sea and practically no cargo. A British curiser, *H.M.S. Newcastle* shadowed the ship upto the Socorro Island causing a delay in its plans. By the time *Maverick* arrived, *Annie Larsen* after waiting for forty-five days at the rendezvous point and running short of water had already left without offloading its precious cargo. It was forced to pull in at Hoquiam.

At Socorro Island, *Maverick* vainly tried to connect with the *Annie Larsen* and lingered on hopelessly to transfer the secret shipment. But *Annie Larsen* was nowhere to be seen. On Thursday, May 13th, as the *Maverick* lurked neared Socorro Island, unexpectedly the British cruiser, *H.M.S. Kent* appeared next to it. The Royal British Navy were extra cautious in the wake of German U-boat sinking *R.M.S. Lustitania* on May 7th 1915 off Ireland leading to the death of 1198 passengers and crew. Fresh from a successful mission at Falkland Islands the cruiser was on its way to China when it spotted the *Maverick*. Two British officials from *H.M.S. Kent* entered the ship and after inspecting the papers requested for an inspection by the British marines. Earlier Ghadr patriot Mangu Ram Muggowal had volunteered for the mission on the *Maverick* and boarded the ship at San Pedro with four Indians holding fake Persian names and passports. Accompanied baggage included Ghadr literarture for distribution. On seeing the British officials, one of the Ghadr patriots who had assumed the name, Jehangir, informed Captain Nelson that the two sacks and six suitcases full of Ghadr literature were on the ship and had to be concealed from the British marines. The Captain wanted to burn the entire lot but Jehangir did not like the idea of destroying the literature and proposed that it should be noiselessly taken ashore and hidden there, pending the departure of the *H.M.S. Kent*. Overruling Jehangir, Captain Nelson ordered that the entire lot of literature stored in the six suitcases and two sacks be immediately burnt in the boiler room. Jehangir did manage to save a few copies for future reproduction. The next day the British officials returned with marines of *H.M.S. Kent*. Starr-Hunt later reported, "They made a thorough search of the vessel this time and returned to their ship. (Captain) Nelson returned the call. On his return Nelson told me that the *Kent's* commander had questioned him rather closely as to what the *Maverick* was doing there and that in reply he had told him that he could not disclose his real purpose but in a roundabout sort of way hinted that she was there in connection with the Mexican troubles."

After the *H.M.S. Kent* has vanished into the Pacific and as the planned rendezvous with *Annie Larsen* did not happen on May 26th the *Maverick* left without its cargo. It managed to reach Hawaii on June 14th. By then all British and Australian fleets were alerted by the British Secret Service to be on the lookout for ships carring warriors and weapons to India. With fresh instructions the *Maverick* was supposed to take the non-existing arms consignment first to the neutral Dutch East Indies and then to India. During the journey, Jehangir, (real name Hari Singh) in a conversation with Starr-Hunt, spoke about the mission of the Ghadr Party. Starr-Hunt recollected, "He was evidently an exile, for he said that 'during the many years of his exile from India' he had at various times written a good deal against the British rule in India. He gave me to understand that formerly he belonged to the (British) Indian army. He said his home was in the far interior of the country inhabited by ignorant classes, and that if he could only succeed in getting to them, he would easily incite them to revolt against the British Government by promising to provide them with arms and ammunition."

After a three-week journey the ship finally reached South East Asia on July 20th with the five Ghadr patriots but no guns. Here the crew gradually split up. *Maverick* was eventually seized in Batavia, Dutch East Indies. The Ghadr

Party abandoned the mission as a lost cause. Auswärtiges Amt suffered a loss of over $300,000 in this failed mission.

Another shipment of 7,300 Springfield rifles and 1,930 pistols along with million rounds of ammunition was to be shipped on the Holland America steamer *Djember* by the Germans. In addition the German Consul at Shanghai purchased five thousand revolvers for the Indian revolutionaries and a schooner *S.S. Henry S* was cleared from Manila with two German Americans, Albert Wehde and George Paul Boehm, on board.

In April 1915, the Indian revolutionary Narendra Nath Bhattacharya (1887–1954), popularly known as Manabendra Nath Roy, arrived in Batavia as an agent of Harry and Sons, under the assumed name of Charles Martin to take delivery of the arms. The shipment would then be transported to Siam and hidden inside hollow teak logs that were towed routinely upriver without suspicion for initiating a revolution. On September 9th, 1915, M. N. Roy was in Batavia for the second time, when the Imperial Police surrounded his compatriat Indian revolutionary 'Bagha' Jatin Mukherjee (1879–1915) along with a party of five Ghadr patriots in India. 'Bagha' Jatin was to be the recipient of the weapons being transported from San Francisco. An unequal battle that lasted seventy-five minutes began. The revolutionaries armed only with pistols fought against an overwhelming number of riflemen. In the end, 'Bagha' Jatin made the supreme sacrifice and faced a heroic death.

Meanwhile the *Djember* mission did go as planned and in his memoirs M. N. Roy, recorded; "The plan was to use German ships interned in a port at the northern tip of Sumatra, to storm the Andaman Island and free and arm the prisoners there, and land the army of liberation on the Indian coast. The ships were armored, as many big German vessels were, ready for wartime use. They also carried several guns each. The crew was composed of naval ratings. They had to escape from the internment camp, seize the ships, and sail... Several hundred rifles and other small arms with an adequate supply of ammunition could be acquired through Chinese smugglers who would get then onboard the ships... At the last minute, money for the conduct of the operation failed to materialize..." After M. N. Roy's attempts to secure arms ended in a failure, he did not return to India and eventually landed in San Francisco on June 15th, 1916. Here he befriended Har Dayal's supporters, David Starr Jordan and Professor Arthur Pope from whom he learnt about the revolutionary activities of the Indian intellectual.

A few months later, on Saturday, December 4th, 1915, after an investigation covering the entire country, United States Secret Service men entered the apartment of Military Attaché Wilhelm von Brincken at the Palace Hotel in San Francisco. The German diplomat could not be arrested as he was attached to the consulate and was just served with a subpoena. Suspected of bombings in Seattle and Canada, the justice department of the United States had targeted, the German consulate and identified Vice-Consul Eckart von Schack and Irish agents Charles Crowley and Margaret Cornell. Even Consul-General Franz Bopp who was in Germany when the war broke out was prosecuted on his return even though he was overseas at that time the ships were making their journey. It was later discovered that German intelligence agents in league with Irish activists and suspected Ghadr Party plotters with operational leadership provided by Har Dayal had engineered the *Annie Larsen* and *Maverick* mission from Berlin and San Francisco. But no Indians were arrested due to lack of evidence.

Later Ambassador Bernstorff in his book *My Three Years in America* remarked, "Besides, even if it be admitted that the schooner in question was actually sent by the Indian Nationalists with her cargo of arms, it is absurd to regard the dispatch of this small supply of war material as a crime, and gloss over the fact that whole arsenals and ammunition columns were being shipped every day to France!"

The Bravest of the Brave

In India, on a mid-November morning in 1915, Kartar Singh Sarabha stood alone in the visitor's room as his grandfather Badan Singh, who had raised him due to the early death of his father, came to meet him for the last time. The Hukumat-i-Britannia had pronounced him, "the most dangerous of all rebels", and sentenced him to death.

On seeing the nineteen-year-old young man about to be hanged, his grandfather began to weep like a baby. "Kartar Singh," he cried, "We are not even sure that the country will benefit from your death…" Kartar Singh Sarabha calmly consoled his grandfather and assured him that he had accepted his fate as he was being hanged for the crime of working for the liberation of thirty crore (three hundred million) suppressed and enslaved people.

On November 16th, 1915, Kartar Singh Sarabha sang a poem he had composed as he was led to the gallows, "O Mother India, If my head is offered, My life is sacrificed, In your service, Then, I would understand, Even in my death, I will attain, A life of eternity."

In their martyrdom, Kartar Singh Sarabha and the Ghadr patriots inspired the next generation of young Indians who were determined to wage war to death against the might of the Hukumat-i-Britannia and create the utopia in India that Har Dayal and Ghadr Party had promised.

Berkeley-Berlin-Baghdad-Bengal Axis

On December 1ˢᵗ, 1915, the first Provisional Government of India – 'Hukumat-i-Moktar-i-Hind' in exile was announced in a room in the palace of Bagh-e-Babar, the last resting-place of the first Mughal Shehenshah Babur located on the slopes of Kuh-e-Sher Darwaza, southwest of the city of Kabul. Mahendra Pratap was declared as the head and Barkatullah as the Prime Minister of the Provisional Government. An army of Indian prisoners of war called the Revolutionary Voluntary Corps was planned with military expeditions into India through Afghanistan via Turkey. At the instance of the Berlin India Committee, the German mission in Kabul was activated to contact Afghan tribal elders and support the smuggling of weapons into India. The delegation also hoped to involve the Russians in their endeavor. The great game was afoot.

Months before in March 1915, Kaiser Wilhelm II had given an audience to the Berlin India Committee delegation led by Mahendra Pratap and Har Dayal at the Imperial Palace in the Tier-Garten. The Indian Prince was conferred with 'the Order of the Red Eagle (Second Class) at the special banquet. Mahendra Pratap reminisced in his memoirs, "Kaiser hailed me up once again and said, 'Don't forget to give my greetings to the Amir of Afghanistan…" Cousins or no cousins, the Kaiser Wilhelm II hated the British. They weakened his stature. He too dreamt of leading millions of Indian sipahis and Turkish troops through Persia to Afghanistan towards India. The Deutsches Reich would then enter India wounding the British Empire where it hurt the most while hitting Russia at the same time.

The thirty-year-old Har Dayal operating from Berlin and Constantinople was confident of accomplishing his fantastic vision of the Indian sipahis with the help of Germans crossing Khyber Pass at the North-Western border into India and the whole nation rising in revolt. Decades later in *The Tribune* (August 16ᵗʰ, 2003), Khushwant Singh observed, "What made his (Har Dayal) reputation impregnable was the fact that he was also a revolutionary who spurned government patronage, directed the Ghadr Movement in its early years in the United States and Canada, became the principal advisor of the German Government's attempt to foment a revolt against the British Raj during World War I..."

On April 10th, 1915, Mahendra Pratap accompanied by Barkatullah had boarded a train from Berlin Hauptbahnhof to travel to Constantinople via Vienna and Budapest on a transcontinental secret assignment. Along with them were a posse of Indian sipahis and two young German officers, Oskar Ritter von Niedermayer, Werner Otto von Hentig, a German diplomat Dr. von Hentig plus some German soldiers. Their objective was to convince Amir Habibullah Khan (1872–1919) of Afghanistan to enter into a treaty with the Deutsches Reich and Turks in waging a war with the British Indian army on the North-Western frontier of India.

Har Dayal with a new German passport in the name of Professor Mirza Osman coordinated the mission from the Berlin India Committee's new outpost in Constantinople - 'Bureau du Parti National Hindou'. Initially, he was to lead the Afghan mission but he declined to make the arduous trip to Kabul on account of his health. He furthermore felt the exiled aristocratic Mahendra Pratap would be more appropriate due to his princely status, patriotic zeal and philanthropic nature in dealing with the Afghan royalty. The Indian Prince claimed to have the support of various Indian princely states that were willing to revolt against Hukumat-i-Britannia.

The Afghan mission exhibited remarkable courage and resolve in crossing one of the most pitiless deserts in Central Asia. Undaunted by the shortage of water and danger of ambush by dacoits while crossing the Dasht-e Kavir salt desert in Persia they were received as state guests in Kabul. The team reached Kabul on October 2nd, 1915. But by December 1915, despite heading the first Provisional Government of India, Mahendra Pratap and Barkatullah were unsuccessful in influencing the wily Amir Habibullah Khan. He remained non-committal to any treaty with Deutsches Reich after numerous meetings. Resentful towards the British Empire, the Amir accepted their bribes and gifts to supplement the subsidies from Hukumat-i-Britannia but made no promises.

Under the banner of Ghadr Party, masterminded in Berlin and unleashed from Constantinople, Har Dayal's idea came to naught. Much to his disappointment, the plan to reduce the British India army's forces in Europe by waging war on the North-West Frontier of India failed. The idea of recruiting Indian prisoners of war for the operation was scrapped. The Indian sipahis instead became research subjects for German anthropologists, linguists, and musicologists who recorded their words and songs for the Royal Prussian Phonographic Commission's museum of voices from around the world. The Provisional Government in exile served only propaganda purpose and Mahendra Pratap was eventually requested by the Berlin India Committee to return to Berlin from Kabul.

A Breakdown in Berlin

After spending almost a year in Berlin the visionary Berkeley-Berlin-Baghdad-Bengal axis created by the efforts of Har Dayal had not brought any significant results. The grand Afghan mission as well as the clandestine shipment of arms from the United States to India initiated by Har Dayal had misfired.

In Turkey, the Auswärtiges Amt rejected Har Dayal's proposal for taking over as the editor of the *Jehan-i-Islam*. Perceiving it to be motivated by religious and sectarian ideology he strongly objected to the discrimination. He complained against the communal strife caused by the Auswärtiges Amt in Turkey by choosing the editorship of the Jehan-i-Islam based on religion rather than merit. But his protest fell ON deaf ears.

Then as he had always done in challenging situations in the past, an extremely disappointed Har Dayal without any notice or justification left Constantinople. In his hastily written account, (*Forty-four months…*), he captured his state, "The Bosphorus, perhaps the most beautiful spot on earth, was a haven of calm and peace in the midst of this warring world of brute force and more brutish intrigue. But it was my business to watch the operation of political forces and to meet all types of characters in the course of the daily routine, for I was supposed to carry on political propaganda. I should have liked to live on the Bosphorus as a poet or a painter, but as I was neither the one nor the other; I had to make the best of the situation and figure as - a politician."

Abruptly, without the knowledge of the Berlin India Committee or the Auswärtiges Amt, Har Dayal once again using the pseudonym 'Israel Aronson,' risked travelling to Netherlands to connect with his comrades in the Anarchist movement. From the seaside resort of Scheveningen, on October 24th, 1915, the desperate revolutionary wrote two letters to Alexander Berkman at his New York address, Another Earth Office West 125th Street, near Sixth Avenue, proposing that the latter find him "some real fighters, IWWs or anarchists." From there he traveled east via Berlin and reached Damascus. Here he distributed seditious literature in Arabic and Persian among the Indian sipahis and explored the possibility of opening another Ghadr center there.

On his return to Berlin at the end of 1915, he still got access to the powerful diplomats of the Auswärtiges Amt yet his views were discarded. He realized that Virendranath was now the undisputed livewire within the Berlin India Committee and his role was marginalized. His fresh ideas and proposals strangely met with negative responses. There was a whisper campaign against him in the corridors of power. There was also a huge trust deficit between him and the other Indian revolutionaries who perceived him to be an intellectual bully, egotistical, unhinged and a loner. Commenting on the atmosphere later, Har Dayal himself chronicled in his book, (*Forty-four months...*), "With regard to the Indian Nationalists in Berlin, I observed that the greater part of their time and energy was spent in quarreling among themselves and telling lies against one another. They had not much work, and idle hands always find mischief to do. Some of the leading members came from words to blows on one occasion, and each party averred that the other had commenced the attack. Such a combination of pugilistic and patriotic activity caused quite a scandal in Berlin... These gentlemen were supposed to be members of an association, or Gesellschaft; but they could never work together harmoniously."

M. N. Roy who was now in New York observed in the memoirs, "Before long he (Har Dayal) clashed with Chattopadhyaya who backed by the Germans bossed the show". In the book, *Life and Myself - Dawn approaching the noon*, by Harindranath Chattopadhyaya, his brother Virendranath described Har Dayal as "a veritable genius during the first half of every hour and a pretty polly prating nonsense, as dull as ditch-water creature during the second half. When he was inspired Har Dayal was a phenomenon of intellectual sparkle and crystalline vision... but gradually even the brilliant first half brain began to wear out and become ordinary. This slowly led his footsteps away from revolution to reaction, which the whole group of his contemporaries resented."

The atmosphere in Berlin was stifling for the independently minded Har Dayal. With complete non-cooperation by the Berlin India Committee members and the negative attitude of the Auswärtiges Amt, Har Dayal, who was not a team player, increasingly began to feel that he had overstayed his welcome in Germany. He was unusually critical of Germany since the loss of *Weltgeist* (world spirit) in the wake of *Weltreich* (world empire) and *Weltmacht* (world power). Besides questioning German intentions he announced that he now looked forward to working independently as the freelance Secretary-General of the Ghadr Party.

Not a free agent

In early 1916, WWI was evenly poised. The German's attack on Verdun in North-Eastern France was underway and a million troops led by Prince Wilhelm, eldest son of Kaiser Wilhelm II faced two hundred thousand French defenders. The longest battle of WWI had begun.

At the beginning of February 1916, the Auswärtiges Amt became impatient with the much ado about nothing at the Berlin India Committee. Concerned about Har Dayal's arrogant assertions and lack of commitment he was now suspected to be a mole. Consequently, the Auswärtiges Amt informally dismissed Har Dayal from the Berlin India Committee. His German passport in the name of Professor Mirza Osman was withdrawn and his movements were limited to just Germany. He was unable to correspond with his family in India and friends around the world.

In his book, (*Forty-four months...*), he recollected, "During the winter of 1915–16 I twice asked the responsible German official for a passport for the journey to Switzerland, politely adding that I wished to return to Switzerland for the benefit of my health." He was emphatically told that he would not be allowed to leave Germany. He added, "I found myself in a very dangerous position, as I was evidently regarded as an 'anti-German' Oriental. In the summer of 1916, even my local correspondence was intercepted by the Berlin police. I was, of course, very anxious about the future, as these German bureaucrats might treat me as an enemy, and I was completely in their power...." He added, "During three years, from February 1916 to February 1919, I was compelled to resort to falsehood and dissimulation in self-defense', and I look back upon that time as a period of utter degradation. But I was not a free agent."

Describing those dreadful days, he recalled, "As I was detained in Germany for nearly one and a half years, and could not go to a neutral country, my health suffered very much on account of the scarcity of food in Germany.... The German Government inflicted all this loss of time and health on me by keeping me against my will in Germany after the winter of 1915–16." Writing about the activities of the Berlin India Committee, Jawaharlal Nehru confirmed in his *Autobiography,* "Har Dayal who had come over from America had long been discarded. He did not fit in with the committee at all and both the committee and the German Government considered him unreliable and quietly pushed him aside." Much later on, Har Dayal wrote off the Berlin India Committee and remarked that these were "the foolish intrigues of unprincipled adventurers."

In that stress-filled period, a nearly starving Har Dayal discovered he was afflicted with a nervous ailment in his eyes. Unable to travel outside Germany, he sought sanctuary in various Spas in Wiesbaden and Garmisch-Partenkirchen in Bavaria in the interest of his deteriorating health.

Human society prizes intelligence. A genius like Har Dayal was from childhood onwards viewed with awe and it was assumed that he would be guaranteed prosperity and success. He had a rage to master everything that came his way – languages, economics, history, philosophy, spirituality, poetry, politics, writing, lecturing, and numerous other fields. He was aware of his strengths and flaws. He consciously chose a lifetime of sacrifice and rebellion to live a life with a difference and to make a difference. He succeeded in the launch of the Ghadr Party in the United States and his mind had powered an international anti-colonial consciousness that fearlessly challenged the British Empire across the planet. That was the high point of his revolutionary life. In several parts of the world, he was admired for his special abilities but in Germany, during WWI his life and abilities were constrained. The next few years were to be the lowest period for Har Dayal and his genius was more like a curse than a blessing at that moment.

Har Dayal's decade of revolutionary endeavor that started in 1906 concluded ten years later by early 1916. Distant from all kinds of anarchist and rebellious occupations he was poised to move into the next phase of his life as a prolific author, keen academic and erudite lecturer. He spent many solitary months reading, and writing at the Deutsches Orient Institute in Berlin. As weeks turned into months for Har Dayal in Germany, on November 22nd, 1916, his friend Jack London, the author, suddenly died at his Glen Ellen ranch north of San Francisco. In his last novel, *The Little Lady of the Big House*, published in April 1916, Jack London eternalized the Indian intellectual as a character named, 'Dar Hyal'. In the novel, the writer correctly predicted the future of 'Dar Hyal' who barely escapes deportation and hides out at a camp in the forest with a group of social outsiders who spend their time understanding and discussing philosophies of the world.

His Majesty's Secret Service in California

On July 30th, 1916, in New Jersey, sixty-nine railroad freight cars were storing more than a thousand tons of ammunition on the Johnson Barge No. 17. They awaited shipment to Britain and France. Despite the United States's claim of neutrality, it was no secret that it was hawking massive quantities of munitions to the British army. Just after two in the morning, a massive explosion lit the skies, the equivalent of an earthquake measuring up to 5.5 on the Richter scale. Nearly everyone in Manhattan and Jersey City was jolted awake and several were thrown from their beds. Even the heaviest plate-glass windows as far as Lower Manhattan and Brooklyn were shattered. The falling shards of glass preceded a mist of ash from the fire that followed the explosion. Immigrants on nearby Ellis Island had to be evacuated. Some historians regard the explosion at the ammunition dump at the Black Tom Island as the first major terror attack on the United States by a foreign power. It was rumored to be an Indo-German-Irish conspiracy but no Ghadr Party involvement could be established. The explosion in New York was enough to alert the vigilant British Secret Service and they were determined to shut down the Indo-German-Irish network on the West Coast. There was no greater threat to the British Empire than the Ghadr patriots inducing Indians to revolt and smuggling them weapons. Now the synergetic relationship and the three-way alliance between the Germans, Indians, and Irish had to be destroyed.

Alarmed by the events in India, Singapore, Japan, Germany, Canada and the United States the top talent from the Indian Civil Service, Imperial Police and Military was drafted to defeat Ghadr Party's vision and mission statement. The recently formed British Secret Intelligence Service created special sections MI5 (g) and MI5 (d) to operate counter-espionage networks. At IPI in London, Wallinger was provided with an assistant, Philip Crawford Vickery (1890–1987), an Assistant Superintendent of Police of Punjab who had joined the Imperial Police in 1909. His duty at the IPI was to watch anti-British conspiracies in Britain and Europe, so far as they affect Indian interests and Indian conspirators attempting to attack the Hukumat-i-Britannia.

British Consulate San Francisco served as a forward base for British Secret Service's cloak-and-dagger operations. Cambridge graduate Robert Nathan, (1868–1921) a retired ICS officer and former Commissioner of Police of Dacca known for successfully fighting sedition, was dispatched to New York in February 1916 as Hukumat-i-Britannia's representative to work in close coordination with Counsel-General Ross in San Francisco. He took control of all of Ross's informers among the Indian students. Two of the best police officials of Hukumat-i-Britannia, George Denham who had worked with Petrie on the Lord Hardinge bomb case and Alexander Marr, a military intelligence officer who once served with Indian Police in Bengal CID, were posted in North America to assist Nathan.

In United States, Nathan reported to William Wiseman, the adventurous Cambridge man with strong family connections who was recruited to run the British Secret Service operations in North America from October 1915 onwards. He covertly worked in the Transport Department of the British Ministry of Mutions. His assistant was the well-networked war hero Captain Norman Graham Thwaites of the Royal Army Service Corps who had served as private secretary to newspaper publisher Joseph Pulitzer.

Between 1915–1917, more than two hundred British Secret Service agents, informers, and recruits were operating in the United States. Besides keeping the Ghadr patriots in check, they also kept a close watch on the sympathy for India's independence in America among the Jewish and the Irish community. Private detectives were hired to track the champions of Ghadr Party and a small group of faculty members of UC Berkeley that included Thomas Harrison Reed, Fritz Konrad Krueger, Arthur Ryder and most prominently, Arthur Pope. Other prominent Americans who supported the Ghadr cause and independence of India were suffragist Sara Bard Field, political commentator Walter Lippman, President of Stanford, David Starr Jordan, publisher Fremont Older, journalist John D. Barry, and Lemuel Parton the editor.

Soon Nathan code-named Charles Lamb infiltrated the Ghadr Party network and reported on meetings between Ram Chandra, Larry de Lacey, the Irish Republican leader and German diplomat von Brincken along with his assistant Charles Latendorff. British cryptanalysts had broken the secret dictionary of codes used in communications between the Indians and the Germans. With the help of decoded intercepted communications between the Ghadr patriots and the Auswärtiges Amt, British Secret Service successfully penetrated the Das Indische Unabhängigkeits komitee in Berlin and the Ghadr Party in the United States. They checkmated all the future plans of sending arms and ammunition to India for a revolution and of engineering rebellions in the British colonies in the Middle East and South East Asia. Through the British spy network, they also raised valuable sources of information and scuttled the imminent plans of the Ghadr patriots.

Aware of the shenanigans of the British Secret Service, a shrewd Ram Chandra had earlier invited his acquaintance, Vaishno Das Bagai from Peshawar to support him in San Francisco. Bagai arrived in San Francisco on September 6th, 1915 with his wife Kala and their three young sons, Brij, Madan, and Ram. Kala Bagai was one of the very few South Asian women in the entire country. Her arrival as the "first Hindu woman to enter the city in ten years" was reported in the *San Francisco Call*. On arrival in the United States, Bagai immersed himself in the Ghadr Party counter-intelligence operations and smartly fed misinformation to the British spies.

Arresting the Ghadr

On the morning of Saturday, April 7th, 1917, Gobind Behari Lal attended to the furious knocking on the main door of his dormitory. On opening the door, to his shock, he discovered a group of Federal Marshals and detectives from the San Francisco Police Department on his doorstep with a warrant to arrest him and several other Ghadr patriots. The policemen also stormed the Ghadr Party offices on Wood Street, Hill Street and Valencia Street and arrested sixteen Indians that day.

Just the day before on April 6th, 1917, the United States had joined its allies Britain, France, and Russia to fight against Germany in WWI. Earlier on January 16th, 1917, British Secret Service code breakers in London known as "Room 40" intercepted the notorious encrypted telegram from Foreign Secretary Zimmermann, intended for Heinrich von Eckardt, the German ambassador to Mexico. The secret communiqué informed the ambassador that the Deutsches Reich would provide military and financial support for a Mexican attack on the United States, and in a give-and-take deal, Mexico could annex "lost territory in Texas, New Mexico and Arizona." In addition, Von Eckardt was told to contact Mexico's president with an offer to forge a wartime alliance and to persuade the Japanese to join the Germans in WWI.

In early March the discovery of a large store of German bought rifles, swords, revolvers and cannon parts in a Houston Street warehouse in Manhattan led leading American newspapers on March 10th, 1917, to report on the front pages the unearthing of a "Worldwide German plot to instigate rebellions and uprisings against British rule in India." Simultaneously the senior diplomatic staff of the German Consulate in San Francisco was arrested. Among those accused in the conspiracy was the New York based Chandrakant Chakarvarty along with his German confidante Ernest Sekunna. In February 1916, Heramba Lal Gupta had relocated to Tokyo and Chakarvarty had replaced him as the Berlin India Committee coordinator in United States. Chakravarty who was arrested from his home at 384 East 120st street in New York by Captain Thomas Tunney, head of the top secret Bomb Squad of the New York Police Department, told American newspapers that he would like to see Britain out of India.

The Zimmerman cipher and evidence of German support to Indian agitation coupled with the German U Boat attacks forced President Wilson's hand. On April 2, 1917, the United States abandoned its policy of neutrality and asked Congress to declare war against Germany and the Central Powers. At this time the anti-German hysteria had spread all over the United States and any Ghadr Party propaganda against the British Empire was viewed as a front for Germany. The Ghadr patriots almost overnight lost American approval.

Charles Warren, the Assistant Attorney General (later a Pulitzer Prize winner) sent a telegram to John White Preston (1877–1958), the United States Attorney for the Northern District of California commanding him to straightaway take into custody the Indians workers of the Ghadr Party. Included in this secret telegram were special orders for the arrest of Gobind Behari Lal. He was charged with violation of the Neutrality Act, indicating that he had allegedly participated in a "conspiracy to set afoot a military expedition against an ally of the United States." Along with Gobind, the right-hand man of Har Dayal, thirty-four suspected Indians were overnight taken into custody in New York, Chicago, and San Francisco. Bhai Bhagwan Singh, considered by most Ghadr patriots as second in command, was arrested on April 18th, 1917 while trying to cross the border into Mexico at Naco, Arizona.

Lenin brings Revolution to Russia

On April 16th, 1917, after seventeen years in exile, Communist revolutionary Vladimir Lenin joined by twenty-nine other Russian exiles, a Pole and a Swiss, was on his way to Russia to try to seize power from the government and declare a "dictatorship of the proletariat". This was a phrase coined and adopted by Karl Marx in the mid-19th century. Besides backing the revolution in India, Auswärtiges Amt had supported Lenin for his planned transformation of Russia. They had allowed him and his deputies to cross Germany en route from Zurich to Russia

292 | The Great Indian Genius Har Dayal

via Sweden in a sealed railway car. The Germans wanted the Russian army to back off on the Eastern front and were keen on fermenting revolution in Russia. The train finally arrived at the Finland Station in Russia's former capital of Petrograd (modern-day St. Petersburg).

In a now-historic speech, Lenin climbed atop an armored train car and argued that the Bolshevik Party must use armed force to seize control from the provisional government that had been formed after Tsar Nicholas II's abdication. Lenin's triumphant return to his home country marked a turning point in Russian history and he changed the course of world history in ways that is still being reckoned with.

The Birth of the Civil Disobedience Movement of India

As the inhuman war raged on the European continent, the Ghadr Party faced an enormous crisis in North America and Russia headed in the direction of a violent communist revolution under the leadership of Lenin, in distant India in April 1917, a Gujarati Barrister was ordered to leave the Champaran district of Bihar for refusing to obey the official order of Hukumat-i-Britannia.

Previously at the Lucknow session of the Indian National Congress on December 26th and 27th, 1916, Mahatma Gandhi had been familiarized with the sordid condition of the farming community in Champaran. In Lucknow, he met his future disciple, Jawaharlal Nehru for the first time. In his *Autobiography*, Nehru remarked, "All of us admired him for his heroic fight in South Africa, but he seemed very distant and different and unpolitical to many of us young men. He refused to take part in Congress or national politics then and confined himself to the South African Indian question...." Four months after the Congress session, Mahatma Gandhi reached Champaran in April 1917 to help the suffering villagers. He visited various villages and cross-examined about eight thousand cultivators to record their statements. He reached an exact understanding of their grievances and the causes underlying them. On April 15th, the Deputy Commissioner gave him an ultimatum to leave Champaran by the first available train or face arrest.

Mahatma Gandhi's mission in life was the peaceful solution of human conflicts and this was his first attempt to employ his strategy of truthful and non-violent means to resolving a disagreement in India. He claimed before the court that he had come to render humanitarian and national service. He added that he wanted to make Champaran his home and end the suffering of the people. To the

Hukumat-i-Britannia's order, he responded that he wouldn't leave, but was ready to bear "the penalty of civil disobedience". Unexpectedly Hukumat-i-Britannia was suitably impressed by the incredible inner strength and devotion of the man. The case was withdrawn and he was allowed to remain in the district. Mahatma Gandhi later put down in his autobiography, "The country, thus, had its first direct object-lesson in Civil Disobedience..." And Nehru added, "Soon afterward his adventures and victory in Champaran, on behalf of the tenants of the planters, filled us with enthusiasm. We saw that he was prepared to apply his methods in India also, and they promised success..."

The news of Mahatma Gandhi's defiance of the Hukumat-i-Britannia reached the Gujarat Club in Ahmedabad on a hot sleepy afternoon in April 1917. British Historian David Hardiman in his book, *Peasant Nationalists of Gujarat: Kheda District 1917–1934*, has recorded that, 'the legal fraternity at the Gujarat Club leapt to their feet', and decided to have this 'brave man' as the next President of their Sabha. Among the lawyers of Ahmedabad who were elated by the news was forty-one-year-old Vallabhbhai Patel (1875–1950). He eventually quit his prosperous legal practice to work full-time with Mahatma Gandhi for the next thirty years in the civil disobedience movement. With Nehru and Patel as his able lieutenants Mahatma Gandhi set out to build the largest mass movement in India's history.

The Indo-German Conspiracy Trial

The Indo-German conspiracy trial also known as the 'Hindoo German conspiracy trial' commenced in the District Court in San Francisco on Tuesday, November 20th, 1917, following the uncovering of the Indo-German plot for initiating an uprising in India. British spies, German representatives, American Bureau of Investigation agents, Irish republicans, private detectives and Indian revolutionaries were assembled in the San Francisco courtroom as the case was argued between United States attorneys, who were assisted by the British Secret Service, on one side, and Irish-American defense attorneys on the other. In the prisoner's dock, Gobind sat next to the Indians and the German diplomats including Franz Bopp and Wilhelm von Brincken. As with the others who were arrested, Gobind was able to raise bail from fellow Indians and the Ghadr Party's funds. He was arraigned on July 10th, in the Federal District Court at 6th and Mission in San Francisco, as he pleaded not guilty. With the June 15th, 1917, passage of the Espionage Act, any kind of negative interference with the American military and support of the enemy among other things was punishable by thirty years in prison or death.

It was a picturous scene in the American courtroom. A map of half the world displaying India, Germany, and the United States marked with red dots and routes of travel was painted on the wall of the courtroom for a better understanding of the global reach of the crimes being discussed. In his book *Fighting Germany's Spies*, French Strother, recounted, "Among the polyglot evidence were Hindoo publications in six Oriental languages, including Persian; cipher messages which, when deciphered, proved to be an Indian revolutionist's letters which had to be translated by reference to page and line of an American's book about Germany and the Germans; enciphered code, written in Berlin by the German Foreign Minister, transmitted to Stockholm and thence by the Swedish Government to Buenos Aires and thence by Count Luxburg to (Ambassador) Bernstorff in Washington, telling him to pay an East Indian in New York money for use in San Francisco to send arms to revolutionists near Calcutta - besides other oddities of men and places and documents too numerous to mention."

Preston, the United States attorney, in his opening argument alleged; "One hundred and five men are involved; ninety-eight have been indicted and seven named as co-conspirators." Preston claimed "the object and purpose of this conspiracy reached the entire world" and its mission "was to engage the assistance of every Hindoo and every sympathizer in every neutral country in the world". He added, "We will show you that they had for their further object seducing from their loyalty to the British Government the troops that were in operation on the British fronts and the French fronts".

Preston positioned the commencement of the 'conspiracy' with the arrival of Har Dayal in the United States whom he described as "an out and out anarchist" who believed in "not only revolution in India but revolution everywhere". He added, "Hindoos on the Pacific Coast were canvassed and those willing to take part in the revolt were registered… shortly thereafter what is known as the India Committee an adjunct of the German Foreign Office was created in Berlin. Among them was Har Dayal, a fugitive from the United States in 1914".

An interesting prosecution witness who appeared in San Francisco was Ernest Dowes Dekker who after being detained in Hong Kong by the British Secret Service agreed to uncover the Indo-German plot at the trial. Another surprise Government witness was Frieda Hauswirth now Mrs. Sarangadhar Das who spoke extensively against Har Dayal and Tarak Nath Das. She also identified the two letters produced by Preston, written by Har Dayal from Holland to the famous anarchist of the United States, Alexander Berkman.

In 1919, a book titled, *Throttled, the detection of the German and anarchist bomb plotters,* authored by Inspector Thomas Tunney of the New York Police Department with twenty-three years of experience revealed specifics about Har Dayal and his involvement in the Indo-German plot in United States. According to the book Har Dayal wrote from Amsterdam, Holland, to Berkman in New York stating, "Dear Comrade: I am well and busy and sad. Can you send me some earnest and sincere comrades, men and women, who would like to help our Indian revolutionary movement in some way or other? I need the cooperation of very earnest comrades. Perhaps you can find them in New York or at Paterson. They should be real fighters, IWW's or anarchists. Our Indian party will make all necessary arrangements. If some comrades wish to come, they should come to Holland. We have a centre in Amsterdam, and Dutch comrades are working with us. If some comrades are ready to come, please tele-graph me from New York to the following address: Israel Aaronson, c/o Madame Kercher, 6 Oude Scheveningerweg, Scheveningen, Holland. My assumed name is Israel Aaronson. Kindly don't telegraph in your own name. The word 'yes' will suffice. The Rotterdam-Amerika Line will receive instructions from us here to give tickets, etc., to as many persons as you recommend. All financial arrangements will be made by our party. Yours for the Fight, Har Dayal. P.S. Kindly be very careful in keeping everything secret and confidential."

Two more letters written by Har Dayal were presented and in one he insisted, "Please keep this matter strictly secret and confidential. Kindly don't discuss it with too many people.... This is a great opportunity for our party. I need the cooperation of earnest comrades for very important work. Several of our comrades have come from India with encouraging news and messages...". The United States Department of Justice used these letters as evidence against Berkman and Emma Goldman. The two were detained in June 1917 and sentenced to prison. Emma Goldman was recorded as stating that she knew Har Dayal from his days in Berkeley, and she called him a "great idealist". Preston quoted extensively from the *Ghadr* newspaper and correctly estimated the membership of the party at ten thousand members. The newspapers reporting the trial even described Har Dayal the former Stanford Professor as a 'German Spy'.

The *Maverick* and the *Annie Larsen* episode also occupied a large place in the trial. The prosecution demonstrated that the funds for the acquisition of the

Maverick and for the charter of the *Annie Larsen* were furnished by the German Consulate's bank accounts in San Francisco. The transactions were masked by complicated jugglery through a string of American attorneys and shipping agents in San Francisco, Los Angeles, and San Diego.

To oppose Preston and defend the Ghadr patriots, a battery of some of the most brilliant San Francisco attorneys were in the battle array. Prominent Irish American lawyer, George A. McGowan who was also the father-in-law of von Brincken along appeared with Charles Sferlazzo for defendants Ram Chandra and Godha Ram. Robert Royce of Oakland defended Gobind and Timothy Healy of San Francisco appeared on behalf of Bhai Bhagwan Singh.

The persuasive McGowan opened with the statement that the sole motive for the Ghadr Party prosecution came from the British government. He maintained, "the whole case is being tried at the initiation of the British Government. The United States Government has never found anything seditious in the writings of these defendants." McGowan revealed that the British Secret Service operative Nathan had been allowed semi-judicial status by United States Government and Denham had actively aided the prosecution He then provided a picture of India under British rule as a land of famine, oppression, and cruelty, The defense strategy was to present the atrocities of British India and argue that it would be criminal to 'not' fight against the oppression. McGowan dramatically produced copies of the *Ghadr* newspapers, quoting liberty appeals made by George Washington and Abraham Lincoln. All the American heroes, Washington, Lincoln, Wilson, and Patrick Henry had graced the covers of Ghadr publications as the symbols of epic triumph against the British Empire immediately prior to the trial. In his appeal, McGowan even quoted from a recent address of President Woodrow Wilson and added the words of Patrick Henry, "Give me liberty or give me death."

Prosecutor Preston was so exasperated by McGowan's stance that he called his utterances, "scurrilous, defamatory, unpatriotic, and almost treasonable".

Yet American writer and journalist, Robert Morss Lovett in his autobiography, *All Our Years*, recorded his protest against His Majesty's Government's role in the Indo-German conspiracy trial; "Apart from personal reasons, however, I have been more deeply irritated by the treatment of the Indians in the United States by British Agents, acting through our authorities than by any other instance of foreign interference in our affairs".

In the index to the transcript of the trial, there are over sixty entries devoted to Gobind. The British Secret Service had noticed that the spirited

Ghadr patriot traveled to New York to meet journalist Lippmann of the New Republic. Then Gobind mysteriously reached Liverpool on March 20th, 1915. They claimed he was present at a dinner in London in April 1915 and had claimed to be in Britain to induce someone to kill Lord Kitchener. He was also suspected to be plotting explosions at the British docks besides contacting Indian sipahis on their way to the frontlines. After failing to give shape to the assassination conspiracy he went back to the United States in April 1915. Before he returned, he had according to British Secret Service set up a cell of Ghadr patriots in Britain. In May 1916 Gobind was reported to have taken part in the German Relief Bazaar held in San Francisco and sold copies of the German edition of William Jennings Bryan's *Die Englische Herrschaft in Indien* (British Rule in India). Bryan had served as United States Secretary of State from 1913–1915.

As disclosed by the British Secret Service reports, on the third anniversary of the *Ghadr* newspaper on November 1st, 1916, Gobind had addressed a gathering in San Francisco and claimed, "Japan says that this a golden opportunity for Asiatics to free themselves from the European nations and to enjoy a free life. But what are the leaders of India doing at home and abroad! It is the Ghadr Party alone that does everything... We should not care for our religion and for old useless things when the fate of our country is at stake. The Government is quite ready to use the opportunity to make us quarrel through our religions, and we should take care that it does not succeed..." In early March 1918, Gobind in his defense detailed his family ties to the Hukumat-i-Britannia and continued to deny any knowledge of the 'Hindoo Plot' when cross-examined. He, however, admitted being at Ghadr Party and IWW meetings.

Professor Arthur Pope was accused of sympathizing with the Ghadr patriots and and the anti British revolutionary movement. He was forced to testify in court and admitted: "there are certain grievances in India against the British government and they warrant aggressive action on behalf of the interests of the Hindoo people." His left leaning stance and the Presidency of the Cosmopolitan Club at the UC Berkeley was also held against him.

All the evidence provided by the prosecuton proved that Har Dayal and Ghadr Party's enormous global efforts to start a revolution against British rule in India had eventually amounted to zilch.

But Har Dayal was still unassailable.

298 | The Great Indian Genius Har Dayal

Shots in the Courtroom

On Wednesday, April 24th, 1918, the Indo-German Conspiracy trial ended. It was one of the longest and most expensive state trials in the history of the United States. Even the transcript of the trial ran into six thousand pages and cost $3,600. It had involved three Governments, thirteen attorneys and five hundred pieces of evidence. The characters involved included senior officials such as Zimmermann, Deutsches Reich's Secretary of State for Foreign Affairs, German diplomats including Papen, Bopp and Wilhelm von Brincken, known anarchists Berkman and Emma Goldman and many Indian revolutionaries led by Har Dayal. The entire Indo-German project cost the Auswärtiges Amt millions of dollars, and the net receipts were a deficit. The scenes of the global action were laid in Berlin, Constantinople, Geneva, Zurich, New York, Washington, Chicago, San Francisco, Socorro Island, Honolulu, Manila, Java, Tokyo, Bangkok and India.

The last act was in a San Francisco courtroom.

Since the departure of Har Dayal from the United States, the Ghadr movement became poorly structured and furthermore breached by British Secret Service. Earlier, Marie Leonhauser, wife of a German Buddhist priest in San Francisco, in a letter on April 11th, 1916, to Har Dayal had sought his intervention in reorganising the leadership of Ghadr Party in California. There was factionalism over financial and administrative issues and the original constitution of the Ghadr Party was destroyed. As a result of the differences engineered by the British Secret Service amongst the Ghadr patriots, the sensational trial concluded in a dramatic climax.

That Wednesday morning all the defendants including Gobind, Tarak Nath Das, Bhai Bhagwan Singh, and Ram Chandra knew that a prison term and possibly deportation to India awaited them. District Attorney Preston finished his closing statement with his wife present in the courtroom. United States District Judge William Cary Van Fleet announced that he would charge the jury in the afternoon and left the bench to enter the chambers.

In the recess, Ram Chandra, the key man in the Ghadr movement in California slowly arose from his seat and started across the room to talk to his attorney. At the same time his adversary a fellow defendant Ram Singh also got up. Since the beginning of the trial, there was such animosity among the defendants that they were searched for weapons every day while entering the courtroom. Ram Singh who had managed to smuggle a handgun past the guards during the morning break forced his way towards Ram Chandra. He suspected Ram Chandra of having embezzled funds and abused his power. There was a loud flash and sound of handgun shots in the courtroom as Ram Singh fired four bullets at Ram Chandra from close range. Ram Chandra staggered and fell dead in front of the witness chair with a bullet in his heart and two others in his body. Terrified spectators, defendants, counsels and others in the room darted for protection toppling tables and chairs in the rush. Almost immediately US Marshal James H. Holohan raised his arm high over the heads of the attorneys and fired across the room. Ram Singh was shot through the neck and died instantly. Soldiers and Deputy Marshals immediately blocked the exits. Judge Van Fleet hurried back into the courtroom and ordered all the defendants to be taken into custody. With order restored in the courtroom, the judge and jury returned.

After months of testimonies, the jury made their decision in only ten hours and returned a verdict just before midnight that same day. The recently deceased Ram Chandra and Ram Singh had their names crossed-out in the verdict. Nine defendants had their cases dismissed, three pleaded guilty, and one was adjudged insane and committed to a state hospital. Finally, twenty-nine men charged with conspiracy on American soil to start a revolution against Hukumat-i-Britannia in India were found guilty under the 1917 Espionage and Sedition Acts by a federal grand jury.

At the end of the trial, even though Har Dayal's name was glaringly mentioned in the indictment, Judge Van Fleet characterized the Ghadr patriots as mere catspaws of the "ruthless Prussian military system". He imposed various fines and prison terms and said that the German foreign office, Embassy at Washington and Consulate at San Francisco "were the nerve centers of the world flung plot to wrest Indian rule from England". Bopp was fined $ 10,000 and sent to McNeil prison along with E. H. von Schack. Wilhelm von Brincken was sentenced to serve two years; and his sentence was to run concurrently with a similar judgment as a consequence of his suspected participation in bombing plans against the Government of Canada. All three resigned from their posts and lodged an appeal. In his book, *My Three Years in America*, Ambassador Bernstorff denied any involvement of the Deutsches Reich in the Indo-German conspiracy stating, "Consul-General Bopp and his colleagues if they had in reality committed the offences of which they were accused, were Page 121certainly actuated in no way by the Embassy or any high authorities, but must be held solely and entirely responsible for the course they adopted. In his reports to me, Bopp invariably asserted his innocence, and I am rather inclined to believe that he really fell into one of the traps which the Allied Secret Service were always setting for our officials in America."

Judge Van Fleet indicated that no deportation action would be taken against the Indian defendants if they refrained from revolutionary actions after completing their prison terms. Among the Indians penalized were Tarak Nath Das, twenty-two months, Bhai Bhagwan Singh, eighteen months, Godha Ram, eleven months, and Iman Din, four months, and led off to McNeil's Island penitentiary in Washington. Bhai Bhagwan Singh named the poet of the revolution by the local newspapers, where he stated, "We get our ideas of freedom not from India, but from America. That is why we are here. It is hard that we should suffer for loving the freedom that you teach us…"

Har Dayal's protégé, Gobind too went to prison for ten-months and he served his sentence at the Alameda County Jail in Oakland.

The historic and high profile trial sent a message to distant India that all Indian revolutionaries operating anywhere in the world would be brought to justice by Hukumat-i-Britannia. A bullet hole made on April 24th, 1918, in the Judge's bench of the San Francisco courtroom survives till today.

Lajpat Rai was also in the United States while the Ghadr Party was operational. He formed the India Home Rule League, with its own office in New York, preferring to keep a safe distance from the Ghadr patriots. He remarked, "Wherever I have been in the United States of America I have tried to remonstrate with them (the Ghadr patriots) and to show to them the weakness and rather the hopelessness of their methods. Some have refused to listen to me; others have confronted me with the equal hopelessness of the Congress program and Congress methods and between these, I have failed to convince them of the practicability of the latter." Lajpat Rai believed that the Ghadr patriots were filled with a wild-eyed hope of Germany as the savior of the cause of Indian independence.

Gobind on getting out of prison detached himself from the undertakings of the Ghadr Party. He never spoke about his incarceration in public for not only did he come close to being deported from the United States, there was a possibility of him being hanged by Hukumat-i-Britannia on his return to India. With encouragement from John Barry, he focused on his career as a journalist with the Hearst group of newspapers for the rest of his life. He started by being a drama editor at *The Los Angeles Examiner* in Hollywood in 1919 and interviewed filmmaker D. W. Griffith and filmstar Valentino on the various studio sets besides hanging around with female stars. He was known to be the most well-informed man in Hollywood and the one who knew the odd restaurants. Gobind however later diversified into popular science reporting and wrote daily columns about the latest scientific discoveries that were syndicated throughout the vast Hearst chain.

Amusingly Wilhelm von Brincken became an American citizen in 1920 after his discharge from prison and moved to Los Angeles where he had a long career playing Germans in ninety-two Hollywood features.

After his release, Bhai Bhagwan Singh remained the President of the Ghadr Party and kept the flame lit by Har Dayal burning. He maintained, "Dynamic personalities like Har Dayal and others played a very important part in arousing the masses." Ghadr patriots never forgot the assistance they were provided by the Irish in their darkest hour and they marched in St. Patrick's Day parades across the United States. In the following years, Eamon de Valera visited the Ghadr Party headquarters on Wood Street.

Trapped in Vienna

With the entry of the United States in WWI in the first quarter of 1917, the tide turned against Germany and its allies. As a result, no significant diplomatic or material support for the activities of the Berlin India Committee from the Germans was forthcoming any longer. In the face of a defeat of an exhausted Germany, the Berlin India Committee was on the verge of collapse. As German patronage dried up, Virendranath established contact with the Bolsheviks in Moscow. Virendranath wanted to enter Russia and applied for a visa to Sweden but it was rejected. Eventually, he managed to land in the port town of Trelleborg in Sweden on May 12th, 1917 and announced his intention to apply for a Swedish passport and seek permanent residence. His official engagement was 'literary work for the Indian National Movement and World Peace'.

The British Secret Service operatives had anticipated the move by Indian revolutionaries to move the propaganda business out of Germany to Scandinavia or Russia. They set off A. Yusuf Ali, Indian lawyer, and administrator to give a series of lectures on Indian culture in Scandinavia, including Copenhagen, Stockholm, Uppsala, and Oslo about the 'genius of India being discovered under British rule'. An outstanding public speaker he claimed on behalf of Hukumat-i-Britannia that the Indian revolutionaries were dishonest as there was no desire for independence in India and on the contrary the ties between India and Britain were strengthened during WWI. To argue against Yusuf Ali's British propaganda,

Virendranath convinced Auswärtiges Amt to rush Har Dayal, the best available intellectually skilled speaker, to Stockholm. He suggested that his presence was "absolutely necessary".

Virendranath knew of Har Dayal's association with IWW and his network with the well-known anarchists in Europe and North America was considered an asset in negotiating with the Bolsheviks. A realistic man he patched up his differences with Har Dayal. The German diplomats and the Deutsches Reich accepted Virendranath's suggestion that Har Dayal could still add value to the Berlin India Committee in the Swedish capital. In early November 1917, the official ban on Har Dayal was removed and he was asked to proceed from Berlin for Vienna to serve as a starting point for a trip to neutral Sweden.

Describing his visit to war torn Vienna, Har Dayal recalled afterward, "I happen to spend a few months in Vienna in 1917. It is a beautiful city of historic memories – "the city of my dreams" as the German song puts it. I did not go to Vienna on account of any romantic dreams but for certain very prosaic reasons". In Vienna, Har Dayal refused to travel further to Stockholm on a fake passport. He demanded a proper identity card from the German so that the prestige attached to his name could be exploited in Sweden. However, the Swedish Government was not keen on welcoming the well-known Indian revolutionary to lecture in their nation. Har Dayal was the kind of rebel, His Majesty's Government sought to arrest and the Deutsches Reich had restrained with some effort. Therefore complications were encountered in getting authorization from the Swedish Government to enter the country.

In January 1918, Vienna and Budapest were rocked by riots against food shortages. Without any source of funds and short on even basic food, Har Dayal was forced to starve in Vienna for the Swedish visa for months. During that dreadful waiting period, his health suffered but he managed to contact the aristocrat Umrao Singh Shergil (1870–1954) who was stranded in Europe by WWI and lived in nearby Budapest with his Hungarian wife Marie Antoinette and two daughters Amrita (later a famous painter) and Indira. He knew of the activities of the Berlin India Committee and Mahendra Pratap was his guest during a visit to Budapest in the spring of 1915. Shergil, a man of culture and intellect found a perfect companion in the Indian revolutionary and they spent considerable time together in Vienna and Budapest discussing the events around them and in their homeland. Shergil later remembered, "Har Dayal was much starved in Wein (Vienna), he was with me for several days. I was glad to see him and rub intellectual shoulders with him. When he is in more vigorous health after the more liberal dietary available in Hungary, I hope his wonderful mental powers will be utilized for the benefit of our respective countries India and Germany. He had been and is an extraordinary man and I am glad to find that though in our religious-philosophical ideas we stand far, we have come nearer. If one has love, systems do not matter…"

At the same time in London on November 28th, 1917, Har Dayal's name came up in a debate on publication of Lajpat Rai's *Young India*. In the House of Commons, Conservative politician, George Cave, then the Home Secretary describing the Indian political situation professed, "We have the two movements, one representing force and the other peaceable agitation, side by side as has been the case in the history of similar movements in other countries. One movement represents the more virile section of the population who believe in force, violence and terrorism the other depends upon appeals to reason, justice, and conscience. Then the author *(Young India)* describes various matters, including his transportation and the attempt upon the life of Lord Hardinge, which resulted in the death of a certain number of people, and in particular, the author praises a man to whom the honorable and gallant Gentleman referred, Har Dayal. The honorable and gallant Member represented this man as one who believed in constitutional government". A member interrupted Cave, "Not constitutional - revolutionary." Cave continued, "See what the author himself says about this man: They are to organize rebellion for raising the standard of revolt for carrying on a guerilla war. For the purpose of this rebellion or war, they may do and will do, anything that is necessary to be done. Otherwise, they would neither murder nor loot."

Some Aspects of Spirituality

The spiritual world was a life long attraction for Har Dayal and he increasingly spent time to study Buddhism and other religions in Vienna. He reached out to the well-known Sanskrit scholar Professor Leopold von Schroeder (1851–1920) at the Universitat Wien. Renowned in Europe for his interest in Indian thought, Schroeder's lectures on the *Bhagavad Gita* were broadcasted across Germany. He had jubilantly stated in 1899, "every newspaper wants an essay, every club wants to have a lecture about the Buddha". He was of the view that Buddha had taken the place of Socrates as the idol of the educated elite. While Har Dayal was waiting in Austria for clearance, well versed in several languages, he made five recordings of literary works in Hindi, Urdu, Braj Bhasha and Awadhi for the 'Phonogrammarchiv' of the Austrian Academy of Sciences on February 7th, 1918. Displaying *Ganga-Jamuni Tehzeeb* at its finest, Har Dayal could recite the *Ramacharitamanas*, episodes of *Bhagavata Purana*, Mirabai's *Bhajans* (devotional songs), the couplets of Kabir and proudly sang when he could, the *Tarana-e-Hind*, "*Sare Jahan se accha Hindostan hamara*". He also had a taste for Urdu poetry of Delhi and often quoted many couplets and ghazals of Mir Taqi Mir, Zauq and Insha. He typically concluded with the famous Indian maxim, "*Raghukul rit yahi chali ayee pran jaye par vachan na jaye*" (It has always been the rule in the Raghuclan that one's stated words must be fulfilled even at the cost of one's life).

Har Dayal recollected, almost a decade later in an article for *The People* dated, March 28th, 1926, that during his stay in Vienna he had met a Jewish Professor (Bernhard Geiger) who had a special interest in Sanskrit and Indian literature. He met him in a café and they talked about India and the projected edition of the *Mahabharata*. Har Dayal gained an understanding of the Jewish faith from the scholar over the next few hours. It took him back to his school and college days in Delhi where missionaries used to teach from the Bible. In the article titled, 'Some Aspects of Zionism' published in *The People*, he claimed, "I have met many Jews on different occasions and I may declare once for all that I am a great admirer of the Jews... I am a pro-Semite and I condemn anti-Semitism in all its forms. The Jews will survive all puerile anti Semitism movements..." He told Professor Geiger, "You are a great people, much greater than you know. You have given us Christ, Paul, Maimonides, Spinoza, Marx, and Trotsky; you will produce greater men and women in the future..." Har Dayal prophesied, "You will live not as a small nation but as a great world force. That is your destiny and your mission. You are called upon to lead all great movements for the uplift of humanity. Cease to be mere Jews; be great men and women..."

Coincidentally when Har Dayal lived in isolation in Vienna, on September 23rd, 1918, 15th (Imperial Service) Cavalry Brigade of the British Indian army comprising lancers from the regiments of princely states of Jodhpur and Mysore were tasked with the mission to liberate the Israeli port city Haifa. Ottoman Turks defended the city with advance artillery and machine guns yet the Indian horsemen overran Turkish positions armed with just spears, lances and swords. It has been recorded that the machine gun bullets over and over again failed to stop the galloping horses. They displayed exemplary cavalry skills and valor and liberated the fortified city of Haifa from four hundred years of Ottoman rule.

The two Indian regiments captured almost one thousand three hundred and fifty Turkish-German prisoners. Major Dalpat Singh Shekhawat, who was killed at the start of the battle and has been recognized by the Indian armed forces as the 'hero of Haifa' and awarded a military cross for his bravery. A memorial on Jaffa Street in Haifa honors the victorious Indian sipahis and in the aftermath of the war, British sculptor Leonard Jennings built the Teen Murti Circle in front of Flagstaff House, the Commander-in-Chief's residence in New Delhi in 1922, with three sipahis depicting the regiments of Hyderabad, Jodhpur and Mysore Lancers who were part of the 15th Imperial Service Cavalry Brigade.

A One-way Ticket to Stockholm

After months of waiting for the sunrise in Vienna and enduring stark wartime difficulties, on Monday, September 30th, 1918, the British Secret Service's most-watched Indian revolutionary Har Dayal stood with his newly minted German Personalausweis nr #5066 (identify card as an alternative to a Passport) in the office of the Swedish legion for a visa. The German Personalausweis was issued in the name of Har Dayal. He no longer needed to assume the aliases of Israel Aronson, Ramalingamdass, Ismail Hakki Hassan or Professor Mirza Osman. Here his profession was recorded as 'University Professor' and date of birth was listed as October 14th, 1884. This date remained his official date of birth as the German Personalausweis was one of his official identifications while traveling abroad for the rest of his life. Though now extremely thin and rather unwell, Har Dayal was finally granted a short-term visa number, on application #15.828 valid from October 1st, 1918 to January 1st, 1919 for visiting Sweden for only three months. He paid four Swedish kronor for the visa. The next day the decent and scholarly revolutionary with some of his writings in his hands and his head headed for the Wien Hauptbahnhof. Another journey, another destination and another platform awaited him. For Har Dayal, it seemed, life was an unending battle at every step.

13

THE IDEALIST OF A STRANGE TYPE IN SWEDEN

"He (Har Dayal) was not only probably the brainiest man in the Indian revolutionary party but also the most highly cultured…"

The New York Times
Sunday, June 8th, 1919

On Tuesday, October 8th, 1918, Har Dayal, the man who was once the torchbearer of the Ghadr movement sat in a train on his way to Stockholm from Wien Hauptbahnhof. As the train rolled from Berlin, his sharp mind took note of the absence of young men in the small towns and villages where the train halted; virtually all were at the front or dead. The passing trains all along the journey in Germany were filled with corpses or wounded soldiers returning home. The trains stank of blood, ether and gangrene. The train stations in Europe were overflowing, filled with mutilated, lame and blind men. Men without boots marched asleep on the platforms. In the fall of 1918, after four years of bitter fighting, the slaughter of WWI had not yet ended. It had been the costliest year of the war. The British had taken two million casualties and the French three million. Europe was tired of the war but it was still a fight to the finish. Never before was this ghastly human carnage seen on Earth.

From Rostock, a port city on the Baltic Sea, Har Dayal, boarded a ferry bound northwards to Sweden. The sea was rough and the sting of sea spray washed the observation decks as the sails heaved towards Sweden. The Polisbyrån, the Swedish intelligence service was suspicious of all foreigners that entered the country. Ferry passengers with their baggage were required to go through the identity checkpoint and the Polisbyrån recorded Har Dayal's entry in Sweden. He held his German Personalausweis and the Swedish visa. For further identification he carried his Oxford University documents, a letter from St. Stephen's College and the Stanford yearbook. *The Swedish Government Archives* indicate that he was a "university professor," and the purpose of his visit to Sweden was "literary work". Here he mentioned his date of birth as October 14th, 1918. Swedish officials recorded that "because of his political activities before and during the World War", he did not posses a passport. As specified by his visa, he was granted permission to stay in Sweden for three months.

Finally as his train departed from Trelleborg Centralstation for Stockholm and the mist cleared up, there was the flag with a yellow cross on a blue field waving in a brisk wind. The spectacular and varied scenery through Sweden passed by from the window. The trip was interrupted by fog as well as light rain. It was extremely cold and the days were getting shorter at this time of the year. The official arrival of vintertid (winter time) was to come on Sunday, October 27th, when clocks would move back an hour. The changing of the season meant hearing the Swedish phrase, "*det finns inget dåligt väder, bara dåliga kläder*" (there's no such thing as bad weather, only bad clothing).

On the eve of his thirty-fourth birthday, Har Dayal with the fleeting landscapes of lush meadows and forests visible across his window, reflected on his past life from a distance. He was reminded of his favorite philosopher Socrates' thought, "the unexamined life is not worth living".

In his youth, the passion of nationalism had raged so violently within Har Dayal that despite being the ultimate tour de force in academic feats from India he admiringly walked away from a life of probable luxury. For close to a decade from 1907 to 1917, the Oxford scholar gifted with eidetic memory fought fire with fire. He stormed through the streets of Delhi, Lahore, Oxford, London, Kanpur, Paris, Geneva, Algiers, Fort de France, New York, Boston, San Francisco, Astoria, Sacramento, Washington DC, Constantinople, Berlin, Amsterdam and Vienna in his struggle to free his homeland from the clutches of the Hukumat-i-Britannia. On the Pacific Coast of America and in Europe, at a time of great social and political turbulence, he had taken center stage in the Indian freedom movement's history as one of the founders of the 'Ghadr Party', a global nationalist movement. This sustained campaign of resistance to the British Empire's occupation of the Indian subcontinent had spread its tentacles from the university campuses of Stanford and Berkeley all across the world. His astonishing feats on an international scale in those early years had inspired several Indian patriots.

After WWI the Indian revolutionary movement in the United States and Europe was wrecked. But Har Dayal's fire as a revolutionary had not been extinguished as yet. He was one of the cleverest and wisest radicals that India had produced. The resources of his wide reading and a lifetime of varied experience coupled with terrific eloquence made him an exceptional adversary. His audacity, whether fighting for a belief or against colonization, was unsurpassable. His magnificent brain could pick out the essential points of a complicated socio-political situation with ease and provide logic-driven solutions. Many of his writings were a testimonial to his prescience.

In the past years employing realpolitik he had successfully outwitted British Secret Service operatives, engineered dangerous operations, risked his life, disguised himself, slipped into the shadows, lived under assumed names, traveled incognito, escaped across continents, faced multiple treacheries, befriended radicals, enthralled intellectuals, overwhelmed politicians, meditated in North Africa, Caribbean and the Pacific, existed meagerly like a wandering émigré in Europe and endured the darkest days of WWI when he was practically interned in Germany during the past three years and could not even correspond with his friends. He was no longer welcome anywhere within His Majesty's dominion. He was on the proscribed list of Hukumat-i-Britannia, his name was prominent in the courtrooms in San Francisco, Delhi and Lahore and if he returned to India he would court a death sentence or penal servitude in the Andamans where the British jailors specialized in torture. Powerless to arrest this force of nature, it was Har Dayal's legacy as a frontline revolutionary that the Hukumat-i-Britannia sought to destroy.

Har Dayal at that time hopeful of an enforced exile in Sweden from India had resided on four continents in a multitude of countries, far removed from the land of his birth, streets of his hometown, friends, close relatives, family and his wife Sunder Rani. Surviving like an ascetic he had forfeited everything for India's freedom movement. The Indian patriot felt that the result of the sacrifice was impractical and fruitless. Though he had won the support of several thousand Indians, except his family in India, no one had funded his revolutionary life. He was fiscally almost broke and left with just thousand German papiermarks (approximately $750 at that time) plus some small savings in Switzerland. All his possessions were reduced to a small bag of essential clothes and another one with some of his favorite books. He had left two boxes containing his prized possession of important books and manuscripts in the Deutsches Orient Institute in Berlin and hoped to retrieve them at a later stage. In his bag he had stored the complete handwritten manuscript chronicling his recent years, *Forty Four Months in Germany and Turkey*, and an unfinished draft of his latest article with the heading, 'My Confession of Faith'.

Harvard graduate, Dr. Anup Singh (1903–1969) who later became a Member of the Parliament in India in an article for *New History* (published in New York in April 1939) analyzed, "This daring political adventure of Har Dayal's failed ostensibly in its immediate objective. He failed because India's political pulse was then beating very feebly. It failed because Har Dayal issued a clarion call for a revolutionary army while Indian leaders at home were marshaling their resources to make the world safe for democracy. It failed because even among the revolutionary elements there was none on the spot dynamic enough to orchestrate these forces."

Nevertheless, Har Dayal's creation of the *Ghadr* newspaper and the ensuing revolutionary incidents in India, the United States, Canada, Germany, Japan, Turkey, Afghanistan, and Singapore between 1913 and 1915 lit the spark for India's freedom. The revolutionaries of that era established something new and those years remain important in the history of India's freedom movement.

On the train to Stockholm, the once ever-smiling face of the bespectacled Har Dayal was now a sad reflection of his disturbed and depressed mental stage. He was physically broken and suffering from nervous trouble in the eyes. Having finally escaped from Germany, his residence in Berlin had convinced him that it was "an absurd country of bureaucrats and snobs" and his estimation of Turkey was transformed after the Armernian genocide. WWI had further outraged Har Dayal's moral sensibilities and he grieved, "Mankind is one house, there is much worth saving in that corner of our house". Additionally his future in Sweden looked rather bleak and chaotic. Later the displaced activist revealed to his friends; "I may say that sorrow and wisdom have grown in me like twin-sisters."

Swedish Intermission

In the fall of 1918, Har Dayal's train pulled into the beautiful city of Stockholm with just around four hundred thousand inhabitants spread over fourteen islands. The city called 'beauty on water' had its grand royal palace, gabled buildings, and razor-thin cobblestone streets. For a traveler, it offered world-class museums and galleries and the impeccably preserved historic center – Gamla Stan, the city's oldest district where the past, present, and future constantly merged.

Har Dayal's colleague Acharya received him at the Stockholm Centralstationen as he stepped off the long and tiring train journey. Since May 1917, Acharya along with Virendranath, with assistance from Deutsches Reich had established the 'Indiska Nationalkommittén' (Indian National Committee) with its office on the first floor, Artillerigatan 28 B, in Stockholm equipped with a reference library and propaganda center. After the Bolshevik Revolution of November 1917 in Russia, peaceful Stockholm became the center of the Indian independence movement in Europe. The pacifist socialist Mayor of Stockholm Carl Lindhagen had made the city a political haven for Indian revolutionaries. The objective of Indiska Nationalkommittén was to carry out propaganda in the Scandinavian newspapers; *Svenska Dagbladet, Aftonbladet, Nya Dagligt, Allehanda Dagens Nyheter* and *Stockholms-Tidningen*. They wanted to spread the information about the repressive British rule in India among the European and Russian socialists in Stockholm.

Eleven months after the Russian Revolution, there was a plan within the Indiska Nationalkommittén to utilize the services of Har Dayal; the man who could have been India's Lenin, as an editor of a bulletin addressing Indian grievances in the appropriate socialist language. He could communicate as a 'socialist' and had previously claimed, "I can write in the regular socialistic style, with quotations from Marx, etc., etc." The Auswärtiges Amt accepted his demand for a thousand Swedish kronor per month for his livelihood and another one thousand Swedish kroner for his winter clothes.

As prearranged Har Dayal on arrival in Stockholm stayed on the top floor of Virendranath's residence at Roséns Pensionat on Grev Turegatan, where he rested, ate and dressed in warmer clothes. He outfitted himself 'like a Swedish nobleman' and also purchased a thick overcoat as the winter in Northern Europe was colder than anywhere he had ever lived before.

Unexpectedly the three month long stay in Sweden got extended and turned into a 'new hope' for him. He lived in Sweden for the next eight years, the longest period of stay in a foreign country for him till then and probably the calmest.

Twilight of the Gods

Within weeks of Har Dayal's relocation to Sweden, Kaiser Wilhelm abdicated on November 9th, 1918 in Berlin and was forced to flee to Netherlands. Two days later, Germany was ready to sign a truce and the guns of the western front fell silent. WWI ended at 1100 hrs on the eleventh day of the eleventh month, in 1918. Germany signed an armistice and one of the deadliest conflicts in human history ended with victory for Britain.

None of the Scandinavian countries had any foreign policy during the Great War. At the commencement of WWI, in spite of Sweden's century-old association with France, a country that had been especially close during the period of Gustav III, strong German sympathies found utterance among the decision-makers. The general population was unwilling to support a Germany steeped in militarism and its use of brutal force. After WWI the new Germany vanquished and mistreated, enjoyed much sympathy in the Scandinavian world. The impact of the war in Sweden was twofold. It was a test of its neutrality policy. Concessions and violations of neutrality had costs in terms of both foreign affairs and the economy. At the domestic level, it meant scarcities and inflation. On the other hand, WWI influenced the democratization process, as the strife at home and abroad made the Swedes demand changes in governence. The Constitutional Reform in 1919 ensued in universal suffrage and the adoption of the principles of parliamentary democracy. Amidst the global economic turmoil of WWI, Spanish flu the worst epidemic since the black death in the fourteenth century, had reached Sweden in June 1918, and at least one-third of the population (then 5.8 million) were infected. Influenza related mortality rate of 693 persons (5.1 per 1,000 people) was reported in the Uppsala region alone.

1918 was an extraordinarily turbulent year. Europe's great empires were breaking apart. The world had never seen such gore and brutality before. More than sixty million soldiers participated in that orgy of violence. Over seventy countries from five continents had joined in it and more than nine million people were killed, twice that number were wounded. Almost one in six men had died. Europeans paid a higher death toll in WWI than in any other war in their entire history. In Britain, Germany, France, and Austria-Hungary, about eighty percent of men fit for military service were sent to the front or sea. Britain's status in the world appeared not only undiminished by WWI but also boosted. British Empire's most powerful asset was its wealth supported by its leading position in the fiscal structure of world business and trade. Later on January 10th, 1920, an intergovernmental organization, 'The League of Nations', was founded as a result of the Paris Peace Conference that ended WWI. It was the first worldwide intergovernmental organization whose principal mission was to maintain world peace.

The diplomat George Kennan correctly defined WWI as "the great seminal catastrophe" of the twentieth century, because it led to so many further catastrophes. WWI was supposed to be the war to end all wars but it contained the seeds of WW2. A whole generation was shaped by the familiarities of the battlefield. It included Winston Churchill, the future Prime Minister of Britain, Charles de Gaulle, the future President of France and Harry Truman, who later became President of the United States. A veteran of WWI, Lance Corporal Adolf Hitler of the German army, who had seen the tattered bodies of his fellow soldiers lying in the trenches of the killing fields of Europe, never recovered from the defeat and went on to become the monstrous tyrant who engineered the WW2 and the Holocaust.

Indian Combatants in WWI

During WWI Indian sipahis served with credit and honor on numerous battlefields around the globe. In France, the Indian intervention was critical in stabilizing the line of control in the critical early days of the war in 1914 and Indians fearlessly fought in the Mesopotamia campaign. The Indian sipahis, who had agreed enthusiastically when the call came for recruits to bear arms for Britain's "King Emperor" in a far-off European war in 1914, earned over 9,200 decorations. Eleven sipahis from India were awarded the Victoria Cross, the highest award for gallantry in Britain. Two of these awards were posthumous. At least ten Indians, who had immigrated to Canada from India, many with the last name 'Singh,' enlisted in the Canadian Army during the war. Of the ten, eight served in Britain and France. Three of these men were wounded, two were killed in action, and one succumbed to his injuries and as he had acquired tuberculosis after his return to Canada.

The young Indian Lieutenant Hardit Singh Malik (1894 – 1985) was one of the four Indians to fly combat missions for the British Empire. Lieutenant Malik survived WWI and as a fighter pilot was credited with shooting down six enemy planes. The other almost-forgotten Indians who flew as combat pilots for the Royal Flying Corps were Lieutenant S.C. Welingkar, Second Lieutenant E. S. C. Sen, and Lieutenant I. L. Roy who was the first Indian to be awarded a gallantry award - the Distinguished Flying Cross. Both Captain S. C. Welingkar and Lieutenant I. L. Roy died in combat missions over Germany.

74,187 Indians, who left their motherland to defend the British Empire, died fighting. But British history books mostly disregarded their heroism and sacrifices. Indian poetess Sarojini Naidu wrote 'The Gift of India' in 1915 and paid tribute to the contribution to the sipahis overlooked in the vast expanse of the WWI's history.

"Gathered like pearls in their alien graves,
Silent they sleep by the Persian waves,
Scattered like shells on Egyptian sands,
They lie with pale brows and brave, broken hands,
They are strewn like blossoms mown down by chance,
on the blood-brown meadows of Flanders and France."

And in Kriegsgäberstätte Hauptalle, Wünsdorf in Germany there is a forgotten cemetery where two hundred and six Indian prisoners of war from WWI are buried. Later a monumental arch was built in New Delhi that recorded India's contribution in blood to the British war effort.

Marooned and Indisposed in Stockholm

As the guns fell silent in Europe, the Berlin India Committee was dissolved on December 6th, 1918. Plans were made for the Stockholm branch to continue working under a one-year contract by the Auswärtiges Amt. The political situation in Europe was fluid and most of the Indian revolutionaries had transferred their hope from Kaiser's Germany to Bolshevik Russia. Some termed themselves Communists and had a new mission - to meet Lenin in Moscow.

In these fast-changing times Har Dayal had still not recovered from his nervous ailment and in due course moved from Stockholm to Bath Hotel, a sanatorium in Saltsjöbaden (the Salt Sea baths), to take care of his declining health condition. Having lived and wandered for the past eleven years without a passport, after his arrival in Sweden, Har Dayal now requested for a Passport from the Utrikesdepartementet (Swedish Foreign Office), stating, "I have come to the conclusion that it would be foolish and useless to carry on revolutionary propaganda against England in the near future..." He requested for a longer stay in Sweden or permission to travel to Holland or Spain and threatened to even commit suicide if the authorization was denied. The Utrikesdepartementet predictably kept him at an arm's length and disregarded his request. Then in December 1918, he applied for a passport as a British subject to the British legation in Stockholm and it was forwarded by telegram to the Foreign Office in London on December 18th. As his visa for Sweden neared the expiry date he made plans to go to Moscow if his request was rejected. Finally the Utrikesdepartementet extended his stay his another three months till March 1919.

Back in India the flame for India's independence was delicately burning. Har Dayal's hometown Delhi was in the throes of a horrible attack of influenza in October 1918. The death toll in Delhi was estimated at 23,000 and the *ghats* (cremation grounds) and burial grounds were swamped with corpses. At the thirty-third session of the Indian National Congress at Delhi on Thursday, December 26, 1918, Madan Mohan Malaviya, was elected as the President. In his address, he announced that the slogan "*Satyameva Jayate*" (truth alone triumphs) from the ancient Indian text, *Mundakopanishad* should be the slogan for the nation.

In February 1919, Har Dayal, with regular access to the British, French, German and American newspapers in Stockholm became cognizant of the latest events in India, Britain, Sweden, and Germany. Way before other Indian leaders, in 1907, he was the first person to formulate and execute the strategy of 'disobedience' with the Hukumat-i-Britannia. Now at the beginning of 1919 after the catastrophe of WWI, he needed to decide on his future course of action. In a life full of experiments he took another risk to achieve three objectives – firstly, to return to India at any cost to lead the freedom movement, secondly to reunite with his mother, wife and daughter, and lastly to enroll for his Doctorate on Buddhism. Undoubtedly the idealist revolutionary within him was still alive. It was time to rebel once again and on this occasion he was up against the might of the combined might of Hukumat-i-Britannia, the Utrikesdepartementet and Auswärtiges Amt. But events moved faster than he anticipated.

On February 19th, 1919, Har Dayal heard from his friends in Stockholm that the British Secret Service had leaked his private letter (written to Lajpat Rai before armistice) in which he had expressed his reservations about German officials. The letter first appeared in the *San Francisco Call* and then on January 31st, the London based British Committee of the Indian National Congress published it in their weekly newspaper *India*. The newspapers in London had commented, "It has always been a matter of regret that a man of such brilliant parts as Har Dayal should have followed the will of the wisp of violent revolutionary methods in order to serve his country."

In an instant all hell broke loose. The Indiska Nationalkommittén and Auswärtiges Amt reacted immediately. The Auswärtiges Amt sent threatening letters and demanded a written retraction for immediate publication in the newspapers. But Har Dayal refused and lost the promised ten thousand German papiermarks from Auswärtiges Amt as a one-time settlement after the Berlin India Committee was wound up. He left his temporary residence and separated himself from all radical activities including Virendranath led Indiska Nationalkommittén. He later claimed, "Circumstances beyond my control also prevented me from writing, speaking, or working openly according to my real convictions during four months after my arrival in Stockholm on October 10th, 1918. At last, I was happy to be able to sever all connection with the German Government on February 20th, 1919, when I voluntarily returned my German passport to the German Legation in Stockholm."

Admitting his current political position in favor of the British Empire, Har Dayal dispatched a telegram to the editor of *India* in London: "Acknowledge letters recently quoted as my authentic personal communications, avow publicly my conversion to principle of Imperial unity with progressive self government for all nations of the Empire, send you open letter for publication, regret this necessary step has been delayed by uncontrollable circumstances during four months".

Remaining in Sweden, Har Dayal continued to use his old Oxford certificate as an official document to prove his identity. Finding Stockholm extremely expensive without monetary backing from Indiska Nationalkommittén and the Auswärtiges Amt he sent for the small savings he had parked in Switzerland for a rainy day. He additionally sought help from friends in Sweden to get him to deliver lectures at Uppsala University. An accomplished writer he intended to start a small journal, titled, The Indian Student's Guide.

Har Dayal then reopened correspondence with London based Orientalist scholar Professor Thomas Walker Arnold (1864 - 1930) who had previously taught philosophy at Government College, Lahore. In a series of messages between December 1918 and March 1919, he requested Professor Arnold for assistance in urgently obtaining a British passport. More importantly he hoped that due to Professor Arnold's intervention the Hukumat-i-Britannia would grant him amnesty. He also sought some financial aid while he was looked for a publisher for his newly written book *Forty-Four Months in Germany and Turkey.*

Additionally, he was keen to get news from his family back in India and commence communication with them with letters transmitted via Professor Arnold. He asked that a message be forwarded to his brother Kishan Dayal in Delhi and added: "I wish to enquire how my mother, wife, and daughter are. They will also be glad to have news of me and learn that I have got rid of my old revolutionary ideas." Professor Arnold now with University College, London, understood Har Dayal's predicament and offered to intercede on his behalf with the India Office.

In March, Har Dayal handed over two manuscripts in a sealed cover to Sir Coleridge Kennard, Secretary at the British Legation in Stockholm to be forwarded to Professor Arnold for his comments. Though he was fully prepared for controversy with the Germans, he feared a reprisal after the publication of his views. The NAI records confirm that he disclosed to Professor Arnold, "I don't want to be the victim of some kidnapping plot, etc. I am quite alone here and all Swedish officials are very pro-German. I have received several threatening letters already". He requested for a British Passport, "so that I may leave this country now. Besides I can't afford to live here, as life is very expensive. I have nothing to do here…"

Later in 1926, Har Dayal disclosed in a message to the British Legation that in 1918 he wanted "to work in India and with the Empire on constitutional and constructive lines" and he had put himself in a very difficult situation by "acting on his conviction and lost the help and protection of German Government".

Once more, "a free and honest man" as Har Dayal was before the war, he was now ready to reinvent his life. The gamble he undertook this time was far greater than anything he had done before in his entire life.

Alea Iacta Est

On Saturday, March 22nd, 1919, the die was cast.

In London, *The New Statesman*, a prominent weekly magazine of Britain, published, 'The Future of the British Empire in Asia', an article written by Har Dayal. Its second part was published in the next edition on March 29th, 1919.

In a shocking confession of faith, after introducing himself as a man who was "a convinced and consistent opponent of British imperialism," he accepted he was "led to modify his views on account of the tremendous events of the great world war". The article reaffirmed Har Dayal's commitment to the British Empire stating, "The day of small States is gone" and added that the break-up of the British Empire in either Asia or Africa would only lead to a change of masters for the people there. British conquest was a misfortune, he wrote, "but that is now a matter of history." By cooperating with the British, the Indians could influence them in the direction of "greater efficiency and equality. He declared that the great things that Britain had secured were order, peace, religious freedom, civil rights, and higher education.

Claiming that "no thinking man can remain the same after this great war as he was before", the man who had opposed "the social conquest of the Hindu race" now declared that the British Empire could be cemented from within if a common basis of intellectual training were supplied, to include English literature, English history, and English law. He even called for the teaching of Greek and Latin in the schools. Very suspicious about German ambition and a recent convert to the cause of the British Empire, Har Dayal openly declared, "Imperialism is always an evil, but British and French Imperialism in its worst form is thousand times preferable to German or Japanese imperialism". He expressed his hope that the "British Empire" of today will be converted into the "British-Oriental-African Commonwealth" of the future. In a carefully nuanced argument, he asserted, "We stand for India as against England, but we stand with England against the world".

Based on the articles in *The New Statesman*, Har Dayal with assistance from Professor Arnold also pressed forward in publishing his first book, *Forty-Four Months in Germany and Turkey (February 1915 to October 1918)*.

The crudely written book issued by P.S. King and Son of London recorded Har Dayal's impressions of Germany and Turkey and provided a devastating critique of German foreign policy and the character of the German people. In this strange document and a sort of memoir he divulged; "I spent about forty-four months in Germany and Turkey from February 1915 to October 1918. I went from Switzerland to Berlin in the last week of January 1915 and worked earnestly till February 1916 with the Germans and Turks for what I then believed to be the common cause of India and Germany." The visionary political thinker critiqued German nationalism and predicted the rise of antisemitism in Germany far ahead of everyone else. The book was equally critical towards Turkish nationals.

Overflowing with praise towards British imperialism, the book was Har Dayal's desperate attempt to endorse Hukumat-i-Britannia and an attempt to somehow reach India. He even complimented the British for their reputation for truthfulness and recalled a conversation with a hotel proprietor in Martinique who told him, "The English are different from other people. If an Englishman says he will do a thing, you may be sure that he will do it." He rejected his previous purpose of Indian independence in favor of a longer British link with India and Dominion status within the Empire. Politically, he associated himself with the concept of Home Rule and was almost utopian in assuming that Britain would live up to her moral tasks, especially in the treatment of the non-white races. He determined that "It is, therefore, best to accept the principle of Imperial unity, and work for the establishment of democratic institutions with the help of Englishmen."

Har Dayal concluded with a grand vision of a one-world state, an idea that stayed with him for the rest of his years. He penned, "England is free and great, and we can share in this freedom and greatness as worthy citizens of the greatest State that the world has yet seen. England will achieve what Alexander dreamed of and what Rome partially accomplished. We, too, are called to this work. If we help to realize this ideal, generations yet unborn will bless our names. The future keeps its secret, but we must do our duty in this spirit, looking forward to the advent of the time - When the war-drum throbs no longer, and the battle-flag is furled In the Parliament of Man, the Federation of the World."

As one of the first prose writers from India to be published in Britain the book by the famous Indian scholar was surprisingly poorly written. Additionally it was quite unbecoming of the intellectual that its author undoubtedly was. He had overstated his case with admiration for British rule, civilization, and values. Within months of his arrival in Sweden Har Dayal had disowned much of his past political career and activities. The reaction around the world was fairly dramatic.

The British Empire Strikes Back

Hukumat-i-Britannia that had dutifully monitored Har Dayal's correspondence from Sweden noticed the publication of his articles in *The New Statesman* and ordered several copies to circulate in India, Britain, France, the United States and even as far as Japan. It was propaganda material in favor of the British Empire and was even translated into Indian languages to be distributed free. The massive publicity blitz given to Har Dayal's newspaper articles and writings was also recognition of the fact that he was a fearless and successful leader of the Indian independence movement overseas.

It was time for the Hukumat-I-Britannia to rub his nose in the dirt.

The news of Har Dayal's desertion spread like wildfire and newspapers in London, India and on both coasts of the United States published the *volte-face* by the known revolutionary. On June 8th, 1919, *The New York Times* in a news story titled, "HAR DAYAL REBEL, RECANTS HIS VIEWS" reported: "Remarkable effect of forced sojourn in Berlin upon an Indian Revolutionist. Wants no new masters and sees the indolent oriental unable to stand-alone at present. He seeks autonomy within the Empire." The paper devoted most of the page to "the most influential of the agitators", and added, "In the opinion of many Englishmen the conversion of Har Dayal is one of the important events of the last few months, as affecting the peace of the British Empire." Similar stories appeared in the *New York Tribune* and *San Francisco Chronicle*. In London, *The Times* in a review of his book remarked, "The author has been for the last ten years one of the most active leaders of the Indian Revolutionary Party... an interesting study in the psychology of an ardent and impressionable Oriental... one of the most curious literary products of the War."

Exitus Acta Probat

After the publication of the articles and his book, Har Dayal had a fall like a Greek tragic hero and lost respect and prestige among sections of educated Indians. Har Dayal's reputation as a tenacious revolutionary built over a decade by rock solid hard work and personal sacrifice was in tatters within the revolutionary circles. Strength of character was considered the *sine qua non* of the leadership of the Indian freedom movement and Har Dayal seemed to have staggered. The millions of followers and supporters of the idealist and noble revolutionary were outraged by his *volte-face*. Har Dayal had turned his back on the Ghadr movement and the Ghadr patriots across the world felt severely betrayed. The change in his political belief came at a time when many of his associates had been hanged by Hukumat-i-Britannia, his closest compatriots Sohan Singh Bhakna, Savarkar and Bhai Parmanand were languishing in the dark chambers of Cellular Jail in the Andamans and several of his comrades like Krishna Varma, Madame Cama, S. R. Rana, Rash Behari, Barkatullah, Pillai, Hanwant Sahai, Bhupendranath Dutta, and Tarak Nath Das had continued to rebel against the British Empire all over the world. Evidently, even his protégé Gobind who had spent ten months in Alameda jail in California alleged that this act of Har Dayal was "reprehensible'".

Many nationalist leaders like Nehru who respected Har Dayal were left wondering what had brought about the complete reversal of opinion. M. N. Roy recorded in his memoirs, "(Har Dayal) wrote a book describing his experiences in Germany. The experience had embittered him. He appeared to be an apologist of the British rule in India and advocated Dominion Status as against complete independence. He wrote something, which, though true, ought not to be said by a revolutionary Indian nationalist. Pointing out the fact that the fighters for Indian freedom had learned their political lesson from Britain, Har Dayal made the declaration that, if India was the mother, Britain was the grandmother. That naturally scandalized all Indian nationalists. It was alleged that he had written the book with the object of getting permission to return to Britain and subsequently to India...."

In India, the newspaper *Leader* of Allahabad published, "Many strange things have been happening these days, but the complete conversion of Lala Har Dayal once the most uncompromising foe of British rule in India to a faith in British Imperialism accompanied by a loss of faith in educated Indians is perhaps the strangest of all". The paper concluded, "Lala Har Dayal has been disillusioned...". And added, "if he has been." It then argued, "But having regard to his multiform transformations, no one can or will take him seriously. His libels on his countrymen are therefore beneath contempt."

Conversely Lajpat Rai, the only national leader who had known Har Dayal since his university days concluded, "Nobody, however, knows what changes are yet to take place in his views. He is quite an uncertain item. He is an idealist of a strange type. He is simple in his life and apparently quite indifferent to the opinions of others about him. He does not court favor at the hands of anyone and would go out of his way to help others. He is loved and respected by hundreds and thousands of his countrymen, including those who do not agree with his views or his propaganda or his program. Even the late Mr. Gokhale admired him..."

After the armistice, countless careers were destroyed and this was certainly seemed the tragic end of Har Dayal's radical political career. Har Dayal probably knew this recantation would haunt him for the rest of his life. On his part, he had tried to play a game of clever deception. He had risked his sterling reputation and his standing as a frontline leader of the Indian freedom movement to accomplish a larger goal. His recantation was a case of *exitus acta probat*: the outcome justifies the deed.

For Har Dayal now living in Sweden all means were justified to realize the ultimate objective of independence of India.

A Strategic Lie

Notwithstanding the obvious propaganda value of Har Dayal's statements Hukumat-i-Britannia quickly saw through the shrewd revolutionary's plan. They regarded his overt writings and pro British Empire leanings as a strategic lie. A series of letters regarding the Indian revolutionary were exchanged between the Secretary of State in London and the British Viceroy's office in Simla making it clear that they had very cleverly grasped Har Dayal's googly. Har Dayal's gamble to convince the Hukumat-i-Britannia that he was now on their side didn't pay off.

On the contrary, the Home Department of Hukumat-i-Britannia worked overtime to have Har Dayal expelled from Sweden. Hukumat-i-Britannia was convinced that the Indian revolutionary despite renouncing his opinions was secretly running an underground movement for Indian independence from the relative safety of Sweden.

Since his successful escape from San Francisco in April 1914, Har Dayal who always outwitted his captors, had now catapulted to the top position in the secret list of thirty Indian revolutionaries who threatened the British Empire. The NAI records reveal that the list included Virendranath, Barkatullah, M. N. Roy, Rash Behari Bose, Mahendra Pratap, Chenchaia among others. The Hukumat-i-Britannia wanted to prosecute Har Dayal in the United Kingdom or extradite him to India for incitement to wage war against His Majesty for his Ghadr activities. As punishment for his audacity, they intended to sentence him to the sazaa-e-kalapani or just hang him.

Instructions went out from the India Office to Sir Arthur Grant Duff, Envoy Extraordinary and Minister Plenipotentiary to the King of Sweden at the British Legation in Stockholm not to issue a passport to Har Dayal. Instantaneously, the police in Britain was directed to arrest him should he ever come within British jurisdiction. Efforts were made to charge him for high treason and condemn him to capital punishment. The legal guidance offered to Hukumat-i-Britannia was that Har Dayal's offenses would be difficult to prove in Indian courts. They were advised to put him on trial in Britain rather than India as local agitation could prevent him from being sentenced to death as in the matter of Bhai Parmanand in the Lahore Conspiracy Case of 1915.

But Har Dayal could never be convicted by Hukumat-i-Britannia. A few months later despite unusual diplomatic pressure from His Majesty's Government in London, the Swedish Government refused to deport Har Dayal, as there were no formal charges against him. The Utrikesdepartementet confirmed to Whitehall that they had no objection to his stay in Sweden without papers. The Polisbyrån continued to keep a watch on his activities and communicated that he was 'giving no trouble'.

Hukumat-i-Britannia had to live with the fact that the arch conspirator of the Ghadr movement had managed to slip through their fingers.

14

THE INDISK PROFESSOR OF GOTEBORG

"Har Dayal stayed on in Sweden and during the last years of his life taught Indian philosophy in the old University of Uppsala. That was a recognition of his learning and intellectual caliber."

Manabendra Nath Roy
Indian Revolutionary and Radical Humanist

Sunday, April 13th, 1919, is a day Indians will never forget.

On that day of 'Baisakhi', one of Punjab's largest festivals at just 1710 hours, an open-topped motorcar pulled up near the Jallianwala Bagh, an irregular six and a half-acre area of waste ground in the ancient city of Amritsar where a peaceful meeting of about twenty-five thousand people was taking place. Many of them who came in from the countryside for the Baisakhi festival, attended out of idle curiosity to listen to the poets and politicians ardently addressing the audience from a platform. An aircraft hovered overhead after the fifth speech was completed and briefly unnerved the crowd.

The short-tempered chain-smoking Brigadier-General Reginald 'Rex' Dyer (1864–1927), of the 45th Infantry Brigade and the face of the brutal Hukumat-i-Britannia, arrived at the Bagh. Dyer attempted to bring an armored car, with its machine gun, into the area but was thwarted by the narrowness of the street. He then marched to a raised bank within a walled garden with his bodyguard Sergeant William John Anderson of the 1/25th Battalion, London Regiment and Captain F. C. C. Briggs, a young officer of the King's Regiment who had won the DSO. An armed party of fifty British Indian armymen followed them. The armymen rapidly fortified the two narrow exits. Dyer's military objective was dispersing the prohibited seditious meeting.

This was war for the military-minded man.

In the months gone by Dyer's superior officer Lt. Governor O'Dwyer had been concerned that the rise of Ghadr movement that professed an end to British rule had gained ground in North India. The veterans of WWI had begun to return home and amplified political awareness and determination across the length and breadth of the country. News about Britain and Germany's conflict in WWI had brought a transformation in people's ideas of equality and liberty amongst Indians who were earlier unfamiliar with international events. Further, the tyrannical administration under O'Dwyer had alienated the citizens. The time tested *divide et impera* strategy was failing as all the religious communities were uniting against the authority of Hukumat-i-Britannia. Hindus and Muslims were witnessed drinking water from the same cup.

To make matters worse, based on the contentious report of Justice Sidney Rowlatt's committee of 1918, the Anarchical and Revolutionary Crimes Act, better known as the Rowlatt Act (1919) The provisions of the Rowlatt Act grew from measures in the Defense of India Act of 1915 to arrest the Ghadr patriots who were defined as a threat to the security of the state while it was involved in fighting the Great War. The tyrannical Rowlatt Act was enacted to deal with acts of sedition that were inspired by the Ghadr Party. It was an emergency legislation that allowed political cases to be tried without juries and permitted internment of suspects without trial with the suspension of habeas corpus. An aroused Indian public resented the proposed act.

At this moment Mahatma Gandhi unleashed his first nationwide *satyagraha* in India against the authoritarian act. In different regions of India, there were political strikes and voluntary closure of shops and schools. On March 30th, 1919, Hindus, Muslims, and Sikhs came out in a joint protest against the Rowlatt Act at the Town Hall in Delhi. Both the British Indian armymen and the Police fired at the protestors. Many Indians died in the macabre bayonet charge and due to bullet wounds. This was just a precursor to the events that followed. Prompted by the Delhi firing, O'Dwyer who ruled with an iron hand managed to keep Mahatma Gandhi away from Punjab and had him detained in Palwal near Delhi to be sent back to Bombay.

In Amritsar, the city of Madanlal Dhingra, two prominent young leaders, Barrister Dr. Saifuddin Kitchlu (1888–1963), educated at Peterhouse, Cambridge and Dr. Satyapal (1885–1954), a medical doctor were arrested on April 9th and deported to Kangra valley on O'Dwyer orders. Their case had many similarities to the deportation of Lajpat Rai and Ajit Singh in 1907. Incensed by the expulsion

Dr. Kitchlu and Dr. Satyapal on April 10th, 1919, a mob in Amritsar killed four British men and attacked Marcella Sherwood who supervised the Mission Day School for Girls. Hukumat-i-Britannia's police had fired at the protestors leading to many deaths. In the midst of an increasingly tense situation in Punjab, the threat of a nationwide insurrection on the lines of the dreaded 1857 revolt loomed large. O'Dwyer was determined to impose martial law to avoid the repeat of Ghadr of 1857. He moved Dyer from Jalandhar to decisively take over control of the challenging law and order situation in a city where the Civil Government of the Deputy Commissioner Miles Irving had lost control. O'Dwyer's words to Dyer were, "if troops were to be used and they were forced to open fire, they should make an example". On his arrival in Amritsar, Dyer issued a proclamation ordering a total curfew and a ban on any kind of gathering of more than four men.

What followed is now part of the world's annals of the worst state-led totalitarianism.

Dyer claimed later that at the Jallianwala Bagh, he had stumbled upon the epicenter of "the rebellion that was in the air" and he had already made up his mind. Within thirty seconds of his arrival and without issuing a single warning to the considerable size of unarmed and defenseless demonstrators, on Dyer's direct orders, his band of armymen unleashed hell. Their .303 Lee Enfield rifles freely sprayed the bullets at defenseless and unarmed targets barely a hundred and fifty yards away.

The sound of fire filled the air. Initially, the crowd thought that the armymen were firing blanks and cried aloud, *"phokian phokian"* (empty) but then bodies began to fall. Then there was pandemonium. The deadly rifle fire at first was directed upon the center so the trapped gathering frantically darted to the sides. The firing was then focused on the sides resulting in a fierce stampede. Dyer's armymen reloaded their smoking guns several times and as they squeezed the triggers repeatedly they were ordered to shoot to kill. "Fire low, for what else have you been brought here?", a man heard Dyer command.

Many threw themselves down on the ground as the gunfire trailed them. The Bagh was filled with the loud rifle cracks, sounds of bullets thumping into human bodies, echoes of shots ricocheting off the walls and the desperate shrieks of twenty-five thousand people in horror.

Afterwards the arch imperialist Winston Churchill, in the House of Commons debate of July 8th, 1920, described the incident as; "The crowd was unarmed, except with bludgeons. It was not attacking anybody or anything... When fire had been opened upon it to disperse it, it tried to run away. Pinned up in a narrow place considerably smaller than Trafalgar Square, with hardly any exits, and packed together so that one bullet would drive through three or four bodies, the people ran madly this way and the other. When the fire was directed upon the center, they ran to the sides. The fire was then directed to the sides. Many threw themselves down on the ground, the fire was then directed down on the ground...."

This ghastly drama of military precision continued unabated for ten minutes and 1,650 rounds of ammunition were fired. After almost all the bullets were exhausted and the noise of the gunfire had subsided, over a thousand dead and wounded Sikhs, Hindus and Muslims lay on the ground. Many had died while seeking refuge in the small well within the premises in the mayhem that followed. After the shameful atrocity, the calm and composed Dyer left as abruptly as he had arrived. The six and a half acres of the enclosed garden were saturated with blood and flesh.

Back at his headquarters after the monstrous undertaking, the acting military commander for Amritsar, Dyer communicated to his superiors without remorse that he was "confronted by a revolutionary army". He claimed to have brought the troublesome city to heel. The next morning, at the Court House in the Civil Lines, he received O'Dwyer telegram, "Your action is correct Lieutenant Governor approves".

Martial Law was imposed in Punjab on April 16th, 1919 and then backdated to March 30th. There was suppression on all news going out of Punjab. Other atrocities followed, such as bombing and machine-gun fire from RAF combat aircraft over the main bazaar and the villages surrounding the town of Gujranwala eighty kilometers north of Amritsar. Subsequently, the insensitive O'Dwyer argued, "the Amritsar business cleared the air, and if there was to be a holocaust anywhere, and one regrets there should be it was best at Amritsar. Speaking with perhaps a more intimate knowledge of the situation than anyone else, I have no hesitation in saying that General Dyer's action that day was the decisive factor in crushing the rebellion, the seriousness of which is only now being realized."

To this day no one knows how many died that day. As claimed by the official records of the Hukumat-i-Britannia, the low casualty number of 379 people was agreed upon. These comprised 337 men, 41 boys, and one six-week-old baby. Civil Surgeon Dr. Williams DeeMeddy indicated that there were 1,526 casualties.

Indians put the casualty figures much higher in the worst atrocity perpetrated by Hukumat-i-Britannia since the Ghadr of 1857.

Cold-blooded Mass Murder

Months after the carnage, Dyer boarded the first class compartment of a night train from Lahore bound for Delhi. Loudly boasting to fellow British army men about the calculated brutality he vividly re-created the chaos and terror of the day. The 'butcher of Amritsar' had remained defiant and unrepentant of his actions. By sheer coincidence traveling on an upper birth in the same compartment was the twenty-nine-year old Nehru returning from a fact-finding mission of the carnage in Amritsar. He was within an earshot of the boisterous army officer and inadvertently overheard the entire conversation.

Describing the incident, Nehru recalled, "He (Dyer) pointed out how he had the whole town at his mercy and he felt like reducing the rebellious city to a heap of ashes, but he took pity on it and refrained". Nehru was furious with the man's overwhelming sense of entitlement as Dyer descended from the train at the Delhi railway station, "in pajamas colored in bright pink stripes and a dressing gown".

Set to inherit the flourishing legal practice of his multimillionaire father, the incident on the train changed the course of Nehru's life. Proud of being educated at Harrow and Cambridge, the Anglicized Nehru barely spoke a word of Hindi but the Amritsar debate marked the point of no return for him. No British action, during the whole course of British Empire's history in India, had struck a severer blow to his faith in British justice than the butchery at Amritsar and the subsequent appalling approval by the Hukumat-i-Britannia. Nehru reflected: "This cold-blooded approval of the deed shocked me greatly. It seemed absolutely immoral, indecent; to use public school language, it was the height of bad form. I realized then, more vividly than I had before, how brutal and immoral imperialism was, and how it had eaten into the souls of the British upper classes." Enraged by the racial hatred displayed at the Jallianwala Bagh, the angry young man gave up his aristocratic lifestyle and legal practice to plunge into the uncertainty of the Indian freedom movement.

Millions of moderate Indians and steadfast backers of the British Empire were outraged by Dyer's action at Jallianwala Bagh while Hukumat-i-Britannia took its time to appoint a seven-member commission under Lord William Hunter (1865–1957), the former Solicitor-General and the Senator of the College of

Justice in Scotland. Sir Chimanlal Setalvad, Pandit Jagat Narayan and Sardar Sultan Ahmed Khan were the three Indian members of the committee. Dyer appeared before it not only to defend himself but saw himself as the hero of the hour. He bluntly told the commission that when he heard a crowd was gathering, it was "my duty to immediately disperse it by rifle fire... I had made up my mind that if I fired I must fire well and strong so that it would have full effect". He told the eminent jurist, Sir Setalvad, that he would have taken the armored cars with machine guns inside if the entrance were not so narrow. Dyer was strongly censured, forced to resign from the British Indian army and reverted to the rank of Colonel. However, Dyer never once expressed regret in public for his crime and was forever upgraded in public imagination as a General.

The Saviour of India

On May 3rd, 1920, Dyer returned to Britain and in an interview with *Daily Mail*, he claimed, "I shot to save the British Raj – to preserve India for the Empire, and to protect Englishmen and Englishwomen who looked at me for protection... I had to shoot. I had thirty seconds to make up my mind what action to take, and I did it."

After winning the WWI, the British Empire was at the zenith of imperial power and glory. Both O'Dwyer and Dyer were designated heroes in Britain who had taught the 'bloody browns' a lesson. They even praised Dyer's own 'crawling order' after the massacre, under which dozens of blameless Indians were forced to crawl on their bellies along the lane where the English mission schoolteacher Marcella Sherwood was hit. In London, major newspapers hailed the bloodthirsty Dyer as 'The Man who saved India' and single-handedly prevented a second mutiny. There were a large number of Dyer supporters who justified his action as, "It was Prussianism, but, then, Prussianism is necessary". They agreed with imperialists like Sir John Kaye's view, "India had been won by the sword and must be retained by the sword."

The House of Lords including one hundred and twenty-nine Lords and a similar number of Members of the House of Commons of the British Parliament lauded the massacre man for his 'feat' and honored him. *Morning Post*, a London based newspaper presented Dyer a purse of £26,317. Nobel Laureate Rudyard Kipling was among those who heaped praise upon Dyer and contributed to the purse.

Later in an article, 'India's Path to Suicide', published in *The Globe* (January 21st, 1921), Dyer declared the attempt to overthrow the Hukumat-i-Britannia was 'well planned'. He suggested that an Eleventh Commandment should be applied to India, "Thou shalt not agitate". Eventually, the man did not have a night's sleep since Jallianwala Bagh and lived out his days in sickness and isolation. He died quietly in his bed at Long Ashton near Bristol on July 23rd, 1927 and was given a military funeral. Startlingly, like a national hero, he had a second ceremonial funeral through the streets of London. His body was carried on a gun carriage draped in the Union flag, from the Guards' Chapel to St Martin-in-the-Fields. Rudyard Kipling's wreath bore the tribute: 'He did his duty as he saw it.' And in Will Podmore's *British Foreign Policy since 1870*, it is confirmed that General Henry Rawlinson, India's Commander-in-Chief, declared in 1920, "You may say what you like about not holding India by the sword, but you have held it by the sword for one hundred years and when you give up the sword you will be turned out. You must keep the sword ready to hand and in case of trouble or rebellion use it relentlessly. Montagu (Edwin Samuel Montagu, Secretary of State for India) calls it terrorism, so it is and in dealing with natives of all classes you have to use terrorism whether you like it or not."

Amritsar Became India

The fifteen minutes on that fateful April 13th, afternoon changed the course of human history. In that short period, Amritsar became India. The heartless massacre shook the nation like never before.

For millions of Indians, the bloodbath in Amritsar uncovered the true face of British imperialism – an empire built on a mountain of human skulls. This was a moment in history more vital even than the Ghadr of 1857. It had no parallel until the Nazis wiped out the Czech village of Lidice in June 1942. British historian Percival Spear commented that with the Jallianwala Bagh carnage, "a scar was drawn across Indo-British relations deeper than any which had been inflicted since the Mutiny". And another British historian Alan John Percivale Taylor called it, "the decisive moment when Indians were alienated from British rule".

A twenty-two-year-old Nanak Singh was in Jallianwala Bagh with two of his colleagues but returned home alone as they fell to Dyer's bullets and the ensuing mayhem. He poured out his heart in the form of a book, *Khooni Baisakhi* published in May 1920 that was banned by Hukumat-i-Britannia. That April day an Indian teenager Udham Singh (1899–1940), who was being raised at the Khalsa Orphanage was deeply affected by the massacre. News traveled all across India of the shattered skulls and body parts of innocent Indians ripped apart by British bullets. These were a description of scenes from hell - heaps of dead bodies lying there some on their backs and some with their faces upturned. The stories from Jallianwala Bagh traumatized Udham Singh. It is said that he picked up blood-soaked earth from Jallianwala Bagh with his hands and smeared it across his forehead. Then he swore to slay the men responsible, no matter how long it took.

The protests that broke out in the country were exemplified by the renunciation of the British Knighthood by Nobel Laureate Rabindranath Tagore conferred to him on June 3rd, 1915. In a message to the British Viceroy Lord Frederic Thesiger Chelmsford (1868–1933), the poet wrote: "The time has come when badges of honor make our shame glaring in their incongruous context of humiliation... I for my part wish to stand, shorn of all special distinctions, by the side of my countrymen who, for their so-called insignificance, are liable to suffer a degradation not fit for human beings." And he asked of the Viceroy Lord Chelmsford, "relieve me of the title of knighthood".

Former President of the Indian National Congress, Sir C. Sankaran Nair (1857–1934) resigned in disgust from the membership of British Viceroy's executive council and during the final interview, when Lord Chelmsford asked if he could suggest somebody as his successor he pointed to his peon Ramprasad for, "he will say yes to whatever you say." In his book, *Gandhi and Anarchy*, Nair wrote, "Before the reforms it was in the power of the Lieutenant-Governor (Sir Michael O'Dwyer of Punjab), a single individual, to commit the atrocities in the Punjab we know too well." O'Dwyer sued him for libel and won damages of £500 and costs of about £7,000. Justice Henry Alfred McCardie summed up the case and ruled: "I express my view that Dyer, under the grave and exceptional circumstances, acted rightly, and in my opinion, upon his evidence, he was wrongly punished by the Secretary of State for India."

Overcome by pain and horrified by the actions of his countrymen, Charles Andrews in a public speech declared, "English honor had departed". Har Dayal's friend added, "I could not sleep or eat or even speak to anyone after what I saw. I wanted to go apart, and be alone... it was a massacre, a butchery." And Lajpat Rai declared, "If the administration of Sir Michael O'Dwyer and the Punjab tragedy enacted by him awakens the Indians to a sense of their duty in the matter, the blood of hundreds (including children) who died at Jallianwala Bagh, Gujranwala, Lahore, and other places would not have been spilled in vain."

For Mahatma Gandhi, the massacre at Jallianwala Bagh in 1919 was the turning point. Alarmed by growing violence, he called off the *satyagraha*. A few years ago, on his return to India in 1915 he was still loyal to the Crown and believed that a reformed British commonwealth and Indian nationalism would be ultimately compatible. On August 11th, 1918, he had written to Professor Herbert Stanley Jevons of Allahabad University, "that India can deliver her mission to the world better through England". The slaughter by Dyer transformed him into an irreconcilable opponent of British rule. He channelized the mass awakening and the feeling of helplessness in a peaceful direction. His message of *ahimsa* resonated with a population traumatized by the ferocity of WWI and slaughter at the Jallianwala Bagh. He emerged as a major political leader of mass nationalism in India and paved the way for the next phase of India's independence struggle.

The End of the Ghadr Experiment

The darkness at the heart displayed by Hukumat-i-Britannia at Jallianwala Bagh marked the end of the Ghadr movement inspired second Indian war of independence much like the fall of Delhi had concluded the Ghadr of 1857 over sixty-two years ago.

Over half a century later, on May 9th, 1973, Gobind described Jallianwala Bagh's impact on the Ghadr movement in a talk at UC Berkeley. Gobind modestly acknowledged that he, "had some thing to do with the initiating of the Ghadr experiment" and recalled, "What kind of an experiment was the Ghadr? It was based upon a theory, which had to be tested by a test. Crudely stated theory was even that the pre-learned Indians can be instructed politically, and become motivated by modern freedom. The idea of self-government, which is political freedom, can be transmitted from the learned to the unlearned to the unlearned common people, farmers, factory and other sorts of routine workers and so forth…" Gobind claimed that Har Dayal, the leader of the Ghadr Party at the time, was very effective in carrying out this experiment, appreciably "changing nonpolitical Indian minds." He maintained that in those early years, the Indian masses lacked political agency by being pre-political and "pre-modern in their cultural experiences".

Soon thereafter, the Ghadr Party became an international network of political solidarity committed to radical political change in India. It was an expression of cosmopolitanism and a unique struggle that depended upon the employment, élan, and emotional investment of countless individuals. It was also serious and important aspect of India's freedom movement, full of adventure and high drama – inflamatory propaganda, secret societies, assassination plots, dramatic bombings, powerful intrigues by spies, ships loaded with guns commandeered to India and secret armies heading to India. In the years that followed, several thousand young men including the top leadership of the Ghadr Party were killed, arrested, hanged or banished to the darkness of 'Sazaa-e-Kalapani' in the Andamans.

In *Dr. Emily Brown's biography*, Gobind recollected that he had interviewed Sir James DuBoulay, former Home Secretary in London, thirteen years after the Jallianwala Bagh tragedy in August 1932. In that conversation, DuBoulay exposed the motivation of Lt. Governor O'Dwyer and Dyer behind the brutal massacre. The senior official confirmed that Hukumat-i-Britannia had fired because they were frightened by the Ghadr propaganda printed from San Francisco. Gobind recalled, "He startled me by saying that the Amritsar massacre could be traced to the Ghadr movement... I had never thought of it that way. If we had achieved that much, to make those idiots believe, then we had done something. They took us seriously, so seriously that they blew our heads off." Till the end of his life, Gobind asserted that there were enough reasons to believe that was a kind of revenge out of fear, on account of the Ghadr Party in India.

Eventually, the selfless exertion and sacrifices of several thousand non-resident Indian patriots had exposed the carefully nurtured image of Hukumat-i-Britannia from a benevolent regime with a belief in fair play romanticized as 'British Raj' to a despotic dictatorship that needed to be gotten rid off. After the Jallianwala Bagh, the Ghadr Party continued its operations in the United States and other parts of the world but it was never the lethal force it once was. Gobind believed that the Ghadr experiment "prepared the way indirectly, for the Great Gandhi Experiment".

By the middle of 1919, Hukumat-i-Britannia had severely crushed the Ghadr movement in India, but one major threat remained at large and was ensconced in Sweden - the architect of the Ghadr movement - Har Dayal.

The agreeable climate of Goteborg

On a summer afternoon, in 1919, an awkwardly dressed and unshaven Har Dayal holding on to some Swedish newspapers and his notes overlooked his shoulder once and then unlocked the door at Tågmästaregatan 6, Goteborg. The stateless and nearly penniless man had walked back from the local university and its bibliotek to his two-room apartment. He was now alone. Disconnected from the heat, dust, and politics of India, Har Dayal who had once labeled the British Empire as 'British Vampire' and failed to outmaneuver the Hukumat-i-Britannia by claiming to change sides was now stranded in Scandinavia. He was gradually learning to survive in the difficult weather conditions and rugged wilderness of Sweden. Despite minuscule professional income, despite the cold weather, despite the language barrier and despite the difficulty in finding vegetarian food in grocery stores, Har Dayal's fragile body, titanic mind, and exemplary spirit were intact.

After leaving Stockholm in March 1919, Har Dayal first went to Uppsala, the university town and Gävle and secured some lectures. Sweden had founded the University at Uppsala in 1477 before Coumbus sailed in search of a route for India. As the largest university in Sweden, it had almost three thousand students. From Uppsala Har Dayal moved to Goteborg (Gothenburg), the second largest city in Sweden with about two hundred thousand inhabitants and located on the western coast. Har Dayal finally found solitude in the city of canals, culture, and cuisine that he had previously sought in Algiers, La Martinique, and Honolulu. Goteborg's geographical location exposed Goteborg to foreign influences - related to production technology, consumer goods, and politics. It was initially characterized by fishing and foreign trade but evolved into an industrial metropolis. The Svenska Ostindiska Companiet (Swedish East India Company) was founded here in 1731 and ended up importing tea from China. Warmer than Stockholm, it had cultural vibrancy with neoclassical architecture and tram rattled streets. Finding the climate of Goteborg suitable he afterwords stressed in a book, "Don't you think that the climate of Sweden is the best in the world?" I (Har Dayal) replied, "Yes; and in Sweden, I prefer the climate of the town of Goteborg where I live at present…"

Separated from his home and all alone Har Dayal was funded in part by his family and friends in India. Since his arrival in Goteborg, he regularly wrote letters to Sunder Rani and Shanti Devi in India once a month and made plans for them to join him in Sweden if circumstances permitted.

For the first time in his life, Har Dayal had ample time and divided it between reading, teaching and meeting new people in Sweden. This marked a return to the easy-going life of a scholar and he had a soft existence of writing on Indian economics, philosophy, art, and literature. He also studied music, painting, and sculpture at the Goteborgs Universitet. Har Dayal connected with Professor Tours

Algot Johnsoon Arne of the National History Museum who was one of the founders of the Swedish Orienteering Society. He informed Professor Arne in Swedish that he hoped to begin his philosophical publications soon, "I have finished political activities of all kind, as I think, I must devote my self to intellectual education". Professor Arne helped him get his work published in *Dagens Nyketer* and made him a member of the society. He also initiated communication with the great explorer-scholar, Erland Nordenskjold, Professor of ethnography and the famous Swedish Indologist Professor Jarl Hellen Charpentier at Uppsala and met them frequently.

Over the next few years, Har Dayal continued to earn a living by lecturing in Swedish on India (using lantern slides) before large audiences all over the country. Initially, he got English lectures translated in Swedish but soon he was comfortable in the language and could read, write and teach in it fluently. Har Dayal had an astonishing talent for languages and now at thirty-four, he had gained complete command over English, Sanskrit, Hindi, Punjabi, Urdu, Persian, Pashto, Arabic, Turkish, French, Italian, German and Swedish. He now began taking classes in basic Latin and Greek, both of which he considered indispensible for his future philosophical work. He devoted time to studying Confucius, Mencius, Plato, and Aristotle, and recommended to his friends Diogenes Laertius's *Lives of Greek Philosophers*. He dreamt of a time when he would have founded a school of Philosophy at Athens.

From the local Swedish newspapers Har Dayal learnt about Nobel laureate Tagore's arrival at Stockholm centralstationen on May 26th, 1921, with his traveling companions. According to press reports, large number of people had assembled on the platform and "the surging crowd" outside the station "received Tagore in silence and with bare heads". In Sweden, he was mainly regarded as a personification of eastern wisdom. Tagore drove with Dr. Erik Axel Karlfeldt, the Swedish poet and secretary of the Swedish Academy to the Grand Hotel. Eight years after he had been awarded the Nobel Prize he gave the customary acceptance speech at the Swedish academy in Stockholm where he laid stress on global cooperation and harmony. Har Dayal consciously did not meet Tagore during his stay in Stockholm as the Polisbyrån continued their surveillance on him and the permission to stay in Sweden was still being renewed on a four and six-monthly bases.

In the summer of 1922, Har Dayal was a featured speaker at the Goteborg Labor Institute, a venue for adult education. Hjalmar Pehrsson, the former teacher at Mölnlycke's folkhögskola (Folk High School) was in the audience and invited the well-educated Indian to a suburb called Mölnlycke about twelve kilometers southeast of Goteborg to teach on a regular basis. Four years since his arrival in Sweden, in September 1922, Har Dayal accepted the offer to be a teacher at the folkhögskola and moved to Mölnlycke. Here he lived his usual ascetic life and rented a room from a local gardener and his wife. As was his practice it was sparsely furnished with a locally made Indian style cot and thousands of books, mostly in Swedish. At night in Mölnlycke, Har Dayal often spent time observing the billions of stars in the Scandinavian skies and developed an interest in Astronomy. He wondered, "Astronomy introduces us to the realm of mystery and magnificence which is inexhaustible in its perennial fascination and its never-ending challenge to human intellect". During the day, he spent his leisure time rowing a boat in the lake or meandering around the numerous paths. He was always reading and almost dipping his nose in the book. When asked by his gardener friend what was he thinking all the time, he softly replied "freedom of my country".

Newer Leaders and Younger Men

From the relatively secure environment of Scandinavia, Har Dayal kept his secret code messaging system active and was in communication with many of his former colleagues in India, Germany, Japan and California. But in the process of escaping from the clutches of the Hukumat-i-Britannia, the self-motivated Indian revolutionary had lost several years in exile. In that period the Indian freedom movement had bypassed him. Newer leaders and younger men had replaced him. He had overtly cut himself off from the mainstream Indian politics while new organizations emerged as rivals to the Indian National Congress in his motherland in the 1920s.

On October 17th, 1920, Har Dayal's admirer, M. N. Roy who had reached Russia after living in the United States and Mexico, founded the Communist Party of India at Tashkent, with seven members attending the meeting. Roy had been elected to the executive committee of the Communist International at its Congress in Moscow and played an important role in the early days of the party. The Communist Party of Great Britain aided the Indian communist movement despite its financial limitations.

In November 1920, His Majesty King Emperor George V had ordered Hukumat-i-Britannia to grant general amnesty to a few political prisoners including Bhai Parmanand after five years of 'Sazaa-e-Kalapani' in the Andamans. In May 1921, after ten years of being locked in the dreadful dark world of the Cellular Jail, both the Savarkar brothers had been brought back to the Yerawada Prison on mainland India. Finally on January 6th, 1924, Har Dayal's colleague Vinayak Savarkar was set free by Hukumat-i-Britannia from Yerawada Prison on the condition that he would not participate in politics for the next five years. Subsequently, Savarkar focused on social reform, writing and became a strong proponent of Hindu culture in India by heading 'Hindu Mahasabha'.

On September 27th, 1925, on Vijayadashami day, Dr. Keshav Hedgewar (1889–1940) launched the 'Rashtriya Swayamsevak Sangh' (RSS), in Nagpur with the words, "All of us must train ourselves physically, intellectually and in every way so as to be capable of achieving our cherished goal". Four other doctors attended the inaugural meeting and these included Vinayak Savarkar's elder brother Dr. Ganesh Savarkar, Dr. Balakrishna Shivram Moonje, Dr. Laxman Vasudev Paranjpe and Dr. B. B. Tholkar.

All these organisations survived beyond the independence of India, but largely due to Har Dayal's exile in Europe, the important chapter of Ghadr Party and the second Indian war of independence, when he was one of the forerunners, remained a footnote in Indian history books.

California Dreaming

Har Dayal had fond memories of his incomparable life and work at Stanford and Berkeley in the years 1912–14. He had developed lifelong friendships in California and had matured into a worldclass leader. Not forgetting his former comrades in India, Europe, and the United States, Har Dayal kept up his correspondence with Brooks at Stanford among others as he made plans to return to the United States in the future for his old propaganda work.

Faraway in San Francisco, Har Dayal's outstanding reputation remained undamaged amongst his friends and large group of supporters. At a dinner in honor of New York based Indian political leader Syud Hossain by the American Women's Independence Committee at the Palace Hotel in San Francisco, journalist John D. Barry recalled, "Friends! It is a great pleasure for me to preside at the dinner and to have the honor of introducing our guests to our honored speaker Mr. Hossain - The occasion has many happy associations for me. It makes me think of the Hindoo (Indian) friends I have had here for the past dozen years of my life. It makes me think of my friend, Har Dayal who, for many years, lived here and was a great figure here. I occasionally get a letter from Har Dayal, now in Sweden, as you all know, where he has made a place for himself. I am very proud to know a man like Har Dayal… Mr. Hossain is going to tell us about India… and he is going to show us those forces that are behind the struggle of the people that we know and the people who are so ably represented in men like Har Dayal and who are so fine represented in the Hindoo (Indian) types that we have in our midst are great forces and that therein lies the hope of a world peace…"

Intriguingly on June 19ᵗʰ, 1921, Paramount Pictures released a sixty-minute Hollywood silent drama film (six reels), *The Bronze Bell*. Its plot centered on the Oxford-educated 'Har Dyal Rutton', a young prince of Khandawar in India in the 1850s, who promised his dying father he would lead a revolt against the English colonial masters of India but escaped to America, to live in obscurity. Here he met a messenger sent from India to remind him of the promise he made to his father and realized that he could not give up his responsibility. Coincidentally in the original story, Har Dyal Rutton is described as, "a singular man, an exotic result of the unnatural conditions we English have brought about in India… As the young Maharaja, he was sent to England to be educated. I'm told his record at Oxford was a brilliant one…" Hollywood actor Courtenay Foote played the part of Har Dyal Rutton. And the second mutiny is explained as "…such is the belief of every thinking man in India who is at all informed. The entire country is undermined with conspiracy and sedition; day after day a vast, silent, underground movement goes on, fomenting rebellion against the English rule. The worst of it is, there's no stopping it, no way of scotching the serpent; its heads are myriad, seemingly…"

Our Educational Problem

As months became years in peaceful Sweden in 1922, Har Dayal's second book, *Our Educational Problem*, a compilation of essays he had written previously was published in Madras. With a preface by Lajpat Rai, in this book Har Dayal discussed the issue of national education in India and attacked British Empire's education system and its aims as one which "de-Hinduizes us and causes the decay of our national institutions thereby hindering the growth of the feeling of Hindu unity and national life". He called for making Sanskrit the link language for national integration of India and rebuked himself for being inept in communicating with his fellow countrymen in this ancient cultural language. He declared, "Sanskrit is the only national tongue for all India, the language of our noble religion and the tongue associated with India's highest hopes and happiness. It is the medium of intercommunication among the various States. And it is the language of science and scholarship. It speaks to us of our common past and can furnish the only solid foundation for a genuine national movement... No Hindu who is ignorant of Sanskrit can have any pretentions to culture..." He added, "...some people say that Sanskrit is a dead language and that it cannot be commonly used for purpose of national business. This idea is altogether erroneous. It is easier for a Hindu to learn Sanskrit than English. Sanskrit is not dead – it is we who are dead..."

From his home in Mölnlycke, Har Dayal proposed to write a series of books in Urdu and Hindi on democratic movements in Europe and the lives of great leaders. He also wanted to translate the major political works in Indian languages. He sought the help of the spiritual leader, Swami Satya Devaji, who he had first met in Boston in February 1911 with his plan since, "Here in Europe the public mind is first trained and elevated by many such books which are sold at a cheap price".

Knowing that his mail would be interecepted by the British Secret Service, Har Dayal informed Swamiji that he was no longer interested in working with revolutionary Indian nationalists in Berlin and California. He did not think they could "accomplish anything". His disappointment was visible as he disclosed, "I devoted myself to Indian movements fifteen years ago and sacrificed everything for them. But what has been the result? Only sickness and waste of time and energy... no one helped me with money when I was ill in foreign countries and nothing could be done for the movement". *(Letters of Lala Har Dayal)*

A supporter of vegetarianism for most of his adult life, Har Dayal was invited by Swedish Vegetarian Society to lecture at the fifth annual Vegetarian Congress held in Stockholm on May 19th - 21st, 1923. He delivered a paper on 'Vegetarianism in India' in Swedish and English with his usual panache and sense of humor. In the peace and calm of Goteborg, the spiritually inclined thinker revisited Buddhism and began learning the Pali language. Writing extensively he published an article in *The Modern Review*, entitled 'Three Ideas on Education', arguing for reinstating Pali language to Indian university curricula. He also denounced the dreaded Caste system of India, "Caste is the curse of India. Caste, in all its forms, has made us a nation of slaves... Caste must go, and it must not go slowly and gradually, but immediately and completely and irrevocably. This should be our vow: No compromise". He added that during the Buddhist period, "India achieved her greatest triumphs in science, ethics, education, art, and international prestige. India has produced few greater men than Buddha, Asoka, Mahinda, Buddhagosha, Kumarajiva and other immortal representatives of the Buddhist period".

Charles Andrews, who was now a prominent British compatriot of Mahatma Gandhi in India in his reminiscences of Har Dayal's transformation in *The Modern Review* (1940), recalled, "Lala Har Dayal wrote to me many times while he was in Scandinavia and told me how much he had changed in his mentality about the use of violence to attain political ends. I think that it was the study of Buddhism that converted him and also some of his experiences with men of violence that had destroyed his belief in it. I never had any doubts about the sincerity of his conversion because Har Dayal was the soul of truth and always strictly followed his own conscience." Dr. Gurdev Singh Deol's article titled, 'Lala Har Dayal as a revolutionary', published in *Madhya Pradesh Chronicle* on June 2nd, 1966 revealed Har Dayal's evolving thought process, who claimed, "when I was a child, I believed as a child, when I became young, I believed as a young man and when I grew old, I did as an old man..."

The news of the passing of his benefactor Principal Rudra on June 29th, 1925 reached Har Dayal in Mölnlycke via a note from Andrews. Rudra too had remained a close confidante to Mahatma Gandhi who stayed at his house at Kashmiri Gate on his visits to Delhi.

The Lost Generation of Indian Revolutionaries

In March 1926, prominent Indian leader Jawaharlal Nehru, the controversial leader of the Congress Party who had already been jailed three times (totaling to 366 days) by Hukumat-i-Britannia checked into Hotel Roseraie in Geneva. He had reached Switzerland along with his eight-year-old daughter Indira (1919–1984) and his ailing wife Kamla for her treatment at the Swiss sanatorium in Montana. During this moderately slow period, Nehru took the opportunity to meet many older political radicals of all 'shades, flavors and colors' of the early part of the century who now lived in exile in Europe.

Away from the latest political developments in India, in the post-WWI Europe the former associates of Har Dayal and the important revolutionaries of the India House, the Paris India Group and the Berlin India Committee lived a dreary life. From once playing an exciting and vital role in the historic freedom movement of

India they were now reduced to a life of regrets. In the 1920s, most Indian exiles were banned from entering India and didn't possess any proper identification papers or passports. They lived as refugees scattered across Europe and there was no adventure left for them in Europe after the war.

Madame Cama had lived in Paris for decades and had become old and infirm. Debarred by Hukumat-i-Britannia from returning to her motherland and realizing that the end was approaching, she had selected for herself a grave in the famous Pere-La Chaise cemetery, in the East section of Paris. In his *Autobiography*, Nehru detailed his European meetings: "In Paris, we saw old Madame Bhikaji Cama, rather fierce and terrifying as she came up to you and peered into your face, and pointing at you asked abruptly who you were... the answer made no difference (probably she was too deaf to hear it) for she formed her own impressions and stuck to them despite facts to the contrary".

Among the other important revolutionaries of the era, Nehru met was Raja Mahendra Pratap. He later recalled, "Another well-known person whose name I had often heard, but whom I met for the first time in Switzerland, was Raja Mahendra Pratap. He was a delightful optimist, living completely in the air and refusing to having anything to do with realities... He appeared in strange composite attire which might have been suitable in the highlands of Tibet or in the Siberian plans but was completely out of place at Montreux in the summer."

"Long ago," he told Nehru solemnly, "I lost a valuable dispatch box in China. Since then I have preferred to carry all my papers on my person." Seeing all kinds of papers stuffed in his bulging pockets Nehru thought it was difficult to take him seriously for "he seemed a character out of medieval romance, a Don Quixote who had strayed into the twentieth century. But he was absolutely straight and thoroughly earnest." Raja Mahendra Pratap in his memoirs recorded that they had met in a palatial hotel and detailed, "we sat alone in his sitting room, we two talked long exchanging our mental notes... I could see he had socialistic views. He even condemned religion while I thought it was necessary for humanity... we could find no program of common action in the foreign lands."

Nehru along with Indira went to meet Krishna Varma in Geneva who was still in contact with old associates such as Madame Cama, Har Dayal, and Ajit Singh. Nehru chronicled in his *Autobiography*, "In London, we used to hear also of Shyamji Krishna Varma and his India House but I never visited that house... Long afterwards, in 1926, I saw Shyamji in Geneva."

At sixty-eight years, Krishna Varma had more of less retired and ceased the publication of his journal *The Indian Sociologist* back in 1922. Nehru described the once fierce and fearless revolutionary as a broken man suffering from acute paranoia and recalled: "There was Shyamji Krishna Varma living with his ailing wife high on the top floor of a house in Geneva. The aged couple lived by themselves... their rooms were musty and suffocating and everything had a thick layer of dust (Krishna Varma) was suspicious of all comers presuming them, until the contrary was proved, to be either British agents or after his money. His pockets bulged with ancient copies of his old paper, *The Indian Sociologist*... His talk was of the old days, of India House at Hampstead, of the various persons that the British Government had sent to spy on him and how he had spotted and outwitted them. The walls were covered with shelves full of old books, dust laden and neglected, looking down sorrowfully on the intruder... the whole place there hung an atmosphere of gloom, an air of decay...with relief one came out of that flat and breathed the air outside."

Four years later, at 2330 hrs on March 30th, 1930, the great Indian patriot, Shyamji Krishna Varma, after several health problems passed away at Clinique La Colline in Geneva. He could never return to India. His wife Bhanumati donated his collection of Sanskrit books to the Indian Culture Institute of the Sorbonne University of Paris. She also donated 10,000 Swiss Francs to Geneva University and 10,000 Swiss Francs to a local hospital in his memory.

In August 2003, Narendra Modi, as then Chief Minister of Gujarat, took his ashes from Geneva to Mandavi, the birthplace of Shyamji Krishna Varma. In November 2015, the Benchers of the Honorable Society of the Inner Temple reinstated the former Indian lawyer and nationalist Shyamji Krishna Varma 'in recognition of the fact that the cause of Indian home rule, for which he fought, was not incompatible with membership of the bar and that by modern standards he did not receive an entirely fair hearing'.

Notwithstanding Har Dayal's recantation, his name was often heard within the Indian political circles. Consequently, during his tour of Switzerland, Nehru also tried to locate Har Dayal in Europe and claimed, "Years later when I was in Europe in 1926 and 1927, I was surprised to find with what bitterness and resentment most of the old Indian residents thought of Har Dayal. He lived at the time in Sweden. I did not meet him."

An Internationalist without a Nationality

Living in the backwaters of the world at the end of 1926, the Oxford educated forty-two-year-old scholar who had lectured at Stanford and was once a force to reckon with in the intellectual circles of North America, now subsisted as a teacher in Swedish folkhögskolas. His superhuman single-mindedness had broken nearly every barrier he encountered and carried him through all the isolation of the years. Confined to Mölnlycke and away from home for close to two decades, Har Dayal knew that though Sweden was an attractive place, the real political action, and academic accomplishment was elsewhere. The world was getting interesting after the official end of the Great War in 1918 and the Treaty of Lausanne in July 1923 and Sweden was comfortably dull for his active mind. Loosing hair like his forefathers and with weaker eyes, he lived all alone in a small two room flat in Langedrag, south of Goteborg. He was in a dark frame of mind and a mood deepened by over a decade of physical absence of Sunder Rani and Shanti Devi in his life. His return to India was uncertain and retirement still far away. But he still viewed himself as an Indian political leader living in exile, an academic and was a respected revolutionary within some secret societies in India.

To keep himself occupied, Har Dayal wrote extensively at this time. He published 'Modem India and European Culture' (in English) in *Svenska Orientsdllskapet*. Here he introduced for the first time his concept of "three R's": Renaissance, Reformation, and Revolution, promulgating that all three had come to India through her contact with Europeans. Europe "thundered" at India's gates with the "fearful message: Awake! Learn! Or die!". The Indians, he emphasized, could not borrow European culture wholesale, but had to be selective. He similarly contributed series of thought-provoking essays in the Lahore based *The People*, about unique aspects he had witnessed in Europe including the Farmer's High Schools in Sweden, the Temperance Movement in Sweden, rural lectures across the nation. He also composed short articles on the birth of Lithuania, Latvia, and Estonia. In other essays, he described the politics in Finland and gave a detailed introduction to the new world language – Esperanto.

In his last article for *The Modern Review* titled, "The Shame of India", Har Dayal attacked those social customs of India that he said he could not endorse when he delivered lectures to Western audiences. While writing against child-marriage, purdah, caste, polygamy, and illiteracy he called for complete national independence as the ultimate goal of all Indians. He admired Mahatma Gandhi as a man of ethics but did not approve of his disenchantment with modern machinery. He observed: "who condemns machinery and railways in the genuine Tolstoyan spirit, travels all over the country with the aid of scientifically constructed locomotives, and telegraphs his fiery orders to his colleagues by means of a current of electricity. Thus Science takes a noble revenge on her thoughtless detractors!"

The Indian mind, Har Dayal claimed was "synthetic and philosophical" and capable of wanting more than the fruits of the industrial revolution, thus great theoretical scientists were emerging from Indian intellectual ranks.

Family Time in Sweden

In this period, Har Dayal's brilliant nephew Raghubar Dayal (1900–1991), son of Bhairon Dayal, after completing his Bachelor's and Master's degrees in Science at the Muir Central College in Allahabad, unlike his rebellious uncle, qualified for the ICS in 1923. He proceeded to join Sidney Sussex College in Cambridge. On his way to India to serve in the ICS at Marseille, he received an affectionate letter from his uncle Har Dayal on October 27th, 1925. His uncle wished the young Raghubar a very successful and useful career and offered the advice of an elder, "Put duty first and you will always be happy". After thirty-five years of service to the nation, Raghubar Dayal, ICS rose to become a Judge of the Supreme Court of India. (*Letters of Lala Har Dayal*)

Har Dayal's eldest brother Kishan Dayal along with his son Bhagwat who was a student at the London School of Economics, and nephew Raghubar briefly visited him in Mölnlycke. Bhagwat spent an entire month with his uncle. All along his tumultuous life, no single individual was a more trusted confidante for Har Dayal than Kishan dada. The foundation of their friendship went well beyond the kinship of blood and rested ultimately on mutual respect and admiration. Kishan Dayal probably shared the latest news and pictures of family and home from India and brought back millions of memories for Har Dayal of his childhood days, his old home in Cheera Khana, household, family and neighbours. Emotionally Har Dayal had paid a heavy price by living in exile.

Kishan Dayal had mastered the craft of British law and acquired status as an eminent lawyer in Delhi and Lahore that enabled him to gain the confidence of Hukumat-i-Britannia's civil servants of the highest ranks. It was left to him to rescue his youngest brother from being emotionally marooned and financially ruined in Sweden. On the advice of Kishan Dayal he made yet another attempt to end his loneliness that bore down his spirit. Har Dayal first planned to move to Stockholm and yet again apply for a Swedish passport. In his official correspondence with Swedish Government, Har Dayal listed his old address, Tågmästaregatan 6, Goteborg as his home and his occupation as 'university professor', although he was never officially associated with any of the Swedish universities. At one stage he even joked that he may call himself, "Dayalson" once he became a Swede. The Utrikesdepartementet aware of his record and revolutionary activities did not let him formally settle down in Sweden or grant him a passport and kept extending his permission to stay just a few months at a time.

Scholar not a Schoolboy

James Leishman Dodds, the Oxford educated First Secretary at the British Legation in Stockholm received a letter from Har Dayal that was dated, May 11th, 1926. The NAI records divulge that in the letter, he asked for permission to travel to London. He intended to study at the British Museum and promised not to participate in any unconstitutional movement in the future. Refused a Swedish Passport once again, he now requested for a British Passport. In the message, he stated that he was now forty-two-years-old and stressed "I am also a scholar and a political leader and not a schoolboy".

The British Legation unswervingly informed Har Dayal that he would be "traveling to India or England at his own risk".

Five days later, the revolutionary identified with the Ghadr Party shot off another note to the British Legation and expressed: "No man wishes to be hanged or put in prison. It is not worthwhile to spend my own money and travel all the way in order to be hanged to put in prison... if the Government does not intend to prosecute me they may intimate their intention to me without granting me a formal and public amnesty. I wish to know if I shall be prosecuted or not. No intelligent person can be asked to take a leap in the dark." Not clear about the stance of the Hukumat-i-Britannia he added: "If I must live in foreign countries for the rest of my life, I shall ask my wife to come and join me. We have not seen each other since 1908 and something must now be done for this personal problem. Every man must live his life and do his work. So I humbly request the Government to inform me that they intend to prosecute me or not. That is all. I do not ask for a formal amnesty at present.... Bygones must be bygones". He requested the British Legation to forward his letter to the Hukumat-i-Britannia.

But the venomous Hukumat-i-Britannia was in no mood to accede.

John Wallinger had retired as head of the secret network IPI in April 1926 and Philip Vickery, who had worked in close co-ordination with British military intelligence in Europe and also in the United States succeeded him in October

1926. Historian Patrick French's *Liberty or Death* corroborates that Vickery, who ran the surveillance operation for twenty years, did "as much as any single person to prolong British rule in India."

In spite of the changes at the top, the British Secret Service continued to keep an eye on Har Dayal in Sweden. For them he was still a notorious Indian revolutionary and his history was well known. As maintained in official noting, he could be given "no assurance of immunity from prosecution for his past deeds which might induce him to return to India." Far from granting amnesty, the Hukumat-i-Britannia frantically wanted to indict him for anti-imperialist subversion on Indian soil even after such lapse of time. The British Secret Service operatives had intercepted a message from Har Dayal addressed to Professor Junjiro Takakusu (1866–1945), a Sanskrit scholar at the Tokyo Imperial University, stating that he had become an ardent convert to Buddhism and wanted to travel to Japan. The NAI documents expose that the Foreign Office in London was alarmed as they discovered Har Dayal's plan to link up with Rash Behari Bose in Japan. Since his escape from India in 1915, Rash Behari was living in Tokyo. He had got sanctuary at the house of Toyama Mitsuru, an extremely powerful pan-Asian leader who belonged to the secret *Genyosha* (Black Dragon) society. In July 1918, Rash Behari had married a Japanese citizen, Soma Toshiko daughter of Soma Aizo, proprietor of the Nakamura-ya restaurant in the Shinjuku district of Tokyo. The marriage between an Indian and a Japanese was exceedingly rare and a radical act for both. He was fluent in Japanese and founded an 'Indian Club' in Tokyo. He had established contact with Sun Yat-Sen, then also in exile in Japan, where he went under the name of Sun Zhongshan. Furthermore, Rash Behari was still a supporter of the Ghadr movement. The British Secret Service quickly connected with the British Embassy in Tokyo and made sure Har Dayal's plans to leave Europe were nipped in the bud. Professor Takakusu who was a well-known Esperantist on the advice of the British Embassy in Tokyo urged Har Dayal to continue his studies in Europe and drop the idea of visiting Japan.

Earlier Kishan Dayal on his visit to Sweden had offered to buy a cottage for his younger brother in Mölnlycke but the plan was abandoned as the possibility of amnesty emerged. Being in financial doldrums, Har Dayal now appealed to Kishan Dayal, "I hope you are not tired of helping me with money in this difficult situation. It is a question of only a few months more as I shall go either to London (if amnesty is granted) or to Moscow (if it is refused"). On 28th, June 1926, Har Dayal yet again approached the British Legation with the added information that his brother Kishan Dayal had been informed by Lajpat Rai that Sir Alexander Phillips Muddiman, home member of the British Viceroy's executive council and Leader of the Legislative Assembly, had confirmed Hukumat-i-Brittania's intention not to prosecute him as long as he "behaved as a law abiding person in England or India."

Ultimately on September 17th, 1926, Dodds at the British Legation officially notified Har Dayal that "no facilities can be accorded you for a journey to the United Kingdom and that no guarantees can be given of the kind suggested in your letter of June 28 last." Har Dayal promptly replied that there may have been a misunderstanding and he was not going to trouble Hukumat-i-Britannia again with such a petition before 1926 and added a mystifying footnote "thus following Swami Satya Deva's wise advice."

Prevented from reaching India by any means necessary, Har Dayal was once again consumed by the dreams of India's independence and setting up the university of the East in the foothills of the Himalayas. Unable to travel to Japan or Britain, he seriously considered traveling to Moscow and then after crossing the Himalayas in Tibet enter Nepal where imaginably Sunder Rani and Shanti Devi and his family could join him. He thought Nepal could be the site for a world class university of the East because it was free of Western influence and that the Nepalese had "new blood, new life in them." He drew up a detailed plan to travel to Nepal. Eventually, he gave up the idea since it was a time and money-consuming scheme. But he did not give up the desire of visiting Nepal in the future.

Next, a chance meeting with a Swedish woman forced Har Dayal to change his plans for the future.

Agda Erikson from Borås

In November 1926, an attractive blue eyed and dark haired Swede Agda Erikson heard the exiled Indian revolutionary deliver a lecture in Swedish in his usual humorous manner at Hammarby in Vasterhanginge, a rural district thirty kilometers southeast of Stockholm. The Swedish heiress, social worker, and philanthropist was spellbound by the depth and breadth of the knowledge of the multilingual Indian scholar.

Agda stood at just five feet two inches and was born on December 18th, 1884, a month after the birth of Har Dayal, in the picturesque town of Rydboholm sixty odd kilometers east of Goteborg. She belonged to an eminent family of Sweden and was the great granddaughter of Kerstin Andersdotter *"Mother Kerstin"* (1774–1856) one of Markbygden's most famous persons who was honored in 1842 with the gold chain by His Majesty the King as a reward. Agda's grandfather Sven Erikson established Rydboholmsbolaget, the first spinning mill of Sweden in 1853. The eighth child of the textile magnet Johannes and Selma Erikson, Agda grew in an enormous house with twenty-five people helping the household every day.

As stated by Tina Collins of the Rydals Museum at Kinna in Sweden, after initial home schooling Agda attended the Higher Elementary School for Female Youth in Halmstad, Sweden and in a French school in Lausanne, Switzerland and finished her schooling in 1905. Her health condition forced her to spend several winters in Egypt and Biskra in North East Algeria and this affected her education. In 1906 she enrolled at Uppsala University for three years but had to drop out because of tuberculosis. She convalesced after spending time at Romanäs sanatorium in Tranas in Sweden in 1910. Agda's father Johannes, also a member of the Parliament, had died on January 11th, 1912, leaving her with a considerable annual income of 54,000 Swedish kronor. Unattached Agda lived in Kinna for a while with her sister Disa whose husband Edvin Leffler was the CEO of Kinnastrom's plants since the death of Johannes.

Agda with a heart for philantrophy had a dream of starting the Viskadalen folkhögskola (the folk high school for Viskadalen area), and wanted to give the young people of the working classes the opportunity to grow and develop. She often acted on impulse and never took long to translate thought into action.

With a grant of 85,000 Swedish kronor by Agda, the Viskadalen folkhögskola opened on November 21st, 1926 in the middle of Sjuhäradsbygden and Allan Degerman became its first principal. In the first winter course it registered six students who studied Swedish, mathematics, history, geography, literature, municipal and political science, international issues, economics and English or Esperanto. Agda handed out scholarships to students from her own pocket and purchased a new Chevrolet for the use of students and teachers. Additionally she went about in her T-Ford motorcar in the town of Kinna and recruited people to knit blankets for the folkhögskola. Agda expressed her vision for the school: "I imagined it as a pioneer of Christian Social Life spirit." And she defined her role as, "I wanted to somehow participate in the work of the school, and wanted by the personal participation in the lowest chores, make them understand that all chores are equally good. Of course, I had hoped to take lessons over time, too."

A scholarly 'Indisk professor' (Indian professor) who was fluent in Swedish and also fourteen other languages was recommended to her for teaching at the folkhögskola. During her interaction with Har Dayal, as he accepted the offer to teach, they discovered that they shared a common mission in life: to leave the world a better place than they had found. Har Dayal enthralled Agda with his presence of mind, sense of humor, zest for life, the quest for knowledge, passion for work, compassion for the living and a heart for giving and forgiving. She enjoyed having long discussions with the erudite Indian on world affairs and on solving the problems of the world.

Har Dayal, now in his forty-second year, was more than attracted to the lively Agda who was similar in age, outlook, and understanding. Gradually the unusual friendship between the Swedish heiress and Indian intellectual blossomed into a romantic liaison.

But unknown to Agda, Har Dayal was a married man and a father. Shanti Devi at eighteen had remained single beyond the usual marriageable age in India at that time, largely due to her father's controversial record as a revolutionary. Frustrated by the negative responses of the British Legation to his multiple appeals he had earlier requested Sunder Rani to divorce him, as his return to India despite his pleading now seemed to be blocked forever. For Sunder Rani, divorce and remarriage were impossible due to prevalent social norms in India. His appeals had come to naught. Ensconced in his tiny home in Goteborg, Har Dayal had been a loner living overseas for almost two decades. At Stanford, he had a disastrous relationship with his student Frieda Hauswirth that became a subject of gossip. He thought it wise not to inform his family and friends about his association with Agda as he anticipated a scandal in India. For similar purposes he kept the continuation of his formal marriage with Shanti Devi, a secret from Agda.

In their conversations, Har Dayal gave the impression to Agda, that as a teenager he had an arranged marriage to Sunder Rani, as was the tradition in India. However being in exile he had not seen his wife since 1908; so they were as good as separated. Disconcertingly he maintained his persona of self-denial and celibacy to his family and close associates in India who remained oblivious of his association with Agda till the end of his life. Officially Har Dayal and Agda remained unmarried though he later acknowledged Agda as his wife – 'Agda Erikson Dayal', but never before Indians.

Agda's strange relationship with 'the Indisk professor' caused disquiet in her conservative neighborhood of Goteborg and within her family. Additionally, local law in Sweden ruled that Swedish women who married non-Swedish men could not obtain a passport and would become women without a country. The severe Swedish climate did not suit Agda. Breathing was difficult for her as she had a history of tuberculosis. With her health impaired and Har Dayal's interest in retrieving his unfinished education in Britain, they now envisaged a comfortable life in London for the two of them, as they grew older. He once again asked Kishan Dayal to intercede on his behalf to get him permission to study in London.

Full and Complete Amnesty

In the winter of 1927, on Har Dayal's insistence Kishan Dayal sought a meeting with David Petrie, who had succeeded Lt. Colonel Cecil Kaye, the sixth Director of DCI in October 1924. The senior Indian Police official was an old acquaintance and Kishan Dayal brought up the issue of amnesty for his brother. He described to Petrie, that in Har Dayal's absence from home, his wife was as good as widowed. There was a discussion on clemency but Petrie expected Har Dayal to make the first move. Kishan Dayal told Petrie that he would ask his brother to admit freely the error of his ways and throw himself at the mercy of Hukumat-i-Britannia. Later Lajpat Rai also met Petrie to get a pardon for Har Dayal citing his financial problems and was offered the same rationale.

On March 30th, 1927, eight years after his public recantation, Har Dayal, the revolutionary who was once cherished by millions of Indians for his patriotism and self-denial addressed a long letter to the British Viceroy of India, Edward Wood, (1881–1959), styled as Lord Irwin (who later became Lord Halifax), and dispatched it to the British Legation in Stockholm. In the missive to the twentieth British Viceroy of India, he requested, "I humbly and respectfully beg to apply for full and complete amnesty on account of certain wrong ideas and through lack of political experience". He asked for permission to live, work, study and write in London and added that he would never take part in any unconstitutional, seditious and revolutionary movement of any sort. In the end, he concluded, "Riper years always confer experience, moderation, poise, and breadth of views on unselfish idealists like my humble self. I know that I can render valuable services to the cause of Indian progress and imperial unity. I therefore beg and pray that the past may be forgotten and forgiven."

For Hukumat-i-Britannia, Har Dayal was "a man of brilliant intellect in the very highest sense of a much-abused adjective" but he was never known for stability and consistency. As disclosed by the British Secret Service reports, he exhibited bitterness for the British in his Ghadr publications and was directly or indirectly involved in the Lahore bomb outrage as well as the attack of British Viceroy Lord Hardinge in 1912. They assumed he was quite prepared to advocate cold-blooded murder as a means to affect his ends. His seditious activity in Germany to injure British Indian army's efforts during WWI was held against him. There were uncorroborated reports of his clandestine communications with various revolutionary groups and secret societies in North India.

The NAI records uncover that Hukumat-i-Britannia estimated Har Dayal's plan to go to London as just a stopgap arrangement. They felt he would eventually relocate to India. The DCI and the Government of Punjab forcefully opposed Har Dayal's return to India registering, "a strong protest against the proposal to give this dangerous and unscrupulous man any assurances which would render it possible for him to return to India". Hukumat-i-Britannia categorically rejected Har Dayal's plea for amnesty and retained the option of prosecuting him for his past conduct anytime in the future. On Ju ly 1st, 1927, in concurrence with both the Government of Punjab and Delhi administration, Hukumat-i-Britannia finally concluded; "if Lala Har Dayal (who belongs to Delhi) does not return to India it will be to the interest of everyone including Lala Har Dayal".

An Apostle of Human Freedom

In the same month, across the Atlantic, Har Dayal's old comrade, Barkatullah, still rebellious against the Hukumat-i-Britannia, disembarked in New York. On July 15th, 1927, he spoke to the Indian community at a dinner event hosted at one of the oldest Indian restaurants in the United States, 'Ceylon India Inn', located at 148 West, 49th street in New York. He then proceeded to California where he was given a rousing welcome at the Yugantar Ashram on 5 Wood Street in San Francisco. At that time, Bhai Bhagwan Singh was the President and a few months later, on the first day of 1928, he retired from the Ghadr Party activities to focus on academic and scholarly life in the United States.

Barkatullah also attended a mass meeting held in his honor at Marysville near Yuba City and the hall was packed with eight hundred Ghadr patriots who had come to hear the treasured revolutionary. The entire space resounded with triumphant shouts of *'Bande Matram'* as Barkatullah and Mahendra Pratap Singh entered. Disregarding medical advice of the American doctors, Barkatullah rose to speak at the meeting and in a feeble voice reminded the audience of the stars of the Ghadr movement who had sacrificed their lives for the freedom of India. He said, "As I look around, I fail to see my co-workers of 1914. Where are they? Where are those apostles of human freedom? Dead? Guillotined? Confined in solitary cells? Yes, they must be, for they were guilty of love for their country. I have been spared, perhaps to witness a little longer, the woeful suffering of my people. Countrymen we owe those heroes, who have taken their places in the Pantheons of martyrs a heavy debt, shall we pay?"

Barkatullah's chronic diseases caught up with him and he passed away on September 20th, 1927 (some newspapers recorded it as September 12th). The Bhopal born Ghadr patriot and Indian revolutionary was buried in the Old City Cemetery of Sacramento. Indians from all faiths performed their respective religious rites at the burial as a significant expression of religious solidarity envisioned by Har Dayal within the Ghadr Party.

Barkatullah's gravestone in Sacramento reads, "World famous scholar and patriot – great leader of Indian nationalism and reformer of modern Islam – may his soul rest in peace."

National Army of Indians

A few weeks later, the news of the passing of Barkatullah reached Har Dayal in eastern Sweden. In a bitter mindset and aware of the adverse reaction by Hukumat-i-Britannia to his request for a full and complete amnesty, an incensed Har Dayal penned a sensational article for Lahore based journal *Sudharsan*. Published on October 5th, 1927, Har Dayal's article boldly laid out the roadmap for India's path to freedom through a national army – the kind he had planned with Barkatullah and Acharya during his Berlin and Constantinople days in 1915–16. Gifted with foresight that was years ahead of his contemporaries, the revolutionary declared that ten million educated youth of India should be enlisted in a national army. These should be men of firm resolve who would sacrifice their persons and properties under the orders of their officers. The united national party would carry 'Swaraj (freedom)…to London and raise a *"quami dal"* (national army) that will lay foundations of an independent Government in India. He added, "If you today organize this party I will tomorrow send you from Geneva and England the parcel of swaraj. From my experience, after my travels in Europe and America, I can say in a word that India cannot get swaraj without *Sangathan* (united party).... The task is a difficult one but it will be accomplished by exertion. You will then see what happens in ten years' time"

David Petrie in Simla at once took note of this provocative article by a known insurrectionary now back with his revolutionary zeal. *Dr. Emily Brown* in her biography has divulged that, "After independence the secretary of the Indian Embassy in Stockholm was to say of Har Dayal's decade in Sweden: For official purposes he was supposed to be doing research work, but in reality, as some of his contemporary Swedish friends are able to recollect, he worked underground against the British domination over India".

Before the Hukumat-i-Britannia could react to his seditious writings, the mastermind of the Ghadr movement and the most dangerous Indian revolutionary outside India had left Goteborg forever. After staying in exile in Sweden for nine years, from October 1918 to October 1927, the perpetual risktaker took a leap in the dark and headed directly to His Majesty's capital accompanied by his partner, Agda.

Har Dayal as usual had unnerved the British Secret Service.

15

THE BUDDHIST PHILOSOPHER
IN LONDON

"Har Dayal was a man of high principle and strong character. I greatly admired
him. He was, of course, a rebel against the British Government of India…
despite all that he had suffered from the English, he spent much of his time
in trying to show Indian students in this country what he considered the best
aspects of English characters and actions…"

Sir Ralph Turner
Chair of Sanskrit, University of London

As the sun rose on the cold morning of Monday, December 19th, 1927, inside
the Central Jail at Faizabad in North India a deeply religious Indian patriot
sentenced to death completed his prayers in his solitary cell. The twenty-seven-
year-old fine-featured and fearless poet was escorted to the hanging platform. As
his chains were released, he reached for the hanging rope calmly and kissed the
noose. He recited one of his own poems:

"Tang aakar hum unke zulm se bedaad se,
chal diye sooye adam zindaane Faizabaad se"

(Tired of enduring their oppression, their cruelty,
We are setting off for the beyond from the Faizabad)

The hangman tied the noose around his neck and pulled it tight against his ear.
Then suddenly the stillness of death pervaded everything and the revolutionary
movement of India lost one of its shining stars.

The name of that brave revolutionary was Ashfaqullah Khan (1900–1927)
a member of the Hindustan Republican Army, which became, by 1928, the
Hindustan Socialist Republican Army (HSRA). Inspired by the Ghadr Party,
Kartar Singh Sarabha's hanging, the Jallianwala Bagh massacre and in response to

the general frustration with the slow pace of Mahatma Gandhi's mass movement, HSRA brought back a resurgence of anticolonial agitation in North India.

Two years earlier, on the evening of August 9th, 1925, Ashfaqullah under the leadership of Ram Prasad Bismil (1897–1927), along with Rajendra Lahiri (1901–1927), Chandra Shekhar Azad (1906–1931) and a few more daredevils, had participated in one of the most daring actions committed by the young revolutionaries in India. The courageous revolutionaries armed with four German Mouser C96 semi-automatics boarded the train Number 8 Down traveling from Saharanpur railway station to Lucknow. When the train reached the right spot near Alamnagar station between Kakori and Lucknow, the revolutionaries in the second-class compartment pulled the communication cord of the alarm signal and forced entry into the section holding the locker. They informed the passengers that their object was not to injure them but to take '*Sarkari property*' (Government property). Then the men overpowered the guard and removed the cash safe from the train. In thirty minutes flat the revolutionaries successfully looted from Hukumat-i-Britannia's treasury an amount of Rs. 4,679 and 16 paise.

The train hold-up at Kakori got tremendous publicity in India and the Hukumat-i-Britannia started an intense manhunt.

Following the incident, the thirty-nine-year-old Superintendent of Police, Ralph Albert Horton was made in-charge of the special inquiry into the Kakori Conspiracy Case. After his investigation, he heard that the so-called dacoits had only looted the Hukumat-i-Britannia's safe and not stolen anything from the passengers. Horton concluded that this was not a case of a train robbery by criminals but revolutionary activity by educated young men to fund their secret society. He turned his attention to the city of Shahjahanpur where the police had traced some of the stolen currency notes. It was soon discovered that an underground meeting of HRSA was to be held on September 13th, 1925 at an orphanage in Meerut. The British Secret Service kept a close watch on the orphanage and some men were observed visiting the place after sunset. One of the men that evening was Ram Prasad Bismil, a devout Hindu and member of the Arya Samaj sect. Bismil was inspired by Har Dayal's writings and there were reports of his secret communication with his mentor in Sweden. At a time of religious strife in India, Bismil and Ashfaqullah's unique friendship within the HRSA went far beyond their faiths and both were united in their quest for freedom for their land. Bismil gave voice to the burning patriotic zeal amongst the youth of India using poetry.

"*Sarfaroshi ki tamanna ab hamaare dil mein hai*
Dekhna hai zor kitna baazu-e-qaatil mein hai"

(The desire for revolution is in our hearts,
Let us see if there is any strength in the arms of our executioner)

Afterwards, the Hukumat-i-Britannia's police used the tried and tested methods of finding traitors and Crown witnesses from among the conspirators. They arrested most of the members who participated in the raid including Bismil and Ashfaqullah but could not capture Chandra Shekhar Azad. They were charged with conspiracy to divest the King-Emperor of the sovereignty of British India; as also the conspiracy to commit robberies to collect finances for that end. In 1928, Hukumat-i-Britannia rewarded Horton for his swift investigation and King George V appointed him Companion, Order of the Indian Empire. He later ended his career in the police as Prime Minister to His Highness Yashwant Rao Holker II, the Maharaja of Indore.

For the moment the entire galaxy of Indian political leadership and legal luminaries from Motilal Nehru, Madan Mohan Malviya, Lajpat Rai to Muhammad Ali Jinnah came out in support of the young revolutionaries. In the court, Gobind Ballabh Pant led the defense assisted by Mohan Lal Saksena and Chandra Bhan Gupta.

Hukumat-i-Britannia repeatedly tried to bribe Ashfaqullah and turn him into an approver to save his life but he rejected the offers. His brother Riyasatullah rushed to the office of the eminent lawyer Kripa Shankar Hajela to defend the case. For eighteen months Hajela brilliantly represented the accused. But eventually, after spending months in dark and hot cells the four revolutionaries including Bismil, Ashfaqullah, Lahiri and Thakur Roshan Singh were sentenced to death. Petitions to commute the death sentences of the young men to life sentences were rushed to Lord Irwin, the Viceroy and even sent to London. But the Hukumat-i-Britannia was resolute and gave orders to execute the four patriots.

On December 19th, 1927 in the Gorakhpur Central Jail, Ram Prasad shouted "*Bande Mataram*", "*Bharat Mata ki Jai*" and recited a Vedic prayer before he placed the noose around his neck like a garland. By choosing death over dishonor, Bismil and Ashfaqullah became icons amongst the youth of India.

At His Majesty's Doorstep

Just two months before the martyrdom of the young revolutionaries, on Monday, October 10th, 1927, a smiling Har Dayal and Agda Erickson had alighted from the train at St. Pancras station in London. On the day of their arrival, London was typically dull, cloudy and rather cold. The weather threatened to remain unsettled over the next few weeks. Having received no assurances from the India Office, Har Dayal, while in Stockholm, had anticipated mischief by British immigration officials and had informed them that they should not embarrass him as he crossed over into Britain, as Swedish friends would accompany him. Agda, the Swedish friend accompanying him was coached to state that she was going to pursue further studies at the University of London under his guidance and that they were not related. Though as audacious as ever in his undertakings, Har Dayal was over-cautious and wanted to avoid Agda's entanglement, in case His Majesty's Government arrested him.

For the moment Har Dayal's principal tormentors His Majesty's Government in its internal correspondence recorded: "there was no evidence of any change in Har Dayal's conduct which gave him any claims to as exception a concession as indemnification for his previous offenses and the India Office were asked to inform him that no assurance would be given and that if he returned to India it must be at his own risk". Though he was allowed to proceed to Britain as a British subject, without a passport, Hukumat-i-Britannia had not been able to find enough legal reasons as yet to prosecute the most prominent Indian in exile.

A British Secret Service report recorded, "Arrived in London after much correspondence with the India Office; came to London at his own risk; no amnesty granted". They also made a note that "though Agda's replies to His Majesty's immigration authorities were not strictly truthful, no proceedings were taken against her. There is no evidence that Har Dayal has married her but she is apparently financing him".

In London, Har Dayal initially stayed at the Westway Hotel on Endsleigh Street within walking distance of St. Pancras station. He avoided meeting his close relatives at the station since he was travelling with Agda. The day after his arrival he met his elder brother Kishan Dayal and his nephew Bhagwat (student at the London School of Economics) and got the latest news from India. Back home, Har Dayal and Sunder Rani's daughter Shanti Devi was married to Bishan Narain, Barrister at Law and the son of Suraj Narain, a well-to-do gentleman in Lahore. A few months after his arrival in London on June 1st, 1928, Har Dayal became a grandfather as a daughter named Shubh was born to Shanti Devi. In the past, Shanti Devi had written to her father pleading for his intervention, as the family wanted to get her married rather than let her continue her higher studies. He had forcefully defended his daughter's decision to study further rather than being married off earlier as was the norm in India in the 1920s. She completed her college education at Allahabad University before her marriage.

Kishan Dayal's insistence and money had enabled Har Dayal to undertake the hazardous journey from Sweden to Britain. Aware of Har Dayal's nationalistic passion and clandestine revolutionary activity, his eldest brother's adviced him to steer clear of the extremist activities while in Britain as the Hukumat-i-Britannia were still keen to produce a cast-iron case against him. Har Dayal was told that if he resigned from all overt and covert political pursuits during his stay in London there was still hope that he may be able to return to India someday. Kishan Dayal wanted him to apply for complete amnesty at the appropriate time.

Every life has within it elements of conflicts and uncertainty; 'the could have been' and 'the might have been'. On his return to London, Har Dayal was now determined not to be a 'has been'.

Agda and Har Dayal at No. 34

Soon after their arrival in Britain, Har Dayal and Agda searched for a suitable home and finally settled down in a two-bedroom modest cottage on the outskirts of London, at 34 Churchill Road, a short walk from the Edgware train station on the northern line.

It was 1928 and London was booming once again. It was a time when Londoners had Bertie Wooster and other specimen of leisurely wealth and recklessness. After the return of soldiers from WWI coupled with the decline in the agricultural nature of Britain's economy had led to London's borders developing even greater than they had in the previous century. The city extended beyond the boundaries of London County into surrounding Middlesex, Surrey, Kent, Essex, and Hertfordshire. This compelled the modernization of the city's roads as the population drifted further from the city center. The middle-class suburb of Edgware was situated five kilometers northwest of Hendon. It had a few streets of terraced houses and a sea of detached houses built since 1927. The Dayal's home had a white-colored wicket fence that led to the small front door. In the main room, some racks held a large collection of books, a globe and straight-backed chairs. This room additionally served as Har Dayal's study. The dining area and kitchen were in the back and there was a large backyard with a garden. The two bedrooms were on the first floor. It was vastly different from Har Dayal's poverty-stricken exile in Sweden and the couple settled down quicker than anticipated in the new environment of a bustling city. Agda went around London using public transport and Har Dayal would be seen pacing outside their home by the neighbours anxiously awaiting her return and worried that she may get lost in the large city.

Agda enrolled as a student of Psychology at the Kings College in London. In a message to a friend in Sweden, she wrote, "I am very pleased with the whole thing, and I think that through lecture and books I get more clear about what I have previously thought about". While living in London with Har Dayal, Agda visited some schools and admired the city as a whole. In another note she penned, "I think London, on the whole, is beautiful with all its public buildings and squares, and so the Thames are really quite stately... The English are good much more hardened than we. The kids still have half socks, at least the poor ones, they also have so thin bad cotton dresses, and hardly any gowns, but they do not look all the way frozen in any case".

From her new home in London, Agda was in regular correspondence with Allan Degerman, the principal of the Viskadalen's folkhögskola in Seglora. In a letter dated January 10th, 1928, she informed him that she was now formally engaged to Har Dayal. In another message on January 29th, 1928, she announced that since she had decided to spend the rest of her life with Har Dayal, she would not ever return to the school. Accordingly, she decided to close the Viskadalen's folkhögskola in Seglora. On March 8th, 1928, the new school association, Västra Sverges Arbetares folkhögskola VSAF was constituted and the school was rescued from impending closure. Later she even left her entire collection of books for the school library.

Heaven is a Large Library

In Edgware, every morning, a forty-three-year-old Har Dayal, dressed in his usual odd clothes, like a university student, would wave Agda goodbye and depart from his home, holding on to an umbrella, books, notes and a small tiffin to take the train to the British Museum. Here he usually spent twelve to fourteen hours a day studying, writing summaries and researching in the tranquil atmosphere of the reading room. A skilled mind such as Har Dayal's absorbed as much as he could from millions of books that surrounded him with only a short break to quickly finish his homemade meals. Pioneering psychologist William James (1842–1910) examined the basic experience of reality and his description of the human mind at work is apt for Har Dayal at this stage: "Geniuses are commonly believed to excel other men in their power of sustained attention... Their ideas coruscate, every subject branches infinitely before their fertile minds, and so for hours they may be rapt."

The man who had passed by death multiple times in his revolutionary days now had moved a great distance away from the torture of exile and the thoughts of rebellion and reinvented himself as a keen academic. Following upon his prior correspondence with Professor Arnold, Har Dayal enrolled at the newly established School of Oriental (later SOAS) at the University of London for a doctoral program in April 1928. His return to the world of academics at a University in Britain was a dream for him since he walked away from his degree in Oxford twenty years ago. Har Dayal was now a scholastically inclined man keen to complete his doctorate on his favorite subject 'Buddhism'.

Har Dayal's guide was Sir Professor Ralph Lilley Turner, MC, the Chair of Sanskrit in the University of London. A former lecturer at Queens College in Benaras he had served in the Palestine Campaign during WWI and won a Military Cross. He also gained a deep affection for the Gurkhas and became profoundly interested in their language. His inscription adorns the Gurkha memorial in Central London. Turner decades later informed biographer, Dr. Emily Brown, that after WWI when his student Dr. Raghu Vira, who later became a member of the Parliament in India, had visited Kaiser Wilhelm II in Huis Droom in the Netherlands, the former ruler of Germany had inquired about his friend 'Har Dayal'.

At the same time in Britain, the women's suffrage movement gained much momentum and the right to vote was open to all women over the age of twenty-one in 1928. Although academic activities kept him fairly engaged, Har Dayal's radical views on feminism found a voice in his regular letters to the newspapers.

On September 21st, 1928, he emphasized, "As a man and a subscriber to *The Vote* may I suggest that your journal should discontinue the use of the titles, "Miss" and "Mrs"? There are no such titles for married and unmarried men. Your readers are not interested in the personal relations of the women named in your columns. A progressive woman's journal should set the example of only the names and the women and discarding these medieval badges of domestic slavery, "Miss" and "Mrs". Even in the Bible, we read of Abraham and Sarah, not of Mrs. Abraham. Whatever name a woman chooses to be known by there is no necessity of prefixing "Miss" or "Mrs" to it. I also desire to enlist your active sympathy for another cause. It is high time that the author of "Adam Bede" and other immortal novels should be called by her real name in all books dealing with literature (also "George Sand" and other great women writers). It is surely barbarous and meaningless to use a masculine pseudonym, "George Eliot", in these days. I think that this change is overdue." Many readers wrote back to *The Vote* endorsing Har Dayal's viewpoint.

In 1928, British Secret Service under orders to unearth clinching evidence of revolutionary activity against Har Dayal kept a close watch on the unpredictable rebel especially since his recent article in India about founding a 'national army'. They regularly read his correspondence and wrote, "he was engaged in intellectual pursuits and writing a history of Western civilization" and also requested for membership to the 'Friends of Soviet Russia'. Then the British Secret Service operatives' intercepted two separate letters penned by Har Dayal to Lajpat Rai and posted to his 12 Court Street address in Lahore. From Edgware, Har Dayal aware that his mail would be opened by the British Secret Service revealed to Lajpat Rai stating; "I am still living a quiet life. I have received the money from 'the man'. I thank you very much for all the trouble you have taken for me...." He thanked Lajpat Rai for the consent he had helped obtain to live in London and "for all the trouble that you have taken on my behalf. My dear brother Lala Kishan Dayal told me all about it when he was with me in Sweden..." He furthermore informed Lajpat Rai that he lived in a suburb and was working at the first volume of a series of Hindi books on the history of western civilization. He added that he visited the British Museum in London daily and studied history, science, and philosophy.

In May 1928, Har Dayal heard that there was some idea of his being prosecuted and in a letter to India Office reiterated that he had withdrawn from politics altogether. He further asked for permission to be allowed to study in London until April 1930. British Secret Service operatives concluded: "From his letters to his friends in India it would appear that he is at present occupying himself in purely literary pursuits and there seems to be no evidence to the contrary".

It was obvious that Har Dayal following the wise counsel of Kishan Dayal had deliberately kept aloof from Indian politics in London and later disclosed to

S.R. Rana, his old friend and benefactor in Paris, "I do not see many people here in London. There are no old friends here except a Ceylonese professor whom I knew at Oxford. All the Indians are new young people. I often go to the British Museum library for my work. I am writing a book on the history of Buddhism…" *(Letters of Lala Har Dayal)*

The Last Nails in the Coffin of British Rule in India

While Har Dayal was lost in the chambers of the British Museum library and academia in London, India was in conflict with Hukumat-i-Britannia over the proposed constitutional reforms. A group of seven British Members of Parliament under the chairmanship of Sir John Simon traveled to India to study constitutional reform in the British colony. On arrival in India in Bombay on February 3rd, 1928 they faced black flag protests and they were subsequently boycotted in all major cities.

In Lahore, on Tuesday, October 30th, 1928, Lajpat Rai led a silent march in protest against the Simon Commission. The thirty-two-year-old, Superintendent of Police of Lahore, James Alexander Scott, who was awarded the Police Medal in 1926, ordered the policemen to attack Lajpat Rai. The policemen mercilessly rained blows on the leader of the peaceful march at the Lahore railway station. The severely hurt veteran nationalist asserted, "I declare that the blows struck at me today will be the last nails in the coffin of British rule in India." Lajpat Rai could not fully recover from his injuries and died on November 17th, 1928 after a heart attack.

At the time of Lajpat Rai's death in November 1928, Har Dayal and Agda were on an organized tour to Greece and the Mediterranean with the Hellenic Travellers' Club. The trip featured a schedule of lectures by prominent British academics led by one of its directors and chairman, Mortimer Wheeler (1890–1976), a former Director-General of the Archeological Survey of India and associated with Institute of Archaeology at the University of London. On his return to London, Har Dayal received the dreadful news of the sudden passing of his guide and ardent supporter. His reaction has not been recorded though he admitted to S. R. Rana in a letter a few months later, "I am sorry that I could not see Lala Lajpat Rai lately". *(Letters of Lala Har Dayal)*

Across India, it was widely believed that the blows Lajpat Rai, the former Congress Party President and the founder of India Home Rule League in New

York, had received at the hands of the Hukumat-i-Britannia's police were the real cause of his death. Lajpat Rai's death was a huge setback to the nationalist fire that had arisen after the Jallianwala massacre. The fierce nationalist had predicted at the onset that Mahatma Gandhi's non-violent movement would fail.

In North India, a brave twenty-one-year-old revolutionary, Bhagat Singh (1907 – 1931) was the leader of HSRA. Nephew of the legendary Indian nationalist Ajit Singh (who was in exile in South America), the young Bhagat Singh was deeply inspired by the revolutionary activity of his uncle and his ideas were partly shaped by the Ghadr Party. His father Kishan Singh had welcomed the Ghadr patriots from the Pacific Coast at their home during WWI. The Ghadr Party was a source of motivation for Bhagat Singh and he believed the Ghadr newspaper articulated the voice of the revolutionary movement. Har Dayal and Bhagat Singh never met but there exist several connections between the two patriots, including textual citations besides familial friendships. Bhagat Singh quoted from Har Dayal's pamphlets in his publications. A strong advocate of violence for the eradication of the Hukumat-i-Britannia, his HSRA was non-sectarian and broadly leftish in thought. He also reportedly always carried a picture of the young patriot Kartar Singh Sarabha on his person and about whom he said: "One is amazed to think of what he at the age of nineteen was able to do... Such courage! Such self-confidence! So much of self-denial and passionate commitment has been rarely seen earlier... *Ohnan di rag rag vich inquilabi jazba smaya hoya si*". (Every vein of his was embedded with a revolutionary passion)

Bhagat Singh, the former student at National College in Lahore, saw Lajpat Rai's demise as a blot on the nation's dignity and decided to avenge his death.

Exactly a month after Lajpat Rai's death, on the late afternoon of December 17th, John Poyntz Saunders, the Assistant-Superintendent of Police, stepped out of the District Police Lines. Mistaking him for Superintendent James A Scott, Bhagat Singh and Shivaram Rajguru (1908–1931) pumped loads of bullets into his body on the streets of Lahore. Faiz Ahmed Faiz, who later became a prominent poet was at the New Hostel of the Government College, Lahore and is reported to have heard the shots. An alarm was immediately sounded throughout Lahore but Bhagat Singh and his crew strode through the Lahore Railway station right under the eyes of the British Secret Service and escaped. The next morning the police discovered several posters pasted on walls at different places in the city, with the bold printed heading in red: "The Hindustan Socialist Republican Army," below which was written out in thick letters: "Saunders is dead, Lalaji is avenged." The

British Secret Service and the Hukumat-i-Britannia's police force ran from pillar to post to identify the men who killed Saunders.

All of a sudden in March 1929, His Majesty's Government unearthed a Communist plot to deprive King George V of the dominion of British India, and for such purpose to use the methods and carry out the program and a plan of campaign outlined and ordained by the Communist International. In a trial that came to be known as the Meerut Conspiracy Case, Shripad Amrit Dange, Shaukat Usmani and Muzaffar Ahmad along with twenty-nine persons including British communist activists Philip Spratt, Benjamin Francis Bradley, and Lester Hutchinson were arrested. The main charges were that Dange under the influence of M. N. Roy had entered into a conspiracy to establish a branch of Comintern in India and various persons, including the British members of the Communist Party of Great Britain, were sent to India by the Communist International to assist them. British military intelligence was aware that some communist sympathizers came to India from Britain under assumed names guided by Rajni Palme Dutt and worked in the trade unions and other organizations.

On Monday, April 8th, 1929, Chaman Lal, a journalist with *Hindustan Times* and an activist, arranged two passes to the visitor's gallery of the central legislature in New Delhi for his colleagues from HSRA - Bhagat Singh and Batukeshwar Dutt (1910–1965). As the assembly opened both of them took their seats next to him. Chaman Lal later in 1975 in a recorded interview with the University of Cambridge, recalled the incident; "Bhagat Singh wanted to shoot but his pistol got jammed... B K Dutt threw the two bombs but they were crude bombs and only two bricks fell down from the ceiling. But the entire house was in a panic and everybody ran away. Hundreds of shoes were left behind. Even the police left the place and went away... Everybody thought the whole building is going to fall... there was so much panic". The two revolutionaries flung a few leaflets, claiming that it took "a loud voice to make the deaf hear." When the smoke subsided, both Bhagat Singh and Dutt courted arrest willingly and cheerfully. Sergeant Terry arrested both of them and Bhagat Singh put down his pistol on the nearby desk.

The Hukumat-i-Britannia did not accept any challenge to its rule. It had a well-defined policy to mercilessly crush the young nationalists with an 'iron hand' and Bhagat Singh and his compatriots were immediately imprisoned. A case was instituted against Bhagat Singh and Rajguru for depriving His Majesty of the Sovereignty of India. They refused to defend their actions in court just like Madan Lal Dhingra. Instead, Barrister Asaf Ali read out a statement on their behalf on June 6th, 1929, "We have only marked the end of an era of utopian non-violence of whose futility the rising generation has been convinced beyond the shadow of a doubt."

Across India, the brave revolutionary Bhagat Singh was seen to have defended Lajpat Rai's honor. By now a large section of the youth of India, frustrated with Mahatma Gandhi's non-violence agenda, were strongly driven to Bhagat Singh's methods. The meticulously planned attacks on Hukumat-i-Britannia's Police officers and the courageous activities of his HRSA with their cry of *'Inquilab Zindabad'* (long live the revolution) for demanding freedom from the Hukumat-i-Britannia became a rage.

Bhagat Singh, the young public intellectual and revolutionary, by his act redeemed and somewhat exceeded the anticolonial objectives of the Ghadr of 1857 and the Ghadr movement in California. In this process, he acquired the status of a national celebrity and became a serious challenger to the popularity of Mahatma Gandhi in India. Nevertheless, on December 19th, 1929, sixteen years after the Ghadr Party first raised its demand for independence from San Francisco, the Indian National Congress voted for *'purna swaraj'* (complete independence) and an official draft by Mahatma Gandhi declared, "The British government in India has not only deprived the Indian people of their freedom but has based itself on the exploitation of the masses and had ruined India economically, politically, culturally and spiritually… therefore India must sever the British connection and attain 'purna swaraj' or complete independence'.

The Significance of December 23rd

On Monday, December 23rd, 1929, the Viceroy's train headed back to the capital city of Delhi from Hyderabad after an official visit. It was a frosty winter morning and there was thick fog between Nizamuddin and New Delhi. Wrapped in heavy blankets Indians slept on the platforms of the railway station or sprawled dozing around small fires on the grassy farms, the doorways of Government buildings and in the verandas of the homes of the sahibs. Inside the train on waking up, the six feet five inches tall British Viceroy Lord Irwin sat down to read a book of faith. Twelve years before his birth, his grandfather Sir Charles Wood, the Secretary of State for India was told by a Hindu sage, that, "your grandson will one day rule India." The deeply religious forty-five-year-old Lord Irwin whose word was law in India was possibly even more powerful than the Prime Minister of Britain and traveled around India in his own private gleaming white train.

Unexpectedly a loud explosion startled him. The train braked furiously as armymen with guns drawn jumped off to inspect the track. A bomb had damaged the track on the embankment and if it had detonated as intended the train would have fallen thirty feet down crushing everyone aboard. Instead, it had damaged the British Viceroy's dining saloon and one attendant received minor injuries. The attempt by Indian revolutionaries to derail the train of the British Viceroy by triggering off bombs on the railway tracks was unsuccessful. Lord Irwin had a narrow escape.

Replying to questions in the House of Commons in London, later that day Captain Wedgewood Benn, Secretary for India read out Lord Irwin's message received via telegram; "I regret to have to inform Your Majesty that an attempt was made this morning to wreck my train by exploding bombs under it as we were approaching Delhi. Luckily no harm was done and few of us realized what had occurred. I hope Your Majesty will not be disturbed by exaggerated reports."

But Petrie, the Director of DCI in Delhi was disturbed. He had grasped that the Viceregal train outrage was timed perfectly – it occurred on December 23rd, exactly seventeen years since the day an assassination attempt was made on British Viceroy Lord Hardinge in Chandni Chowk as he too had entered the city of Delhi. The revolutionary groups and secret societies were actively working against Hukumat-i-Britannia and kept the memories of the past alive.

In the meanwhile, Lord Irvin arrived at the Viceregal Palace in New Delhi in time for a previously arranged meeting with Mahatma Gandhi and leaders of the Congress Party including Motilal Nehru, Sir Sapru and Vithalbhai Patel (1873–1933). At the meeting with the Indian leaders, Lord Irvin was in a jovial mood and discussed the bomb incident for nearly forty-five minutes. Indian leaders then demanded freedom not in the language of charity but injustice. The meeting came to nothing.

Unlike Mahatma Gandhi, Motilal Nehru had no inhibitions about revolutionaries. According to *Truth about the Indian Press*, written by Jogendra Nath Sahni, editor of the *Hindustan Times* from 1926 to 1933: "He considered them misguided but treated them with affection. Once when these boys were being trailed from one rat hole to another, spending their time in jungles and low down slums, living sometimes on the roasted gram and dry bread, he called me and gave me a thousand rupees to be passed on secretly to the revolutionaries…" On being informed by Sahni that the money was being spent on buying revolvers rather than food, "the elder Nehru, his eyes filled up with moisture, in a hoarse voice full of emotion, he said, One thing is sure even if we fail, these boys will see to it that India is free."

Then on the midnight of the last day of 1929, on the banks of a freezing river Ravi in Lahore, Jawaharlal Nehru unfurled the Indian tricolor and told the assembled party members, that the national flag of Hindustan, "must not be lowered so long as a single Indian lives in India."

The March to Dandi

Three months later, on Wednesday, March 12th, 1930, after the Indian National Congress had resolved to fight for *Purna Swaraj* Mahatma Gandhi began a march from his base, the Sabarmati Ashram with seventy-eight followers to a coastal village Dandi, some three hundred and ninety kilometers away. He was protesting against Britain's Salt Acts that prohibited Indians from collecting or selling salt, a staple in the Indian diet. The sixty-year-old trudged along at an average speed of sixteen kilometers per day and his travels were followed with zeal by millions of Indians. When simple peasants thronged to see him (many tried to kiss his feet), Mahatma Gandhi tried to stop 'the craze for darshan.'

After the Jallianwala massacre, Mahatma Gandhi was the leading man in the Indian freedom movement and the central figure of Indian National Congress as the champion of the Indian masses in the quest for 'Swaraj'. In fifteen years since his arrival in India, the former Barrister at Law was now a nationally recognized social activist, an upright fundraiser, and a ruthlessly sharp political negotiator. He successfully worked out the method of *ahimsa* and *satyagraha* upon which his world-renown was later established.

On the eleventh anniversary of the Jallianwala Bagh massacre, Mahatma Gandhi reached the sea and broke the law by scooping up a little seawater and publicly evaporating it to recover a mere pinch of salt. In one simple stroke, he had defied the British salt act. Towards the evening a huge, blood-red papier-mâché monster, symbolizing the salt tax, was dumped into the Arabian Sea. The salt crusade was an economic war against the Hukumat-i-Britannia. Across India, while Mahatma Gandhi walked to Dandi, white-capped Gandhians had stretched themselves full-length in front of boycotted shops, trams and trains. Hukumat-i-Britannia's police beat the unresisting volunteers and fractured their arms and wrists. As fast as they were brutally beaten by the police and carted away, others took their places. And on May 5th, 1930, Mahatma Gandhi now considered a dangerous and seditious agitator by His Majesty's Government was arrested and held in a furnace-like prison cell in Yerwada Jail in Poona to be only released on January 26th the next year.

Simultaneously in Chittagong, a small town in East Bengal on Friday, April 18th, 1930, at around 2200 hrs, a clutch of boys, most of them still in their teens, inspired by the famous Easter Uprising in Dublin (1916), confronted the might of the British Empire through a series of raids on the armories of the police and the Auxiliary Force of Chittagong. Their actions stunned the colonial powers and ignited a spark of upheaval throughout Bengal. Their charismatic leader Masterda Surja Sen (1894–1934) was later executed after being brutally tortured by the Hukumat-i-Britannia.

Dr. Har Dayal's Masterpiece on Buddhism

On July 16th, 1930, completely detached from the turbulent Indian political scene Har Dayal in a deliberate effort to divert his attention from India after just two years of unperturbed study fulfilled one of his ambitions. He leisurely mastered the ancient Pali language and submitted a well-researched thesis for a Doctorate. As expected, under the guidance of Professor Turner he chose an extremely complex spiritual subject, *The Bodhisattva Doctrine in Buddhist Sanskrit Literature*.

At forty-five, Har Dayal was granted a *'Philosophiae doctor'* (Doctor of Philosophy) from the Faculty of Arts, the University of London for his thesis on Buddhism. He dedicated his thesis to "Sankta Agda (Saint Agda in Swedish) in token of friendship and esteem". In those academic years in London, his relationship with Agda had deepened. He learned to discipline himself and she provided financial stability that he desperately needed for survival.

Two years later in 1932, his thesis was published in London by Kegan Paul, Trench, Trubner and Co. Ltd. The end result of Har Dayal's intellectual pursuit was considered a masterpiece of Buddhist studies. With his third book, Har Dayal became a pioneering author of Indian origin in Britain and a recognized brandname in the exclusive literary clubs of London.

In the introduction to the book, he claimed that he had attempted to discuss the Bodhisattva doctrine as it is expounded in the principal Buddhist Sanskrit treatises. He thanked his Professor Ralph Turner, two British scholars of Pali language, Dr. Thomas William Rhys David and Dr. William Stede as also

Dr. Nalinaksha Dutt and his own brother-in-law Gukul Chand who was a lawyer, for their help and support during his research.

The 392-page book contained seven precisely written chapters: chapter one analyzed the different factors including the influence of Persian religio-cult, Greek art and Christian ethics that contributed to the growth of Bodhisattva doctrine. In chapter two he expounded his theory on the advent of the thought of enlightenment for the emancipation of all creatures. Chapter three explained the thirty-seven practices and principles prerequisite for the attainment of enlightenment. Chapter four illustrated the ten perfections (paramitas) that lead to the welfare, rebirth, serenity, spiritual, cultivation and ultimate knowledge. Chapter five described the distinctive stages of the spiritual rise along the aspirant's extended passage to the final emancipation. Chapter six recounted the events of Gautama Buddha's past lives and earlier incarnations as Bodhisattva. Chapter seven studied how the ideology and contributions of Bodhisattva intermingled with society.

In his scholarly study of Buddhism, Har Dayal incorporated some of his own beliefs, writing "A great religion is not a dead static formula of salvation and ethics it is always a living, dynamic, self-evolving and self-adjusting spiritual movement." He further spelled out his viewpoint: "It is the personality that secures the triumph of a religious movement; the dogmas and precepts shine in the light reflected from personality," and added, "Hinduism is a national religious and social system, like Confucianism and Judaism." His distinctive style of writing of making an extremely complex philosophical subject easy to understand is visible in the final paragraph, "Our task is done. The bodhisattva, who commenced his career with 'the thought of Enlightenment' many eons ago, has now become a perfectly enlightened Buddha. Wherefore we respectfully and regretfully take leave of him."

Renowned British authority in the history of Buddhism, Edward Joseph Thomas reviewed Har Dayal's work and remarked, "Within the limited time he has imposed on himself he gives a well-documented account, remarkable for the thoroughness with which the work of previous investigators has been examined… There is no doubt that the whole work forms the most systematic and extensive study that we possess in English on this important development of religion."

Other reviewers were equally gracious in their appreciation of the first extensive study in English of the Bodhisattva doctrine. Dr. J. Michael Mahar, in his critical bibliography of India, recorded, "A scholarly survey of the Bodhisattva, or Buddha-to-be, a concept initially formulated in relation to Gautama Buddha, later elaborated into a major tenet of Mahayana Buddhism. Bodhisattvas are enlightened ones who perform acts of kindness and mercy during their final series of transmigrations." A raving review claimed, "Dr. Dayal's work has brought him success at London University which his unflagging industry and exploitation of a hitherto unmapped field so richly deserved." Yet another identified, "Dr. Dayal has written what seems a compendium of pure Buddhism".

Scholars around the world are still widely using the celebrated thesis that appeared in 1930 and it remains an open question if anything more could be added to this excellent study. As the thesis approaches the centenary of its publication, Professor Christopher Key Chapple, currently at the Theological Studies Department, Loyola Marymount University, Los Angeles, USA, even now in 2019 maintains, "Har Dayal's book *The Bodhisattva Doctrine in Buddhist Sanskrit Literature* on the bodhisattva still towers above other research on the topic. In the textbooks on Buddhism and the then-available translations of Buddhist texts in the late 20th century, it was nearly impossible to find any specifics on the nature of the bodhisattva... It was only in Har Dayal's work could granular descriptions be found, particularly in regard to the progressive states known as the Bodhisattva Bhumi. For scholars of the Yoga Sutra as well as practitioners of Yoga, Dayal's work holds the key to understanding an important part of the Yoga path. The stage of Dharmamegha Samadhi, mentioned in Yoga Sutra IV:29, gives cogency to whole system of Yoga. And, as can be learned from Dayal, it is also the tenth and final attainment of the Bodhisattva. Har Dayal's book, remains a classic and profoundly informed my own work."

From the glowing reviews, it was clear despite a life of hardship, Har Dayal's powerful intellect was still intact and capable of doing wonders. *The Bodhisattva Doctrine in Buddhist Sanskrit Literature* was the second act of genius in Har Dayal's life after the formation of the Ghadr Party.

Inquilab Zindabad

By the end of 1930, after almost three-quarters of a century of Hukumat-i-Britannia's rule in India, their communal strategy of *divide et impera,* had begun to provide impressive dividends. On December 29th, 1930, Har Dayal's former Professor at Government College in Lahore, Sir Muhammad Iqbal, was elected as the President of All India Muslim League. In his acceptance speech, the poet who penned the patriotic poem, "*Saare jahan se achcha Hindustan hamara*", shockingly proclaimed, "I would like to see Punjab, the North-West Frontier Province, Sind and Balochistan amalgamated into a single State. Self-government within the British Empire, or without the British Empire, the formation of a consolidated North-Western Indian Muslim State appears to me to be the final destiny of the Muslims at least of north-west India…" The idea of creation of a separate state for Indian Muslims covertly encouraged by Hukumat-i-Britannia subsequently led to the bloodstained partition of India and the creation of Pakistan – an idea opposed in Har Dayal's Ghadr philosophy.

Then two months later on February 27th, 1931, Bhagat Singh's twenty-four-year-old daring compatriot Chandra Shekhar Azad, encircled by the Hukumat-i-Britannia's police at Alfred Park in Allahabad, shot himself in the head with his last bullet as per his own vow, not to be ever taken alive. And after ignoring pleas from Indians, Hukumat-i-Britannia on March 23rd, 1931, hanged Bhagat Singh along with his team members Shukdev Thapar (1907–1931) and Rajguru.

These ghastly acts of the Hukumat-i-Britannia agitated the entire nation. The courageous young men had distinguished themselves in a manner that none before them had dared, becoming true Indian heroes. Across India, men and women wept like children on hearing the news of the hanging of the three young nationalists. Their capsuled expression *'Inquilab Zindabad'* (Long live the revolution) was to reverberate as the war cry of the youth.

In 1931, unknown to Har Dayal, the Ghadr Party published a curious pamphlet in Punjabi from San Francisco. It juxtaposed Bhagat Singh's famous portrait in a hat photographed at a studio at Kashmiri Gate in Delhi and an article *'Barabary de arth'* (The Meaning of Equality) with the author's name: Lala Har Dayal. The images of the two figures - one the foremost political figure of the day placed along with the "most dangerous of all the Indian agitators", confirmed the logical association in public mind of the two most powerful and popular men of anti-colonial activism in India though separated by twenty years.

The Emperorship must go

The Congress Party held its annual session at Karachi from March 26th to 31st, 1931, under the dark shadow of the tragedy of the hanging of the three fearless patriots. The young leader from Bengal, Subhas Bose who had observed the revolutionary activities at close distance stole the moment and announced, "Bhagat Singh had become the symbol of the new awakening among the youths." At this time, Nehru who along with his father Motilal Nehru had visited Bhagat Singh in prison recorded, "Bhagat Singh's amazing popularity rivaled that of Gandhi." Even, Horace Williamson, the highly decorated and the newly appointed Director of DCI, concurred, "his photograph was on sale in every city and township and for a time rivaled in popularity even that of Mr. Gandhi himself."

In reality, no Mughal Shehenshah ever had more power in India than Mahatma Gandhi. He held no rank or post but his faith and leadership had made the Indian National Congress the single largest resistance force against the British Empire. Mahatma Gandhi accompanied by disciples arrived in London on a rainy night on September 12th, 1931. Besides meeting important political leaders Mahatma Gandhi met George Bernard Shaw and even Charles Chaplin. Har Dayal deliberately kept away from all political visitors from India still hopeful of returning back to India.

On a visit to Oxford University, Mahatma Gandhi spoke at the Majlis that was founded by Har Dayal in 1906 and was asked, "How far would you cut India off from the Empire?" Mahatma Gandhi's reply was precise: "From the Empire, entirely; from the British nation not at all, if I want India to gain and not to grieve." He claimed: "The British Empire is an Empire only because of India. The Emperorship must go..." Hukumat-i-Britannia was not amused. The newly appointed British Viceroy Earl of Willingdon (1866–1941) ordered Mahatma Gandhi's detention. He was arrested on his return from Europe on January 4th, 1932.

It all looks like a dream

Indifferent to Mahatma Gandhi's civil disobedience movement, Har Dayal, much against his nature consciously disconnected himself from all political activities. During the Christmas holidays of 1931, he was in the Mediterranean town of Menton in the South of France with Agda. Every time he left Britain, he was scrupulous in notifying his movements to India Office. The British Secret Service observed that each year in the summer months from July to September and sometimes over the New Year holidays Agda and Har Dayal would travel to Europe. Concerned about the precarious condition of Agda and the illness of her lungs, Har Dayal took her to the Alpine region of Montreux, Geneva, and Chamonix and similarly to the coastal town of Menton in South of France to seek better weather. She also received guests; relatives and friends from Sweden at their home in London and on one occasion went off to Oxford with Har Dayal and her family for a picnic. Deeply in love with Har Dayal, she never hid the fact that she was in a relationship with an Indian and was addressed by neighbours and local folks as Mrs. Dayal.

From Menton in 1931, Har Dayal sent a letter of condolence to S. R. Rana in Paris on the passing of Therese Listz. Possibly free from the interception of his mail by the British Secret Service and it being a local letter in France he admitted, "As I grow older, I feel that it is necessary for one's happiness to be in the company of younger people and help them along. This will be one way of defeating old age and loneliness and you will be serving the cause of India...." A bit nostalgic, Har Dayal for the first time inquired about their past comrades from the Paris India Group, "I would like to know what has become of our friends (Madam Cama, etc.). Yes, life changes so much that it all looks like a dream!"

16

THE WORLD OF HAR DAYAL

"Regardless of his political views and personal philosophy, Har Dayal is a genius whom no intelligent individual can fail to admire... Judged from all points of view, Har Dayal proves that India undoubtedly is a great country that produces geniuses in all spheres of activity..."

Dr. Kharaiti Ram Samras
Historian, Department of State, USA

In early August 1932, on a summer day, a neatly dressed Gobind Behari Lal holding on to his briefcase followed by a porter walked into the luxurious Savoy Hotel in London. He had left New York on August 3rd 1932 on the *S.S. Leviathan* and reached London on a holiday as well as a business trip.

Though Gobind had lived in the United States for twenty years he was still not accepted as an American citizen. Earlier on March 16th, 1928, Vaishno Das Bagai, a Ghadr patriot and an art dealer in San Francisco had committed suicide in protest after feeling betrayed, when the United States Government revoked his citizenship. Gobind had served a jail sentence in 1918 for his participation in the Ghadr Party activities and thereafter completed his education at the University of California. By 1932 he was a respected journalist in the United States specializing in science. He had lived in San Francisco, Los Angeles and New York working as a reporter for the Hearst Group of Newspapers. It was an exciting time for a science news reporter with radio waves becoming a new communication model, television making its debut in the labs in San Francisco and aviation becoming a transport tool of the future. There were talks about exploring outer space already.

Gobind efficiently and persistently tracked down the world's distinguished scientists and obtained first-hand reports on their latest theories and discoveries. On his visit to Britain, he visited the laboratories of Cambridge University where he interviewed Nobel Prize-winning Physicists Ernest Rutherford, Frederick Gowland Hopkins, and future Nobel Prize winner John Cockcroft. While in

London, Gobind also interviewed writer H. G. Wells who complimented him for interpreting the mystical East to the West. From London, he was to travel to interview yet another world-famous scientist, Albert Einstein at his home near Potsdam.

In the British capital, he had scheduled an important meeting with his mentor Har Dayal. They were to meet after a gap of eighteen and a half years. Recollecting the meeting with Har Dayal in *Dr. Emily Brown's biography*, Gobind recalled that his relative and mentor arrived at the Savoy in his usual scruffy clothes, unshaven with a receding hairline with worn-out rotten shoes. In addition, Gobind saw "a piece of string hanging from his pocket which he said was tied to his key". Gobind though thrilled to meet him was upset at the upkeep of the man he held in such high esteem. He immediately drove Har Dayal to an exclusive hair-cutting saloon for a shave and proper hair cut. Then he got a couple of new suits and shirts stitched for him at an expensive tailoring shop on Savile Row and bought him a few pairs of decent shoes.

The Urdu speaking Dilliwallahs then proceeded to have a sumptuous dinner at the finest Indian restaurant in London (possibly Sir William Steward's 'The Veeraswamy' that had opened on Regent Street in 1926). Gobind still retained the traces of his hometown in accent and taste for the famed gastronomic culture of Delhi, 'Dilli ka khana' as he called it. He ordered the best in the house announcing to the owner that his guest was a famous leader of India. Though they had corresponded regularly they had eighteen years of life and work to cover over dinner. Har Dayal had spent his years in Geneva, Constantinople, Berlin, Vienna, Stockholm, Goteburg and now London while Gobind had made New York his home and journalism his calling. Gobind noticed that his mentor had retained his charming personality but with age, the fire in the belly had more or less disappeared.

Har Dayal who preferred a low profile existence in London must have been overwhelmed by Gobind's affection and generosity. He naturally wanted to reciprocate and later took Gobind to a workingman's eatery for a meal. Gobind was disgusted at the quality of the servings and returned to the Savoy with Har Dayal for a proper dinner. An embarrassed Har Dayal profusely apologized for his choice of restaurant and Gobind wondered why Har Dayal lived in such appalling conditions. Gobind divulged to *biographer Dr. Emily Brown,* "I told him, though, that he still meant the same to me and he was very much moved."

The next day Har Dayal invited Gobind to his home in Edgware and showed him his proud possession – his life's only major investment – the library of five thousand-books that he had built over decades with his miniscule personal income. Gobind was astonished to learn that even after receiving a Ph.D. from the University of London, Har Dayal was studying Botany, Zoology, Physics, Astronomy besides Painting and Sculpture and conducting experiments in science at the university as an enthusiastic undergraduate student. His quest for knowledge was insatiable. Gobind realized that his mentor was truly unique, as no one would ever take undergraduate work once they had finished a Ph.D. He told him that he could not respect him more for his intellectual integrity!

But in his personal matters, Har Dayal was not that honest. He kept his relationship with Agda a secret from Gobind and did not mention her.

The British Secret Service has recorded that Har Dayal once again met Gobind in Paris in September 1932. Then on the morning of Saturday, September 22nd, 1932, Gobind sat across from Professor Albert Einstein still clad in a pair of blue pajamas at his residence at Caputh-on-the Havel. The scientist was interviewed for three hours out of which two hours were spent discussing India, the independence movement and the dissolution of the caste system. Gobind walked out of that interview with the feeling that Einstein the great scientist was also a great lover of humankind. Gobind returned from Europe on October 1st, 1932 and later interviewed Einstein again on March 28th, 1958 in Princeton, the United States, but found him a different and sadder man.

The Vanishing Empire

In London on the remarkably bright morning of Wednesday, July 5th, 1933, an Indian journalist and revolutionary Chaman Lal accosted Har Dayal at the travel agency Thomas Cook's office in Mayfair. Lal had miraculously managed to reach London despite the British Secret Service reports that revealed, "his movements are under surveillance and it is considered that he is undoubtedly in touch with revolutionaries... Mr. Chaman Lal is an excitable character who is capable of doing any wild act under the stimulus of his feelings and I feel that to give him a passport to England at the present time might lead to undesirable incidents."

During his stay in London, it had been impossible for Chaman Lal to locate Har Dayal for a very specific reason. Aware of British Secret Service's surveillance techniques, Har Dayal completely avoided the company of Indians especially due to a fairly bad experience in one instance with some Indian students. He still hoped to return to India someday and kept his reputation with the India Office as a non-political resident of Britain undamaged.

After that brief encounter with Har Dayal, Chaman Lal changed his career path and authored many books, including *The Vanishing Empire* (published in 1937) that accurately prophesied the collapse of Hukumat-i-Britannia within the next ten years. In, *The Vanishing Empire*, Chaman Lal wrote that as they parted that July morning after their serendipitous meeting (detailed in chapter one), Har Dayal provided him with introductions to his associate Rash Behari Bose who lived in exile in Japan and the address of Godha Ram Chanon, the editor of the *Ghadr* newspaper in San Francisco. Lal later recalled, "In the United States I met dozens of Lala Har Dayal's disciples and admirers in California."

Chaman Lal's other book, *Hindu America* (issued in 1940), revealed the forgotten story of the imprints of Hindu and Buddhist cultures on the ancient Americas. In this book he revealed, "Godha Ram Chanon was introduced to me by the late Lala Har Dayal, the father of the Indian Revolutionary Party living in England in 1933. The credit for my researches goes to the two respected compatriots and I salute them". Conceivably influenced by his chance meeting with Har Dayal, Lal took Buddhist vows in December 1955 and became a 'Bhikshu', moving from country to country bearing the message of truth. In the final years of his life, he settled down in Modern School, Barakhamba Road, New Delhi.

Sou Sonar Ki: Ek Lohar Ki

Har Dayal's decision to settle down in London made it easier for his old friends to visit him. Another confidante from India, Charles Andrews, the Principal of St. Stephen's College met Har Dayal in London. Andrews called 'Deshbandhu' by the Indian masses was now a well-known supporter of Mahatma Gandhi and recalled, "He (Har Dayal) had brought a Professor of Pali with him to see me with whom he was collaborating in bringing out some Pali texts. After that he met me many times over and we had many talks together about Buddhism. He had become a convinced Buddhist in his general outlook, so he told me" (*The Modern Review*). Seeing the transformation, Andrews decided to convince the Hukumat-i-Britannia to allow Har Dayal to return to India; "I was very impressed by the change that had come over him and his long for inward peace. When I had returned to India I did everything I could to get the ban against him removed."

Around the same dates in the summer of 1933, Bhai Parmanand and his son-in-law Dr. Dharmavira (Har Dayal's biographer) arrived in London to attend the hearings of the Joint Parliamentary Committee, whose work resulted in the Government of India Act of 1935. Bhai Parmanand, as a leader of Hindu Mahasabha, also attended the World Monetary and Economic Conference. During their visit to London both of them spent many hours with Har Dayal almost every single evening.

Overcome by emotion on meeting Har Dayal after decades, Dr. Dharmavira as recorded in Dr. Emily Brown's biography recollected, "He was a lovely personality. You needed only to sit with him for three or four hours to know that no other person could be like him. I love to remember those evenings with him — those times. It was a treat to be with him and to listen to his conversation. One of the things about him that was most striking was his sincerity - his earnestness about anything he took up. You will not find this in ordinary persons." Dr. Dharmavira in his *biography*, has divulged, when Har Dayal was questioned by Bhai Parmanand about his *volte-face*, he is reported to have explained, "In politics, you have to think of so many things; one has to look at a particular problem from various angles. It was a move from my side at that particular moment. Again, it is not necessary that you succeed in each and every move. The die was cast. I thought that it would get through but it did not succeed. I was however not at all sorry…".

In the absence of Adga, after carefully sanitizing his living room of her belongings, Har Dayal invited both Bhai Parmanand and Dr. Dharmavira to his home in Edgware to proudly show his large personal library. Dr. Dharmavira thought, "this was the product of his life of contentment". Later Har Dayal wrote to Dr. Dharmavira, "If out of love, you want to write an article about my personal library, you can. Before me there have been two principles objects - 'knowledge and service' – such an article by you will not harm me in any way."

The other subject Har Dayal touched upon was Mahatma Gandhi - the man of the moment who was drawing large crowds across India and dominating the newspaper headlines in India, Europe, Asia and North America. Comparisons were drawn at that time by Dr. Dharmavira between Har Dayal's work as a revolutionary between 1907–1917 and Mahatma Gandhi's civil disobedience campaign. It is reported that Har Dayal using a popular Hindi proverb humbly claimed, *"Sou sonar ki: ek lohar ki"*. It loosely translated, as 'a hundred hits by a goldsmith were equal to a single stroke by an ironsmith'. In other words, he believed that the Ghadr movement had accomplished a lot more in a shorter period than the much more widespread Gandhian *satyagraha*.

Months before on Tuesday, May 9th, 1933, veteran Indian nationalist leader Vithalbhai Patel and the young trailblazer, Subhas Chandra Bose had issued a strong-worded joint statement, the Patel-Bose manifesto from Switzerland saying that, "The events of the last thirteen years have demonstrated that a political warfare based on the principle of maximum suffering for ourselves and minimum suffering for our opponents cannot possibly lead to success. It is futile to expect that we can ever bring a change of heart in our rulers merely through our sufferings or by trying to love them. And the latest action of Mahatma Gandhi in suspending the Civil Disobedience Movement is a confession of failure as far as the present method of the Congress is concerned. We are clearly of the opinion that as a political leader Mahatma Gandhi had failed."

In London during the summer of 1933, British Secret Service had sighted Har Dayal with Ranchhodas Bhavan Lotwala (1876–1971), a rich merchant and the proprietor of the journal, *Sunday Advocate*. Lotwala spent every summer in London and was engaged in communist propaganda at his home at Beaufort Gardens. Lotwala had become disillusioned with the non- cooperation movement and was instrumental in helping the early communists. As disclosed by the British Secret Service report, Har Dayal "considered Gandhism must go but Congress must adopt organizational programs which all reasonable men could join and there must be good leadership; no good forming new parties".

Har Dayal's Hints for Self-Culture

In March 1934, the postman dropped the usual mail at the Van Wyck Brooks residence on 87 Kings Highway in Westport Connecticut. Brooks was surprised to receive a dispatch posted from France and read with great interest a letter from his old friend Har Dayal after a gap of eight years. He was pleasantly surprised to learn that his Indian revolutionary friend had settled in London and read all his books.

Brooks resumed his correspondence with Har Dayal and shortly heard back that the former Stanford lecturer used his leisure in London to write a book on Buddhist philosophy, for which he received his Ph.D. in 1930. Har Dayal updated his friend that he was in Germany during WWI, then retired in Sweden and stopped working against the British Empire. Now in complete isolation in London suburbs, he concentrated on his next book that contained his philosophical and ethical propaganda (including economics and politics). Har Dayal felt that the spiritual vacuum, in which most modern "advanced" people passed their lives, must be filled up. He had also dropped a hint beforehand about his next book to Bhai Parmanand, and told him that the book is for the "Hindu youths" obsessed with communalism and "pseudo-nationalism".

This book that aimed at preaching the ideal of free thought constructively was to be his tour-de-force in the decades to come.

In April 1934, Watts and Company, publishers based on Fleet Street in London brought out *Hints for Self Culture*, the fourth book written by Har Dayal. Founded in 1864, by Charles Watts, the London based publishing firm encouraged freethinkers and secularists and his son, Charles Albert Watts, developed the Rationalist Press Association in Britain.

Once again Har Dayal affectionately dedicated the book to, "Sankta Agda (Saint Agda in Swedish) in token of friendship and esteem". In his preface, he did not accept the Christian calendar and datelined April 6934 A.H. - Anno Historiae stating, "...I may tentatively fix 5000 BC as the starting point of historical era." The 363-page book itself was a reflection of the writer's wide reading and his depth of understanding of a vast universe of subject material. It was like a summary to a world encyclopedia, that invited the readers to head out further for their betterment. The book was the sum total of Har Dayal's enormous reservoir of global knowledge after almost five decades of learning and living on planet earth as also his final thesis as a philosopher, politician, and propagandist.

Har Dayal confirmed, "In this little book I have tried to indicate and explain some aspects of the message of Rationalism for the young men and women of all countries," and added, "If it helps them in their efforts for self-improvement in the least degree, I shall be amply rewarded." He then addressed himself at greater length to the prospective reader: "To a young fellow rationalist. These short hints on Self-Culture are addressed to you in the hope that you will try to make the best use of your life according to the philosophy of Rationalism" and encouraged the reader, "It is for you to blaze the trail for great movements that will build up a happier world."

A reviewer from Miami wrote, "This valuable book presents a wide survey of nearly every branch of human culture from the earliest to modern times. The author challenges those who would mislead men with false god near or distant. These short hints on self-culture are intended to aid the growth and development of the reader's personality in its four aspects: Intellectual, Physical, Aesthetic and Ethical. The volume is recommended as stimulating reading for all who desire to polish these four facets of a complete life."

Continuing his quest for a philosophic synthesis between the east and west, Har Dayal divided the book into four sections. In the first titled 'Intellectual Culture' he incorporated science, history, psychology, economics, philosophy, sociology, languages and comparative religions. The second section dealt with the 'Physical Culture' in which he reviewed diet, proper health habits, exercise, and sports and concluded with the remark that "a happy mind makes a healthy body". In the third, he covered the 'Aesthetic Culture' and examined the theory and function of art, architecture, sculpture, painting, music, dancing, oratory and poetry. While the fourth one was called the 'Ethical Culture' he examined the personal ethics, personal service, the five circles (family, relatives, municipality, nation, world state), economics and politics. Har Dayal determined; "with these four facet development of human personality a man can live and enjoy his life fully".

Among the groundbreaking English prose writers of Indian origin, Har Dayal's individuality emerges in the book as a total cosmopolitan detached from the 'Indian nationalist' that he was perceived for decades. He drew influence and inspiration from the eminent thinkers, scientists, humanists, rationalists, religious mystics and authors of outstanding caliber and quoted them considerably. He wished the readers, "to be wise and independent in our religion and in our politics not to be doped and duped by selfish priests and the scheming politicians of capitalism and so-called socialism". He quoted, Sheikh Saadi, "Like a taper one should melt in pursuit of knowledge, this is thy duty even if thou has to travel over the whole earth. It is our duty to train and develop our mind and acquire as much knowledge as we possibly can obtain".

Arguing for the significance of science, Har Dayal exhorted, "one should pay attention towards science. We have already been scientists in a general way ever since we are born". While explaining superstitions he quoted Lucretius a Roman poet-philosopher; "superstition is put underfoot and trampled upon in turn. This terror and darkness of mind must be dispelled not by rays of the sun and glittering shafts of the day but by the aspect and the law of nature".

Though scientific temper has been the hallmark of Indian thought over the millennia, Har Dayal was the first Indian thinker to expound the idea of the study of modern science as an essential part of education in his book, *Hints for a Self*

Culture. Har Dayal insisted on the study of the history of science writing, "You will learn to love Truth and Fact more than gold and silver. You will acquire that stern intellectual integrity and incorruptible spiritual veracity which no amount of merely ethical and religious training can ever bestow upon you". He added the general ideas about Nature and the Universe should be thoroughly comprehended and inwardly digested, "Your personal religion should be based on them; otherwise you will fall headlong into the bottomless pit of superstition."

Considering superstition as an enemy to be faced and foiled, Har Dayal was convinced that, "Superstition was the ubiquitous enemy of Man in the infancy of civilization. But science, and science alone, can liberate and enfranchise your mind from the corroding and demoralizing influence of superstition in all its ghastly shapes and disguises. Superstition means belief in the reality of that which does not exist; it assumes a thousand forms and enslaves humanity with a thousand fetters. It has led to cruel exploitation and infamous barbarities in the history of the race."

Rationalism was a dominant thought in his life and he made a connection between a rational mindset and working democracies stating in his book, "Without Rationalism, Democracy will never win, as the people and their leaders will always be deluded into chasing the empty phantoms of salvation and nirvana. But if Democracy is attired in the armor of Rationalism, then it will be invincible in all the combats and jousts to which it may be challenged... Rationalism again can never be suppressed this time, because it is the necessary outcome of Science and scientific education... Science and scientific education will cure the people of the somnolence induced by theology and superstition: and when the people are fully awakened then woe to all the oligarchs and their vile brood."

Today Article 51A of the Constitution of India, states that among the fundamental duties of every Indian, to develop the scientific temper, humanism and the spirit of inquiry and reform is essential and desirable. The careful cultivation of a scientific outlook has remained Har Dayal's principal contribution to twenty-first-century India. Har Dayal wanted to establish the supremacy of science in the autobiography of the world.

Communicating in the same first-person plural like the texts of *Ghadr-di-Gunj*, Har Dayal inspired young rationalists in the making, "Great man of the past - they despised money and property. You can do the same. They sacrificed everything for the good of their fellow men. You can do the same. They cultivated extreme simplicity in food, drink, and dress, you can do the same, they loved and served the poor and the humble, you can do the same. They were free from lust and craving, you can be the same, they were always patient and gentle, you can be the same, they inspired their friends and comrades with zeal for perfection, you can do the same."

The man without a passport claimed, "The World-State needs its pioneers now. You can be such a pioneer. Do your duty within the nation-state today, but do it in the spirit of a world-citizen of the future. Eschew all hatred and contempt for other nations and races. Study world-history, travel as often as you can, learn a world language, read world-literature, cultivate the society of foreigners and strangers, and thus make yourself and your friends worthy of world-citizenship. Establish a Cosmopolitan Club in your town. Join an international correspondence society. Preach peace, when others howl in hate or rage for revenge. Welcome, all to your home and your heart... all men and women and children without distinction of race or color. Eat and drink with all. Love and serve all. Do good to all... Work thus, and wait for the World-State. It shall come, not today and not tomorrow, but in its own good time. But if you live in the light of its ideal now and here, you are already a citizen of that State. You belong to it. You may be born in the present nation-state, but you are not of it. Your heart is elsewhere. Waking and sleeping, you think of the World-State and long for its advent. When the Sun is still below the horizon in the early morning, he cannot be seen; but he sends before him sister Dawn, holy Ushas, radiant Aurora, who has also been deemed worthy of adoration. Such a slow-brightening Dawn you are privileged to witness in this age, though your eyes cannot behold the Sun. Your children and grandchildren will rejoice in the light and warmth of the Sun that shall illumine the Earth in the days to come, the serene and spacious World-State, one and indivisible."

By August 1933, Har Dayal had spent a quarter of a century away from home. He was the product of the British Empire's social and intellectual conquest of India and a first-hand witness to both Hukumat-i-Britannia's brutality and the horrors of WWI. Forced by circumstances not to resist British imperialism directly and still hoping that His Majesty's Government would one day allow him to be reunited with his family and friends in India, he had written a book that covertly opposed the idea of the British Empire. Har Dayal in his radical outlook created a utopian vision of an optimistic new world for the future generations of humankind. In the book he focused on the development of a World-State as an alternative to imperialism, a utopian community "with the Earth as its territorial basis. One State, One Flag, One Language, one Ethics, one Ideal, one Love, and one Life: that is our goal."

This was the central hint in Har Dayal's book for future world citizens and he pursued it with great passion.

In California, his friend John Barry reviewed the book in *The San Francisco News* and remarked, "Reading this book is like having an intimate talk with a character mellowed by a knowledge of the world and the best the world has to offer... His book ought to have a wide reading. I shall be surprised if it does not place him among the best of the popular philosophers." The review in the *Palestine Post* was equally glowing, "Such an assembling together of advice in every realm of life and knowledge is not common. Here is the cream of the world's thinkers and teachers".

The literary works of Indian leaders, including Aurobindo Ghosh's *Life Divine*, Mahatma Gandhi's *My Experiments with Truth*, Nehru's *Autobiography*, *Discovery of India* and *Glimpses of World History* and Subhas Chandra Bose's *An Indian Pilgrim* were all products of the freedom struggle. Har Dayal too had aggressively participated in the elimination of Hukumat-i-Britannia and the formation of the Ghadr Party was a miraculous moment in his life as a revolutionary followed by the doctorate in Buddhism by the University of London. Now with the publication of *Hints for Self Culture*, he had firmly established himself as an outstanding author and a world-class philosopher with original ideas. Here was a man who could see the world and its civilization through the lens of time and created a work that would be enjoyed for generations.

Philiospher Schopenhauer once argued, that while talent speaks brilliantly to the moment and is of the moment, genius speaks of the eternal and to eternity and wrote, "The genius, on the other hand, lights on his age like a comet into the paths of the planets, to whose well-regulated and comprehensible arrangement its wholly eccentric course is foreign."

The commonly read book, *Hints for Self Culture* was the third act of genius in Har Dayal's life.

Apka Vayaktitva Vikas Ke Sutra

At his home in Edgware, reports were reaching Har Dayal that Hukumat-i-Britannia wanted to ban his book. It was an instant hit in India and Frederick Watts, the publisher confirmed in a note to him' "the sales for India are going fairly well". The book was also published in its Hindi version, *Apka Vayaktitva Vikas Ke Sutra*.

Har Dayal concerned about the impact of the book on his future ability to return to his family tried to stop the review and sales of the book in India. In a letter to the India Office he clarified the non-political nature of his writings, "The book is a philosophical treatise, in which I have expounded a complete new system of philosophy somewhat on the model of Plato's *Republic* and More's *Utopia*." In this communication to the India Office, Har Dayal, emphasized, "I have decided to abstain from direct or indirect participation in contemporary Indian movements, as I am now domiciled in England. But I intend to carry on my philosophical propaganda in Europe and America, where the book will be sold and circulated. I hope that the Government of India have no objecting to such intellectual activity on my part."

The NAI records unveil that the recently knighted Sir Horace Williamson, Director of DCI still considered prosecuting Har Dayal should he return to India. His department reviewed the book instantly, noting, "The chapter on politics is mainly made up of arguments against militarism and war and India has been left out of the picture not only in this chapter but throughout the book. The book is not as fiery as it might have been coming from the pen of Har Dayal and taken as a whole it is doubtful whether we should be justified in banning its importation into India under the Sea Customs Act."

Later on June 21st, 1934, the British Viceroy's office in an official communication to the Secretary of State for India in London wrote, "Government of India have examined Har Dayal's book and do not consider that any action to prohibit circulation in India is necessary."

On his desk at his home library in the suburbs of London, Har Dayal unmoved by the success of his immense undertaking was already working on writing a companion volume titled, *History of Civilization*. He had read some Greek and all of Plato and Aristotle for a revival of Hellenism. He wanted to distill the best teachings of the Greek philosophers with the working title, *The Wisdom of Hellas*. He also had plans to write *The New Gospel of Jesus* and to present Christianity and its history in a modern form for the benefit of modern rationalists.

The East Meets West in Dayalism

At the onset of summer on a pleasant Sunday evening of May 1934 in a London suburb, a crowd of freethinkers, rationalists, humanists, leftists, spiritually-minded individuals, utopian socialists and other fellow travellers from Britain's highbrow society gathered inside the small living room of a home in Edgware to attend a free lecture by an extremely interesting Indian. They congregated on every first and third Sunday at 1900 hrs to hear the distillation of thoughts by a civilized man from the east and of all that he held of value in the Western civilization. One of the men present in the room posing as a socialist quietly took notes of the talk. He represented the British Military Intelligence Section 5 of His Majesty's Government that kept an unobtrusive watch on the notable Indian and reported on his close friendships.

After the success of his book, *Hints for Self Culture*, Har Dayal and Agda established the Modern Culture Institute at their home in Edgware. This was similar in nature to societies started by other forward-looking writers and philosophers such as an H. G. Wells Society and Bertrand Russell. In this multicultural mix, Har Dayal added his own Modern Culture Institute that was a modern version of the Viskadalen's folkhögskola.

To advertise his Institute, Har Dayal had posters printed and plastered at rail stations.

MODERN CULTURE INSTITUTE

FOR RATIONALISM, SOCIALISM, AND SELF-CULTURE
(Physical, Mental, Aesthetic and Ethical)
MEETINGS and Lectures at 7 pm on the First and Third Sundays
in each month at 34, CHURCHILL ROAD, EDGWARE
(Reached from Whitchurch Lane and Montgomery Road)

Free Study Classes, Library, Health
Advice Center, Social Service Department

Har Dayal held lectures based on the ideas of Self Culture outlined in his book. Besides lectures, there were study classes, social service, a sun-ray clinic, political propaganda for socialism and ethical sermons. In the official sketch of the Modern Culture Institute, (see annexure), Har Dayal claimed that it was "established for the promotion and realization of the philosophy of Dayalism, theoretical and practical," and continued: "This movement aims at the progressive fulfillment of the complete ideal of personal and social life expounded by Dr. Har Dayal's book, *Hints for Self-Culture* (Watts and Co., London)."

During his stay in London, the polyglot along with Agda had mastered yet another language – Esperanto. Amazingly Har Dayal could now fluently read, write and teach in seventeen languages. He also offered classes in Esperanto and put out advertisements in the London newspapers, "*Modern Culture Institute Oni invitas petojn por la Agda Emilia Vojagpremio, kiu estos aljugita a1 Esperantista Socialisto dum 1937. Detalojn de Dro Har Dayal, 34 Churchill Road, Edgeware, Middlesex*". (Applications are invited for the Agda Emilia Travelling Scholarship for 1937, which will be awarded to an Esperantist).

On that May evening in the interwar years of London, Dr. Har Dayal, M.A., Ph.D.; the nearly fifty-year-old speaker with penetrating eyes, sharp intellect and an arresting aura dressed in a formal suit and tie, addressed the small audience on his chosen subject 'development of self-culture'. He opened his talk by stating, "Ethical culture includes and embraces all the other branches of self culture. Ethics teaches the men their duty. It is sole mistress of life. All your thought actions belong first and foremost to the domain of ethics. Nothing in your life can escape ethics which is omnipresent and omnipotent".

Har Dayal brought strong counter-arguments to the philosophies expounded by Lord Macaulay and his variety besides invalidating Rudyard Kipling's classic notion, "twain shall never meet". Har Dayal stood for and argued that the future lay in world citizens adopting the combination of the finest qualities of the spiritual East and scientific West to construct a modern civilization. He was trying to create a new map toward total liberation through the path of his philosophy of 'development of self-culture'. His temperate personality and light manner of speaking represented the finest Indian attributes - the gentleness of a mature mind and respect for all of humankind. The author insisted, "You should be meliorist, meliorism should be your creed, and meliorism is the gospel of progress plus personality".

Living in exile away from his land of birth, Har Dayal was consumed with the idea of a one-world synthesis of human civilization on Earth. He was now in pursuit of his life's quest of a nobler and utopian holistic goal – the liberation of all mankind and one world. He reasoned, "Destroy imperialism, establish a world federation then alone can you have democracy and peace". In a composed manner he went on to unfold his vision of new world order and a paradigm shift that would be the synthesis of the best in all the cultures of the world. He stressed, "Philosophy is the theory of the best life for individuals and communities, while ethics is practical philosophy which applies the theory and embodies it in social customs and institutions - now the world state cannot be created and maintained without a common system of ethics."

It was immediately evident that there was a mind-blowing orator in the room. As is apparent in his writings, cerebrally Har Dayal stood head and shoulders above his contemporaries - the very Everest of erudition. One of his guests was a young man and a world-famous Buddhologist, Edward Conze who later recalled his association with Har Dayal; "I cherished him as a truly lovable person… who befriended me at a time when I was a rather bewildered refugee in the huge city of London". A. F. Dawn, who was a regular at the Self Culture Institute, recalled in *Dr. Emily Brown's biography*, "he certainly had a sense of humor, I remember asking him when he intended to take up Russian and Chinese. He remarked humorously, the doctrine of reincarnation is very convenient, I can leave the studies of those to my next life."

The Government of India Act of 1935

In June 1935, Sir Tej Bahadur Sapru, one of the most sought-after Indian lawyers arrived in Britain to discuss The Government of India Act of 1935 with His Majesty's Government. Originally a member of the Indian National Congress, he opposed the civil disobedience movement of Mahatma Gandhi and was considered a close advisor of British Viceroy Lord Irwin. His arrival in London was well publicized in the local newspapers.

Sir Sapru received a letter from Har Dayal written in Urdu at his Central London hotel requesting for a meeting. He remembered that he had met Har Dayal as a first-year student at St. Stephens College in Delhi over thirty years ago and was surprised to hear from him after a gap of so many years. He invited Har Dayal for lunch and had a long discussion about upcoming The Government of India Act of 1935. Together they examined the proposed Bill and the distinguished lawyer was immediately struck by the comprehensive knowledge Har Dayal possessed of the proceedings of the Joint Parliamentary Committee and the Round Table Conferences. Hukumat-i-Britannia intended the Bill as a partial measure that could defuse the rising nationalist sentiment, and it was strongly opposed by conservatives in Britain. But Har Dayal believed that it was an important event in the closing stages of British rule in India and gave Indians a chance of political unity after centuries, so must be accepted. To a finely tuned legal mind such as Sir Sapru, Har Dayal's analysis of the finer points was "a great surprise". Sensing that the amazing intellect of Har Dayal could be tremendously useful within the national discourse in India, Sir Sapru immediately offered, "if he thought of coming out to India I would be glad to speak on his behalf".

Remarkably Har Dayal made no appeal to Sir Sapru to intercede for him. Sir Sapru recalled, "one thing, however, I could see and that was his obvious desire to meet his wife and daughter who he had not met for nearly thirty years."

However, Har Dayal accepted the advice of Kishan Dayal, Sir Sapru and Charles Andrews and appealed to the India Office on December 30th, 1935, declaring clearly "I beg to apply for a full legal amnesty. I shall not participate directly or indirectly in any unconstitutional movement".

The letter was officially received only on February 22nd, 1936 and months later on July 19th, 1936, Lord Zetland, the Secretary of State for India, forwarded a letter regarding Har Dayal to Lord Victor Linlithgow (1887–1952) the newly appointed British Viceroy. Lord Zetland testified in favor of Har Dayal, "His conduct has been exemplary for a long time now and he has gone out of his way to keep the authorities informed of his movements and activities. For some past years, he has been devoting himself largely to the study of philosophy in which he is I believe quite genuinely interested. The occasion of my perusal of his papers was an inquiry from him if he might now have the ban of official displeasure against him lifted."

The British Viceroy Lord Linlithgow, after conferring with J. M. Ewart, the newly appointed Director of DCI, voiced a different sentiment in his reply to Lord Zetland on August 2nd, 1936. He informed Lord Zetland that though he was in favor of Har Dayal's return to India given that he had settled down peacefully on a literary career, however, Hukumat-i-Britannia's officials did not recommend any relaxation of the prohibition against his return. He was advised by his civil servants that, "peaceful and uneventful as Har Dayal's record has now been for so many years there were the gravest potentialities of danger if he returned, more particularly at a time when the Punjab situation is one of so much delicacy." The original Ghadr Party initiated by Har Dayal had by now soared into major communism inspired movement for independence of India and Hukumat-i-Britannia felt his arrival in Delhi would be akin to adding fuel to the fire.

After six months of deliberations, Har Dayal's second application for amnesty and permission to return to India was rejected by Hukumat-i-Britannia. Lord Zetland regretfully informed Har Dayal that he could not accede to his request.

Interestingly at this time a former Scotland Yard detective and a member of the Special Branch, Harold Brust, began writing his memoirs 'Authentic Adventure Stories' that were printed as columns in the Australian newspapers and detailed Indian revolutionary movement highlighting Har Dayal and Savarkar's activities in UK, France, and the United States in the decade 1905–1915.

International Secretary of the World Fellowship of Faiths

On Friday, July 3rd, 1936, as Har Dayal with a wide smile on his face stood up to speak on Buddhism at the World Congress of Faiths held at the University College, London he was greeted with a sustained applause. By mid 1930s, Har Dayal had carved a niche for himself as a formidable speaker and public intellectual in the academic society and clubs of Britain and was regularly invited to speak at Caxton Hall, Oxford Street Settlement, Vedanta Society, Lancaster Gate, Ethical Society, Besant Hall, the Hendon Public Library, Economic Reform Club, International Friendship league and Mahabodhi Society of London on a variety of subjects ranging from religion, ethics, rationalism and socialism to dialectical humanism and Chinese art. His lectures in London were extensively advertised, well attended and widely appreciated. He continued to earn decent sums of money from his speaking engagements as well as his articles and the sale of his books.

The World Congress of Faiths was a successor to the Parliament of Religions Congress held in September 1893 in Chicago, addressed by Swami Vivekanand. It was organized by Kedarnath Dasgupta (1878–1942) a former activist for India's freedom based in New York and the hero of the Indian renaissance in Britain and the United States. He along with peace activist Charles Frederick Weller of New Jersey's League of Neighborhood had raised the status of Indian spiritual traditions in the eyes of the West. The British National Chairman of the Congress was Sir Francis Younghusband, the famous British army officer, explorer and writer also described as 'the last great imperial adventurer'. Defending the charge that this Congress was promoting neo-Hinduism, Sir Younghusband stressed that the primary aim of the initiative was to promote fellowship between faiths, "We must have these kinds of gatherings so that in the streets of London they shall know that our Parliament for Peace is meeting here".

At the World Congress of Faiths, after his speech on Buddhism, Har Dayal was in great demand and in august company. The Congress drew eminent religious scholars from all faiths and from across the world, including Dr. S.

Radhakrishnan, Professor Mahendranath Sircar and Professor S. N. Dasgupta on Hinduism, Sir Abdul Qadir and Salim Yusuf Ali on Islam, Professor Malasekara from Ceylon on Buddhism, Professor Nicolas Berdiaeff on Christianity and Dr. Suzuki on Zen Buddhism.

Noting the reaction of the international delegates and speakers to Har Dayal's profound talk and his cultured bearings, Kedarnath Dasgupta took the initiative and appointed Har Dayal as the International Secretary of the World Fellowship of Faiths with a mission to organize the Fifth Parliament of Religions of the World Fellowship of Faiths. This was quite a leap for Har Dayal, author of the revolutionary Ghadr movement.

Intimidated by the Indian thinker's elevation at his event, Sir Younghusband later gave his estimation of Har Dayal to the India Office, stating; "I came across Dr. Har Dayal a few years ago in the World Fellowship of Faiths. I knew something of his former activities as I had been working in the India Office during the war. I found him in his philosophical and religious activities to be very brilliant but very unattractive... I believe he knows several languages and he is certainly well versed in Indian philosophy..."

Twelve Religions and Modern Life

Har Dayal invigorated by his experience at the World Fellowship of Faiths, authored his fifth book, *Twelve Religions and Modern Life*, which was privately published in 1938, bearing the imprint, 'Edgware (Middlesex) England: Modern Culture Institute'.

In the preface of the book, he acknowledged: "In this essay, I have attempted to indicate some elements of permanent value in twelve religious systems from the standpoint of modern Humanism. The new gospel of Constructive Humanism comes to fulfill all the old dispensations. Their objectionable features are noted very briefly, but their merits are explained and expounded for the benefit of the Humanists and others. The twelve religions discussed are Zoroastrianism, Judaism, Shinto, Taoism, Confucianism, Hinduism, Jainism, Buddhism, Christianity, Islam, Sufism, and Positivism." He carefully selected striking elements from various religions of the world and presented them as an intellectual gift to the humanists.

The book revealed his spiritual depth and his profound understanding of various mystical paths. He believed in a universal spirit stating, "There is one energy, one universal force, one eternal tao, everywhere in the electrons, protons, and molecules. In the cells and the tissues in starlight and cosmic rays and in the mind of man. So all things and beings are the same in their innermost essence. The universe is one. This is the truth of truths, the secret of all secrets. The Taoist and the humanist feel and know that all things, and beings, are sparks from the same fire, drops, from the spray of the same waterfall."

The Curse of the Extraordinary

On October 2nd, 1936, Mahatma Gandhi's sixty-seventh birthday, Dr. Kharaiti Ram Samras, a former student of University of California at Berkeley and a historian with the Department of State in the United States profiled Har Dayal in the journal *Indian Opinion* (founded by Mahatma Gandhi).

The article, 'Lala Har Dayal, Revolutionary Becomes Philosophic', gave a long overview of Har Dayal's life as a revolutionary and his transformation concluding, "...He is friendly and affable by nature. As the late Lajpat Rai says, he would go out of his way to help others without ever expecting or courting favors from them. In his personal habits, he is simple to the extreme, often presenting the appearance of the proverbial absent-minded philosopher and cares little what others think about him. His remarkable mastery of a number of languages including French, German, Persian and Swedish, his forceful writings, his keen interest in the field of research, and his magnetic oratory all combine to earn him the title of genius. In his youth, he was impulsive and emotional and took pleasure in an unrestricted activity in an extremist and anti-British campaign. Extremism became a passion with him, and its expression was his only means of satisfaction and pleasure. With the warm blood of youth in his veins, he was rash and emotional and an idealist... Undoubtedly, there have been many changes in this remarkable man's views and there may be more to come, but his virtues and talents stand out so prominently that none can fail to be impressed by them. His days of unrest and rash propaganda are over and he has scars of the wounds inflicted on him by the changing times. As a result, he has turned philosophic... In this cultural field, he can use his talents to great ends and in the future, he may become a leading figure of his school of thought."

Dr. Samras was correct in his assessment of Har Dayal. He was unquestionably one of the most charismatic figures to emerge on the global stage during the first few decades of struggle for the independence of India. This marvelous man had previously impressed Gokhale, Tilak, Lajpat Rai, Sir Mohammed Iqbal, and Sir Sapru, enthralled Jawaharlal Nehru, M.N. Roy and John Barry, befriended Reverend Charles Andrews, David Starr Jordan, Professor Arthur Pope and Van Wyck Brooks, toiled with Shyamji Krishna Varma and Madame Cama, captivated Savarkar, Bhai Parmanand and Guy Aldred, inspired Amir Chand, Avadh Behari, Rash Behari Bose, Chaman Lal and Gobind Behari Lal, collaborated with Fremont Older, Sohan Singh Bhakna, Mahendra Pratap, Barkatullah and Virendranath and studied under Professor Sir Ralph Turner and Professor James Wood. All major international newspapers had publicized his activities and Somerset Maugham and Jack London eternalized him as a fictional character.

Living in Europe in exile since 1914, Har Dayal evolved from a radical propagandist and an apostle of the bomb to a staunch pacifist and the champion for new world order. The man was deprived of a nationality, yet found his identification as an internationalist. Owing to the transnational life enforced upon him by Hukumat-i-Britannia this extraordinarily talented public intellectual was constrained to plow a lonely furrow all his life. The curse of the extraordinary, as philosopher Schopenhauer submits, is a certain loneliness with which the person of genius walks through life, continuously somewhat apart from the ordinary world in being slightly above it. Schopenhauer held, "The man of genius, on the other hand, whose excessive power of knowledge frees it at times from the service of will, dwells on the consideration of life itself, strives to comprehend the idea of each thing, not its relations to other things; and in doing this he often forgets to consider his own path in life, and therefore for the most part pursues it awkwardly enough. While to the ordinary man his faculty of knowledge is a lamp to lighten his path, to the man of genius it is the sun which reveals the world… The man in whom genius lives and works is easily distinguished by his glance, which is both keen and steady, and bears the stamp of perception, of contemplation."

Such was Har Dayal.

Thirty Years in Exile

On Monday, August 15th, 1938, the fifty-three-year-old, Har Dayal completed three decades in exile. He was far away from the once familiar heat, dust, and noise of the bazaars and havelies of his hometown Delhi. As life was passing him by, he longed to walk through the familiar territories of Dariba Kalan, Katra Neel, Moti

Bazaar, Ballimaran Market, Khari Baoli and relish the rich delicacies of Delhi's famous cuisines at Ghantewala. He missed all his close friends in India he had not seen in years including Hanwant Sahai, Khudadad Khan, and several others. He wanted to visit his colleges, St. Stephens College as well as Government College in Lahore where he had studied decades ago. Most of all he longed to meet his three brothers, their families and warmly embrace Sunder Rani, Shanti Devi, and his grandchildren.

A year earlier in the summer of 1937, Sir Sapru had once again met Har Dayal at his hotel in London over lunch and discussed the Indian political situation. Besides his astonishing knowledge of world affairs, Sir Sapru observed, "it is my belief that he has sincerely changed and indeed he seemed to me from all that he said to me to be full of admiration for practical genius of the British people. I did not find a trace of bitterness in him and altogether the impression left on my mind was that of a highly cultured and scholarly man who had moral courage to admit his error. He knows so many languages and knows them so well. His one great obsession seemed to be taught elements of Greek culture and civilization and that our education in India should be remodeled so as to provide foundation for our political greatness in the future".

Sir Sapru concluded, "He is a man of highest intellect but also of the highest character. I do not think that he is a revolutionary any longer and I would strongly urge that whoever else may or may not be allowed to come back, no hindrance should be placed in his way". On his return to India, he made a public statement and it was published in *The Tribune* on September 19th, 1937, with the title, "Allow Dr. Har Dayal to return to India - he is no longer a revolutionary - Sir. T.B. Sapru greatly impressed by his intellectual attainments."

Sir Sapru's comments initiated a public debate in India led by Charles Andrews about Har Dayal's return. On October 5th, 1937, Bhai Parmanand, Mohan Lal Saxena and Sham Lal took the matter to the Legislative assembly. As per the records of the Delhi Archives, Har Dayal's relative, Kripa Narain, a senior advocate of the Federal Court of India, approached Sir Henry Craig, the Home Member in New Delhi on February 2nd, 1938, on behalf of by Mrs. Har Dayal (Sunder Rani), for the grant of permission and amnesty to Har Dayal who was outside India for the last thirty years or so. He added that it was his understanding that after the statements of Sir Sapru and Charles Andrews the Hukumat-i-Brittania was reexamining Har Dayal's request.

But the vindictive Hukumat-i-Britannia was unmoved.

Further, in due course, Hukumat-i-Britannia produced several facts before the India Office to put forward its case that Har Dayal was a revolutionary of the worst possible type. Hukumat-i-Britannia's civil servants in New Delhi believed; "Har Dayal is at heart as much of a revolutionary as ever and believes in ultimate independence but he has not the courage to execute his convictions. As his record shows he lacks resolution and is liable to change his views at any time. It is doubtful whether his remarks to Sir Tej Bahadur Sapru represent other than provisional opinions."

In a confidential note, DCI added, "Har Dayal is now about fifty-three years of age and although he still enjoys good health he has lost practically his former fire and vigor. He never introduces his Swedish wife on whom he is dependent for his support to other Indians although in English circles she passes as Mrs. Har Dayal. It cannot be said whether he would take her to India with him; he already has a wife and grown-up daughter in India". In an official statement Hukumat-i-Britannia disclosed its final position, "If Government were clearly satisfied on good authority that Mr. Har Dayal had entirely changed his attitude of mind and was no longer dangerous, there would be much more reason for considering opportunities which he asked for to come to India". In the interim Hukumat-i-Britannia also deliberated upon the cases pertaining to other Indian revolutionaries stranded abroad besides Har Dayal.

However Hukumat-i-Britannia's harsh decision-making held Har Dayal back from leading India's freedom movement or any other worldwide movement in the prime of his life.

Invitation Letter from the United States

In mid August 1938, Har Dayal along with Agda proceeded to the Chateau du Moncel, Jouy-en-Josas (Seine-et-Oise) outside Paris. In addition to his position as the International Secretary of the World Fellowship of Faiths, he had accepted to be the President of the Peace Academy Summer School at the request of pacifist and author Bartholomeus de Ligt. The conference was held from August 16th to 29th, 1938 in France and a few weeks later Bartholomeus passed away with the entire responsibility of the future of the Peace Academy falling on the shoulders of Har Dayal.

On his return from France, Har Dayal received an invitation from the Ethical Culture Movement for a fully paid lecture tour in Philadelphia and New York that winter. Founded in 1876, the Ethical Culture Movement was a humanistic, socially active attitude that combined teachings from various philosophies and religions to encourage the knowledge, love, and practice of the 'right'. The society held its meetings at the two adjoining residences at 1906 and 1908 South Rittenhouse Square in Philadelphia.

Excited about returning to the United States, Har Dayal informed Brooks in a message dated October 3rd, 1938 that he would be visiting the United States that winter along with his wife (Agda) and would like to meet him. He also informed Gobind that he would be in New York in November and planned to stay in Philadelphia during the winter.

In October 1938 as Agda and Har Dayal packed their bags for sailing across the Atlantic a newer and deadlier threat had emerged. There was the smell of gunpowder in the air and everyone feared that Nazi Germany was getting ready for a war with Britain. These war clouds were threatening to soon engulf Europe and impact Hukumat-i-Britannia's control over India. On the eve of his trip to the United States in 1939, British Secret Service documented Har Dayal's political views and maintained; "he also takes considerable interest in Independent Labour Party politics and recently became the Secretary of the Left Book Club. His views as to the ultimate necessity for a revolution in India have not changed in the least; all that he has changed are his tactics…."

For three decades Har Dayal had experienced triumph and disaster, love and loss amid a chaotic and turbulent life. The writer, whose wisdom was more powerful than any sword once again stood on the brink of international acclaim and his followers in India anticipated his return sooner than later. At this stage of his life, Har Dayal had only one unfinished mission in a deeply divided world - to unify humanity and our planet under one flag, one ethic and one state using the power of peace and the supremacy of knowledge. His first trip to the United States in 1911–1914 had been a gamechanger for him and now on his second trip in 1938, it seemed the final victory lap awaited the great Indian genius.

17

THE GREAT INDIAN GENIUS

"Such was Har Dayal, the great scholar, the socialist, the internationalist, the humanist, and the pacifist. The wave of life had carried this voyager onto the highest crest of human endeavors. He was a man of genius, not to be confounded with the man of talent. He was one of those who surpass the level of their contemporaries and are often misunderstood. But they project a light that shines on generations to come…"

Dr. Anup Singh
Member of Parliament of India

On the early Tuesday morning of October 18th, 1938, the Cunard Line's 81,235-ton *R.M.S. Queen Mary* reached New York, after a journey of three days, twenty hours and forty-two minutes from Britain. The 1,018 feet passenger ship under the command of Captain Robert Beaufin Irving, an imposing figure more than six feet tall, entered the New York harbor with a flurry of twelve tugs fuming out to ease her into her mid-Manhattan berth at West 50th Street. The wind was down and the tide was slack. The lights of Brooklyn, Staten Island and the tip of Manhattan formed a festive garland to welcome them to the United States. Some Americans returning home sang the Star-Spangled Banner as the zigzag of the world-famous skyscrapers and New York Skyline came into view. Many pointed to the Statue of Liberty – the symbol of hope, freedom, and peace for millions around the world.

Across the Atlantic all over Europe, the lamps were going out. American newspapers in the previous months were filled with momentous stories drawing readers' attention to happenings in locations across the globe and the possibility of another war. After the victory speech at Karlsbad, the rise of Adolf Hitler and Nazi Germany was being felt. All German passports held by Jews were invalidated. The ship was filled with Jewish refugees fleeing the stifling Nazi persecution.

The Queen Mary was snug in her berth and gangplanks were in the position to land her approximately one thousand six hundred passengers. One of the passengers onboard the Queen Mary was the former Stanford University lecturer and the architect of the Ghadr Party, Har Dayal, now a published writer and a public intellectual living in London. Dressed in a thick overcoat and a well-cut dark suit with a white turban that covered his nearly bald-head the bespectacled and clean-shaven Har Dayal escorted an equally elegantly attired Agda. They had first departed from London on September 21st, 1938 for Sweden and then journeyed to New York from Cherbourg.

As documented in the passenger records of the Statue of Liberty, Ellis Island, in his interview with the US Immigration Service, Har Dayal happily confirmed that he was an author, had lived in the United States from 1911 to 1914 and his last date of departure was April 1914. He mentioned that he had arrived from London and that he was single. Interestingly in response to a question by the Immigration officer, Har Dayal categorically confirmed that he was not an anarchist and was never deported. Unknown to the Immigration officer, Har Dayal had reached the high point of his revolutionary life and gained worldwide recognition during his last stay in the United States. Now in 1938, Har Dayal was a changed man. He was no longer the young vibrant anarchist but a well adjusted, erudite and serene man.

Agda confirmed her marital status as single and declared herself as a Scandinavian citizen. Her age recorded on the passenger manifest is fifty-three which corresponds to her birth date and year but Har Dayal's age was written down as fifty-four that contradicts his date of birth on his Oxford entrance form.

After a day in New York the couple proceeded to Philadelphia to stay at the luxurious Hotel Walton, located on the southeast corner of the Broad and Locust Street. Later they rented a small apartment at 701 Park Manor Apartments, 40th Street and Girard Avenue.

In the United States, Har Dayal was the guest of the Ethical Culture Movement. Additionally, as the International Secretary of the World Fellowship of Faith, Har Dayal had traveled to the United States to organize the Fifth Parliament of Religions of the World Fellowship of Faiths. He had planned a series of lectures on the topic "Hints of Self-Culture", at Bryn Mawr College and other organizations.

The Road to India is Open

Then on a cold afternoon in early November, as Har Dayal collected his mail from his post office box in Philadelphia, he found an official-looking dispatch from the India Office, Whitehall, London forwarded from his Edgware address. He quickly opened it and sat down to read the contents.

The NAI records reveal that the formal letter from Aubrey Dibdin, Secretary, to the Public and Judicial Department, India Office, dated Tuesday, October 25th, 1938, addressed to Har Dayal indicated, "With reference to your letter received on 22nd February 1936, I am directed to inform you that, subject to what is stated in paragraph 2 below, the Government of India are willing to allow you to return to India and that the Secretary of State for India concurs in this decision."

The second paragraph of the formal intimation from Dibdin clearly specified, "I am to say neither the Government of India nor the Punjab Government will prosecute you or take other action against you in respect to past events so long as you faithfully observe your assurance not to participate directly or indirectly in any unconstitutional movement. But in the event of a breach of your undertaking, the Punjab Government will not hesitate to take action…"

The official communiqué had a strange stipulation that Har Dayal will have to surrender his passport on his return to India and would not be allowed to travel overseas again.

Over a month earlier, on September 17th, 1938, Hukumat-i-Britannia after relentless urging by Sir Sapru, Charles Andrews Bhai Parmanand and Mohan Lal Saksena had decided to permit Har Dayal to return to India because of his having given an undertaking not to take part directly or indirectly in any unconstitutional movement. On September 22nd, 1938, Sir John Andersson Thorne, ICS, Secretary, Home Department of Hukumat-i-Britannia informed Mohan Lal Saksena, at his Amoniddaila Park address in Lucknow, the "Government of India have decided to permit him to return to India…" It took over a month for the India Office to issue a formal letter to Har Dayal.

Har Dayal received the unexpected news with pleasure.

He had been under tremendous pressure for over thirty years. For decades his task had been to overtly and covertly preach revolution in India and he had worked in exile because the Hukumat-i-Britannia would not let him work in India. Now it was possible to go back to India. But the letter from London also created a new set of complications for him specially the precondition that on reaching India his passport would have to be returned. It was unlikely that Agda would accompany him to India and in any case, Sunder Rani, Shanti Devi (Narain), his brothers and other relatives knew nothing about her.

Har Dayal was aware that three years ago, in 1935 Hukumat-i-Britannia had lifted the ban on his colleague Acharya and he relocated to Bombay from Berlin with his Jewish wife Magda Nachman. While he pursued journalism in India, she was a well-known painter. Even the ailing Madame Bhikaji Cama at the age of seventy-five was forced to sign a guarantee that she would not hold or make any speeches on her return from France to India. She had landed on her native soil in November 1935 after thirty-four years of exile, to go straight to the Parsi General hospital in Bombay. Here the brave lady lingered for eight months and passed away on August 16th, 1936.

On the other hand, M. N. Roy, the Communist leader and a friend of Lenin was elected to the Presidium of the Comintern International but in July 1929, the Comintern expelled him and declared that he "was no longer a comrade of the communists." He returned to India in December 1930 using a forged passport to be arrested by Hukumat-i-Britannia for a case that dated back to March 1924, and sentenced to six years imprisonment. On his release in November 1936 he had joined the Indian National Congress.

Sadder fate awaited Har Dayal's former teammate and rival Virendranath Chattopadhyaya considered 'one of the most dangerous international anarchist by the Polisbyrån. He was denied permission to return to Stockholm from Berlin in March 1921 and formally expelled from Sweden. Ten years later he fled to Russia and worked at the Institute of Anthropology and Ethnography in Leningrad. No one had heard of him since. It was later revealed that the Indian patriot was charged with having been a German spy on Soviet soil and arrested for treason on July 17th, 1937. He was probably executed by a firing squad in Moscow under unclear circumstances in one of Stalin's purges on September 2nd, 1937. A man of enviable abilities and an indomitable passion for India's freedom, Virendranath had lived an amazing life.

Nevertheless Har Dayal wanted to end his exile and return to India but was not sure of the timing as yet. Being in excellent health he was keen on completing his current assignments in Europe and the United States and had countless ideas and plans in his head for India. He had received an invitation for another lecture tour in America by the World Fellowship of Faiths in the winter of 1939–40. He planned to return to London in the last week of April 1939, and to again preside at the Summer School of the Peace Academy in Switzerland in August 1939.

Irrespective of the dilemma that the permission presented, Har Dayal wrote back to Lt. Colonel Anthony Moorhead, the Under Secretary of State for India in London on November 10th, 1939, from the United States expressing thanks to "the Government of India and the Punjab Government for their kindness and magnanimity in granting him a legal amnesty. I shall return to India in course of time in accordance with the stipulations which I beg to accept…". He requested the passport office for endorsement of visas for Ceylon, Siam (Thailand) and Burma (Myanmar) as he intended to study some manuscripts of the Buddhist scriptures before proceeding to India. In a subsequent letter to the India Office, he applied for additional endorsements on his passport for Egypt and New Zealand for a proposed lecture tour.

A month later, Dibdin acknowledged the receipt of his letter.

The news of the permission to return to India was widely published in Indian newspapers. Charles Andrews one of the prime motivators behind Hukumat-i-Britannia's decision reminisced, "His daughter and her husband came to see me and it was a great joy to me when I heard that the efforts of his friends were successful and the ban was lifted."

Bhai Dharmavira sent him a cable congratulating him and welcoming him to India. Har Dayal replied from Philadelphia that he was apprehensive about employment in India. He was moreover concerned that it may be difficult for him to manage a livelihood. He was open to the idea of becoming a member of the Central Legislative Assembly but as an independent member and being elected unopposed from any constituency. In another note written on November 15th, 1938, his last one to Dharmavira, Har Dayal stated that he would be "so pleased to meet all friends in Delhi and Lahore." *(Letters of Lala Har Dayal)*

The same day Har Dayal also sent a postcard to Sant Ram of Lahore in reply to his letter, supporting him in rooting out the nuisance of the caste system in India adding, 'it will be a pleasure to meet you and all other friends when I return to the country…"

Lectures by a remarkable Hindu visitor

The World Fellowship of Faiths organized lectures and dinners and presented their International Secretary Har Dayal as a featured speaker in New York. A special address by Har Dayal followed by dinner was held on Armistice Day on

November 10th, 1938, at Hotel Iroquois, 49 West 44th Street. The advertisement for the event specified that 'Dr. Har Dayal, M.A. Ph.D. (London)', would speak on 'Psychology and World Peace' and the cost of the dinner was priced at $1. That night Har Dayal was introduced as 'Noted Oxford and London University Scientific thinker', 'a most remarkable Hindu visitor'; 'A brilliant public speaker, author of many books in English'. Press opinions were added to reflect his international reputation. *The San Francisco News* was quoted as: "An extraordinarily original and sympathetic mind", *Palestine Post* (Jerusalem): "Dr. Dayal's private reading is truly colossal" and *Freedom* (London): "Dr. Dayal is in the direct line of the Encyclopedists."

In New York, Har Dayal's career as a public speaker peaked as once he got on the stage to speak he would electrify an audience with the power of his words. His lectures in the United States in the winter of 1938–39 were extensively published and the newspaper devoted several columns to his ideas reporting: "Dr. Har Dayal is as will be seen, a declared pacifist... this is what Dr. Dayal says; I hold and believe that all men and women are naturally and fundamentally pacifists, for they love a peaceful life."

Making Philadelphia his base Har Dayal traveled often to New York for the day and occasionally stayed overnight at the Hotel Iroquois to reconnect with some old-timers from the Ghadr days in New York. He met Basanta Koomar Roy, who was once the editor in chief of the bulletin of the *Hindustan Association of the USA*, in Chicago in the 1910s and was now a distinguished journalist credited with popularizing Tagore in the United States. Dr. Haridas T. Muzumdar, a prominent Gandhian who had participated in Mahatma Gandhi's famous Salt March, met Har Dayal in New York in November 1938, decades after his role in the Ghadr movement and found him to be "an urbane gentleman, deeply devoted to philosophic research and burning desire to service all mankind". It is not known if Har Dayal met his old colleague Dr. Tarak Nath Das who was a University Professor in New York.

In New York, an Indian student at Harvard University and one of the founders of 'The India League of America', Dr. Anup Singh, attended a talk by Har Dayal at the Caravan Hall in New York that was supported by the Bahai community. He was captivated by the words of the famous Indian intellectual as he proclaimed 'Each for all and all for each" and remarked, "The crowning race of those that eye to eye shall look on knowledge under whose command is Earth and in their hand is nature like an open book".

Singh asserted, "Har Dayal, the man! No one who once met him could ever forget this genial soul. So simple, so sincere, so real. A man whose heart encompassed the whole of humanity." According to Singh, at the lecture Har Dayal, "...had boundless admiration for the vitality and the dynamic spirit of America. Here, humanity is on the march, he often observed. Here a ceaseless search for the new permeates the atmosphere. The future man, predicted Har Dayal, would not be a Hindu, not a Chinese, not a European, not an American, but a happy blending of all – a noble cosmopolitan." The young Indian student who was fascinated with Har Dayal's thoughts and later wrote, "Har Dayal was a rebel; a born rebel; a noble rebel. Oppression anywhere in any form shook his whole being to its very core... He played with his life to liberate his land. He later sought to regenerate mankind through love and compassion. But he always gave his all. His was a life of complete self-effacement. Discipline, Development and Dedication', three D's in his own words always guided the career of this patriot, humanist, socialist and pacifist."

Motivated by the syncretistic passion of Har Dayal, Mirza Ahmad Sohrab, the founder of *The Caravan of East and West* in New York endeavored to discover the better elements of nine major religions. He invited Har Dayal to write an introduction to Buddhism in a book titled, *The Bible of Mankind* (1939), edited by Sohrab himself. In addition to Har Dayal, Dr. Haridas Muzumdar wrote a chapter on Hinduism, Mr. Chih Meng on Confucianism, Dr. Mousheng H. Lin on Taoism, Rabbi Louis I. Newman on Judaism, Reverend Elliot White on Christianity and Dr. Edward J. Jurji on Islam.

The First Asian American to Win the Pulitzer Prize

In late November, Har Dayal wearing a white turban and a decent winter coat and suit reached the residence of his relative, colleague, and protégé at 1 University Place near Washington Square Park in New York. He had previously informed Gobind that he had arrived in the United States and made Philadelphia his temporary home.

After arriving in United States in 1912, Gobind had emerged, as one of the most successful immigrants from India. Gobind by now was a renowned journalist and science writer who was read across America. A year and a half earlier, on May 3rd, 1937, Dr. Nicholas Murray Butler, President of Columbia University announced the Pulitzer Prize, "for the most distinguished example of a reporter's work". Five members of the National Association of Science Writers including Gobind Behari Lal shared the prestigious award and he became the first Asian American to win the Pulitzer Prize. Gobind had moved from San Francisco to New York in 1930 as the science editor of media giant William Rudolph Hearst's *International News Service* and was also the editor of the *American Weekly*.

Receiving his mentor Har Dayal at the doorstep of his small heated bachelor's pad in New York, Gobind was overcome with emotion. The forty-nine-year-old Gobind attired in his usual formal dark suit and looking a bit solemn in his big glasses greeted his guru with the familiar salutation *'Bande Mataram'*. Har Dayal and Gobind shared an emotional bond and shared similar family history in Cheera Khana and Shahjahanabad. Though they had met in Europe in August 1932, Gobind was delighted to see him again after a gap of six years. This was special since they were meeting in the United States where they had worked for India's freedom decades ago.

Gobind was pleased and relieved to see that Har Dayal had gained some weight and was much better attired than ever before. They settled down in the small living room that had hundreds of books stacked up from the floor to the roof. Among the pictures on the wall hung the framed 'Pulitzer Prize 1937', the award of $1,000 given in recognition of Gobind Behari Lal for his accomplishments.

Gobind told Har Dayal that he was a bit disappointed that he had not contacted him on arrival in New York in October and only much later got to know that his guru wanted to conceal his association with Agda. Since Gobind was related to his wife, Har Dayal was extra cautious about the news of Agda reaching his wife and family in India. Har Dayal gave Gobind signed copies of his latest books including his best-known book, *Hints for Self Culture*. As recorded by *Dr. Emily Brown in her biography*, Gobind while recognizing Har Dayal's intellectual honesty was critical of his book. He felt his guru had lived his entire life under the impression that he was some kind of a messiah or modern-day Buddha who had to give a message to the world. Gobind felt that Har Dayal as a writer was competent in several areas like history, literature, and economics but had limited knowledge of other fields such as science that was advancing every second. Har Dayal humbly accepted the constructive criticism and agreed to modify his book in a revised version.

The two non-resident Dilliwallahs who had made a name for themselves overseas then went out for 'Dilli ka khana' (Delhi cuisine) at an Indian restaurant, in New York that winter day and reminisced in (possibly Ceylon India Inn) about the past and the future. Following Har Dayal's advice, Gobind did not smoke or consume liquor and never got married. Gobind wanted to learn about the latest developments in Har Dayal's life.

Har Dayal first shared the good news that after years of trying he had received the permission to finally return home from the India Office. He confessed to Gobind that he had bowed considerably before the Hukumat-i-Britannia in order get their consent and was repulsed by his own conduct. Unlike the educated elite in India, Har Dayal had moved from a fully paid scholarship to decades of hardship and accepted a lifetime of asceticism and self-denial. Discussing his own future, Har Dayal disclosed to Gobind his desire to get involved in academics in India but was apprehensive, as there were not too many financially sustainable options available. Har Dayal aspired to establish a modern university in Kashmir and felt India needed modern and trained leaders and a world-class university set in beautiful surroundings that could serve the needs of India as well as the East. Har Dayal also revealed that he was diligently writing his sixth and seventh books, *Man and Movements in History (History of Great Movements)*, and *History of India*.

They talked about the events in India and in the world of science with references to Mahatma Gandhi, Bose, Nehru, Einstein and the possibility of war in Europe. 1938 was a tumultuous period in Indian politics. The young firebrand and the rising star of India, Subhas Chandra Bose had been elected as the President of the Indian National Congress Party even though Mahatma Gandhi had previously opposed him. While Gobind had reservations about *ahimsa*, Har Dayal, a lifelong revolutionary himself, believed, that Mahatma Gandhi was a man of very great character. Gobind informed Har Dayal that he had in August 1938 finally received permission from Hukumat-i-Britannia to visit India after twenty-six years and had plans to interview Mahatma Gandhi as also to meet all the frontline leaders of the Indian freedom movement. As Har Dayal boarded the train for Philadelphia, Gobind offered to help his mentor and meet a few important Indians on his forthcoming trip to work out a viable professional life for him in India. Har Dayal who never asked for any favors from younger Gobind was deeply moved.

It is not known if the two Ghadr patriots met again in United States and a few months later, on February 4th, 1939, Gobind departed for India for the first time since arriving in United States. In the past year he had lost his older brother Brij Mohan Lal and had not met his family in years. The British Secret Service had taken its time to grant Gobind permission to tour India. They were apprehensive of the Ghadr patriot from the United States and posted a detective from DCI to trail him during his stay. In Delhi, Gobind interviewed Mohammed Ali Jinnah and Jawaharlal Nehru. Impressed with Nehru's global outlook, he invited him to visit the United States. The Hearst newspapers were eager for an interview with Mahatma Gandhi but Gobind's request was turned down. The Pulitzer Prize winning Indian journalist settled in the United States made his protest public claiming that he would get an interview instantly if he was a 'White' person.

Eventually, with great difficulty, he was able to meet Mahatma Gandhi in the presence of Vallabhbhai Patel. The Ghadr patriot who had served time in a Californian jail for India's independence during the Ghadr days was not enthusiastic about *ahimsa* and *satyagraha*. Unable to hold back his emotions, Gobind ended the conversation by telling Mahatma Gandhi what he believed, "Mahatmaji, here are two hundred thousand Englishmen, and you have four hundred million Indians - drive them out! What are you waiting for?" After the interview, Gobind remained unconvinced of Mahatma Gandhi's philosophy of 'non-violence'. For the rest of his life, Gobind appreciated the great soul as a philosopher and a man of the future but not as a freedom fighter.

Mankind is One in Spirit

On November 23rd, 1939, Professor William Norman Brown (1892–1975), who had taught Sanskrit at the Prince of Wales College in Jammu and founded the Department of Oriental Studies in 1931 at the University of Pennsylvania received a letter from Har Dayal.

The writer in a note on his personal letterhead had given a short introduction to his book, his career as a scholar and his acquaintance with the masters in the field of Philosophy including Professor von Schroder (Vienna), Professor Geiger (Erlangen), Professor Lanman (Harvard), Professor K.F. Johansson and Professor Jack Charpentier (Upsala), Profesor Hehmutt von Glasenapp (Konigsberg) and Professor Ryder (California). He also mentioned that he had given lectures at the University of California in the Department of Philosophy. He informed Brown that though he lived in London permanently he would be spending the coming winter in Philadelphia and was hoping to return the following year too. He ended his note with a '*Sadar Namasharam*' in Hindi script and signed his name at the bottom in both in English and Hindi.

The University of Pennsylvania was one of the first American academic institutions to offer courses in Sanskrit during the 1880s.

Professor Brown who later mentored Professor Stanley Wolpert, a distinguished historian and expert on South Asia, realized that Har Dayal was keen on pursuing his passion for academics. He wrote back on December 14th, 1938, that Har Dayal could call him on his telephone number and they could lunch together.

Just before the winter and Christmas break Har Dayal visited Professor Brown at the University and presented him with a few of his books. But he failed to impress Professor Brown who later noted that the famous Indian author had lost his fire and vigor. Consequently, Har Dayal took no part in teaching on the campus.

Over Christmas of 1938, Har Dayal sent greeting cards to all his friends from his Philadelphia address, that read, 'Love All' and "Mankind is one in spirit".

Reunion with Van Wyck Brooks

One of the things that Har Dayal really looked forward to on his trip to the United States was to reconnect after twenty-five years with Van Wyck Brooks, his friend from the California days.

At 1110 hrs on Sunday, January 8th, 1939, Har Dayal made the two-hour train journey to Westport, Connecticut from Grand Central Station in New York to visit his friend from Stanford. Interestingly Har Dayal's friend and confidante the fifty-two-year-old Van Wyck Brooks had also been awarded the Pulitzer Prize for the best book of the year upon the history of the United States, *The Flowering of New England 1815–1865*, in the same year as Gobind. The celebrated critic, biographer and historian beset by bouts of depression had moved to Westport in 1920. His circle of associates and neighbors included famous writers like Sherwood Anderson, F. Scott Fitzgerald and Robert Frost. He became the literary editor of a magazine called *The Freeman*, and worked there with novelist John Dos Passos. Brooks was considered one of the key American writers and literary historian who shaped a national literary consciousness in the twentieth century. For "not to be writing a book was not to be alive at all," Brooks wrote in his autobiography.

Har Dayal landed at the station and held a copy of the Sunday edition of *The New York Times* for easy recognition. Brooks had a headmaster's thick white mustache and wore his white hair en brosse. The man with warm blue eyes was less grand in speech but delighted to meet his old friend. Later in the afternoon, at Brooks' home, 87 Kings Highway, Westport, Har Dayal presented him autographed copies of of his recent books.

Brooks reminisced in his *Autobiography* that he sat upright in his chair with a bunch of red roses for his wife and with his white teeth still gleaming in his dusky face. He was delighted that he would be able to return to India after all these years, Brooks added, "That week the British Government had given him permission to go home again and he murmured, half incredulously, over and over - the road to India is open." After consuming thousands of books, his intellectual caliber and width of scholarship on politics, philosophy, religion, and literature were visible in his five books and several articles. Yet Har Dayal told Van Wyck Brooks that life was much too short to accomplish all that he wanted to do and hence he wanted to live up to one hundred.

The next day Har Dayal dropped a short note from Philadelphia, thanking Brooks and his wife Eleanor for their kindness and hospitality. Har Dayal also enjoyed meeting Brook's twenty-two-year-old young son Kenyon, who was attending Harvard like his father and his elder brother Charles. In the years to come Brooks remembered his friend as the elegantly loquacious firebrand who introduced him to the world of the professional revolutionist enlivening his quiet days in California. Brooks faithfully preserved all his correspondence with his Indian friend, which later found a permanent home at the University of Pennsylvania, Philadelphia, USA.

"I Am at Peace with the World"

In the first few months of 1939, Har Dayal remained a much sought after speaker in New York and Philadelphia and he retained his dynamism in public speaking.

On January 20th, 1939, Har Dayal surprisingly appeared and addressed the dinner gathering for 'Friends of the Duke of Windsor in America' at the Town Hall Club in New York. Julia Chanler, wife of a prominent politician and defense attorney of New York, Lewis Stuyvesant Chanler, organized the event. The active socialite Julia was a proponent of the Bahai faith and started the New History Society in New York. Julie formed the 'Friends of the Duke of Windsor in America' to support Edward VIII who became the first monarch in British history to voluntarily abdicate his throne after assuming it only to marry his love, Wallis Simpson.

The New York Times published a short notice about the dinner and Dr. Har Dayal got the top billing as a speaker. In a photograph of the speaker's table taken on that evening, and published in April 1939 issue of *New History*, a smartly attired, clean-shaven and slightly bulky Har Dayal can be seen smiling and dressed in a dark jacket, bowtie with an Indian style white turban covering his almost bald head. At the conclusion of the dinner, a hundred and eighty people present sent a cable to the Duke of Windsor that he be appointed "First Secretary of Peace to the Democracies of the World – an Ambassador at Large – salesman of Goodwill, Representative of True Friends of Humanity".

On January 27th, 1939, from his home in Philadelphia, Har Dayal informed his friend S. R. Rana about his plans to return to India after completing his literary work in Europe and the United States. He noted, "I came here in October for a lecture tour and shall stay here until April. I hope to see you in the summer. I have now obtained amnesty, but I don't know when I shall go back to India… But I am glad that the way is clear now, and I can return whenever I like. I may be able to do some good work there, for my health is quite all right, and I have many ideas and plans in my head. I don't feel old at all. I hope that Europe can maintain peace this year…" He also disclosed that he was planning a comprehensive book on *New India. (Letters of Lala Har Dayal)*

Rabbi Leon Hurwitz, Chairman of the World Fellowship of Faith, invited Har Dayal to speak at the Bay Ridge Jewish Center located on 4th avenue and 81st street in New York on the night of February 24th, 1939. Here he contended that race prejudice is based on ignorance of history. With systemic barbarity being unleased in Nazi Germany, he identified that the three chief causes of strife in the world were problems of race, intolerant creeds and nationalism. In the presence of three hundred people he added, "Intolerant religion is worse than none for the dogma of exclusive salvation leads to hatred, persecution, and war".

On February 26th, 1939, Har Dayal delivered yet another speech at the Congregation Rodeph Shalom on Broad and Mt. Vernon Street in New York for a morning lecture on 'India and America'. His speech was published in the newspapers where in he also indicated: "The building of schools and hospitals is beneficial to India but the teaching that salvation is obtained through membership in a particular denomination is religious intolerance even if well-intentioned".

The well-read Indian with an encyclopedic memory on March 3rd, 1939, lectured at the Ethical Culture Society in Philadelphia and conducted a class in meditation. He eloquently spoke about the philosophical synthesis that drew the best elements from both Eastern wisdom and Western scientific thought. He affirmed that he stood for direct pacifism; never again to lift his sword, never! That was his irrevocable choice. He felt pacifists must be content to be humble pilgrims in this crusade and they alone could secure a just peace.

Har Dayal had evolved from a true blue revolutionary nationalist to an ultra pacifist internationalist with his loyalty to planet Earth. This is what the philosopher and political leader Har Dayal stood for. That night, with a big smile on his face, the man with revolutionary thoughts ended the evening by joining his hands, bowing and telling the gathering, "I am at peace with the world".

A Death in Philadelphia

On the particularly cold night of Friday, March 3rd, 1939, Har Dayal kept the bookmarked volume he was reading on the side table and took off his steel-rimmed glasses to relax his eyes in his small bedroom at his temporary residence at 701 Park Manor Apartments in Philadelphia. The handwritten notes for his upcoming book, *Man and Movements in History*, lay beside him. Next, he drank his usual glass of milk and recited a short shloka in Sanskrit, "Om Shanti Om", as he always did at the end of the day. Then he put his colossal mind to rest. He peacefully went to sleep never to wake up again.

That night Har Dayal's heart stopped beating due to a sudden cardiac arrest. And in his unexpected death, the humankind lost one the most brilliant minds the world had ever produced. He was just fifty-four years old far less than the hundred years he had endeavored for. It is fitting to cite a tribute to Har Dayal from his book, *Hints for Self-Culture* where while emphasizing knowledge he quoted historian John Richard Green, "I knew what men will say of me. He died learning". And as we respectfully take leave of this unique individual an appropriate homage to the eminent Dilliwallah would be a couplet of Sheikh Ibrahim Zuaq, a poet from his hometown Delhi;

"Kahte hain aaj Zauq jahan se guzar gaya;
Kya khub admi tha, khuda magfirat kar"

(They say Zauq left this world today,
What a man he was, God pardon him)

Two days later on March 6th, 1939, a grief striken Agda collected Har Dayal's certificate of death (file number 22100 registration number 1971), from the Commonwealth of Pennsylvania, Department of Health and the Bureau of Vital Statistics. On the certificate, Agda mentioned that he was married and was her husband. His profession was recorded as an author and his business was lectures. She also noted his birthday as September 2nd, 1884 (changed from November 18th, 1884 on the Oxford University enrollment form and October 18th, 1884 printed on the German Passport). At the bottom, in her handwriting, she signed "Agda E. Dayal". The invoice issued by the funeral home listed her name and added, "Widow".

On learning about Har Dayal's sudden demise, a stunned Kedarnath Dasgupta reached Philadelphia to assist Agda in the paperwork and funeral related activities. Har Dayal was cremated on March 7th, 1939, at 1030 hrs at the Oliver Bair funeral home on 1820 Chestnut Street in Philadelphia. W. E. Collier conducted the service. At the cremation ceremony arranged by the Philadelphia Ethical Society, Hindu, Christian, Jewish, and other religious heads paid compliments to him. Har Dayal's friend Rabbi Leon Hurwitz arrived from New York to join in the funeral services. None of his family members in India could be informed.

On March 7th, a short obituary appeared in *The New York Times* stating: 'HAR DAYAL OF INDIA, AUTHOR, LECTURER, 54; Dies on Tour Here - He Planned Indian Revolt During War'. The paper described him as Dr. Dayal and that his widow, Agda Erickson of Sweden as the survivor. The newspaper also mentioned that the body will be cremated and the ashes taken to Sweden. In the short biography, it was mentioned that for years Dr. Dayal was one of the most influential of the agitators seeking to foment revolution in India and he helped found the powerful Indian revolutionary party on the Pacific Coast. A short, three-paragraph article on page 2 of the *Evening Bulletin of Philadelphia* also reported Har Dayal's passing. The news about his funeral services 'Funeral today for Dr. Har Dayal' was published in *The Philadelphia Inquirer* on page 30.

The following Sunday, March 12th, 1939, special memorial services were held in New York under the auspices of World Fellowship of Faiths in honor of Har Dayal organized by Kedarnath Dasgupta. Indumati Marathi sang a Sanskrit hymn and prayers in eleven great faiths were read. Leaders of many faiths gave tributes to the memory of Har Dayal. A picture from that day shows the presence of Agda, Kedarnath Dasgupta (Hindu) Julia Chanler, Indumati Marathi, Rev. John Haynes

Holmes (Christian) Rev Dr. Charles Francis Potter (Humanist), Mirza Jafer Khan (Muslim), Dr. Anup Singh (Sikh), Mirza Ahmed Sohrab (Bahai), Rustom Wadia (Parsi) and Nandu from Ceylon (Buddhist).

Agda dressed in black got up and spoke poignantly about her life companion. To pay respect to the departed soul services ended with the singing of 'Bande Mataram' and the Universal Anthem. It was a perfect send-off for the rationalist, the nationalist and the internationalist.

Dr. Har Dayal Dead

It took surprisingly a month for the news of Har Dayal's death to reach India. On Tuesday, April 4th, *The Hindustan Times*, published a letter from Hilda Wierum Boulter, a supporter of India's freedom and a resident of 401, East 91st Street, New York, that informed its readers about the death of the 'Famous Indian Revolutionary Lala Har Dayal'. The news item included an excerpt from the letter, "On March 4th, he suddenly died of a heart attack, leaving his friends stunned" and mistakingly added that "For a number of years he was in Vienna. He went to the United States of America a few years ago."

On that Tuesday morning Har Dayal's relative, Kripa Narain after reading the shocking news at his residence on Court Road in Delhi's Civil Lines, quickly sent a handwritten note addressed to Sir Aubrey Metcalfe, the Foreign Secretary, and sought confirmation of the death on behalf of Har Dayal's wife Sunder Rani. The NAI documents reveal that on April 4th, 1939, the Home Department of the Hukumat-i-Britannia in New Delhi sent two urgent telegrams to the British Embassy in Washington DC and Godfrey Haggard, the Consul-General in New York seeking to confirm the reported death of Har Dayal on March 4th, 1939, at Philadelphia. The Consul-General Haggard's office in New York replied, "Report of death of Har Dayal March 4th in Philadelphia is correct". Three days later Hukumat-i-Britannia in a confidential internal correspondence disclosed that it was ascertained informally by the External Affairs Department that the report of the death of Har Dayal was confirmed. It also indicated that the India Office was aware of the fact and no further action was called for in this regard. Hukumat-i-Britannia decided to close the file relating to Har Dayal's return to India.

Cecil Savidge, ICS, Under Secretary, External Affairs Department, following an exchange of telegrams with the His Majesty's Consul in New York, confirmed Har Dayal's death on March 4th at Philadelphia. Subsequently, Kripa Narain was also informed about the existence of his widow "Mrs. Agda Har Dayal and that this lady was with him at the time of his death and made all the arrangements thereafter". The External Affairs Department even forwarded a confirmation from N. R. Checker, an Indian businessmen in New York and the founding President of the India League of America, that Har Dayal's only estate was a collection of books at his house in Edgware in London. The travel agency Thomas Cook and Company was assigned to transfer Har Dayal's ashes from Philadelphia back to Sweden. There was also a request received from India to send the cremated remains to Har Dayal's land of birth to be scattered in the River Ganges.

Two days later, on April 6th, 1939, the Indian newspaper, *The Statesman* quoting Reuters news agency published the news with the headline, "Dr. Hardayal Dead - Indian Exile Who Revised His Politics". It stated "Dr. Hardayal, described as a man who had the moral courage to revise his opinion and admit his error had been exiled from India for about twenty-seven years when last September, the Government of India announced that he would be allowed to return". The news report added, "Dr. Hardayal had an extraordinarily eventful career in India, in the USA, and in Germany during the Great War..." Other newspapers including *Indian Express* and *The Tribune* also published the news on the front page.

After the news appeared in India, Har Dayal's family member Kripa Narain in a letter to Cecil Savidge, Under Secretary, External Affairs Department demanded a detailed inquiry, "It is a matter of great regret that the intimation of his death could not reach India for such a long time. It is a matter of great necessity that the Government of India should make definite inquiries from Philadelphia about the circumstances of his death and the reason and circumstances why his death was not communicated in India for such a long time."

Little is known of Har Dayal's family relationships other than that he did not break off his connection with his brothers and dutifully wrote to his wife Sunder Rani each month. It is reported that on hearing about his sudden death from the Hukumat-i-Britannia, his wife Sunder Rani who had not met him for thirty-one years claimed, "He was married to the country. His duty lay there and there was nothing I could do to persuade him otherwise". Sunder Rani resided with Har Dayal's brothers and nephew Rajeshwar Dayal for the rest of her life and passed away in 1975.

Shanti Devi's (Narain) husband Justice Bishan Narain became a Judge in the Punjab High Court from 1954 to 1961. Shanti Devi passed away before her mother in 1973 at the relatively young age of sixty-four years. Lala Har Dayal's granddaughters Shubh Paul, Malti Nehru and Indu Sen now live in Delhi while his grandson Pradeep Narain lives in Paris.

There was once a Har Dayal

Unaware of Har Dayal's unexpected demise in Philadelphia, Gobind boarded a ship to return back to United States from Europe. Gobind during his twelve-day trip to Delhi in March 1939 had met several family members, neighbours in Cheera Khana and admirers of Har Dayal who not knowing about his demise were enthusiastically waiting for him after a gap of thirty-one years. He discussed his mentor's future occupation in India with Hanwant Sahai, Bhai Parmanand, Sir Sapru and his brother Jugal Behari Lal, who was a director of Education in Bharatpur State in India. He even ensured that Har Dayal's supporters arrange for funds for his passage to India and there was great enthusiasm in India about his anticipated return in the future. But sadly that was not to be.

After disembarking from the *Queen Mary* in New York on Saturday, April 15th, 1939, Gobind looked forward to getting together with his guru. He was excited about sharing with Har Dayal his Indian experiences as well as the latest news and meetings with India's political leaders. But the shocking news of Har Dayal's sudden passing awaited him at his Manhattan apartment. He was saddened beyond words since Har Dayal was in good health and showed no signs of illness during their last meeting. He was also greatly distressed to learn from *The New York Times* obituary about the existence of 'Agda Erikson Dayal'. His friends in New York confirmed the fact but Har Dayal had hidden it from him.

Decades later Gobind recollected in *Dr. Emily Brown's biography:* "Har Dayal's patriotic activity in the early part of his adult life accelerated in an explosive manner the departure of English rule from his country, India. He was one of the outstanding leaders of the so-called extremist phase of the Indian independence movement, which was the pre-cursor of the Mahatma Gandhi wave... Har Dayal used to say...that for the Modernization of India, all the 'Three R's had to be accelerated. He meant these R's: Renaissance (intellectual), Reformation (of social institutions) and Revolution (political-economic, etc.). He was a synthetic thinker...anticipating both Gandhi and Nehru in many ways."

The news of Har Dayal's passing hit Bhai Parmanand like a bolt from the blue as he received the news at the Central Legislative Assembly. Biographer Dr. Dharmavira recorded Bhai Parmanand's reaction as, "If they had said the sun or moon were gone out of the heavens it could not have struck me with the idea of a more awful and dreary blank." Dr. Dharmavira himself felt, "Har Dayal would not only be of service to the motherland but a source of inspiration to millions… Lala Har Dayal could not have died on a sickbed. Martyrdom was the only way in which the significance of his life could have been completed".

On April 6th, a telegram was dispatched to Subhas Chandra Bose, the President of the Indian National Congress, from Sreemati Chandoo Bibi, President of the Workers League with a request for observing a 'Har Dayal Day' in India. Eventually on May 10th, 1939, Sarvarkar now the elected President of Hindu Mahasabha ensured that 'Har Dayal Day' was observed in Bombay and all across Maharashtra in Poona, Nasik, Nagar, Sholapur, Satara, Karhad, Dhulia, Darva, Nagpur, Barshi, Jalgaon and Amravati. Savarkar who had not seen Har Dayal since March 1910, spoke poignantly about his friend at a well-attended memorial meeting held at the Chowpati in Bombay. He recounted the story of the continuing struggle that had begun in London when he worked with Har Dayal and Virendranath Chattopadhyaya as co-revolutionaries of the India House group.

At the other end of the political spectrum, Puran Chand Joshi, a prominent leader of the Indian Communist Party, recognized, "Lala Har Dayal belongs to the early valiant band of Indian revolutionaries. He played a leading role among the Indian revolutionary exiles abroad but ultimately fell out with the national movement itself. His heroic life and tragic end are typical of the worth as well as the limitations of the revolutionary pioneers. Born in the 1880s, Lala Har Dayal awoke to national consciousness in the first decade of the present century."

The ailing British missionary, Charles F. Andrews who supported Har Dayal's return to India briefly gathered himself against his illness to pay his tribute in an article titled, A Noble Patriot and truth lover, in *The Modern Review* (April 1940). A year after his friend's passing, on the morning of April 5th, 1940, Andrews died at Dr. Riordan's Nursing Home in Calcutta.

The Modern Review in its May 1939 issue published a short tribute to their former contributor in two columns that paid him the supreme homage and added, "His book, *Hints for Self Culture* published in 1934 by Watts London, although bearing a very modest title is one of the finest, most comprehensive and eloquent books he wrote, embracing the entire circle of modern social, intellectual emotional problems." The obituary was accompanied by the reprinting of Har Dayal's article 'The Social Conquest of the Hindu Race', that had originally appeared in September 1909.

After the abrupt end of Har Dayal's life, Dr. Anup Singh was among the first Indians in the United States to focus on Har Dayal as one of the most noteworthy, but almost entirely ignored figures of the 20th century. He penned a long essay titled, 'Har Dayal: A Stalwart Champion of Peace is Gone' that appeared in the April 1939 issue of the journal *New History*, edited by Mirza Ahmad Sohrab and Julie Chanler. In the essay, Dr. Singh identified Har Dayal as: "he belongs to the galaxy of patriots of the world. Like them, he dared. Like them, he chose the methods that had the hallowed sanctions of history. The sacrifices of his comrades constitute a brilliant chapter in India's fight for freedom. Their policy is now superseded by another. But Gandhi did not build on nothing. Har Dayal and his coworkers were legitimate precursors who laid the corner-stone." Dr. Singh ended by writing, "His countrymen have lost an illustrious patriot, whose place in their hearts is secure. There his earlier dream of political emancipation for India is being fast realized. But, his greater dream of World Emancipation – to make that dream come true is his legacy to us".

Har Dayal's sudden death came as a jolt to his friends in London. The South Place Ethical Society in its *Monthly Record* printed a long obituary detailing his life, work, writings and association with the group. The tribute claimed, "He was a fluent speaker and was especially interesting when dealing with Eastern subjects. His lectures were remarkable for their humor and humanity." It recalled that Har Dayal had written to the editor of the *Monthly Record* from Philadelphia on January 31st, about the contacts he was making with ethical leaders in New York and Philadelphia. The South Place Ethical Society extended their deepest sympathy to Mrs. Har Dayal (Agda).

The radical humanist, M. N. Roy, observed, "I never met him (Har Dayal); but from whatever is known about his life, one can come to the conclusion that his was a remarkable personality. He was a misfit in politics; but when at last he found the profession congenial to his character, premature death put an end to his life. Perhaps that was a blessing in disguise. Successful nationalism is not particularly grateful to its heroic and martyred pioneers who today live in obscurity as embittered old men."

Even after his passing, Har Dayal had many detractors in Britain notably among the historians who rejected the man's magnificent achievements largely due to his revolutionary past. British historian, Percival Spear assumed, "Har Dayal was a rudderless individual with a passion for liberation but an unorganized though powerful mind... He was a stimulator rather than a leader, the gadfly on

416 | *The Great Indian Genius Har Dayal*

the horse rather the steed itself." Unable to grasp the singular qualities of the man, Spear concluded Har Dayal was a strange personality and a lonely mind. Other writers indulged in similar character assassinations and subsequently Har Dayal's role was entirely ignored in the accounts of the India's freedom movement.

Death comes to Agda

A heart-broken Agda left New York alone by ship in March 1939 and returned to her empty home in Edgware in London surrounded by the memory of Har Dayal and his collection of five thousand-books. Agda was a brave woman much ahead of her time to have the courage to challenge the social conventions of Europe in associating and living with an Indian revolutionary without a formal marriage. There exists a literal portrayal of her by the author Ingrid Alfvén in the novel *Arvedelen* (Heritage). The novel describes the reaction from Agda's family and from the village to her connection with Har Dayal.

According to *Dr. Emily Brown's Biography*, Agda while going through Har Dayal's papers in London, discovered to her astonishment that as specified by his will, he had bestowed all that he owned to his Indian wife Sundar Rani who he had to leave in 1908 and their daughter, Shanti Devi (Narain), who he never saw. From his earnings as a lecturer and the royalty received from his books he had also left £200 for the boy who lived in the neighborhood of Edgware and often accompanied them on their holidays to Europe. Har Dayal's indifference to Agda in his will hurt her immensely. This relationship and partnership was one aspect of Har Dayal's personal life that remains a mystery. As is evident in his worldview, wealth was of little importance. But Har Dayal by lovingly dedicating his thesis and books to Agda in his own way made her part of his life's most important work.

For Agda after the death of Har Dayal, living in London was meaningless and she put the house in Edgware on sale. She first moved to Chamonix for health reasons and then according to Bo Scharping, a former teacher at Viskadal folkhögskola, she finally returned to the cold and snow of her native home in Kinnastrom, Västra Götaland County, in Sweden to settle down with her sister Disa Leffler. On her homecoming, the privately wealthy Agda published an obituary for Har Dayal in Swedish newspapers: "I hereby announce that my beloved husband Har Dayal, born in Delhi in India, has left for the invisible world. Death does not separate it unites. Agda Erikson Dayal".

With a premonition of her end, Agda formalized her will on June 18th, 1939 and left most of her assets to her nephews and donated 1,000 Swedish kronor to Birkagården. As stated by Tina Collins of the Rydals Museum she thanked Kedarnath Dasgupta in her will and signed it as Agda Dayal. After the passing of the man she passionately loved, Agda was reported to be ailing but still exceptionally sparkling in her conversations. Less than a year after Har Dayal's untimely demise, Agda, the daughter of Johannes and Selma Erikson passed away on Saturday, January 13th, 1940 after a bout of pneumonia and tuberculosis in Kinnastrom.

At the time of Agda's death, her estate was worth approximately five million Swedish kronor in financial terms today. Her family issued an obituary in the newspapers and put down her name as Agda Dayal. She was buried at Kinna Kyrkogård on January 20th, 1940. Workers at Kinnaströmsfabriken and the Viskadal folkhögskola were also represented, and "thanked her for the school". Gillis Hammar, Rector at Birkagarden folkhögskola later remembered Agda, "She did not belong to the people who say to others: Go and do! She belonged to the rather rare group of people who say to others: Come, let's do this thing together!"

Her gravestone reads Agda Erikson Dayal.

18

THE WORLD AFTER HAR DAYAL

"Har Dayal had a unique devotion to the cause of India and humanity, as well as
a fundamental humility – so much so that he never thought of writing anything
about himself. He avoided the limelight like plague. This was only natural.
There was altruism in his marrow. His life proclaimed the legend of pain and
ritual of suffering in that he underwent exile, imprisonment, torture and passed
by death several times. That is why his name has so proud a sound…"

Professor Ramesh Chandra Majumdar
Indian Historian

On the chilly late afternoon of Wednesday, March 13th, 1940, a joint meeting
of the Royal Central Asian Society and the East India Association was in
progress at Caxton Hall in London. It was a venue where Har Dayal had delivered
talks on numerous occasions.

Spring 1940 was a difficult time for Britain. Since September 1939 the nation
was at war. Neville Chamberlain's appeasement policy with Nazi Germany had
failed yet he struggled on as British Prime Minister. German Fuhrer Adolf Hitler
had met his Italian counterpart Benito Mussolini at the Brenner Pass in the Alps
and consequently, the Wehrmacht, Luftwaffe and the Kaiserliche Marine were
poised to launch an offensive in the west. Just two days before on March 11th,
1940, the French battleship Bretagne and cruiser Algerie had departed with one
hundred and forty-seven tons of gold bound for Canada to deposit the reserves
for safekeeping.

In India the political atmosphere was quite vitiated by the communal politics
of All India Muslim League. The demand for the creation of a separate state
of Muslim majority areas in India had gained tremendous momentum. At the
same time, Mahatma Gandhi undeterred planned a renewed *satyagraha* while the
firebrand nationalist and former President of the Congress Party, Subhas Chandra
Bose drew huge crowds to his meetings in Bengal. To counteract the popularity

of Bose and his followers, the Hukumat-i-Britannia imposed restrictions on the press, disallowing publication of any news about him.

On that late afternoon, the Tudor Room inside the Caxton Hall, with its heavy drapes, and the wooden beamed ceiling was packed with little standing space left for the people who had turned up to listen to a lecture on 'Afghanistan: The Present Position', delivered by Brigadier-General Sir Percy Sykes.

Lord Zetland, the Secretary of State for India occupied the Chair. He was the former Governor of Bengal and the aide-de-camp to the British Viceroy Lord Curzon. Others on the stage included high-powered former British civil servants Charles Cochrane-Baillie, 2nd Baron Lamington, the former Governor of Bombay, Sir Louis William Dane, ICS, former Lt. Governor of Punjab from 1908 to 1913, and Sir Michael Francis O'Dwyer, ICS, the fire-spitting former Lt. Governor of Punjab till 1919. The hundred and fifty-odd mostly bespectacled members of the audience in tweeds and pinstripes were mainly retired administrators of the Hukumat-i-Britannia who had a history of serving in Afghanistan and India.

Udham Singh (1899–1940) a thirty-nine-year-old Indian with a steely gaze wearing a trilby hat and dressed in a blue lounge suit like a perfect English gentleman took up a position in the right-hand passage near the front row of seats. The eyes of the fiercely patriotic Indian were fixated on one man - O'Dwyer.

Most Indians believed that as the Lt. Governor of Punjab O'Dwyer the man who loathed the Ghadr movement had set Brigadier-General Dyer to open fire on an unarmed gathering in Jallianwala Bagh on April 13th, 1919. Later O'Dwyer had even defended the mass shooting as a 'correct' action.

Udham Singh, born to a Sikh peasant family from Punjab's Sangrur district was about to accomplish his lifelong mission. For the past twenty-one years, he lived with only one overpowering obsession - to avenge the Jallianwalla Bagh bloodbath by killing O'Dwyer since General Dyer had already died. His quest to deliver justice took him to Europe and North America. While in California, he even established contacts with the elements of the Ghadr Party. In July 1927, he returned to India to be arrested for the illegal possession of two revolvers, ammunition, and copies of prohibited *Ghadr* newspapers. He was prosecuted and sentenced to five years in prison to be released on October 23rd, 1931. He finally made it to Britain in 1934, after securing a passport on March 20th, 1933 in Lahore, and lived at 8 Mornington Terrace, Regent's Park, in London doing a series of odd jobs. Intriguingly, he also worked as an extra in two feature films, *Elephant Boy* (1937) and *The Four Feathers* (1939). The unexpected death of Har Dayal, the architect of the Ghadr movement in Philadelphia exactly a year ago had conceivably convinced him that the British Secret Service operatives could kill him at the time, place and manner of their choosing. Possibly time was running out for him too. On that March day at the lecture, Udham Singh was absorbed in the thoughts of the horrific event of April 13th, 1919 in Amritsar in Punjab. The sound of bullets fired by Dyer's men had thundered in his mind for years. Right through his life, he had waited for the right moment and on March 13th, 1940, that moment finally arrived.

Earlier that day, the seventy-five-year-old O'Dwyer had left his nine-roomed flat in Prince of Wales Terrace, Kensington, decorated with Indian weapons and mementos, and informed his wife that he would be back in time for tea at 1700 hours.

At about 1630 hrs, Lord Lemington closed the meeting after the conclusion of the lecture by Brigadier-General Sir Sykes. The talk was formally wrapped up and the dignitaries started to leave, and Udham Singh sprung into action. From his coat pocket, he pulled out the loaded .45 Smith and Wesson revolver that was purchased from a British soldier in a pub at Bournemouth. Next, he pulled the trigger in rapid succession.

Six bullets tore through the Tudor Room in the Caxton Hall. The sound was unmistakable – a meaty thumping as if someone was beating a dusty carpet. Then there was a strong smell of burnt powder and a blue haze of smoke enveloped the hall. Suddenly there was considerable commotion. A mass of people surged and heaved. Some were too mesmerized and shocked to even flinch. This was followed by an uproar of protesting shouts and cries.

On the stage, the sixty-three-year-old Lord Zetland toppled three feet from the platform to the main floor as a bullet slightly grazed his chest. His steel-rimmed spectacles flew away. Sir Louis Done who was in the front row was shot in the right forearm and fell bleeding. Lord Lamington whirled around wounded in the right hand in a state of collapse. O'Dwyer who had just walked in the direction of the platform to have a word with Lord Zetland fell to the ground as two shots punctured his kidneys and right lungs. Doctor Grace Mackinnon, a retired missionary, with several years of experience in India, instantly knelt beside Sir O'Dwyer and realized that he was dead.

Two worlds collided at Caxton Hall in London that day. Udham Singh's shots were a final echo of the firing in the Jallianwala Bagh.

When Lady O'Dwyer returned to her home in Kensington that evening hoping to see her husband, the maid burst into tears and said that there was a report of a bad accident. Lady O'Dwyer telephoned her daughter and then called for a taxi to drive straight to Caxton Hall where her husband lay dead in a pool of blood.

O'Dwyer's death was retribution for his role in imposing martial law in Punjab, carried out almost exactly twenty-one years later. His killing marked the end of a chain of events that began in Amritsar on April 13th, 1919. Udham Singh's fearless action swiftly shrunk the distance between Amritsar and London and collapsed the time between 1919 and 1940. Resistance to the Hukumat-i-Britannia had reached the epicenter of Britain – a stone's throw from Westminster Abbey, within minutes of the Houses of Parliament.

Next, the British police quickly apprehended a smiling Udham Singh. At 2200 hrs on March 13th, 1940, Udham Singh was charged with the murder of O'Dwyer. During his trial, Udham Singh gave his name as Ram Mohammad Singh Azad, symbolizing that all the major religions in India were united in their opposition against British rule. Udham Singh's heroism nevertheless brought back memories of the bloody scenes at Jallianwalla Bagh, where hundreds of innocent men, women, and children had died. The Ghadr Party in California contributed substantial funds for his defense in the court of law.

At the height of the colossal military disaster - the evacuation of the British army from Dunkirk, Udham Singh was convicted and sentenced to death, for his violent resistance to the terror perpetrated by Hukumat-i-Britannia. He achieved martyrdom on July 31st, 1940 at London's Pentonville Prison and was buried within the prison grounds. In July 1974, his remains were exhumed and brought to India to be cremated in his home village of Sunam. India's top political leadership lined up to honor him as the coffin of Udham Singh, draped in garlands and carnations, moved slowly along the flat, wet roads of Punjab. The crowds shouted slogans for their hero, "Long live Udham Singh!"

Udham Singh's sacrifice was not the last Ghadr Party inspired event in the freedom struggle of India.

Dilli Chalo

Just four years following the passing of Har Dayal at a packed meeting in the Cathay Theatre on July 4th, 1943, in Singapore, Rash Behari, the old revolutionary and former colleague of the Indian revolutionary, got up to speak, "You might now ask of me what I did in Tokyo for our cause, what present I have brought for you?" With those words, Rash Behari Bose, the man behind the bomb attack on Lard Hardinge in December 1912, passed on the baton and leadership of the Indian National Army (INA) to his younger colleague - Subhas Chandra Bose.

Bose reprised the adaptation of one of Har Dayal's mission – the theme of an armed rebellion against the Hukumat-i-Britannia. Bose had many parallels with Har Dayal. The brilliant Cambridge graduate had also rejected the Indian Civil Service in his youth (though he had qualified), dramatically escaped from the clutches of the Hukumat-i-Britannia and sought a strategic alliance with Germans against the British Empire. Bose declared, "Our task will not end until our heroes hold the victory parade on the graveyard of the British Empire, at the Lal Qila, the Red Fort of ancient Delhi". The INA like the Ghadr movement belived in the multiculturalism of India and gender equality. Thus began the final phase of India's independence movement and the third Indian war of independence after the Ghadr of 1857 and the Ghadr movement.

Bose picked up the fragments of the Ghadr Party in Japan, Hong Kong, Singapore and South East Asia to form a larger Indian National Army. He revived the war cry, *'Dilli Chalo'* (Onwards to Delhi), the famous call of the brave warriors of the Ghadr of 1857. Then on October 21st, 1943, Bose established 'Arzi Hukumat-e-Azad Hind', the second Provisional Government of India in exile, after Mahendra Pratap and Barkatullah's futile attempt in Kabul in December 1915. As head of the provisional Government, he also planted the INA flag on the Japanese-occupied Andaman and Nicobar Islands in December 1943.

The INA inspired by the charisma of Bose took on the Hukumat-i-Britannia on the battlefields of Imphal and Kohima in the summer of 1944. The British Indian army contemptuously termed the Bose's INA as, 'Japanese Inspired Fifth Columnists' (Jiffs). At the end of the WWII, Bose mysteriously disappeared and was declared dead much to the disbelief to the nation while the INA ended as prisoners of war. They returned to the Red Fort in Delhi not as victors but as captives. The hometown of Har Dayal once again became the central focus of India's independence movement.

On November 4th, 1945, the intense Indian National Army trials charged the former members of the British Indian army and three patriots of the INA - Captain Shah Nawaz Khan, Captain Prem Kumar Sahgal and Lieutenant Gurbaksh Singh Dhillon with "waging war against the King-Emperor". There were many similarities between the INA trial and the trial of Bahadur Shah Zafar in 1858, the Indo-German conspiracy trial in the United States in 1917, the Lahore Conspiracy trials in 1915 and the trial of Bhagat Singh.

The INA trials in Delhi united the entire country like never before and recreated the atmosphere of the Ghadr of 1857. Sir Tej Bahadur Sapru, Jawaharlal Nehru and Asaf Ali were among the nationalist lawyers who joined the legal team to defend the three patriots and Hanwant Sahai, who was sentenced to seven years imprisonment in the Hardinge Bomb Case led the protests outside the Red Fort. Subhas Bose's national salutation; *'Jai Hind'* became the nationwide slogan once again. He emerged as the most popular Indian leader of that period and thereafter especially among the youth. However, the court-martial held the three INA men guilty and sentenced them to deportation for life, but the chief of the British Indian army, General Claude Auchinleck, was reluctant to endorse the decision. There was a colossal public outcry against the court's verdict and the British Indian army dangerously favored the three men. General Auchinleck's father Colonel John Auchinleck (1835–92) had served in India during the Ghadr of 1857 and he knew the consequences of a widespread revolt. General Auchinleck was strained to commute the judgment and set the three patriots free. Within months, there were mutinies (Ghadrs) in the major naval establishments, air force bases and at the army cantonment of Jabalpur. The INA trial was the moment when the INA prisoners of war finally won the battle for India's freedom from the Hukumat-i-Britannia and finished the British Empire. With the threat of a nationwide rebellion looming across India, the Hukumat-i-Britannia had no choice but to bolt in a hurry. In due course without the support and loyalty of Indian armed forces, the entire universe of the British Empire collapsed and all the colonies were declared free.

End of the British Vampire

At the stroke of midnight on Friday, August 15th, 1947, India emerged as a free nation.

African-American writer W.E.B. Du Bois argued that August 15th, 1947, deserved to be considered, "as the greatest historical date" of modern history and believed the event was of "greater significance" than even the establishment of democracy in Britain, the emancipation of slaves in the United States or the Russian Revolution. He claimed India's independence signified, the time "when the white man, by reason of the color of his skin, can lord it over colored people" was finally drawing to a close.

In October 2018, Economist Utsa Patnaik in a reaseach paper published by Columbia University Press has revealed that India was the goose of the Hukumat-i-Britannia that laid the golden egg. As per the new calculations, the despotic rule of Britain drained a total of nearly $45 trillion from India during the period 1765 to 1938. Cambridge historian Angus Maddison has recorded that India's share of world income shrunk from 22.6% in the year 1700, almost equal to Europe's share of 23.3% at that time, to as little as 3.8% in 1952. During the history of Hukumat-i-Britannia in India, there was no growth recorded in the per capita income. The jewel of the Crown was the poorest country in the world in terms of per capita income at the beginning of the 20th Century. Even the average life expectancy dropped by a fifth from 1870 to 1920. Millions died in a policy-induced famine while it drew the blood of over hundred thousand Indian sipahis who sacrificed their lives fighting for king and country in WWI and WWII. It was truly the 'British Vampire' as renamed by Har Dayal.

On the morning of Saturday, August 16th, 1947, some thirty hours after India gained its independence, the handsome silver-haired fifty-seven-year-old Nehru, the first Prime Minister of India, swiftly climbed up the ramparts of Red Fort in Delhi, the city Har Dayal once called home and unfurled the tricolor to thunderous applause. After raising the tricolor in August 1947, Nehru made a special mention of Subhas Bose on the occasion and recalled his dream of seeing the national flag unfurled at the Red Fort.

It was almost ninety years since that fateful Monday, September 21st, 1857, when with the support of an army of retribution Hukumat-i-Britannia had flown the Union Jack at the same spot on the blood-stained battlements of Red Fort. In those ninety years, countless patriots ranging from the heroic Indian sipahis of the Ghadr of 1857 to the fearless Ghadr patriots along with the valiant women and men of the Indian National Army and members of the Indian National Congress had dreamt the dream of a free India and sacrificed everything to witness the unfurling of the tricolor on the Red Fort. Har Dayal and all his comrades including Rash Behari Bose, Madame Cama, Shyamji Krishna Varma, Abdul Hafiz Barkatullah and Virendranath Chattopadhyaya did not live to see the sunset of the British Empire.

Among the thousands of Indians who were present at the Red Fort on that historic moment was Hanwant Sahai. Savarkar hoisted the Indian tricolor and the Bhagwa flag at Savarkar Sadanto in Bombay, to celebrate India's independence. In the distant hill station of Dalhousie, Ajit Singh who had finally returned to India in 1946, passed away on August 15th, 1947, with the knowledge that India had finally gained independence. The seventy-six-year-old Bhai Parmanand survived to see the demise of Hukumat-i-Britannia and departed from this world a few months later on December 8th, 1947. The fifty-eight-year-old, patriot Asaf Ali who had spent eight years in jail was appointed India's first Ambassador to the United States in 1947.

In San Francisco, Kesar Singh, the Executive Secretary of the Ghadr Party dissolved the organization and handed over the headquarters to the new Government of India. Many Ghadr patriots and Indian revolutionaries who had spent a lifetime in exile returned to India. After an exile of more than forty years, S. R. Rana returned to his native Limbdi in India in 1947. Among his first acts on landing on Indian soil was to kiss the motherland and say, *'Bande Mataram'.* He was bestowed with national honor 'Chevalier' in 1951 by the *Gouvernement de la République française.* A hundred years since the Ghadr of 1857, on May 25th, 1957, S. R. Rana at the age of eighty-seven met his end at the Circuit House, Veraval, Gujarat.

The Men Who Knew Har Dayal

Two years after India had attained its independence, on Saturday, October 15th, 1949, Prime Minister Nehru, already a colossal figure on the international stage accompanied by his sister Vijai Laxmi Pandit and daughter Indira Gandhi landed at La Guardia airport in New York. Nehru had met Dr. Gobind Behari Lal, the science editor emeritus for the Hearst newspapers in the United States who had been conferred with an honorary doctorate, at the Prime Minister's residence in New Delhi in January 1949. Over lunch Nehru had divulged that he had not forgotten Gobind's suggestion to visit United States and would be going there in October 1949. Gobind, a long-time resident of the United States but a Dilliwallah at heart, was made part of Nehru's delegation. Ahead of Nehru's arrival, Gobind revealed, "The Prime Minister is himself a scientist and his range of scientific studies is amazing, his personal library which I saw in his great mansion in New Delhi contains some of the most notable writings on every scientific subject and on scientific philosophy."

Indians like Har Dayal and Lala Lajpat Rai had lived in United States in the first half of the twentieth century and had created a favorable impression among Americans with their intellectual capital. The correspondence between

US President, Franklin D. Roosevelt and British Prime Minister Churchill has revealed the serious strains that developed between the leaders over independence for India. Roosevelt exasperated Churchill by trying to prod him into promising independence for India during the war rather than after, and wrote on April 11th, 1942. "American public opinion cannot understand why, if the British Government is willing to permit the component parts of India to secede from the British Empire after the war, it is not willing to permit them to enjoy what is tantamount to self-government during the war."

Then a year before India's independence on July 2nd, 1946, President Harry Truman signed 'The Luce-Cellar Bill' to grant the United States of America citizenship to Indian immigrants. It was the joint effort of Jagjit Singh of India League of America, Mubarak Ali Khan of the Indian Welfare League, Dr. Anup Singh, Haridas Muzumdar, Dr. Tarak Nath Das and Dalip Singh Saund (1899–1973) of the India Association of America. On July 2nd, Luce-Cellar Bill became law as the Immigration Act of 1946, conferring rights of American citizenship on the natives of India. This day, in essence, could be considered as the Independence Day for Indian Americans. This was the culmination of the pioneering initiative of the three-member delegation of Dr. Sudhindra Bose, Dr. Bishan Singh and Har Dayal in February 1914. Later in November 1955, Dalip Singh Saund became the Asian American to be elected to the United States Congress representing Riverside and Imperial County of Southern California as a Democrat.

During his first trip to the United States, on the night of October 20th, 1949, Nehru met over two hundred American intellectuals, supporters and friends of India who in the past had worked towards India's cause. At a reception at the Waldorf-Astoria Hotel in New York, the Indian Prime Minister, now wearing a three-piece British tailored suit seemed official, natural and boyish. His baldness emphasized the noble cast of his face, with its high cheekbones and sharply sculptured nose; he had the demeanor of a prince who spoke to the guests in his low, Cantabrigian voice, which carried only traces of Asian inflections. The guests included writers, journalists and among them was Van Wyck Brooks, the eminent American literary critic who had graced the cover of *Time* magazine on October 2nd, 1944. Brooks stepped forward to be presented to the visiting Prime Minister. Consul-General Ramji Ram Saxena introduced him, as he had been for several years, "The man who knew Har Dayal".

Brooks in his memoirs, *Scenes, and portraits: memories of childhood and youth*, recalled, "What could I possibly say that might interest this great man? Casting about for something, I heard myself uttering the phrase, "Do you remember Har Dayal?" and, with a wan smile, the great man said, "We all remember Har Dayal," though just how he was remembered I forebode to ask. The overtones of Nehru's reply seemed to speak volumes…and I reflected that some of these volumes I had read in California when Har Dayal and I were still in our twenties."

Brooks died on May 2nd, 1963, in Bridgewater, Connecticut and residents of his village, added a new wing to the Burnham Public Library in his memory.

Contribution of the Revolutionaries

After India attained independence it took some time for post-colonial governments to acknowledge the revolutionaries as part of the freedom struggle. The new Government of India - Bharat Sarkar was reluctant to embrace those who had deployed violence against the state. Nehru spoke at the centenary of the Ghadr of 1857 at a large public meeting at the Ram Lila Grounds in New Delhi on May 10th, 1957. Nehru appealed to Indians, "to think of all those brave warriors who had lit the torch of India's independence. That torch continued to burn for a century until India became free. Let us pay homage to those brave heroes and the others who came after them and carried the torch…" At the end of his speech, Nehru asked the audience, "Let us stand up and observe two minutes' silence in memory of all those who laid down their lives in 1857 and since then for India's freedom." Coincidentally the newly constituted *Lok Sabha* (Upper house of the Indian parliament) had met that day to take the oath of office to serve a free India.

On December 13th, 1958, at the All India Old Revolutionaries Conference in New Delhi, Bhupendranath Dutta, the President of the conference in his opening speech claimed that the Ghadr patriots and other Indian rebels had extended the struggle to foreign countries and that therein lay their contributions. Dr. Rajendra Prasad, the President of India, in his message to the old revolutionaries, admitted, "though the nation was wedded to non-violence, the contribution of the revolutionaries to the movement for independence was no less valuable".

As stated in *Sites of Asian Interaction: Ideas, Networks, and Mobility*, by Tim Harper and Sunil Amrith (Editors), there were divergence of views emerged between the revolutionaries and Nehru at the official tea. After India gained its independence Sohan Singh Bhakna was involved with the Kisan Sabha and was a leading light of the Communist Party of India and Mahendra Pratap on his return to India in 1946 had as an independent candidate defeated the debutant thirty-three-year-old Atal Behari Vajpayee in the 1957 Lok Sabha Election from Mathura. Both Sohan Singh Bhakna and Mahendra Pratap confronted Nehru and candidly told him that India's independence had not been achieved without shedding a drop of blood as was being propagated by his Government – immense sacrifices were made by Indians and the nation must respect its martyrs.

On learning about Har Dayal's childhood friend Hanwant Sahai's health and financial difficulties, Nehru sent him some money from his personal account. In a letter, the Prime Minister observed, "He is rather old and weak. He is one of the few survivors of the old revolutionaries of Delhi…" A few days later, on December 22nd, Dr. Tarak Nath Das died of a stroke at the Flowers-Fifth Avenue Hospital at the age of seventy-four. In 1935, he had set up 'The Mary Keatinge Das Fund' to help promote educational and cultural ties among nations. It is now known as the 'Tarak Nath Das Foundation' at the Columbia University, New York.

On February 26th, 1966, Har Dayal's compatriot, Veer Savarkar the fearless revolutionary, social reformer, writer, dramatist, poet, historian, political leader, and philosopher died at the age of eighty-three. Prime Minister Indira Gandhi, in her message on Savarkar's death in 1966 remarked: "It removes from our midst a great figure of contemporary India. His name was a byword for daring and patriotism. Mr. Savarkar was cast in the mold of a classical revolutionary and countless people drew inspiration from him."

In India decades after his passing, Har Dayal's magnificent influence was unmatchable. His intellectual output including his book *Hints for Self Culture* inspired a range of Indian political leadership from extreme right to extreme left. His glorification of Karl Marx made a deep impact on intellectuals and countless remained admirers of Marxism all their life. Major General Sir Sahib Singh Sokhey (1887–1971), a military physician and a member of the Indian parliament, who was knighted by the Hukumat-i-Britannia, was captivated by Har Dayal's writings especially his article on Marx rather than any other source. India's first Economic advisor, Dr. Gyan Chand (1893–1983), who represented the country at the World Bank, admitted that he had read Har Dayal's note on Marx as a student. He was to become among the first Marxists in India and proudly preserved the copy of Har Dayal's pamphlet in his library.

Marxist leader P.C. Joshi spent three days with Sohan Singh Bhakna, in his village of Bhakhna in Punjab in 1965. He later recorded that, "Babaji talked long, both enthusiastically and sadly about Har Dayal, He (Har Dayal) was a good man and a well-read intellectual, while we Sikh peasant members of the Ghadr

Party were illiterate or semi-illiterate. He described how they all felt inspired when Har Dayal talked to them about Marx and his ideas in the Yugantar Ashram, headquarters of the Ghadr Party, where all the full-time functionaries of the Party lived together on a commune basis." One of the founders of the Ghadr Party Sohan Singh Bhakna passed on in 1968 at the age of ninety-eight.

And veteran revolutionary turned parliamentarian Mahendra Pratap once nominated for the Nobel Peace Prize died on April 29th, 1979. He was ninety-three. By then Hanwant Sahai too had passed away at the age of ninety-six on August 5th, 1975. Till the end of his life, he never revealed who threw the bomb at Viceroy Hardinge on that fateful December morning.

The End of an Era

By 1978, Gobind Behari Lal, the eighty-nine-year-old Ghadr patriot had lived for sixty-six years in the United States. Having officially retired in 1958 he had accepted an invitation to write for the *Herald-Examiner* in Los Angeles and then moved to be a columnist back in *San Francisco Examiner*. Age was catching up with the courtly newspaperman and he now walked with a cane, bent forward to hear clearly the other person but as always was immaculately dressed in a dark suit. Still alert and striking he retained his unmistakable Delhi accent and the sophistication of the *Ganga-Jamuni Tehzeeb*. His American friends called him Dr. Lal or informally 'Gobi' and he invariably greeted everyone with "Hello Brother".

On Friday, June 9th, 1978, Gobind the nearly ninety-year-old journalist who had interviewed Mahatma Gandhi, Einstien and Roosevelt and knew Nehru on the occasion of Prime Minister Morarji Desai's visit to California wrote about the important roots of Indian independence that had begun in the Bay Area. In his article in the local newspaper, Gobind observed, "This segment of modern history has remained largely unknown. Let the river of history be traced backward, to the period 1912 to 1922. The University of California at Berkeley and the City of San Francisco became the cultural and political field in which a cutting of the movement for the independence of India was planted, in which it grew rapidly. To the university came a few Indian students and scholars for scientific and other modern studies. Some of them were converted to the faith of the American Revolution, and became determined to apply it to India; it is enough to give one Indian name, Dr. Har Dayal. He had come from Oxford University to Stanford. He became the leader. He had the brain and the emotive fire to gather around him hundreds of Indian immigrants. But even the Indian mind, nourished and inspired by the university, and the Indian workers' young brawn, taken together, would have accomplished little. What brought historic results was the arousing of sympathy and support from influential Americans at the University of California." Gobind added that the seeds of Indian independence, that were nurtured in San Francisco, in Berkeley, and Stanford, had bloomed a generation later.

Gobind continued to tell the story of the Ghadr movement as a journalist at all the Indo American social events. After a celebratory dinner, he informed a friend, "What I did was to talk about Har Dayal – the forgotten man, the founder of the Ghadr Party whom everybody wants to forget". He always recalled the friendliness of the American people over a long period in supporting the Indian freedom movement and often mentioned the names of Fremont Older, Cora Miranda Older, and Barry White.

Thursday, April 1ˢᵗ, 1982, marked the end of an era as, Gobind Behari Lal passed away in San Francisco, the city he had first arrived on August 26ᵗʰ, 1912. He was ninety-two. The cremation and memorial services were held at 1100 hours on April 5ᵗʰ, 1982, at Halsted N. Gray and Co., 1123 Sutter Street, San Francisco. He had no surviving relatives in California but Indian diplomats and his close friends were present.

The New York Times in an obituary mentioned his role in the Indian independence movement and quoted his interview of March 1982, "My interest is to create among the reader's lust for the knowledge of science, which destroys superstition and all kind of false assumption and raises the power of the human brain". Other obituaries appeared in *San Francisco Chronicle, San Francisco Examiner* and *California Monthly.*

In his action-packed life, the soft-spoken popular science writer had seen the complete transformation of India from being the jewel in the Crown of the British Empire to the largest democratic republic on Earth. Besides being the first Asian American to win the Pulitzer Prize, Gobind won the 1946 George Westinghouse Award from the American Association for the Advancement of Science, a 1958 distinguished service award from the American Medical Association and a Guggenheim fellowship in 1956. Gobind was among the first Indians to be honored both in the United States and his land of birth. The Government of India bestowed him with a Padma Bhushan in 1969 and Prime Minister Indira Gandhi presented him a Tamra Patra in 1973 in appreciation of his distinguished record of service to the nation.

Suzanne Riess of the Regional Oral History Office of the Bancroft Library, UC Berkeley, conducted four long interviews of Gobind between June and December 1981 at his San Francisco apartment detailing many aspects of his remarkable life as well his view about Har Dayal. It was later issued as a book titled, *A Journalist from India – at Home in the World* with an introduction by William Randolph Hearst Jr.

Like his guru, Har Dayal, Gobind Behari Lal, has left us with a rich legacy of his writings and his thoughts for the future: "Progress with militarism has been in history; peace, with no progress, has been in history; but the combination of peaceful progress has been god-damn not realized yet. I pin my faith upon the educated man of the world."

In Memory of Har Dayal

On a winter afternoon, in my search for the legacy of the original firebrand from Delhi, driving non-stop from Los Angeles, I reached 5 Wood Street in the heart of San Francisco. This is the location of *The Ghadr Hall* that was formerly known as the Yugantar Ashram. After India became independent, the Ghadr building was handed over to the Indian Consulate in San Francisco in 1949. The Ghadr Memorial was partially rebuilt in 1974, at a cost of $183,000 by Bharat Sarkar. India's Ambassador Triloki Nath Kaul performed the inauguration ceremony in March 1975. At present it houses a museum displaying various memorabilia of the Ghadr Party and a digital archive. However the thousands of speeches of Har Dayal were never recorded on camera or tape. They are lost forever. Future generations did not hear the man who could transform people's thinking with the force of numerous languages at his command.

In nearby Stockton, in California, there is a *Ghadr Hall* at the Sikh Temple complete with the illustrated history of the Ghadr movement and the pictures of the Ghadri babas (the elderly revolutionaries) including Har Dayal. The original hand-operated printing press of the Ghadr movement is preserved here.

From October 4th to 5th, 2013, the City of Astoria in Oregon, the United States, hosted a centenary commemoration of the founding of the Ghadr Party and a sign commemorating its birth was erected at the former site of the Finnish Socialist Hall to mark it as the birthplace of "the shot heard around the world."

In 1916, four years after British Viceroy Lord Hardinge had survived an assassination attempt by Har Dayal's compatriots (December 23rd, 1912,) a library building was erected in Delhi to commemorate the event. Donations were received from several Indian Maharajas, Nawabs and leading Dilliwallahs including Hakim Ajmal Khan, Haji Abdur Rehman, Lala Minamal Dhuliyawala, Lala Lakshmi Narayan, Lala Radha Krishan, and Lala Sultan Singh. The books from the Lawrence Institute and the Delhi Public Library in Kaccha Bagh were shifted to the new Hardinge Municipal Library. In 1970, as an afterthought, the Bharat Sarkar renamed the Hardinge Municipal Heritage Library in Delhi as *Har Dayal Municipal Library*. Today, the dark and dingy library in fairly bad shape holds a collection of 1,700,000 books, including twenty editions of exquisite books and around seven thousand rare books. Later all the public libraries in the city of Delhi were renamed *Har Dayal Public Libraries* as a mark of respect to the great nationalist and Dilliwallah. The small lane where he was born in Cheera Khana was also renamed *Har Dayal Street* to honor the man of letters. And close to the spot where the bomb was launched on Lord Hardinge in 1912, just off Nai Sarak, there exists a *Katra Har Dayal*.

On March 18th, 1987, the India Department of Posts issued a commemorative stamp to honor Har Dayal, the inexhaustible letter writer who had consistently refused to use Hukumat-i-Britannia's postage stamps. A commemorative postage stamp was also issued on December 26th, 1916, to mark the centenary of the Har Dayal Municipal Heritage Library. On the occasion of the centenary of the Ghadr Movement, Prime Minister of India Dr. Manmohan Singh issued a postage stamp honoring the Ghadr Party on January 8th, 2012.

A double-story building called *Ghadar Party Martyrs Memorial* stands on the Grand Trunk Road, in Jalandhar in Punjab. A Ghadr veteran, Amar Singh Sandhwan, laid its foundation stone on November 17th, 1959 with the sole aim to preserve the Ghadr Party's legacy through time. The Ghadr Party's inspiration and its Ghadr-di-Goonj continued to reverberate in India for long and found favor among the new Communist Party of India (Marxist-Leninist).

The campuses of Berkeley and Stanford where Har Dayal once lectured and the Silicon Valley where his ideas were shaped is now home to over a hundred thousand bright Indians enriching the world like never before. And on September 27th, 2015, on an official visit to the United States, Narendra Modi, Prime Minister of India, during a speech to the Indian community at SAP Center in San Jose, rightly highlighted the historical role of the Ghadr Party of California in India's freedom, "How can we ever forget the Ghadr that was formed here thousands of miles away from India and lit the flame of India's independence movement?"

Ever since Har Dayal passed away, it is clear that the history of the Indian freedom movement produced no greater enigma than him. In the short time allotted to him, Har Dayal did make a mark on this planet. At the time of his death he left two unfinished books - *Man and Movements in History* and *The History of India*. And his vision of establishing a modern university in India for training the entire East was left unfulfilled. In Har Dayal's passing the world possibly also lost a future Nobel Prize winner and it is quite probable that if he had lived longer he would have been a candidate for the Bharat Ratna. And writer Kushwant Singh argued, "One may well ask, if Veer Savarkar's portrait can be hung in our Parliament, why not Har Dayal's?"

Nonetheless for millions who sought to emulate this quintessential Dilliwallah, he was *The Great Indian Genius.*

The world has moved on since Har Dayal's departure. The mighty British Empire ultimately collapsed, the racist Nazis were defeated, the atom was split, the United Nations was formed, Yuri Gagarin orbited the Earth, Neil Armstrong stepped on the moon, Apartheid ended, Nelson Mandela was released, the Berlin Wall came crashing down, the Internet was invented, Hubble space telescope began working, Olympics Games were held successively, major discoveries were made in medical science, billions of smartphones emerged, President Obama entered the White House, Kim Jong-un and Moon Jae-in shook hands, spacecrafts reached Mars and the land where Har Dayal's genius was first discovered emerged in the postcolonial world, as the largest working democracy humankind has ever known. Simultaneously, our planet populated by over seven billion humans, faces overwhelming problems including bad governance models, severe inequality, climate change crisis, lethal wars, unending poverty, deplorable human rights, shocking discrimination, dubious technological advancements, uneven economic growth, relentless racial hatred, growing religious fanaticism, rising gun violence, horrific terror attacks and wall-to-wall fake news that dominates twenty four news network headlines. At this crucial juncture, humankind can turn to the thoughts and ideas of a humanist and internationalist like Har Dayal. Decades after his demise, his philosophies and writings are still valid and alive.

An advocate of world citizenship, Har Dayal decades ago, comprehended in his lifetime that by virtue of our birth on Planet Earth we are all automatically world citizens on arrival. He also understood humankind may have many faiths and nations but only one planet to live. And today despite all the challenges, the world is a much smaller place with global travel, Internet and social media.

Conceivably, Har Dayal's dream of a cosmopolitian one-world state is not far. And one-day not so far in the future we will peacefully vote to have a global leadership that is spiritually elevated, intellectually gifted and ethically strong to solve the planet's greatest problems and resolve all kinds of discrimination created by ignorance. Hopefully on a future date we will integrate ourselves into a world without borders and achieve our quest for world peace, global prosperity, and international egalitarianism.

As humankind launches itself into the future, the life and work of Har Dayal, the exceptional public intellectual, revolutionary thinker and uncompromising internationalist, will remain significant. In the centuries to come, the unique legacy of this *Great Indian Genius* will be recalled with admiration in the knowledge led borderless digital world society for his lifelong belief in the ancient adage, "The dash of a pen is more significant than the counter use of a lance."

GLOSSARY

Ahimsa	Non voilence
Auswärtiges Amt	German Foreign Office
Azad Hind Fauj	Indian National Army
Badshah	King Emperor
Bagichis	Enclosed gardens
CID	Criminal Investigation Department
DCI	Department of Criminal Investigation
Diwan	Chief Minister/Chief Secretary
Durbar	Royal Court
Dar-ul-Insha	Department of letters
Ganga-Jamuni Tehzeeb	Composite culture
Ghadr of 1857	Rebellion of 1857
Firangi	Foreigner/British
Firanghi Fauj	British armed forces in India
Firman	The letter of consent
Haveli	Mansion
HAPC	Hindustan Association Pacific Coast
Howdah	Seat on an elephant
HSRA	Hindustan Socialist Republican Army
Hukumat-i-Britannia	Government of British India
ICS	Indian Civil Service
INA	Indian National Army

IPI	Indian Political Intelligence
IWW	Industrial Workers of the World
Kaghazi Raj	Paper Empire
Kartoos	Cartridges
Kayathas	The community of scribes in India
Kotwali	Police station
Mughliyah Saltanat	Mughal Sultanate
Mughal Shahzadas	Princes
Mughal shahi- gharana	Mughal Royal family
Munshis	Indo-Persian state secretaries
Munshi khana	Office and secretariat
Pagri	Turban
Sazaa-e-Kalapani	Punishment to the black waters
Shayari	Poetry
Shehenshah	Mughal Emperor
Sipahis	Soldiers/Sepoys
Satyagraha	Soul force
WWI	World War One
WWII	World War Two

ANNEXURE

Ethical Culture Institute

I. The Universe

We believe in the existence of an eternal and universal energy, from which all phenomena proceed. The Universe is uncreated and an indestructible. Space, Time, Casualty and Flux - these three govern all phenomena. Nature is autonomous in its Evolution. There is no Absolute or Unconditioned. It is also necessary to postulate metaphysical entities like life-force, spirit, etc. We are Humanists and Rationalists. We promote Science and the scientific spirit. We are neither spiritualists nor materialists, but simply scientists. We investigate all natural phenomena without making the division into Spirit and Matter.

II. Two Principles

The Universe, as observed and judged by Man, manifests two principles, Good and Evil. The Good consists of Life, Growth, Truth, Beauty, Happiness, Love, Knowledge, Health, Wealth, Virtue, Liberty, Equality, Fraternity, etc. The Evil is the opposite of these. But these principles are immanent in Nature and in Humanity; but they are not external to Nature and Humanity. We do not pray to any deity; we meditate on the Principle of Good.

III. Triumph of Good

This principle triumphs slowly but surely in biological evolution and in human civilization. Its complete fulfillment depends entirely on the development of

Human Personality, and not on any impersonal natural law. We are Personal Energists, not theological or pseudo-scientific fatalists.

IV. Human Personality

Our ideal is the complete and harmonious development of Human Personality in all its aspects: physical, intellectual, aesthetic, ethical, etc. Human Personality is creative and progressive. It is the supreme manifestation of the Divine Principle of Good. Man is the highest being known to us at present.

We do not base Ethics and Conduct on the dogma of personal survival after death, rebirth, resurrection, etc. We must grow and do our duty, whatever may happen after death. Young people should avoid this morbid theme and concentrate their thoughts on the problems of this life and this world. Philosophical speculation on this subject may be permissible in old age, when some may welcome the prospect of rebirth on this earth for further development,, but not for any reward or punishment. But this is not essential or important. Above all, we are truly and certainly immortal, physically and mentally, in our children and their descendants.

V. Fourfold Development

We promote the fourfold development of Human Personality by all means in our power.

  a. Physical Culture: We tear the natural methods of maintaining health and caring disease (without drugs, sera, vaccines, etc.). We proclaim the gospel of Health and Healing through sunshine, water, pure air, gymnastics, sport, eugenics, wholesome food and drink, proper breathing, thought-control, optimism, etc., etc. We discourage the use of meat, alcohol arid tobacco.

  b. Intellectual Culture: We exhort and help all to acquire some knowledge of Science, History, Comparative Religion, and other subjects. We insist on an all-round education. We also promote scientific and literary research.

  c. Aesthetic Culture: We teach all persons to appreciate the beauties of Nature and good Art in all its farms. We condemn sensationalism and sensualism in Art, and encourage only serene, sublime and sympathetic Art.

d. Moral Culture: We honor and revere all the great teachers of the past... We use suitable selections from their writings for our moral progress. We attach special importance to the works of the Hellenic philosophers.

We believe profoundly in the Unity of Humanity, and promote friendly intercourse and co-operation among all peoples. We combat all prejudices based on race, color and nationality. We are consistent cosmopolitans. We teach Esperanto as an auxiliary language for world-unity. We teach self-discipline and condemn sexual license and improper self-indulgence. The sexual impulse should be gratified in accordance with strict ethical rules, and a few may even sublimate it. We proclaim a new and noble code of sexual ethics for all men and women.

VI. Social Institutions

We work for the gradual establishment of social institutions based on Justice, Liberty, Equality and Fraternity in a World-State without sovereign national governments and without War.

VII. Festivals

We celebrate a festival each month in commemoration of the great events and personalities of World-History. Thus, in April, we remember Shakespeare and the great poets of all countries and nations. In September, we commemorate Comte, Bradlaugh and all pioneers of Rationalism. In July, we celebrate all democrats. And so on. Our festivals are truly international and universal, and they are related to all aspects of human progress and civilization. We may also retain some old festivals like Easter, Christmas, Vesak, Id, etc.; but we interpret them in a new way.

VIII. Solemnities

We appreciate informal social functions on such important occasions as Birth, Name-giving, School-going, Economic independence, Marriage, Death, etc.

IX. Apostles

Some enthusiastic men and women are trained as apostles. They must give their whole time to the Service of the Movement. They receive no salaries and have no home. They are given simple food, clothes, etc., for maintenance. They must live at our Institutes. Some of them also renounce marriage and parenthood.

X. Twelve Precepts

Our precepts abolish and supersede all old commandments:

1. Discard superstition and strive for the triumph of the Principle of Good by developing Human Personality.
2. Take care of your body and enjoy good health and long life.
3. Develop your intellect and acquire Knowledge.
4. Cultivate and ennoble your Emotions, and learn to appreciate the beauties of Nature and good Art.
5. Love Humanity, do your Duty, and build up a noble character.
6. Work for social progress and establish institutions on the basis of Justice, Peace, Liberty, Equality, and Fraternity in a democratic World-State.
7. Be gentle and peaceful and refrain from violence and murder.
8. Be just and honest, and do not gamble, cheat or steal.
9. Be truthful and polite in speech.
10. Be pure and chaste and shun lewdness and adultery.
11. Abstain from narcotics and stimulants, or be very moderate in their use.
12. Be humane to all useful or harmless animals.

Thus the foundations of a new civilization are well and truly laid.

Thus begins a new era in the history of the human race.

SOURCES

I have consulted several sources across three continents on the subject and I would very sincerely regret, inadvertence, any matter has been used in this book without due acknowledgement, for which I wish to offer my most sincere apologies should such an omission be found.

Archives and Libraries

National Archives of India (NAI), New Delhi, India

Delhi Archives, Government of Delhi, India

Nehru Memorial Museum and Library (NMML), New Delhi, India

Oxford University Archives, Bodleian Library, Oxford, UK

India Office Records (IOR), British Library, London, UK

Senate House Library, University of London, UK

St John's and The Queen's Colleges, Oxford, UK

Stanford University Archives, USA

Bancroft Library, University of California, Berkeley, USA

Statue of Liberty-Ellis Island Foundation, Inc., USA

Historical Society of Philadelphia, Pennsylvania, USA

Anneberg Rare Book and Manuscript Library and Penn Library, University of Pennsylvania, Philadelphia, USA

National Archives and Records, USA

Rydals Museum, Borasvagen, Rydal, Sweden

Gothenburg Film Office, City of Gothenburg, Sweden

Swedish Government Archive, Stockholm, Sweden

Politisches Archiv des Auswärtiges Amt, Berlin, Germany

Library and Archives Canada, Ottawa, Canada

Collectvite Territoriale de Martinique, Fort de France, Martinique

Writings of Har Dayal

Har Dayal was the author of the following books:

1. Forty-Four Months in Germany and Turkey, February 1915 to October 1918, A Record of Personal Impressions. London: P. S. King and Son Ltd., 1920.

2. Our Educational Problem. Madras: Tagore and Co., 1922.

3. The Bodhisattva Doctrine in Buddhist Sanskrit Literature. London: Kegan Paul, Trench, Trubner and Co., Ltd., 1932.

4. Hints for Self-Culture. London: Watts and Co., 1934.

5. Twelve Religions and Modern Life. Edgware (Middlesex): Modem Culture Institute, 1938.

6. He also contributed a chapter, 'A Preface to Buddhism' to The Bible of Mankind, ed. Mirza Ahmad Sohrab (New York: Universal Publishing Co., 1939).

From 1909 through 1926 the following articles by Har Dayal were published in *The Modern Review* (Calcutta) including during his time in the United States and Sweden.

Public Life and Private Morals, The Hindustan Review, XVIII: 12 (December 1908),

The Social Conquest of the Hindu Race, VI:3 (September 1909),

Woman in the West, X:I (July 1911).

India in America, X:l (January 1912),

Education in the West: A Suggestion, XI:2 (February 1912),

Karl Marx: A Modern Rishi, XI:3 (March 1912),

Indian Philosophy and Art in the West, XI:4 (April 1912),

The Wealth of the Nation, XII:1 (July 1912),

Some Phases of Contemporary Thought in India, XII:5 (Nov1912),

Mr. Har Dayal's Rejoinder, XII:6 (December 1912), Optimism, XIII: 1 (January 1913),

India and the World Movement, XIII:2 (February 1913), The Indian Peasant, XIII:5 (May 1913),

Class-Psychology and Public Movements, XV:2 (February 1914),

Twenty-Five Hundred Years of Humane Education in India, XV:5 (May 1914),

What the World is Waiting For, The Open Court (Chicago), XXVI:3 (March 1912),

Mr. Har Dayal's Confession of Faith, India (London), March 28, 1919,

The Future of the British Empire in Asia; The New Statesman (London), XII:311 (March 22, 1919) and XII:312 (March 29, 1919),

Modem India and European Culture, Svenska Orientsallskapet, Arsbok IV (1926/1927),

The Inevitability of Pacifism, New History (New York), VIII:3 (December 1938),5–8.

"X.Y.Z" was a pseudonym Har Dayal used in writing for *The Modem Review* from Sweden.

The Buddha-Gaya Problem, XXXVIII:2 (August 1925),

Three Ideas on Education, XXXVIII:6 (December 1925),

The Shame of India, XL:3 (September 1926)

Books Recommended for Further Reading

Ali, Asaf – The Emergence of Modern India,

Andrews, C. F – Lala Har Dayal: A Noble Patriot and Truth Lover, The Modern Review,

Aspengren, Henrik Chetan – Indian Revolutionaries Abroad, Revisiting their silent moments.

Banerjee, Kalyan Kumar – Indian Freedom Movement, Revolutionaries in America,

Barooah, Nirode K. – Chatto: The Life and Times of an Indian Anti-Imperialist in Europe,

Basu, Shrabani – For King and Another Country: Indian Soldiers on the Western Front, 1914–18,

Barry, John D. – Sidelights on India. San Francisco: The Bulletin.

Chirol, Valentine, Indian Unrest,

Bose, Arun Coomer – Indian Revolutionaries Abroad, 1905–1922

Bose, Sugata – His Majesty's Opponent: Subhas Chandra Bose and India's Struggle Against Empire,

Brown, Emily – Har Dayal: Hindu Revolutionary and Rationalist,

Brooks, Van Wyck – An Autobiography,

Brückenhaus, Daniel – Policing Transnational Protest,

Dharmavira – Lala Har Dayal and Revolutionary Movements of His Times,

Gandhi, M. K. – The Collected Works of Mahatma Gandhi,

Gaor, Amit – Contribution of Lala Har Dayal as an Intellectual and Revolutionary,

Gould Harold – Sikhs, Swamis, Students and Spies: The India Lobby in the United States,

Guha, Ramachandra – Gandhi: The Years that Changed the World

Lord Hardinge of Penhurst – Indian Years, 1910–1916,

Isemonger F. C. and Slattery J. – An Account of the Ghadr Conspiracy, 1913–1915

Jordan, David Starr – The Days of a Man,

Kapila Shruti (Editor) – An Intellectual History for India,

Krüger, Horst. – Har Dayal in Deutschland,

Lajpat Rai, Lala – Young India: An Interpretation and a History of the Nationalist Movement from within,

Liebau, Heike – The German Foreign Office, Indian Emigrants and Propaganda Efforts Among the Sepoys,

London Jack – The Little Lady of the Big House,

Majumdar, R. C. – History of the Freedom Movement in India,

Nehru, Jawaharlal – Toward Freedom: The Autobiography of Jawaharlal Nehru,

O'Connor, Daniel – A Clear Star: C. F. Andrews and India,

O'Dwyer, Sir Michael Francis – India As I Knew It, 1885–1925,

Omissi, David – Indian Voices of the Great War: Soldiers' Letters, 1914–18,

Parmanand, Bhai – The Story of My Life,

M. N. Roy – Memoirs,

Paul, E Jaiwant, and Shubh Paul – Har Dayal: The Great Revolutionary,

Petrie, David – Communism in India 1924–1927,

Popplewell, Richard J. – Intelligence and Imperial Defence: British Intelligence and the Defence of the Indian Empire 1904–1924,

Pratap, Raja Mahendra – My Life Story of Fifty-five Years,

Ramnath, Mala – The Haj to Utopia: How the Ghadar Movement Charted Global Radicalism and Attempted to Overthrow the British Empire,

Sareen, Tilak Raj – Indian Revolutionary Movement Abroad (1905–1920),

Savarkar, Vinayak Damodar – The Indian War of Independence,

Savarkar, V.D. – The Story of My Transportation for Life,

Sawhney, Savitri – I Shall Never Ask for Pardon: A Memoir of Pandurang Khankhoje

Sen, N. B. (ed.) – Punjab's Eminent Hindus,

Captain Amarinder Singh – Sepoys in the Trenches: The Indian Corps On The Western Front 1914–15,

Captain Amarinder Singh – Honour and Fidelity: India's Military Contribution to the Great War 1914–1918,

Singh, Anup – Nehru: The Rising Star of India,

Singh, S. Kesar, Gadhar di dee – Gulab Kaur,

Singh, Ganjendra – The Testimonies of India Soldiers and the Two World Wars (War Culture and Society),

Smedley, Agnes. Daughter of Earth

Sohi, Seema – Echoes of Mutiny: Race, Surveillance, and Indian Anticolonialism in North America,

Wolpert, Stanley – Tilak and Gokhale: Revolution and Reform in the Making of Modern India,

Yajnik, Indulal Kanaiyalal – Shyamji Krishnavarma: Life and Times of an Indian Revolutionary

Zachariah, Benjamin – A long strange trip; The lives in exile of Har Dayal

ACKNOWLEDGEMENTS

Over the years my parents **Vijai Laxmi Lal** and **Sharan Behari Lal**, who are no more on Earth, discussed every chapter of my life and they supported me in more ways than I can tell. By kindling my love for books and exploring the world culture with me they made me who I am. So I must first acknowledge their love, support and kindness in helping me discover the writer within me.

While working on this project since 2004, I have received the support of many individuals and institutions across several countries. First and foremost I must thank the members of the Har Dayal family especially to Shubh Dayal, E Jaiwant Paul and their daughter Nisha Grover. I must thank Beth and Dr. Raj Bhatnagar who shared their stories relating to the incredible life of Gobind Behari Lal and showed me the medals and other awards he received in his long career in the United States at their home in Burlingame in California. Thanks is also due to Narendra Nath, grandson of Hanwant Sahai who recounted in great detail the life and times of his forefathers. I also got valuable assistance from Rajendrasinh Rana, grandson of S. R. Rana.

I must additionally single out Late Stanley Wolpert (UCLA) and his wife Dorothy for their consistent encouragement and inspirational conversations. Gratitude is due to my history teachers at Modern School and at the University of Delhi specially Late Dr. Biswamoy Pati, for inculcating my interest and making me a lifelong student of the history of India with their illustrative lectures to our class. I have also had fruitful discussions about various aspects of India with learned Professors such as Christopher Chapple (LMU), Dilip Basu (UC Santa Cruz), Sugata Bose (Harvard), Mark Juergensmeyer, (UC Santa Barbara), Roger Connah (Carleton), Amitanshu Das (Univ of Penn), Ruhi Khan (UC Riverside) and Fuad Chowdhury and Farat Bashir Khan (Jamia MCRC).

It is my bounden duty to acknowledge the help and assistance that I have received from researchers, archives and libraries around the world in accumulating information for the book, the important among them are Sanjay Garg, Delhi Archives, Tilly Burn, Oxford University Archives, Bodleian Library, Oxford, Richard Temple, Senate House Library, University of London, Michael Riordan FSA, St John's and The Queen's Colleges, Oxford, Jenny Johnson, Stanford University Archives, Dean Smith, Bancroft Library, University of California, Berkeley, Cheryl Desmond, Ethical Society, Philadelphia, David Haugaard, Historical Society of Philadelphia, Tina Collins, Administratör Museum, Rydals Museum, Bo Scharping and Maria Dimander, Viskadalens folkhögskola, Henrik Chetan Aspengren, PhD, Research Fellow (South Asia), Swedish Institute of International Affairs, Moa Nordendag, Uppsala University Library and Heinrich Koppensteiner, Verlag der Österreichischen Akademie der Wissenschaften, and Austrian Academy of Sciences Press. Samip Mallick, Executive Director, South Asian American Digital Archive has done laudable work in preserving and documenting the Ghadr.

There are some close friends in California who have passed on in the last decade and I would like to acknowledge the terrific support of Robert Friedman, Beeta Grover, Jagmohan Mundhra, Krishna Shah and Inder Singh who were never short of words in praising my writings and work. I must acknowledge close associates across the world who have always encourgaged me in all my professional endevours, Ashok Amritraj, Vijay Amritraj, Anil Baijal, Manoj Bajpayee, Parveen and Kabir Bedi, Jeff Berg, Colin Brown, Nandita Das, Tushar Gandhi, Meghna Ghai, Subhash Ghai, Gulshan Grover, Ashutosh Gowariker, John Irvin, Christian Jeune, Dr. Gareth Jones, Andy Kaplan, Kiran Karnik, Manisha Koirala, Jim Landmark, Nina Lath, Tim McGovern, Ketan Mehta, Sudhir Misra, Narayan Murthy, Mira Nair, Paula Wagner and Rick Nicita, Laura Trombley and Bruce Raben, Rakesh Roshan, Chuck Russell, Deepa Sahi, Ronnie Screwvala, Vipin Sharma, Sasha Shapiro, Deep Sethi, Ken Silverman, Vijay Singh, Anubhav Sinha, Sundaram Tagore, Tarsem, David S. Ward and Gil Zobda.

This book would not have been complete without the inspiration drawn from my conversations with Dr. Harbeen Arora, Suman Kalra Bajaj, Major General Dr. G. D. Bakshi, VSM, Dr. Anurag Batra, Radhika and Kapil Batra, Billa Bhandari, Nisha and Sumeet Bawa, Abhinav Chaturvedi, Raman Chawla, Tarun Dalaya, Dr. Vijay Datta, Sharmila and Jayant Dua, Arvina Gadre, Anil Godhwani, Ramchandra Guha, Urmila and Anil Gupta, Nigar Hussain, Shazia Ilmi, Dr. Bashyam Kasturi, Pramod Kapoor, Priya Kapoor, Dr. T. S. Kler, Nitash and Rukn Luthra, Captain Manmohan Singh Kohli, Abha and Satish Kumar Modi, Dr. Bhupendra Kumar Modi, Sangeeta and Murali Nagarajan, Ajit Naidu,

Surina and H.S. Narula, Ashok Ogra, Nadir Patel, Gitu and Prashant Pathak, S. Ramanathan, Vinay Rai, Major Maroof Raza, Gauri and Harsh Sehgal, Ashish Joginder Singh, Dheerendra Singh, Pratap Singh, Chandrakant Singla, Mohammed Syeduzzman, Neville Tuli, Sushil Tyagi and Ratna and Shashank Vira.

Special thanks to all my school friends from Class of 1983 of Modern School, Barakhamba Road, New Delhi, Kendriya Vidhyalaya, Bhopal and Kendriya Vidhyalaya GCF, Jabalpur, as also my classmates, teachers and professional colleagues from AJK Mass Communication Research Center, Jamia Millia Islamia University in New Delhi who have been immensely supportive of all my ventures and writings over the years.

All my family members were encouraging as I explored the territory of Indian history and special recognition is due to Late K. K. Singh, Late Krishan Deish, Hari Babu Johri, Kusum and Shyamjee Saxena, Jyotsna Deish, Vikram Deish, Alok Deish, Surendra B. Lall, Subhash B. Lal, Gobind B. Lal, Kamal Nath, Veenu Shah, Aruna and Shailendra Hajela, Ranjana, Mike and Gautam Pandey and Meeta and Atul Lall. I will be failing in my duty if I do not thank the original community of Dilliwallahs for whom Har Dayal was much more than just a celebrated family member. I would specially like to thank my in laws Sudha and B. N. Mathur along with Ashok Narayan, Rasika Narain, Sajan Narain, Tilak Narayan, Abhilash Mathur, Rakesh Mathur, Raj Mathur, Gita Mathur, Umesh Mathur, Natwar Mathur, Vijay and Bharti Mathur, Veer and Sarita Mathur, Gopal and Panam Mathur and their families.

It is my duty to acknowledge the extraordinary care that my life partner, Arti Mathur, Associate Professor, University of Delhi, took in reading the manuscript and for her constant guidance on the importance of thinking through words and meanings. I am grateful to my brothers Vivek and Akshay for countless great days spent together and my niece Niharika and nephew Avinash for helping me remember that there is a world beyond work.

Finally thanks is due to my son Satyajit for keeping me both entertained and informed during the years of writing this book.

"He thinks too much. Such men are dangerous."
William Shakespeare
Julius Caesar, Act 1 Scene 2

CPSIA information can be obtained
at www.ICGtesting.com
Printed in the USA
LVHW091549230321
682224LV00044B/613